Marty Robbins

Fast Cars and Country Music

Barbara J. Pruett

The Scarecrow Press, Inc.
Lanham, Maryland • Toronto • Plymouth, UK
2007

SCARECROW PRESS, INC.

Published in the United States of America
by Scarecrow Press, Inc.
A wholly owned subsidiary of
The Rowman & Littlefield Publishing Group, Inc.
4501 Forbes Boulevard, Suite 200, Lanham, Maryland 20706
www.scarecrowpress.com

Estover Road
Plymouth PL6 7PY
United Kingdom

Frontispiece: Photo by Joan Goodwin

British Library Cataloguing in Publication Information Available

The hardback edition of this book was previously cataloged by the Library of Congress
as follows:

Pruett, Barbara J., 1942–
  Marty Robbins : fast cars and country music / by Barbara J. Pruett.
    p.   cm.
  Discography: p.
  Includes index.
  1. Robbins, Marty—Bibliography. 2. Robbins, Marty—
Discography. 3. Robbins, Marty. I. Title.
ML134.5.R6P8 1990
016.78242'1642'092—dc 20
                              90—8709

ISBN-13: 978-0-8108-2325-9 (cloth : alk. paper)
ISBN-10: 0-8108-2325-X (cloth : alk. paper)
ISBN-13: 978-0-8108-6036-0 (pbk. : alk. paper)
ISBN-10: 0-8108-6036-8 (pbk. : alk. paper)

The paper used in this publication meets the minimum requirements of
American National Standard for Information Sciences—Permanence of
Paper for Printed Library Materials, ANSI/NISO Z39.48-1992.
Manufactured in the United States of America.

DEDICATION

This book is dedicated to two people whose love, faith, and friendship made my life better. Both are gone now but their memory and influence will always remain.

First, I want to thank my aunt, Ruth Keel Barkman. Her love, encouragement, and faith in my ability to achieve the goals I set for myself gave my life direction when it was needed. She was a traditional schoolteacher from Indiana who cared about the future of those she taught and I was fortunate to have had her as part of my family.

This book is also dedicated to Philip Brouwer, a close friend who died in December of 1989. Philip was a successful Canadian businessman who emigrated from the Netherlands in the 1950s and for many years spoke of Marty Robbins as being a major inspiration in his life. Their lives were strikingly similar; my description of Marty in the introduction of this book could be written, with minor changes, about Philip. Both were born in 1925, each broke away from working for others to carve out a career as his own boss; sad to say, they had the same health problem. Both men were "believers" in God, independent in action, untiring workers who put in long days, and gentlemen. At one time, Marty said he wanted to be remembered as "a good person" and Philip agreed that this was the best one could hope for. They both succeeded.

CONTENTS

PART II: MARTY AND HIS MUSIC
(Including Discography)

ACKNOWLEDGMENTS

Were it not for Henry Johnson this book would never have been written. For years now he has acted as mentor and advisor to me, pushing me from my life as an inexperienced scribbler to that of a seasoned writer. His hard-core, honest, junkyard dog approach to teaching writing skills brings with it the assumption that you want to learn and are willing to work at it. He's rough, but he's good. He's also the reason I'll have the pleasure of writing for the rest of my life.

My thanks to all of the people who helped with this book during the six years it took to put it together. Bob Allen provided the interview with Marty, thereby giving readers a touch of Marty's magic. Three people from the Country Music Foundation Library were crucial to the successful completion of this book: Ronnie Pugh helped with hundreds of details over the years and introduced me to people I needed to know, Bob Pinson gave me the earliest entry in the bibliography when he called my attention to a 1948 *Billboard* mention of Marty, and Jay Orr saw to it that I started my research right by providing a nine-page list of country music periodicals that were worth searching. In addition, Gillian Anderson of the Music Division of the Library of Congress provided extensive assistance in educating me about their collection. Both the Country Music Association and The Academy of Country Music supplied support and assistance every time they were asked; my thanks to their staffs. I'm especially indebted to Pat and Billy Galvin, who acted as mentors and were instrumental in providing the first professional recognition of my work. Kathy

McClintock Harris (of The Oak Ridge Boys staff) also provided practical advice and professional encouragement. The time she took to tell me about the Nashville country music community helped me set the direction of my future work.

My thanks also to Joan and Gordy Goodwin and the photographers who let me use their work. And to Gail Andrews, Sandy Daens, and my *Pen Friends* friends who helped with the research and gave me encouragement.

Lastly, I'd like to pay a special tribute to a lady who has helped many people over the years, Donnie Jennings. Anyone who has done Marty Robbins research in the last ten years knows Donnie. Her unselfish willingness to help everyone who asks for assistance has made countless articles better, information more accurate, and museum exhibits more complete.

Barbara J. Pruett
Washington, D.C.

CHRONOLOGY

9/26/25   Martin David Robinson and a twin sister, Mamie,
                 were born near Glendale, Arizona.

Age 1–12   Marty lived in the desert area near Glendale.

Age 12   Marty's mother and father divorced. His mother
                 moved to Glendale with the children. There were
                 nine children in the family, including half-brothers
                 and sisters.

Age 14–15   He spent part of the year with his brother herding
                 goats and breaking wild horses in the Bradshaw
                 Mountains near Phoenix.

Teen yrs.   Attended high school in Glendale, but didn't
                 graduate.

1943–45   He was in the Navy for three years and saw action in
                 the Pacific. One of the campaigns he participated in
                 was the landing at Bougainville.

1946–51   Marty started singing in a local nightclub and on the
                 radio. He briefly used the name "Jack Robinson"
                 before becoming "Marty Robbins."

Late 1940s   Started at KTYL in Mesa, AZ.
                 Had a radio show at KPHO in Phoenix called
                 "Chuck Wagon Time," Monday through Saturday at
                 7:30 a.m.
                 He also had a TV show at KPHO-TV: "Western
                 Caravan."

	He had his own band at Fred Kares, a local nightclub.
9/27/48	Married Marizona Baldwin.
7/16/49	Son, Ronald Carson Robinson, born.
7/20/50	"H-E-A-R-T-S-I-C-K" and "I wish somebody loved me" were the first songs he wrote to be copyrighted.
1951	Marty signed a contract with Columbia Records.
11/14/51	Marty attended his first recording session, for Columbia Records, held in Los Angeles.
1952	Signed a songwriting contract with Acuff-Rose.
Apr. 1952	His first record, "Love me or leave me alone/ Tomorrow you'll be gone," was released.
1/19/53	Marty officially joined the Grand Ole Opry. He had previously appeared as a guest.
Mar. 1953	"I'll go on alone" was his first record to make the charts, reaching No. 10.
Apr. 1953	"I couldn't keep from crying" entered the charts on this date and went to No. 6.
9/26/54	Glendale proclaimed a "Marty Robbins Day."
9/12/56	"Singing the blues" entered the charts on this date and became a No. 1 hit for Marty on both the country and pop charts. It stayed on the charts 30 weeks.
1957–58	Marty held a series of recording sessions in New York with Ray Conniff and his Orchestra which resulted in several teen love song hits.
Jan. 1957	"Knee deep in the blues" entered the charts and went to No. 5.
4/10/57	"A white sport coat (and a pink carnation)" entered the charts and went to No. 1 on both the country and pop charts. It stayed on the charts 22 weeks.

Sept. 1957	Started Robbins Records. The first recording artists signed for the label were the Glaser Brothers.
1957	His first album, "Song of Robbins," was released.
11/16/57	"The story of my life" entered the charts and became another No. 1 hit.
1/29/59	His daughter, Janet, was born.
Oct. 1959	"El Paso" was released, entered the charts in early November, and became a No. 1 hit for many weeks in late December and early January. It spent 26 weeks on the charts.
Late 1950s	Marty built and drove micro-midget cars at a local track.
Early 1960s	Started his own music companies: Mariposa Music, Maricopa Music, Maricana Music, Marizona Music.
1960	Marty was awarded a Grammy for "El Paso." It is popularly recognized as the first Grammy ever awarded to a country song.
2/12/61	"Don't worry" entered the charts and went to No. 1.
1960s	Marty started racing at the Nashville Speedway at the Fairgrounds in Nashville. He was successful enough to win sportsmanship awards at the track in 1966 and 1967.
8/4/62	"Devil woman" entered the charts and became a No. 1 hit, staying on the charts 21 weeks.
12/8/62	"Ruby Ann" entered the charts and went to No. 1.
11/30/63	"Begging to you" entered the charts and went to No. 1.
1964	Marty supported Barry Goldwater for President.
4/17/65	"Ribbon of darkness" entered the charts and went to No. 1.

Mid-1960s   During 1965 he started performing on the last seg-
                   ment of the Grand Ole Opry (the 11:30 p.m. time
                   slot) so that he could race regularly at the Nashville
                   Speedway.
                   Also during this time period, he toured Australia,
                   New Zealand, and Japan.

Late 1965   Marty filmed a TV series called "The Drifter."

1966   Wrote a western paperback novel titled *The Small
                   Man*.

7/30/66   Marty entered his first NASCAR Grand National
                   race at the ½-mile at the Fairgrounds Speedway in
                   Nashville. He finished 25th.

6/3/67   "Tonight Carmen" entered the charts and became
                   No. 1.

6/16/67   The movie premier for "Hell on Wheels" was held
                   in Nashville.

Summer 1968   Marty started consistently going past his time in his
                   Opry time slot, a practice that became a regular oc-
                   currence (and grew in length) over the years any
                   time he appeared.

1968   Marty ran his first NASCAR Grand National Circuit
                   race, The Charlotte National 500 at the Charlotte
                   Motor Speedway, finishing 12th and winning
                   $1525.00.

1968   Supported George Wallace for President.

10/5/68   "I walk alone" entered the charts and went to No. 1.

Mid-1969   Marty filmed some segments of a TV series called
                   "The Marty Robbins Show."

8/1/69   Marty had a heart attack on his tour bus near
                   Cleveland, Ohio.

Nov. 1969   Marty appeared at the Fremont in Las Vegas.

1/20/70   Marty entered St. Thomas Hospital in Nashville for tests.

1/27/70   Marty underwent bypass surgery.

1970   Started Charger Records. (Source: *Who's Who in America, 1982–83*)

3/21/70   "My woman, my woman, my wife" entered the charts and went to No. 1.

Apr. 1970   Marty began a four-week appearance at the Fremont Hotel in Las Vegas.

4/13/70   Marty received "The Man of the Decade" Award from The Academy of Country Music in Los Angeles.

10/11/70   After passing his physical, Marty returned to NASCAR racing at the Charlotte Motor Speedway in North Carolina.

Oct. 1970   Marty appeared on the CMA Awards program and sang "My woman, my woman, my wife." He was nominated for three awards.

3/16/71   He won his second Grammy for "My woman, my woman, my wife." The award was presented in 1971 for the 1970 year.

June 1972   Left Columbia Records and signed with Decca/ MCA Records from 1972–1974.

1972   Marty was named Rookie of the Southern 500.

9/12/72   The film "Country Music" was released.

June 1973   The film "Guns of a Stranger" was released.

7/19/74   NASCAR paid tribute to Marty with a "Marty Robbins Night."

10/6/74   Marty was involved in a crash at the NASCAR National 500 race in Charlotte, North Carolina.

1/11/75	A "Marty Robbins Day" was held in El Paso.
2/16/75	Marty was involved in a crash during the NASCAR Daytona 500 at Daytona Beach, Florida.
3/29/75	Marty made his Wembley (England) debut.
5/4/75	Marty was involved in a crash during the NASCAR Winston 500 at Talladega, Alabama. After this wreck, he announced he was giving up racing.
7/19/75	The Nashville Speedway held a "Marty Robbins Night."
10/12/75	Marty was inducted into the Hall of Fame of the Nashville Songwriters Association.
11/17/75	Marty was named the "Entertainer of the Year" by the Great Britain Country Music Association.
Dec. 1975	Marty left Decca/MCA Records and returned to Columbia Records.
2/19/76	Marty hosted the 11th Annual ACM Awards show. The show was taped in Los Angeles and nationally televised in early March.
4/17/76	"El Paso City" entered the charts and became a No. 1 hit.
Apr. 1976	Marty won the "Best International Vocalist" award at the Wembley Festival in London.
5/30/76	Marty drove the pace car for the "Indianapolis 500" race in Indiana.
7/2/76	El Paso held a tribute to Marty at its Sun Bowl. The Mayor declared July 2 as "Marty Robbins Day" in the city.
9/4/76	"Among my souvenirs" entered the charts and went to No. 1.

3/19/77	The Grand Ole Opry presented Marty with the George D. Hay Award for his contribution to country music.
6/19/77	Marty returned to NASCAR racing at the Michigan International Speedway in Brooklyn, Michigan.
10/16/77	The first "Marty Robbins World Open 500" was run at the Nashville Speedway.
1977–78	Marty appeared in the TV series "Marty Robbins' Spotlight." 48 episodes were made.
6/17/78	Marty drove his brand new car, a Panther DeVille, onto the Opry stage to show the fans.
4/7/79	Marty was given a special Golden Trustee Award from the National Cowboy Hall of Fame and Western Heritage Center in Oklahoma City for his contributions to western music. The award was presented to him by Gene Autry.
6/9/80	The MCN Awards show was telecast and Marty won two awards: Male Artist of the Year, and Songwriter of the Year.
1/1/81	Marty suffered a mild heart attack during the first days of 1981. He was admitted to the hospital January 5th for the illness.
June 1981	The Marty Robbins Band was voted Band of the Year at the MCN Awards.
7/4/81	Marty performed at the White House for President Reagan.
Early 1982	"Some memories just won't die" appeared on the charts and went to No. 10.
Apr. 1982	Marty appeared at the Silk Cut Festival in London (previously named the Wembley Festival) and toured England.

May 1982	Marty toured Canada.
6/5/82	The Marty Robbins Museum opened at Hermitage Landing near Nashville.
6/7/82	Marty was voted "Male Vocalist of the Year" at the MCN Awards.
6/10/82	The "Marty Party" was held at the Opryland Hotel during Fan Fair.
10/11/82	Marty was inducted into the Hall of Fame during the CMA Awards program.
Nov. 1982	Marty toured the west coast.
11/7/82	Marty raced in the NASCAR Atlanta Journal 500.
12/1/82	Marty's last concert was held in Cincinnati, Ohio.
12/2/82	Marty suffered a heart attack and underwent surgery.
12/8/82	Marty died. His funeral was held December 11th.
12/15/82	The film "Honkytonk Man" was released.
1/24/83	The Music City News Songwriters Award Show paid tribute to Marty during a special section of the show.
5/7/83	CBS Records and NASCAR paid tribute to Marty with the running of a special race, the "Marty Robbins 420" in Nashville.
5/9/83	The Academy of Country Music paid tribute to Marty on their show and announced the renaming of their annual charity golf tourney after him.
5/17/83	Groundbreaking ceremonies were held for "The Marty Robbins Memorial Showcase" at Music Village in Hendersonville.
5/18/83	The television special "Country Comes Home" paid tribute to Marty with a special segment by Glen Campbell.

6/6/83	Marty won three awards during the telecast of the MCN Awards Show: Male Vocalist of the Year, Single of the Year, and Album of the Year. The awards were accepted by Marizona and Ronny Robbins.
7/4/83	Marty was named the first member of the Arizona Songwriters Hall of Fame.
7/4/83	"Marty Robbins Day" was held in his home town of Glendale, Arizona.
1984	KRPT Radio in Anadarko, Oklahoma established the "Marty Robbins Lifetime Achievement Award."
5/18–19/85	Douglas, Arizona celebrated "Marty Robbins Days" as a tribute to Marty.
6/15/85	Marty was posthumously awarded the Metronome Award from the city of Nashville.
Summer 1986	The television special, "Marty Robbins—Super Legend," was produced and syndicated around the country.

Photo of Marty Robbins and Barbara Pruett, October 10, 1982.

INTRODUCTION

> I would like to be remembered as a good entertainer, a good person . . . I think maybe better as a good person.
>
> —Marty Robbins, *PM Magazine* interview, November 29, 1982 (syndicated television show).

Marty Robbins died December 8, 1982 at the age of 57. He never wrote his life story and that's a shame because it robs us of hearing, from his viewpoint and in his own words, what his life was like and how he faced his problems and enjoyed his success.

But if you bring together as much of forty years of American and foreign literature about Marty as possible, and present it in chronological order, a life story will take form. There's a lot there. The excitement, he said, was something he felt every day of his career. Marty was interviewed frequently over the years and he was a very open person in talking to the press. He didn't try to gloss over the problems and he was at times candidly honest about his frustrations and disappointments. He was both the common man and the uncommonly talented entertainer. He faced the normal problems the rest of us have: he had to deal with frustrations of home ownership (when a house he bought had structural problems), he worried about balancing family and career needs, he fought with the IRS over taxes. But he also tackled unusual life stresses: three heart attacks and bypass surgery when it was in the experimental stage, destructive wrecks while racing stock cars, and the emotional highs and lows that face any per-

1

former who is forcefully pushing for career success. The core of Marty Robbins was his natural enthusiasm about everything he did. If you were to string together a list of terms that defined the man, they would have to include: songwriter, auto racer, entertainer, family man, a lover of the Old West, religious "believer." The force of his energy kept his life running on high nearly 24 hours a day. By his own admission, he rarely slept more than two or three hours a night from the time his career started right up to the time his life ended.

Marty was a rebel in the entertainment industry. I've heard people say that he could have been the biggest star in the industry if he had listened to other people or did things the way others wanted him to do them. He didn't. But his refusal was based on his determination to do things his own way, not on ignorance about the price he would have to pay. He was stubborn, independent, and a tireless worker. He called himself a modern-day drifter, often saying if he had been born a hundred years ago he would have been a cowboy. He admitted to a love of touring and said he felt hemmed in if he stayed in one location too long.

Early on, he decided to manage his own career and handle his own bookings. He also started music companies to market the music he wrote, started a record label, and bought a recording studio. He spoke openly and honestly about what he felt to be music industry problems at a time when few others did. He was known as a loner who rarely mixed socially with industry people, participated in industry events, or sought out industry advice. Despite this, he had as full a schedule of tours and concerts as he wanted. Over the years, he had developed good relations with the "small people" in the industry, the county fair bookers and venue owners in the everyday American towns who were more than glad to give him all of the return bookings he wanted. Regardless of his status in the industry, he always maintained a high popularity in mainstream America. That's where his fans were and his concerts usually sold well, without receiving much industry notice. His audience read *Reader's Digest* and *TV Guide* rather than *Billboard* or *Variety*.

Equally independent on a personal level, he rejected the words of the doctor who told him after his first massive heart attack in 1969 that he would have to lead a quiet life. Marty spoke about that conversation with continued anger and emotion the rest of his life, declaring that the doctor had no right to say that . . . no right to tell him how to lead his life. He started regular big-time NASCAR circuit stock car racing in the early 1970s, at an age when most drivers start thinking about slowing down, and raced (at times against the wishes of his family and business associates) throughout the rest of his life. More than one writer has drawn the analogy that he seemed to be living out the code of ethics and the lifestyle of the Old West in a modern-day setting.

At 57, Marty was still very much in the game. The last year of his life saw a resurgence of his popularity and he was outdistancing the younger artists who were the attention of the industry media campaigns. He was winning awards, had been voted into the Hall of Fame, his concerts were sellouts, and his records were once again going to the top of the charts. He continued to race and was appearing on more television programs. In fact, he had cut back on his usually full tour schedule for the coming year; his explanation was that he wanted to give some attention to trying to find some film roles.

This compilation of historical information is not simply a celebration of the past; it's the key to the future for those people smart enough to learn from the past. As such, this book is not intended to be an end in itself. It's designed to provide the foundation for new beginnings, to be used as a resource book for industry professionals and researchers who need direction in finding information for writing books, articles, background information for TV productions, or other projects that require an in-depth knowledge about Marty Robbins. This book provides names, places, events, facts, and other information needed for such activities. It's also a book for fans, to provide a source of guidance to extensive readings about Marty, the events of his life, and his music.

By the nature of its format, a bibliography doesn't easily let in warmth and personality, sad to say. But if you look for that personal feeling and style, you will find it in the titles of the articles and in their abstracts. The history of a performer's life and career is written every day in local papers, radio and television interviews, notes in news columns, and in the photographs that are taken constantly by professionals and fans alike. The interviews, particularly, are of tremendous value because they represent the story in the performer's own words. Excitement, humor, love, faith, disappointment, and hardship: these are the life events and emotions all of us face. But in the life of a performer they become public and are recorded in print, sight, and sound. They become a part (albeit, though minor) of American history.

This bibliography is designed to highlight the special qualities that made Marty Robbins such a unique entertainer. He was, so many people have said, an entertainer and a showman rather than just a singer. But he was also a composer, a businessman, a comedian, a movie star, a lover of the Old West, a stock car racer, a friend of his fans, a family man, and a "believer" to whom religion had everyday meaning. The citations chronicle his professional accomplishments: his record releases, performances, TV and film appearances, and his awards. Also, his health problems, his positive attitude, and especially his love of life.

A detailed bibliography arranged in chronological order can present an effective biographical overview only if sufficient care and effort have been devoted to finding the materials most expressive of that particular life and personality. Of course, a sufficient number of entries have to be collected to provide the depth of reporting needed to accomplish this purpose. That's why I've included a wide variety of material. In attempting to compile the historical record of Marty's career, I have included the things that I feel accurately portray Marty's personality and professional history. For example, where he was featured on the cover of an issue of a periodical, this is noted by use of the term "cover photo." It is an important status symbol in the entertainment business to be featured on the cover, recognition as the most important feature in the issue. I have also included such information as ads for new record releases and products featuring Marty. Also included are notes about photographs and items from news columns. The news columns especially serve to document the small everyday activities that happen in the life of a performer but are not important enough to warrant a separate article. Auto racing activities, photographs that identify events, people, places, etc. are also among the citations.

Stories about his awards chronicle his success in the industry, the accolades he received for his writing, and, finally, the tributes he received after his death from the people who shared the special categories of his life.

The compilation of interviews throughout this work will make available Marty's story from his own perspective and in his own words. He gave a number of candid interviews during the last few years of his life. The most personal televised interview took place on a local Nashville television program, "Miller and Company," in 1981. These interviews tended to cover his professional and public life, though he was more circumspect about his personal life, his family, and his problems. And the citations cover his private passion—it could almost be called an addiction—for stock car racing.

It has been my experience in working with people in the entertainment industry that large amounts of information about the activities of performers are most helpful when arranged by date. Questions frequently arise about the various stages of a career and the facts that surrounded a particular event or events. There is a distinct relationship, for example, among record releases, concert tours, performance reviews, television appearances, awards, and personal activities. One caveat: the accuracy of any print information should occasionally be questioned. That which is in print is not always correct.

There are certain characteristics in the field of country music that are relatively unique to this area of entertainment. Country music performers, when they reach the point in their careers where they can afford to do so, tend to be involved in businesses related to the support of their careers: music publishing houses, recording studios, public relations firms, management agencies. Many are successful songwriters. Marty had his hand in all of these activities.

Country music fans often have close emotional ties and easy

access to the performers. They're not kept at arms-length (or shunned) as is the frequent case in the pop music or film industries. Fan clubs are formed, or newsletters are issued, from every performer's office for his or her fans. Fan Fair, an event held in Nashville each June, brings performers and their fans together for a week-long gathering of shows, parties, and meetings. Often, the performers themselves spend considerable amounts of money and time on this event as a way of recognizing and thanking their fans for their support throughout the year. No other part of the entertainment business so openly recognizes the value of fans.

And of all of the bonds between artists and fans, the bond between Marty and his fans was openly acknowledged to be the closest and strongest. Marty and his fans were in close harmony with each other; the strength and dedication that flowed back and forth between the two sides has been covered frequently in articles, and especially in interviews with Marty. The relationship existed, in large part, because he felt so strongly about the audience he called "My people!" The rest of the world named them "Marty's Army." He gave much of himself to them and received the same in return. In an industry where fans are noted for unusually strong loyalties, his are the most loyal.

Marty's fans were the most able of information hunters; they had information "networking" fully developed long before anyone else. And Marty was the most cooperative of performers. Throughout his career, he answered every piece of fan mail that requested an answer . . . and some that didn't. He opened and read it all; his staff was instructed to leave the fan mail untouched in his office when he was on tour. Eventually he got to each letter.

If you never saw Marty in a live concert, you really missed something! Marty in person was nothing like the more restrained and normal person you saw on television or in the movies. He hit the stage with speed and took control from the very first strings of a fast-paced song. He followed one hit with another in rapid-fire succession. He joked with the audience, took requests, and became emotionally higher as the evening wore on. He was excited, he was silly, and he was in love with his audience as much as they were with him. He often stayed on stage far longer than his contract required. And Marty's concerts were always one long photo session; fans were allowed to take pictures non-stop as he performed . . . with Marty's encouragement and approval. He sang beautifully, told awful jokes (his comedy style was at various times compared with Red Skelton's, Flip Wilson's, and Jerry Clower's), and held poses for photos without missing a word of the song he was singing. And frequently he stayed for hours afterwards, signing autographs and talking to "his people."

WORKING WITH COUNTRY MUSIC LITERATURE

A number of problems exist for anyone trying to compile this sort of publication. The good news is that there is an immense body of literature covering the country music field. The bad news is that virtually none of it is indexed. There is no easy access, therefore, to the information contained in the hundreds of country music journals that cover decades of history.

There is a lack of understanding on the part of both the industry professionals (including the artists) and the public, a mistaken belief that once something such as an interview is in print, it is forever available for the public to read. This is not the case at all. For all practical purposes, information is "lost" if it can not be identified, found, and retrieved. Accessibility is the issue; if it can't be found, it does not exist.

Most country music periodicals come and go every few years. The only ones to last for a long period of time are *Country Song Roundup, Music City News,* and *Country Music People.*

There are a number of good country music journals from around the world: *Country Music People* (England), *Country Corner* (Germany), and *Kountry Korral* (Netherlands) are three of the more popular titles. There are others from England, and from Sweden, Australia, Japan and Europe.

No one library or research center has a complete collection of every country music periodical. The work on this book was done primarily in The Country Music Foundation Library and Media Center in Nashville and in two divisions of the Library of Congress (the Music Division and the Copyright Office). These two research centers contain the major collections covering the field of country music. However, complete sets of some journals simply do not exist in either place.

The country music industry is fortunate to have the Country Music Foundation Library and the staff members who work there. Not only does the library have the most extensive collection of print materials, photographs, and recordings available, the staff makes an ongoing attempt to find and collect this valuable history from every source possible. Most of the newspaper clippings cited in this book came from their extensive collection. And they are most helpful to researchers. At the start of my research they provided me with a nine-page compilation of journal titles from their collection they believed to be most likely to contain information about Marty Robbins. (See Appendix A.) I am indeed indebted to the staff of that Library, particularly Ronnie Pugh, the Head of their Reference Section. Others who provided assistance were Jay Orr, Alan Stoker, and Bob Pinson.

RESEARCH PROBLEMS

Information technology has been slow in coming to the entertainment field and where it has arrived, it is most often found in the market research part of the business. In the age of automation, most research in the entertainment field has to be done by hand— and a page at a time at that. Some information can be found in automated newspaper indexes, but none of the country music periodicals have been included in automated databases.

A major problem in conducting research about any performer and his career is the need for an in-depth background about that person before starting. This is absolutely necessary in order to set the parameters of the research and to identify the areas to be included in your work.

As much as possible, one needs to decide what to look for before starting: names, events, dates, associates, businesses, etc. The headline of an article may feature one of these topics (not the name of the performer) even though the article may be about the performer himself. For Marty, I decided to include as much as could be found on every aspect of his life: friends, associates, business activities, career, auto racing.

TECHNICAL PROBLEMS ENCOUNTERED

First, inaccurate information. It is common in the entertainment industry to announce forthcoming projects and/or appearances. Publicity, photos, and a variety of announcements are released, and dates set. Unfortunately, it's also common for performers to cancel these plans for a variety of reasons. Often, no public announcement of these changes are made. The artists involved simply move on to other projects. The consequence (for bibliographers striving for accuracy) is serious; you are left with "false" citations in the literature, noting an event that never occurred. For instance, I found two references in my research to an appearance Marty was supposed to have made on the "Ed Sullivan Show" in the late 1950s. Yet, my correspondence with Sullivan Productions attempting to verify this information brought back the response that they could find no record that Marty was ever on the show. With any luck, the bibliographer will be familiar enough with the career of the artists to know that the announced event never happened. If this is not the case, and no additional citation exists to indicate the change, there is always the danger of creating false history!

When I could identify such false citations, I opted to keep them and added an editorial note at the end explaining that the event never took place. This, I felt, was a service to future researchers. The citing of inaccurate information is still providing accurate information. And sometimes this false information is included in an interview or article that is of considerable value for many other reasons.

There are also problems with title changes, name spellings, volume and issue number errors from the periodicals themselves. The *Country Music Reporter* became *The Music Reporter,* Hillous

Butrum is spelled differently in separate articles, Shirell Milete is Shirl Milete on different copyright records. A film initially planned to be called "The Drifter" was renamed "Guns of a Stranger" at the time it was released, but a 13-episode television series was named "The Drifter." Even *The Nashville Tennessean* became *The Tennessean*. And Marty's name was in the Copyright Office records in a total of 11 different variations of his stage name (Marty Robbins), his personal name (Martin David Robinson) and a pseudonym (Lobo Rainey). Marty's son, Ronny Robbins, himself a singer and songwriter, previously spelled his name "Ronnie" and this is the way it is spelled in earlier publications. He also went under the stage name "Marty Robbins, Jr." for a very brief time, and his first album uses that name.

To make matters worse, at times Marty gave away the music he wrote to other people; and this music is copyrighted under the name of the person to whom he gave the song! A very personal and heartfelt example of this generosity is the song, "Two Little Boys." Marty had been close friends with country singer Hawkshaw Hawkins, who died in the plane crash with Patsy Cline and Cowboy Copas on March 5, 1963. Hawkshaw was married to Jean Shepard at the time; she was expecting twins and two little boys were born shortly after their father's death. Marty's song is about a woman whose husband has died; she sings about how proud he would have been of his sons had he lived to see them. But Marty is not listed as the writer of the song; the writers are listed as Don Robin Hawkins and Harold Hawkins. And the song can be found on the Jean Shepard album, "The Best of Jean Shepard" (1975, distributed by Gusto Records).

Publicity photos that accompany an article are frequently older than the date of the interview or the article—sometimes by many years. For example, Marty had different racing numbers on his cars over the years (and many different cars) and at times the racing photo used in an article showed a different number or car than the one referred to in the story.

Marty's activities were covered in three different newsletters over the years. He had a fan club from the early 1950s until the late 1970s and their *Journal* provided regular news of his work and occasionally reprinted articles. In addition, a newsletter titled *Pen Friends,* started in 1975 by Doris Fjelstad, provided monthly coverage of Marty's tour schedule and media appearances. And Marty's own office published a monthly newsletter; it was available to anyone who provided a SASE (self-addressed, stamped envelope). All of these publications contain a considerable amount of valuable historical material, including older newspaper clippings and articles. In some cases, the information is undated or lacks the name of the newspaper or magazine which originally published the item. By searching back issues of these newsletters, you can identify the names of his band members of many years ago, read reviews of his Las Vegas appearances, or discover a letter he wrote that was printed in his local newspaper while he was a teenager overseas during World War II.

Titles of songs are sometimes incorrectly cited in an article; sometimes they are even wrong on the record jacket itself.

Journal volume numbers, issue numbers, or even the date of publication are sometimes printed incorrectly on the publication. And some journals intentionally publish a cover date for use on the newsstands that bears little relationship to the actual date of publication. As a consequence, information from publicity releases appearing in the December issue of one journal may appear in the March issue of another; and both titles may be on the newsstand at the same time. While this problem is serious to the bibliographer who is trying to correctly identify a citation, little can be done beyond adding an editorial note explaining the inconsistency where it exists.

How to Use This Bibliography

Information in each citation is arranged in the same order: author, title of article, journal title, date, volume number, issue number (in parentheses), paging, technical note, abstract. Therefore, a sample citation will read like this:

Author   *Title*   *Journal*

Minsky, Betty. Robbins offers solution. *Music City News;*
1980 June; 17(12): 36.
Note: Illus.
Interview comments include his ideas about how to handle the
Iranian crisis, his feelings about CMA, and other topics.

Note   Date   Abstract   Volume   Issue   Paging

Brackets ([ ]) indicate information added to make something
clearer. For example, advertisements and photographs generally
do not have titles; I therefore included them in the bibliography
by using brackets. I also found it necessary occasionally to add
explanatory notes, and these are also enclosed in brackets.

In the 1950s and 1960s, the words to the songs Marty wrote
and recorded were frequently reprinted in popular song magazines such as *Country Song Roundup.* These are included in the
bibliography with Marty listed as the author, followed by the
song title. I've consistently used the phrase "lyrics to the song"
to describe these entries because only the words to the song were
published; the music itself was not.

CONCLUSION

Did this project accomplish what it set out to do? Only in part. It
was impossible, of course, to find and cite everything about
Marty. But the bibliography does provide a fairly detailed outline
of his life and career, to the extent that someone without a working knowledge of Marty's life can come away with an understanding of the important events of his career and a feeling of
what he was like as a person.

There is still much to be done in order to complete a thorough
documentation of Marty's life. An international discography
should be compiled, hundreds of radio shows should be indexed,
and additional effort must be made to find and save such things as
correspondence, film, interviews, etc., etc.

Unexpectedly, the most personally satisfying part of the work was assembling all of the tributes that were written about Marty immediately after his death. Although I had gathered them over a three-year period, it was the first time I had read them all at one time. Instead of creating a feeling of sadness or remorse, they create a pensive feeling of warmth and optimism that people appreciate the virtues of their friends. There were so many people

Eddy Arnold presenting the Hall of Fame Award to Marty, October 11, 1982. (Photo courtesy of the Country Music Association)

who wrote about the positive aspects of Marty; his love of life, and how he had affected their own lives. It is in these eulogies that the depth of their feeling is expressed. The tributes came from all parts of his life—from colleagues in the music industry, auto racing drivers, fans, friends and neighbors.

I never knew Marty Robbins personally. I don't pretend to know what he thought or how he would have wanted to be remembered. By all accounts, he never discussed this in great detail with anyone, beyond saying that he would like to have his music remembered. As I said at the beginning of this introduction, it's a shame he didn't write his own story. Now he has no opportunity for first-person response to what is written or said about him; no rejoinder for the accounting of events by someone else.

If artists want their life stories to be told their way, they had better take the opportunity to set that personal version in writing while they can. Therein lies the best reason for performers to write their own life stories. After all, history is in the perspective of the person telling the story. Marty's story will never be told his way. But some of it has been written throughout the years in interviews and in his actions, and this chronology brings a lot of that together.

The words on the Hall of Fame Award (presented to him during the CMA telecast in October, 1982) sum up the industry's recognition of his career:

> Marty Robbins is the quintessential entertainer, whose music has delighted audiences everywhere. His Arizona heritage greatly influenced the western ballads he was later to write and record. He won the first Grammy Award for a country song, "El Paso"; was the first Nashville artist to appear in Las Vegas; and was the first person to perform at the new Opry House. One of country's most successful stars, he has won innumerable awards for his recordings, songwriting, and performing.

PART I

BIBLIOGRAPHY

Photo of Marty by Donnie Jennings

1

BIBLIOGRAPHY, 1948–1959

Entertainer Marty Robbins was born Martin David Robinson on September 26, 1925 near Glendale, Arizona and started life with a struggle. By all accounts his early life was impoverished and lacked direction. He had little to say about these days in later years, only noting that they were frequently unhappy. He felt that his father showed little love for him and, while Marty was still a young child, his father abandoned the family, leaving Marty's mother to care for him and his nine sisters and brothers. During a televised interview on a local Nashville show called "Miller and Company" in 1981, Marty recalled that his family had lived in a tent on the desert for a while and that other children at the small school they attended had brought them food so that they would have enough to eat. It had left a lifelong impact on him, he said, because "If you were poor when you were small, and knew what it was like, you don't want to go back to what it was like." And, with characteristic honesty softened with humor, he said that all of this had led him to feel that he would never be financially secure, but he would be sure to buy three tents if he felt himself slipping.

He attended grammar school in Peoria, Arizona and high school a few miles away in Glendale. By his own account he was nearly a juvenile delinquent by the time he was a teenager, skipping school and barely staying on the right side of the law. He said that although he attended several years of high school, he rarely finished a course. He joined the Navy during World War II at the age of 17 and served in the Solomon Islands. During this

Marty at one of his first recording sessions in the early 1950s at the Jim Beck Studio in Dallas. Band members (left to right): Marty, Jimmy Rollins, Joe Knight, and Joe Vincent (seated). (Photo by Joe Knight)

time, he learned to play the guitar and became an amateur boxer. Returning home after his service with no particular ambition for the future, he worked as a laborer in a series of jobs that paid little and usually lasted no longer than it took to collect his first paycheck. He did meet an attractive young lady, still in high school at the time, named Marizona Baldwin. She fondly relates that at that first meeting Marty said to a friend, "I'm going to marry that girl." And he did, on September 27, 1948. The marriage lasted a lifetime.

Marty's entry into show business in 1947 was inauspicious. A country music band leader at a local bar needed a guitar player and Marty was asked to join the group. Shortly after, he also began to sing. At first, he was so shy and embarrassed that he looked down at the floor instead of at the audience. But he soon found he loved the work and to his amazement the pay was more than he could ever have hoped to make in any other job. At first, he performed briefly on the radio under the name of Jack Robinson before taking the permanent stage name of Marty Robbins. In explaining the name change, he always said it was so that his mother wouldn't know what he was doing; his family didn't quite accept singing in bars as proper employment.

Marty joined radio station KTYL in Mesa, Arizona in 1947 and later moved to KPHO in Phoenix in 1948. He was quickly successful in his own radio show, which led to his television show for KPHO-TV called "Chuck Wagon Time." Later, another show called "Western Caravan" followed on the same station. Happy being on radio, his initial reaction to the offer of a television show was adamant: he wanted nothing to do with live television, and he accepted the job only after the station management made the radio show contingent upon his agreement to do the television show as well. His fear of live television lasted a lifetime and he avoided it as much as possible, doing only a few shows and always admitting to overwhelming nervousness.

All of this activity made him a popular personality in the Phoenix area, but he had yet to establish a reputation beyond the local boundaries. The big break Marty needed came in 1951 when national recording star Little Jimmy Dickens stopped by to make an appearance on Marty's television program to publicize a concert. He listened to Marty sing and offered to help. The offer was substantial; he said he would talk to Columbia Records when he got to Los Angeles and see if he couldn't get them to come down and listen to Marty and give him a recording contract. Jimmy was as good as his word and Columbia Records had a new artist on its roster later that year. However, it wasn't until the next year that his first recording was released— "Love me or leave me alone" (April, 1952). A second break came after songwriter/publisher Fred Rose of Acuff-Rose Publishing heard another of Marty's early releases, the self-penned "I'll go on alone" (October, 1952), and flew out to Arizona to sign him to a contract as a songwriter for the music publishing firm. Rose's reputation as one of America's greatest songwriters was so renowned that Marty often said he regarded Rose's attention as the greatest compliment he had ever been paid.

By this time, Marty was attracting a growing following of fans and had made a number of guest appearances on the Grand Ole Opry. On January 19, 1953, he became a permanent member of the prestigious show and moved his family to Nashville soon after. By this time he had a son, Ronny, who had been born July 16, 1949. (A daughter, Janet, would be born in January of 1959.)

From the very first, many of Marty's recordings were his own compositions. By the mid-1950s he was winning "favorite artist" polls. In April, 1955, he was the winner of the Ralph Emery radio poll on WSIX in Nashville as the "Favorite Artist" of his listeners. Along with some of the other country stars such as Johnny Cash, he was an early writer and recorder of rock and roll. Several articles in this bibliography focus particularly on his contributions to the "rockabilly" music style. By now he was also a popular and established headliner on the concert tour circuit; sometimes newcomer Elvis Presley was his opening act.

Marty was recognized as a man of many styles. This versatility made him one of the first "crossover" artists. He released his first Hawaiian recordings in 1954 with the single, "My Isle of Golden Dreams," backed by "Aloha Oe." In 1956 one of the most important stories in the music industry was a song Marty recorded called "Singing the Blues," a huge success that put him at the top of the charts in a big way and won him a coveted "Triple Crown Award" from *Billboard*. Written by a then unknown songwriter named Melvin Endsley, the song was "covered" by Guy Mitchell (also a Columbia Records artist) and both versions vied for airplay and sales in the pop market. Marty followed this success by releasing another Endsley tune, "Knee Deep in the Blues." Surprisingly, this Robbins recording was also immediately covered by Mitchell. Angered at this unexpected repetition, Marty had some heated discussions with Columbia executives and this practice was brought to an end. Then, in 1957, Marty released another of his own compositions, "A White

Marizona and Ronny visited the recording studios to listen to Marty. (Photo by Joe Knight)

Sport Coat (and a Pink Carnation)." It became what today would be called a "monster" hit and was the first of a number of hit teenage-type love songs. Still the premier prom song, it's probably known to every teenager who ever attended a prom. The success of these teen romance songs led to appearances on popular television programs such as The Today Show, The Steve Allen Show, and the Eddie Fisher Show.

By the late 1950s, he had also established his own businesses in Nashville, including Robbins Records (1958) and his own music publishing company. He became one of the first country music artists to hold recording sessions in New York.

The last part of the 1950s brought out two particularly strong loves in Marty's life, his romance with the Old West and his fascination with auto racing. Building and racing micro-midgets occupied much of his free time and served as the basis for a stronger involvement and the larger NASCAR stock cars he would race in the future. Themes of the Old West, however, fitted into his performing style and forever became his favorite music. His first three motion pictures were all low-budget westerns: "Raiders of Old California" (1957), "Badge of Marshall Brennan" (1957), and "Buffalo Gun" (1958). The first two involved straight acting jobs; "Buffalo Gun" was made with Carl Smith and Webb Pierce as co-stars and included a number of songs. Years later, when western songs lost popularity and virtually disappeared for a time, he was often credited with keeping the music alive during a period when no other popular performer would touch it. He finished out the decade with the release of the album "Gunfighter Ballads and Trail Songs" in September of 1959 and the release of the legendary single, "El Paso," in October. By the end of December, the latter recording was nearing the number one position on the charts.

BIBLIOGRAPHY, 1948–1959

Sippel, Johnny. Folk talent and tunes [news column]. *Billboard;* 1948 August 14; 60(33): 31.
Earliest mention of Marty in a national publication. The news column mentions that Martin Robinson is a newcomer to KOY [Phoenix radio].

I'll go on alone / You're breaking my heart. *Billboard;* 1952 November 8: 49.
Single review.

Dee Jay Jamboree [news column]. *Country Song Roundup;* 1952 December; 1(21): 6. Photo included.
Short article about Marty mentions that he wrote his first song, "Heartsick," at age 17 and that it was recorded on the Tennessee label. In the following nine years, the article says, he's written 75 songs. He currently has two radio shows at KPHO in Phoenix and a popular television show at KPHO-TV called "Western Caravan." The article goes on to say that Marty started his career in 1947 with a group of local musicians and then organized a trio with Jimmy Farmer on steel and Floyd Lanning on guitar. KPHO was the first television station in Phoenix and

Marty was the first western singer to appear. His first show, "Chuck Wagon Time," ran 30 minutes a day for a year and a half before being replaced with his current show. He's described as "five feet ten, sandy hair, brown eyes with a flashing smile and the whitest teeth you've ever seen. His personality matches his good looks. He's one of those rare types that both men and women find appealing."

Disc jockey roundup [news column]. *Cowboy Songs;* 1953 March; 1(25): 9.
Note: Illus.
Notes that Marty is from KPHO radio and television in Phoenix; includes information about his early TV program. Includes publicity photo. Among topics covered: the shows "Chuck Wagon Time," "Western Caravan," and early appearances on the Grand Ole Opry. Also mentioned, the "Hollman Hayride."

A half-way chance with you / A castle in the sky. *Billboard;* 1953 May 30: 32, 34.
Single review.

Robbins, Marty. I'll go on alone. *Cowboy Songs;* 1953 May; 1(26): 3.
Note: Lyrics to the song.

Robbins, Marty. I'll go on alone. *Country Song Roundup;* 1953 May; 1(23): 3.
Note: Lyrics to the song.

From the four corners [news column]. *Country Song Roundup;* 1953 June; 1(24): 26.
News column notes that Marty joined the WSM Grand Ole Opry January 19th [1953].

Robbins, Marty. I'll go on alone. *Country Song Roundup;* 1953 June; 1(24): 13.
Note: Lyrics to the song.

Robbins, Marty. I'll go on alone. *Cowboy Songs;* 1953 July; 1(27): 14.
Note: Lyrics to the song.

Popularity poll winners. *Country Song Roundup;* 1953 August; 1(25): 4.
Marty was listed as no. 13 in the poll.

Robbins on the range. *Country Song Roundup;* 1953 August; 1(25): 7.
The article covers Marty's early career; he's called a "new find." It
notes he attended grammar school in Peoria and high school in Glendale. It says his first song, "Heartsick," was written while he was a
teenager, recorded on an independent label, and gained considerable
local popularity. His first radio job was at KTYL in Mesa, Arizona.
From there he went to KPHO, where he organized his own band called
the "K-Bar Cowboys."

Robbins, Marty. I couldn't keep from crying. *Country Song Roundup;*
1953 August; 1(25): 5.
Note: Lyrics to the song.

Artist of the month: Marty Robbins. *Hillbilly and Cowboy Hit Parade;*
1953 Fall; 1(3): 3.
Note: Illus.
Full-page story and large publicity photo. Article notes that Marty has
just completed his first year with Columbia Records, is now on the
Grand Ole Opry, and has his own radio show on WSM, 5:45–6:00 a.m.
The first song he ever wrote was "Heartsick." Additional coverage
about his early professional career in Arizona includes the story about
how Marizona got her name (a combination of the state and county
where she was born).

Robbins, Marty. After you leave. *Cowboy Songs;* 1953 September;
1(28): 24.
Note: Lyrics to the song.

Robbins, Marty. I couldn't keep from crying. *Cowboy Songs;* 1953
September; 1(28): 3.
Note: Lyrics to the song.

Sing me something sentimental/At the end of a long, lonely day. *Billboard;* 1953 September 5: 24, 28.
Two reviews of the single.

[Advertisement]. *Country Song Roundup;* 1953 October; 1(26): 23.
A Columbia Records ad for several singles, including Marty's single,
"A Castle in the sky/A half way chance with you."

Robbins, Marty. Castle in the sky. *Country Song Roundup;* 1953 October; 1(26): 11.
Note: Lyrics to the song.

One of Marty's first publicity pictures after joining the Grand Ole Opry in 1953.

Robbins, Marty. A half way chance with you. *Country Song Roundup;* 1953 October; 1(26): 5.
Note: Lyrics to the song.

Don't make me ashamed/It's a long, long ride. *Billboard;* 1953 November 14: 32.
Single review.

Mr. Teardrop. *Cowboy Songs;* 1953 November; 1(29): 5.
Note: Illus.
This article covers Marty's early life and career.

Robbins, Marty. Castle in the sky. *Cowboy Songs;* 1953 November; 1(29): 27.
Note: Lyrics to the song.

Robbins, Marty. A half way chance with you. *Cowboy Songs;* 1953 November; 1(29): 6.
Note: Lyrics to the song.

Robbins, Marty. I couldn't keep from crying. *Cowboy Songs;* 1953 November; 1(29): 29.
Note: Lyrics to the song.

Robbins, Marty. I've got a woman's love. *Cowboy Songs;* 1953 November; 1(29): 11.
Note: Lyrics to the song.

Robbins, Marty. I'll go on alone. *Country Song Roundup;* 1953 December; 1(27): 11.
Note: Lyrics to the song.

Robbins, Marty. Sing me something sentimental. *Cowboy Songs;* 1953 December; 1(30): 4.
Note: Lyrics to the song.

[Photograph]. *Country Song Roundup;* 1954 January; 1(28): 18.
Small early publicity photos.

Robbins, Marty. At the end of a long, lonely day. *Country Song Roundup;* 1954 January; 1(28): 5.
Note: Lyrics to the song.

Robbins, Marty. At the end of a long, lonely day. *Cowboy Songs;* 1954 January–February; 1(31): 9.
Note: Lyrics to the song.

Robbins, Marty. Sing me something sentimental. *Country Song Roundup;* 1954 January; 1(28): 7.
Note: Lyrics to the song.

Robbins, Marty. Sing me something sentimental. *Cowboy Songs;* 1954 January–February; 1(31): 14.
Note: Lyrics to the song.

1953 in review. *Country Song Roundup;* 1954 February; 1(29): 18.
Marty is one of the artists included in the review.

My isle of golden dreams / Aloha oe. *Billboard;* 1954 February 20: 38.
Single review.

Questions and answers [column]. *Country Song Roundup;* 1954 February; 1(29): 27.
A reader wanted to know if Marty Robbins and Marty Roberts were the same person. Answer: no.

Dee Jay Jamboree [news column]. *Country Song Roundup;* 1954 March/April; 1(30): 18.
Marty just missed getting into the top ten in their recent popularity poll.

Robbins, Marty. Don't make me ashamed. *Country Song Roundup;* 1954 March/April; 1(30): 6.
Note: Lyrics to the song.

Robbins, Marty. It's a long, long ride. *Country Song Roundup;* 1954 March/April; 1(30): 5.
Note: Lyrics to the song.

[Photograph]. *Country Song Roundup;* 1954 May; 1(31): 18.
Photo of Marty and Eddy Arnold with several disc jockeys.

Robbins, Marty. Don't make me ashamed. *Country Song Roundup;* 1954 May; 1(31): 24.
Note: Lyrics to the song.

Robbins, Marty. Don't make me ashamed. *Cowboy Songs;* 1954 May; 1(33): 8.
Note: Lyrics to the song. Cover photo.

Robbins, Marty. It's a long, long ride. *Cowboy Songs;* 1954 May; 1(33): 8.
Note: Lyrics to the song. Cover photo.

Your favorites and mine [news column]. *Cowboy Songs;* 1954 May; 1(33): 26.
Note: Lyrics to the song. Cover photo.
Marty is having success with his new release, "It's a long, long ride."

[Advertisement]. *Cowboy Songs;* 1954 June; 1(34): 25.
An ad for Columbia Records, including Marty's "My isle of golden dreams/Aloha oe."

Pretty words/Your heart's turn to break. *Billboard;* 1954 June 12: 46.
Single review.

Popularity poll. *Country Song Roundup;* 1954 July–August; 1(33): 10–11.
Marty ranked number 10 in the poll.

[Letter to CSR from Marty]. *Country Song Roundup;* 1954 July–August; 1(33): 13.

[Photograph]. *Country Song Roundup;* 1954 July–August; 1(33): 22.
Small publicity photo.

[Small ad for fan club]. *Country Song Roundup;* 1954 July–August; 1(33): 33.

I'm too big to cry/Call me up. *Billboard;* 1954 August 21: 44.
Single review.

[Photograph]. *Country Song Roundup;* 1954 September; 1(34): 4.
Small early photograph.

Robbins, Marty. Pretty words. *Country Song Roundup;* 1954 September; 1(34): 7.
Note: Lyrics to the song.

Robbins, Marty. Pretty words. *Cowboy Songs;* 1954 September–October; 1(37): 4.
Note: Lyrics to the song.

Robbins, Marty. Your heart's turn to break. *Country Song Roundup;* 1954 September; 1(34): 13.
Note: Lyrics to the song.

Robbins, Marty. Your heart's turn to break. *Cowboy Songs;* 1954 September–October; 1(37): 5.
Note: Lyrics to the song.

It's a pity what money can do/Time goes by. *Billboard;* 1954 November 20: 48.
Single review.

Robbins, Marty. Pretty words. *Country Song Roundup;* 1954 November; 1(35): 32.
Note: Lyrics to the song.

WSM talent. *Down Beat;* 1954 November 17; 21: 17.
Article includes Marty.

[Photograph]. Pin up [monthly feature]. *Cowboy Songs;* 1954 December; 1(38): 10.

Robbins, Marty. Call me up (and I'll come calling on you). *Cowboy Songs;* 1954 December; 1(38): 9.
Note: Lyrics to the song.

Robbins, Marty. I'm too big to cry. *Cowboy Songs;* 1954 December; 1(38): 6.
Note: Lyrics to the song.

Robbins reels 'em in. *Hillbilly and Cowboy Hit Parade;* 1954 Winter; 1(8): 2.
Note: Illus.
Article about early recording hits, professional activities in Arizona, and his hobbies (cross-country motorcycle racing and hot rods).

The presidents report on your favorite stars [news column]. *Country Song Roundup;* 1955 January; 1(36): 15.
Reports by fan club presidents include one by Peggy Ann Munson, Marty's fan club president. Her report includes comments about a planned Marty Robbins Day in Glendale, Arizona on September 26, 1955 [Marty's birthday].

Review of 1954. *Country Song Roundup;* 1955 January; 1(36): 18–19.
On the list of Top Male Artists, Marty is number 9.

Robbins, Marty. Call me up (and I'll come calling on you). *Country Song Roundup;* 1955 January; 1(36): 5.
Note: Lyrics to the song. Illus.
Photo included along with words to the song.

Robbins, Marty. I'm too big to cry. *Country Song Roundup;* 1955 January; 1(36): 12.
Note: Lyrics to the song. [Editorial note: Song title incorrectly noted as "To big to cry"].

That's all right/Gossip. *Billboard;* 1955 January 15: 58.
Single review.

Robbins, Marty. Call me up (and I'll come calling on you). *Cowboy Songs;* 1955 February; 1(39): 26.
Note: Lyrics to the song.

That's all right/Gossip. *Billboard;* 1955 February 5: 43.
Single review.

Dee Jay Jamboree [news column]. *Country Song Roundup;* 1955 March; 1(37): 28.
Marty listed as a favorite of a guest disc jockey.

Presidents report on your favorite stars [news column]. *Country Song Roundup;* 1955 March; 1(37): 20.
Article includes a report from Marty's fan club president.

Robbins, Marty. It's a pity what money can do. *Country Song Roundup;* 1955 March; 1(37): 4.
Note: Lyrics to the song.

Robbins, Marty. My funniest experience. *Country Song Roundup;* 1955 March; 1(37): 17.
Note: Illus.
Article includes two stories: 1) When Marty first met his future wife, he mistook Marizona's name for Arizona; 2) hearing himself on the radio for the first time.

Robbins, Marty. Time goes by. *Country Song Roundup;* 1955 March; 1(37): 4.
Note: Lyrics to the song.

That's all right/Gossip. *Country and Western Jamboree;* 1955 March; 1(1): 20.
Single review.

[Photograph]. *Country and Western Jamboree;* 1955 April; 1(2): 33.
Photo of Marty and Ralph Emery. Caption under photo notes that Marty is receiving a scroll for winning "The favorite artist poll" that Ralph conducted on WSIX radio in Nashville.

Pray for me, mother of mine/Daddy loves you. *Billboard;* 1955 April 16: 44.
Single review.

Robbins, Marty. It's a pity what money can do. *Cowboy Songs;* 1955 April; 1(40): 4.
Note: Lyrics to the song.

Robbins, Marty. Time goes by. *Cowboy Songs;* 1955 April; 1(40): 4.
Note: Lyrics to the song.

Presidents report on the stars [news column]. *Country Song Roundup;* 1955 May; 1(38): 23.
Article includes a report from Marty's fan club.

Robbins, Marty. Gossip. *Country Song Roundup;* 1955 May; 1(38): 4.
Note: Lyrics to the song. Illus.
Small photo included along with words to song.

Robbins, Marty. Time goes by. *Country Song Roundup;* 1955 May; 1(38): 26.
Note: Lyrics to the song.

Robbins, Marty. Gossip. *Cowboy Songs;* 1955 June; 1(41): 4.
Note: Lyrics to the song.

TV hits the Opry. *Cowboy Songs;* 1955 June; 1(41): 6.
Note: Illus.
Filming of the TV series, "Stars of the Grand Ole Opry."

It looks like I'm just in your way/I'll love you till the day I die. *Billboard;* 1955 July 9: 44.
Single review.

Robbins, Marty. Pray for me, mother of mine. *Country Song Roundup;* 1955 July; 1(39): 56.
Note: Lyrics to the song.

Rita Robbins. *Country Song Roundup;* 1955 July; 1(39): 38.
Note: Illus.
Story and photo of Rita. [She was Don Winter's sister; no relation to Marty. Don was a long-time member of Marty's band.]

Robbins, Marty. Daddy loves you. *Country Song Roundup;* 1955 July; 1(39): 20.
Note: Lyrics to the song.

Cross country jamboree [news column]. *Country and Western Jamboree;* 1955 August; 1(6): 11.
Marty topped a radio poll from KYOU, Colorado, as the most popular male singer.

[News column]. *Cowboy Songs;* 1955 August; 1(42): 12.
Both sides of Marty's new single, "Pray for me, mother of mine/Daddy loves you," are getting strong air play.

[Photograph]. *Country and Western Jamboree;* 1955 August; 1(6): 28.
Photo of Marty, Ferlin Husky, Carl Smith and part of their bands at the end of a road tour.

Robbins, Marty. Daddy loves you. *Cowboy Songs;* 1955 August; 1(42): 5.
Note: Lyrics to the song.

Robbins, Marty. Pray for me, mother of mine. *Cowboy Songs;* 1955 August; 1(42): 28.
Note: Lyrics to the song.

Cross country jamboree [news column]. *Country and Western Jamboree;* 1955 September; 1(7): 9.
The column notes that "Colonel Tom Parker came through with a top notch show down this way." The show included Marty, Ferlin Husky, and Elvis Presley in Orlando, Florida.

Maybelline/This broken heart of mine. *Billboard;* 1955 September 10: 46.
Single review.

Presidents report on the stars [news column]. *Country Song Roundup;* 1955 September; 1(40): 28.
Fan club reports.

Pretty mama/Don't let me hang around. *Billboard;* 1955 October 29: 48.
Single review.

Maybelline/This broken heart of mine. *Country and Western Jamboree;* 1955 November; 1(9): 23.
Single review.

Tennessee Toddy/Mean mama blues. *Billboard;* 1955 December 31: 32.
Single review.

On the spot [news column]. *Cowboy Songs;* 1956 January; 1(44): 8.
One-page interview with Marty includes photo. Highlights include his early personal life. He joined the Navy at age 17 and saw duty in the South Pacific. He learned to play the guitar while there as a way to pass the time. He provides details on his first jobs. His KPHO-TV show was 15 minutes long, four nights a week. He credits the "great Harry Stone" with giving him his first big break. Hobbies include motorcycles, cars,

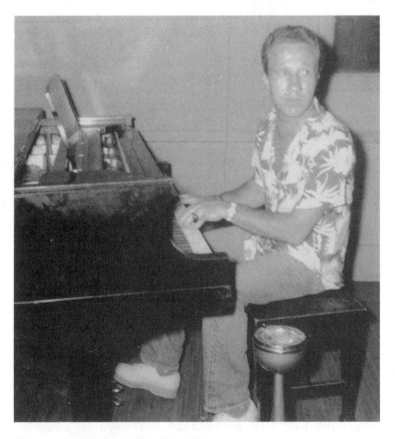

Marty at the piano, 1956. (Photo by Jean Scotte)

boxing, and working out with the WSM softball team. In answer to the question about his greatest honor to date, he responded it was when his hometown (Glendale) declared "Marty Robbins Day" in his honor on his birthday (September 26th).

Pretty mama/Don't let me hang around. *Country and Western Jamboree;* 1956 January; 1(11): 29.
Single review.

Robbins, Marty. This broken heart of mine. *Cowboy Songs;* 1956 January; 1(44): 10.
Note: Lyrics to the song.

Presidents report on the stars [news column]. *Country Song Roundup;* 1956 February; 1(42): 14.
Marty's fan club president reports that he has just toured Canada and that his son Ronnie is in his first year at school.

Reader's choice; the top 20. *Country Song Roundup;* 1956 February; 1(42): 9.
Marty listed as number 13 in the poll.

Mister Teardrop/Long tall Sally. *Billboard;* 1956 March 24: 50.
Single review.

Maybellene goes west. *Hillbilly and Cowboy Hit Parade;* 1956 Spring; 1(14): 23.
Note: Illus.
Standard article on Marty. Phoenix had a "Marty Robbins Day" last year on September 26th; two couples were thanked for helping with the event.

Gillis, F. B. Marty Robbins, the voice of many styles. *Country and Western Jamboree;* 1956 May; 2(3): 7.
Note: Illus.
Recording and career history to date. The article recounts how Marty got his start by filling in for an ailing band member with Frankie Starr's band. He was given a job as a regular member as a guitar player but quickly became popular as a singer with the group. Marty credits three other people with having an influence on his success: Harry Stone of KPHO, Fred Kare (a Phoenix night club owner), and disc jockey Fred Wample, who helped Marty get national attention with his first record, "I'll go on alone."

Robbins, Marty. Don't let me hang around if you don't care. *Cowboy Songs;* 1956 May; 1(46): 23.
Note: Lyrics to the song.

Robbins, Marty. Mean mama blues. *Cowboy Songs;* 1956 May; 1(46): 9.
Note: Lyrics to the song.

Robbins, Marty. Pretty mama. *Cowboy Songs;* 1956 May; 1(46): 14.
Note: Lyrics to the song.

Robbins, Marty. Tennessee Toddy. *Cowboy Songs;* 1956 May; 1(46): 14.
Note: Lyrics to the song.

Respectfully, Miss Brooks/You don't owe me a thing. *Billboard;* 1956 June 23: 54, 58.
Single reviews in both pop and country review sections.

Robbins, Marty. Tennessee Toddy. *Country Song Roundup;* 1956 June; 2(44): 13.
Note: Lyrics to the song.

Mister Teardrop/Long tall Sally. *The Hillbilly-Folk;* 1956 July/September; 3(3): 30.
Single review.

Singing the blues/I can't quit. *Billboard;* 1956 August 18: 68.
Single review.

Singing the blues/I can't quit. *Billboard;* 1956 September 15: 61.
Single review.

Arlene Francis recognizes talent in TV Home Show. *The Country Music Reporter;* 1956 October 6; 1(3): 3.
Arlene Francis in Nashville September 25 with her NBC TV show to tape Opry stars; Marty is included on the list of those performers taped.

Charlie's country chatter [news column]. *Country Song Roundup;* 1956 October; 2(46): 10.
Marty is listed as one of several stars making an unnamed film.

The cracker barrel [news column]. *The Country Music Reporter;* 1956 October 20; 1(4): 5.
Marty's manager, Eddie Crandall, notes that he and his newly named band are on a tour of Texas with Lee Emerson.

Robbins rigs special bus with showers. *The Country Music Reporter;* 1956 October 6; 1(3): 7.
Short piece about interior of the tour bus.

Robbins, Marty. It won't do no good. *Country Song Roundup;* 1956 October; 2(46): 4.
Note: Lyrics to the song.

Robbins, Marty. Mister Teardrop. *Cowboy Songs;* 1956 October; 1(48): 28.
Note: Lyrics to the song.

[Advertisement]. *The Country Music Reporter;* 1956 November 10; 1(5): 5.
Half-page ad by Marty, thanking DJ's for playing "Singing the blues." Includes photo.

[Billboard top chart lists]. *Billboard;* 1956 November 17: 51.
"Singing the blues" tops most of the charts.

[Billboard top country charts]. *Billboard;* 1956 November 24: 47.
"Singing the blues" at the number 1 spot on all country charts.

Cross country jamboree [news column]. *Country and Western Jamboree;* 1956 November; 2(9): 26.
Notes that Marty and Lee Emerson received a lot of attention this past summer with their duet of "I'll know you're gone," backed by "How long will it be."

Marty Robbins 'Blues' near top; thanks DJ's. *The Country Music Reporter;* 1956 November 10; 1(5): 16.

Singing the blues/I can't quit. *Country and Western Jamboree;* 1956 November; 2(9): 20.
Single review.

Singing the blues/I can't quit. *Billboard;* 1956 November 24: 40.
Single review; record listed as a strong pop release.

[Advertisement]. *The Country Music Reporter;* 1956 December 8; 1(7): 3.
Small ad from Marty thanking people for a great year.

[Advertisement]. *The Country Music Reporter;* 1956 December 22; 1(8): 2.
Ad for Marty's new single, "Knee deep in the blues."

[Billboard top charts]. *Billboard;* 1956 December 1: 41.
"Singing the blues" remains at the top of three charts (retail, jukebox, disc jockey charts).

[Billboard top charts]. *Billboard;* 1956 December 15: 60.
"Singing the blues" remains at the top of all three charts.

[Billboard top charts]. *Billboard;* 1956 December 22: 47.
"Singing the blues" remains at the top of all three charts.

Don Law and Marty Robbins have been working hard to rush out Marty's new album. *The Country Music Reporter;* 1956 December 22; 1(8): 2.

Fats and Marty coronations. *Billboard;* 1956 December 1: 14.
Marty won the Billboard Triple Crown Award for "Singing the blues" when it topped all three charts last week (retail, jukebox, and disc jockey charts).

Marty Robbins has new 'Blues' album. *The Country Music Reporter;* 1956 December 8; 1(7): 4.

Robbins, Price, Cash grab lead on Elvis, Singing the blues at top of charts. *The Country Music Reporter;* 1956 December 8; 1(7): 1.

Robbins, Marty. It won't do no good. *Cowboy Songs;* 1956 December; 2(49): 23.
Note: Lyrics to the song.

Robbins, Marty. Lucky, lucky someone else. *Country Song Roundup;* 1956 December; 3(47): 22.
Note: Lyrics to the song.

Robbins, Marty. Lucky, lucky someone else. *Cowboy Songs;* 1956 December; 2(49): 20.
Note: Lyrics to the song.

Robbins, Marty. Respectfully, Miss Brooks. *Country Song Roundup;* 1956 December; 3(47): 11.
Note: Lyrics to the song.

Marty with the producer of most of his early hits, Don Law. (Photo by Joe Knight)

Robbins, Marty. Respectfully, Miss Brooks. *Cowboy Songs;* 1956 December; 2(49): 24.
Note: Lyrics to the song.

Robbins, Marty. You don't owe me a thing. *Country Song Roundup;* 1956 December; 3(47): 17.
Note: Lyrics to the song.

Robbins, Marty. You don't owe me a thing. *Cowboy Songs;* 1956 December; 2(49): 12.
Note: Lyrics to the song.

[Billboard top charts]. *Billboard;* 1957 January 5: 43.
"Singing the blues" still tops all three charts in country music.

Knee deep in the blues/The same two lips. *Billboard;* 1957 January 5: 42.
Single review.

Knee deep in the blues/The same two lips. *Billboard;* 1957 January 12: 46.
Single review.

No "blues" for Marty Robbins. *Folk and Country Songs;* 1957 January; 2(1): 5.
Note: Illus.

Marty Robbins. *Country and Western Jamboree;* 1957 January; 2(11): 46.
Brief biography. Good detail.

[Photograph]. *Country and Western Jamboree;* 1957 January; 2(11): 47.
Early publicity photo.

Marty Robbins almost gave away 'Singing the blues' that won him triple crown. *Nashville Banner;* 1957 January 12; Saturday: 6.
Note: Illus.
Good article about the finding of the song. The award referred to is the Triple Crown Award from *Billboard.* Basic history about Marty's early career and his move to Nashville from Arizona. It says Marty showed up for his first job (with Frankie Starr) with a guitar owned by an older sister. The next day Frankie hired him full time, and took him out and

bought him his own guitar. Photo of Marty and his current band: Jimmy Farmer, Shorty Lavender, Louis Dunn, Hillous Butrum, and Jack Pruett.

[TV appearance] NBC's "Today Show"; 1957 January 22.
Information from the NBC Index to Television Shows. Marty sang "Singing the Blues" on the show.

[Advertisement]. *Country Music Reporter;* 1957 February 2; 1(11): 4.
Ad for the single "Knee deep in the blues."

[Advertisement]. *Country Music Reporter;* 1957 February 16; 1(12): 3.
Ad for "Knee deep in the blues."

Endsley, Melvin. Singing the blues. *Country Song Roundup;* 1957 February; 4(48): 4.
Note: Lyrics to the song.
Words to Marty's biggest hit to date.

Endsley, Melvin. Singing the blues. *Cowboy Songs;* 1957 February; 3(50): 3.
Note: Lyrics to the song. Cover photo of Marty.

Robbins given royal treatment in New York stay. *Country Music Reporter;* 1957 February 2; 1(11): 4.
The article lists the television and radio programs Marty appeared on during his stay in New York.

Robbins, Marty. I can't quit (I've gone too far). *Country Song Roundup;* 1957 February; 4(48): 4.
Note: Lyrics to the song.

Robbins, Marty. I can't quit, I've gone too far. *Cowboy Songs;* 1957 February; 3(50): 3.
Note: Lyrics to the song. Cover photo.

Ackerman, Paul. C & W booms as vital force in music-record business. *Billboard;* 1957 March 23: 79, 86.
Marty, "Singing the blues," and Guy Mitchell included in the article along with others.

[Advertisement]. *Country Music Reporter;* 1957 March 16; 1(14): 6.
Quarter-page ad for "A white sport coat/Grown up tears" release.

[Advertisement]. *Country Music Reporter;* 1957 March 30; 1(15): 2.
Ad/photo for "A white sport coat" single.

[Advertisement]. *Country Music Reporter;* 1957 March 30; 1(15): 5.
Ad for the Robbins/Emerson duet, "Where d'ja go?" Other side is "I
cried like a baby" by Lee Emerson. Photos included.

Country crowds Cindy's Carnegie. *Country Music Reporter;* 1957
March 16; 1(14): 7.
Information about a show featuring Marty, Johnny Cash, and Lee
Emerson.

Country style, USA. *Country Music Reporter;* 1957 March 30; 1(15): 3.
Article about the television series. One of the publicity photos includes
Marty when he was on the program.

Knee deep in the blues/The same two lips. *Country and Western Jamboree;* 1957 March; 2(12): 20.
Single review.

Nash, Murray. Singing the blues. *Country and Western Jamboree;* 1957
March; 2(12): 16, 26.
Article covers Marty's huge success with his latest record. Good publicity photo. Information included: many of Marty's records have been
covered in the pop field; Eddie Crandall is his new manager; he just
made a movie with Web Pierce and Carl Smith for Gannaway Productions; and background information about Guy Mitchell covering his
music.

News from the Grand Ole Opry [news column]. *Country and Western
Jamboree;* 1957 March; 2(12): 10.
Notes Marty's record "Singing the blues" has topped all three *Billboard*
charts for some time. It also notes that Guy Mitchell covered the record
and is also covering Marty's new hit, "Knee deep in the blues."

Grand Ole Opry hits the hit parade. *Folk and Country Songs;* 1957
March; 2(2): 11.
Note: Illus.
Article about the Opry includes information and photo of Marty.

[Photograph]. *Billboard;* 1957 March 23: 79.
Caption under photo says that "Singing the blues" was the top-selling
country record in the first three months of 1957.

Pop and nets grab country talent. *Country Music Reporter;* 1957 March 16; 1(14): 8.
Marty included in article about country stars who are making the pop charts and appearing on television shows.

Robbins named top artist in deejay poll. *Country Music Reporter;* 1957 March 2; 1(13): 1, 4.

Robbins, Butrum team in pubbery. *Country Music Reporter;* 1957 March 30; 1(15): 3.
Marty and Hillous Butrum form Be-Are Music. The article notes they published "Where d'ja go" by Marty and Lee Emerson.

White sport coat/Grown up tears. *Billboard;* 1957 March 9: 52.
Single review. The release is listed as an upcoming pop hit.

White sport coat/Grown up tears. *Billboard;* 1957 March 9: 59.
Single review.

A white sport coat/Grown up tears. *Billboard;* 1957 March 30: 79.
Single review.

Young, Robbins, Cash and Dickens on tour. *Country Music Reporter;* 1957 March 16; 1(14): 7.

[Advertisement]. *Billboard;* 1957 April 6: 45.
Ad for "A white sport coat," with photo.

[Advertisement]. *Billboard;* 1957 April 20: 56.
Ad for "A white sport coat," with photo.

[Advertisement]. *Billboard;* 1957 April 27: 53.
Full-page ad for a Johnny Desmond release of "A white sport coat."

G-G award to Price, Robbins. *Billboard;* 1957 April 6: 20.
Marty Robbins and Ray Price were presented with Golden Guitar Awards from Columbia Records for the sale of a record exceeding $250,000.

"Singing the blues," Marty Robbins. *Hillbilly and Cowboy Hit Parade;* 1957 Spring; 2(18): 2.
Note: Illus.
A half-page article and photo. Mentions Ronnie as singing "Jesus loves me" with Marty.

Acuff-Rose firm boasts stable of 'Hit' writers. *Music Reporter;* 1957 May 11; 1(18): 3.
Marty is included in the article for the songs he has written and the artists who have recorded them.

[Advertisement]. *Billboard;* 1957 May 20: 123.
Full-page ad for Columbia Records artists, including Marty.

Future for country music rosy, says 'Wes' Rose. *Music Reporter;* 1957 May 25; 1(19): 7.
Marty is one of five artists mentioned as having teen popularity.

Green, Ben A. Millions hear Melvin's love songs but . . . he hasn't a girl friend. *Country and Western Jamboree;* 1957 May; 2(14): 8–9, 20, 22–23, 30.
Article about Melvin Endsley and his songwriting. Includes background to writing "Singing the blues" and Marty's discovery of the song and willingness to help Melvin. Photo of Marty and Wesley Rose, among others. Cover photo of Melvin Endsley.

Knee deep in the blues / Same two lips. *Folk and Country Songs;* 1957 May; 2(3): 23.
Single review.

New sound vogue here; takes buyers by storm. *Music Reporter;* 1957 May 25; 1(19): 1, 3.
Marty is one of the performers noted as being successful in the pop field.

[News item]. *Music Reporter;* 1957 May 25; 1(19): 2.
Marty Robbins, Anna Maria Alberghetti, Errol Garner and Martha Raye to guest on Steve Allen Show, May 26.

Pop poop [news column]. *Music Reporter;* 1957 May 25; 1(19): 14.
Marty will be on Steve Allen's show May 26, singing "A white sport coat."

[TV appearance] NBC "The Steve Allen Show"; 1957 May 26.
Information from the NBC Index of Shows.

Charlie's column [news column]. *Music Reporter;* 1957 June 8; 1(20): 2.
The Jimmy Rogers Memorial Day Celebration was held last week and Marty was given the Jimmy Rogers Achievement Award as outstanding male entertainer in country music for the year.

Charlie's column [news column]. *Music Reporter;* 1957 June 22; 1(21): 2.
An item mentions that Marty plans to vacation in Arizona for several weeks to get rid of an asthma condition.

Cross country jamboree [monthly feature]. *Country and Western Jamboree;* 1957 June; 3(3): 13.
Marty and Johnny Cash lead the list of country stars appearing on network television from New York.

Endsley, Melvin. Knee deep in the blues. *Country Song Roundup;* 1957 June; 6(50): 28.
Note: Lyrics to the song.
Words to a hit song recorded by Marty.

Endsley, Melvin. Knee deep in the blues. *Cowboy Songs;* 1957 June; 4(52): 3.
Note: Lyrics to the song.

Green, Ben A. Opry launches greatest season. *Country and Western Jamboree;* 1957 June; 3(3): 22–23.
Article notes that Marty and Ray Price won Golden Guitar Awards from Columbia Records, Marty for "Singing the blues." Photo of Marty, Ray, Hal Cook, and Don Law with the Awards.

New stars soar in '57 DJ poll. *Country and Western Jamboree;* 1957 June; 3(3): 8–9.
Marty is listed as the "number one" Male Singer in poll.

Robbins, Marty. The same two lips. *Cowboy Songs;* 1957 June; 4(52): 3.
Note: Lyrics to the song.

Robbins, Marty. Sugaree. *Country Song Roundup;* 1957 June; 6(50): 30.
Note: Lyrics to the song.

Robbins, Marty. You don't owe me a thing. *Country Song Roundup;* 1957 June; 6(50): 4.
Note: Lyrics to the song.

Robbins, Marty. You don't owe me a thing. *Cowboy Songs;* 1957 June; 4(52): 6.
Note: Lyrics to the song.

A white sport coat/Grown up tears. *Country and Western Jamboree;* 1957 June; 3(3): 24.
Single review.

[Advertisement]. *Music Reporter;* 1957 July 20; 1(23): 6.
Ad, including photo, thanking DJ's for two awards: 1) Most programmed record of the year (for "Singing the blues"), and 2) Most programmed vocalist of the year.

[Advertisement]. *Billboard;* 1957 July 29: 39.
Full page ad for Columbia Records artists, including Marty and Ray Conniff. Includes photos.

C & W cleffers spot six tunes on BB's H.R. of H. *Billboard;* 1957 July 8: 21.
Marty is listed as having several songs on the Pop Honor Role of Hits.

The cracker barrel [news column]. *Music Reporter;* 1957 July 20; 1(23): 6.
Marty made his first Washington (DC) appearance two years ago at the Glen Echo Ballroom; he returned to town last week courtesy of Don Owens of WARL.

First new triple crowns go to Robbins, Coasters, Cole. *Billboard;* 1957 July 15: 21.
New *Billboard* awards to artists who have number 1 songs on charts for three weeks in a row. Marty won for "A white sport coat."

Nets track top artists as audiences cry 'more'. *Music Reporter;* 1957 July 6; 1(22): 1, 3.
Marty among the performers listed; he will appear on the Steve Allen show on NBC-TV.

[News item]. *Music Reporter;* 1957 July 20; 1(23): 6.
The Army has turned "Country Style, USA" into a television series; Marty among artists listed as guests.

[Photograph]. *Hillbilly and Cowboy Hit Parade;* 1957 Summer; 3(19): 26.
Photo of Marty singing.

Teen-age dream/Please don't blame me. *Billboard;* 1957 July 22: 68, 73.
Single reviews. Record reviewed in both the Pop and Country sections.

The early famous publicity photo that went along with his hit of 1957, *A white sport coat (and a pink carnation)*.

1957—Country music's boom year. *Country Song Roundup;* 1957 August; 7(51): 17–18.
Note: Illus.
Article includes photo and mention of Marty.

[Advertisement]. *Music Reporter;* 1957 August 3; 2(1): 9.
Ad for Marty, with photo.

Army's Country Style television series assists in bringing music to the people. *Country and Western Jamboree;* 1957 August; 3(5): 18–19.
Page 19 of article contains a photo of Marty and his band. Band members are identified as Jim Farmer, Shorty Lavender, Louis Dunn, Hillis Butrum, and Jack Pruett.

Dressed up for stardom. *Hit Parade;* 1957 August. n.p. Illus.
Article covers Marty's popularity with teen fans in pop music. It's expected that "A white sport coat (and a pink carnation)" will be his first million seller and biggest hit to date in the pop field.

Music trade paper snobbery for birds; sales show difference. *Music Reporter;* 1957 August 3; 2(1): 1, 3, 8.
Article about the success of country music in the pop area; it says that country artists are now among the best money makers for record companies. Marty listed as one of the most successful artists.

Nita, Rita, and Ruby are singing the new ballad by Marty Robbins called "You came to the prom alone." *Music Reporter;* 1957 August 17; 2(2): 6.
Marty wrote the song.

[Photograph]. *Music Reporter;* 1957 August 31; 2(3): 7.
Photo of Marty and the Glaser Brothers. Caption information mentions that Marty has Robbins Records and is his own A&R man for his companies. The Glasers will record for Robbins Records.

Robbins heads three firms in new trade twist. *Music Reporter;* 1957 August 17; 2(2): 1.
Marty will start his own recording company, music publishing firm, and booking agency in cooperation with Hillous Butrum and Lee Emerson.

Robbins, Marty. The tears behind the smile. *Country Song Roundup;* 1957 August; 7(51): 5.
Note: Lyrics to the song.

Marty at his LEEMART Agency office in Nashville, 1956. (Photo by Jean Scotte)

Robbins, Marty. The tears behind the smile. *Cowboy Songs;* 1957 August; 5(53): 3.
Note: Lyrics to the song.

Robbins, Marty. A white sport coat. *Country Song Roundup;* 1957 August; 7(51): 4.
Note: Lyrics to the song.

Robbins, Marty. A white sport coat and a pink carnation. *Cowboy Songs;* 1957 August; 5(53): 3.
Note: Lyrics to the song.

[Advertisement]. *Music Reporter;* 1957 September 21; 2(5): 7.
A Robbins Records ad for a Glaser Brothers release.

[Advertisement]. *Music Reporter;* 1957 September 28; 2(6): 3.
A half-page ad for Robbins Records and a Glaser Brothers release.

[Advertisement]. *Music Reporter;* 1957 September 30; 2(7): 4.
A half-page ad for Robbins Records and the Glaser Brothers.

Charlie's column [news column]. *Music Reporter;* 1957 September 30; 2(7): 2.
Photo of Marty and information about his new record company.

The country's toast from coast tò coast (top ten hitmakers). *Folk and Country Songs;* 1957 September; 2(5): 18.
Marty is included in the article.

The cracker barrel [news column]. *Music Reporter;* 1957 September 14; 2(4): 6.
Marty, George Jones, Johnny Horton, Bobby Helms, and Jimmy C. Newman are all being booked by the Lee-Mart Agency headed by Lee Emerson (and co-owned by Marty). The Lee-Mart name is a combination of their two names.

Cross country jamboree [news column]. *Country and Western Jamboree;* 1957 September; 3(6): 17.
A news item mentions that "A white sport coat" has been on *Billboard*'s top charts recently and that Marty recently toured Canada.

First Robbins artist goes on Godfrey show. *Music Reporter;* 1957 September 28; 2(6): 7.
The Glaser Brothers appeared on Arthur Godfrey's show September 23rd.

Labels ride country talent "gravy train." *Music Reporter;* 1957 September 14; 2(4): 1, 4.
Marty is listed among the country artists who have become big money makers in the pop field.

Music's segregation fades into oblivion. *Music Reporter;* 1957 September 28; 2(6): 1, 7.

[Photograph]. *Hillbilly and Cowboy Hit Parade;* 1957 Fall; 4(20): 26.
Photo of Marty holding the Golden Guitar Award.

[Advertisement]. *Music Reporter;* 1957 October 28; 2(21): 7.
One-half-page ad for the Emerson-Shucher Agency, including a photo of Marty and a listing of the talent booked through the agency.

CSR's 1957 popularity poll winners. *Country Song Roundup;* 1957 October; 8(52): 14–15.
Marty is listed as number 5 in the poll.

Emerson-Shucher form new agency. *Music Reporter;* 1957 October 14; 2(9): 6.
Lee Emerson has formed a new talent agency; he will continue to manage Marty Robbins, and others.

Marty sports a hit. *Country Song Roundup;* 1957 October; 8(52): 11.
Note: Illus.
Article about Marty's current hit, "A white sport coat"; also mentions earlier hits. Noted, his appearance on Steve Allen's NBC Sunday night television show.

Robbins, Marty. The tears behind the smile. *Country Song Roundup;* 1957 October; 8(52): 6.
Note: Lyrics to the song.

Robbins, Marty. A white sport coat. *Country Song Roundup;* 1957 October; 8(52): 9.
Note: Lyrics to the song.

Story of my life/Once a week date. *Billboard;* 1957 October 7: 62, 67.
Single reviews in both the pop and country sections.

[Advertisement]. *Billboard;* 1957 November 4: 27.
Marty is one of several artists featured in a Columbia Records ad.

[Advertisement]. *Music Reporter;* 1957 November 11; 2(13): 23.
Half-page ad from Marty thanking DJ's for their support.

Merged singing styles now bring joy to music feudists. *Music Reporter;* 1957 November 11; 2(13): 20.
Marty among those listed as being in the forefront of the change.

The story of my life/Once a week date. *Billboard;* 1957 November 11: 124.
Single review.

Charlie's column [news column]. *Music Reporter;* 1957 December 16; 2(18): 2.
Rosalind Ross recently signed Marty to a GAC pact.

Cross country jamboree [monthly column]. *Country and Western Jamboree;* 1957 Winter; 3(7): 16.
Marty Robbins and others have recently appeared on feature television shows.

Robbins, Marty. Please don't blame me. *Country Song Roundup;* 1957 December; 9(53): 4.
Note: Lyrics to the song.

Robbins, Marty. The tears behind the smile. *Cowboy Songs;* 1957 December; 6(54): 10.
Note: Lyrics to the song.

Robbins, Marty. Teen age dream. *Country Song Roundup;* 1957 December; 9(53): 5.
Note: Lyrics to the song.

Robbins, Marty. A white sport coat and a pink carnation. *Cowboy Songs;* 1957 December; 6(54): 6.
Note: Lyrics to the song.

Marty Robbins. *Country and Western Music Stars;* 1958; 1(1): 15.
Note: Illus.
Good basic facts about early career. It notes that Marty's idol was Gene Autry and his desire to become a western singer came from this.

[Advertisement]. *Music Reporter;* 1958 January 6; 2(21): 4.
Half-page ad from Robbins Records featuring Phil Gray and the Go-Boys.

[Advertisement]. *Music Reporter;* 1958 January 20; 2(23): 7.
Large ad from Robbins Records for Phil Gray and the Go-Boys.

Charlie's column [news column]. *Music Reporter;* 1958 February 3; 2(25): 2.
Small photo of Marty and comments about his new album, "Songs of the islands."

Robbins, Marty. Please don't blame me. *Country Song Roundup;* 1958 February; 10(54): 17.
Note: Lyrics to the song.

Robbins, Marty. Teen age dream. *Country Song Roundup;* 1958 February; 10(54): 13.
Note: Lyrics to the song.

Songs of the islands. *Music Reporter;* 1958 February 3; 2(25): 6.
Album review.

The story of my life, by Marty Robbins. *Country Song Roundup;* 1958 February; 10(54): 6.
Note: Illus.
Marty gives details about his early life, saying he sometimes calls himself a "desert rat" and that he has a twin sister five minutes older than himself.

[Advertisement]. *Country and Western Jamboree;* 1958 Spring; 3(8): 87.
An ad by Marty thanking fans for their support for the year; includes photo.

[Advertisement]. *Music Reporter;* 1958 March 3; 2(29): 6.
Full-page ad for Robbins Records and the Glaser Brothers.

Charlie's column [news column]. *Music Reporter;* 1958 March 3; 2(29): 2.
Marty will sing "The story of my life" on the Eddie Fisher Show on NBC-TV March 4, and will appear on the Ed Sullivan Show on CBS-TV March 3rd. [Editorial note: a letter from Sullivan Productions in February of 1988 indicated they could find no record that Marty ever appeared on the "Ed Sullivan Show."]

Marty Robbins, Opry part. *Nashville Banner;* 1858 March 3.
Marty was fired from the Opry in a dispute with the management.

Maples, Bill. Marty Robbins fired from Opry; argument brings "prima donna" charge from management. *The Tennessean;* 1958 March 3.
Long article detailing the dispute.

Charlie's column [news column]. *Music Reporter;* 1958 March 3; 2(29): 2.
The Wilburn Brothers recorded "My baby ain't my baby no more," published by Marty's Be-Are Music.

Just married / Stairway to love. *Billboard;* 1958 March 10: 50, 56.
Single reviews in both the pop and country sections.

Maples, Bill. Marty, the Opry together again! *The Tennessean;* 1958
March 7.
Marty is back on the Opry after settling the dispute with Opry
management.

Marty Robbins, 'Opry' bosses bury hatchet. *Billboard;* 1958 March 10:
4, 12.
Marty was fired Saturday (March 1) after heated discussions with the
Opry management. The dispute was settled and he was re-hired on
Thursday, March 6th.

Robbins, Marty. Please don't blame me. *Cowboy Songs;* 1958 March;
7(55): 4.
Note: Lyrics to the song.

Robbins, Marty. Teen age dream. *Cowboy Songs;* 1958 March; 7(55):
21.
Note: Lyrics to the song.

[Photograph]. *Hillbilly and Cowboy Hit Parade;* 1958 Spring; 6(22):
25.
Photo of Marty Robbins and Ferlin Husky.

Sholes, Steve. The new stars determine evolution of C & W music.
Country and Western Jamboree; 1958 Spring; 3(8): 42–43, 92.
Note: Photo of Marty on p. 43.

Story of my life / Once a week date. *Cowboy Songs;* 1958 March; 7(55):
15.
Note: Illus.
Single review.

Top management agency sets tours for country music stars. *Country and
Western Jamboree;* 1958 Spring; 3(8): 46–47, 92.
Note: Photo of Marty on p. 47.
Marty briefly included in article.

[Advertisement]. *Music Reporter;* 1958 June 2; 2(42): 13.
Photo and ad for Marty and record "Just married."

[Advertisement]. *Music Reporter;* 1958 June 16; 2(44): 4.
Half-page ad for Robbins Records and the Glaser Brothers.

[Advertisement]. *Music Reporter;* 1958 June 30; 2(46): 7.
Full-page ad for three Robbins Records releases.

Charlie's column [news column]. *Music Reporter;* 1958 June 2; 2(42): 14.
Marty will be a guest on Red Foley's radio program June 7th.

Jubilee TV'er looms as big "country" biz. *Music Reporter;* 1958 June 2; 2(42): 13.
Article about the Country Music Jubilee TV show out of Springfield, Missouri. Marty listed as one of past guests.

The man with a heart. *Cowboy Songs;* 1958 June; 8(56): 13.
Note: Cover photo.
The article includes a description about starting Be-Are Music with Hillous Butram. The name is a combination of Butram and Robbins. It also recounts how Marty discovered the Glaser Brothers while on a tour. An early photo of Marty and the Glaser Brothers is included.

Marty Robbins signs with Denny Bureau. *Music Reporter;* 1958 June 2; 2(42): 14.

Robbins gains strength; Nashville hub of indies. *Music Reporter;* 1958 June 30; 2(46): 4.
General overview of Marty's businesses and details about Eddie Crandall's job. Photo of Robbins Records office.

Robbins team . . . torrid. *Music Reporter;* 1958 June 30; 2(46): 1.
Front-page photo of Marty and Eddie Crandall, new manager and vice-president of Robbins Records.

Robbins, Marty. Miss me just a little. *Cowboy Songs;* 1958 June; 8(56): 12.
Note: Lyrics to the song. Cover photo.

Country clippings [news column]. *Music Reporter;* 1958 July 7; 2(47): 14.
Jerry Mason signed to Robbins Records.

Nelson made sales, promotion manager at Robbins. *Music Reporter;* 1958 July 7; 2(47): 13.
Pat Nelson of Robbins Records.

Marty guesting on Red Foley's show. (Photo from the Country Music Foundation)

[Photograph]. *Country and Western Jamboree;* 1958 Summer; 4(1): 33.
Photo of Marty in performance.

She was only seventeen (he was one year more)/Sittin' in a tree house.
Billboard; 1958 July 14: 36, 45.
Single review; release covered in both the pop and country sections.

Sittin' in a tree house/She was only seventeen. *Music Reporter;* 1958
July 14; 2(48): 10.
Single review.

Robbins, Marty. Sweet lies. *Cowboy Songs;* 1958 August; 9(57): 23.
Note: Lyrics to the song.

"Country America" on film to get national exposure. *Music Reporter;*
1958 September 15; 3(7): 13.
Produced by KABC-TV; to be syndicated nationally. Marty is announced as a future guest.

Ain't I the lucky one/The last time I saw my heart. *Billboard;* 1958
October 27: 44.
Single review (in the pop music section).

Cigarettes and coffee blues. *Music Reporter;* 1958 October 13; 3(11):
10.
Single review. The song, written by Marty, is the latest release by Lefty
Frizzell.

[Advertisement]. *Music Reporter;* 1958 November 17; 3(16): [10].
Half-page ad, including photo, for new release.

Charlie's corner [news column]. *Music Reporter;* 1958 November 10;
3(15): 2.
Eddie Wolpin of Famous Music Corporation is heavily promoting Marty's new single, "The last time I saw my heart."

Marty doesn't miss. *Cowboy Songs;* 1958 November; 10(58): 7.
Note: Illus.
Interview includes comments about forming Robbins Records. A photo
of Marty with Ferlin Husky is included.

MR "Hit" awards prime interest at CMDJ Convention. *Music Reporter;* 1958 November 24; 3(17): 1, 14.

Photos of the 12 top money makers for the year on p. 1; Marty is included.

Music Reporter recaps '58's top country money-makers. *Music Reporter;* 1958 November 17; 3(16): [48].
Article includes photo of Marty and mentions that he was one of the top artists.

Pin up of the month [Photograph]. *Country Song Roundup;* 1958 November; 10(57): 24.
Note: Illus.
Full-page photo of Marty.

Robbins, Marty. She was only seventeen. *Country Song Roundup;* 1958 November; 10(57): 4.
Note: Lyrics to the song.

None mightier than Marty, the music maker. *Hillbilly and Cowboy Hit Parade;* 1958/1959 Winter; 6(25): 25.
Note: Illus.

Vito's real hoss on the Opry stage. *The Tennessean;* 1958 December 28: 7F [Music City Beat column].
Marty is included in the article.

The hanging tree / The blues country style. *Billboard;* 1959 January 19: 50.
Single review in the pop music section.

[Photograph]. *Country and Western Jamboree;* 1959; Yearbook(v. 5): 49.
Full-page photo.

Pure country music. *Country Song Roundup;* 1959 January; 11(58): 18–19.
Note: Illus.
Article includes photo and comments about Marty.

Robbins, Marty. She was only seventeen. *Country Song Roundup;* 1959 January; 11(58): 13.
Note: Lyrics to the song.

Robbins, Marty. She was only seventeen, he was one year more. *Cowboy Songs;* 1959 January; 11(59): 6.
Note: Lyrics to the song.

Charlie's corner [news column]. *Music Reporter;* 1959 February 23; 3(30): 20.
Marty sang "The hanging tree" on 'Country America' recently.

How country music fared in 1958. *Country Song Roundup;* 1959 March; 11(59): 10.

[Photograph]. *Hillbilly and Cowboy Hit Parade;* 1959 Spring; 7(26): 17.
Photo of Marty and a DJ at a station interview.

I say—"Grand Opera!" *The Tennessean;* 1959 May 10: 8G [Music City Beat column].
Marty is included in the article.

Cap and gown/Last night about this time. *Billboard;* 1959 June 1: 50.
Single review.

Last night about this time/Cap and gown. *Music Reporter;* 1959 June 1; 3(44): 8.
Single review.

Marty Robbins hangs up a hit. *Cowboy Songs;* 1959 July; 11(62): 4.
Note: Illus.
Article highlights the success of "The hanging tree" single.

Marty Robbins, mile of smile (Marty, a smile and a song). *Country Song Roundup;* 1959 July; 11(61): 12.
Note: Illus.
Article includes photo of Marty, Mitch Miller, and Faron Young.

Pick country music king for 1959. *Country Song Roundup;* 1959 July; 11(61): 22.
Note: Illus.
Marty one of top artists listed; photo included.

[Advertisement]. *Music Reporter;* 1959 August 3; 4(1): 31.
Full-page ad, with photo, for Marty and his new release, "Cap and gown."

Swingin' with Marty. *Folk and Country Songs;* 1959 August; 4(17): 26.
Note: Illus.

Robbins, Marty. Baby, I need you. *Cowboy Songs;* 1959 September; 11(63): 26.
Note: Lyrics to the song.

Filming starts on "Country America." *Music Reporter;* 1959 October 5; 4(10): 12.
The TV series is being filmed at KABC-TV in Hollywood by Mobile Video Tape, Inc. for national distribution. Marty is listed among guests.

Saga of the sports coats. *The Tennessean;* 1959 October 19: 9F.

[Advertisement]. *Music Reporter;* 1959 November 9; 4(15): 12.
Half-page ad, including photos, for Marty and his new release, "El Paso."

Country clippings [news column]. *Music Reporter;* 1959 November 2; 4(14): 14.
Marty and the Glaser Brothers completed a tour through Texas last week.

Country music's king for 1959 is Johnny Cash. *Country Song Roundup;* 1959 November; 11(63): 26–27.
Note: Illus.
Article includes photo of Marty.

Country stars lead the "pop" music parade. *Cowboy Songs;* 1959 November; 11(64): 16–17.
Note: Illus.

El Paso/Running gun. *Billboard;* 1959 November 2: 43.
Single review.

Jordanaires, prisoners of ability. *The Tennessean;* 1959 November 8.
Article includes background information about their work with Marty on his recordings.

[Photograph]. *Cowboy Songs;* 1959 November; 11(64): 20.
Photo of Marty being interviewed by WSM DJ Joe Rider.

Robbins, Marty. Sugaree. *Country Song Roundup;* 1959 November; 11(63): 11.
Note: Lyrics to the song.

Robbins, Marty. Sugaree. *Cowboy Songs;* 1959 November; 11(64): 11.
Note: Lyrics to the song.

Pat A. meets Pat B. again. *The Tennessean;* 1959 December 6.

Ray Price stays faithful to "Country." *The Tennessean;* 1959 December
13: 19 F.
Article includes Marty.

Marty Robbins is going up-up. *The Tennessean;* 1959 December 27.

Country artists hot on "Hot 100" chart. *Billboard;* 1959 December 28:
3.
Article covers several artists. Notes that "El Paso" is number 2 on the
pop chart this week and that "Gunfighter ballads and trail songs" is on
the top part of the album chart.

2

DON WINTERS REMEMBERS
MARTY ROBBINS

I had a chance to visit with Don Winters on his farm last October. It was a cold, brisk, sunny late afternoon. A typical fall day. I drove out to Don's place and met him as he was coming down from the hill where his house was under construction. It seemed to me that everything was knee-deep in mud, and I was wearing tennis shoes when boots were clearly called for. Don suggested we sit in an open shed where he stores some of his performing equipment. The shed had electricity there and I could plug in my tape recorder. The interview went for about an hour and by the time we finished, I knew what it felt like to be chilled to the bone, and so did he. So this interview runs as long as we could both stand the cold and discomfort of sitting on various pieces of farm equipment.

Don's easy to interview. You can hand him a microphone to a tape recorder and ask him to talk into it and give you good sound. He's cooperative and relaxed about the whole thing. Not all performers are so accommodating about the interview process. Don worked with Marty for many years and was one of the few people to spend time with Marty both on and off the stage.

BP: Don, how did you meet Marty?

Don: I met him at WSM when I went to audition for the Grand Ole Opry. They had Georg D. Hay. They called him "The Judge"; he used to take care of people who came to audition for the Opry. And I was one of those people . . . didn't know any-body. When I auditioned, I was standing around talking to Judge Hays and Marty walked in.

BP: What year was this?

Don: 1953. The Judge introduced me to Marty and I'd heard Marty's record "I'll Go On Alone" at home in Florida before I'd come up to Nashville. And I'd told my wife, "That guy's gonna be your next super star right there. The next big country singer is going to be Marty Robbins because he's got that feeling in his voice."

Anyhow, Marty, the Judge, and I talked for about 30 minutes. A few days later I went back home to Miami and then came back about six months later. I ran into Marty and what really impressed me was that Marty hollered at me and remembered my name and everything. We began to hang out a little bit together and we would go places where Marty's friends had little night spots. Marty didn't drink but he always went to the night spots. He would play steel guitar and I'd sing. He loved to play steel guitar. We'd do this two or three nights a week sometimes.

BP: Were you married then?

Don: Oh, yes. I got married in 1949.

After we met, Marty and I became "big brothers." Spent a lot of time together. He'd tell me about songs he was writing and I'd tell him about songs I was writing. We'd get together and sing songs to each other. I'd just got a contract with Decca Records—it's MCA Records now—and I'd recorded a song with Webb Pierce called "I Ain't Never" which turned out to be one of the biggest records Webb ever had. It got me the contract with Decca. I had just recorded it when I went to work for Marty. A thing came out called "Too Many Times," which was another top ten record for me. About a year after I went to work for him, people tried to get me to go out on my own, do my own thing. I said,

"No, I like working with Marty too much." So, I hung in there with him.

I probably had four or five records in the top 20–25 for several years in a row. But I loved working with Marty; he and I had a good time and enjoyed working with each other, I guess. I enjoyed it because of the fun we had. We probably laughed more than any other two men in the world.

In 1960 he asked me to go to work with him and I did. It was September and "Don't Worry" had just come out. We had an agreement that I could sing my records on his show. He made me a featured artist on his show from day one.

I was gonna play guitar with him and sing harmony. The first time I played rhythm guitar on stage, he turned around to me and said, "Back up a little bit." So I backed up a little and he said, "Back up a little more, I can still hear you!" (Don is laughing at this point.) I finally backed up until I was off stage, and he said, "That's better." He told me, "Sing from now on and forget about playing guitar!" He didn't like my rhythm playing at all!

BP: Who were the band members then?

Don: At that time it was Joe Babcock; he sang harmony with us. Bill Johnson, who is a friend of mine. We went to work for Marty at the same time. He played steel guitar and actually sang some harmony with us. Jack Pruett was working with us. Louie Dunn was playing drums.

Bobby [Sykes] was not with us then. He had worked with Marty a few months before for a little while. Not very long. Sometimes they didn't see "eye to eye," and Bobby would quit or get fired a few times. They were both kind of hot tempered and neither one would give in. But they both loved each other. They would always make up right quick. Marty was one of these guys, if he had something to say, he'd say it. I guess we were both like that. I guess Bobby was too, you see. The only difference was that Bobby would get mad and pout about it. And I'd be the kind to say it and that was it. Marty the same way. We'd never really get mad at each other. We would have some strong arguments. But we never really got mad at each other.

Marty would never say, "I'm the boss and we'll do it my way." We knew he was the boss and we tried to do it his way. But if we thought it was wrong, well, I'd tell him.

BP: Can you give me an example?

Don: Well, like on the farm. If Marty wanted something done and it was wrong, like cutting hay, I'd argue with him.

BP: Argue over cutting hay?

Don: Yeah. We'd argue over cutting hay a lot!

BP: What was there to argue about?

Don: The time to cut it. The time to get it up. The way we cut it. He had his own way he wanted to do things. But I think I showed him in the long run. 'Cause I'd get out and ask these farmers about the best way of doing it.

BP: You lived on Marty's farm?

Don: Yes, I lived on the farm with Marty for 12 years.

BP: When did you start living out there?

Don: We moved out there about 11 years after I went to work for him. Had our own house on the farm. In 1970, right after his first heart attack and operation. He asked me to come out there because he and I practically went everywhere together. My wife once said that he and I spent more time together than we did with our wives, which is just about the truth. Just about everywhere Marty went from 1970 I was with him, right up to when he died.

We went to California, to Florida, and went racing, and would hang out here in town. We'd go shopping here in town for Christmas gifts. Go downtown and sit around restaurants and chat with people. It was good public relations for Marty. He made lots and lots of very good friends, like with the college kids. They all loved him very much. We'd go to some of the restaurants where the college kids were. We'd sit around and talk with football players, basketball players. I remember one time at an old Lums, we had probably 15 to 20 tables full of college kids talking to Marty. They were a great bunch of kids.

BP: What was touring like in 1960? What did you tour in?

Don: What did we tour in? I shall never forget! We toured in a Mercury station wagon. A blue Mercury station wagon.

BP: All of you in one car?

Don: All of us. You talk about miserable! We probably traveled in that thing two and a half to three years. Pulled a trailer behind it. We went from one side of the country to the other and across Canada.

I remember the Glaser Brothers, when they got out of the army they came back and toured with us for a while. I think we rented another automobile or Marty bought it. We traveled in two cars then, but it didn't last long. They wanted to go on to different things.

BP: Who drove?

Don: All of us. We'd take turns driving. I'll never forget one night, I'd just quit driving and Jack Pruett had started his turn driving. I'd dozed off to sleep in the front seat and all of a sudden he pulled off the road at a place to get a cup of coffee and he was circling around looking for a parking place. I came up off that seat just screaming bloody murder! I thought we were going off a cliff, the way it felt going in a circle! I believe that was one of the scariest times I ever had in an automobile, coming out of a sleep and him circling around and the lights flashing in my face.

We were always, always laughing. With Marty it was like a 23-year vacation. We spent a lot of time having fun. Everything was fun. Marty told me one time, "When it gets to be work, I'm quittin'." I agreed with him; in fact, we made a pact on it.

BP: Was it true that Marty slept very little, only two or three hours a night?

Don: From the time I knew him until he died he was that way. He'd sleep an hour or two and that would be it.

BP: Why do you think he was that way?

Don: I've always thought Marty had one of the most creative minds in the world. People never really recognized that. I think that Marty wrote the greatest song that was ever written and I think he was the greatest songwriter, bar none, that ever lived.

Now you can talk about these other guys who have hit songs, but they're just songs that happen to "catch on" a little bit as far as I'm concerned. But Marty wrote stories. And the other guys, God bless 'em, I'm behind them 100%, but I still don't think there's a songwriter in the world that can compare to Marty Robbins in writing a good, interesting story. And I'm talking about a song that tells something from beginning to end.

Most songs tell a little bit; they've got their "kick" lines in 'em and that, to me, is about it. I don't see a whole lot of story in the songs these days. Or, for that matter, too many of the songs back in the old days. Marty started writing his western stories; that's when it all came together.

BP: Which do you consider his best songs?

Don: El Paso; El Paso City; Devil Woman; Don't Worry; My Woman, My Woman, My Wife; You Gave Me A Mountain. I think one of the greatest songs Marty wrote in his career was one called "Life." It never did get off the ground (as far as sales went). That was when he was with MCA Records. It was one of the prettiest, one of the greatest songs ever written. But it never did go anywhere. It never got the chance, I don't guess, that the rest of them got. Of course, nowadays if you don't have the money behind the song to get it played, nothing happens. Probably more hit records hit the trash can than hit the air, if you stop and think about it. And I've had a lot of DJ's tell me the same thing. Without that money behind you, and certain magazines, you aren't going to get anywhere in all this. That's the pitiful part about it.

BP: What was the difference between touring back then and doing the same thing now?

Don: Well. If a guy had a hit record then, he done it on his own. Most of the DJs back in those days gave a record a chance. I agree that there are more records these days than back then, but they could still review them today if they wanted to. They're getting paid to review them enough to tell whether or not it's got hit potential. But if a record is on a new label or a small label, they won't even listen to it, much less give it air play. If you're a new label, you've got to do something to call attention to your records because they won't even listen to them. It's all major label stuff. It's not near as good today as it was back in the old days, the 1950s and 1960s. Because back in those days, a song made it because it was good. Nowadays it's because the song's got money behind it. I guarantee you that most of the records in the top ten are there because they got money behind them. The public don't know. Some of them are getting wise. It's helping the cassette tape business. If the people don't hear what they want on the radio, they will go and buy a cassette tape of what they do want to hear, and listen to it at home or in the car. They won't even listen to the radio. I don't listen to it much any more.

The "Top 10" is supposed to be a combination of air play and sales. But the big companies will only give radio stations certain records to play. That way they make sure they will get certain

songs on the charts. Pay-play. They were supposed to have
stopped payola years ago, but it's bigger today than it ever has
been.

BP: What was Marty's typical audience like?

Don: We mostly played clubs and concert halls or arenas. Sometimes we even played school gyms. We played lots of state and
county fairs in the summer. Boy, were they hot! Once in a while
we would get caught in the rain, but you had to stay and complete
the show because that's what the fans came for. Marty would play
out in the rain under an umbrella if he had to. The fans usually
stayed so we had to. And by the end of the show we would all be
wet! It was fun.

As to what Marty's fans were like, when Marty hit the stage
they would go crazy! They just loved him. I think Marty's popularity was as high as it had ever been when he passed away. I
always thought Marty had the most loving fans in the world.

BP: Why do you think that was?

Don: It wasn't a put-on with Marty like it is with some people.
He loved his fans very much. I guess when you look at it, everyone is peculiar in some way. Marty was no exception. Marty was
a peculiar type person; he had his own little pet peeves and all.
He never could stand somebody coming around and really making over him real big. It bugs me too. You don't want that,
especially from somebody you don't even know. That's one of
the few things I've ever seen Marty get mad about. That and
somebody bugging him while he was on stage. He would tell
them to sit down and shut up! But you get those kind of people
anywhere you go.

BP: What was Marty's attitude toward his fans?

Don: Marty *always* appreciated the public and the fans making
life easy for him, giving him a good life. We talked about that so

much. They gave him the things he wanted in life, and his family too. And he loved them for it. And I loved them for it. At the same time they made it nice for me too. But that's not just it. I love them because they're good people. I've made some good friends from the people who came to see us over the years.

Marty came from a poor family and when he started getting the nice things in life, he really appreciated it. He's not like a lot of those people who get a chance to do something in life when they don't have anything, and the first thing they will do is get greedy. Sometimes they mess up their lives and other people's lives too. They're never satisfied.

Marty always wanted to give people a good, clean show. He never allowed drinking before a show. He didn't drink himself. He got high on stage and sometimes people thought he had been drinking. But he would just get a little silly because he was enjoying himself so much.

BP: Did you play the Las Vegas dates with Marty?

Don: Oh, yes. Marty was the first country music star to headline in the big hotels in Las Vegas. And then he started breaking all the records on top of that. When Marty and Elvis worked there at the same time, they would complement each other crowd-wise. Marty's first crowd would go see Elvis' second show . . . and the same way with Elvis. His first crowd would come and see our second show. We set all kinds of attendance records. I guess some of them still hold.

BP: When I talked to Tommy Thomas, who owned the Palomino Club in Los Angeles, he said that Marty was one of the few stars who would come and listen to the newcomers. But he said, "Marty always brought his two boys with him and one sat on each side of him." Why did you and Bobby do that?

Don: I always stuck close to Marty in case anyone got smart with him. They could hit on me while he was running! (Laughs). I had a few little scraps with Marty now and then. Nothing major.

When we were touring, Marty would always stand back by the curtain in the back and listen to the acts that opened for us. He wanted to hear newcomers and see what they were doing, to hear their songs. He cared. And he always tried to be of some help to them. I know there was a whole bunch of them he tried to help years ago. He must have recorded fifty or sixty sessions of newcomers. He would give them the tapes, after spending all that money on them. I never knew what happened to most of them. Some of them put him down because nothing got done after that. But all he said he would do was try. They got bitter because they didn't make it, rather than being thankful that someone tried. But he wouldn't let it bother him and would go right on trying to help the next one that come along.

BP: Were you with Marty during his foreign trips?

Don: Yes. Neither Marty nor I was much of a tourist. We wouldn't go out much and look around. We never took pictures.

BP: How did you like England?

Don: Great! Marty would get a standing ovation every time! We had great fans over there. I'd like to go back myself some day.

BP: You went to a lot of the auto races with Marty?

Don: That's right. All of them over the years. As a matter of fact, I've got one of his old midgets out back in the shed. He built a track and raced midgets on weekends years ago.

BP: Did you ever want to race stock cars yourself?

Don: Never! They're too fast for me. The big ones go pretty fast. In the little cars you never got a chance to go that fast. The danger was not that great.

BP: What did you do when you went along?

Don: Just company. I'd take care of him. Pals. We just enjoyed each other's company. I would do some of the running around for him if something needed to be done and he had to be at the track.

BP: How did Marty get along with the drivers?

Don: He was friends with all of them. Darrell Waltrip, Richard Petty, I think, was one of his favorite people because Richard was a gentleman, and Marty respected that. Marty never liked smart aleck people. Marty was a gentleman. He liked Bobby Allison, Donnie Allison, Cale Yarborough, David Pearson, Bill Elliott. But I think his favorite was Richard Petty.

We would sit around the motel or pool at night with them and the pit crews and sing for them until two or three in the morning.

BP: You were with Marty when he had his worst wrecks?

Don: The one that scared me the most was the one where he turned into the wall to keep from hitting the other driver. Going into a wall at 150 miles an hour . . . that car exploded! And they took him down there to the hospital at the race track and I took off down there. They knew I was upset when I came in. I remember one of the guys stopped me and kept saying, "Don, don't worry, he's all right. He's all right!" I said, "Well, where is he!" He said, "He's in the other room; you can go in." I opened that door and all I could see was his head and he had a big gash over his eye . . . and all that blood. I passed out cold. Just fainted. They had to give me a shot and get me revived.

And then after that, when he had a wreck and went to the field hospital, the first thing the doctors and nurses would do was stop me from getting to him. They made the mistake one time and weren't going to do it again!

I never had a brother, but if I had one, Marty would have been it.

BP: When you and Marty would go out late at night around Nashville, what did you do?

Don: Most of the time we would just go out and have a sandwich. It depended on how tired he was. If he wasn't sleepy we would talk to people. Then go home.

Marty liked to go visit those late night radio shows. He had his favorites: Ralph Emery, Bill Mack, and a guy in Louisiana. But mostly Ralph and Bill. I guess that just about covers the whole country. Most radio stations had a piano in them and he would play that. Or, he would carry his guitar with him. A lot of them would have a guitar for him if they knew he was coming.

BP: What was life like on the tour bus?

Don: Every night when we finished a show date we would get on the bus and take off to the next place.

We *all* liked to play poker. I did, so did Marty, and Jack Pruett. Jack and Marty would really take after each other. They would get so mad at each other . . . raise each other and try to break each other. Funny stuff. "Go ahead, let me see what you are going to do now!" Jack would say to Marty. "I'll show you what I'll do!" Marty would say. "I'll raise you 10!" And Jack would say, "That's just what I thought! I'll raise you back 10!" And it would last all night, sometimes until we would get to where we were going. Marty was a lucky poker player. Jack was a smart poker player, but so was Marty. On top of that, Marty was lucky; he would really get the cards. Even when other people were dealing! Jack was more of a bluffer, but he was a good bluffer. I remember there were times when Jack would win the game and I had the better hand! I used to get so mad!

BP: Did you play for money?

Don: Oh yes! Sometimes $400 or $500 would change hands a night. I was always the sucker, I'm the one who got caught in the middle all of the time. But when those two got to betting against each other, it was time to get out. I wasn't that good. It was a way to make it through the night. Then we would get to our hotel the next morning and check in and go to sleep.

BP: How do you think Marty's heart problem affected the way he looked at life?

Don: After Marty's open heart surgery, I think he became a lot more compassionate than he was before.

BP: More compassionate towards whom?

Don: Towards everyone. I think anyone would have done the same thing. You know, if you get a second chance in life, you're going to try to make a little more of it than you did the first time. Most people take life for granted. When you stop and think about it, it doesn't last very long. That's one thing that Marty learned.

BP: Did Marty slow down at all?

Don: No, Marty didn't slow down at all; I think he was back performing about a month after he got out of the hospital. In fact, I think Marty got in high gear. I believe he worked *more,* more days than before. His attitude definitely changed. He thought a lot more about your needs and feelings. He made a lot more friends, which made him happy.

BP: Were Marty's shows planned as much as other performers' are?

Don: We had a set show in that there were certain songs we usually did. But he would put one in or take one out whenever he wanted to. You could usually tell what he was going to do next. But you had to be on your toes!

BP: You could tell what he was going to do next?

Don: Well, you never really knew. You just followed the rhythm of it all. But he would do songs a lot of the guys had never heard. But we would follow along and get it done. He would pull something out of left field once in a while. Call up an old song he hadn't done in five, ten, or 15 years. Everyone in the band would be looking around. "What is that! How do you do it?" But they would catch it right quick.

Marty could probably remember the words to more songs than anybody else in the world. Him and Bobby Sykes both. I have to hear a song a few times before I can remember it. Marty remembered people's names better than anyone I've ever known. Like I said, I met him one time, went home and came back six months later, and he called me by my name. I've seen him do it to many people.

BP: Marty seemed to genuinely like to sign autographs.

Don: Yes, he did. He had a good time doing it. If Marty had time, he would always sign autographs after a concert. If he didn't have time, he wouldn't sign any. If you sign one, you've got to sign them all.

BP: Why did he do it?

Don: So he could talk to people, carry on, and keep people laughing. Mainly, he just liked people.

BP: How do you think Marty would have wanted to be remembered?

Don: He wanted to be remembered as a man who sang songs people liked; someone who had a good time. He wanted to be loved. I think that's happened. People had a good time with him and loved him.

BP: And you, how would you like to see him remembered?

Don: As a compassionate man. A great singer. A great songwriter. I don't think he ever got the credit he deserved as a songwriter. Once he did, that's all. He understood how to put a song together.

3

BIBLIOGRAPHY, 1960–1969

The 1960s started and ended with two of the most important events in Marty's life. The meteoric ascent of "El Paso" on the charts signaled a new high in Marty's career; it not only became the most important recording hit of his career, it also became known and loved worldwide. It topped all of the charts in January of 1960, stayed there for weeks, and won the first Grammy ever awarded to a country music song. Once again, Marty was the songwriter. Marty used the occasion to move more fully into western songs and started regular trio and harmony work with Don Winters and Bobby Sykes. These two long-time colleagues sang harmony with Marty on many of his western recordings.

By this time, he had expanded his business activities and become his own manager. He started, and sold, several music publishing companies: Marizona Music, Marty's Music, Maricana Music, and Mariposa Music. And in addition to maintaining a heavy tour schedule, he also found time to star in several more films and do two short-lived musical television series. And, of course, during it all he increased his racing activities. He moved up to modified stock cars in the early 1960s and frequently raced at the Nashville Speedway on Saturday nights before he performed the last show of the evening at the Grand Ole Opry. He once owned a race track for micro-midgets but sold it when it took up too much of his time. He moved briefly into the big league with a NASCAR stock car race in 1968, but this was only a preview for the next decade.

The hit songs continued with such titles as "Don't Worry" in

1961, "Devil Woman" in 1962, "Begging to You" in 1963, "Ribbon of Darkness" in 1965, and other titles. "Don't Worry" found a place in musical history with the accidental development of the "fuzz" sound. The sound occurred when a piece of equipment blew a fuse and went undetected until after the recording was made. The musicians and Marty liked the sound, it was left on the finished product, and a new sound was born. One of Marty's most popular songs, "You Gave Me a Mountain," was a big hit for Frankie Laine in 1969 but was never released as a single by Marty himself. Written by Marty with biographical overtones, it has been recorded by a number of artists over the years and appears on several of his albums. His album work continued to showcase a variety of styles: more western songs, Hawaiian tunes, religious hymns, pop and rock releases, and even one jazz-based album ("Marty After Midnight"). He became vocal in the political arena and openly supported Barry Goldwater for President in 1964. His music reflected his beliefs and several of the songs he wrote during this period expressed his ideas and feelings for America. Columbia Records was more cautious in its approach and refused to let him release a song called "Ain't That Right," a strong right-wing protest against Communism and against what he considered anti-American war protesters. The song was eventually released on Sims Records with Bobby Sykes the singer under the pseudonym of Johnny Freedom. A copy of Marty's recording can now be found on a 1983 Bear Family Album (BFX 15212) release titled "Pieces of Your Heart."

Always anxious to get out among his fans, Marty maintained a heavy tour schedule. And by now, he was also traveling to foreign countries and completed highly successful tours of Japan and Australia.

During the summer of 1968, Marty's racing accidentally inspired a new tradition at the Grand Ole Opry. As he tells it, he was running with the leaders at the Speedway in a race that had been plagued by delays, and time was fast approaching for his 11:30 p.m. Opry performance. Forced finally to pull out of the race and head for the Opry, he arrived to find the Opry programming itself running late. In a pique of temper over not only having to leave the race unnecessarily but also over the possibility of losing some of his time on stage, Marty decided to take all of the time he was supposed to have on stage . . . and more. He stayed and stayed, and the audience loved it. And WSM radio stayed with him instead of cutting to the following program. From that time on, whenever he appeared on the Opry, he stayed until he wanted to leave. At first, it was only fifteen or twenty minutes longer but as the years passed he gradually worked his Opry appearance up to an hour. No one complained.

In August of 1969 Marty Robbins' life changed permanently. He suffered a massive heart attack in Ohio on his way to a concert. He was hospitalized in Cleveland for several weeks and then flown back to Nashville, where he spent several more weeks resting and recovering. Medical science lacked the sophistication in technique available today and the extent of Marty's illness was not fully detected. His doctors allowed him to return to a reduced concert schedule and he was back to playing Las Vegas by November. More serious trouble followed in January, 1970.

BIBLIOGRAPHY, 1960–1969

[Music Reporter charts]. *Music Reporter;* 1960 January 4; 4(23): various paging.
"El Paso" is number 1 on several charts.

Archie can also sing well. *The Tennessean;* 1960 January 10: 6E.
Article includes Marty.

[Billboard charts]. *Billboard;* 1960 January 11: 42.
El Paso is No. 2 on Pop chart and No. 1 on Country and Hot 100 Charts.

Robbins' "El Paso" stirs c & w revival. *Billboard;* 1960 January 11: 30.
Photo and short biography.

Jim Reeves is still a satisfied man. *The Tennessean;* 1960 January 17: 31 C.
Article includes Marty.

Marty in *Buffalo Gun*, 1961.

Big iron/Saddle tramp. *Billboard;* 1960 February 22: 41.
Single review.

Marty. *Country & Western Record Review;* 1960 March; 2(12): 17.
EP review. Songs include: Judy, Wedding bells, (Nothing but) sweet
lies, Then I turned and walked slowly away.

[Popularity charts]. *Country & Western Record Review;* 1960; 2(12):
14.
The charts show "El Paso" to be number 2 on both the British and
American charts.

Gunfighter ballads and trail songs. *Country & Western Record Review;*
1960 April; 3(1): 19.
Album review.

Saddle tramp/Big iron. *Country & Western Record Review;* 1960 April;
3(1): 6.
Single review.

Is there any chance/I told my heart. *Billboard;* 1960 May 23: 35.
Single review.

Robbins, Marty. El Paso. *Country Song Roundup;* 1960 May; 12(66): 9.
Note: Lyrics to the song.

Robbins, Marty. Big iron. *Country Song Roundup;* 1960 July; 12(67):
4.
Note: Lyrics to the song.

Songs of the islands. *Country & Western Record Review;* 1960 July;
3(4): 16.
Album review.

Marty unhurt in crash. *The Tennessean;* 1960 August 22. Marty's wreck
was in a micro-midget car crash during a race in Bartlesville,
Oklahoma.

Marty Robbins unhurt in crash. *Nashville Banner;* 1960 August 22.
Midget car racing wreck in Oklahoma left Marty unhurt.

Ballad of the Alamo/A time and a place for everything. *Billboard;* 1960
September 26: 43.
Single review.

Five brothers/Ride, cowboy ride. *Billboard;* 1960 September 5: 31.
Single review.

Country clippings [news column]. *The Music Reporter;* 1960 September 12; 5(7): 24.
The column notes that Marty, whose hobby is racing micro-midgets, has
built a track for them south of Nashville near Stewart Air Base.

They go ape [monthly column]. *Hillbilly & Cowboy Hit Parade;* 1960
Fall.
Photo of Marty and Johnny Horton.

[Photograph]. *Hillbilly and Cowboy Hit Parade;* 1960 Fall; 8(29): 22.
Photo of Marty and Johnny Horton.

[Advertisement]. *The Music Reporter;* 1960 October 31; 5(14): 20.
Full-page ad with photo of Marty in a western outfit from one of his
movies. The ad thanks DJ's for their support.

Marty at a micro-midget race track, 1960. (Photo by Jean Scotte)

Top c & w moneymakers for 1960. *The Music Reporter;* 1960 October
31; 5(14): 14.
"El Paso" included in the top ten.

[Advertisement]. *Billboard;* 1960 November 7: 47.
Full-page ad, with photo, for "The Ballad of the Alamo."

Ballad of the Alamo/Five brothers. *Country & Western Record Review;*
1960 November; 3(8): 17.
Single review. British release; the B side is different from American
release.

Robbins, Marty. Is there any chance. *Country Song Roundup;* 1960
November; 12(69): 10.
Note: Lyrics to the song.

Songs of the Islands. *Country Western Express;* [1960 November]; (1
NS): 7.
Album review.

[Billboard 13th Annual C/W D/J Polls]. *Country & Western Record
Review;* 1960 November; 3(8): n.p.
Marty is listed as no. 3 male artist, "Gunfighter ballads . . ." is listed
as top album, and "El Paso" is no. 3 for favorite record.

[Yearly popularity charts]. *Country & Western Record Review;* 1960
December; 3(9): 13–14.
Marty is in the top ten on the male artist, LP and single charts.

Ballad of the Alamo/Five brothers. *Country Western Express;* 1961
January/February; (3 NS): 9.
Single review.

Country clippings [news column]. *The Music Reporter;* 1961 January
16; 5(25): 27.
Note: Illus.
Comments on the "sax" sound on "Don't worry." The sound is the
guitar used by Grady Martin.

More gunfighter ballads and trail songs. *Country Western Express;*
1961 January/February; (3 NS): 11.
Album review.

Robbins, Marty. I told my heart. *Cowboy Songs;* 1961 January; 12(65):
8.
Note: Lyrics to the song. Cover photo.

Robbins, Marty. Is there any chance. *Country Song Roundup;* 1961
January; 13(70): 28.
Note: Lyrics to the song.

Robbins, Marty. Is there any chance. *Cowboy Songs;* 1961 January;
12(65): 3.
Note: Lyrics to the song. Cover photo.

Lamb, Charlie. Charlie's column [news column]. *The Music Reporter;*
1961 January 30; 5(27): 2.
The column notes that Tony Martin has covered "Don't worry."

Country clippings [news column]. *The Music Reporter;* 1961 February
20; 5(30): 61.
Marty plans to open his micro-midget race track, located near
Murfreesboro, on April 1, when the season begins.

[Advertisement]. *The Music Reporter;* 1961 February 20; 5(30): 3.
Full-page ad for "Don't worry." Good publicity photo.

Country clippings [news column]. *The Music Reporter;* 1961 February
27; 5(31): 21.
Marty headlined a benefit to buy uniforms for the Sheriff's deputies of
Nashville.

[Advertisement]. *The Music Reporter;* 1961 March 27; 5(35): [20] back
cover.
Full-page ad featuring Marty and Gloria Lambert, who recorded a song
he wrote called "Each time I hear (Don't worry)."

[Advertisement]. *The Music Reporter;* 1961 April 3; 5(36): 24.
Full-page ad for "The hands you're holding now," noted as "from the
pen of Marty Robbins," as recorded by Skeeter Davis.

[Top country charts]. *Country & Western Record Review;* 1961 April;
4(1): 5.
"Don't worry" is number 1 on the chart.

[Advertisement]. *The Music Reporter;* 1961 May 8; 5(41): 7.
Full-page ad for the new single, "Jimmy Martinez/Ghost train," and the album, "More greatest hits."

Jimmy Martinez/Ghost train. *Billboard;* 1961 May 8: 21.
Single review.

No glad togs for M. Robbins. *The Music Reporter;* 1961 June 12; Extra edition: 52.
The article is about Marty wearing business suits to perform.
Also included: background on his music companies, Marty's Music and Marizona Music.

Robbins, Marty. Don't worry. *Country Song Roundup;* 1961 July; 13(73): 14.
Note: Lyrics to the song.

Why "our" stars stay on top. *Country Song Roundup;* 1961 July; 13(73): 4–5.
Note: Illus.

[Advertisement]. *The Music Reporter;* 1961 August 14; 6(3): 19.
Full-page ad and large publicity photo for new single, "It's your world/You told me so."

More greatest hits. *Country & Western Record Review;* 1961 September; 4(6): 16.
Album review. Photo included.

Robbins, Marty. The hands you're holding now. *Country Song Roundup;* 1961 November; 13(74): 4.
Note: Lyrics to the song. Cover photo.

I told the brook/Sometimes I'm tempted. *Billboard;* 1961 December 4: 27.
Single review.

Jimmy Martinez. *Country-Western Express;* 1961 [?] December [?]; N S(5): 10.
Single review.

Just a little sentimental. *Country & Western Record Review;* 1961 December; 4(9): 14.
Album review.

[Photograph]. *Country-Western Express;* 1961 [?] December [?]; N S(5): 16.
Photo of Marty and Ferlin Husky.

Just a little sentimental. *Country-Western Express;* 1962 [?]; N S(7): 14.
Album review.

More greatest hits. *Country-Western Express;* 1962 [?]; N S(6): 11.
Album review.

Marty Robbins: an all time great. *Country Song Roundup;* 1962 February; 14(75): 8–9.
Note: Illus.
Early career information; mentions early television show in Phoenix and first recordings.

Robbins, Marty. It's your world. *Country Song Roundup;* 1962 February; 14(75): 5.
Note: Lyrics to the song.

Robbins, Marty. You told me so. *Country Song Roundup;* 1962 February; 14(75): 27.
Note: Lyrics to the song.

Love can't wait/Too far gone. *Billboard;* 1962 March 24: 27.
Single review.

Axton, Mae B. Riding high: country caravan. *Country Song Roundup;* 1962 May; 14(76): 18–19.
Mentions performances by Marty and Johnny Cash.

[Photograph]. *Country & Western Record Review;* 1962 May; 5(1): [back page].
Full-page publicity photo.

Robbins, Marty. It's your world. *Country Song Roundup;* 1962 May; 14(76): 31.
Note: Lyrics to the song.

Devil woman/April Fool's Day. *Billboard;* 1962 June 30: 49.
Single review.

Robbins, Marty. I'll go on alone. *Country Song Roundup;* 1962 August;
14(77): 16.
Note: Lyrics to the song.

Robbins, Marty. Sometimes I'm tempted. *Country Song Roundup;* 1962
August; 14(77): 9.
Note: Lyrics to the song.

[Biography, photo]. *Cashbox;* 1962 September 1: 18.
Brief biography and photo.

Today's top record talent. *Billboard;* 1962 September 22: 65.
Brief biography.

Just a little sentimental. *Country and Western Roundabout;* 1962
November; 1(2): 38.
EP review.

Ruby Ann/Won't you forgive. *Billboard;* 1962 November 10: 43.
Single review.

The voices behind the voices. *Country Song Roundup;* 1962 November;
14(78): 8–9.
Note: Illus.
Article about The Jordanaires; mentions that they back Marty on his
records.

[Advertisement]. *Country-Western Express;* 1963 [?]; N S(9): 19.
Ad, with photo, for "Ruby Ann."

Devil woman. *Country-Western Express;* 1963 [?]; N S(9): 12.
Album review.

Hawaii's calling me. *Country-Western Express;* 1963 [?]; N S(11): 10.
Album review, photo included.

Marty Robbins—the girl he didn't marry. *Country Music Stars;* 1963:
50–51.
Personal story, good photos.

No signs of loneliness here/I'm not ready yet. *Country-Western Express;* 1963 [?]; N S(10): 12.
Single review.

Not so long ago / I hope you learn a lot. *Country-Western Express;* 1963 [?]; N S(11): 8.
Single review.

Portrait of Marty. *Country-Western Express;* 1963 [?]; N S(10): 9.
Album review.

Ruby Ann. *Country-Western Express;* 1963 [?]; N S(9): 10.
Single review.

U K readers poll results. *Country & Western Record Review;* 1963 January; 5(8): 5.
Marty is number 4 Male Artist; "Devil woman" is listed as number 2 Favorite Single for the year.

Cigarettes and coffee blues / Teenager's Dad. *Billboard;* 1963 February 23: 6.
Single review.

Ruby Ann / Won't you forgive. *Country and Western Roundabout;* 1963 February; 1 (3): 37.
Single review.

Marty Robbins. *Country & Western Record Review;* [1963] March; 5(10): 8.
Note: Cover photo.
One-page article.

Marty Robbins. *Country & Western Record Review;* [1963] March; 5(10): 13.
Note: Cover photo.
Album review.

Marty Robbins; talent in action. *Cowboy Songs;* 1963 Spring: 19–20.
Note: Illus.
The article highlights the many styles of Marty and includes a photo of him dancing with a girl in Hawaiian costume. The article says *Trail* magazine's readers voted him "Best Male Singer" and *Billboard* has awarded him four "Triple Crown Awards" for his music.

Devil woman. *Country and Western Roundabout;* 1963 May; 1(4): 40.
UK album release.

I'm not ready yet/No signs of loneliness here. *Billboard;* 1963 May 4: 24.
Single review.

Portrait of Marty. *Country and Western Roundabout;* 1963 May; 1(4): 43.
UK album release.

Cigarettes and coffee blues/Teenager's Dad. *Country & Western Review;* 1963 June; 6(2): 14.
Single review.

Portrait of Marty. *Country & Western Review;* 1963 June; 6(2): 12.
Album review.

Marty Robbins: thinking man's musician. *The Music Reporter;* 1963 June 29; 7(48): [66].
Note: Illus.
Interview covers his dislike of live TV appearances because he doesn't believe a singer can project his talent in just three to five minutes. He believes it has to be built up before live audiences in arenas or auditoriums. He loves touring and the open road, spending at least ten days a month there. He sold his midget car race track. His "boys" participate in his music publishing businesses (Lee Emerson, Louis Dunn, Jack Pruett, Joe Babcock, and Jim Farmer); he has them listen to incoming tapes so he won't hear them and be accused of stealing the ideas of other people. The three music companies named are Marizona, Marty, and Maricana Music.

Is western wear flashier? *Country Song Roundup;* 1963 August; 15(81): 10–11.
Marty is listed as conservative and continental in his style.

Not so long ago/I hope you learn a lot. *Billboard;* 1963 August 3: 18.
Single review.

Trigg, Ellyn. Hobbies of the stars: tracking Marty Robbins. *Music City News;* 1963 August; 1(2): 2.
Note: Illus.
The article covers Marty's dirt-track racing activities at Highland Rim Speedway at Ridgetop, Tennessee. About five years previously Marty had become interested in micro-midgets and had owned up to six of them at one time. Last year he started racing modified cars. The car he

is now driving is number 777 and named "Devil Woman." He's sold the race track he owned that was located between Nashville and Murfreesboro. When he has the time, he races at tracks in the immediate several-state area, but does most of his racing on Friday nights at Ridgetop. Two photos of Marty with 777 are included: one at Ridgetop and one at the Fairgrounds Speedway in Nashville.

Begging to you/Over high mountain. *Billboard;* 1963 October 19: 24.
Single review.

[Photograph]. *Music City News;* 1963 October; 1(4): 5.
Photo of Marty with DJ Andy Anderson of Sioux City, Iowa.

[Photograph]. *Country Song Roundup;* 1963 November; 15(82): 16.
Photo of Marty and Minnie Pearl.

[Photograph]. *Country Music Report;* 1963 November; 1(3): 2 [inside front cover].
Full-page photo and ad for an appearance at the Palomino Club in Los Angeles.

[Photograph]. *The Music Reporter;* 1963 November 2; 13(14): 82.
Two photos: one of Marty with Paul and Paula, and one taken on the Opry stage with a Hawaiian dancer.

Hollywood, a last frontier. *The Music Reporter;* 1963 November 2; 13(14): 68–69.
Note: Illus.
Article about films made by country-western stars; Marty included in the article.

[Photograph]. *Hillbilly and Cowboy Hit Parade;* 1963 Winter; 11(32): 14.
Photo of Marty and Minnie Pearl.

[Advertisement]. *Country Music Review;* 1964 January; 1(5): 35.
Half-page ad from Marty wishing "Merry Christmas to all my friends."

[Annual yearbook]. *Country Music Review;* 1964/65; Annual Yearbook(1st): unpaged.
The volume contains several items on Marty: "Marty Robbins," an article about Marty with a photo of the LeGarde Twins; another article is titled "Marty Robbins Australian style." Also included is a half-page photo.

Marty in *Ballad of a Gunfighter*, 1963.

Island woman. *Country-Western Express;* 1964 [?]; N S(15): 15.
Album review.

Marty Robbins. *Country-Western Express;* 1964 [?]; N S(15): 10.
EP review.

[Photographs]. *Country Music Review;* 1964 January; 1(5): 25, 35.
Photo of Marty and Don Law on page 25. Page 35 has a half-page ad
from Marty (with photo), wishing all of his friends a Merry Christmas.

Return of the gunfighter. *Country-Western Express;* 1964 [?]; N S(13):
13.
Album review.

Girl from Spanish town/Kingston girl. *Billboard;* 1964 February 8: 22.
Single review.

Axton, Mae. Top country stars of 1963. *Hillbilly and Cowboy Hit Parade;* 1964 Spring; 12(34): 6–7.
Note: Illus.
Marty included in article as one of the top stars; photo on p. 7.

Return of the gunfighter. *Country and Western Review;* 1964 March/April; 6(6): 9.
Album review.

[Advertisement]. *Country Music Review;* 1964 May; 1(8): 31.
Note: Cover photo.
One-half-page ad for "Girl from Spanish town," including photo.

The cowboy in the continental suit/Man walks among us. *Billboard;* 1964 May 30: 22.
Single review.

Marty Robbins. *Country Music Review;* 1964 May; 1(8): 24.
Note: Cover photo, illus.
Article about Marty and his tour of Australia includes photo of LeGarde Twins.

[Photograph]. *Music City News;* 1964 May; 1(11): 5.
Photo of Marty and Ralph Emery.

[Photograph]. *Music City News;* 1964 May; 1(11): 8.
Photo of Marty receiving an award from radio station WBMD; Golden Award as number 1 recording artist.

Robbins, Marty. Not so long ago. *Country Song Roundup;* 1964 May; 16(84): 23.
Note: Lyrics to the song.

The cowboy in the continental suit. *Music City News;* 1964 June; 1(12): 13.
Record review.

The grandest birthday party of all. *Cowboy Songs;* 1964 June; 15(74): 4–5.
Note: Illus.
A Grand Ole Opry celebration; Marty is listed as one of the performers attending.

Starday buys catalog from Marizona Co. *Billboard;* 1964 June 20: 32.
Starday publishers bought Lee Emerson's catalog from Marizona Music, one of Marty's publishing companies.

Robbins, Marty. Begging to you. *Country Song Roundup;* 1964 August; 16(85): 26.
Note: Lyrics to the song.

Robbins, Marty. Girl from Spanish town. *Country Song Roundup;* 1964 August; 16(85): 10.
Note: Lyrics to the song.

The night I knew I was going to die. *Country Music Stars;* 1964 Fall: 42–43.
Note: Illus.
The story comes from an experience during his life in the Navy during WW II. He was on a landing craft in the Solomon Islands during a Japanese bombing raid, with no place to seek cover when the bombs started to drop. He was sure he was going to die, but the bombs fell all around him and he survived, shaken but unhurt. He also told of a racing accident where he thought he would be killed, but survived, he felt, by the grace of God. He acknowledges that his wife doesn't want him to race, but he feels he's a careful driver and he doesn't press to win. He switched from micro-midgets to modified cars and now mostly races at Highland Rim Speedway. He sold his micro-midget race track because he lost money on it. He takes his 14-year-old son Ronnie to the races with him, but admits he doesn't want him driving until he's 21. Ronnie also sings and plays the guitar. Daughter Janet is five years old. Good photos.

Robbins, Marty. Girl from Spanish town. *Cowboy Songs;* 1964 September; 16(75): 13.
Note: Lyrics to the song.

Robbins tops Goldwater entertainers. *Nashville Banner;* 1964 September 12.
Marty supported Barry Goldwater for President. Campaigned and performed for him.

[Advertisement]. *Music City News;* 1964 October; 2(4): 16.
Note: located on back page of journal.
Half-page ad supporting Barry Goldwater for President. Marty listed as Chairman of Stars for Barry Goldwater. Photo included.

Robbins seeks no limelight. *The Tennessean;* 1964 November 5.

Your cowboy favorites [monthly feature]. *Country Songs and Stars;* 1964 December; 15(76): 14–15.
Includes a photo and section on Marty.

I-eish-tay-mah-su/A whole lot easier. *Billboard;* 1965 January 9: 12.
Single review.

R.F.D. *Country and Western Express;* 1965 [?]; N S(17): 13.
Album review.

Robbins, Marty. The cowboy in the continental suit. *Country Song Roundup;* 1965 February; 17(87): 22.
Note: Lyrics to the song.

[Advertisement]. *Country Music Review;* 1965 March/April: 20.
Half-page ad for "I-eish-tay-mah-su."

Ribbon of darkness/Little Robin. *Billboard;* 1965 April 10: 48.
Single review.

Benefit features Robbins. *The Tennessean;* 1965 May 2.
Benefit for the Arthritis Foundation.

Robbins, Marty. One of these days. *Country Song Roundup;* 1965 May; 17(88): 8.
Note: Lyrics to the song.

The award winning Marty Robbins. *Country Songs and Stars;* 1965 June; 16(78): 10.
Note: Illus.
The article is a general review of Marty's recordings. It does mention that he has several gold records and that in November of 1964 he won BMI awards for nine of his songs. Included are photos of Marty and the Glaser Brothers, Mitch Miller, Ernest Tubb, and others.

Grand Ole Opry-1965. *Music City News;* 1965 August; 3(2): 4.
Photograph of Opry members, including Marty.

Marty Robbins sings to live . . . lives to race. *Country Music Review* (Anaheim, CA); 1965 August/September: 29–34.
Note: Cover photo of Marty and Car 777. Illus.

Good, in-depth article and photos of Marty at the race track. The article calls racing more than a hobby; it's an obsession. It identifies Marty's cars as: 1) the modified special is a 1934 Ford. 2) the late model modified is a 1959 Plymouth. He's currently building a 1962 Plymouth. He says that when he's racing, it's the one time he can truly relax; he lives for the racing season. He also admits his family and friends have asked him to give up his hobby more than once.

News from the Opry [news column]. *Country Song Roundup;* 1965 August; 17(89): 16.
The column notes that Marty is just back from a tour of Japan.

Old Red/Matilda. *Billboard;* 1965 September 11: 79.
Single review.

News from the Opry [news column]. *Country Song Roundup;* 1965 October; 17(90): 15.
Notes that Marty is negotiating a new movie contract.

Marty Robbins busy man—even when "hobbying." *The Tennessean;* 1965 October 21.
Article about auto racing.

While you're dancing/Lonely too long. *Billboard;* 1965 October 30: 16.
Single review.

Martin, Harris. 40th Grand Ole Opry celebration. *Music City News;* 1965 November; 3(5): 4–5,9,18–19,38.
Marty included in the article.

Brittain, William D. Out of the mouths of babes. . . *Music City News;* 1965 December; 3(6): 25.
Note: Illus.
Story about four-year-old Carolyn Binkley and Marty. Ad for her record also appears on page 35 of same issue.

Marty Robbins has style. *Country Songs and Stars;* 1965 December; 16(80): 10.
Note: Illus.
The brief article covers the many styles of Marty: ballads, blues, country, western, Hawaiian, Spanish, and gospel.

Marty Robbins tapes TV series "The Drifter." *The Tennessean;* 1965 December 9: 4 [TV Section].
About taping the series.

Buz 'n beat [news column]. *Music City News;* 1966 January; 3(7): 10.
Note: Column includes news about Marty's new television series. The show has a western setting, a plot for each show, and eight songs per segment. Debut scheduled in Wichita this month and Nashville next month. [Show was called "The Drifter"].

Private Wilson White/Count me out. *Billboard;* 1966 January 22: 16.
Single review.

Marty Robbins speaks his mind. *Country Song Roundup;* 1966 April; 18(93): 8.
Note: Illus. Cover photo.
Personal comments on people and musical styles. Discusses creating the "fuzz" sound on the recording "Don't worry."

Nashville notes [news column]. *Country Music Life;* 1966 May: 8.
Marty is backing his movie "Road to Nashville" and has a new TV series, "The Drifter."

. . . Alias Marty Robbins. *Hoedown;* 1966 June; 1(2): 8–12.
Note: Cover photo of Marty from "The Drifter." Illus.
Article includes information on early life and career, including youth, Navy, Frankie Starr, radio shows; good selection of photos.

Written in the stars [monthly feature]. *Country Song Roundup;* 1966 June; 18(94): 24.
Note: Illus.
One-page article about Marty; photo included.

In person or on record, Marty is always a hit. *Country Songs and Stars;* 1966 July; 17(83): 8.
Note: Illus.

Robbins, Marty. Private Wilson White. *Country Songs and Stars;* 1966 July; 17(83): 24.
Lyrics to the song.

Charon, Ruth. Nashville movies: The road to Nashville. *Country Music Life;* 1966 August: 30–33.
Note: Illus.
Article about the making of the film, "The Road to Nashville."

The raging controversy of Marty Robbins. *Country Song Roundup;* 1966 August; 18(95): 14–15.
Note: Illus. Cover photo.
Photos include Janet and Ronnie at a very young age. Interview covers auto racing, family life, his life in the armed forces. and his television series. The long article points out the contradictions in Marty's life. For example, his openness to his fans and his completely secluded family life, his conservative lifestyle as a nondrinker and nonsmoker and his insistence on auto racing, his charm and great sense of humor and his bluntness and stubbornness. The article also mentions that he briefly did some professional boxing just after he left the Navy.

Robbins, Marty. Private Wilson White. *Country Song Roundup;* 1966 August; 18(95): 28.
Note: Lyrics to the song. Cover photo.

Nash, Melodie. Marty Robbins races to top of the charts. *Music City News;* 1966 September; 4(3): 1,4.
Note: Illus.
Article provides information about "The Drifter" television series and "The Road to Nashville," a film Marty has just completed. The motion picture will premier in Bakersfield in September. Bobby Sykes and Jim Glaser were the people who sang harmony with him on the recording of "El Paso." He has just finished writing a book called *The Small Man;* it's a western story and will be available for sale soon. Photos from the film and series are included in the article.

Columbia says no to Marty Robbins! *The Georgia World of Country Music;* 1966 October: 1. Illus.
This headline article provides details about the refusal of Columbia Records to let Marty release a song he wrote and recorded titled "Ain't that right." Marty calls it a patriotic song against communism and recent un-American activities in our nation and says Columbia won't let him release it because it's too political. Don Law, speaking for the Nashville office, verified that the song was turned down as being too controversial and said he agreed with the decision of the New York Office. He added that he felt Marty Robbins was a great artist and that material of that nature would not be an asset to his popularity. The article goes on to say that Marty has produced the record himself, using a singer called "Johnny Freedom" on Sims Records. The song is currently receiving heavy air play in the South.

Franchised coffee service organized. *The Tennessean;* 1966 October 4: 20 [Nashville business notes].

Robbins to entertain at GOP dinner. *The Tennessean;* 1966 October 14: 48.

Mr. Shorty/Tall handsome stranger. *Billboard;* 1966 October 29: 16.
Single review.

The Drifter. *Hillbilly;* 1966 December; (20): 20.
Album review.

The Drifter. *Country-Western Express;* 1966 [?]; (21): 14.
Album review.

[Photograph]. *Music City News;* 1966 December; 4(6): 24.
Photo of Marty at a San Antonio performance.

[Photograph]. *Country Music Life;* 1966 December: 19.
Photo of Marty after a live performance in San Antonio.

My kind of country. *Country-Western Express;* 1967 [?]; (22): 14.
Album review.

Robbins, Marty. The shoe goes on the other foot tonight. *Country Songs and Stars;* 1967 January; 18(86): 11.
Lyrics to the song.

Tonight Carmen. *Country-Western Express;* 1967 [?]; (23): 15.
Album review. Photo on page 23.

[Photograph]. *Country Song Roundup;* 1967 February; 19(98): 45.
Photo of Marty getting his hair cut.

Stonemans, Connie in Robbins movie. *Music City News;* 1967 February; 4(8): 11.
Article about performers in movie, "Hell on Wheels."

Hall of Fame opening star-studded occasion. *Music City News;* 1967 March; 4(11): 1,28–29.

Robbins, Marty. Mister Shorty. *Country Songs and Stars;* 1967 March; 18(87): 14.
Lyrics to the song.

[Advertisement]. *Music City News;* 1967 April; 4(10): 5.
Full-page ad, with photo, for album "My kind of country."

Robbins, Marty. Mister Shorty. *Country Song Roundup;* 1967 April;
19(96): 23.
Note: Lyrics to the song.

Wilson, Maggie. Boss of the gunfighter songs and trail ballads. *Arizona
Republic;* 1967 April 2; Sunday Magazine section ("Arizona Maga-
zine"): 6–9.
Note: Cover photo, illus.
Long article about Marty as one of Arizona's most successful natives.

Charon, Ruth. Nashville movies: Hell on wheels. *Country Music Life;*
1967 June: 38–44.
Note: Illus.
About the making of "Hell on Wheels." Includes photos.

No tears milady. *Country Song Roundup;* 1967 June; 19(100): 29.
Note: Illus.
Brief article about Marty.

Premiere attracts 3000 here. *The Tennessean;* 1967 June 17: 1.
Article about the premiere of "Hell on Wheels."

Marty Robbins. *Country Songs and Stars;* 1967 July; (89): 4.
Note: Cover photo.

Robbins, Marty. No tears milady. *Country Songs and Stars;* 1967 July;
(89): 9.
Note: Cover photo.
Lyrics to the song.

Tompall and the Glaser Brothers. *Country Song Roundup;* 1967 August;
19(101): 38–39.
Note: Illus.
Article includes background information about how Marty gave then
their start.

Hell on Wheels. *Variety;* 1967 September 27.
Film review.

My kind of country. *Hillbilly;* 1967 September; (23): 13.
Album review.

Song of Robbins. *Hillbilly;* 1967 September; (23): 29.
Album review.

Tonight Carmen. *Hillbilly;* 1967 September; (23): 29.
Album review.

The Glaser Brothers [Part 2 of the series]. *Music City News;* 1967
October; 5(4): 6.
Note: Illus.
They recall working with Marty and Robbins Records.

Letters to the editor [monthly feature]. *Country Song Roundup;* 1967
October; 19(102): 6.
Fan letter.

Robbins, Marty. Tonight Carmen. *Country Song Roundup;* 1967 October; 19(102): 32.
Note: Lyrics to the song.

[Photograph]. *Music City News;* 1967 November; 5(4): 14.
Photo of Ronny accepting a Special Columbia Records Award for Marty
from Columbia VP Bill Gallagher.

Cackett, Alan. Marty Robbins. *Record Collector* [Kent, England]; 1967
November; Number 4: 1–24.
Note: Cover drawing.
The complete issue is about Marty and his recordings.

Robbins, Marty. Tonight Carmen. *Country Songs and Stars;* 1967
November; 18(91): 5.
Lyrics to the song.

Hilburn, Robert. Marty Robbins. *BMI* [monthly newsletter]; 1967 December: 18.
Note: Illus.
The article is a brief review of his career, with an emphasis on his
songwriting. It notes that Marty's record release "I'll go on alone"
caught the attention of Fred Rose, and quotes Marty as saying, "When
Fred Rose flew out to Arizona to see me, it was the greatest compliment
of my life. He was really a great songwriter, probably one of the
greatest of all time." Rose signed Marty as a songwriter for Acuff-Rose
Publications.

Pillow, Ray. Pillow talk [news column]. *Country Song Roundup;* 1967
December; 19(103): 22.
The news column mentions the "Hell on Wheels" movie premier in
Nashville.

By the time I get to Phoenix. *Country-Western Express;* 1968 [?]; (24): 14.
Album review.

Hell on Wheels. *Filmfacts;* 1968 January 15: 10(24): 404.
Film review.

NBC to present color special on C&W music. *Music City News;* 1968 January; 5(7): 1, 18.
Show to be a one-hour news special about country music. Marty is listed as one of the performers to be on the February 10, 1968 show.

[TV appearance] NBC "American Profile"; 1968 February 9. Information from the NBC Indexes to Shows.
Marty appeared on a Grand Ole Opry film clip during the show.

[Photograph]. *Country-Western Express;* 1968 [?]; (23): 21.

Tonight Carmen. *Country-Western Express;* 1968 [?]; (23): 15.
Album review.

Highlights of Marty. *Music City News;* 1968 March; 5(9): 11.
Note: Illus.
Photo and short story about an appearance at Jamboree at WWVA, Wheeling, West Virginia.

Nashville Notes [news column]. *Country Music Life;* 1968 March: 43.
The column recounts an interview Marty gave on a radio program in which he discussed how Jimmy Dickens helped him get a recording contract.

Marty Robbins; likable guy. *Country* [Philadelphia, PA]; 1968 April: 15–19.
Note: Illus.
Long article about Marty's racing activities. Good racing photos. Back cover [p.50] has nice color western photo.

Emery bombed with ad libs. *Music City News;* 1968 May; 5(11): 35.
Article about radio show. Mentions Marty dropped by to play the piano and answer questions.

Letters to the editor [monthly feature]. *Country Song Roundup;* 1968 June; 20(108): 26.
Fan letter.

Pillow, Ray. Pillow talk [news column]. *Country Song Roundup;* 1968 June; 20(108): 30.
Mentions that Marty is recording in New York.

King, L. L. The Grand Ole Opry. *Harpers Magazine;* 1968 July; 237: 48–50.
Marty included in the article.

Pillow, Ray. Pillow talk [news column]. *Country Song Roundup;* 1968 September; 20(110): 30.
Notes that Marty's next movie will be "From Nashville with Music."

Robbins, Marty. Love is in the air. *Country Song Roundup;* 1968 September; 20(110): 22.
Note: Lyrics to the song.

9 new buildings slated in Music Row plans. *The Tennessean;* 1968 October 16.

Spring construction set on music row. *The Tennessean;* 1968 October 18: 12.

Arnett, Larry. Human dynamo of Music Row. *Country Song Roundup;* 1968 November; 20(112): 42–43.
Note: Cover photo. Illus.
Interview. Photo of Marty with race car no.777.

By the time I get to Phoenix. *Hillbilly;* 1968 November; (28): 12.
Album review.

Corbin, Everett. Robbins, Cash hit of Columbia party. *Music City News;* 1968 November; 6(5): 31.
Note: Illus.
Photos in article include one of Marty and Ronny Robbins. It mentions that Marty has just started a television show at WSIX, Nashville.

Blu, Hal. Las Vegas notes [monthly feature]. *Country Music Life;* 1968 December: 5+.
The column notes that the Marty Robbins Show at the Thunderbird Hotel is a first for Las Vegas. Ronny also performed.

Columbia has best year: tops charts. *Music City News;* 1969 January; 6(7): 2.
Marty is listed as one of the top artists for the label.

Above: Marty kidding around with driver Tiny Lund, 1968. Below: Marty inspecting his car at the Charlotte race in October 1968. (Photos from NASCAR News Bureau)

Powell, Tom. So it's a mountain! . . . Marty Robbins tries to climb it. *The Tennessean;* 1969 February 23.
The newspaper article covers his early life, the writing of "You gave me a mountain," the recording by Frankie Laine, and gives a lot of detail about Marty's early interest in auto racing in Arizona. It notes he ran a (NASCAR) race in Charlotte, N.C. last year. Illustrated with racing photos.

I walk alone/Lilly of the valley. *Hillbilly;* 1969 March; (29): 13.
Review of Marty's new single.

Letters to the editor [monthly feature]. *Country Song Roundup;* 1969 March; 21(116): 26.
Fan letter.

[Photograph]. *Music City News;* 1969 March; 6(9): 13.
Photo of Marty and Johnny Cash.

Marty Robbins. *Country Music Hits;* 1969 Spring: 45. Illus.
General review of Marty as a person and a performer.

Winters, Audrey. Bush climbs his mountain. *Music City News;* 1969 March; 6(9): 3.
Article about Johnny Bush recording "You gave me a mountain." Additional comments about the recording on p. 2 in the "Late Bulletin" news column.

3700 fans jam WJRZ cavalcade. *Music City News;* 1969 May; 6(11): 8.
Note: Illus.
Marty noted as the main performer of the show.

The million sellers in country and western. *Music City News;* 1969 May; 6(11): 6.
Note: Illus.

I walk alone. *Hillbilly;* 1969 June; (30): 12.
Album review.

Loretta, Marty, Flatt & Scruggs top WSM poll. *Music City News;* 1969 June; 6(12): 6.
Note: Illus.
Article includes photo of Marty, Loretta, and Ralph Emery.

Myers, Judy. A talk with Marty Robbins. *Country Song Roundup;* 1969 June; 21(119): 8–11.
Note: Cover photo. Illus.
In this long interview, Marty talks about "The Drifter," saying he made the TV series in black and white, the summer before color came in. The segments were hard to sell, so he just put them in the vault and took the loss. He's now making "The Marty Robbins Show" and has 18 filmed; he plans to make at least 26. At the moment, they're being shown locally in Nashville, and maybe Denver. He discusses his plans for auto racing. He says he played piano on his album, "I walk alone," and on the singles, "I walk alone" and "It's a sin." He recalls his Navy years, saying he was on the boxing team for two years during that time.

I walk alone. *Country Music People;* 1969 July; 1(2): 4.
Album review.

[Performance review].*Variety;* 1969 July 2; 255: 61.
Review of Marty's show at the Bonanza Hotel in Las Vegas.

Marty Robbins in Ohio hospital with severe exhaustion. *Nashville Banner;* 1969 August 5; (Tuesday): 8.
Note: Illus.
Marty was hospitalized last Friday while traveling from an engagement in Warren, Ohio to Greenville, South Carolina.

Hurst, Jack. Marty Robbins in Ohio hospital. *The Tennessean;* 1969 August 5; (Tuesday): 1,2.
Marty is in the Cleveland General Hospital after a heart attack last week (last Friday). A hospital spokesperson said Marty was in fair condition in the coronary care unit. His wife and son left Saturday to see him.

Hurst, Jack. Robbins may be moved to Nashville hospital. *The Tennessean;* 1969 August 6; (Wednesday).
Marty may be moved to a Nashville hospital in a week or two, but plans are uncertain at this time. He reportedly suffered a heart attack after a Warren, Ohio concert last Thursday night. Members of the band were quoted as saying he became ill on the bus after they had left the concert and were on their way to South Carolina for another engagement. A spokesperson for Marty described him as exhausted from a heavy schedule. They say he had just completed three weeks in Las Vegas, one nighters in Illinois and Ontario (Canada), and taping of his syndicated television show before leaving on his current trip.

Marty, Marizona, and Janet see Ronny off on the plane as he leaves for
military duty overseas in late 1960s. (Photo from the Country Music
Foundation)

Robbins to stay in Ohio hospital. *The Tennessean;* 1969 August 9.

Cleveland hospital says Robbins "fair." *The Tennessean;* 1969 August
11.

O'Donnell, Red. Robbins returning to city. *Nashville Banner;* 1969
August 13.
Marty will be released from the hospital Saturday morning and flown to
Nashville in the National Life and Accident Insurance Company's private plane (arranged by the management of the Grand Ole Opry; the
company is one of their major sponsors). He will be taken to Park View
Hospital, where he will be under the care of Dr. William Ewers. The
doctor estimated he would be there for about two weeks and then spend
a month or more at home resting.

Opry star Robbins to return tomorrow. *The Tennessean;* 1969 August 15.
Marty will return to Nashville from the hospital in Ohio.

Marty Robbins back in Nashville. *The Tennessean;* 1969 August 18.

Robbins, Marty. You gave me a mountain. *Country Song Roundup;* 1969 August; 21(121): 19.
Note: Lyrics to the song.

Dubro, A. Gunfighter ballads and trail songs. *Rolling Stone;* 1969 September 20: 35.
Album review.

Marty Robbins in fair condition after recent heart attack. *Music City News;* 1969 September; 7(3): 2.
Mentions recent heart attack and current television series.

[Photograph] *Country Music.* 1969 October; (3): 19.
The magazine published a full-page photo of Marty with a caption under it wishing him a speedy recovery.

Columbia's Epic's review, a parade of exciting artists. *Music City News;* 1969 November; 7(5): 10.
Note: Illus.
Photo of Marty. Marty and Ronny both mentioned in article.

Marty Robbins returns to Opry. *Country Hotline News;* 1969 November; 1(1): 3.
Brief article about Marty's return to the Opry stage after his August heart attack.

[Performance review]. *Variety;* 1969 November 26; 257: 58.
Review of performance at the Fremont Hotel in Las Vegas.

[Photograph]. *Country Song Roundup;* 1969 November; 21(124): 20.
Small publicity photo.

It's a sin. *Hillbilly;* 1969 December; (32): 20.
Note: Illus.
Album review.

4

BOBBY SYKES TALKS ABOUT WORKING WITH MARTY ROBBINS

Bobby Sykes worked for Marty Robbins for 24 years, first as a band member and harmony partner, and later as his booking agent out of the Marty Robbins Enterprises office in Nashville. I had called Bobby a few days before my March trip to Nashville for the Country Music Radio Seminar meeting and asked him for an interview. He was able to meet me for a while during one of the afternoons I was in town. He's a friendly, casually dressed middle-aged man in his early 60s, and he was looking a little tired from filming a TV commercial for a local truck dealer.

BP: I'm especially pleased that you could take the time to talk to me today because you played such an important part in Marty's career for so many years.

Bobby: I'm glad to see Marty's memory kept alive and to help anyone who's doing it.

BP: When did you start working for Marty?

Bobby: It was either August or September of 1958; I forget the exact month. Just after "White Sport Coat." I stayed with Marty 24 years, up to the day he died.

BP: How did you meet him?

Bobby: The way I met Marty, I'd been on a local television show here in town on WSIX-TV (now WKRN, Channel 2). They had a live show from noon until 1:00 pm called "Home Folks." We also had an hour show every Saturday night on the ABC network with a different guest host every week—people like Carl Smith, Webb Pierce, Farron Young. I think they were trying to compete with Red Foley and his "Ozark Jubilee." It didn't last too long because no one could compete with Red Foley. At any rate, I'd been on that daytime show for two years and that's why I remember it was August or September, because it lasted two years to the month. I had been out of work for about two weeks.

I was going into the old Clarkston Hotel, which has since been torn down. That old hotel used to have a coffee shop where all of the musicians, entertainers, songwriters and everyone used to gather because it was next to the old WSM studios. I was going in one day and Marty was coming out. Of course, I'd met him just in passing before, so we knew each other by name. Evidently he must have been watching the program because he knew the show had been taken off the air. He asked me what I was doing now that the show was off and I said, "Nothing." He said: "How would you like to come to work for me?" And I said: "Sure, I'm looking for work." So, he said: "I have an 18-day tour coming up. Why don't you go with me on this one tour and it will give you a chance to see if you like me, and me a chance to see if I like you. When we get back, we'll talk about it." When we got back, I figured I was hired and he never did say anything about it. And I stayed 24 years.

BP: What was your job with Marty and the band?

Bobby: I played rhythm guitar and sang. I was what they called back then a "front man"; they don't have them very much any more. A front man would take the band out and do 15 or 20 minutes as a sort of a warm up.

BP: An opening act?

Bobby: Yes, an opening act for the star. I'd go out and do that and introduce Marty. That was my job. When the Glaser Brothers were with us, they would also do about 20 minutes before Marty. Then, when he started to do the western songs, I'd sing harmony with him. He always loved The Sons of the Pioneers. Of course, we all know by now that Marty wrote some of the greatest western songs that were ever written. Absolute classics.

BP: How did you travel back then?

Bobby: We would tour in cars and station wagons. Back then, about the only person who had a bus was E.T. [Ernest Tubb]; he was the first. The best I can remember, his was the first bus I ever saw that had a name on it. We traveled in cars and station wagons pulling trailers.

BP: What about the western music? How did that start?

Bobby: Marty had written some cowboy songs and wanted to start rehearsing them. I don't know how it came about as to why he didn't rehearse them with the Glaser Brothers, but it came down to where Jim [Glaser] wanted to rehearse them and Marty asked me one day if I sang harmony. I said: "Sure, I love to sing harmony." He said, "Well, rehearse a few of these songs with us." And we started with just plain old working songs like "Tumblin' Tumbleweed," "Cool Water," and "Little Green Valley." When he heard that I did know harmony, could switch harmony, and had a good high voice and a low voice, from then on it was Marty, myself, and Jim Glaser. I had just the type of voice he was looking for. And remember, this was before Don Winters joined us.

BP: What about recording the "Gunfighter" album?

Bobby: Our first time in the studio singing harmony was when he went in and did the first "Gunfighter" album ("Gunfighter ballads and trail songs"). "El Paso" was on it. It was the first time we did trio work on an album. From then on, it was Marty, myself, and whoever else was there at the time on the western albums. The one exception was a record called "Five Brothers"; the Glaser Brothers did that one with him. We had two or three different members of the trio. Joe Babcock was there for a while, and I think Bill Johnson did some trio work with us. He also played steel for Marty.

And then he had a young man named Don Winters. Don was it from the time he started working. Don had a very high voice and he knew harmony real good. You couldn't hardly get it too high for Don. There was no limit to Don's range as far as going high; he couldn't go too low, but he could go as high as you wanted him to go. So, from then on, it was Marty, Don, and myself.

BP: When did Don start working for Marty?

Bobby: Don started about two years after I did, about 1960. And about that time he started the trio work with us too.

BP: What was it like to do a recording session back then?

Bobby: Recording was *so much more fun* back then.

BP: Why?

Bobby: Well, number one, Marty made it fun. And the recording methods were different then. You would take into the studio the amount of songs and musicians you were going to use. You would work up an arrangement and everyone would do it all at once. Now they do it on "tracks." They lay down a basic track, drums, bass, piano. Then they bring in one instrument at a time and after all of this is done, they bring in the singer and he will put his voice down.

We used to do three or four songs in three hours. Now it takes six weeks for them to do it. And we had just as big hit records back then as they do now! If not more so. The old was more spontaneous and felt more live . . . real . . . believable. Because everything was happening all at once. Today, they will bring in one guy to do one "lick" or a brief fiddle part. Everything else may already be there. And he's sitting in the studio all by himself with a pair of earphones on, and when it comes to his time to play, he does his part and goes home. To me, that leaves out the spontaneity of it. You can't do a good job without reacting to everyone else. The natural vibrations from one person to another is what makes creative work. I think we did better back then. It certainly was a lot quicker, and a lot cheaper.

BP: What about the costs?

Bobby: You could turn out a good three-hour session for $1500 to $2000. Now, to get those same songs, there's still a three-hour session, but it may only be one person sitting in the studio. Now it takes you six weeks and can cost $50,000 to $100,000.

BP: Who produced the recordings?

Bobby: Don Law was Marty's producer. It was called A & R then (for Artist and Repertoire). The same person is now called a producer. Don worked for Columbia Records; now producers are independent. But the sessions were always a meeting of the minds between Marty and Don. If Marty didn't like it [an arrangement or a song] he would say: "I don't like that and I will *not* do it." And it wouldn't get done. Don always had somebody working for him on the sessions trying to get the right sound, the right arrangement. In many of Marty's sessions, that man was Grady Martin. I know I heard Don say many times before a session started: "Grady, get me a good sound on this." And he more or less left it up to Grady. Don would go into the control room and when he heard what he wanted to hear, then he would say: "O.K., that sounds good, let's do a take." Then they would play it back for Marty. If it was what Marty wanted to hear, fine. If Marty would say; "Let's change this or do that a little different," I don't care who spoke up, that's the way they would do it.

BP: When you recorded "El Paso," did anyone realize at the time it would be the hit it became?

Bobby: Marty didn't think it would be a big record. As to his reasons for the way he thought, I don't know. By the way, we did that entire album in one night ["Gunfighter ballads and trail songs"], in just a little over eight hours. It was fun! I heard Marty tell Don that night: "Don, this album won't sell 500 records, but it's something I've always wanted to do and I think Columbia Records owes it to me." Don said: "That's fine, Marty, you never know. Let's do the best we can and see what happens."

We did three takes on "El Paso" and Don wanted to stop and listen to it. So, we listened to it and Don said: "Marty, I think that's *pretty good,* but we can do it over if you want to." Marty said: "Don, I told you the whole album won't sell 500 records. That's as good as I can make it; let's keep that one." He didn't know it would sell five million! If he thought it in his own mind, he sure kept it from everyone else! He just wanted to do a western album. The album sold three million at the time and the single, five million. It's one of the great classics of all time and still selling.

BP: How many people did you use at the session?

Bobby: For that session, we didn't have that many people in the studio: Marty, myself, Jim Glaser, the Jordanaires, and perhaps five musicians. The Jordanaires were there because Marty wanted a certain sound on things like "The Master's Call"—he wanted a bigger sound. I think they were on three or four songs in that album.

Everyone was having such a good time that night! Because, like I say, Marty wasn't really serious about the album because he didn't think it was going to sell. Of course, when the lights went on, we all got serious. But we joked in between takes. In just about any session with Marty, he would clown around so much, he would put you at ease. But then, if you got too loose, he would snap you back into shape in a second, I guarantee you! But, that's the way it should be. Somebody has to take control or you come out with nothin'. You don't get anything done. It was his career and one way or another he was paying for it. It didn't come out of his pocket right then, but eventually it would. Back then, the company paid for the recording session, but then they would deduct it from your royalties. The way it is now, many of the artists use their own money and produce their own sessions or hire their own producer.

I have my doubts about how much independent producers know. That's just about all hindsight! If it's a flop, no one wants to take credit for it. If it's a hit, then they say: "Look what I did!" A whole lot of it is just a matter of luck. I think any producer can tell when they have an absolute hit song, because there's songs and then there's songs. If it's a true hit, it will slap you in the face and will not be denied. But you still have to match the right song to the right singer to make a hit. If you've got that, then the producer can go out and hire an arranger. He doesn't think all that up in his own head.

BP: And now?

Bobby: The way they do it now, someone like Kenny Rogers or Willie Nelson might go out and spend $50,000 to $100,000 to make each album. They're tied to a label, but have a free hand in doing their own sessions. But they put out their own money and contract with the record company: "I record them, I deliver them, and you pay me." Not including royalties. Recording today is a fabulous money business! People come down here [to Nashville] and they have $5,000 to $10,000 in their pocket, and this town is full of people who will take every penny you've got away from you and give you nothing. What these people don't know is, number one, you've got to have a "name" to sell a record. No DJ is going to play a record if you don't have a name, unless you want to slip a lot of money to them, which people still do. Payola's not dead. It hid, and upped it's price . . . that's all. The DJ's won't play it unless you've got a big name, and then you had better expect to spend $50,000 to produce that album. $5,000 to $10,000 will get you nothing and somebody will just take your money. Marty spent $30,000 to $40,000 on each album, and he wasn't as extravagant as a lot of them are.

BP: Who gets the most royalties from a recording?

Bobby: There's three people who get paid by the record company for each recording: the writer, the publisher, and the artist. So, if you write the songs, publish them, and record them yourself, you get it all. And that's frequently what Marty did. And Marty was very good at songwriting. I've seen him listen to songs from other people until he was blue in the face and come up with nothin'. He listened to thousands of songs. I do think he found one, once. "Jenny" came from Australia. It was a great song, but it still wasn't a great "hit" single. It was a beautiful song, but "beautiful" and what sells isn't necessarily the same thing. Some of the songs that sell, that are big hits, I can't see anything in them. But somebody must, because they sell a lot of records. I've heard a lot of people say, "I can't see what anyone sees in Johnny Cash." I'm just using him as an example . . . you can hear the same thing said about *any* artist. I like Johnny, he's a friend. I love the man, but there's lots better singers. But there's something about him that somebody likes or he wouldn't be as big as he is. And he wouldn't sell the millions of records he's sold. A lot of that's sour grapes, professional jealousy, because he made it and someone else didn't. Well, I think I can outsing a lot of people and I didn't "make it." There was a time in my life I almost got bitter about it. And then I said, "Hey, if everyone in the music business became a star, *everyone* would be in the music business. So, be happy with the role you've got." I didn't get rich, but I made more than some people made. Pretty decent job . . . it was good to me: I didn't make millions, not even close to that. I just thank God that I got what I got. I thank Marty Robbins for being the instrument that God let me have what I got. I thank God first, then I thank God for using Marty Robbins as the instrument to give me what I got. I give a lot of praise and a lot of love to Marty Robbins; he was a brother, a friend. He was as good to me as family, probably better to me than I deserve. And I love the man. Still do. I still miss him.

BP: What do you miss most?

Bobby: Just him. The fact that he was Marty. Everyday he was an exciting man. Everyday was something new. He would think of things to do. He had a lot of "devilment." He was "devilish" in the fun sense of the word. He liked to play tricks.

It's very ironic but the one place we always had trouble with selling tickets was El Paso! I've had other people tell me that as far as music is concerned, El Paso is a wash-out. Sports events they like and will go to. Some rock concerts. But country music, it should stay out of El Paso. That's the only thing I can tell you. Because I'd hate to think it was jealousy. Because Marty did more to put the city of El Paso on the map than any one person I know of.

We did a show there when "El Paso" was number one on the charts. They held a ticker-tape parade down main street. The streets were lined with people on both sides. We went up the steps of the court house and the Mayor presented Marty with the keys to the city. They held two different celebrations in town for him. "El Paso" was number one all over the charts . . . pop and country. And then when we went to do our show that night, there were only 400 or 500 people. You couldn't explain it!

BP: When was that?

Bobby: Late 1959 or early 1960. It was released in late '59. It stayed number one for a while. Which records don't do now. It's hard enough just to get a song to number one. Today, if it stays there two weeks, you've got a monster hit.

BP: I talked to Tommy Thomas [long-time owner of the Palomino Club in Los Angeles] a couple of years before he died and he told me about the "Marty Robbins Door" that is at the back of the stage and opens directly into the parking lot outside. There's a plaque with Marty's name on it nailed over the door. He said Marty made him build it so he named it after him.

Bobby: That's true. I was booking Marty then. And Marty and Tommy were close friends. This was when Marty was just coming up, when he had his first record or two, and only two or three people in his band. Tommy would use Marty when Marty needed the work. So, when Marty got where he was a big star, he never forgot that. He always told Tommy, "Yeah, I'll work for you."

The place had a room, I used to call it the "holding pen," like in a rodeo where you hold all the animals. It was supposed to be the musicians' room but anybody and everybody could walk in and out of it. The entertainers had no privacy whatsoever.

One time when we worked there, I noticed Marty was outside in the parking lot, walking around and waiting for the show to start. Let me say that we never had any problems with Tommy paying Marty for his work. Because Tommy always made money. I don't care what the price was, he made money off of Marty. That was one of the things about Marty; he'd say, "I want this much," which was actually very low compared to most of the other big stars, the stars of his stature. He would be getting about one-third of what they were getting. He'd say, "That's enough for me. I pay my band good, everybody who works for me good, you travel right, and I make all I want to make. Let the man who hired me make some money. And then we can go back." Which we could . . . we did. There were no problems with Marty because everybody who knew him wanted him back. He drew a lot of people. People who read this may think it's outrageous, but he actually did get less than other performers who were drawing the same numbers [of audience size]. Tommy would take in $30,000 and say, "I had someone else a few weeks ago and he charged me twice what you did, and he didn't bring in half the people you did."

By the way, as Marty's agent I never misrepresented him. Because Marty always told me, "This year, this is what we are going to charge." Every year, I'd try to get him to go a little higher, yes, because I thought he deserved much more than what he was gettin'. So, he would set the price, "This is it." And we never had any problem. Marty could work as much as he wanted to.

Anyway, Marty was outside standing around. The holding pen was located at the back of the club by the kitchen. The building is long in shape, with the stage at one end and the holding pen at the other. And in between is the bar and the audience. So when we opened the show and I'd introduce Marty, he'd have to walk the length of the building through the audience to get to the stage! And the audience would be jam-packed. Even the dance floor had tables and chairs. They had people there like Jack Lord and Dale Robertson and a whole bunch of movie stars who had come to see him. And it would take Marty 15 minutes to get from that room through the crowd to the stage.

Marty had been outside looking around. He said if he ever worked there again, he was going to rent a house trailer, pull it up on the outside of the building by the bandstand [the stage], knock a hole in the wall and hang a drape over it so he could step right out of the trailer and on to the stage. He said, "Otherwise, I will not work here again."

So, a short time later Tommy called me and wanted to know when Marty could come out and work for him again. I told Tommy, "This is what we want. We'll come for the same money as last time, *but* here's what we want: You've got to rent a trailer, pull it outside the building by the stage, and knock a door in the wall so Marty can step out on the stage. "What!" Tommy says. I said, "That's it. I'm sorry. I'm just telling you what Marty wants if he works there again." Tommy said, "You're kidding me."

Tommy called Marty because they were friends. He tells Marty, "You know what that Sykes told me I had to do?" And he told Marty exactly what I had just told him. And he said, "Marty, what are we going to do about that?" And Marty said, "You're going to have to talk to Sykes. Whatever he said is what you're going to have to do." So, Tommy called me back and said, "O.K., I'll knock a hole in the wall!" He knew we had him! And he did it and it's still there as far as I know.

BP: Yes. I've seen the door. It's behind a curtain, with Marty's name over it—"Marty Robbins' Door."

Bobby: Some of the other entertainers saw it and said, "Hey, this is what we want! We want to use it too! We don't want to have to walk through that audience either!"

Marty wouldn't ignore anybody. He would walk through that audience and they were always grabbing at him, yelling, wantin' his autograph on something. They wouldn't wait until afterwards! Marty was always very good at signing autographs. I've seen him stand in the same spot for an hour and a half, signing autographs and taking pictures with the fans. But people didn't want to wait.

BP: Tommy told me that Marty was the only one of the big stars to come back and sit and listen to the newcomers. But he said Marty wouldn't come alone. He always came with "his boys" (meaning you and Don Winters) to sit on each side of him.

Bobby: There's a reason for that. If you're a "Marty Robbins" and have a big name and everybody knows you're pretty well off, there's always somebody that wants to approach you for something or somebody's always wanting to test you.

Marty wasn't a physically big man but he was *all* man. Marty would take anybody on. I'm not a fighter, but I look big. And Don Winters; well, he's an ex-professional fighter. He's just as nice a person as you'd ever want to meet. But you get him riled and he will "clean your whistle" in a minute, and clean it good! So, Marty used to say, "If I take the two of you with me, you're big and look mean. And if that doesn't work, then I'll sic the one that's really mean on 'em!"

We used to go with him a lot of places simply because if we were there, people might not be in such a hurry to go up to him and test him or challenge him. Everybody has their bodyguards. We never thought of ourselves as bodyguards but I'll guarantee you I'd "go to the wall" over Marty and I know damn well Don would. I think Don did a couple of times.

I've seen Marty fight a couple of times. I remember once on a movie location he whipped the dog manure out of a long lean cowboy twice his size. Marty worked him over good.

BP: Why?

Bobby: He called Marty a "son of a bitch." I think Marty hit him about three or four times and it took them about five minutes to bring the guy to. And the guy never did hit Marty once! Marty was a nice guy, and easy going, but he did have a temper and he wasn't afraid of nothin'. He was *not* afraid of *anything*. He wasn't even afraid of death. He was not.

BP: Do you think he knew how sick he was just before he died?

Bobby: I think about the last year we all had an inclination. But we didn't know at the time how serious it was. But I'm pretty sure Marty knew. Heart bypass surgery is usually good for seven to ten years. Marty got 12 years out of his.

The last year we could see Marty got tired pretty easy. Especially the last two or three months. But he'd wear himself out on stage and then collapse on the bus. And I've seen that. But he would go out and give people what he thought they'd spent their money to see. He would always be tired. But as tired as he was, he'd see people gathering around the bus and he'd say, "Give me ten minutes to get out of my stage clothes." And he'd change and sit down and relax for five or six minutes and then go out and stand for an hour signing autographs. And he didn't feel like doing it, but he did.

BP: He didn't slow down very much.

Bobby: No. He didn't want to slow down. He loved life and loved to live it.

I'm not trying to paint a picture of Marty Robbins as a saint.

He wasn't. Who is? No one is. He respected and took care of the people who worked for him and were loyal to him. He respected and loved fans and *absolutely* loved the business he was in. He enjoyed every minute of it. How many of us don't complain once in a while? Even say things we don't mean? That's human. He was human. He was not a saint, but he was a damn good man.

BP: What were Marty's feelings about winning the "Hall of Fame" Award in October of 1982?

Bobby: He didn't think he was going to win it, to tell you the truth. He almost left before it was presented to him. We had to think up excuses to keep him backstage so Eddy Arnold could do it. He had no idea he would win it.

He was very happy about it. When he won it and got up on stage to accept it, he said to Eddy Arnold something like, "There's a lot of people who deserve it more than I do, but it may not get offered again, so I'm going to take it tonight!" He didn't know how true that was.

BP: Were you on the bus in August of 1969 when Marty had his first heart attack?

Bobby: Yes, I was. We had worked Toledo, Ohio the night before and we had an engagement in Youngstown, Ohio. I believe it was a Sunday. The King Sisters were on the bill to open for us. We stayed the night in Cleveland. It's not that far a drive. We got up fairly early, about 8:00 am. Back then, Marty was sort of heavy, ate a lot. We got on the bus and were just about half-way there. Marty had a small room on the bus and said he was going to the room. After a short period of time, Marty came out of the room and said, "Guys, I don't feel good." He was real gray, like burnt cigarette ashes. We took a look at him and said, "Marty, what's wrong?" He said, "I don't know. I feel like maybe I'm having a heart attack."

We had him lay down and started rubbing his arms and legs. We didn't know how to handle a situation like that. So, one of us went and told Okie, the bus driver, to go to the hospital. So he did. Got off the Ohio Turnpike to go to a hospital in this little town.

We got to the emergency room of the hospital; it was on a Sunday and there wasn't one single doctor on duty. Not one. The lady in charge of the entire hospital was a head nurse. So she took him in, took his blood pressure, and found his heart was irregular. Marty told me, "Go call the stadium where we were supposed to be appearing and tell them we're not going to be able to make it." The promoter's name was Mike and we had worked for him before. So I did; it took a few minutes for them to round him up and get him to the phone. But I finally got him on the phone and he said, "What's wrong?" I said, "I don't know, but I think Marty may have had a heart attack." Marty would never miss a show unless it was an absolute emergency, the man knew that.

The head nurse gave him a shot of Demerol. Now, Marty had just had a massive heart attack but she didn't know it. And that's the worst thing in the world she could have given him! That's like taking a whole hand of pep pills! So he got to feeling better and said, "Go call Mike back and tell him we'll be there for the night show." It started at 8:00 pm.

We kept telling this nurse, "Go get a doctor or something! Get him in here!" She couldn't find one. She wouldn't let us leave without signing a form releasing the hospital from responsibility for what might happen. By this time, Marty was dancin' around, feelin' high on this shot of Demerol she had given him. He said, "Sure, I'll sign it," and he did. He got back on the bus and we went to the show. He got dressed up and things were going great and he was feeling great. But by the time he got on the stage the shot was beginning to wear off. And we got down to "El Paso," which was always his closing song. We had our eyes on him and could see he was beginning to get ashen-looking, white, again.

Marty turned to me and said, "Bobby, go find Mike and tell him that I don't want to speak to nobody, I don't want to be stopped. As soon as I come off this stage and get to the bottom of this grandstand, I want to go immediately to the bus. I don't feel good." So, I went and got Mike and he got 24 or 25 cops, security people. When he got through "El Paso" he turned to me and handed me his guitar and said, "I like not to have made that." He got out to the bus and went to his room . . . and he didn't want to let any of us in. We made him let us in and he was in pretty bad shape. And we had a show date in South Carolina and we were going back to Cleveland to pick up a different interstate to go down through North Carolina. Just before we got to Cleveland we said, "You're going to go to the hospital." He didn't want to go. So we took him to a big hospital in Cleveland and they run an EKG on him and said he had had two massive heart attacks that day. *Two!* We spent the bigger part of that night with him there while the doctors came in and ran tests. They had him in intensive care. They told us we might as well go home; we couldn't do anything there. We came on to Nashville. He spent about a week to ten days there before they flew him back to Nashville.

That was in August. He rested up for several weeks and then went back working. At the end of the year, we worked four weeks in Las Vegas and twice in that four-week period they had to call the doctors while he was on stage. They had to call the doctors to be waiting for him when he came off. But they hadn't really found out what was wrong with him yet. Because the blockage to his heart valves had not shown up yet on any of the tests. And then, after we got back from Las Vegas, they put him in the hospital and really ran some extensive tests on him. And that's the first time the blockage showed up. They told him. "You've got two choices: either have the surgery or die." Actually, he only had *one* choice. And the surgery was still very new. He was probably one of the first dozen people to have it. He came through it like a trouper.

Now, about heart operations. For your first operation, the chances of surviving are about 90% in your favor. The second operation, it's about 52% against you. That's how Bobby Darin died, from his second bypass surgery. Marty knew he had already had more than they told him he would get out of the first one. But he didn't know for sure he could survive a second one. He tried very hard to survive that last operation but he would have been a very sick person if he had.

Maybe I spent more time on these questions than I should have, but I wanted to be as thorough as I could so people could understand. I have to go now because I have another appointment, but I'll be glad to talk to you again whenever you want. I'd like to see more being done to remember Marty and will be glad to help where I can. Say "Hi" to all my friends for me.

5

BIBLIOGRAPHY, 1970–1979

Marty entered the hospital in late January of 1970 for tests to determine the condition of his heart. He was still ill and on a reduced performance schedule, but he wanted to resume auto racing if possible. To do that, he had to pass a medical exam. Instead of receiving good news, he was told that his heart problem was more serious than had been realized. Two main arteries in his heart had become completely blocked and the other one nearly so. He had just finished a three-week engagement in Las Vegas, a series of recording sessions, and an exuberant performance at the Opry the previous Saturday night.

The doctors told him he had two choices: he could look forward to perhaps only a few months more of life or he could have experimental bypass heart surgery. But even with the operation, they said, he would have to lead a quieter life. Without the operation he had no chance at all. A week later, on January 27, he became one of the first people to undergo the surgery. It was a painful experience, but one that strengthened his religious faith. He waited for years to tell the story, but finally said that while he was on the operating table, he had seen Christ and had started to cross a stream to go to Him, only to see Christ hold up His hand and say, "Not yet."

His hospital ordeal was softened by thousands of heartfelt cards, letters, and gifts from fans wishing him well. He had been surprised and deeply moved. Until that time, he said, he hadn't realized how close his fans felt to him or how much he was loved in a personal way. The caring had gone much deeper than he had ever thought about. Unable even to think of answering the over-whelming volume of mail personally, he wrote a song, "A very special way," for the fans, one that expressed in his own way the love affair he shared with them. It appears on the album "My woman, my woman, my wife."

He didn't stay in bed long. He was home by early February and, much to the amazement of everyone, returned to the Opry stage March 30th for a rousing and love-filled evening. And despite vigorous objections from his doctors, family, and business associates, he took and passed his race driver's physical in July and resumed racing a few weeks later. The desire to race, he said, was behind the will to live. But his doctors refused to let him resume a vigorous tour schedule, so he confined his concerts largely to the Nevada night club circuit for the next several years. Soon after he returned to the stage, he did television shows such as "Hee Haw" and two locally televised specials on WSM-TV with Ralph Emery.

He won his second Grammy for "My Woman, My Woman, My Wife," a song he wrote as a tribute to his own wife. And in April, the Academy of Country Music named him the first recipient of its "Man of the Decade" Award at its annual awards program.

He continued to make films that centered around his personal interests. A 1972 film, "Country Music," was simply a chronicle of Marty Robbins. It followed him through a performing and racing schedule of several weeks, ending with a typical Saturday night Opry show. The following year he starred in "Guns of a Stranger" and realized his lifelong dream of becoming a singing cowboy.

After his heart operation, he resumed racing with a passion. He moved up into NASCAR Grand National Circuit racing and loved it. Now he had the chance to race with the best in the business, and found out that he could hold his own. Although he never won a race, he finished in the top ten several times and was considered a well-liked and respectable racer by the other drivers. His love of the sport frequently dominated the interviews he gave. And the racing industry paid tribute to him in 1974 with a "Marty Robbins Night" at the Nashville Speedway. In late 1974 and early 1975 a series of three major accidents in a row caused him to reconsider his participation in the sport. The last wreck, May 4th at Talladega, left him dazed and his car destroyed. He announced his decision to quit. But he was unable to stay away and by June he was talking about returning. He tried to quit on other occasions over the years, and sometimes the announcements of his "retirement" reached the public through the media after he had already resumed his activity. It was an addiction he could never conquer; his last race was the Atlanta 500, just three weeks before his final heart attack.

He changed record companies briefly in the early 1970s, leaving Columbia for Decca/MCA. But he soon became disappointed with the agreement and returned to Columbia.

By 1975 his doctors allowed him to resume touring again as long as the schedule lasted only a few days in length. In addition, he made his first trip to England on Easter weekend for the Wembley Festival, and was popularly received. He returned to England frequently thereafter, and sometimes combined the trip with show dates in other European countries.

Highlights of 1976 included hosting duties on the February Academy of Country Music Awards Show, driving the pace car at the Indianapolis 500 Memorial Day race, and making a promotional film for the Convention and Visitor's Bureau of the city of El Paso.

He started a series of successful concert tours with Merle Haggard in the Spring of 1977. The two performers had strikingly different stage styles but the combination worked and they repeated the tour several times over the next three years. Merle's son (now a performer in his own right) had been named after Marty and the Marty/Merle friendship went back many years. In fact, Merle had written "Today I Started Loving You Again" for Marty, but had ended up recording it himself. It became one of Merle's own biggest hits.

During the latter half of the 1970s, Marty appeared frequently on such popular talk shows as The Dinah Shore Show, The Merv Griffin Show, and the Mike Douglas Show. On one of the Douglas shows in 1979, Marty paid tribute to Elvis Presley by singing "The Performer." It was a song he wrote for Elvis, who died before he could hear it. It's the only known tape of Marty performing the song, a rare piece of film indeed.

Marty made three television series, the most popular of which was "Marty Robbins' Spotlight." It started production in late 1977 and aired for two years. The concept was simple and effective: each show highlighted one guest and Marty. While it managed to catch some of the magic of his personality and stage persona, he soon tired of the show because of the time it took. He called it quits on his own accord.

In June of 1978, Marty created chaos at the Opry when he drove his brand new Panther deVille on stage to show the car to the fans; it had been flown over from England only a few days before. Roy Acuff (always the showman and unofficial "boss" of the Opry) went after the police and Marty received, on stage, his first parking ticket for the car!

Another brush with the Opry management occurred when Marty became the first person to take horns on the Opry stage. Although horns had always been rejected for use on the Opry stage (because they were not considered to be a traditional country instrument), they had been a part of Marty's band for some time. Marty was "fired" and the public argument over the dispute between Marty and Opry officials lasted for three or four weeks before it was settled and Marty was allowed back on the stage.

At the close of the decade, the western influence on Marty was stronger than ever. He was wearing brightly colored stage suits with Spanish designs made by Nudie in California. They were uniquely his and frequently of his own design. During the mid-seventies he had worn stage clothes with a strong western or American Indian style. Just as often, he would wear business suits; he had worn business suits over the years and this set him apart from most other country music performers. In April of 1979, Marty received another honor which gave him particular pleasure, a special Trustees' Award from the Cowboy Hall of Fame. The person bestowing the honor at the Museum in Oklahoma City was Gene Autry.

Publicity photo from the early 1970s after Marty decided to lighten his hair a bit.

BIBLIOGRAPHY, 1970–1974

[Photograph]. *Music City News;* 1970 January; 7(7): 27.
Photograph of Marty and Ronnie at the plane as Ronnie is leaving for
military service in Germany. The photo was taken in late 1969.

Thru the looking glass [monthly column]. *Country Song Roundup;* 1970
January; 22(126): 46.
The column notes that Marty had been ill and hospitalized in Cleveland,
Ohio.

Opry star Marty Robbins hospitalized for tests. *The Tennessean;* 1970
January 23; (Friday): 16.
Marty entered St. Thomas hospital in Nashville Tuesday to undergo
routine diagnostic tests to see how badly his heart was damaged from
his August heart attack.

Hurst, Jack. Robbins considers heart operation. *The Tennessean;* 1970
January 24: 1, 5.
Note: Illus.
The article quoted Mary as saying: "I've got a 1969 Dodge Dart ready
and I wanted to race it. I didn't want to start racing again until I took
these tests and found out everything was all right, so I came and took
them and found out nothing was all right." The tests showed that two of
the three of the main arteries to his heart were completely blocked and
the other one was 75% clogged. His doctor, Dr. William Ewers, is
leaving the decision about the bypass operation up to him. Marty main-
tains the attack hasn't affected his career too much, saying he's felt fine
since his August attack and has just finished a two-and-a-half-week
engagement in Las Vegas.

Robbins may have open heart surgery. *Nashville Banner;* 1970 January
24.

O'Donnell, Red. Robbins will have heart operation. *Nashville Banner;*
1970 January 26: (Monday) 2, 8.
Note: Illus.
The operation is set for Tuesday morning.

Surgery on Robbins set today. *The Tennessean;* 1970 January 27: 1.
The surgery will start at 8:30 am and the doctors will use arteries from
Marty's legs to bypass the clogged arteries.

O'Donnell, Red. Robbins makes plea for prayers. *Nashville Banner;* 1970 January 27.

Robbins surgery success. *Nashville Banner;* 1970 January 27: 1.
The five-hour operation was termed a success. He will be in intensive care for approximately three days and then be in the hospital for another week.

O'Donnell, Red. Robbins in satisfactory condition. *Nashville Banner;* 1970 January 28: 1.
The operation consisted of bypassing three clogged arteries by using veins from his legs. The doctors said that he would be very uncomfortable during the healing process; "He'll feel like a truck hit him," said the doctor, explaining that chest discomfort would be the worst problem of all. The condition was caused because they had to split the breastbone to get to the heart. Marty was the 17th to have bypass surgery at the hospital, but the first to have all three arteries bypassed. Only about 300 people in the U.S. have had such an operation.

Hurst, Jack. Singer Marty Robbins' unique heart artery operation successful. *The Tennessean;* 1970 January 28: 1, 2.
The operation took four hours and his blood pressure is the best it's been since his heart attack. He'll be under sedation for the next several days and in the cardiac intensive care unit. He's the first at the hospital to have all three arteries bypassed and only about 300 such operations have been performed in this country. It's a very new operation that's only been performed in the last two years. The test that disclosed the degree of congestion in the arteries (a muscle arteriogram) is also a very recent medical advance. The doctor at the press conference was quoted as saying a movie was made of Marty's operation, but it would be several weeks before the film would be ready. Assessing Marty's condition when he entered the hospital, the doctor said "he was hanging by a thread."

Marty Robbins "resting well." *The Tennessean;* 1970 January 29; (Thursday).
All of his vital signs are good and he'll be moved from the cardiac care unit in two days, and may be able to leave the hospital in two weeks.

Robbins shaves self, sits in chair. *The Tennessean;* 1970 January 30: 4.
The hospital spokesperson said Marty was resting better, sat up in a chair for a while, and helped shave himself today.

Recuperating Robbins gets private room. *Nashville Banner;* 1970 January 31: 10.
Marty was moved from the cardiac care unit to a private room. He's said to be progressing well and may be able to go home by Valentine's Day (February 14th).

Marty Robbins heart operation a success; may resume his career soon. *Country Hotline News;* 1970 January: 1, 6. Illus.
Large-print headline and long article cover Marty's operation and future plans. [Editorial note: although the cover date of the journal is January, the article was written after Marty left the hospital.]

Robbins to leave care unit. *The Tennessean;* 1970 February 1.

Robbins moved to private room. *The Tennessean;* 1970 February 1.

O'Donnell, Red. Marty has short walk at hospital. *Nashville Banner;* 1970 February 3: 2.
Marty walked up and down the hall several times Monday morning; the only ill effects seemed to be bad headaches. He hopes to go home before too long and resume his career by early Spring, when he has a month long booking at the Fremont Hotel in Las Vegas starting April 16th. "I'll never be able to answer all of the mail," he said, "but I'll read every bit of it."

Columbia's Robbins under knife. *Billboard;* 1970 February 7: 42.
Article about heart surgery two weeks ago. Marty Robbins heart operation a success; may resume career soon.

Marty Robbins on mend following heart surgery. *Music City News;* 1970 February; 7(8): 1, 24.

O'Donnell, Red. Marty will go home Tuesday. *Nashville Banner;* 1970 February 9: 1, 2.
Note: Illus.
Marty is scheduled to check out of the hospital Tuesday morning and may resume his career in about three weeks. Marty said the first order of business is to finish an album he had started before entering the hospital; then he plans to return to the Opry stage, possibly as soon as March 14th. His first road trip will be to Las Vegas in April. He admits he's already been singing the past several days—"to myself and not too loud. I don't want to disturb the other patients." He says he is now able to take a full deep breath, "something I haven't been able to do for

almost a month." He said he will use some of his time to read some of the more than 10,000 pieces of mail he's received over the past three weeks.

Opry star Robbins out of hospital. *The Tennessean;* 1970 February 10: 1.

Robbins recovering from heart surgery. *Variety;* 1970 February 4; 257: 51.

Country Hotline News; 1970 March; 1(4): 1, 6.
Note: Illus.
Article includes interview with the doctor and details of the operation. Doctor quoted as saying a film was made of the operation.

The Drifter. *Country Corner;* 1970 March/April; 5(23): 21.
Album Review.

Letters to the editor [monthly feature]. *Country Song Roundup;* 1970 March; 22(128): 29.
Fan letter.

Marty's on the mend. *Music City News;* 1970 March; 7(9): 1.

My kind of country. *Country Corner;* 1970 March/April; 5(23): 21.
Album review.

[TV appearance] NBC "The Dean Martin Show"; 1970 March 5.
Information from the NBC Index of Shows.

[Photograph]. *The Tennessean;* 1970 March 6: 14.
A photo of Marty and Chet Atkins at a fundraiser held for the American Cancer Society.

[Photograph]. *Nashville Banner;* 1970 March 12: 55.
Photo of NASCAR racer Bobby Allison and wife with Marty at Grammy Awards banquet in Nashville.

Robbins heart surgery gave national coverage to our cardiac program. *St. Thomas Scope;* 1970 March; 5(2): 1, 4.
St. Thomas Hospital's monthly journal article about Marty's surgery and how the press was handled.

Thompson, Jerry. They stayed on and on for Marty. *The Tennessean;*
1970 March 30: 1, 2.
Note: Illus.
Long article about Marty's first time back at the Grand Ole Opry after
his heart attack, with details about his performance and the wild crowd
reaction to his return. With characteristic modesty, about midway
through the show he sat at the piano and said: "I had so many things I
was going to say tonight. I want to thank all my friends for their concern
and I want to thank God for letting me be here. Now I can't think of
anything else to say, so I guess I'll have to sing for you." And he did,
going overtime until about 12:30.
Throughout the show fans crowded up to the front of the stage to take
pictures, and the result is described as resembling a fireworks display at
a small country fair. He's quoted as saying he's learned a lot [from
living through the operation]: "I've learned to accept a lot. I'm just so
glad to be alive. Used to, I wouldn't even come into town if the sun
wasn't shining. I loved the sunshine. Now, every day is a good one."
He plans to confine his activities to Las Vegas and television shows.
He's scheduled to appear on the Johnny Cash, Dean Martin, and Andy
Williams shows. He will appear tonight from midnight to 1:00 am on a
special WSM television show with Ralph Emery.

Hotline around Nashville [monthly feature]. *Country Hotline News;*
1970 April; 1(5): 4.
Photo and comments that Marty was at the Grammy Awards (in
Nashville) recently.

12th annual Grammy Award winners named. *Music City News;* 1970
April; 7(10): 1, 11.
Note: Illus.
Marty listed. Article includes photo of Marty on p. 11.

[Performance review]. *Variety;* 1970 April 29; 258: 223.
Review of Marty's engagement at the Fremont Hotel.

Robbins top C & W Man of the Decade. *Nashville Banner;* 1970 April
14: 22.
Note: Illus.
Marty received the Man of the Decade Award from the Academy of
Country Music at its 5th annual awards program and dinner.

Robbins, Marty. Camelia. *Country Song Roundup;* 1970 April;
22(129): 21.
Note: Lyrics to the song.

Marty receiving the "Man of the Decade" Award from the Academy of Country Music in 1970. Presented by Herb Alpert and Linda Crystal. (Photo from the Country Music Foundation)

Haggard sweeps west coast with 5 awards. *Music City News;* 1970 May; 7(11): 1, 31.
Note: Illus.
Fifth Annual ACM Awards. Marty received Man of the Decade Award. Photo of Marty on p. 31.

Winters, Audrey. Around town in Hollywood. *Music City News;* 1970 May; 7(11): 12.
Includes Marty's comments on winning the ACM Man of the Decade award.

Marty in person; returns to ovations. *Country Hotline News;* 1970 May; 1(6): 8.
Note: Illus.

Backstage at the ACM Awards program with Waylon Jennings, 1970.
(Photo by Jasper Dailey)

Full-page story with photos of Marty's appearance Easter weekend on a Ralph Emery Special. Article also mentions appearances on the Opry stage and the Johnny Cash TV Show (set for May 13th). The live telecast was simulcast on WSM radio and WSM-TV as a "welcome back" for Marty. Marty alternated singing and playing the piano and exchanging jokes and comments with Ralph Emery, the host of the program. He told how he would play jokes on the WSM late-night DJ by driving to Murfreesboro so he could place a long-distance call, disguise his voice, and pretend he was a trucker calling in. He'd ask Hill to play a Marty Robbins song and talk to him until he realized who it was. On the serious side, Marty talked about God and prayer. He said that right after the operation, the pain was so intense that he prayed to God to take the pain away or take him, because it was almost unbearable. He quickly realized he had said something stupid, and prayed again to live. Shortly after that the pain began to go away.

Haggard wins awards. *Country Hotline News;* 1970 May; 1(6): 3.
Note: Illus.
Academy of Country Music Awards program. Marty was honored as "Man of the Decade"; small photo included.

[Advertisement]. *Country Music People;* 1970 June; 1(5): 38.
Ad for the Marty Robbins Fan Club in England.

Around Nashville [news column]. *Country Music People;* 1970 June; 1(5): 8.
Much of the column covers the Man of the Decade Award won by Marty at the Academy of Country Music Awards, April 13th. Quote from Marty at the time he won the award.

Word of prophesy; editorial opinion. *Country Hotline News;* 1970 June; 1(7): 7.
Note: Illus.
One-half page article giving the reasons why neither Marty nor Merle Haggard was selected to replace Johnny Cash for the summer. Apparently, the network felt that if either became instant hits, it would be harder for Cash to return in the fall.

Breakdown of an album; My woman, my woman, my wife. *Country Music People;* 1970 July; 1(6): 25.
Album review of "My woman, my woman, my wife."

Myers, Bob. Racing saved his life. *The Charlotte News;* 1970 July 3.
The story is out of Daytona Beach, Florida, where Marty is in town to

be Grand Marshal of the 400-mile stock car classic tomorrow at the Daytona Speedway. The story says that a major factor in Marty's recovery from his heart operation was his strong desire to race again. He raced in 1968 at the Charlotte Motor Speedway and finished 12th; it had been a thrill. But it was his last race before his heart attack and he wanted to race again. It was this desire that got him to the hospital for tests and gave him hope through the hospitalization. Although he won't race tomorrow, he plans to race again as soon as he can.

Marty Robbins rarin' to go, passes physical for racing. *The Tennessean;* 1970 July 4: 18.
Note: Illus.
Dateline, Daytona Beach, Florida. Marty says he passed his physical yesterday and hopes to race in September. His plans for 1971 include dates in Las Vegas, Lake Tahoe, and Reno. The rest of the year may be spent racing. Marty served as Grand Marshal for today's Firecracker 400.

[Photograph]. *The Tennessean;* 1970 July 21: 11.
Photo of Marty with beauty contestants. Marty, Grand Marshal of the NASCAR 420 race at the Nashville Speedway, is holding the trophy for the winner of the Miss Nashville contest.

Robbins, Marty. My woman, my woman, my wife. *Country Song Roundup;* 1970 July; 22(132): 20.
Note: Lyrics to the song.

[Advertisement]. *Music City News;* 1970 August; 8(2): 5.
Half-page ad for album: My Woman, My Woman, My Wife. CS9978.

Marty Robbins to race again? *Country Hotline News;* 1970 August; 1(9): 2.
Note: Illus.
Marty may plan to resume racing.

New country music film. *Country Music People;* 1970 August; 1(7): 10.
Film review, "From Nashville with Music". Film rights to Ember Records.

[Performance review]. *Variety;* 1970 August 26; 260: 47.
Review of Marty's engagement at the Fremont Hotel in Las Vegas.

Sharpe, David. "The Gunfighter" wins his toughest fight. *Country Music People;* 1970 August; 1(7): 9.
Note: Illus.
Article about recovery from heart attack and surgery.

Thru the looking glass [news column]. *Country Song Roundup;* 1970 August; 22(133): 46.
Notes that Marty is recovering from a heart operation.

Marty's message to mankind: how to love a second-hand heart! *Country Music Star Life;* 1(1): n.p. Illus.

Around Nashville [news column]. *Country Music People;* 1970 September; 1(8): 6.
The Nashville 420, a NASCAR race, was held July 25; Marty was Grand Marshal. The race was won by Bobby Isaacs.

Cash returns on September 23. *Music City News;* 1970 September; 8(3): 1.
Marty listed among guests to appear the coming year.

A country Christmas. *Hillbilly;* 1970 September; (35): 12.
The article, about country music Christmas albums, includes "Christmas with Marty Robbins."

Around Nashville [news column]. *Country Music People;* 1970 October; 1(9): 7.
Quotes Marty's comments on the imitation Merle Haggard does of him on a current album.

Country Song Roundup salutes Marty Robbins. *Country Song Roundup;* 1970 October; 22(135): 14–15.
Note: Illus. (Photos by Bill Grine)
Most of the article covers his heart attack and surgery.

Lloyd, Harry. Marty Robbins, racer. *The Charlotte Observer;* 1970 October 9.
Marty will resume racing with a recently purchased Dodge Charger after two years away from the track. If he qualifies, he will race in the National 500 at the Charlotte Speedway on Sunday. Two years ago he drove the same race, starting in 33rd place and finishing 11th. Marty goes on to discuss how he became interested in racing and his plans for the future.

Marty Robbins races again. *Country Hotline News;* 1970 October; 1(11): 2.
Note: Illus.
Article about the October 12th NASCAR National race at Charlotte, North Carolina.

Marty tackles his mountain today. *The Tennessean;* 1970 October 11: 16. Illus.
Marty returns to racing, in the Charlotte 500, for the first time after his heart attack nine months ago. Some racing history given.

[Photograph]. *Billboard;* 1970 October 17: n.p.
Photograph of Marty and Ralph Emery from their recent TV special.

[Photograph] in article: Gospel men meet. *The Tennessean;* 1970 October 25.
Photo of a delegation to meet participants in the gospel convention includes Marizona and Janet Robinson.

Robbins-Haggard do TV Special. *Country Hotline News;* 1970 October; 1(11): 8.
Note: Seven photos from program accompany the article.
Detailed article on the Ralph Emery simulcast TV/Radio Special. The show brought out such a large crowd that security men had to block off the studio after 1000 fans crowded into space designed for 250 people. Merle's song, "Today I started loving you again," was originally written for Robbins. When Marty was slow to record it, Merle recorded it himself and had a huge hit. Haggard performed impersonations of other artists, including one of Marty. Two guests from the audience also got some attention: Tex Ritter and Roy Rogers. Marty did a number of songs at the piano.

BMI Awards dinner. *Music City News;* 1970 November; 8(5): 32, 34.
Note: Illus.
Marty among citation winners, October 13, 1970.

Haggard sweeps CMA awards show. *Music City News;* 1970 November; 8(5): 24, 25.
Note: Illus.
Marty performed his nominated song, "My Woman, My Woman, My Wife."

[Photograph]. *Music City News;* 1970 November; 8(5): 5.
Photo of Marty at a Charlotte, North Carolina race.

6,000 attended DJ Convention, Opry Birthday celebration. *Country Hotline News;* 1970 November; 1(12): 2, 7–8.
Note: Illus.
The article mentions a Kraft Music Hall show (the CMA Awards show); a photo of Marty singing on the show (seated on the steps of the stage) is included.

[Information on Marty]. *Kountry Korral:* 1970 December: Issue No. 4.
Provides an update for its European readers on Marty's health.

Academy of Country and Western Music Awards. *Country Song Roundup;* 1970 December; 22(137): 8–11.
Note: Illus.
Marty received The Man of the Decade Award; small photo on p. 8. This is the first "Decade" award to be given; ACM will present one each ten years to the performer of the decade.

Columbia Records presents Marty Robbins, Jr. *Country Corner;* 1971 February; 6(27): 12–13.
Note: Illus.
Album review. Ronny Robbins' first album. Marty joins him for two cuts on the album.

Padre. *Country Corner;* 1971 February; 6(27): 14.
Single review.

Everything beautiful for Stevens; also Miss Anderson, Robbins, Price. *The Tennessean;* 1971 March 17.
NARAS Awards.

[Advertisement]. *Country Music People;* 1971 April; 2(4): 32.
Ad for the movie, "From Nashville with Music," showing at a theater in London.

Grammy awards highlight of music business year. *Music City News;* 1971 April; 8(10): 26.
Note: Illus.
Best Country Song Award to "My Woman, My Woman, My Wife."

Letters to the editor [monthly feature]. *Country Song Roundup;* 1971 April; 23(141): 33.
A letter mentions the television simulcast with Marty, Merle Haggard, and Ralph Emery. The show was broadcast October 13, 1970.

[Album review] Greatest Hits, vol. III. *Billboard;* 1971 April 24;
33(17): 58.

Marty Robbins returning to Fairgrounds Speedway. *Nashville Banner;*
1971 April 29.
Note: Illus.
His appearance May 6th will be his second here since heart surgery.

[Performance review]. *Variety;* 1971 April 7; 262: 55.
Review of show at Harrah's in Reno.

[Advertisement]. *Country Music People;* 1971 May; 2(5): 2.
Ad for movie, "From Nashville with Music," playing in several theaters
in the London area.

The Chair. *Billboard;* 1971 May 8; 83(19): 66.
Single review.

Hurst, Jack. Visiting newsmen check out Opry. *The Tennessean;* 1971
May 10: 20.
Note: Illus.
Article includes photo of Marty and Am. Rosenthal, managing editor of
the *New York Times.*

Marty Robbins qualifies 19th in World 600 race. *Nashville Banner;*
1971 May 29.
Note: Illus.
The race to be held in Charlotte, N.C.

[Photograph]. *The Tennessean;* 1971 May 23.
Photo of Eddy Arnold, with Marty, Roy Clark, and John Davidson in
the background, in just-completed television production, "Sound
America."

[Advertisement]. *Country Music People;* 1971 June; 2(6): 2.
Ad for movie, "From Nashville with Music," playing in London area
theaters.

Letters to the editor [monthly feature]. *Country Song Roundup;* 1971
June; 23(143): 37.
Fan letter.

"Sound America" special taped. *Music City News;* 1971 June; 8(12): 1.
To be shown on prime-time television in the fall. Eddy Arnold host,
Marty a guest.

Executive House becomes totally home owned. *Nashville Banner;* 1971 July 21: 43.
Marty was one of the businessmen involved in the purchase.

Marty Robbins will drive in Dixie 500. *Atlanta Constitution;* 1971 July 24. Illus.
The race will take place August 1st at the Atlanta International Raceway. The article notes that Marty competed in the Grand American 250-mile race at AIR in 1967, in the National 500 at Charlotte, N.C. in 1968, finishing 12th, and this past May he finished 15th in the World 600 (also at Charlotte).

[Advertisement]. *Kountry Korral;* 1971 August; (4): 8.
Full-page ad for the movie, "From Nashville with Music."

From Nashville with Music. *Country Corner;* 1971 August; 6(29): 41–43.
Note: Illus.
Motion picture review.

Browning, Wilt. Robbins likes El Paso and auto racing, too. *The Atlanta Constitution;* 1971 August 2.
Note: Illus.
Auto racing story.

[Performance review]. *Variety;* 1971 August 4; 263: 47.
Review of show at the Fremont in Las Vegas.

Today. *Billboard;* 1971 September 4; 83(36): 22.
Album review.

Early morning sunshine. *Billboard;* 1971 September 11; 83(37): 55.
Single review.

Nashville scene [news column]. *Billboard;* 1971 September 11; 83(37): 52.
Marty brought along a large cake and coffee for the fans while he appeared on Ralph Emery's all-night radio show.

[Advertisement]. *Music City News;* 1971 September; 9(3): 5.
Full-page ad for album "Today."

Lane, Geoff. El Paso to Phoenix. *Country Music People;* 1971 September; 2(9): 16–17.

Marty at a performance in the early 1970s. (Photo from the Country Music Foundation)

Letters to the editor [monthly feature]. *Country Song Roundup;* 1971 September; 23(146): 39.
Two fan letters, one from Peggy Ann Munson, fan club president.

From the Heart. *Music City News;* 1971 October; 9(4): 22C.
Album review.

Hurst, Jack. Marty: the Opry's different balladeer. *The Tennessean;* 1971 October 10; (Sunday): 10–11.
Note: Illus.
In-depth interview; good photos.

The World of Marty Robbins. *Billboard;* 1971 October 23; 83(43): 50.
Album review.

TV promotes c-m month. *Music City News;* 1971 October; 9(4): 13A.
The David Frost Show included country music artists in October; Marty listed as a guest.

[Advertisement]. *Music City News;* 1971 October; 9(4): 5A.
An ad for the album, "The world of Marty Robbins."

[Performance review at the Fremont, Las Vegas]. *Variety;* 1971 November 24; 265.

Winters, Audrey. Around town [news column]. *Music City News;* 1971 November 9(5): 11.
The column includes a news item about a long recent *Esquire* article covering the country music industry. Marty is included in the article.

[Photograph]. *Music City News;* 1971 November; 9(5): 20.
Photo of Marty with Bill Anderson and CMA officials before a CMA show at Municipal Auditorium.

Marty Robbins sings theme songs in "Moonfire." *Overdrive;* 1971 December; 51. Illus.
Marty will sing two theme songs from the movie "Moonfire": "Get you off my mind," and "Wheel of life."

The Best Part of Living. *Billboard;* 1971 December 11; 83(50): 64.
Single review.

Opryland Iris halt Robbins. *Billboard;* 1971 December 11; 83(50): 49.
A fan sent thousands of iris bulbs to Opryland to establish the Marty

Robbins Iris Garden, but Marty is allergic to the flowers and won't be able to go near them.

Country music film slated here. *Nashville Banner;* 1972 January 6. Announcement that the movie "Country Music" will start filming February 15th at the Opry. Marty wrote the script and will back it financially and star in it; Bob Hinkle will be the director.

[Advertisement]. *Billboard;* 1972 January 22; pg. 55.
Note: Illus.
A one-half page ad for Marty's new single, "The best part of living."

Robbins writes and bankrolls "rush" country music movie.
Billboard; 1972 January 22; 84(4): 52.
The article is about Marty's movie, "Country Music." It says Marty wrote the script. The closing scenes of Marty on the Opry stage were filmed February 19th.

Jones, Bill. DJ's corner [monthly column]. *Music City News;* 1972 February; 9(7): 28.
A new movie, written and produced by Marty, is scheduled to shoot some scenes at the Opry this month. Sammy Jackson of KLAC to have a role in the movie. [Ed. note: Movie was "Country Music."]

Marty Robbins to make movie. *Country Hotline News;* 1972 February; 3(2): 2.
Note: Illus.
Details of the movie "Country Music."

Mayer, Louise. Marty Robbins. *Kountry Korral;* 1972 February; (1): 14–15.
Note: Illus.
Alternate title: Louise Mayer presents Marty Robbins. Louise was vice-president of Marty's fan club at the time.

Glick, Shav. Sound of racing engines is music to Marty Robbins. *Los Angeles Times;* 1972 March 1; (Part 3): 1, 8.
Note: Illus.
Good quotes and historical detail. He plans to drive this week in the Miller High Life 500 at the Ontario Raceway. "Nobody likes the idea except me," he said. "My wife, my doctor, my agent, and all my friends think I'm crazy. But I just can't resist the urge to race. If I was afraid of something happening to me, I'd get in a closet and forget about

life. If I did that, though, I'd probably be afraid of the dark and scare myself to death." Marty is also quoted as saying, "I just want to make the race. That's what I love, driving against those fellows. There are some I don't even try to run with. I know who I can pass and who I can't. I'm just in it for the fun of it." His biggest thrill came the day he outran Bobby Allison in qualifying for a race. Bobby, in turn, takes credit for Marty's entry into the world of NASCAR racing. He had been impressed with Marty's ability on the tracks around Nashville and encouraged him to move up to the big cars. Marty also plans to use the Ontario track while he's in town to shoot some footage for a movie he's making.

Foyt wins Ontario; Marty Robbins 8th. *The Tennessean;* 1972 March 6. Note: Illus.

Glick, Shav. Country music, roaring engines; sweet sounds to Marty Robbins. *Annison Star* (AL); 1972 March 4.

Hillburn, Robert. Marty Robbins still writing hit songs. *Los Angeles Times;* 1972 March 4.
General article: Includes comments about Marty being limited to playing Nevada clubs since his heart attack. At that time, his doctors wouldn't let him tour. His concert tonight at Long Beach for KLAC radio is his first appearance outside of Nevada night clubs. He also plans to start his own mail order service in order to get his records to his fans. Marty says, "I feel it is the best way to reach my fans, to make sure they can get my records. I've had so many people write me and say they can't find my records in the stores that it seems time to do something about it."

Nashville writers mold the sound. *Music City News;* 1972 March; 9(9): 17B, 26B.
Marty mentioned as one of artists recording rock and roll.

[Performance review]. *Variety;* 1972 March 22; 266: 71.
Review of show at the Fremont in Las Vegas.

NASCAR [news column]. *Area Auto Racing News;* 1972 April 19.
Marty to enter the May 7 Winston 500. To be his first Alabama International Motor Speedway appearance.

Hotline around Nashville [monthly feature]. *Country Hotline News;* 1972 April; 3(4): 6.

Note: Illus.
Photo and racing news that Marty finished 8th in the Ontario, California, race.

Racing sweet music to Marty Robbins. *Akron Beacon Journal* (OH); 1972 April 4.

Robbins Winston entry. *National Speed Sport News;* 1972 April 19. The race will take place Sunday, May 7th.

Marty Robbins will run in Winston 500. *The Sylacauga Advance;* 1972 April 20; Thursday.

Bolton, Clyde. High notes, high banks for Robbins. *The Birmingham News;* 1972 April 21; (Friday).
Auto racing stories.
The article mentions Marty's racing history and notes he was voted Rookie of the Southern 500 at Darlington last year after his 7th place finish there.

Granger, Gene. His values changed. *Spartanburg Journal* (SC); 1972 May 15.
Racing interview.

Granger, Gene. Marty just likes it. *Southern Motor Sports Journal;* 1972 May 26.
Marty talks about his race at the Winston 500, when his carburetor restrictor was set in an illegal manner and allowed him enough speed to run with the leaders. He finished 18th and was voted "Rookie of the Race." He declined the award, turned himself in and was fined and dropped to last place. Marty said of the race, "The only time I've ever gone faster was when I was in a jet." He's raced the Grand National Circuit for three and a half years now; his best finish to date was 7th in the Southern 500 last September, where he was voted "Rookie of the Race."

Bibb, John. An honest day's work. *The Tennessean;* 1972 May 9.
Racing story.

Marty visits with fans. *Music City News;* 1972 May; 9(12): 4.
Note: Illus.

"Moonfire" premiere set for "The biggest little town in Ohio." *Overdrive;* 1972 May: 1.

Premiere set May 12 for the movie "Moonfire." Marty to attend. Sings two songs on the soundtrack: "Wheel of life," and "Get you off my mind."

[Performance review]. *Variety;* 1972 May 31; 267: 55.
Review of show at the Fremont in Las Vegas.

[Performance review]. *Daily Variety;* 1972 May 31.
Review of show at the Fremont in Las Vegas.

"Sinner" Robbins confesses; car had no carburetor ring. *National Speed Sport News;* 1972 May 10: 21.
Marty ran the race without the required restrictor in place. Asked why he did it, he said, "Ever since I started racing, I wondered if I could drive as well as the best drivers in the race. My car wouldn't go fast enough with the restrictor ring in the carburetor for me to find out if I was really a racing driver or not. By finishing where I did, I proved to myself I can drive with the best of them."

Song writers corner [news column]. *Country Song Roundup;* 1972 May; 24(152): 43.
Comments on Marty's singing "My woman, my woman, my wife" on a televised awards show last year.

Four styles of Marty Robbins. *Kountry Korral;* 1972 June–August; (3–4): 49–50.
Album review. Two-record set. Photo on p. 50.

Hotline around Nashville [monthly feature]. *Country Hotline News;* 1972 June; 3(6): 5.
Note: Illus.
Notes that Marty plays the Fremont Hotel in Las Vegas regularly, and quotes West Coast manager Marty Landau.

Letters to the editor [monthly feature]. *Country Song Roundup;* 1972 June; 24(155): 35.
Fan letter from Louise Mayer, vice-president of his fan club.

Marty "serious" about 'Cracker. *Southern Motor Sports Journal;* 1972 June 23.

Racing "top ten" singer's target. *Democrat and Chronicle* (Rochester, NY); 1972 June 14.
Marty will enter more races.

Wyant, Martin. Gentlemen . . . start your engines [racing news column]. *Chicago Tribune;* 1972 June 19.
Marty finished 8th in this year's Miller 500 at Ontario and 7th in the 1971 Southern 500; he will enter more races now that he has a better car.

Marty Robbins "Favorites" (Harmony KH 31257). *Billboard;* 1972 June 24; 84(26): 58.
Album review.

[Photograph]. *Nashville Banner;* 1972 June 28.
Caption: "Marty gets a Decca welcome." Photo of Marty and Decca record executives at a luncheon where Marty signed a new recording contract with them.

"Firecracker 400" set Tuesday for Daytona. *Southern Motoracing;* 1972 June 29.
Marty is making his first Daytona start.

Marty Robbins. *Kountry Korral;* 1972 June–August; (3–4): 27.
Album review.

Decca signs Marty. *Music City News;* 1972 July; 10(1): 3.
Note: Illus.

Marty Robbins signs Decca pact for records and movies. *Billboard;* 1972 July 15; 84(29): 34.
Marty was honored at a luncheon last week at which he signed a five-year contract and revealed his recording and film plans. His son, Ronny, also signed with Decca under the name of Marty Robbins, Jr.

Jack and Chill get into act. *Arizona Republic;* 1972 July 22.
Note: Illus.
About the filming of the movie "The Drifter." Photos include Marty and Chill Wills. [Ed. Note: movie title was later changed to "Guns of a Stranger."]

Marty Robbins; I'll keep racing. *Country Hotline News;* 1972 July; 3(7): 2.
Note: Illus.
Article includes racing story about a carburetor problem and a previous announcement that he would quit racing. Because of the carburetor incident at the Winston 500, Marty declined the Rookie of the Year

award at the race. Marty went on Ralph Emery's all-night radio show to explain the incident to his fans. He said he had been illegal, but hadn't deliberately cheated. He said at that time he was quitting racing because that event had embarrassed too many people. During the program, more than 500 calls and letters encouraged him to continue racing.

Mathews, Doris J. Despite blazing sun, there's a Chill at Apacheland. *Apache Sentinel;* 1972 July 27: 1, 6–7.
Note: Illus.
Filming of "Guns of a Stranger." Photos of Marty, Chill Wills, producer Bob Hinkle, and other cast members.

[Photograph]. *Music City News;* 1972 July; 10(1): 12.
Photo of Marty and Ronnie. Ronnie identified as just out of the service and starting a singing career.

Sonny James and Marty Robbins in label change. *Country Music People;* 1972 July; 3(7): 4.
Note: Illus.
Marty signed a new recording contract with MCA/Decca, leaving Columbia after a number of years. Photo of Marty and his band included.

Will the real Marty Robbins please stand up? *Country Song Roundup;* 1972 July; CSR Annual (156): 6–23.
Note: Illus.
Interview includes comments on auto racing, Ronnie's coming into the business, preparations for a new movie ("Country Music"), and song writing.

Browning, Wilt. Robbins likes El Paso and auto racing, too. *The Atlanta Constitution;* 1972 August 2 (Monday). Illus.
Racing interview.

Marty moves to Decca. *Country Music Review;* 1972 August; 1(6): 26.

Marty Robbins signs Decca Record-movie pact. *Country Hotline News;* 1972 August; 3(8): 3.
Note: Illus.
The article briefly discusses Marty's signing with Decca. It also notes that Marty owns considerable real estate in Nashville, including a 400-unit apartment complex with Eddy Arnold. Photos of Marty and Owen Bradley, and Marty and Marty Robbins, Jr. (Ronny Robbins) accompany article.

Mathews, Doris J. Star of "The Drifter" is also down-to-earth humorist. *Apache Sentinel;* 1972 August 3: 6, 7.
Note: Illus.
Long interview with Marty and information about the filming of "The Drifter" [later renamed "Guns of a Stranger"]. Includes stories about Marty's early life and starting his career. Good location photos.

All time greatest hits. *Billboard;* 1972 August 19; 84(34): 49.
Album review.

[Advertisement]. *Music City News;* 1972 September; 10(3): 27.
Ad for new single, "This much a man." (Decca 33006).

Capsule reviews of films playing in the area. *Ottawa Citizen* (Ontario, Canada); 1972 September 23.
Brief review of "Country Music."

A Glaser fan . . . is a Glaser fan. *Country Song Roundup;* 1972 September; 24(158): 11–13+.
Note: Illus.
Interview includes comments about Marty helping the Glasers get started in the business.

Uncle Sam's Ramble [monthly column]. *Country Music Review;* 1972 September; 1(7): 22.
The column says that part of Marty's agreement with Decca/MCA calls for television shows and motion pictures.

[Advertisement]. *Music City News;* 1972 October; 10(4): 14C.
Ad for Decca artists (includes photo of Marty).

[Photograph]. *Dallas Morning News;* 1972 October 14.
Photo of Marty with the caption "Music Visitor," saying Marty will visit Dallas for the opening of his movie "Country Music."

Wuntch, Philip. Marty Robbins plays perfect film role. *The Dallas Morning News;* 1972 October 18.
Long review of the movie "Country Music."

Claypool, Bob. Marty: music, motors, movies. *The Houston Post;* 1972 October 19.
Note: Illus.
Interview about the opening of the movie "Country Music" in area theatres and his racing interests.

Millar, Jeff. Singer Robbins dresses mod. *Houston Chronicle;* 1972 October 19 (Thursday); Sect. 4, page 9.
Something of a tongue-in-cheek interview in connection with "Country Music."

Claypool, Bob. "El Paso" to Vegas. *Houston Post;* 1972 October 29.
Note: Illus.
In-depth interview covers his Las Vegas performances, love of the old west, his all-night radio sessions with Ralph Emery, and opinions about trends in country music. Even though he uses a big orchestra sound in Las Vegas, he says it doesn't change the way he sings.

Four styles of Marty. *Country Music Review;* 1972 October; 1(8): 33.
Album review of a two-record set titled "Four Styles of Marty." Identified as a German issue: Country Music History CMH 108/9.

Marty Robbins at Fremont Hotel. *Las Vegas Sun;* 1972 October 29.

Pugh, John. "I hope people like my singing" says Jeanne. *Music City News;* 1972 October; 10(4): 38C.
Note: Illus.
Jeanne Pruett includes comments about songwriting for Marty and how he helped her get a recording contract.

Robbins, Marty. Kate. *Country Song Roundup;* 1972 October; 24(159): 24.
Note: Lyrics to the song.

Wuntch, Philip. Marty Robbins plays perfect film role. *Dallas Morning News;* 1972 October 18.
Review of the movie "Country Music."

Country music film slated. *The Sun* (Colorado Springs, CO); 1972 November 9; (Thursday): 19.
Note: Illus.
Review of the film "Country Music."

[Performance review]. *Variety;* 1972 November 15; 269: 70.
Review of show at the Fremont in Las Vegas.

[Photograph]. *Music City News;* 1972 November; 10(5): 1.
One of front-cover photos of "Marty Robbins, Jr." (Ronny Robbins) and Lynn Anderson.

Powel, Bob. Pete Drake talks to Bob Powel. *Country Music People;*
1972 November; 3(11): 16–18.
Note: Illus.
Part of interview covers the time Pete worked with Marty. Recounts
creating the "fuzz" sound on the record "Don't Worry."

[Advertisement]. *Music City News;* 1972 December; 10(6): 11.
Decca ad for several albums, including "This much a man."

This much a man. *Billboard;* 1972 December 2; 84(49): 69.
Note: Illus.
Album review for Marty's first Decca (MCA) release.

Four styles of Marty. *Country Corner;* 1972 December; 7 (33): 29.
Album review for "The four styles of Marty," CMH 108/109.

I've got a woman's love. *Billboard;* 1972 December 16; 84(51): 52.
Album review.

Letters to the editor [monthly feature]. *Country Song Roundup;* 1972
December; 24(161): 34.
Fan letter from Doris Fjelstad.

[Photograph]. *Music City News;* 1972 December; 10(6): 24.
Photo of Marty Robbins, Jr. (Ronny Robbins) signing BMI agreement
with Frances Preston.

Ronny Robbins inks Decca recording pact. *Music City News;* 1972
December; 10(6): 6.

This much a man. *Music City News;* 1972 December; 10(6): 26.
Album review.

Borsten, Orin. Singing western's coming back; Marty's happy. *Post
Crescent* (Appleton, WI); 1973 January 26.
Note: Illus.
Interview about the movie, "The Drifter" [editorial note: the movie title
later changed to "Guns of a Stranger"]. Marty says of Gene Autry: "He
was to me one of the greatest cowboy singers. I saw his movies over and
over. All I wanted to be from the age of 12 was a singing movie star like
Autry." About country music fans: "The warmest, friendliest people in
the world. Once they accept you, you're in the family. They keep
buying you. They don't forget you. Once you have a fan in the country-

western field, you have to hurt him to get rid of him. And who wants to do that?"

Las Vegas Country [news column]. *Country Song Roundup;* 1973 January; 25(162): 26.
The column says Marty is supposed to move from the Fremont Hotel to the Landmark.

NASCAR's own ballader. *Stock Cars* [annual]; 1973 [January?]; (1973): 83-94, 97-98, back cover.
Note: Illus.
Yearbook published annually by Magnum-Royal Publishers, N.Y. Long article with excellent photos about Marty and his racing career. Topics covered: his childhood, Navy life, his entry into show business through local radio and television, and his interest in auto racing. Marty provides some detailed information about his racing activities in the 1960s in Nashville. He recounts that he only ran about nine races in 1966, but one was special because he won the race, beating Coo Coo Marlin. In 1968, Marty raced his first Grand National (NASCAR) race at Charlotte and finished 12th. He also ran five races in NASCAR's GT circuit. Good detail about Marty's start in NASCAR racing. His first race in his new car was at the Darlington 500, Labor Day (1971); he finished 6th and won the Fireball Roberts Memorial Trophy, which goes to the best rookie of the race.

Bound for Old Mexico. *Billboard;* 1973 January 27; 85(4): 114.
Album review.

Nashville publishers. *Billboard;* 1973 January 27; 85: 57-68.
Marty and his publishing companies included in article.

[Photograph]. *Nashville Banner;* 1973 January 30.
Photo of Marty at piano. Caption says he is celebrating his 20th year at the Grand Ole Opry. Marty has a new mustache in the photo.

York, Max. Guitars and fast wheels: Marty Robbins loves both. *The Tennessean;* 1973 January 30.
Good interview at the race track.

Powel, Bob. Bob Powel interviews Marty Robbins. *Country Music People;* 1973 January; 4(1): 18-20.
Note: Illus.
Long interview. Marty talks about the first time he ever heard himself on

the radio and jukebox, and about songwriting. Marty mentions that he has the last half-hour of the Opry and usually runs over about 15 minutes. [Ed. note: the film "Guns of a Stranger" is called "The Drifter" in this interview.] Marty credits Jimmy Dickens with getting him on Columbia Records. Jimmy told Columbia how good he was and they sent Art Satherly to listen to him, and Art signed him to a recording contract. He talks about writing "Ain't I right," which Bobby Sykes recorded under the name of Johnny Freedom when Columbia wouldn't let Marty release it. He talks about doing different kinds of music: using an orchestra in Las Vegas, using a small jazz group to record the album "Marty After Midnight." Other comments about the singers he likes, his change to Decca, why he left Columbia, making films, and his plans for the future.

[Advertisement]. *Country Music People;* 1973 February; 4(2): 31.
Note: Illus.
Ad for coming British tours; part of ad features Marty's tour.

[Advertisement]. *Country Music Review;* 1973 February; 1(12): 20.
One-page ad, with photo, for Marty's "debut" tour in England.

Country western greatest hits. *Kountry Korral;* 1973 February; (1): 23.
Album review. Marty has several cuts on this two-album set.

Robbins honored, Cash welcomed at two shows. *Billboard;* 1973 February 10; 85(6): 45.
Marty celebrated his 20th anniversary at the Grand Ole Opry. After the show, he stayed around to sign autographs.

Pearce, Al. Marty Robbins to try Daytona. *Times-Herald* (Newport News, VA); 1973 February 13.
Marty will race in the Daytona 500 on Sunday in his Bobby Allison-built car.

Nashville's renovation stirs old memories. *NASCAR Newsletter;* 1973 February 15; 18(4).
Note: Illus.
Long interview with Marty on the renovation site at the Nashville Speedway. Good detail on early racing stories. He says that when he beat Coo Coo Marlin and won the race, he kept the checkered flag. He says, "Well, they gave me the checkered flag. I took it and kept going, out the back gate. I've still got that flag. I won some heat races after that, but they wouldn't trust me with the flag. They gave me one of those small ones, the kind you can buy in the store for a dime."

Marty sings the blues. *Indianapolis News;* 1973 February 19.
Marty crashed in the Daytona 500 yesterday.

[Photograph]. *Illustrated Speedway News:* 1973 February 20.
Photo of Marty when he hit the wall in a spectacular crash.

Durden, Chauncey. It takes all kinds. *Richmond Times Dispatch* (VA);
1973 February 25: Sports, 1+.
Editorial includes comments about Marty's racing.

Everett, Todd. Marty Robbins [concert review]. *Hollywood Reporter;*
1973 February 27.
Note: Illus.
Performance review, Palladium, February 23. The review notes that
Marty's long-time friend and personal manager, Marty Landau, had
died the morning of the concert date.

Five kings of the country world. *Country Music People;* 1973 February;
4(2): 24.
Album review. Marty has two cuts on the album, "El Paso" and "By
the time I get to Phoenix."

Marty Robbins to tour. *Country Music People;* 1973 February; 4(2): 5.
Short article and schedule for upcoming British tour.

Robbins honored, Cash welcomed at two shows. *Billboard;* 1973 February 10: 45.
Marty's 20th anniversary at the Grand Ole Opry celebrated.

Robbins, Marty. I've got a woman's love. *Country Song Roundup;* 1973
February; 25(163): 20.
Note: Lyrics to the song.

Robbins, Marty. This much a man. *Country Song Roundup;* 1973 February; 25(163): 24.
Note: Lyrics to the song.

This much a man. *Country Music Review;* 1973 February; 1(12): 27.
Album review.

This much a man. *Kountry Korral;* 1973 February; (1): 23.
Album review.

This much a man. Records; Marty Robbins on a new label. *Country Music;* 1973 February; 1(6): 58.
Album review.

[Photograph]. *NASCAR Newsletter;* 1973 March 1: 18(5) 1, 6.
Photo of Marty hitting the wall in Daytona 500 on page 1; story on page 6.

[Advertisement]. *Country Music People;* 1973 March; 4(3): 27.
Full-page ad for album "This much a man."

[Advertisement]. *Country Music Review;* 1973 March; 2(1): 9.
Full-page ad for "This much a man" album.

DJ's corner [monthly column]. *Music City News;* 1973 March; 10(9): 31A.
Marty recently headlined the 2nd annual KLAC Radio Jamboree.

Marriott, Martin. Next month Marty Robbins will make his British debut. . . *Country Music Review;* 1973 March; 2(1): 4–5.
Note: Illus.
Article about Marty's upcoming British tour.

Marty Robbins celebrates 20th Opry Anniversary Saturday night, January 27. *Country Hotline News;* 1973 March; 4(3): 7.
Note: Illus.
Marty's first appearance on the Opry is noted as January 24, 1953.

Marty Robbins escapes race crash injuries. *Country Hotline News;* 1973 March; 4(3): 3.
Note: Illus.
Marty had a serious wreck at the February 18th race at the Daytona 500.

Marty Robbins tour off! *Country Music People;* 1973 March; 4(3): 4.
Dates for British tour change from March to September.

[Photograph]. *Country Song Roundup;* 1973 March; 25(164): 16.
Photo of Marty and Billy Walker.

Robbins will continue with racing circuit. *The Tennessean;* 1973 March 29.
Note: Illus.
Interview covers the details about his Daytona wreck. Marty had decided to quit racing after the wreck, but now says, "I had some second

thoughts about racing after my wreck in the Daytona 500, and decided to quit. But now I have had time to think it over, and my third thought is to continue when my schedule will allow." He lost control of his car coming out of the fourth turn and hit the wall, sliding 1000 feet backward. He wasn't hurt, but was unable to continue in the race because of extensive damage to his car.

Marty Robbins new movie, "The Drifter." *American Sound;* 1973 March/April; 1(4): 24–27.
Note: Illus.
Article about the movie is illustrated with both b/w and color photos. To be released in the fall. [Editorial note: the film was later renamed "Guns of a Stranger."]

Down home and around [monthly column]. *Country Music;* 1973 April; 1(8): 8.
Note: Illus.
The column notes that Marty recently celebrated his 20th anniversary at the Grand Ole Opry. Photo from "Guns of a Stranger" included.

Jeanne will soon have "satin sheets." *Music City News;* 1973 April; 10(10): 16, 24.
Includes comments about Jeanne Pruett working with Marty and writing for him.

Marty Landau, top agent, dies. *Country Music People;* 1973 April; 4(4): 4.
Article notes that Landau represented Marty Robbins and had negotiated Marty's scheduled British tour.

[Photograph]. *Country Corner;* 1973 April; 7(34): 13.
Note: Cover photo.
Photo of Marty and editor of this magazine at the Grand Ole Opry. Cover photo of Marty also on issue.

The road to Nashville. *Country Music Review;* 1973 April; 2(2): 42.
Motion picture review.

Cotterman, Dan. Return of the singing cowboy. *Horse and Rider;* 1973 May: 30–34.
Note: Illus., Cover photo.
Long article covers Marty as a western singer and the making of the movie, "Guns of a Stranger." Location photos. Biographical information about Bob Hinkle, producer of the film.

Marty in *Guns of a Stranger,* 1973.

Las Vegas Country [news column]. *Country Song Roundup;* 1973 May; 25(166): 48.
Notes that Marty remained at the Fremont and didn't move to the Landmark as previously announced.

Marty Robbins in "Country Music." *Bedford Daily Times-Mail* (IN); 1973 May 16.
Motion picture review.

[Performance review]. *Variety;* 1973 May 23; 271: 69.
Review of show at the Nugget in Sparks, Nevada.

The rise and fall of the Nashville sound. *Country Music Review;* 1973 May; 2(3): 10–12.
Note: Illus.
Marty included in the article.

Bound for old Mexico. *Country Music;* 1973 June; 1(10): 54.
Album review.

Left to right: Merle Haggard, Marty, Burt Reynolds, Dinah Shore in 1973. (Photo by Jasper Dailey)

Dean Martin Summer taped. *Country Hotline News;* 1973 June; 4(6): 8.
The summer show, "Dean Martin Presents Music—Country," will feature country music artists; Marty is listed as one of the guests.

Down home and around [monthly column]. *Country Music;* 1973 June;
1(10): 6.
Marty has said that he won't quit racing.

[Photograph]. *Country Hotline News;* 1973 June; 4(6): 8.
Photo of Marty signing an autograph for Barbara Mandrell.

This much a man. *Country Music People;* 1973 June; 4(6): 20.
Album review.

Robbins, Marty. Walking piece of heaven. *Country Song Roundup;*
1973 July; 25(168): 19.
Note: Lyrics only.

Marty Robbins. *Billboard;* 1973 July 21; 85(29): 22.
Album review.

Four styles of Marty Robbins. *Kountry Korral;* 1972 June–Aug.; No.
3–4.
Album review of "The four styles of Marty Robbins," a two-album set.

Country "Midnight Special" August 24. *Country Hotline News;* 1973
August; 4(8): 6.
Note: Illus.
Marty and Loretta Lynn will host the show.

Laney, Randy. Marty's ultra-fast practice lap puts him to "Singing the
blues." *Southern Motor Sports Journal;* 1973 August 17.
Racing interview; Marty's qualification for the Talladega 500.

Nashville scene [news column]. *Billboard;* 1973 August 18; 85(33): 30.
The column said Marty was preparing for a motorcycle movie, had a
motorcycle accident and hurt his hand.

Marty Robbins. *Music City News;* 1973 August; 11(2): 31.
Album review.

Midnight Special features country. *Music City News;* 1973 August;
11(2): 2.

Note: Illus.
Marty and Loretta Lynn, hosts. To be shown August 24; show taped in mid-July.

Music city hotline [monthly column]. *Music City News;* 1973 August; 11(2): 10.
Three items about Marty are included in the column: 1) Marty will be the first person on stage at the new Opry location, 2) He just filmed a segment (at the new Opry) for the Dean Martin summer replacement television show, and 3) Marty and Loretta Lynn just hosted a segment of the "Midnight Special" television show.

Race stars run tonight; Marty Robbins among Twin 100 race drivers. *Jackson Daily News* (MS); 1973 August 18.
Marty will race in the NASCAR Pepsi Twin 100 at the Jackson International Speedway at Clinton, a late model stock car race. The article says he was running 7th in the NASCAR Talladega 500 last Sunday before engine problems forced him out.

Bound for old Mexico. *Country Music Review;* 1973 September; 2(7): 33.
Note: Photo on p. 32.
Album review.

Country music chronolog [new column]. *Country Song Roundup;* 1973 September; 25(170): 34–35.
The column notes that Marty is continuing to race and is growing a mustache for a movie role.

Talent in action [concert review]. *Billboard;* 1973 September 1; 85(35): 16.
Concert review of Marty, Merle Haggard, and Charlie McCoy at the Hollywood Bowl in Los Angeles.

Granger, Gene. Throwing the bull. *Southern Motor Sports Journal;* 1973 September 7.
Detailed article about a bull Marty gave race driver Elmo Langley, and the problems that followed when it broke loose on Elmo's farm.

Nashville Scene [news column]. *Billboard;* 1973 September 15; 85(37): 30.
The column includes a kidding note that Marty fell asleep during a late-night interview on Hairl Hensley's show.

Lindberg, Jack. Racing milepost may be ahead for Robbins. *Kansas City Star* (MO); 1973 September 16.
Note: Illus.
Detailed racing interview. Marty is scheduled to race at the I-70 Speedway in the Mid-America Stock Car Racing Association 300 on Friday and Saturday.

Singer, Pat. Memo. . . [news column]. *Area Auto Racing News;* 1973 September 5.
Story about a bull Marty gave Elmo Langley.

Bound for old Mexico. *Country Music Review;* 1973 September; 2(7): 33.
Note: Photo on p. 32.
Album review.

Bound for old Mexico. *Country Music People;* 1973 October; 4(10): 17.
Album review.

Chapin, Kim. Will the real drifter please suit up? *Sports Illustrated;* 1973 October 8; 39(15): 80–90.
Note: Illus.
Major article about Marty and auto racing. Excellent photos. Words and music to the song, "Twentieth century drifter," included at beginning of article.

Fan time [monthly column]. *Country Song Roundup;* 1973 October; 25(171): 36.
The movie "Guns of a Stranger" set for Fall release. Previous title was "The Drifter."

Marty Robbins. *Country Music;* 1973 October; 2(2): 52.
Note: Cover photo. Illus.
Album review.

Reinert, Al. What makes Marty Robbins run against Richard Petty? *Country Music;* 1973 October; 2(2): 26–33.
Note: Illus. cover photo.
Long article and good photos. Mostly covering Marty's racing career.

Stafford, John. One of the great stylists in country music. *Country Music People;* 1973 October; 4(10): 28–29.

Note: Illus.
In-depth review of Marty's life and career. [Editorial note: the author incorrectly says Marty's last name is Robertson.]

This much a man. *Country Corner;* 1973 October; 8(36): 30–31.
Album review.

From the heart. *Country Music People;* 1973 November; 4(11): 13.
Album review. A Pickwick release in England, Hallmark CHM 757.

From the heart. *Country Music Review;* 1973 November; 2(9): 32.
Album review.

Marty Robbins. *Country Music People;* 1973 November; 4(11): 17.
Album review.

Marty Robbins. *Country Music;* 1973 November; 2(3).
Album review.

[Photograph]. *Music City News;* 1973 November; 11(5): 16.
Photo of Marty at the October MCA show during DJ Week in Nashville.

[Photograph]. *Country Music;* 1973 November; 2(3): 8.
Photo of Marty in racing clothes.

[Photograph]. *Country Music Review;* 1973 November; 2(9): 33.
Early photo of Marty.

Robbins, Marty. A white sport coat. *Country Song Roundup;* 1973 November; 25(172): 26.
Note: Lyrics to the song.

[Advertisement]. *Music City News;* 1974 January; 11(7): 27.
Note: Illus.
Full-page ad for "Midnight Special" Television program, hosted by Marty, to be broadcast December 28, 1973. Ad includes photos of Marty in racing clothes and notes that his new single is "Twentieth century drifter."

Hotline around Nashville [monthly feature]. *Country Hotline News;* 1974 January; 5(1): 7.
Note: Illus.
Marty received a shoulder injury last month trying to get a cow out of a ditch, and save it from drowning, after it fell off a bridge on his farm.

Insurance firms must assist buyers or risk changes. Report. *The Tennessean;* 1974 January 18.

Letters to the editor [monthly feature]. *Country Song Roundup;* 1974 January; 26(174): 36.
Fan letter.

Star gazing [monthly column]. *Music City News;* 1974 January; 11(7): 20.
Marty will resume concert tours in 1974. He has not been doing road shows since his heart attack.

Footsteps leave big tracks in country music. *Country Song Roundup;* 1974 February; 26(175): 29–32.
Note: Illus.
Article about several performers includes the information that Ronnie is dropping the "Marty Robbins, Jr." name; photo of Marty on p. 32.

Jeanne Pruett's satin stardom. *Country Music;* 1974 February; 2(6): 72–77.
Note: Illus.
Jeanne's songwriting for Marty mentioned in article.

Scott, Jim. A singer tuned to racing. *Grit* (Williamsport, PA); 1974 February 24.
Note: Illus.
Detailed racing interview.

Songs of Marty Robbins. *Kountry Korral;* 1974 February: 24.
Album review for "The songs of Marty Robbins," volumes 3 and 4.

Country music chronolog [news column]. *Country Song Roundup;* 1974 March; 26(176): 37.
Notes that Marty has signed to star in a movie titled "Motorcycle Joe." [Ed. note: this movie was never made.]

[Photograph]. *The Tennessean;* 1974 April 28.
Photo of Marty in racing clothes for Nitro fuel additive advertisement.

Have I told you lately that I love you. *Music City News;* 1974 May; 11(11): 12.
Album review.

Adamson, Dale. Marty Robbins still going strong 15 years after "El Paso" biggie. *Houston Chronicle;* 1974 June 22.
Performance review.
In describing his style, the writer says: "With no opening act to delay the show or distract the audience, the slightly gray-haired Robbins bounded onto the revolving stage right on cue with all the anxious-to-please charm of a bright-eyed amateur at his first audition. His obvious enthusiasm—he whooped it up between verses, kicking the show quickly into high gear and keeping it there—won over the near-capacity crowd in an instance." It goes on to say, "Robbins' voice—low and smooth, sliding up to a yodel—was clear, always pronouncing the lyrics distinctly rather than letting them trail off as so many popular singers do. Between songs he kept things alive with his non-stop stage patter and horribly corny jokes." He was wearing a new mustache described as "an overgrown walrus mustache."

Carr, Patrick. Nashville's biggest weekend; farewell to the Ryman, hello to Opryland. *Country Music;* 1974 June; 2(10): 32–34, 67–68.
Note: Illus.
Includes photo of Marty.

Jeanne Pruett; a real winner. *Country Song Roundup;* 1974 June; 26(179): 16–18.
Interview includes comments about writing "Love me" and other songs for Marty.

Marty Robbins gets more out of life. *The Oakland Press* (Pontiac, MI); 1974 June 22.
Note: Illus.
Good interview while racing at a track in Michigan. It quotes Marty as saying, "I get more excitement out of life than the average person. I do music for fun because I love to be on the stage. Out here, it's kind of like being on stage but it's a different kind of excitement. There's people in the stands and they're looking and enjoying. It's the same as singing a song."

Munro, Neil. Country music and race driving [news commentary]. *The Oakland Press* (Pontiac, MI); 1974 June 27.

Robbins, Marty. Twentieth century drifter. *Country Song Roundup;* 1974 June; 26(179): 23.
Note: Lyrics to the song.

Success hasn't changed the real Jeanne Pruett. *Music City News;* 1974
June; 11(12): 19A, 36A.
Article mentions her writing for Marty and his publishing house.

[Advertisement]. *Country Music;* 1974 July; 2(11): 7.
Full-page ad for the album "Own Favorites." Offer in conjunction with
promotion by Vaseline hair tonic. Same ad also appears in the August,
1974 (v. 2, no. 12) issue.

DJ's corner [monthly column]. *Music City News;* 1974 July: 33.
Marty recently headlined the WMC radio show concert in Memphis.

Koval, Johnny "K". Mini-view. Marty Robbins, part 1. *Country Song
Roundup;* 1974 July; 26(180): 30–31.
Note: Illus.
Interview includes comments about childhood, early career, auto rac-
ing, and other subjects.

Letters to the editor [monthly feature]. *Country Song Roundup;* 1974
July; 26(180): 33.
Fan letter.

Marty Robbins. *Country Music People;* 1974 July; 6(7): 9.
Album review. MCA MCF 2545.

Music city hotline [monthly column]. *Music City News;* 1974 July;
11(13): 10.
Marty recently finished 5th in a NASCAR race at Irish Hills, Michigan,
after starting 22nd.

Robbins, Marty. Twentieth century drifter. *Country Song Roundup;*
1974 July; 26(180): 24.
Note: Lyrics to the song.

Timms, Leslie. Superstars at the fair. *Spartanburg Herald-Journal*
(SC); 1974 July 7.
Note: Illus.
Racing interview. Marty says, "I'm not trying to race to get to the top. I
just enjoy the sport and I enjoy the people connected with it. People that
like country music usually like racing." He started working as a construction worker before he began recording in 1951 and says, "I just
decided that wasn't what I wanted to do, to work for a living. I know
that you have to work for a living, but I also knew that I wanted to do
what I liked."

[Photograph]. *The Tennessean;* 1974 July 12.
Photo of Marty and Governor Dunn as Marty is made an honorary Colonel on the Governor's staff. It's part of the recognition for "Marty Robbins Night," scheduled at the Nashville Speedway July 19 to honor Marty for his contributions to stock car racing.

Good 'n country. *Country Music People;* 1974 August; 5(8): 33.
Album review. MCA 421.

Koval, Johnny "K". Mini-view. Marty Robbins, part 2. *Country Song Roundup;* 1974 August; 26(181): 32–33.
Note: Illus.
Interview includes comments about the Grand Ole Opry, winning the Man of the Decade Award from ACM, early movies, and other topics.

Marty Robbins night in Nashville. *Country Hotline News;* 1974 August; 5(8): 12.
Note: Illus.
July 19th was Marty Robbins Appreciation Night at the Nashville Speedway.

Good 'n country. *Country Music;* 1974 September; 2(13): 49.
Album review.

Hee Haw viewers to see Buck on the MCN cover. *Music City News;* 1974 September; 12(3): 2.
The article covers a variety of topics, including the fact that a new show with Ralph Emery called "Pop goes the country" will debut in September. Marty will be a guest on the program.

Hotline around Nashville. *Country Hotline News;* 1974 September; 5(9): 7.
Note: Illus.
Marty's last NBC "Midnight Special" was so successful, he has signed to host more.

Marty. *Country Music Review;* 1974 September; 3(5): 40.
Album review.

Vaseline tonic promotion strikes a country note. *Journeyman Barber and Beauty Culture;* 1974 September.
Note: Illus.
Promotional tie-in with Marty's album, "Marty Robbins' Own Favorites."

Good 'n Country. *Country Hotline News;* 1974 October; 5(10): 11.
Note: Illus.
Album review.

Good 'n country. *Kountry Korral;* 1974 October/December; (7): 28.
Album review.

Marty, George, Tammy, Dolly make Wembley debut. *Country Music People;* 1974 October; 5(10): 5.
Information regarding the Wembley show of March 29, 1975. This show to be Marty's British debut. Pages 24–25 are ads for this show, including lists of expected performers.

Pearson edges Petty; Robbins hurt in crash. *Chicago Sun Times;* 1974 October 7.
Marty was injured Sunday in the National 500 race in Charlotte when he turned his car into the wall to avoid wrecked cars in front of him.

Robbins ok after crash. *Billboard;* 1974 October 19: 34.
Marty crashed in the Charlotte 500 race.

Roden, Jim. Marty's modern oldie. *Dallas Times-Herald;* 1974 October 1974.
Note: Illus.

Star gazing [monthly column]. *Music City News;* 1974 October; 12(4): 14A.
Marty has a new Fleetwood Cadillac, upholstered completely in black and white.

Fan time [monthly column]. *Country Song Roundup;* 1974 November; 26(184): 37.
Marty is appearing in a series of ads for Nitro 9 automotive products.

Have I told you lately that I love you. *Country Music Review;* 1974 November; 3(7): 30.
Album review.

Letters to the editor [monthly feature]. *Country Song Roundup;* 1974 November; 26(184): 35.

Marty hurt, but O.K. in race crash. *Country Hotline News;* 1974 November; 5(11): 2.
Note: Illus.

Details of Marty's crash and injuries at Charlotte, North Carolina October 6th.

Marty injured, but O.K. *Country Music People;* 1974 November; 5(11): 6.
Auto racing accident.

Wembley '75. *Country Music Review;* 1974 November; 3(7): 7.
Marty is one of the artists to appear.

Write in [letters to the editor]. *Country Music People;* 1974 November; 5(11): 23.
Fan letter.

Jimmy Payne's Nashville News [news column]. *Country Music People;* 1974 December; 5(12): 7.
Short paragraph on racing accident.

Jones, Mike. Robbins' singing survives crash. *Evansville Press* (IN); 1974 December 7.
Performance review. Marty still showed signs of injury from his Charlotte wreck, but performed well.

Scott, Susan. Ronnie Robbins: If I'm not good, it won't make any difference who I am. *Country Song Roundup;* 1974 December; 26(185): 29–30.
Note: Illus.

Star gazing [monthly feature]. *Music City News;* 1974 December; 12(6): 6.
The Oklahoma Music Association held its annual convention recently and Marty received the "Entertainer of the Year" award.

BIBLIOGRAPHY, 1975–1979

Marty Robbins—modern day cowboy. *Country People* (formally the *Illinois Music Country Magazine*); 1(2): 31–33.
Illus. Cover photo.

[Advertisement]. *Country Music Review;* 1975 January; 4(1): 2 [verso of cover].
Full-page ad for 7th Wembley Festival.

Marty Robbins brings country music to E.P. *El Paso Herald-Post;* 1975 January 8.
Photos of Marty and Ronnie Robbins accompany article.

[Photograph]. *El Paso Herald-Post;* 1975 January 4.
Marty to appear in concert; show also features Ronnie Robbins and Jeanne Pruett.

[Advertisement]. *Country Music People;* 1975 February; 6(2): 34.
One-half-page ad for MCA albums by Marty.

[Advertisement]. *Country Music Review;* 1975 February; 4(2): 35.
One-half-page ad for Marty Robbins albums on MCA Records.

Devil woman. *Country Music People;* 1975 February; 6(2): 15.
Album review.

Famous NASCAR drivers record record album. *Country Hotline News;* 1975 February; 6(2): 7.
Note: Illus.
Marty is included in the article and photos, but did not perform on the album itself.

Marty Robbins El Paso Day. *Country Hotline News;* 1975 February; 6(2): 6.
Note: Illus.
Marty was honored by the city Saturday, January 11, 1975. He received the key to the city, Lama boots, and took part in an airport ceremony.

Marty Robbins in Tahoe. *Herald Examiner* (Los Angeles, CA); 1975 February 5.

Robbins may trade sport coat in on racing jacket. *The Atlanta Journal;* 1975 February 8.
Brief article about NASCAR race drivers recording a record album, "NASCAR goes country."

Robbins racing again; says Petty sings off key. *The Tennessean;* 1975 February 8.
Note: Illus.

Seely, Fred. If a singer can race, then. . . *Jacksonville Journal;* 1975 February 9.

About the recording of the album "NASCAR goes country" by several race drivers. Marty included in the publicity but did not appear on the album.

Willson, Brad. Richard Petty stars at annual victory dinner. *Daytona Beach Evening News;* 1975 February 13.
Note: Illus.
Marty performed at the dinner honoring Petty.

Robbins pans NASCAR crooners. *National Speed Sport News;* 1975 February 19.
Note: Illus.
A light look at the recording of the album "NASCAR goes country"; interview with Marty and a couple of the drivers.

Robbins, Marty. Two gun daddy. *Country Song Roundup;* 1975 February; 27(187): 23.
Note: Lyrics to the song. Cover photo.

Scott, Susan. Marty Robbins . . . myth as man. Part 1. *Country Song Roundup;* 1975 February; 27(187): 16–18.
Note: Cover photo. illus.
Extensive interview mainly covers his relationship with his fans. Lots of fan quotes about Marty. One fan is quoted as saying, "Marty Robbins has always put himself on the same plane as the people in his audience. And over all these years as he got bigger, he hasn't changed one bit. He's always got time for anybody that turns out to see him."

Sontext [monthly column]. *Country Corner;* 1975 February; 9(43): 25.
Words to the song "Cigarettes and coffee blues."

Star gazing [monthly column]. *Music City News;* 1975 February; 12(8): 10.
The column covers two items about Marty; 1) El Paso recently honored Marty with a "Marty Robbins Day" and placed a plaque in the airport. The song "El Paso" is played every 30 minutes; and 2) several NASCAR race drivers recently recorded an album titled "NASCAR goes country" at Bradley's Barn and Marty attended the recording session.

[Advertisement]. *Country Music People;* 1975 March; 6(3): 36.
Full-page ad for Marty's MCA record albums.

Cackett, Alan. Marty Robbins in depth; part 1, (early days).
Country Music People; 1975 March; 6(3): 18–19.
Note: Illus. Cover photo.
Part 1—early days. Part 2 is published in the April, 1975 issue. The
article is a long review of Marty's early life and performing career. It
emphasizes Marty's versatility and ability to handle many styles of
music. The article provides the names of a number of people who
helped Marty start out in Phoenix and discusses his early recordings.

Devil woman. *Country Music Review;* 1975 March; 4(3): 30.
Album review.

Fan time [monthly column]. *Country Song Roundup;* 1975 March;
27(188): 44.
Marty set to appear on NBC-TV's "Midnight Special."

Holiday recipes of the stars. *Country Song Roundup;* 1975 March;
27(188): 28.

Sanders, Rex. Marty Robbins in Boyd's race. *The Chattanooga News
Free Press* (TN); 1975 March 13.
Note: Illus.
Marty will race there April 20th for the Alhambra Shrine Flying Fezz
Twin 50s race.

Kurycki, Mary Rita. Marty Robbins, a long way from '48. *Democrat
and Chronicle* (Rochester, NY); 1975 March 21.
Candid interview about his views of the country music industry, songwriting and politics (he's supported Barry Goldwater, George Wallace,
and will probably support Ronald Reagan if he decides to run). The
article notes that Ronny Robbins has been touring with his father the last
several months.

Kurycki, Rita. Crowd loves Robbins. *Democrat and Chronicle*
(Rochester, NY); 1975 March 22.
Performance review. Jean Shepherd and Joe Stampley also appeared.

LeGrand, Allen. Out in the West Texas town of El Paso, I fell in love
with a Mexican girl. *El Paso Today;* 1975 March; 27(3): 19, 21, 34.
Note: Illus.
Interview with Marty about writing "El Paso," "Feleena," and other
songs. Good photos.

Robbins, Marty. Two gun daddy. *Country Song Roundup;* 1975 March; 27(188): 26.
Note: Lyrics to the song.

Scott, Susan. Marty Robbins, racing driver. Part 2 of interview. *Country Song Roundup;* 1975 March; 27(188): 16–18, 27.
Note: Illus.
The article starts with a quote from race driver Richard Childress about the Oct. 6, 1974 wreck during the Charlotte 500: "There is no doubt in my mind, I wouldn't be here talking to you right now if Marty Robbins hadn't risked his life to save me." Childress had crashed, along with other cars, and his vehicle had come to a stop crossways on the track. Childress continues, "I looked down the track and saw Marty coming right at me. I knew if he hit me in the driver's side I'd either be mangled badly or killed. There was no way of my escaping injury and no way out of his path. Then I saw something I still am not sure I can believe. Marty turned the wheel of the car right and it veered into the concrete wall." Marty suffered bruises and a gash between his eyes that ran down his forehead and eyebrow, requiring 32 stitches to close. The article quotes other drivers about Marty. The article also covers a special honorary event held earlier this year, Marty Robbins Appreciation Day at the Nashville Speedway, in which Marty was thanked for his efforts on behalf of NASCAR racing.

7th International Festival of Country Music, Empire Pool, Wembley. *Country Music Review;* 1975 April; 4(4): 15.
Note: Illus.
The article presents an overview of the artists who appeared at the festival and includes a photo and brief biography of Marty (who performed March 29th), calling him "the most sensational act ever to grace the Wembley stage." It was his British debut.

[Advertisement]. *Country Music People;* 1975 April; 6(4): 37.
Ad for Marty's British fan club.

[Advertisement]. *Country Music Review;* 1975 April; 4(4): 12.
Full-page ad for Marty's MCA albums.

Cackett, Alan. Marty Robbins in depth; part 2. *Country Music People;* 1975 April; 6(4): 20–21.
Note: Illus.
Rock and roll to the gunfighter ballads.

Good 'n' country. *Country Music Review;* 1975 April; 4(4): 40.
Album review.

Hotline around Nashville [monthly feature]. *Country Hotline News;*
1975 April; 6(4): 8.
Note: Illus.
Marty made his first Wembley appearance over the Easter weekend.

Hurst, Jack. Marty Robbins off to Las Vegas. *Lexington Herald* (KY);
1975 April 17.
Interview about performing in Las Vegas (at the Sahara, May 15–28);
Marty says it will be his first time to work with an orchestra there. He
performed previous dates at the Fremont Hotel.

Howell, Walt. Allison, Farmer, Robbins head Boyd's field. *The Chattanooga Times;* 1975 April 20.
Note: Illus.

NASCAR goes country. *Country Hotline News;* 1975 April; 6(4): 10.
Album review. Marty helped with publicity but does not appear on the
album.

Race drivers sing out. *Country Music;* 1975 April; 3(7): 22.
Article about Marty and several NASCAR race drivers at the recording
session of the album "NASCAR goes country." Marty did not sing on
the album.

Wembley acts on B.B.C.2 television and radio. *Country Music People;*
1975 April; 6(4): 6.
Two 40-minute programs were broadcast; Marty included in shows.

Wembley Festival Easter weekend. *Music City News;* 1975 April;
12(10): 2.
Marty is listed as one of the headliners.

Cackett, Alan. Marty Robbins in depth; part 3. *Country Music People;*
1975 May; 6(5): 27–29.
Note: Illus.
Conclusion of three-part series.

Woody, Larry. Last crash did it—Marty turns in keys. *The Tennessean;*
1975 May 6; (Tuesday): 27, 30.
Note: Illus.

Marty to quit racing after experiencing serious wrecks in his last three races: 1) the Winston 500 at Talladega this past Sunday, 2) Daytona Beach in February, and 3) at Charlotte last October. In commenting about the Talladega wreck (where he was knocked unconscious), Marty said, "I climbed out of that car and I couldn't remember a thing." He was rushed to the infield hospital and "I started singing 'El Paso' to myself just to see if I could remember the words. I figured right then it was time to quit."

Woody, Larry. Trail's end; expenses closed door on Marty's racing. *The Tennessean;* 1975 May 9.
In-depth article covers Marty's decision to quit racing after three wrecks, fan response, and other things he plans to do with his time.

Robbins sings a new tune. *Chicago Tribune;* 1975 May 11.
Interview about decision to quit auto racing. Marty is quoted as saying his decision to quit racing is final.

[Photograph]. *The Tennessean;* 1975 May 11.
Photo of Hope Powell receiving an award for her portrait of Marty from the North Carolina Professional Photographer's Association.

[Photograph]. *Illustrated Speedway News;* 1975 May 13.
Marty announced he is quitting racing after his spectacular accident in the recent Winston 500 at Talladega. A description of the accident is included.

Granger, Gene. Will Marty quit? *Southern Motor Sports Journal;* 1975 May 16.
Interviews about the Talladega accident include driver James Hylton and Cotton Owens. Hylton's car was the one that hit Marty, who was briefly knocked unconscious. "I had nowhere to go," Hylton said. "I hit Marty right in the door. I saw him slump over and I thought I had killed him. There was nowhere for me to go but into Marty. Marty was knocked cold." It was the third straight race in which Marty was the victim of wrecks not of his causing.

Hotline around Nashville [monthly feature]. *Country Hotline News;* 1975 May; 6(5): 8.
Marty will produce a recording session on Diane Jordan of Sutton, NB.

Marty Robbins sued. *Country Music People;* 1975 May; 6(5): 4.
Suit accused Marty of not fulfilling contract to tour England in March, 1973.

[Photographs]. *Country Corner;* 1975 May; 11(44): 47–50.
Photos of the Wembley festival. Photos of Marty on pages 47, 49, and back page; photo of Bobby Sykes on page 48.

Review of the 7th International Festival of Country Music at Wembley. *Country Music Review;* 1975 May; 4(5): 33–34.
The review called Marty's performance "a highlight of the festival."

Robbins, Benton headline Sahara. *Las Vegas Review-Journal;* 1975 May 17.
Note: Illus.
The show opened this week. The article also mentions that Marty just completed a successful engagement in Lake Tahoe earlier this spring.

The seventh International Festival of Country Music. *Country Music People;* 1975 May; 6(5): 8–9.
Note: Illus.
Review of the Wembley shows. Marty featured in the article; photo included.

Wembley Festival is a smash. *Music City News;* 1975 May; 12(11): 10.

[Performance review]. *Variety;* 1975 May 28; 279: 85.
Review of show at the Sahara in Las Vegas.

Boyd, Jimmy. Hercules racing biz [Racing news column]. *Motor Racing News;* 1975 May 30.
Details about Marty's Talladega wreck and his decision to quit racing.

[Advertisement]. *Music City News;* 1975 June; 12(12): 23B.
One-half-page ad for the Marty Robbins gift shop.

Robbins in benefit. *The Wichita Beacon;* 1975 June 6.
The benefit performance is for the Wichita Firefighter's Association.

Dickerson, Jim. Robbins—"People here are my kind of people." *North Platte Telegraph* (Nebraska); 1975 June 17 (Tuesday). Illus.
Interview before a concert that night. Marty says his favorite singer in country music today is Merle Haggard; his favorite popular artist is John Denver. His all-time favorite is Gene Autry, "because he was easy to listen to. Every word was clear as a bell and it meant something."

Bob Steward says [newspaper column]. *Wichita Beacon;* 1975 June 19.
Marty Robbins plans to race again.

Marty and Merle Haggard in concert, 1975. (Photo by Jasper Dailey)

Kaler, Janice. Marty Robbins at LGH; admitted for back injury. *Lawrence Eagle-Tribune* (MA); 1975 June 19.
Note: Illus.
A straightforward news story and interview about Marty being treated in the local hospital for a back injury. [Editor's note: A couple of days later, the newspaper found out the man was an imposter. The photo that accompanied the article was that of the imposter.]

Marty Robbins' imposter aided. *The Tennessean;* 1975 June 22: 1, 8.
Note: Illus.
At Lawrence, Massachusetts, an imposter, claiming he was Marty, spent three days in a hospital receiving treatment for an injury.

Huffman, Jim. Singer Robbins to race again. *Omaha World-Herald;* 1975 June 22.
Note: Illus.
Marty has changed his mind and will race again. Interview at North Platte, Nebraska before concert includes racing history.

Granger, Gene. Marty will be back in harness for Talladega. *Southern Motor Sports Journal;* 1975 June 27.
Marty, who will turn 50 in September, will resume racing and may enter the August 10th race at Talladega if his car can be ready by then.

Gunfighter ballads and trail songs. *Country Music Review;* 1975 June; 4(6): 29.
Album review.

Letters to the editor [monthly feature]. *Country Song Roundup;* 1975 June; 27(191): 37.
Three fan letters about Marty.

Marty Robbins quits racing. *Country Hotline News;* 1975 June; 6(6): 2.
Note: Illus.
Detailed article about his three consecutive wrecks. Racing photos included.

Marty tops the Country Club poll. *Country Music People;* 1975 June; 6(6): 5.
Marty rated the top country music performer in a radio station poll in England.

Micmarsus, June. On the wrong track. *Stock Car Racing;* 1975 June: 54–57.
Note: Photos from the recording session accompany article.
Long article about several NASCAR racers who recorded an album of songs about racing. The author interviews the racers/singers and Marty (who was present at the recording sessions as an observer) about recording the album "NASCAR goes country." The racers are Cale Yarborough, Bobby Allison, Richard Petty, David Pearson, Darrell Waltrip, and Buddy Baker.

[Monthly news column]. *Country Music;* 1975 June; 3(9): 11.
Marty was recently presented the key to the city of El Paso.

More gunfighter ballads and trail songs. *Country Music Review;* 1975 June; 4(6): 29–30.
Album review.

Music city hotline [monthly column]. *Music City News;* 1975 June; 12(12): 6A.
Marty quits racing after third accident in Talladega. The cost of wrecking three cars at $35,000 each is too much.

Micmarsus. NASCAR goes country. *Country Song Roundup;* 1975 June; 27(191): 31–33, 46.
Note: Illus. (Photos from the recording session).
Article about Marty and auto racers who recorded an album. Marty does not appear on the album, but was involved in making it.

[Photograph and brief article]. *Music City News;* 1975 June; 12(12): 32B.
Note: Illus.
Photo of Hope Powell with her award-winning photo of Marty. The award was from a North Carolina exhibition and convention of professional photographers.

The return of the gunfighter. *Country Music Review;* 1975 June; 4(6): 30.
Album review.

Robbins, Marty. It takes faith. *Country Song Roundup;* 1975 June; 27(191): 25.
Note: Lyrics to the song.

Robbins, Marty. Life. *Country Song Roundup;* 1975 June; 27(191): 22.
Note: Lyrics to the song.

Scott, Susan. Top country-western singer Marty Robbins tells Tattler how prayer saved son's life. *National Tattler;* 1975 June.
Note: Illus.
The article recounts how Marty believes that God saved his son's life after he promised to give up drinking. He came home late one night after drinking heavily, and found his son very sick and his wife exhausted. When he picked up his son, the boy's heartbeat was very fast and Marty thought he was dying. He said he started to pray and promised a lot of things, but when he said he would quit drinking, a light appeared in the room and his son's heart immediately stopped pounding and he went to sleep. Marty also talked about his heart attack and bypass operation and the fact that he put his life in God's hands during that time too.

Auto racing welcomes Marty back. *The Tennessean;* 1975 July 8.
Marty will resume racing after two months of "retirement."

[News column]. *Nashville Banner;* 1975 July 8.
It appears that Marty has purchased a new car from Cotton Owens and will race again.

Singer Robbins may be back in GN stocker. *The Albuquerque Tribune* (NM); 1975 July 11.
Marty will resume racing.

Entertainment was Fan Fair highlight. *Music City News;* 1975 July; 13(1): 20.
Note: Illus.
Article includes Marty; photo on p. 20.

O'Donnell, Red. Robbins racer to roar again; crash at Talladega just a pit stop. *Arkansas Democrat* (Little Rock); 1975 July 20.
Racing interview; Marty just bought a new car and intends to race again.

Knox, Kirk. Marty Robbins gives warmth to chilled night show crowd. *Wyoming State Tribune* (Cheyenne, WY); 1975 July 24.
Performance review.

Marty and Tammy at Wembley. *Country Music People;* 1975 July; 6(7): 4.
Announcement that Marty has been booked for the 8th annual concert to be held in April, 1976.

Marty Robbins. *CSR Yearbook* [*Country Song Roundup*]; 1975 Spring/Summer: 57–59.
Note: Illus.

Tickertape [news column]. *Country Music People;* 1975 July; 6(7): 5.
Marty has opened a gift shop on Music Row.

Wembley festival; British country explodes. *Country Music;* 1975 July; 3(10): 14.

Marty Robbins back to racing. *Country Hotline News;* 1975 August; 6(8): 12.
Note: Illus.
The article quotes Marty as telling an Opry audience that he had decided to return to racing and had bought a new car.

Nelson, Don. Ex-trucker loves life at the top. *Eugene Register-Guard* (OR); 1975 August 15.
Note: Illus.
Performance review and interview. The article quotes Marty as saying, "I got into this business because I didn't want to work. I like what I'm

doing, so it isn't work." The writer describes Marty during concert: "Robbins appeared to be having a good time on stage, wisecracking at the crowd and mugging for picture takers. After the show, he took a few minutes to sign autographs and pose for more pictures with fans who had waited patiently outside the backstage trailer."

[Advertisement]. *Country Music Review;* 1975 September; 4(9): 9.
Full-page ad for CBS albums includes "The double-barrelled Marty Robbins."

Gilliam, Stanley. Robbins sings a winner; ballads and jokes. *Sacramento Bee* (CA); 1975 September 14: C 10.
Performance review. Calling his show was a "winner" and sold out the four nights, the author says: "Robbins, in many ways, is a throwback to an earlier day. While many of his contemporaries have gone the strict country route, Robbins, a ballad singer par excellence, has stayed with western music."

[News column note]. *Country Music;* 1975 September; 3(12): 8.
Marty Robbins quitting the race track.

Scott, Susan. Marty Robbins and his hobby cars. *Stock Car Racing;* 1975 September: 15–18.
Note: Racing photos by Howard O'Reilly Photography.
Long profile of Marty's racing career; quotes from other drivers.

Country star here Oct. 3. *The Syracuse Herald Journal* (NY); 1975 September 3.
Announcement of a forthcoming concert.

Star gazing [news column]. *Music City News;* 1975 September; 13(3): 4.
Marty has left MCA Records. Also looking for a race car in order to resume racing.

[Advertisement]. *Music City News;* 1975 October; 13(4): 15B. Full-page ad for Marty Robbins; a Hope Powell photo used.

The CMA (GB) nominations. *Country Music People;* 1975 October; 6(10): 6.
Marty nominated for two awards: Entertainer of the Year and Male Vocalist of the Year.

Porter, Seana. Marty lives life to the fullest, then writes it. *Music City News;* 1975 October; 13(4): 14B.
Note: Illus.
Information about the background for his song writing. He gives a detailed account about writing "El Paso" and talks about writing "Fellena," "Man walks among us," and "A very special way." Photo of Marty on a large motorcycle.

Reschke, Andrew. Country music delights fans. *Syracuse Herald Journal;* 1975 October 4.
Note: Illus.
Performance review. "A master showman, Robbins kept things light between numbers through constant clowning with his band members. His set reflected the polish of an experienced entertainer, fast-paced and very enjoyable." Don Williams also appeared.

Country music. *Hartford Courant* (CT); 1975 October 5.
Photo of Marty and an announcement that he will appear in concert October 12.

Lioce, Tony. Marty Robbins presents half a program. *Providence Journal* (RI); 1975 October 12.
Performance review. The reviewer was critical of Marty, saying he sang too few songs and talked too much. "He only sang about seven songs. The rest of the time he was on stage, he was telling jokes, none of which were really very funny, and indulging in fairly weak showbiz routines with the members of his band." He goes on to say, "Marty didn't fool around the whole time he was on stage, but he fooled around about half the time. It's too bad, because whenever he settled down to business, he was tremendous."

Tickertape [news column]. *Country Music People;* 1975 October; 6(10): 6.
Column notes that Marty will return to CBS Records.

Don Williams, Dolly and Marty at Wembley plus Willie and Buffy. *Country Music People;* 1975 November; 6(11): 5.

The double-barrelled Marty Robbins. *Country Music Review;* 1975 November; 4(11): 26.
Note: Illus.
Album review.

Marty Robbins gives up racing! *Country Song Roundup;* 1975 November; 27(196): 8–10.
Note: Illus.
Photos and detailed article describes Marty's recent wrecks and quotes him on his recent decision to stop racing.

Marty Robbins: listens and speaks. *Nashville Sound;* 1975 November: 17. Note: Illus.
Interview.

Music city hotline [news column]. *Music City News;* 1975 November; 13(5): 8.
Marty noted as an inductee into the Nashville Songwriter's Association Hall of Fame. Ronny accepted the award when Marty couldn't attend.

Opry saluted on ABC-TV Nov. 11th. *Country Hotline News;* 1975 November; 6(11): 6.
Note: "The Grand Ole Opry at 50"; Marty listed as a performer on the show.

[Photograph]. *Music City News;* 1975 November; 13(5): 20.
Photo of Ronny accepting Marty's award from the Nashville Songwriter's Association; Marty one of five writers elected to its Hall of Fame. The award was presented to Ronny by Willie Nelson.

CMA (GB) Award winners. *Country Music People;* 1975 December; 6(12): 5.
Marty winner of the Entertainer of the Year Award.

The double-barrelled Marty Robbins. *Country Music People;* 1975 December; 6(12): 27.
Album review for "Double-barrelled Marty Robbins."

Marty leaving MCA records. *Country Music;* 1975 December; 4(3): 6.

Marty Robbins; modern day cowboy. *Country People;* 1975 Winter; 1(2): 31–33.
Note: Cover photo. Illus.
Good photos. Standard article.

Academy of Country awards set Feb. 19. *Music City News;* 1976 January; 13(7): 2.

Eleventh annual awards, to be held Feb. 19, will air on ABC Feb. 27. Marty will host the show.

[Advertisement]. *Country Song Roundup;* 1976 January; 28(198): 45. Full-page ad and photo of Marty thanking the fans for their support.

[Advertisement]. *Nashville Sound;* 1976 January: 7.
Note: Cover photo.
One-page ad.

The CMA (GB) awards. *Country Music Review;* 1976 January; 5(1): 8. Marty won the Entertainer of the Year Award from the Great Britain Country Music Association.

The CMA (GB) dinner. *Country Music People;* 1976 January; 7(1): 6–7.
Awards dinner and celebration. Marty won Entertainer of the Year Award.

David Allan page [news column]. *Country Music People;* 1976 January; 7(1): 9.
Marty called the finest entertainer at Wembley.

Editor's comment [editorial page]. *Nashville Sound;* 1976 January: 6.
Note: Cover photo.

Edwards, Joe. Marty Robbins loyal to Grand Ole Opry. *American-Statesman* (Austin, TX); 1976 January 14.
Note: Illus.
Interview covers current trends in music, current styles in on-stage clothes, and the Grand Ole Opry.

Marty Robbins and Mac Wiseman to tour. *Country Music People;* 1976 January; 7(1): 4.

Marty Robbins back to Columbia. *Country Hotline News;* 1976 January; 7(1): 4.
Note: Illus.
Marty re-signed with Columbia Records.

Marty Robbins listens and speaks. *Nashville Sound;* 1976 January: 11, 41.
Note: Cover photo., illus.
Marty's answers to questions and letters from readers.

Marty's approach—the shotgun. *Lake Charles American Press* (LA); 1976 January 17.
Interview.

Robbins enduring performer. *The Raleigh Times;* 1976 January 17.
Note: Illus.
Interview about changes in the industry, music he records, and the way he dresses on stage.

Woody, Larry. Star Marty Robbins back in the saddle. *The Tennessean;* 1976 January 22.
Marty to resume racing.

Singer Marty Robbins returns to car racing. *Los Angeles Times;* 1976 January 23.

Einstein, Tom. Motor sports [news column]. *Greensboro Daily News* (NC); 1976 January 25.
Marty has changed his mind and will resume racing.

Marty Robbins set. *Hollywood Reporter* (Los Angeles, CA); 1976 January 26.
Marty will be the Master of Ceremonies for the 11th Annual Academy of Country Music Awards program (to be taped February 19th and shown on ABC-TV March 1st).

Scott, Susan. Marty Robbins; it's been a year and a lot more too. *Nashville Sound;* 1976 January: 24–29.
Note: Cover photo by Hope Powell, Illus.

Signing on the dotted line [news column]. *Music City News;* 1976 January; 13(7): 9.
Note: Illus.
Marty is leaving MCA Records and signing again with CBS/Columbia; will work with Billy Sherrill. Photo of Marty and others signing contract.

Songwriters name Hall of Famers. *Country Music;* 1976 January; 4(4): 18.
Marty is one of five people to be inducted into the Nashville Songwriters Hall of Fame.

Star gazing [news column]. *Music City News;* 1976 January; 13(7): 8.
Marty's Christmas gift to wife Marizona was a new home in Williamson
County.

Moore, Pat. Cold couldn't keep 'em down on farm last night. *La Crosse
Tribune* (WI); 1976 February 2.
Note: Illus.
Performance review.

O'Donnell, Red. Marty Robbins to host awards show on March 1.
Nashville Banner; 1976 February 10.

Robbins added to Daytona radio broadcasts. *Illustrated Speedway
News;* 1976 February 10.
Note: Illus.
Marty to serve as a commentator on the Motor Racing Network (radio
network) at the Daytona 500.

Academy of Country Music awards. *Music City News;* 1976 February;
13(8): 32.
Marty to host the awards show.

[Advertisement]. *Country Music Review;* 1976 February; 5(2): 7.
Full-page ad for the 8th Wembley Festival. Marty listed as one of the
performers.

Fastest gun around. *Country Music Review;* 1976 February; 5(2): 31.
Album review.

Marty Robbins stars as host on country music awards show. *Sun-Sen-
tinel* (Ft. Lauderdale, FL); 1976 February 13.

Marty Robbins to race again! *Country Hotline News;* 1976 February;
7(2): 3.
Note: Illus.
In addition to racing again, Marty will drive the pace car at the Indianapolis 500, May 30th.

Country honors set. *Eugene Register-Guard* (OR); 1976 February 29:
TV Guide section.
Note: Cover photo.
Cover photo and article about the ACM Awards show.

[Photograph]. *Los Angeles Times;* 1976 February 29.
Text below photo of Marty notes he will host the 11th ACM awards show Monday night; the show was taped at the ceremonies held February 19th.

Fan time [monthly feature]. *Country Song Roundup;* 1976 March; 28(200): 46.
Marty has ended his association with MCA Records.

The great bootleg bonanza. *Country Music Review;* 1976 March; 5(3): 18–22.
An article about bootleg records includes a photo of Marty and information about one of his albums.

Hensley is joined by Robbins, Sovine at trucking show. *Music City News;* 1976 March; 13(9): 26.

Hotline around Nashville [monthly feature]. *Country Hotline News;* 1976 March; 7(3): 8.
Marty provided the commentary for the radio broadcast of the Daytona 500 last month. He also hosted the 11th annual ACM Awards Show March 1st. The show was taped February 19 at the Hollywood Palladium.

Tuber, Keith. Robbins "returns" to El Paso. *Herald-Examiner* (Los Angeles, CA); 1976 March 20.
Note: Illus.
An interview before a performance at Disneyland covers the writing of "El Paso City."

Wembley Festival TV plans. *Country Music People;* 1976 March; 7(3): 4.

Marty Robbins. *CSR Yearbook* [*Country Song Roundup*]; 1976 Spring.
Note: Illus.

[Advertisement]. *Country Music Review;* 1976 April; 5(4): 8.
Full-page ad for Marty's concert tour in England for Mervyn Conn.

[Advertisement]. *Country Music Review;* 1976 April; 5(4): 14.
Ad for the album "Double-barrelled Marty Robbins."

[Advertisement]. *Music City News;* 1976 April; 13(10): 22.
Ad and small photo for Marty's Fan Club.

Fan time [monthly feature]. *Country Song Roundup;* 1976 April;
28(201): 45.
Marty returned to racing in February in the Daytona 500.

The fastest gun around. *Country Music People;* 1976 April; 7(4): 21.
Album review.

Langefeld, Auggie. Modified Buick V-6 to pace cars at Indy. *Cincinnati Inquirer;* 1976 April 11.
Note: Illus.
Marty will be the pace car driver at this years' Indianapolis 500 in May;
a detailed description of the pace car is given.

Marty Robbins to appear at county fair. *Champaign-Urbana Courier;*
1976 April 16.

Powel, Bob. Hello Dolly. *Country Music People;* 1976 April; 7(4): 27.
Note: Illus.
Article includes photo of Marty and Dolly Parton.

[Advertisement]. *Country Music People;* 1976 April; 7(4): 15.
One-half page ad and schedule for Marty's April/May British tour.

Powel, Bob. The number one country hits of Marty Robbins. *Country Music People;* 1976 April; 7(4): 28–29.
Note: Cover photo of Marty and Dolly Parton. Photos of Marty on stage
in England by Doug McKenzie and Marie O'Connell of the Doug
McKenzie Studio in England.
The article covers Marty's shows on the Grand Ole Opry, his success at
the 1975 Wembley Festival, and his upcoming tour of the British Isles.
It also reviews his recording career in detail.

Rogers, Tom. Dolly, Marty win honors. *The Tennessean;* 1976 April
19: 37.
News from London; Marty won Best International Male Vocalist Award
at the Wembley International Festival of Country Music.

Tickertape [news column]. *Country Music People;* 1976 April; 7(4): 5.
Notes that Marty starts filming a western in June for his production
company.

Wembley; the international festival. *Country Music Review;* 1976 April; 5(4): 10, +.
Article includes a photo of Marty and says he was the "undisputed sensation" of last year's festival.

Marty gets back on track. *The Tennessean;* 1976 April 25.
Last season, Marty gave up racing. "Too expensive, I'm giving it up," he said after three wrecks. But now he says he misses it. "I guess it kind of gets in your blood. I want to get back into it."

[Advertisement]. *Country Music Review;* 1976 May; 5(5): 2.
One-half-page ad for Marty's upcoming British concert tour.

Country artists rock Wembley. *Music City News;* 1976 May; 13(11): 35.
Marty and Dolly Parton won top honors. Marty won Best International Male Vocalist Award.

The Eighth International Festival of Country Music. *Country Music People;* 1976 May; 7(5): 8–9, 40–41.
Note: Illus.
Marty's performance given a great review on pp. 40–41. Photo included.

First International Country Music Awards: Dolly, Marty and Statlers. *Country Music People;* 1976 May; 7(5): 4.
Marty selected as Male Artist of the Year. Awards presented at Wembley.

Marty back racing. *Country Hotline News;* 1976 May; 7(5): 14.
Note: Cover photo of Marty and Tammy Wynette.

No signs of loneliness here. *Country Music Review;* 1976 May; 5(5): 30.
Album review.

Star gazing [news column]. *Music City News;* 1976 May; 13(11): 7.
Marty will be driving the Pace Car at this year's Indianapolis 500.

Von Manfred, Vogel. Marty Robbins. *Country Corner;* 1976 May; 12(49): 7–10.
Note: Cover photo. Illus.
Interview and long discography of European releases.

Was ist Eigentlick . . . Alamo? *Country Corner;* 1976 May; 12(49): 10–11.
Review of the John Wayne movie, "The Alamo," and the soundtrack album. Includes Marty's recording of the "The Alamo."

Fan time [monthly feature]. *Country Song Roundup;* 1976 June; 28(203): 44.
Marty has returned to Columbia Records after ending his contract with MCA/Decca.

Hurst, Jack. El Paso becomes a city in Robbins' reincarnation. *Chicago Tribune;* 1976 June 16.
Note: Illus.
Interview about writing the song "El Paso city." He wanted to write a new song about El Paso. This one, like the first one, ended up writing itself. "I didn't choose a word or anything. I just wrote it until it stopped." It had to do with reincarnation, and is the story of a man flying over El Paso and wondering if he was the cowboy in the earlier song. Robbins himself doesn't believe or disbelieve in reincarnation, noting only that it's a subject nearly everyone thinks about. The interview also recounts how he wrote the original "El Paso." He had driven through the city several years in a row when he and his wife were going home for Christmas. Each time he intended to write a song about the city. Finally, as they were driving through the third time, the words came. He describes the words of the song as coming to him like a movie, in scenes. He wrote the words down the next day and never changed a thing. Marty says that his racing is "probably a substitute for the frontier excitement which happened before my time." He goes on to say, "If I could have been born 100 years ago, when you had open range and could ride wherever you wanted to, I would have made a good drifter."

Marty Robbins at the Hammersmith Odeon. *Country Music People;* 1976 June; 7(6): 17.
Note: Illus.
Performance review.

Funkhouser, Barbara. Country-western star to tout EP in film. *El Paso Times;* 1976 June 17.
Marty will star in a promotional film for the Convention and Visitors Bureau of the city of El Paso. Details of the 15-minute film are given.

Marty Robbins joining field for Michigan. *Southern Motor Sports Journal;* 1976 June 18.
Marty will race in the CAM2 Motor Oil 400 on June 20.

[Photograph]. *Country Hotline News;* 1976 June; 7(6): 13.
Photo of Marty performing at Fan Fair.

Wood, Gerry. Words of wisdom from Cash, Robbins. *Billboard;* 1976 June 19; 88: 44, 62.
Interviews with Marty and Johnny Cash about their years in the entertainment business and their recent success with number one records. Includes their advice to newcomers.

[Billboard top country singles chart]. *Billboard;* 1976 June 19; 88: 60.
"El Paso City" is number one this week.

Weekend of Bicentennial events opens with Marty Robbins show. *El Paso Times;* 1976 June 20.
Note: Illus.
Marty will be honored with a "Marty Robbins Day" and will arrive two days before his concert at the Sun Bowl to take part in various ceremonies.

Wembley and George IV on BBC 2. *Country Music People;* 1976 June; 7(6): 4.
Wembley telecast includes Marty.

Wembley: the international festival. *Country Music Review;* 1976 June; 5(6): 10–13.
Note: Illus.
Article includes a review of Marty's performance on p. 13.

[Photograph]. *Music City News;* 1976 July; 14(1): Front cover.
Marty is one of the artists on the cover of the Fan Fair issue. General articles about Fan Fair also mention his activities during the week.

Crouch, Gene. Marty Robbins thrills 5000 for Bicentennial. *El Paso Herald-Post;* 1976 July 3 (Saturday). Illus.
A Bicentennial Tribute to Marty was held last night at the Sun Bowl. The Mayor proclaimed July 2 "Marty Robbins (Superstar) Day in El Paso" and presented Marty the city's Conquistador Award, the first time it has ever been presented to an entertainer.

Funkhouser, Barbara and Normann, Debbie. Robbins' crowd small, warm. *The El Paso Times;* 1978 July 3: 7-C. Illus.
Article about Marty's show and the tribute to him. In addition to the Conquistador Award, Marty received several gifts, including the key to the city, specially made boots, and a photo of El Paso. Earlier in the day, Marty had visited the El Paso Museum of Art and donated $1000 toward the purchase of a painting.

Rhodes, Larry. Marty Robbins!! Crossover songster comes to Kaintuck. Leisure Scene Edition; *Tribune Courier* (Benton, KY); 1976 July 16 (Friday): 1, 2.
Note: Cover photo. Illus.
An interview (after two local shows) covers Hawaiian music, his relationships with the fans, and his styles of performing. The article recognizes the fact that Marty's fans go beyond country music and notes, "Marty Robbins' fans like him for what he is . . . in spite of the fact that what he is, isn't what all his fans actually like." He's been a crossover artist from the start of his career because of his ability to handle different styles. He spent long periods of time after both concerts signing autographs for his fans. In Nashville, Marty likes his privacy. He says, "I don't have parties and I don't go to parties. In 23 years that I've lived in Nashville, I believe two people have been to my house. Eddy Arnold came for a Mexican dinner; and steel guitar player Roy Wiggins has been to the house seven or eight times."

[Photograph]. *El Paso Times;* 1976 July 27.
Photo of Marty on the international bridge in El Paso during the filming of a promotional film for the city.

Hadler, Nancy; Bray, Jim. "The Golden Teardrop"; Robbins charms 'em with that down home appeal. *The News Gazette* (Champaign, IL); 1976 July 30.
Note: Illus. with photos from concert.
Long, warm review about Marty's performance and the audience response to him and his band.

Mann, Steve. Robbins still going strong. *Champaign-Urbana Courier;* 1976 July 30.
Performance review and quotes from fans.

DJ Corner [news column]. *Music City News;* 1976 August; 14(2): 31.
WIRE picnic at Indy Raceway Park to feature Marty Robbins; crowd expected to be 75,000.

El Paso City. *Billboard;* 1976 August 21: 60.
Album review.

[Photograph]. *Country Hotline News;* 1976 August; 7(8).
Cover photo of Marty.

Sledge, Ransom. Marty Robbins' bedroll is in Nashville, but there's drifting sand in his boots. *Country Style;* 1976 August; (3): 6.
Note: Illus.
Interview about Marty's love of the west and his need to travel. Marty is quoted: "I guess I've always been a drifter. When I was a kid growin' up in Arizona, I hardly ever went to school. I would catch a boxcar every mornin' and go from Glendale to Prescott." He goes on to say, "I never have liked to stay in one place. That's why it's hard for me to work in Las Vegas. I just can't take it, because I have to stay two weeks in one place at a time. Really, I can't take two weeks any place." About the west, "I love the Southwest. I love the desert. Just to be out there. Many times I'll rent a car at midnight or after a show and just go out on the desert. I'll turn the motor off, roll the windows down, and just listen. . ." He says his biggest thrill was seeing where Custer's last stand took place.

Pioneers enter Star's Walkway. *Music City News;* 1976 September; 14(3): 21.
Sons of the Pioneers honored at several functions, one of which was a KLAC Show with Marty as the featured performer.

[Advertisement]. *Music City News;* 1976 October; 14(4): 37A.
One-half-page ad, with photo, thanking DJ's for their support.

[Advertisement]. *Country Music People;* 1976 October; 7(10): 47.
Full-page ad for the album "El Paso City."

[Advertisement]. *Country Music Review;* 1976 October; 5(10): 9.
Full-page ad for the album "El Paso City."

El Paso City. *Country Music People;* 1976 October; 7(10): 30–31.
Album review.

Marty Robbins. *Country Corner;* 1976 October; 12(51): 28–29.
Review of a number of Marty's albums.

The Marty Robbins collection. *Country Music People;* 1976 October; 7(10): 21.
Album review.

Sledge, Randy. El Paso revisited; Marty Robbins squeezes the most out of life and music. *Rambler;* 1976 October 21: 8.
Note: Photo by Hope Powell.
Marty says of his childhood, "I can remember living in a tent on the desert. From the time I was seven to the time I was twelve we moved from a tent to a shack, from a shack back to a tent. We lived off the land. There was no water to grow anything so we survived mostly on jackrabbit, doves, and quail—my mother was a dead shot with a 20-gauge." At one time his father had held a good job, but he took to drink and times got hard.
When Marty wrote "El Paso" he was recording in New York and couldn't get it released as he wanted. Mitch Miller said it was too long and Ray Coniff liked it but wanted him to shorten it. It wasn't until Marty was back recording in Nashville that he was able to put it on an album the way he wanted it. Then, when it was released as a single, it was put out in a shortened version. It was only after Marty and the buying public protested that the complete version was released as a single.

Stilley, Al. The Indianapolis 500: Marty at the helm. *Stock Car Racing;* 1976 October: 28–30.
Note: Illus.
About Marty being at the Indy 500 in May and driving the pace car. He was also Grand Marshal of the parade and took part in other activities. Bob Hinkle accompanied Marty. Some racing stories included.

Two gun daddy. *Country Music People;* 1976 October; 7(10): 22.
Album review.

Drew, Joan. Marty Robbins made a deal with God. *Country Music;* 1976 November; 5(2): 22–24.
Note: Cover photo., Illus.
Interview covers his worst auto racing wreck and playing a show date for physicians two days later, his belief in God, and his writing "El Paso City." Marty talks about the time, approximately ten years ago, when he relaxed enough to start kidding around with the audience at the Grand Ole Opry. Now he kids with the audience on his road shows and tries to have fun on stage. The title of the article comes from a personal crisis. His young son was critically ill and Marty promised God he

would give up drinking if He would let the boy live. His son immediately got better and Marty hasn't had a drink since.

David Allan page [news column]. *Country Music People;* 1976 December; 7(12): 11.
Photos from a recent Wembley festival include Marty.

El Paso city. *Country Corner;* 1976 December; 12(52): 31.
Note: Illus.
Album review.

El Paso city. *Country Music Review;* 1976 December; 5(12): 30.
Album review.

El Paso city. *Country Style;* 1976 December; (7): 43.
Album review.

Robbins, Marty. El Paso City. *Country Song Roundup;* 1976 December; 28(209): 22.
Note: Lyrics to the song.

ACM awards show scheduled. *Music City News;* 1977 January; 14(7): 25.
Marty listed as one of the guests to appear.

Country stars share Christmas with MCN. *Music City News;* 1977 January; 14(7): 11.
Marty's staff gave him two portable heaters as a gift so he wouldn't turn the office heat up so high.

El Paso city. *Country Music;* 1977 January; 5(4): 57, 58.
Album review.

Robbins, Marty. El Paso city. *Country Song Roundup;* 1977 January; 29(210): 25.
Note: Lyrics to the song.

Academy country awards set. *Music City News;* 1977 February; 14(8): 25.
Twelfth annual awards set to air on ABC February 24th; Marty scheduled to appear.

Adios amigo. *Country Music Parade;* 1977 February; 2(1): 6.
Album review.

Border town affair. *Country Music People;* 1977 February; 8(2): 39.
Album review.

El Paso city. *Country Song Roundup;* 1977 February; 29(211): 30.
Album review.

Renney, Tony. The Martin guitar. *Country Music Review;* 1977 February; 6(2): 21–23. Note: Illus.
Marty mentioned in the article and pictured on p. 23 (with others) holding his guitar.

[Performance review]. *Variety;* 1977 March 16; (286): 63.
Review of concert.

Singers Merle Haggard, Marty Robbins will bring the country to the city. *Memphis Press-Scimitar* (TN); 1977 March 18.
Note: Illus.

Hance, Bill. Conway, Loretta take it easy recording in country. *Nashville Banner;* 1977 March 18: 25.
The article also includes a photo of Marty and the background story that led to the writing of "El Paso City."

Adios amigo. *Melody Maker;* 1977 March 19; 52: 30.
Album review.

High-flying Robbins still manages to keep his feet on the ground. *Country Style;* 1977 March 24; (13): 10–11.
Note: Illus.
Interview, mostly about writing "El Paso City."

Dawson, Walter. Country fans couldn't ask for more. *The Commercial Appeal* [Memphis, TN]; 1977 March 20.
Concert review of Marty and Merle Haggard.

Border town affair. *Country Music Review;* 1977 April; 6(4): 33.
Album review.

Kimball one of a kind. *Musical Merchandise Review;* 1977 April.
Note: Illus.
Article about the special checkered piano Marty had designed for his use on his television series, "Marty Robbins' Spotlight."

[Photograph]. *Country Hotline News;* 1977 April; 8(3).
Cover photo of Marty.

Blue and white checkered grand: a new Guinness record. *Music Trades;*
1977 April.
Note: Illus.
The article is about how Kimball made the special piano used on the TV
series, "Marty Robbins' Spotlight."

Star gazing [news column]. *Music City News;* 1977 April; 14(10): 6.
Notes that Marty is currently working on a television series to start next
fall for Show Biz. [Marty Robbins' Spotlight].

Adios Amigo. *Country Music People;* 1977 May; 8(5): 35.
Album review.

Adios amigo. *Country Music Review;* 1977 May; 6(5): 33.
Album review.

Hance, Bill. Marty lives each day for what's in it. *Nashville Banner;*
1977 May 6: 32.
Note: Illus.
Interview about his health and his love of racing. In discussing his
health, Marty said he never slept much at night; he hated to waste his
time that way. He also talked candidly about his religious faith, saying
that prayer is what gives you the faith to go out and get the things you
want. He had his heart operation in 1970 mainly so he could race again,
in spite of the fact that the doctors told him he would have to lead a
quieter life. He says, "I really didn't start living until this happened . . . I can't wait to get up in the morning. Every day is a good
day to be alive whether the sun's shining or not. I've really started
appreciating everything. Life used to be great. But now it's greater."

[News column note]. *Country Style;* 1977 May 5; (16): 7.
Several country music stars, including Marty, participated in a Robert
Redford press conference in Nashville about his campaign to save the
environment.

[Photograph]. *Country Hotline News;* 1977 May; 8(4): 13.
A caption notes (under a photo of Marty pictured with a model airliner
given to him as a gift) that Marty recently wrote the song "Allegheny
Airlines." The song will be used as promotion by the airline.

Robbins undaunted by heart problem. *Augusta Chronicle* (GA); 1977
June 5.
Note: Illus.

Farmer, G. Robert. Marty talks about songs, music trends. *Watertown
Daily Times* (N.Y.); 1977 June 9.
Interview.

He tells Ronnie; believe in God, never give up. *Watertown Daily Times*
(N.Y.); 1977 June 9.
Marty met with Ronnie Donate, who was in a respirator from a hunting
accident.

MacDonald, Jay. White sport coats and blue suede shoes. *CountryStyle;*
1977 June 16: 20–21.
Note: Illus.
The article discusses the forces which produced rockabilly music. Comments about Marty's influence included in the article.

Hotline chatter [monthly feature]. *Country Hotline News;* 1977 June;
8(5): 11.
Note: Illus.
Marty recently sponsored a fiddler's convention in Talladega, Alabama,
with the proceeds going to the American Heart Association.

[Photograph]. *Music City News;* 1977 June; 14(12): 30A.
Photo of Marty and DJ Marty Sullivan, who hosted a show Marty
headlined.

Tickertape [news column]. *Country Music People;* 1977 June; 8(6): 7.
Notes that Marty's new television series will be seen in over 100 markets when it debuts this autumn.

Tom T. Hall benefits children with concert and tourney. *Music City
News;* 1977 June; 14(12): 44B.
Note: Illus.
Good photo of Marty as one of the performers participating.

Airlie, Bob. Rockin' in the country; part 1. The Columbia rockabilly
sound of Marty Robbins. *New Kommotion;* 1977 Summer; 2(6 [Consec-
utive issue no. 16]): 25–26.
Note: Illus.
Detailed article about Marty's contribution to rockabilly.

Flanagan, Mike. "Rainmaker" Marty Robbins pleases fair friends. *Jackson Daily News* (MS); 1977 July 15.
Performance review and interview.

Glen joins star cast for benefit show. *Country Hotline News;* 1977 July; 8(6): 16.
Benefit show for the family of Lloyd Perryman (of the Sons of the Pioneers) at the Shrine Auditorium in Los Angeles. Marty listed as one of the performers.

Woody, Larry. Robbins makes racing return. *The Tennessean;* 1977 July 24.
Note: Illus.
Racing interview. Marty says he was serious when he retired from racing two years ago, "But racing gets into your blood . . . it's a difficult sport just to walk away from." His first race will be at Talladega, which is the scene of his worst wreck in a series of three that led to his retirement from the sport. Marty said he didn't quit because of the danger but because of the expense involved. He says, "When you walk away from a wrecked race car, you are walking away from several thousand dollars. I was racing merely as a hobby, and the hobby suddenly became very expensive. It wasn't a matter of running out of nerve, but a matter of running out of spending money for a hobby."

Marty Robbins back on track. *New York Times;* 1977 July 25.

Robbins to return to auto racing. *Washington Post;* 1977 July 25.

Hightower, James. Sears' electric car. *Atlanta Journal;* 1977 July 28: 17-D, 20-D.
Note: Illus.
The article covers the mechanics of the car; also notes that Marty will drive it at an exhibition in Talladega this weekend.

Marty Robbins interview. *Country Song Roundup;* 1977 July; 29(216): 14–15, 46.
Note: Cover photo. Illus.
A long, in-depth interview covers: the writing of "El Paso City," problems with his MCA contract, the loyalty of his fans, and his frustrations with being misquoted in a book, *Nashville Sounds*. He now feels that leaving Columbia Records was the biggest mistake of his career.

[Photograph]. *Country Corner;* 1977 July; 13(55): 5.
Photo of Marty, Jeannie C. Riley, Tom T. Hall, and Bobby Bare on the set of "Marty Robbins' Spotlight."

Star gazing [news column]. *Music City News;* 1977 July; 15(1): 6.
Notes that Marty recently sponsored a fiddlers' convention in Talladega, Alabama; proceeds were donated to the American Heart Association.

The stars' guitars. *Country Style;* 1977 July 28; (22): 26.
Note: Illus.
A photo of Marty and his Martin guitar is included.

Adios amigo. *Country Music;* 1977 August; 5(11): 48.
Album review.

Morning briefing [news column]. *Los Angeles Times;* 1977 August 1.
Marty drove the Sears electric car at Talladega Sunday and set a world record for electric cars by averaging 67.645 m.p.h.

Parsons takes Pocono. *Chicago Tribune;* 1977 August 1.
Article also includes information about Marty driving the Sears electric car.

Robbins returns to racing. *Music City News;* 1977 August; 15(2): 3.
Marty racing again after a two-year absence; will enter the Talladega 500 on August 7th.

Hurst, Jack. Daring Marty Robbins isn't shying from the "Spotlight." *Chicago Tribune;* 1977 September 7.
Note: Illus.
Detailed interview about doing the television series "Marty Robbins Spotlight."

Marty Robbins. *Country Song Roundup Annual;* 1977 Fall; Annual: 17–19.
Note: Illus.

Marty Robbins headlines Coal Jamboree. *Wheeling News-Register* (WV); 1977 September 18.

Robert Redford in Nashville. *Country Song Roundup;* 1977 September; 29(218): 31.
Note: Illus.

Marty is identified as one of several stars at Redford's news conference on saving the environment.

Rockin' Ronny rambles while papa Marty beams in the wings. *Country Music;* 1977 September; 5(12): 17.
Note: Illus.
Brief article about a performance by Ronny with Marty in the audience. Photo of Ronny included.

Vitt, Janet. Marty Robbins brings state fair to a close. *Wichita Eagle;* 1977 September 19.
Performance review.

[Advertisement]. *Music City News;* 1977 October; 15(4): 5B.
A half-page ad from Marty thanking DJ's for their support. Photo included.

Allen, Bob. Marty Robbins talks about racing and TV. *Music City News;* 1977 October; 15(4): 12-A.
Note: Illus.
Includes mention of "Marty Robbins' Spotlight" and the Marty Robbins Open 500 at the Nashville Speedway.

El Paso. *Kountry Korral;* 1977 October; 10(5): 35.
Album review.

Thomas, Suzanne. Robbins and Davis are institutions. *Monroe Morning World* (LA); 1977 October 2.
Note: Illus.
Article about Marty and former governor Jimmy Davis; both will be appearing at the fair.

Hurst, Jack. Marty Robbins translating onto videotape. *Valley News/ Van Nuys News* (CA); 1977 October 7.
Note: Illus.
The article largely about the television series, "Marty Robbins' Spotlight." Additional story about Marty learning to play the dobro at the Opry.

Thomas, Suzanne. Robbins pleases crowd. *Monroe Morning World* (LA); 1977 October 8.
Flattering performance review.

Hershorn, Connie. Robbins' wit, voice keep them spellbound. *The Dallas Morning News;* 1977 October 11: 6C.
Note: Illus.
Concert review.

Big field ready for "Robbins 500." *The Chattanooga News-Free Press* (TN); 1977 October 13.
The race is to be held in Nashville this weekend.

Caldwell, Joe. North vs. South added sidelight to Sunday's Marty Robbins 500. *Nashville Banner;* 1977 October 15.
Note: Illus.
Story about the Marty Robbins World 500 race to be held at the Nashville Speedway.

Koper, Terry. Marty Robbins thrills country music fans. *Register-Star* (Rockford, IL); 1977 October 15.
Note: Illus.
Performance review and audience reaction. Quotes from fans.

Hurst, Jack. Trying to capture Robbins on the tube. *Philadelphia Inquirer;* 1977 October 16.
Note: Illus.

Woody, Larry. Robbins 500 premiers; top race in Nashville's history. *The Tennessean;* 1977 October 16: 1 (Sports).
Note: Illus.
Information about the race today and an interview with Marty.

[Photograph]. *Music City News;* 1977 October; 15(4): 5A.
Note: Cover photo.
Photo of Marty, Roy Acuff, and Brother Oswald playing dobro.

Singer Marty Robbins' house said sliding down hill; $200,000 asked. *Nashville Banner;* 1977 October 20.
A lawsuit was filed and is scheduled to be heard December 19th. Marty bought the house in December, 1975 and the house has started sliding this year. The situation is so bad it has affected gas and water lines as well as walls and doors.

C & W star favors Fender equipment. *Musical Merchandise Review;* 1977 November.
Marty prefers Fender guitars and other equipment.

Merle Haggard for Wembley; other favorites return. *Country Music People;* 1977 November; 8(11): 4.
Marty among performers announced for the 1978 Wembley.

Johnson, Jimmy. Haggard and Robbins will be returning heroes. *The Sun* [San Bernardino, CA]; 1977 November 4: C1, C5.
Announcement of upcoming concert.

Palmer, Barry. Country music beat [newspaper column]. *Manchester Union Leader* (N.H.); 1977 November 18: 22.
Note: Illus.
Interview and commentary.

Palmer, Barry. Country Music Beat [news column]. *Manchester Union Leader* (NH); 1977 November 18.
Note: Illus.
Long appreciation; calls Marty "The greatest singer in entertainment today."

Robbins hits the top. *The Daily Dispatch* (Moline, IL); 1977 November 27. Note: Illus.
Interview; covers early career and some of his early rock recordings.

Star gazing [news column]. *Music City News;* 1977 November; 15(5): 6.
New house recently purchased by Marty is sliding down hill. Law suit has been filed against previous owner by Robbins' attorney, Jack Green.

Battle, Bob. Marty Robbins; 25 years of solid gold success. *Country Style;* 1977 December; (26): 38–39.
Note: Illus.
Interview.

Entertainer's house suit postponed. *The Tennessean;* 1977 December 20.

Harvey, Robert B. Merle Haggard and Marty Robbins live from Los Angeles. *Mother Trucker News;* 1977 December: 18–19.
Note: Illus.
Performance review and interview with Marty.

Hearing reset in singer's suit. *Nashville Banner;* 1977 December 20.

Marty and Nudie, 1977. (Photo by Jasper Dailey)

Hearing slated today on Robbin's lawsuit. *Nashville Banner;* 1977 December 19.

Oppel, Pete. Robbins—a big talent indeed. *Dallas Morning News;* 1977 December 6: 16A.
Performance review.

[Performance review]. *Variety;* 1977 December 7; (289): 66.
Review of performance.

[Advertisement]. *Country Music People;* 1978 January; 9(1): 51.
Full-page ad for the album "Don't let me touch you."

[Advertisement]. *Music City News;* 1978 January; 15(7): 4.
Full-page ad for Wembley. Marty listed among headliners.

Don't let me touch you. *Music City News;* 1978 January; 15(7): 22.
Album review.

Don't let me touch you. *Country Hotline News;* 1978 January; 9(1): 12.
Note: Illus.
Album review.

Don't let me touch you. *Country Music Parade;* 1978 January: 10.
Note: Illus.
Album review.

Eipper, Laura. Marty's movin'; one of country music's longest running successes, Marty Robbins has got his eye on the next 25 years. *The Tennessean* (magazine); 1978 January: 7–9.
Note: Illus.
Long review article; good quotes and photos. Comments cover current trends in country music, the "outlaw" sound, and what it takes to stay in the business. About talent, Marty says, "Do you know what talent really is? It's being able to please the people. What I do isn't anything great, but I have a good time and so does the audience. Knowing how to please people is the only secret for staying in the business."

Fan time [monthly column]. *Country Song Roundup;* 1978 January; 30(222): 42.
Notes Marty's recent birthday [Sept. 26] and quotes him.

Higgins, Tom. Robbins planning more racing in '78. *The Charlotte Observer;* 1978 January 11 (Saturday).

Interview before a concert covers his racing plans. He also talks in some detail about what it was like to go through his serious wrecks.

Marty Robbins. *Kountry Korral;* 1978; 11(3/4): 34–36.
Note: Illus.

Nashville sounds [monthly feature]. *Country Song Roundup;* 1978 January; 30(222): 37.
In an article about Grady Martin, he mentions that he played on the recording of "El Paso."

[Performance review]. *Billboard;* 1978 January 21; (90): 71.
Review of Marty's performance at the Palomino Club in Los Angeles.

Der Columbia rockabilly sound des Marty Robbins. *Country Corner;* 1978 February; 13(58): 31–33.
Note: Illus.
Long article on Marty's contribution to rockabilly. Includes a discography of his rockabilly recordings.

Don't let me touch you. *Country Music People;* 1978 February; 9(2): 40.
Album review.

Marty Robbins' sliding house suit scheduled. *Nashville Banner;* 1978 February 6.

Singer's house hearing today. *The Tennessean;* 1978 February 7.

Lyons, David. Wouldn't live in Robbins' home, builder says. *Nashville Banner;* 1978 February 8.
Testimony given in suit.

More testimony in Robbins suit slated Saturday. *The Tennessean;* 1978 February 8.

Reid, Dixie. Marty Robbins hits home here. *Houston Chronicle;* 1978 February 12.
Performance review.

Robbins house suit decision due this month. *The Tennessean;* 1978 February 13.

Sliding home case to be decided in three weeks. *Nashville Banner;* 1978 February 13.

Harb, S. H. Robbins steps to two tunes. *The Raleigh Times* (NC); 1978 February 18 (Saturday): 19, 23. Illus.
Interview before a concert centers on his love of cowboy music and his racing activities. He talks about his childhood: "I would pick cotton to earn enough money to go to the movies. I'd walk into town in the mornings and sit in the movie house all afternoon and evening until it closed, watching the same show over and over. It was all cowboy movies then on Saturday. Gene Autry was my hero. At 10 that night I'd have to walk home again through the desert." But he wasn't afraid, he said, because he was Gene Autry that night.

Gladden, Chris. Marty Robbins: man and his music embody spirit of the southwest. *Roanoke Times and World-News* (VA); 1978 February 25. Note: Illus.
Interview and performance review.

Nash, Alanna. Marty Robbins: silly on stage; serious in office. *Louisville Courier Journal;* 1978 February 26: 1, 11.
Note: Illus.
Long interview covers his jokes, early career, taping of the "Marty Robbins Spotlight" and his admiration for Vernon Dalhart.

Robbins suing. *Country Style;* 1978 February; (28): 12.
Marty is suing the builder of a home he bought that is now sliding down a hill.

[Advertisement]. *Country Western Express;* n.d. [1963?]; (9 NS): 19.
Photo and ad for new single.

[Biography and photo]. *Melody Maker;* 1978 March 25; 53: 34.

[Advertisement]. *Country Music People;* 1978 March; 9(3): 28.
Full-page ad for upcoming tour; includes schedule.

British dates set for Merle Haggard and Marty Robbins. *Country Music People;* 1978 March; 9(3): 4.
Schedule for upcoming British tour.

DJ's corner [monthly column]. *Music City News;* 1978 March; 15(9): 27.

The column notes that Marty has taped a couple of episodes of the "Jim Nabors Show" television series, but no air date has been set yet.

Schumann, von E. Reinald. Marty Robbins, life story. *Hillbilly;* 1978 March; (54): 6–17.
Note: Cover photo. Illus.

Marty Robbins diskographie, teil 1 (part 1). *Hillbilly;* 1978 March; (54): 17–21.
Note: Cover photo. Illus.

Marty Robbins out from under sliding house. *The Tennessean;* 1978 March 3.

Robbins, Marty; Sherrill, Billy. Don't let me touch you. *Country Song Roundup;* 1978 March; 30(224): 21.
Note: Lyrics to the song.

Robbins, home builder agreement voided. *Nashville Banner;* 1978 March 4.

Dawson, Ralph. Robbins pleased over court ruling on home. *The Tennessean;* 1978 March 4.

Ridenour, Valerie [Nashville Sounds news column]. *Country Song Roundup;* 1978 March; 30(224): 40–41.
Part of the article for the month quotes Harold Bradley recounting how the "fuzz" sound came into being when Grady Martin's equipment broke while recording Marty's "Don't worry."

Cackett, Alan. Marty Robbins: a song for all musics. *Country Music People;* 1978 April; 9(4): 28–29, 50.
Note: Cover photo. Illus.
The interview covers his British success, his songwriting, his early career, and problems with Columbia and MCA.

Lawrence, Robert P. Keeping with 'W' in C & W; Marty hasn't forgotten. *Country Style;* 1978 April; (30): 64.
Note: Illus.
Much of article about Marty's writing and performing western songs.

The Opry remembers Hank Williams. *Country Song Roundup;* 1978 April; 30(225): 25–27.
Note: Illus.
Article includes a statement by Marty and a photo.

"That's Country" tributes 25 years of music. *Music City News;* 1978 April; 15(10): 26.
A country music film; Marty one of the artists shown.

Country set for TV exposure. *Country Music People;* 1978 May; 9(5): 6.
BBC 2 to broadcast 10th Wembley.

Dawson, Ralph. Robbins must pay rent for living in "sliding house." *The Tennessean;* 1978 May 9.
The court decision voided Marty's contract on the house, but also stipulated that he had to pay rent for the time he lived in it.

Robbins told to pay $21,700 for house rent. *Nashville Banner;* 1978 May 9.

Robbins, Marty; Sherrill, Billy. Don't let me touch you. *Country Song Roundup;* 1978 May; 30(226): 25.
Note: Lyrics to the song.

Wembley celebrates 10th anniversary. *Music City News;* 1978 May; 15(11): 18–19.
Note: Illus.
Two pages of photos from the festival, including some of Marty.

Wembley's 10th: a gigantic gathering of the star names. *Country Music People;* 1978 May; 9(5): 11–12, 14.
Note: Illus.
Marty's performance featured on p. 12.

Marty Robbins diskographie, teil 2. *Hillbilly;* 1978 June; (55): 16–33.
Note: Illus.

Marty Robbins/Don Everly, Hammersmith Odeon, London. *Country Music People;* 1978 June; 9(6): 17.
Performance review.

[Photograph]. *The Tennessean;* 1978 June 19.
Photo of Marty and his custom-made car, a Panther DeVille, on the stage of the Grand Ole Opry.

Robbins, Marty; Sherrill, Billy. Don't let me touch you. *Country Song Roundup;* 1978 June; 30(227): 25.
Note: Lyrics to the song.

Forsyth, Aljean. Marty Robbins loves to look at his fans. *Waycross Journal Herald* (GA); 1978 July 31.
Note: Illus.

Letters [letters to the editor column]. *Country Music People;* 1978 July; 9(7): 53.
Fan letter.

[Photograph]. *Music City News;* 1978 July; 16(1): 26.
Photo of Marty and the Statler Brothers filming a segment of "Marty Robbins Spotlight" show.

[Photograph]. *Country Hotline News;* 1978/July; 9(7).
Cover photo of Marty with Stella Parton.

Nashville every day [monthly feature]. *Country Song Roundup;* 1978 August; 30(229): 36.
The taping of "Marty Robbins Spotlight" is underway; taping moved to WTVF-TV.

Postell, Charles. Robbins' songs, gags delight Opry audience. *Albany Herald* (GA); 1978 August 2.
Performance review that recalls strong audience response.

Star gazing [news column]. *Music City News;* 1978 August; 16(2): 4.
Column includes story about Marty taking new car, the Panther DeVille, on the stage of the Grand Ole Opry June 17th. Description of the car is included.

Stevens, Dale. Marty Robbins talks of Willie Nelson and Parton. *Cincinnati Post;* 1978 August 26: 15.
Interview covers Nelson, Parton, country music trends, and his unhappiness with CMA.

[Advertisement]. *The Tennessean;* 1978 September 17: Showcase section.
Large ad for the upcoming "Marty Robbins World Open 500" stock car race to be held in Nashville.

Belisle, Richard F. From "El Paso" to Frederick, Maryland; Marty wows 'em. *Morning Herald* (Hagerstown, MD); 1978 September 20.
Note: Illus.
Performance review.

Fuhrmann, Georg. Veranstaltungen. In dulci Wembley-O. *Hillbilly;* 1978 September; (56): 33–40.
Note: Illus.
Article about the Wembley Festival includes a review of Marty's performance and a photo on p. 33.

Hicks, Jerry. Marty Robbins overdoes the showbiz sillies. *Louisville Times* (KY); 1978 September 19.
Performance review. While the reviewer acknowledges that Marty was a hit with the crowd ("the second time he's been here this year; they could have him back next week and he'd draw a crowd"). The reviewer didn't care for Marty's jokes and silliness but admitted that no one else in the audience seemed to mind. And he also admitted it was tough not to smile when Marty hams it up for the picture takers.

Marty Robbins says, "racing is hard work." *Florence Morning News* (SC); 1978 September 1: 10C.
Interview about racing.

[Photograph]. *The Tennessean;* 1978 September 29.
Photo of Marty in pace car to be used Sunday in his race at the Nashville Speedway. Qualifying starts today.

Rockabilly rules OK. *Country Music People;* 1978 September; 9(9): 36.
Recent album releases on rockabilly includes some cuts by Marty.

[Advertisement]. *Music City News;* 1978 October; 16(4): 26B.
Full-page ad, with photo, thanking fans for MCN Award nominations.

Forsyth, Aljean. Performing is fun for Marty. *Music City News;* 1978 October; 16(4): 11-A.
Note: Illus.

Top country-western singers will share stage. *Fresno Bee* (CA); 1978 October 6.
Marty and Merle Haggard will appear together.

Rhodes, Larry. Country singers please devoted fans. *Times-Herald* (Newport News, VA); 1978 October 14.
Note: Illus.
Marty and Billy "Crash" Craddock concert performance review. The review on Marty says: "Robbins strolled on stage in an attractive white outfit with colorful embroidery and flirted with and teased the audience

continuously . . . Robbins even appeased the instamatic camera crowd by performing with the house lights on so the fans could take better pictures."

Kanengiser, Andy. Robbins: CMA just "politics." *Albany Herald;* 1978 October 18.
Interview covers, in part, his feelings about CMA. Clearly put, he believes: "The CMA is nothing but politics . . . the people who vote are choosing artists who benefit CMA." He feels the winners are usually artists booked out of Los Angeles or New York and heavily backed by their big organizations. The country music fans are pretty much left out of the picture; that's why he feels the *Music City News* Awards are "the real awards—because the fans vote."

Country singers bring a little Nashville. *Wichita Beacon;* 1978 October 20.
Note: Illus.
Article about an upcoming concert with Merle Haggard.

Marty Robbins; he gambled with death so he could risk his life. *Country Style;* 1978 October; (36): 42, 51.
Note: Illus.
Article about his heart operation and auto racing. Notes Marty talks to others who need the same kind of operation.

Otteson, Jan. Marty Robbins is country charisma. *Music City News;* 1978 October; 16(4): 1.
Note: Illus. Cover photo.
Interview covers Marty's unique stage style of bragging, strutting, humor, cutting up for cameras, and singing. Marty tries to avoid seeing fans before going on stage. He says, "I learned that trick from Gene Autry. He told me 'Don't let anyone see you before a show. Be a surprise to them.' And I've found that if I stay away from people the day of a show, I'm usually so happy to see them when the time comes that the exuberance pours out of me." He's recently disbanded his fan club, but some people have joined together and are calling themselves "Marty's Army," and even wear little patches on their jackets. The article notes that Marty's concerts transmit a one-to-one feeling between him and the audience which gives an intimate feeling between them. Asked to define his charisma, Marty said, "Me and the crowd get along just fine, and that's all that matters."

Rucker, Leland G. Haggard, Robbins: two kinds of style. *Kansas City Times* (MO); 1978 October 23.

Note: Illus.
Performance review. The reviewer calls Marty "the personification of romantic characters that populate those border-town romantic songs that have made him famous. Dressed in a well-tailored cowboy suit, Robbins delivered a relaxed set of his old standards." The review goes on to say, "Robbins is a natural on stage, stopping to mug for the almost steady stream of people trekking to the front to take snapshots of their hero, and talking and laughing almost all the time he isn't singing. It's easy to see he enjoys being the center of attention, and although he merely is reliving his past triumphs, his overdramatic gestures and handsome looks are effective."

Robbins, Haggard on Fresno stage. *Fresno Bee* (CA); 1978 October 27.
Note: Illus.
An article about the upcoming concert, Nov. 3rd.

Tully, Gloria. Robbins shows just why they don't go faultin' him. *San Francisco Examiner;* 1978 November 1.
Note: Illus.
Performance review of concert at the Saddlerack Club. The reviewer notes: "Country singer Marty Robbins hasn't changed a bit. He sang and clowned his way through 20 songs . . . his big beautiful voice as mellow and musical as ever and his ability to take himself seriously nonexistent. If you shut your eyes and listen you would never guess from the sound that the singer is mugging for fans' flash cameras, kidding his own performance, and just generally hamming it up." She goes on to say, "An incorrigible comic, he has been doing it successfully for years. As C'nelia Wallace once said on television, 'Now, don't you go faultin' Marty'."

Palmer, Chuck. Merle Haggard, Marty Robbins party at Swing, Nov. 4. *San Bernardino Sun Telegram* (CA): 1978 October 29.
Announcement of the beginning of their tour.

Nashville every day [monthly column]. *Country Song Roundup;* 1978 November; 30(232): 40.
Marty won a settlement in a suit he had brought against the builder of his home. He had the house for 19 months when it started sliding down the hill it was on.

Palmer, Chuck. Robbins, Haggard—a double dose of country. *San Bernardino Sun Telegram* (CA); 1978 November 6.
Note: Illus.
Detailed performance review, including descriptions of their extreme contrast in performance styles.

Zakem, Marc. Marty Robbins did his best to fill in for Merle Haggard despite hecklers. *Louisville Courier Journal;* 1978 November 12.
Performance review. Merle was ill and missed the concert. The review centers on Marty's excellent rapport with the audience, his joking, and efforts to handle some heckling from disappointed Haggard fans. Marty got high marks for handling a very mixed audience.

[Performance review]. *Variety;* 1978 November 15; 293: 68.
Concert review.

Ralph Emery; country's most famous disc jockey. *Country Music;* 1978 November/December; 7(2): 104–105.
Part of the article covers the taping of "Marty Robbins' Spotlight," which Ralph co-produced.

Stars pay tribute to Ernest Tubb on new LP. *Country Music;* 1978 November/December; 7(2): 21, 22.
Marty has one cut on the tribute album of duets with Ernest.

[Advertisement]. *The Tennessean;* 1978 December 17: Showcase section.
A large ad, featuring Marty, for the Music City Tire Co. and Uniroyal tires.

All star line-up for Wembley '79. *Country Music People;* 1978 December; 9(12): 4.
Marty listed among performers signed to appear.

B J's corner [news column]. *Music City News;* 1978 December; 16(6): 26.
Notes that Marty, Merle Haggard, and the Sons of the Pioneers had two sellouts in Phoenix recently at concerts presented by KNIX Radio.

Deception said cause of concert cancellation. *Charlestown Gazette;* 1979 January 18.

Blackwell, Sam. Marty Robbins recalls path from trucker to country music star. *The Times-Standard* [Eureka, CA]; 1979 January 25.
Performance review and interview.

Orme, Terry. Marty Robbins carries the ball for Haggard. *The Salt Lake Tribune;* 1979 January 28: E9.
Performance review. Merle sang one song, announced he was ill, and left the stage. The reviewer notes that "Friday night he recovered mirac-

ulously because Haggard had one thing going for him: he was sharing the bill with Marty Robbins." The review goes on to give the details of his concert, saying it was "the best country show this town has seen for some time."

20 star studded country hits. *Country Music People;* 1979 January; 10(1): 39.
Album review. Various artists. Cuts by Marty included.

Young, Chuck. Darrell Waltrip came marching home for "his" day. *NASCAR Newsletter;* 1979 January.
Note: Illus.
A home town celebration in Owensboro, Kentucky for Waltrip; Marty was Parade Marshal and attended the dinner. Photo of Marty included.

Condolences [special column]. *CMA Close-up;* 1979 February; 20(10): 3.
Lee Emerson Bellamy died December 4, 1978. Lee worked for Marty Robbins, was a noted songwriter, and wrote "Ruby Ann."

Harris, Stacy. Are the country stars being ripped off? *Country Song Roundup;* 1979 February; 31(235): 8–10.
Note: Illus.

Hasden, Nikki C. Robbins and Twitty thrill crowd. *Chattanooga Times;* 1979 February 4.
Performance review.

Marty Robbins and Hickory Farms. *Country Hotline News;* 1979 February; 10(2): 11.
Eddy Fox recorded a commercial by Marty for Hickory Farms for radio and TV. Eddy had previously made the TV commercials with Marty for Uniroyal Tire.

[Advertisement]. *Hillbilly;* 1979 March; (58): 48 [back cover].
Full-page ad for the First International Festival of Country Music '79, Festhalle, Frankfurt, 21/4/79. Marty is one of the performers scheduled to perform.

[Live special telecast]. The Grand Ole Opry on PBS. *TV Guide;* 1979 March 3.
Marty closed the evening long show, going overtime as usual.

Am 21. 4. 79 in Frankfurt: Talent das ist die Fahigkeit, Leute erfreuen zu konnen, Marty Robbins zieht nach 25 Jahren en Bilanz. *Country Corner;* 1979 March: 6–7.
Note: Cover photo., illus.
Performance review.

B J's corner [news column]. *Music City News;* 1979 March; 16(9): 22.
A news item says Pee Wee King filmed a pilot last month for a one-hour PBS special. Guests included Marty.

The Performer. *Dayton Journal-Herald;* 1979 March 17.
Album review.

Freeders, Al. Robbins cuts a winning LP in "Performer." *Dayton Daily News;* 1979 March 18.
Note: Illus.
Album review for "The Performer." Mentions that Marty wrote the title song for Elvis Presley.

Kool Country Tour announced. *Music City News;* 1979 March; 16(9): 3.
Marty and Merle Haggard to tour together under sponsorship of Kool cigarettes and Brown & Williamson Tobacco.

Wagoner show to tape during Fan Fair. *Music City News;* 1979 March; 16(9): 23.
Marty listed as one of the guests.

Gilson, Nancy. Celebrities coming to western awards. *The Oklahoma Journal;* 1979 April 5 (Thursday): 10.
Note: Illus.
The 18th annual Western Heritage Awards will be held this coming weekend at the National Cowboy Hall of Fame. Marty will be the Master of Ceremonies at the awards presentations and dinner Saturday night.

Reid, H. Spins 'n' needles [record review column]. *Times-Herald* (Newsport News, VA); 1979 April 6.
Review of the album, "The Performer." Also includes information about Marty's writing the title cut.

Hefner, John. Preservers of western heritage win awards. *The Sunday Oklahoman;* 1979 April 8: 1.
Note: Illus.

Gene Autry presents Marty with the Golden Trustee Award, April 7, 1979. (Photo from the National Cowboy Hall of Fame)

Marty was Master of Ceremonies and was given a special Trustees' Award (presented by Gene Autry).

[Advertisement]. *Country Music People;* 1979 April; 10(4): 7.
One-page ad for tour; includes dates.

Byworth, Tony. Wembley's eleventh: crammed full of country. *Country Music People;* 1979 April; 10(4): 9.
Note: Illus.
Includes photo of Marty and performance review.

Country bus drivers: unsung heroes of the road. *Music City News;* 1979 April; 16(10): 15.
Note: Illus.
Okie Jones, driver of Marty's tour bus, is included.

Golden collection. *Country Music People;* 1979 April; 10(4): 52.
Album review.

International country festival in Frankfurt. *Country Corner;* 1979 April: 2–3, 10.
Note: Illus.

Marty Robbins. *Country Music Parade;* 1979 April; 4(4): 12.
Note: Illus.
Article covers early part of career, writing songs, including "The Performer" which he wrote for Elvis Presley. Marty says, "I wrote it for Elvis. He never got to hear it. I finished it on an airplane a month before he died. It says what a performer wants to say to his audience, what a performer feels for his fans . . . 'The Performer' is a love song to my fans."

Marty Robbins: Lied und sanger: erfolg. *Country Corner;* 1979 April: 5–6.
Note: Illus.

The Performer. *People;* 1979 April 23.
Album review.

UK dates set for Marty Robbins. *Country Music People;* 1979 April; 10(4): 4.
Announcement of upcoming tour.

Van Dam, Hans. Marty Robbins, "superstar." *Country Gazette;* 1979 April; (66): 2–3.
Note: Illus.

Kersey, Nancy Bigler. Marty Robbins: a man of note. *Cleveland Plain Dealer;* 1979 May 31: 1D, 2D.
Note: Illus.
Long interview includes comments about Gene Autry, Elvis Presley, the Opry, his support of Ronny, and his feelings about various industry issues and the CMA Awards.

The Performer. *Country Music People;* 1979 May; 10(5): 40.
Album review.

The Performer. *Country Music;* 1979 May; 7(7): 62.
Note: Illus.
Album review.

[Photograph]. *Billboard;* 1979 May 12: 59.
The caption to the photo notes that Marty recently received the Golden Trustee's Medal from the Cowboy Hall of Fame.

Stardom wasn't mirage for "desert rat" Robbins. *Country Hotline News;* 1979 May; 10(5): 6.

Note: Illus.
Interview covers Marty's early career history. Quotes Marty as saying he wrote "The Performer" for Elvis a month before he died and he never got to hear it. It also quotes him as saying, "The Performer is a love song to my fans."

[Advertisement]. *Music City News;* 1979 June; 16(12): 54.
Full-page ad with photo by Marty thanking fans for MCN Award nominations.

By the time I get to Phoenix. *Country Music People;* 1979 June; 10(6): 39.
Album review.

First International Country Music Festival '79. *Country Corner;* 1979 June: 2–5.
Note: Illus.
Marty included in photos and article.

"Grand Ole Ahoy"; Nashville in Rotterdam (music festival). *Country Gazette;* 1979 June; (68): 2–6.
Note: Cover photo. Illus.
Review of Marty's performance on p. 4; photo included.

Greatest hits, vol. 4. *Country Corner;* 1979 June: 27.
Album review.

Robbins is first entry for "Firecracker 400." *News and Press* (Albermarle, NC); 1979 June 5.
The July 4th race to be held at Daytona. Marty's car will be number 36 for the first time; he gave the number 42 to Kyle Petty because it had been Petty's father's number.

Huffman, Bob. Marty A-One. *Southern Motorsports Journal;* 1979 June 15: 3, 4, 7.
The author includes several stories about Marty as a racer, including his giving up his car number 42 to Kyle Petty, running a race without a carburetor restrictor, and his friendship with drivers.

Granger, Gene. Racing [news column]. Marty Robbins, fan. *The Fayetteville Times;* 1979 June 16: 3B.
About Marty's love of racing and the writing of his "Twentieth Century Drifter" song for use in a feature article *Sports Illustrated* was doing about him.

Marty Robbins to race again. *The Sentinel* (Winston-Salem, NC); 1979 June 16.
Note: Illus.
Article includes several racing stories.

Robbins knows victory is out of the question. *South Bend Tribune* (IN); 1979 June 16.
Interview about a race in Grand Junction, Michigan.

[MCN Awards nominees]. *Music City News;* 1979 June; 16(12): 28–29.
Note: Illus.
List of award nominees, with photos, for each category. Marty nominated in seven categories.

Monch, Edward K. Internationales Country Music Festival 1979; Bericht uber die Veranstaltung in der Festhalle, Frankfurt/Main, am 21.4.79. *Hillbilly;* 1979 June; (59): 24–26.
Note: Illus.
Marty was one of the performers at the festival.

The stars gather around Ernest. *Country Music People;* 1979 June; 10(6): 25.
Album review of new Ernest Tubb album. Marty sings one song with ET.

Wembley '79. *Country Music People;* 1979 June; 10(6): 17–20, 46.
Note: Illus.
Marty's performance reviewed on p. 17.

Woody, Larry. Tunin' up . . . Marty Robbins rides again. *The Tennessean;* 1979 July 1.
Note: Illus.
Racing interview. Marty was the first driver to enter the Firecracker 400 at the Daytona International Speedway. He last ran the race in 1973 and finished eighth. Talking about his decision to resume racing, Marty said, "I guess I'm hooked. Guess drivin' is always going to be an attraction for me."

Cunniff, Al. Marty Robbins; the performer. *Country Music;* 1979 July/August; 7(9): 36–38, 80.
Note: Illus.
Interview at a recording session; author says it's a cross between a recording session, a concert, and a Mel Brooks movie. Good photos.

Ernest Tubb—The legend and the legacy, v. 1. *Billboard;* 1979 July 28: 56.
Album review. Marty sings with Ernest on the album.

The Performer. *Country Corner;* 1979 July: 25.
Note: Illus.
Album review.

Robbins, Marty. Walking piece of heaven. *Country Song Roundup;* 1979 July; 31(240): 22.
Note: Lyrics to the song.

Country on the tube [news column]. *CMA Close-up;* 1979 July: 2.
Marty listed as a guest on the pilot of a new Pee Wee King TV show called "King Country." [Editorial note: the series never got past the pilot stage.]

Bragg, Rick. Marty; singer a favorite at AIMS. *Talladega, Alabama Home;* 1979 August 3.
AIMS (Alabama International Motor Speedway).

Lipper, Hal. Marty Robbins will keep playing until it feels like work. *Dayton Daily News;* 1979 August 10.
Note: Illus.
Interview covers early events that got him started in his career.

Caldwell, Joe. Robbins 500 is canceled; Southern 200 still slated. *Nashville Banner;* 1979 August 15.
The date for the race conflicted with another race.

Beck, Ken. Good luck, good Lord fulfill singer's dream. *The Tennessean;* 1979 August 26: Showcase section.
Note: Illus.
The article is about Jeff Chandler, a member of Marty's band who plays and sings harmony with Marty.

Coffey, Betty. Of cowboys, Texas, women and gunfighters; Marty Robbins in concert. *Meridian Star* (MS); 1979 August 31.
Note: Illus.
Good performance review of Marty and his band; with concert and backstage photos.

Faces 'n' places [news column]. *Country Music People;* 1979 August; 10(8): 10.
Notes that Marty has been elected to the International Cowboy Hall of Fame in Oklahoma City.

[Advertisement]. *Music City News;* 1979 September; 17(3): 2.
Full-page ad for Marty. Gives tour schedule and booking/office address. Photo included.

[Advertisement]. *Music City News;* 1979 September; 17(3): 22.
Full-page ad, with photo, thanking fans for his MCN Awards nominations the previous June.

Jarnigan, Bill. Robbins is the all around cowboy. *Birmingham News* (AL); 1979 September 29.
Note: Illus.
Album review for "All around cowboy."

Greatest hits, vol. 4. *Country Gazette;* 1979 September; (70): 27.
Album review.

Jeannie Pruett has time to make a home. *Music City News;* 1979 September; 17(3): 18.
Note: Illus.
Interview includes comments about songwriting for Marty, her husband Jack (a member of Marty's band) and his travels with Marty.

Star gazing [news column]. *Music City News;* 1979 September; 17(3): 4.
Marty was recently honored by the Cowboy Hall of Fame in Oklahoma City.

McNulty, Jim. All around cowboy; album review in the "Country Music" record review column. *Edmonton, Alberta Journal* [Canada]; 1979 September 29.
Album review.

Zakem, Marc. Robbins was a commercial success. *Louisville Courier Journal;* 1979 September 29.
Performance review.

[Advertisement]. *Music City News;* 1979 October; 17(4): 2.
Full-page ad for Marty includes photo of Marty on Brute, his buckskin horse.

All around cowboy. *Music City News;* 1979 October; 17(4): 46.
Album review.

All around cowboy. *Country Music;* 1979 October; 8(2): 63.
Album review.

Andrews, Jenny. Gunfighter balladeer dreams; is Marty Robbins an anachronism? *Music City News;* 1979 October; 17(4): 22.
Note: Illus.
Interview centers around his love for the Old West and films he has made.

Changes and exchanges [news column]. *Music City News;* 1979 October; 17(4): 7.
Column notes that Ronny Robbins has signed with Thunder Records.

Country music chronolog [news column]. *Country Song Roundup;* 1979 October; 31(243): 46.
Note: Illus.
The column quotes Marty about the controversy over his use of horns on the stage of the Opry. Only traditional musical instruments are permitted on the Opry stage, and Marty had taken the horns on stage without approval. This led to a dispute with the Opry management that lasted several weeks. It also says he performed recently for the Governor of Tennessee.

News, views, and previews [news column]. *Music City News;* 1979 October; 17(4): 40.
Column notes that the Marty Robbins' Spotlight will be stopped. It quotes Marty as saying he liked the show but couldn't do it and maintain as active a tour schedule as he wanted.

Palmer, Barry. Country music beat [review column]. *Manchester Union Leader* (NH); 1979 October 5.
Note: Illus.
Album review for "All around cowboy" and interview with Marty regarding Bob Nolan and song writing.

Merle Haggard, Marty Robbins to be in concert together. *Advance Monticellonian* [Monticello, AR]; 1979 October 25.
Announcement of concert.

Best bets [news column]. *Daily Californian* [El Cajon, CA]; 1979 October 27.
Details for a Robbins-Haggard concert to occur at the end of the week.

Nickerson, Marina. Marty and Merle strum spiffy music. *El Paso Times;* 1979 October 27.
Note: Illus.
Performance review of this Robbins/Haggard concert centers on their different styles and ways of relating to the audience. Concert photos.

Dawson, Susan. Haggard-Robbins; a "can't miss" combo. *Fort Worth Star-Telegram;* 1979 October 30.
Marty and Merle to appear November 17th.

The Performer. *Country Song Roundup;* 1979 October; 31(243): 37.
Album review.

Robbins, Marty. All around cowboy. *Country Song Roundup;* 1979 November; 31(244): 20.
Note: Lyrics to the song.

Fan time [monthly column]. *Country Song Roundup;* 1979 November; 31(244): 38.
Marty was recently elected to the Cowboy Hall of Fame in Oklahoma City, OK.

Haggard-Robbins show. *San Jose Mercury* [CA]; 1979 November 1.
Story about the upcoming performance at the Oakland Coliseum with the Sons of the Pioneers as the opening act.

Merle & Marty due here. *Anaheim Bulletin* (CA); 1979 November 1.
Announcement of a concert to be held this coming Saturday.

Robbins, Haggard to give concert here on Friday. *Commercial* [Pine Bluff, AR]; 1979 November 10.
Note: Illus.

Maxwell, Maggie. 2 country stars visit Pine Bluff. *Little Rock Democrat* [AR]; 1979 November 16.
Marty and Merle will give a concert tonight.

Fister, Greg. Country music hits local stage. *Commercial* [Pine Bluff, AR]; 1979 November 17.
Concert review.

Dawson, Susan. Haggard captures C & W hungry crowd. *Fort Worth Star Telegram;* 1979 November 19.

Performance review of a Marty and Merle concert. The reviewer took a dim view of Marty's chatter, saying, "Robbins' recital was in dire need of editing in regard to his off-the-cuff remarks. A gifted writer and performer, he should have sung more and talked less. Histrionics and provocative chatter aside, Robbins gave the audience its money's worth . . . Talent and musical professionalism weren't in question here. They abounded in every number. Robbins' road manager should have slapped a muzzle on him between tunes."

Oppel, Pete. Iran has made us all "Okies from Muskogee." *The Dallas Morning News;* 1979 November 19; (Monday).
A Marty and Merle concert review.

Barnes, Suzanne. Robbins serious about music. *Cedar Rapids Gazette* (IA); 1979 November 25.
Note: Illus.
Interview before a performance with Merle Haggard in Iowa includes Marty's opinion on a variety of topics.

Chute, James. Country stars stir emotions. *The Cincinnati Post* [OH]; 1979 November 26.
A Marty and Merle concert review. The reviewer characterized Marty as "a rare combination of arrogance and humility." Both Marty and Merle were made Honorary Teamsters by the head of the union local at the end of the concert.

Trott, Walt. Robbins digs racing and music. *The Capital Times* (Madison, WI); 1979 November 26 (Monday).
Note: Illus.
Marty and Merle will appear this coming Sunday.

Hogan, Dick. Near legends please crowd of country music fans. *Cedar Rapids Gazette* (IA); 1979 November 30: 13A.
Note: Illus.
Performance review of a Robbins/Haggard concert and the audience reaction to their two diverse styles.

[Advertisement]. *Music City News;* 1979 December; 17(6): 26.
Full-page ad thanking fans for their support during the past year.

All around cowboy. *Country Music People;* 1979 December; 10(12): 44.
Album review.

All around cowboy. *Country Corner;* 1979 December: 42.
Note: Illus.
Album review.

Anthony, Michael. Robbins, Haggard play Met Center concert. *Minneapolis Tribune* (MN); 1979 December 2.
Note: Illus.
Review of an exciting Robbins/Haggard concert on an incredibly cold winter night. The reviewer notes, "This was the kind of crowd that comes not just to listen and see, but to shoot pictures." He goes on to say that Robbins presumably sees blue dots in front of his eyes weeks after a concert tour. He calls Marty one of the funniest men around, and says he probably has the best singing voice in country music among the men singers.

Letters [to the editor]. *Country Music;* 1979 December; 8(4): 7.
Three fan letters regarding Marty are included.

Martin, Chuck. Country duo worth wait for fans. *Wisconsin State Journal* (Madison, WI); 1979 December 3.
Concert review of a Robbins/Haggard concert includes quotes from several fans.

Trott, Walt. Merle 'n Marty show—a winner. *The Capital Times* [Madison, WI]; 1979 December 4.
Concert review. Both went over equally well with the audience.

[Performance review]. *Variety;* 1979 December 19; 297: 68.
Concert review.

Rice, Gary. Robbins' jokes lack rhythm. *Kansas City Star;* 1979 December 5.
Note: Illus.
Concert review. Although the reviewer notes Marty had good rapport with the audience, he felt there should have been fewer jokes and more music.

Robbins, Marty. All around cowboy. *Country Song Roundup;* 1979 December; 31(245): 25.
Note: Lyrics to the song.

6

BIBLIOGRAPHY, 1980–1988

The decade started out routinely enough. Marty continued his tours with Merle Haggard. His popularity with the fans led to the winning of the fan-voted MCN Awards. And he enjoyed success as a songwriter when a Johnny Cash recording of his "Song of the Patriot" became one of the popular songs of the year. Marty sang harmony with Johnny on the recording.

But then, on New Year's day of 1981, Marty suffered another heart attack. It was considered a mild one and he was treated with rest and medication. An operation was considered, but a decision was made against performing one. The attack had been in progress for several days. With characteristic lightness, Marty described how he had been bothered by indigestion and headaches for several days before going to see the doctor, only to be carried out of the doctor's office on a stretcher with his boots on and holding his cowboy hat in his hands! During these days, not knowing how ill he was, he had filmed an episode of Barbara Mandrell's popular television show. Not one to stay quiet long, he returned to touring with a March 6th show in Saginaw, Michigan and a March 7th performance in Warren, Ohio. Also in March, he appeared at the Grand Ole Opry for the first time since his illness, as part of a special live PBS telecast, hosting the last segment of the evening and staying overtime as was his usual practice. The Fourth of July of the same year brought special recognition when he was asked by President Reagan to perform at the White House.

The year 1982 saw a strong revival of his career. Early in the

227

year, he had a hit record with "Some memories just won't die," his concerts were selling out, and he was nominated for several MCN Awards. An article in *Esquire* magazine called his voice "A national treasure." He performed at the Wembley Festival in April. During the June Fan Fair week, he held what would be his last big gathering with his fans, hosting a "Marty Party" at the Opryland Hotel for over 2000 fans at his own expense. He performed for over two hours and then stayed nearly five hours signing autographs. The rest of the summer was spent touring and starting work on a new album. He was also featured in a segment of Charles Kuralt's Sunday morning television show, doing what he loved best, driving race cars and performing in a stage show.

October of 1982 brought increased attention from the music industry. *Billboard* recognized his success in its special Country Music Awards issue by giving him the "Artist Resurgence Award" for the artist who had the greatest career revival during the past year. The Country Music Association paid special tribute to him by voting him into the "Hall of Fame"; the award was presented on the Association's nationally broadcast awards show in mid-October. He toured Canada and the West Coast in late October, and put in long hours on his upcoming album.

November was equally as busy. He started off the month with a November 1st visit to "The Noon Show," a daily local telecast hosted by his friend Chuck Morgan. Roy Acuff was also a guest that day and the viewers were treated to a joint performance and Marty playing dobro for Roy. He raced in the NASCAR Atlanta Journal 500 November 7th, flew to Los Angeles to tape an episode of "The Grapefruit Show" (shown on foreign cable stations), and taped "The Bobby Jones Gospel Hour" show on November 10th.

The morning of December 2, after returning from a concert in Cincinnati late the night before, Marty suffered a heart attack at his home and was rushed to the hospital. Emergency bypass surgery was performed and it was briefly believed that he would survive, but he was unable to recover and died a week later on December 8th.

The citations in the bibliography from 1983 through 1988 reflect the sense of loss of a loved and respected performer, tributes to his talent, and recognition of his lasting popularity. Many radio and television shows have broadcast tributes. His records continue to sell. Articles continue to be written. The most used phrase to describe him and the recognition he continues to receive is the somewhat prophetic title of his last hit, "Some memories just won't die."

BIBLIOGRAPHY, 1980–1982

[Advertisement]. *Music City News;* 1980 January; 17(7): 19.
Full-page advertisement.

Funeral services held for country music pioneer. *Country Hotline News;* 1980 February; 11(2): 3.
The article is about the death of Vic McAlpin. A friend is quoted as saying he had demos of his songs with the late Jim Reeves and Marty Robbins on them.

News, views, and previews [news column]. *Music City News;* 1980 January; 17(7): 27.
The column says that Marty has two movie projects in the negotiating stage; one would cast him as a rock and roll promoter, the other would use his voice in a cartoon of Pecos Bill. The column also notes he will appear this month on the Mike Douglas and Dinah Shore shows.

Olmstead, Rebecca. He's singing the blues . . . all the way to the bank. *The Sentinel* (Salem, NC); 1980 February 13.
An interview, before a concert with Merle Haggard, covers racing, performing, and song writing.

Dawidziak, Mark. Marty Robbins: two decades after "Gunfighter ballads and trail songs" was pressed, this durable singer-composer is still highlighting and celebrating America's western heritage of gunfighters, ranch hands, trail bosses, lawmen and lovely Mexican girls. *Kingsport Times* (TN); 1980 February 15.
Note: Illus.
Detailed interview, in question-answer format, covering a number of his western albums and the inspirations behind his songwriting.

Letters to the editor [column]. *Music City News;* 1980 February; 17(8):
3.
A long letter from Juanita Wolfe giving details of a call Marty made to
her mother, who was suffering with cancer.

News, views, and previews [news column]. *Music City News;* 1980
February; 17(8): 22.
Marty listed among performers set to do an Austin City Limits segment
during the coming season.

Rice, Gary. Haggard and band rattle the rafters. *Kansas City Star;* 1980
February 23.
Note: Illus.
Concert review of a Robbins/Haggard concert; photo of Marty in
performance.

Star gazing [monthly column]. *Music City News;* 1980 February; 17(8):
27.
Marty received an award from the Teamster's Union commemorating
one million miles of safe driving with his tour bus without an accident.
Credit goes to Okie Jones, Marty's bus driver.

All around cowboy. *Country Song Roundup;* 1980 March; 32(248): 35.
Album review.

Wood, Gerry. Nashvillians prefer easy listening music. *Billboard;* 1980
March 1: 6, 36.
Marty one of the artists listed as a favorite.

[Television Special] PBS-TV. 1980 March 1 (Saturday night).
PBS televised a three-hour "Live From the Grand Ole Opry" and Marty
performed in his regular spot the last half hour (and longer).

Mietkiewiez, Henry. Country grab-bag deserves full marks. *Toronto
Star;* 1980 March 21.
Concert review of show starring Marty, Hank Williams, Jr. and Gene
Watson.

News, views, and previews [news column]. *Music City News;* 1980
March; 17(9): 35.
Marty's song, "El Paso," was the subject of a parody on the 2nd Steve
Martin Special on NBC.

[Advertisement]. *Music City News;* 1980 April; 17(10): 13.
Ad for the Wild Turkey Jamboree. Marty one of performers listed.

[Television appearance]. Austin City Limits. Broadcast on PBS stations around the country during the month of April, 1980.
Marty starred in a half-hour episode that had been taped October 23, 1979.

Brooks, Ellen. Patience pays for Jeanne Pruett. *Country Hotline News;* 1980 April; 11(4): 17.
Note: Ilus.
Article includes comments about Marty reviewing her songs and encouraging her writing. He recorded five of the early ones she wrote for his company.

Rhodes, Don. Marty Robbins has no trouble pleasing fans. *Augusta Chronicle* (GA); 1980 April 13.
Note: Illus.
Marty talks about ending his series, "Marty Robbins Spotlight." Photo of Marty, Charlie Collins and Minnie Pearl. Of picking the songs he sings, Marty says, "I try to please myself. I don't try to please other people. I don't think I have the talent to know what people like. I try to sing the songs I would buy. The only pattern I have for a stage show is there are certain songs I have to sing for every show. It depends on the audience."

[Photograph]. *The Tennessean;* 1980 April 20.
Photo of Marty as he appears on "Austin City Limits" television program this week.

Eipper, Laura. Fans favor Marty Robbins for nine "Cover" awards. *The Tennessean;* 1980 April 30: 21,23.
Marty was nominated for nine awards in the Music City News Awards voting. Article includes complete list of nominees.

Backstage at the Opry [news column]. *Country Hotline News;* 1980 April 30; 11(4): 16.
A paragraph of the column covers Marty and Tony Lyons kidding about the Opry clock and Marty's extended time on stage. The recent PBS show went an hour overtime because of Marty.

Wild Turkey Jamboree of Country set for June 7–8. *Country Hotline News;* 1980 April; 11(4): 3.
Marty is one of the headliners.

[Advertisement]. *Music City News;* 1980 May; 17(11): 7.
Full-page ad for the Marty Robbins Recording Studio.

[Advertisement]. *Music City News;* 1980 May; 17(11): 13.
Ad for the Wild Turkey Jamboree. Marty listed among the headliners.

David Allen page [news column]. *Country Music People;* 1980 May;
11(5): 12.
Interview with Marty includes comments about morals in songs, his
love of the old west, and his British fans.

Thomas, Roy. Country singer Robbins doesn't care about winning.
Montgomery Advertiser (AL); 1980 May 4: 1C,8C.
Racing interview; Marty to race in the Winston 500 at Talladega Sun-
day. Marty tells several racing stories.

Stearns, Dave. Robbins paces hits to stay on top; and he sings all the
verses to "El Paso" at every concert. *El Paso Times;* 1980 May 17.
Note: Illus.
Good interview covers his love of travel, the Old West, and his song
writing. About traveling on his tour bus, he says he likes traveling; he
and his band usually drive all night on his tour bus after a concert to the
next performance because they can't sleep. He says, "I'd rather travel
than lay awake until 4 or 5 in the morning and then have to get up at 8.
We have nine bunks, recorded music to listen to, a television, and a very
good poker table. I've spent 12 hours at a time playing poker." In
talking about his love of the Old West and cowboy songs, he says, "I
grew up with that kind of music. In Arizona I used to work on ranches
in the summertime. I used to have books of cowboy songs. . . I like the
desert, and I guess that's why I like cowboy songs. At home, I have
about 12 hours of cowboy songs on tape. If I could live another life, I'd
probably be a cowboy."

Farmer, Bob. City youth believes in Robbins message. *Watertown
Daily News* (NY); 1980 May 23.
Story about a paralyzed youth who had a visit from Marty.

Marty Robbins sweeps MCN Awards nominations. *Music City News;*
1980 May; 17(11): 6, 29.

Palmer, Barry. Marty Robbins is doing quite well. *Manchester Union
Leader;* 1980 May 27.
Note: Illus.

Topics of the interview include writing "Song of the Patriot" and singing harmony with Johnny Cash on his recording of it, the music business, and auto racing.

Souvenir album. *Country and Western Spotlight* (Australia); 1980 May; New Series(23): 39.
Album review.

[MCN Awards nominees]. *Music City News;* 1980 June; 17(12): 20–21.
Note: Illus.
List of award nominees, with photos, in each category. Marty received nine nominations.

[Advertisement]. *Music City News;* 1980 June; 17(12): 43.
Ad for Opryland shows photo of Marty and Roy Acuff.

[Advertisement]. *Music City News;* 1980 June; 17(12): 31.
Note: Illus.
Full-page ad by Marty for his new single release.

Cornett, Linda. Marty Robbins; something unique in country. *The Record Delta* (Buckhannon, WV); 1980 June 4: 1, 2.
Note: Illus.
Excellent lengthy performance review and interview. The review describes in accurate detail Marty's performance style and rapport with his audience.

Versatile Marty Robbins slates fair appearance. *Lubbock Avalanche-Journal* (Texas); 1980 June 8.
Marty is scheduled to appear at the 63rd Annual Panhandle South Plains Fair September 23rd.

Eipper, Laura; Browning, Graeme. Fans cite stars at awards. *The Tennessean;* 1980 June 10; (Tuesday): 21.
Note: Illus.
The article is about the "Music City News Awards" telecast the night before. Marty was nominated for nine awards and won two: Songwriter of the Year and Male Artist of the Year.

[Photograph]. *Wichita Eagle;* 1980 June 10.
Photo of Marty winning Male Artist of the Year at the MCN Awards. He was also named Songwriter of the Year.

Marty receiving one of his Music City News awards, June 1980. (Photo by Neil Pond/Music City News)

Statler Brothers reap acclaim, MCN Awards. *The Marietta Daily Journal;* 1980 June 10; (Tuesday).
Marty quoted in winning two awards.

[Photograph]. *Chicago Sun-Times;* June 10, 1980; (Tuesday): 1.
Large photo of Marty holding an award as "Country Music Male Artist of the Year," won the night before at the Music City News Awards. Awards story on page 54.

Harris, Pat. Robbins is still playing—and he's still talking. *Chicago Sun Times;* 1980 June 13.
Interview includes opinions on politics, Gene Autry, and fan-voted awards. The article starts out: "If you don't know Marty Robbins' opinion on everything, you're just not listening." On politics, he's quoted as saying: 1) If this country had the greatest military power in the world, we wouldn't have the problems plaguing us today; 2) from the first grade on, children are taught not to fear communism in America, which is part of the communist plan; 3) World War III has started—dating from the day the Russians went into Berlin in 1945. In talking about awards, Marty said: "I think the public is best qualified to judge

artists. The music industry doesn't anticipate trends. They don't know what the fans will like. The people are always a step ahead of the industry. That's why I think the only really legitimate awards are the ones given at the Music City News show every year. The awards are based on votes by fans." The writer of the article made it a point to say that Marty made this statement a week *before* he won his MCN awards.

Marty Robbins expresses opinions freely. *The News Diary;* 1980 June 18: 6A,7A.
Interview. Topics cover a number of his political opinions, writing "Song of the Patriot" (released by Johnny Cash), his grandfather, and his thoughts about fan-voted awards.

"Outlaw" at Glendale High is now a major star. *Arizona Republic;* 1981 June 18.
Long article about Marty and his early life in Arizona. Photos.

Letters to the editor [regular feature]. *The Tennessean;* 1980 June 25.
One of Marty's fans feels he didn't receive enough coverage during Fan Fair.

Ramey, Larry. Marty Robbins; the hyped-up country singer brings his carnival of music to Sandusky. *Lorain Journal* (OH); 1980 June 27.
Note: Illus.
Good interview covering Marty's songwriting and the inspirations behind several songs.

Harrison, Susan E. Marty: "you're gonna love the show." *Muskegon Chronicle;* 1980 June 28.
Note: Illus.
Good interview covering his opinions on a variety of topics.

Minsky, Betty Jane. Robbins offers solution. *Music City News;* 1980 June; 17(12): 36.
Note: Illus.
Interview comments include how to handle the Iranian crisis, his feelings about CMA, and other topics.

[Advertisement]. *Music City News;* 1980 July; 18(1): 23.
Note: Illus.
Ad and photo. [Editorial note: The "Open letter to my fans" in the ad is the one read on the televised tribute to Marty, January, 1983, during the MCN Songwriter Awards.]

Hackett, Vernell. Cross country [news column]. *Country Hotline News;* 1980 July; 11(7): 10.
The column says that Marty will race at the Missouri State Fair in the afternoon and perform on the stage at night.

Fans choose winners for the 14th MCN cover awards TV show. *Music City News;* 1980 July; 18(1): 15.
Cover photo. Illus.

Yohnka, Dennis. Robbins plans Kankakee stop. *Kankakee Daily Journal;* 1980 July 6.
Note: Illus.

Carter, Tom. Tammy's record tops; Robbins just keeps rollin'. *Tulsa Daily World* (OK); 1980 July 11.
Note: Illus.
Album review for "With Love, Marty Robbins."

Letters [to the editor]. *Music City News;* 1980 July; 18(1): 3.
Note: Cover photo.
Two letters from fans about Marty.

Lynn, Robbins, Statlers are winners of MCN awards. *Country Hotline News;* 1980 July; 11(7): 3.
Note: Illus.
Marty was voted Male Artist of the Year. Photo of Marty from the show included.

MCN Awards show highlights week of fan activities in Music City USA. *Music City News;* 1980 July; 18(1): 16–18.
Note: Cover photo. Illus.
Article about awards show. Photo of Marty included on p. 18.

Weinstein, Anne. Marty Robbins: he puts pleasing the public first. *Champaign News-Gazette* (IL); 1980 July 14.
Note: Illus.
Interview between shows includes his interest in his fans and the audience and his style on stage.

Wild Turkey fest rocks Columbia. *Music City News;* 1980 July; 18(1): 3.
The Wild Turkey Jamboree included Marty. Concert was filmed by Time to Shine Productions, a subsidiary of Nashville Television Produc-

tions. To be used for a PBS documentary. [Ed. note: The show was never broadcast.]

Wild Turkey Festival may return next year. *Country Hotline News;* 1980 July; 11(7): 6.
Note: Illus.
The festival was filmed by Rise & Shine Productions of Nashville for possible PBS showing. Marty a featured performer.

Orndorff, Bill. Robbins delights audience. *The Duncan Banner* [OK]; 1980 July 28: 8.
Note: Illus.
Detailed concert review and backstage interview. Good photo. The following excerpts from the review comment about Marty's stage persona: "Genial, smiling, and in perfect voice, Robbins mugged for the fans' cameras, cracked jokes, and provided an energetic, rousing show, much to the delight of the audience. Robbins virtually lit up the stage in his yellow floral patterned sequined suit (with matching boots) . . . when he started talking, Robbins provided hilarious patter and assorted comments on age, politics, and profiles of his band members."

15,000 at Nashville Fan Fair. *Country Music People;* 1980 August; 11(8): 6.
Note: Illus.
Review of Fan Fair week. Photo of Marty at MCN Awards included.

Barker, Teresa. Singer Marty Robbins stays close to the country. *Dubuque Telegraph-Herald* (IA); 1980 August 14.
Interview inside Marty's tour bus.

Ware, Jim. Take five [news column]. *Huntington Herald Dispatch* (WV); 1980 August 24.
The column includes section about Debbie Michelle Scott, who wrote "I can't wait until tomorrow," recorded by Marty on his album "With love."

Marty really wants to race. *National Speed Sport News;* 1980 August 27.
Brief article about Marty racing at the Missouri State Fair. Marty wrecked his car during the time trials, but bought another car and finished 10th in the race.

Backstage [monthly column]. *Country Style;* 1980 September; (58): 8.
Marty is still active in racing and entered the Talladega 500 in May.

Estes, Wayne. Robbins: country singer-stock car driver has ride with M. C. Anderson. *Savannah News* (GA); 1980 September 30.
Note: Illus.
Good racing interview. Marty will drive an Anderson car at Charlotte; detailed description and photo of Marty's car. Includes some history of past cars.

The man in black goes red, white, and blue. *Country Style;* 1980 September; (58): 5.
Johnny Cash recorded the song "Song of the Patriot," written by Marty. Marty sings harmony with Johnny on the recording.

News, views, and previews [news column]. *Music City News;* 1980 September; 18(3): 28.
Note: Illus.
Photo of Marty and comments about the possibility of his voice being used in Pecos Bill cartoons. Column also mentions that PBS has started filming a three-hour documentary on Marty. [Ed. note: the first production was never made. The documentary was made, but never shown.]

Shields, Charmaine; Diem, Nadine. Marty Robbins—just give him the wide open spaces. *Country Music Scene;* 1980 Fall: 27–29.
Note: Illus.
Interview and description of a typical Marty Robbins Grand Ole Opry performance.

Star gazing [news column]. *Music City News;* 1980 September; 18(3): 6.
Column notes that Marty recently finished 13th in an auto race.

With love. *Country Hotline News;* 1980 September; 11(9): 19.
Album review.

Smith, Steve. Marty Robbins' style pleases. *Shreveport Journal* (LA); 1980 October 16.
Note: Illus.
Performance review of Marty and his band. While generally praising the performance, the review also says, "Robbins is totally relaxed on stage, at times too relaxed. Often his patter with the audience and mugging for his band got in the way of the music; more than once he was attacked by laughing fits in the middle of a lyric, or he leaned away from the microphone to chat with the crowd." It ends by noting that Marty got a standing ovation and that the crowd left thoroughly satisfied.

People [monthly column]. *Country Music;* 1980 October; 9(2): 14.
Comments from Marty saying he doesn't feel he is risking his life auto racing.

Umbaugh, Nellie. Marty's music fills the house. *Hagerstown Morning Herald* (MD); 1980 October 27.
Note: Illus.
Performance review with photos.

With love. *Music City News;* 1980 October; 18(4): 50.
Album review.

Bishop, Nancy. Marty wants a doctor in the house. *The Dallas Morning News;* 1980 November 9; (Sunday): 4C.
Note: Illus.
Interview before a performance, mostly about auto racing. Good photo.

Miller, Townsend. Robbins hero, friend to Austin teen. *Austin American Statesman;* 1980 November 20.
The commentary is written by guest columnist Diana Zapalac, a teenager who is a fan and friend of Marty's. She recalls phone conversations and visits with him backstage.

News, views, and previews [news column]. *Music City News;* 1980 November; 18(5): 23.
Marty was one of the headliners for the 25th anniversary party for KSOP radio in Salt Lake City, Utah.

Robbins, Marty. Song of the patriot. *Country Song Roundup;* 1980 November; 32(256): 22.
Note: Lyrics to the song.
Recorded by Johnny Cash with Marty singing harmony.

With love. *Country Music People;* 1980 November; 11(11): 40–41.
Album review.

[Television show announcement]. *El Paso Times;* 1980 December 26.
The Sun Bowl football game is to be telecast by CBS; Marty will participate in the half-time show.

Ligon, Betty. Here he is on a hill overlooking El Paso. *El Paso Herald Post;* 1980 December 27.
Article covers press conference at the El Paso Airport, the gift of a

replica of a plaque that was hung in the El Paso Airport in his honor, Marty receiving a pair of Tony Lama boots, and his participation today in the Sun Bowl (he'll narrate the half-time show). The plaque has his picture on it and reads, "El Paso, Texas honors Marty Robbins, entertainer, entrepreneur, great guy. As the man who most singularly made El Paso famous throughout the world. Thank you Marty, we love you. All the citizens of El Paso. December 26, 1980."

Booth, Jim; Albrecht, Jim. Marty Robbins; angry patriot. *Country Style;* 1980 December: 19–20.
Note: Illus.
Interview, mostly about politics, his feelings toward the CMA, changing moral standards, the direction he sees America taking, and the reasons he wrote "Song of the Patriot."

[Advertisement]. *Music City News;* 1980 December; 18(6): 13.
Full-page ad from Marty thanking fans for their support. Photo of Marty at podium with an award.

Marty Robbins; super legend. *National Entertainment News;* 1980 December: 11.
Note: Illus.
General review of all facets of Marty's career.

Hill, Carole. Robbins meets "girl of his song." *The Evansville Sunday Courier and Press* (IN); 1981 January 4. Note: Illus.
The article is about Marty meeting a four-year-old girl named Carmen Falina, named after two of Marty's songs by her parents (both long-time Marty Robbins fans). Included, a large photo of Marty and the girl. The meeting followed the first of three shows Marty performed at Evansville on New Year's Eve.

O'Donnell, Red. Robbins suffers mild heart attack. *Nashville Banner;* 1981 January 7 (Wednesday).
Note: Illus.
Marty was admitted to the hospital Monday (January 5th).

Hill, Laura Eipper. Marty Robbins in high spirits despite heart attack. *The Tennessean;* 1981 January 8 (Thursday): 31.
Note: Illus.
Marty was admitted to St. Thomas Hospital Monday (January 5th) after complaining of chest pains. On Monday, Marty was in his office, felt chest pains, and went to his doctor, Bill Ewers. The doctor ran a

cardiogram, which indicated Marty had suffered a mild heart attack. The doctor sent him to the hospital and they are conducting further tests. They don't yet know the extent of the damage. Robbins is reported to be in good spirits. His most recent appearances were three shows in Evansville, Indiana on New Year's eve. He will cancel the rest of his shows for January but expects to resume work in February.

Country singer stricken; he put El Paso on the map. *El Paso Herald-Post;* 1981 January 8.
Note: Illus.
Marty's daughter, Janet Robinson, was the spokesperson and said her father was in intensive care in the hospital but not in any real pain. The hospital said he was in serious but stable condition and is undergoing tests. The article recaps Marty's link to the city and the times he has visited the city.

Singer has heart attack. *The El Paso Times;* 1981 January 8.
Note: Illus. Marty's daughter, Janet Robinson, was the spokesperson for the family.

Robbins won't have surgery. *El Paso Herald-Post;* 1981 January 9.
Marty's condition was changed from "serious" to "fair" and it was determined that he won't have to have surgery.

Marty Robbins feeling better. *Santa Rosa Press* [CA] 1981 January 14.
Note: Illus.
Marty may be able to go home by the end of the week.

[Photograph]. *Nashville Banner;* 1981 January 17.
The caption under the photo reads "A Robbins' Return." It's a photo of Marty leaving the hospital to go home after a ten-day stay. It notes that he says he will rest for two months before resuming his career.

[Photograph]. *Nashville Banner;* 1981 January 21.
A photo of Bobby Sykes and Jim Anderson carrying a giant get-well card sent to Marty by El Paso fans. The "card" was seven feet long and weighed 100 pounds, according to Sykes.

Giant card wishes Robbins a speedy recovery. *El Paso Times;* 1981 January 23.
A giant 4 × 8 foot get-well card that was signed by thousands of citizens of El Paso was sent to Marty by radio station KHEY and was received at Marty's office in Nashville Wednesday.

Completely out of love. *Billboard;* 1981 January 24: 107.
Single review.

[Photograph]. *The Tennessean;* 1981 January 24.
A photo of Bobby Sykes with a 100-pound get-well card sent to Marty
from his fans in El Paso. Marty had a heart attack earlier in the month
and is still recovering.

Cash, Wynette, Robbins, Spears—all set for Wembley festival. *Country Music People;* 1981 January; 12(1): 4.

With love. *Country Song Roundup;* 1981 January; 33(258): 34–35.
Album review.

[Advertisement]. *Music City News;* 1981 February; 18(8): 21.
Ad for his new album, "Everything I've Always Wanted."

[Performance review]. *Country Gazette;* 1981 February; (86): 14.
Note: Illus.
Performance review in Europe includes photo.

Opry's Marty Robbins the Renaissance Man of country music? *The Tennessean;* 1981 February 6.
Note: Illus.
Detailed review of Marty's career and accomplishments.

Minsky, Betty Jane. Robbins set for comeback. *Lansing State Journal* (MI); 1981 February 14.
Marty's first concert since his heart attack is scheduled March 6th in
Saginaw, Michigan.

Oakey, Bill. Marty Robbins; the dreamer. *Country Song Roundup;* 1981 February; 33(259): 17,26–27,39.
Note: Illus.
A long review of Marty's career, including an interview and stanzas
from several of the songs he's written. Most of the interview covers
western history and music. Good photos, including one of Marty with
Ralph Emery.

Robbins rests, Tubb hits road after brief hospital stays. *Music City News;* 1981 February; 18(8): 4.
Marty had a minor heart attack New Year's day and will rest for two
months.

Tatum, Patricia. EP ballad lures English policewoman. *El Paso Times;* 1981 February 22.
Note: Illus.
This is the story of a woman who was so influenced by the song "El Paso" that she decided to visit the United States.

Weiss, Steve. Balladeers have similar styles. *Beaver County Times* [PA]; 1981 March 1; (Sunday).
A record review column reviews "Everything I've Always Wanted."

[Photograph]. *The Canton Repository* [OH]; 1981 March 5.
Photo with caption about an upcoming concert date in Warren, Ohio.

Everything I've always wanted. *Music City News;* 1981 March; 18(9): 48.
Album review.

Garbutt, Bob. Marty Robbins; twentieth century drifter. *Goldmine;* 1981 March; (58): 197–199.
Note: Illus.
Detailed review and analysis of early recordings. Discography on pp. 198–199.

News, views, and previews [monthly column]. *Music City News;* 1981 March; 18(9): 52.
Marty is listed to be one of the guests on Charlie Chase's new WSM radio show, "On Stage."

Sharpe, Jerry. These albums smooth country [album review column]. *Pittsburgh Press;* 1981 March 1.
Album reviews compare Marty's and Eddy Arnold's styles. Reviews Marty's "Everything I've Always Wanted."

[Photograph]. *Music City News;* 1981 March; 18(9): [56]Back cover.
Full-page color photo of Marty holding an award. [Same photo as the cover photo on the July, 1980 issue.] Text at the heading of the photo thanks everyone for their concern during his recent hospital stay. Text at the bottom of the photo also thanks his fans for his nine nominations to the MCN awards.

[Photograph]. *The Tennessean;* 1981 March 8; (Sunday): Showcase.
Note: Photo of Marty as one of the Opry stars to appear on the PBS Special "Live from the Grand Ole Opry," to be broadcast Saturday, March 14, 1981.

[Cover Photograph of Marty]. *The Corpus Christi Caller-Times* [TX], TV Weekly Log Section, 1981 March 8: 1.
The TV section of the paper spotlights the PBS special broadcast of "Live from The Grand Ole Opry" on Saturday, March 14th.

Marty put his heart into it. *The Saginaw News.* 1981 March 8 (Sunday).
A review of Marty's first performance after his heart attack.

Heart attack fails to stop me. *The Times-Reporter* [Dover-New Philadelphia, Ohio]; 1981 March 13.
Interview with Marty following his second performance upon returning to his tour schedule.

Star gazing [news column]. *Music City News;* 1981 March; 15(9): 6.
Note: Illus.
Marty is home resting after a heart attack. Among his get-well cards is a 4 × 8 foot card from fans and a radio station in El Paso.

Black, Bill. Marty Robbins: always keeping the crowds happy. *Country Music People;* 1981 April; 12(4): 20–21.
Note: Illus. Color cover photo; good pictures accompany article of Marty in England and with Dolly Parton.
An interview with Marty covers a lot about his early life and the poverty his family faced. Marty also talked his performing style, his religious beliefs, his drinking problems when he was younger, his son Ronnie, and Gene Autry.

Marty Robbins. *Country Music Round-up* [England]; 1981 April.
Biography and photo.

Letters [to the editor]. *Music City News;* 1981 April; 18(10): 3.
Letter from one of the fans who attended his first concert after his heart attack in 1981.

[Information about tour]. *Pen Friends;* 1981 April.
Marty will perform at the Wembley festival and tour England April 17–20.

Pickers [monthly feature]. *Country Music;* 1981 April; 9(8): 60–61.
The article is about Buddy Harman, who recorded and played some with Marty. He played on the recordings of "Singing the blues" and "A white sport coat."

Everything I've always wanted. *Country Music People;* 1981 April; 12(4): 49.
Album review.

Robbins recovering from heart attack. *Country Hotline News,* 1981 April; 12(2): 2.
Note: Illus.
Article about his heart attack in January.

'81 Music City News Awards set June 8. *Billboard;* 1981 May 16: 72.
Marty and Barbara Mandrell received the most nominations.

Allen, Bob. Robbins has heart attack, bounces back. *Music City News;* 1981 May; 18(11): 14.
Note: Illus.
Article covers Marty's return to performing after his January heart attack.

Hill, Laura Eipper. Opry's Marty Robbins to open souvenir shop. *The Tennessean;* 1981 May 8: 44.
Note: Illus.
The shop is scheduled to open next month on Division Street.

What's up in Reno: Marty Robbins opens Thursday at Nugget. *Los Angeles Times;* 1981 May 10.
Marty will appear, starting Thursday, through May 27.

Powers, Bob. Robbins pleases a packed palace. *Columbus Dispatch* [OH]; 1981 May 11.
Favorable concert review. Marty's show lasted two hours and fifteen minutes.

Byworth, Tony. Festival pulls in 33,000. *Billboard;* 1981 May 16: 72, 90.
Coverage of the Wembley festival notes that Marty and Bill Anderson were crowd favorites and received standing ovations.

Everything I've always wanted. *Country Hotline News;* 1981 May; 12(2): 19.
Album review.

Everything I've always wanted. *Country Style;* 1981 May; (66): 45.
Album review.

[News note]. *Country Music Roundup* [England]; 1981 May.
The news item says that the society formed to get Marty to change his act is now disbanded.

People [monthly column]. *Country Music;* 1981 May; 9(9): 11–12.
Marty is recovering from a recent heart attack and received a giant get-well card from El Paso.

Provizer, Norman. Marty Robbins rides again to Celebrity Theatre Cantina. *Shreveport Journal* (LA); 1981 May 30.
Concert review.

[Advertisement]. *Music City News;* 1981 June; 18(12): 19.
Full-page ad, with photo, for Marty Robbins Enterprises. He thanks his fans for voting him seven nominations for the MCN awards.

Everything I've always wanted. *Country Music;* 1981 June; 9(10): 67.
Album review.

Fan Fair: 10 years old and always enjoyable. *Billboard;* 1981 June 27: 56.
Note: Illus.
Page of photos of Fan Fair activities includes one of Marty signing autographs.

[List of MCN Awards nominees]. *Music City News;* 1981 June; 18(12): 10–11. Note: Illus.
List of MCN Awards nominees, with photos, by category. Marty has seven nominations.

Mandrells dominate Music City honors. *Billboard;* 1981 June 20: 50.
The MCN Awards; Marty performed on the show and his band was named the Band of the Year.

Robbins to perform for Reagan staff. *The Tennessean;* 1981 June 27.
Marty will perform at the White House on the 4th of July.

Schofield, Erma. Marty Robbins . . . an entertainer for all ages. *Country Connection;* 1981 June: 5, 6.
Note: Cover photo., illus.

Schofield, Erma. Movin' up, Ronny Robbins. *Country Connection;* 1981 June: 14.
Note: Illus.
Interview and history.

Marty performing at the White House, July 4, 1981. (Photo by White House/Mary Anne Fackelman)

Wembley: varied, but not always artistically successful. *Country Music People;* 1981 June; 12(6): 45+.
Note: Illus.
Marty included in review.

Mandrells sweep MCN Cover Awards. *Music City News;* 1981 July; 19(1): 15–18.
Note: Illus.
Article about the MCN Awards show.

Hill, Laura. Marty Robbins gives "command performance." *The Tennessean;* 1981 July 11; (Saturday): 27.
Note: Illus.
Marty performed at the White House for President Reagan on the 4th of July. Marty said the President especially asked to hear "A white sport coat" during his 25-minute show.

[Photograph]. *Music City News;* 1981 July; 19(1): 16.
Photo of Marty and his band receiving the Band of the Year Award at the MCN Awards show.

Robbins opens gift shop. *Country Hotline News;* 1981 July; 12(5): 30.
Marty opened a gift shop at the Marty Robbins Recording Studio on
Division street.

Oppel, Pete. Keep going Marty, they love you! *Dallas Morning News;*
1981 July 19.
Performance review at Granny's Dinner Theater.

Sondergard, Mary. Packed grandstand cheers man in the "white sport
coat." *Janesville Gazette* (WI); 1981 July 29.
Note: Illus.
Favorable performance review and interview; good concert photo.

Price, Mary Sue. Singer Robbins spins tales with country songs. *The
News-Leader* [Springfield, MO]; 1981 August 7.
Performance review and interview. Marty talks about his grandfather's
influence on his life.

Jumper cable man. *Billboard;* 1981 August 8: 67.
Single review.

Millburg, Steve. Robbins delivers what crowd wants. *Omaha World-
Herald News;* 1981 August 15.
Performance review.

[Photograph]. *Country Music People;* 1981 August; 12(8): 47.
Photo of Marty with fans at Fan Fair '81.

Star gazing [news column]. *Music City News;* 1981 August; 19(2): 6.
Notes Marty's White House performance of July 4, 1981 for President
Reagan. Although Marty had campaigned for him, he never met him
until his White House show.

[Information notes]. *Pen Friends;* 1981 September (no. 60).
The newsletter notes that Marty was at a press conference for Sugar Ray
Leonard in Nashville recently.

Morris, Edward. Country concert trail rocky. *Billboard;* 1981 September 12; 93(36): 1, 31, 43.
Marty mentioned in article as one of those successful the past summer,
during a time when the concert circuit was difficult.

The legend. *Billboard;* 1981 September 19: 77.
Album review.

Golden collection. *Country Gazette;* 1981 September; (92): 40.
Album review. K-Tel TN 1601.

Woosnam, Jeff. Audiences keep Marty performing. *Ashland Times-Gazette* (Ashland, OH); 1981 September 25: 9.
Note: Illus.
Long performance review and interview.

Dyson, Ray. Chilly fair goers respond warmly to Marty Robbins. *Mansfield News Journal* (OH); 1981 September 25.
Note: Illus.
Performance review covers Marty's rapport with his audience, his jokes, and his warm reception. Good concert photo. The review says in part: "Robbins was almost constantly talking and mugging even while singing. He is expert at playing with his audience, and the packed house responded warmly as Robbins cracked jokes, ad-libbed asides with individual fans, and swept through an 18-song, 70-minute set with the aplomb of the old pro he is." It goes on to note that one song, "Streets of Laredo," was begun but ended after only about eight bars. "I didn't get enough applause on that one," Marty kidded. "I don't want to bore you with songs you don't care about." Immediately afterwards, he launched into "Don't worry" and smiled appreciatively at the thundering applause the song elicited. Near the end of the concert, the review quotes Marty: "I enjoy life. I enjoy being on stage and I enjoy a nice audience," Robbins said before bidding farewell. "But I didn't pay to get in, and that's what I like most."

[Advertisement]. *Music City News;* 1981 October; 19(4): [56]Back cover.
Note: Illus.
Full-page ad from Marty with wishes for a happy 56th anniversary to the Grand Ole Opry.

Allen, Bob. Marty Robbins doesn't sweat the small stuff. *Country Music;* 1981 October; 2(10th Anniversary Issue): 35–42, 56.
Note: Illus.
Long interview about Marty's faith, heart attacks, and love of life. Detailed recounting of Marty's first performance after his January heart attack.

Border Town Affair. *Country Gazette;* 1981 October; (93): 39.
Album review.

Exotic autos on album jackets. *Billboard;* 1981 October 3: 43.
Marty and his Panther DeVille included in the article.

Legendary Marty. *Lansing State Journal* [MI]; 1981 October 3.
Album review of "The Legend."

Eggler, Bruce. Marty Robbins: no clocks and no ties. *Times-Picayune States-item* (New Orleans, LA); 1981 October 16.
Note: Illus.
Performance review and interview. Marty talks about his first time back on the Opry stage since his heart attack (during the PBS special broadcast). The article makes a special point of acknowledging that Marty ignores the time clock at the Opry.

Country TV special slated. *Country Hotline News;* 1981 October; 12(8): 24.
"A country galaxy of stars" (best of the MCN Awards programs) to be syndicated and shown in September. Marty is one of the stars on the program.

Harris, Stacy. Marty Robbins; the gunfighter shoots straight. *Country Song Roundup;* 1981 October; 33(267): 8–11.
Note: Illus.
Long interview covers Marty's feelings about the "Urban Cowboy" craze, other men's dress styles of other years (the zoot suit, the continental suit, and his stage clothes made by Nudie and Anthony Gasbari). He talks about designing his own stage suits and what goes into the making of them. He also discusses his Columbia recording contract and what he feels the label should be doing to promote his records more vigorously. Photo of Marty in his Nashville office.

Breckenridge, D. P. The Legend. *Kansas City Star* (MO); 1981 October 20.
Note: Illus.
Album review.

It's been a good year for country music. *Country Hotline News;* 1981 October; 12(8): 16–17,25.
Note: Illus.
Marty included in article; photo on p. 17.

The legend. *Music City News;* 1981 October; 19(4): 46.
Album review.

Robbins needs a song tailor. *Milwaukee Sentinel;* 1981 October 10.
Note: Illus.
Album review for "The Legend."

Versatile Marty Robbins plays Sunday at the Palace. *Beaumont Enterprise* [Texas]; 1981 October 15.

Spires, Shari. Fans and Marty Robbins share a special rapport. *Palm Beach Post* (FL); 1981 October 23.
Note: Illus.
Detailed performance review and interviews about Marty. The review admits that "his long-term audience appeal is perplexing to many in the business side of the music industry, since few balladeers and basically western singers like Robbins survived the '60s." Even his record company is quoted as being puzzled by his persisting popularity. A CBS publicist says of Marty's awards at this year's Music City News Awards, "I don't really understand it, especially in an artist who hasn't had a whole lot of chart action in recent years. But Marty just continues right up there with the fans. They love him." The article also says that Marty is one of the few entertainers who is cited as generous and encouraging to new talent. It says that a few years ago he maintained a house next to his office that was jokingly referred to as Robbins Ramada or Robbins Roost. Songwriters or musicians could get something to eat or a place to stay there. About autograph signing, Bobby Sykes says: "He is most definitely an autograph signer. I've seen him stand in one place for more than two hours signing autographs and talking to the fans. In fact, one of the few times you'll see him get mad is if some security guard or policeman tries to cut off the line. He believes an entertainer owes that to the fans." [Editorial comment: the show was never telecast on cable, as the article indicates it would be. However, film from most of the concert was released as two separate videos in 1987: 1) ". . . His Legacy" and 2) "For Fans Only."]

Freeders, Rosie. Marty Robbins appears at ease with place among men, music. *Dayton Daily News;* 1981 November 3.
Album review of "The Legend."

Sharpe, Jerry. Just like "legend," Robbins recovers. *Pittsburgh Press;* 1981 November 8.
Note: Illus.
Album review of "The legend."

Farrell, Christopher. Robbins fan creates quilt of love. *Tallahassee Democrat* (FL); 1981 November 12: 1C, 2C.
Note: Illus.
Article about Judy Burns and a quilt she made for Marty illustrating his career. Photo of the quilt included.

Shefchik, Rick. Robbins broadens "cowboy" image. *St. Paul Dispatch;* 1981 November 12.
Article about Marty and his upcoming performance.

Bream, Jon. Robbins keeps "western" flavor in his old-style country music. *Minneapolis Star;* 1981 November 13.
Note: Illus.
Performance review at the Carlton Theater and long interview; concert photo.

Fan time [news column]. *Country Song Roundup;* 1981 November; 33(268): 42.
Note: Illus.
The column notes that Marty has opened a gift shop on Division Street. Publicity photo of Marty in a business suit and hat included.

The legend. *Country Music People;* 1981 November; 12(11): 46.
Album review.

Letters [to the editor]; Robbins gives entertaining show. *Music City News;* 1981 December; 19(6): 3.

The tune's title tells the story. *Billboard;* 1981 December 26: 49.
A humorous article about country music songs includes mention of "Jumper cable man."

[Advertisement]. *Music City News;* 1982 January; 19(7): 22.
One-half-page ad thanking fans for their support and giving the address of his gift shop; photo of Marty included.

Allen, Bob. Marty Robbins, a country singer's battle to survive. *Hustler;* 1982 January; 8(7): 50–52, +.
Note: Illus.
Alternate title: "Marty Robbins: Country music's crown prince." In-depth personal interview covers Marty's description of his 1969 heart attack, his recording career, and his love of racing.

Edwards, Joe. Country-western music pioneer says "urban cowboy" craze firing blanks. *The Denver Post;* 1982 January 3; (Sunday): 14 R.
Note: Illus.
Interview with Marty includes comments about his opinions on the current trend in country music.

"Urban cowboy" craze branded fake. *The Daily Oklahoman;* 1982 January 8 (Friday).
Note: Illus.
Interview.

Marty Robbins av Rolf Nilse'n. *Kountry Korral;* 1982; 15(1): 17.
Note: Illus.
Short article and photo.

Edwards, Joe. Robbins not impressed by urban cowboy craze. *The Columbus Dispatch* [OH]; 1982 January 10; (Sunday): D 4.
Note: Illus.
The story is the same as the Edwards story listed above.

PCB's favorite; Marty is returning. . . *Beach News and Bay News* [Panama City, FL]; 1982 January 28–February 3; 4(52): 1,3.
Note: Illus.
Marty to perform February 6 at the Ocean Opry.

[Photograph]. *Music City News;* 1982 January; 19(7): 2.
A page of photos from the June, 1981, MCN Awards; Marty included.

Portrait: Marty Robbins. *Country Music Club of Switzerland, Newsletter;* 1982 January; (21): 4+.
Note: Illus.

[Advertisement]. *Music City News;* 1982 February; 19(8): 9.
Full-page ad for the Silk Cut Festival. Marty one of the headliners.

The legend. *Country Gazette;* 1982 February; (97): 38.
Album review.

Kaye. Roger. Marty Robbins still sings and clowns. *Star-Telegram* [TX]; 1982 February 12.
Review of concert at Billy Bob's in Texas.

Claypool, Bob. Music: Marty Robbins. *The Houston Post;* 1982 February 14; (Sunday): 16 D.
Concert review centers on Marty's rapport with the audience and his ability to put them at ease, his showmanship and personality.

McRhaney, Elizabeth. Don't call me country, says Marty Robbins. *San Antonio Light;* 1982 February 15.
Note: Illus.
In an interview between shows, Marty talks about the difference between cowboy and country music, where he thinks the music is going today, and how he got started in the business. Good photo.

Sanderson, Jane. Marty Robbins comes on first at concert tonight. *Memphis Press Scimitar;* 1982 February 26.
Note: Illus.
Interview before a show with Jerry Lee Lewis. Lewis had insisted that he be the last performer on the show and Marty was accommodating, saying that it didn't matter.

[Advertisement]. *Music City News;* 1982 March; 19(9): 16.
One-half-page ad for Marty Robbins Enterprises.

Tubb show set for taping. *Billboard;* 1982 March 13: 56.
Marty is one of the hosts of the television special honoring Ernest Tubb.

Axelsson, Hans och Ingegard. Ronny Robbins. *Kountry Korral;* 1982 March; 15(3): 48–50.
Note: Illus.
Article about Ronny Robbins. Good photos.

Robbins takes shot at urban cowboys. *Aurora Beacon News* (IL); 1982 March 19.
Interview includes comments on his opinions about the "urban cowboy" craze.

Harris, Pat. Marty Robbins: the maverick of music row. *Chicago Sun Times;* 1982 March 21.
Note: Illus.
Interview covers Marty's management of his own career, his business activities, and his future interests. Except for the first three years, Marty has managed his own career. He admits, however, that he would be bigger than he is if he had had a manager all the way. He plans to get in some racing this year and would like to make a western movie. In

explaining that it's the road shows he does that really turn him on, he says, "I come alive on stage. I really love it. Once I get started, I hate to stop. If you like the business, that's the way it is. But you can't fake it like some performers do. I'll tell you, it takes another performer to see through that." And in talking about his life today and his belief in God, he says, "It's like this: Everybody has to believe in something. I believe in God. If I'm right, fine. If I'm not, I haven't lost anything. But I don't go around trying to tell other people what to believe or how to behave. I've got my own ground rules, for me only." He ends by saying, "But I'm really enjoying life these days. I don't even mind winter any more. Each day is just one day closer to spring. And I find time for things I really like."

Harvey, Hank. Country singer Robbins to perform in Toledo. *Toledo Blade* (OH); 1982 March 21.
Note: Illus.
Interview. Marty says he wrote "El Paso" in 1956 but couldn't get his recording company interested in releasing it. He finally got it on an album and it proved so popular that he was finally able to get it released as a single.

Hayman, Edward. No flab, just straight crooning. *The Detroit* News; 1982 March 22: B1,2.
Note: Illus.
Long concert review of Marty's show; Ricky Skaggs was the opening act.

Lane, Marilyn. Robbins brings them to their feet. *Quad-City Times* [Iowa]; 1982 March 30; (Tuesday): 12.
Performance review from a Davenport, Iowa concert. Mel McDaniel opened the show. The reviewer notes that Marty gave his audience a "dynamite" show that went a good half-hour longer than scheduled. Marty was in top form "as he posed and pranced for the gang of photographers who were ever present at the edge of the stage." The reviewer said that "he's a showman, a tease, and he found a very receptive audience, so he played it his way." He's called a funny story-teller with a good comedic touch. Marty told his audience, "I hope you'll forgive me for being foolish on stage. I enjoy it. The reason I enjoy my shows is that I don't have to pay to get in. I can't be foolish like this during the day or people would stare. But when I'm foolish on stage, they just say oh, he's crazy." At one point, Marty asked his audience, "Anything going on in Davenport tonight that you have to get to?" When the audience yelled "No," he said, "We'll go ahead and sing a couple we hadn't planned on."

Oermann, Robert K. Country conquers the tube. *Country Rhythms;*
1982 March; 4: 22–25.
Article about television series and specials mentions "Marty Robbins'
Spotlight."

[Advertisement]. *Country Music People;* 1982 April; 13(4): [56, back
cover].
Ad for Wembley Festival includes photo of Marty.

[Advertisement]. *Music City News;* 1982 April; 19(10): 23.
Note: Illus.
Quarter-page ad for the "Marty Party" to be held during Fan Fair in
June.

Club parties to highlight Fan Fair. *Music City News;* 1982 April; 19(10):
20.
Note: Illus.
Article includes photo of Marty and details of "Marty Party."

Oermann, Robert K.; Lomax III, John. The heavy 100 of country music. *Esquire;* 1982 April: 65–70.
Note: Illus.
A long article about the most important people in the country music
industry. The entry on Marty says, "Perhaps the greatest showman in
country music. Opera-star temperament and refusal to play Nashville
politics have prevented recognition he deserves. Worshipped by fans.
Should be declared a national treasure for his massive repertoire of
songs from all styles and periods of country music."

[Photograph]. *Country Gazette;* 1982 April; (99): Cover.
Cover photo.

Star gazing [news column]. *Music City News;* 1982 April; 19(10): 6.
Notes that Marty still loves racing and plans to race at Daytona July 4th.
Also notes that he likes to listen to Luciano Pavarotti.

Wembley sets artists and events. *Country Music People;* 1982 April;
13(4): 4.
List of artists for coming event includes Marty.

Woodbury, Nola L. Loyal Marty Robbins fans pack Paramount. *Aurora
Beacon News* [IL]; 1982 April 2.
Note: Illus.
Concert review.

[Advertisement]. *Music City News;* 1982 May; 19(11): 25.
Quarter-page ad for the "Marty Party." [Editorial note: This was a party
Marty held (June 10th) for his fans during the June Fan Fair in
Nashville.]

Changes and exchanges [news column]. *Music City News;* 1982 May;
19(11): 7.
The Fireside Recording Studio has been sold. Marty one of the many
artists listed as having recorded there.

International Country Music Festival VII, 1982. *Kountry Korral;* 1982;
15(2): 28–31.
Note: Illus.
Coverage of the April Wembley festival includes Marty. Photo on p. 31.

Kienzle, Rich. The great guitar players of Nashville. *Country Rhythms;*
1982 May; (6): 28–31.
Note: Illus.
The article includes sections on Grady Martin and Ray Edenton, who
played on some of Marty's recordings. Grady ("Don't worry," "El
Paso"); Ray ("Singing the blues").

The legend. *Kountry Korral;* 1982; 15(2): 54.
Album review.

McMillan, Greg. Music and humor notes in Marty Robbins' hit. *The
Spectator* (Hamilton, OH); 1982 May 7.
Note: Illus.
Concert review highlights Marty's successful mix of humor and music;
concert photo included. The review says of Marty, "In his own manner,
he managed to break up his songs with elongated rap sessions that
'broke up' the people sitting in the seats in front of him. And it was his
willingness to kid around with his fans that made his concert something
out of the ordinary. . . . He was never aloof or condescending, rather he
seemed to almost welcome responses from the audience, something
most performers always shy away from."

Some memories just won't die. *Billboard;* 1982 May 8.
Single review. The recording was released April 15th.

Music City News nominees set; Robbins, Mandrell, Statler Bros. lead
list of bidders. *Billboard;* 1982 May 15: 54.

News, views, and previews [news column]. *Music City News;* 1982 May; 19(11): 24.
Marty was one of the performers and hosts for a national radio benefit for the National Kidney Foundation broadcast from the Opryland Hotel.

Stern, Susan. Robbins a man of many styles and songs. *Columbus Dispatch* (OH); 1982 May 20; (Thursday): 3.
Note: Cover photo.
Interview in advance of a show covers his humor, early recordings, opinion on award shows, his band, and the nickname "Mr. Teardrop," which Marty says he never liked.

Stern, Susan. Robbins' tunes, talk delight fans. *The Columbus Dispatch* [OH]; 1982 May 24; (Monday): C 7.
Note: Illus.
Concert review. Good analysis and quotes. The reviewer says of Marty's entrance, "Like the much-awaited hero of a melodrama, Robbins strode out in his white, brightly embroidered get-up with the assuredness of a swaggering sheriff but all the friendliness of a close relative. Even without the comfort of recent radio hits, this man WAS family to his fans. They knew he'd pose comically for pictures and converse with them in calm country talk that would hit home. Yet he kept a warm upper hand as fans noisily hurled requests, and he punctuated the upbeat tunes with a hearty 'hey,' to which the crowd eagerly responded, along with giving him yellow roses and gifts."

Carter, Walter. Mandrell & sisters win most fan-voted awards. *The Tennessean;* 1982 June 8: 31.
The article includes a photo of Marty and notes that he had the most nominations and won the Male Vocalist of the Year Award.

Erickson, Michael. Cars of the stars. *Nashville Banner;* 1982 June 8; (Tuesday): B 8.
Note: Illus.
The article includes a photo of Marty and his racing stock car no.42. It also mentions his 1979 black Cadillac and his 1981 red Corvette.

[Photograph]. *The Tennessean;* 1982 June 9: Front page of Living Section.
A photo of Marty signing autographs at the CBS booth during Fan Fair.

[Program booklet of The All American Country Games]; 1982 June 12.
Marty participated in the "games" held at the Vanderbilt Stadium the morning of the last day of Fan Fair, 1982.

Marty and Barbara Mandrell at the Music City News Awards, June, 1982. (Photo by Don VanPutte)

Marty preparing to sign autographs for several hundred people after the "Marty Party." (Photo by Barbara Pruett)

[Program booklet of the Grand Old Opry]; 1982 June 12 (Saturday). Marty closed the Saturday night show of the Opry, performing in his 11:30 pm slot.

Leach, Hugh. Robbins a hit with small fry. *Lansing State Journal* (MI); 1982 June 12.
Note: Illus.
Concert review and interview covers Marty's relationship with fans before concert, his image onstage versus offstage, and his warm reception of the children in the audience during the show. The reviewer pointed out that Marty offstage wasn't quite the same as he was onstage. Offstage he seemed a bright, but humble man. Onstage he played the clown with the big ego. In talking about his heart problem, Marty said, "I don't worry about it. I'm goin' to be here for so long on this earth and then there's a better world after that when I leave here. I'm goin' to enjoy this one, but I'm goin' to enjoy the next one better."

[Advertisement]. *The Tennessean;* 1982 June 17: 29.
One-half-page ad featuring Marty for Elm Hill foods and Hermitage Landing. Same ad appears in the paper for June 16, 1982 (p. B25).

[Advertisement]. *Southern RV;* 1982 June: 81.
Full-page ad, featuring Marty, for Hermitage Landing lake and camping facilities.

Nixon, Bruce. Marty Robbins races into town for 8-night stand. *Dallas Times Herald;* 1982 June 18: 1F, 4F.
Note: Illus.
Long concert preview and interview. Shows to be at Granny's Dinner Theater.

Kirby, Kip. Mandrell tops Music City fete. *Billboard;* 1982 June 19: 41.
Marty, nominated for seven awards, won "Male Vocalist of the Year" award.

Saxton, Ernie. Auto racing notes [news column]. *Area Auto Racing News;* 1982 June 23.
The column notes that Marty will race at Daytona in the Firecracker 400 on the 4th of July.

Bishop, Nancy. Marty Robbins offers stunning performance. *The Dallas Morning News;* 1982 June 25; (Friday).
Note: Illus.

Above: Marty with son Ronny during Fan Fair 1982. Below: Marty with daughter Janet during the All-American Games, Fan Fair 1982. (Photos by Don VanPutte)

Concert review at Granny's Theater in Dallas. The review begins, "It's easy to be impressed with Marty Robbins, the singer. But you'll be truly awed by watching Marty Robbins, the performer." It points out that while some of his numbers were uninspired, it didn't matter because he had already convinced the audience that his purpose in life was to entertain rather than monotonously sing his hits. Just because he was up on stage in some flashy, expensive outfit, which he designed, didn't mean that people couldn't talk back to him and treat him like one of their friends."

Ask Showcase [question and answer column]. *The Tennessean;* 1982 June 27; (Sunday): p.62, Showcase section.
Note: Illus.
The column provides information about Marty's film, "Hell on Wheels." Photo of Marty from the film.

Country goes international at Silk Cut Festival. *Music City News;* 1982 June; 19(12): 22.
Note: Illus.
Marty noted as a major performer at the festival; photo included.

1982 Country music festival. *Country Gazette;* 1982 June; (101): 22–25.
Note: Illus.
Marty's performance reviewed on pp. 22–23; photos included.

Faces [news column]. *Music City News;* 1982 June; 19(12): 38.
Notes that Joe Babcock used to work with the Glaser Brothers and has been a member of Marty's band. Also notes that Marty has recorded some of his songs.

Hackett, Vernell. Marty Robbins—"people and I get along well." *Country Hotline News;* 1982 June; 13(4): 14–15.
Note: Cover photo., illus.
Interview covering his relationship with his fans, his feelings toward the recording industry, performing in England, and his personal faith.

[Letters to the editor]. *Country Gazette;* 1982 June; (101): 35.
Letters about Marty's performance at the festival. Photo included.

Wembley days were back again. *Country Music People;* 1982 June; 13(6): 24–25, 28, 42.
Note: Illus.
Festival review. Marty reviewed on p. 28.

[Advertisement]. *Music City News;* 1982 July; 20(1): 30.
Full-page ad thanking the fans for his MCN Awards.

Edwards, Joe. Finalists selected for "Hall." *The Tennessean;* 1982 July
3: 29.
Note: Illus.
Good recent photo of Marty and article announcing the nominations for
the Hall of Fame; Marty was one of the nominees.

Long, Gary. They're taking a NASCAR short course. *The Miami Her-
ald;* 1982 July 3; (Saturday): D1,3.
An article about the Daytona Firecracker 400 includes a section on
Marty and his racing experiences.

Smith, Terry. Robbins picks his pastime, and he prefers to be racing.
Times-Union and Journal [Jacksonville, FL]; 1982 July 4; (Sunday): D
5.
Note: Illus.
Interview and some racing history. Marty to race in the Firecracker 400.
Photo of Marty and Neil Bonnett.

Huston, Lucille. Performing: Robbins' greatest love. *The Evening Review* [East Liverpool, OH]; 1982 July 13; (Tuesday).
Note: Illus.
Interview and performance review of a concert at Ponderosa Park in
Salem, Ohio. The reviewer notes that Marty was very popular with the
audience and that many of the people stayed for the second show, which
went nearly two hours instead of the scheduled one hour. He signed
autographs for an hour between the two shows.

C-T makes Lodi woman's dream come true; she meets Marty Robbins
in person. *Madison Capital Times* (WI); 1982 July 19.
Note: Illus.
The newspaper arranged for a long-time fan to meet Marty; coverage of
the meeting included.

Trott, Walt. Tomfoolery disappoints true Robbins fans. *Madison Capital Times* (WI); 1982 July 19.
This reviewer would have liked less kidding with the audience and more
music, saying, "Fans took advantage of the artist's good nature Saturday night, causing him to slow down his show's pace, a real irritant to
those who enjoy hearing Robbins' still-strong vocals. Those lengthy
pauses between numbers, as the star indulged in a lot of silliness with

those wandering up to the stage, added up to a waste of valuable performing time."

Country music questions [news column]. *Country Music People;* 1982 July; 13(7): 48.
A correspondent asked if Marty had a "live" album. Answer: no.

Events surrounding Fan Fair week. *Music City News;* 1982 July; 20(1): 26–29. Note: Illus.
Photo of Marty at the "Marty Party" on p. 29.
[Editorial note: The "Marty Party" was held the evening of June 10th (Thursday) at the Opryland Hotel. Marty performed a two-and-a-half-hour show for his fans and then stayed around to sign autographs until around 2:00 am.]

Fans pick Mandrell and Robbins country's top 1982 vocalists. *Music City News;* 1982 July; 20(1): 10–14.
Note: Illus.
Article covers awards show; photo of Marty on p. 14.

[Photograph]. *Music City News;* 1982 July; 20(1): [40] Back cover.
Full-page color photo of Marty and Barbara Mandrell together.

Tackett, Dan. Robbins show was great attraction for fairgoers. *Lincoln Courier;* 1982 August 2.
Detailed concert review. The reviewer would have liked less talk, but admitted the crowd loved Marty's chatter. The review covers his humor and music, noting that he signed autographs for a long line of waiting fans after the show. It said, in part, "Robbins, it can be safely said, is the Mohammed Ali of the country music world. He'll handle a song in grand fashion, then be the first to applaud. He literally struts and prances on stage, and yells 'Ain't it great!' For those who haven't seen the veteran performer before, the flashy ego-trip on stage might be a turn-off. But to his many fans (and he had plenty of them here), it's all part of Robbins' dynamic personable stage presence that has helped earn him the reputation as a legend."

[Advertisement]. *Music City News;* 1982 August; 20(2): 9.
Three-quarter-page ad for the album, "Come back to me."

CMA Announces Country Music Hall of Fame finalists. *CMA Close-up;* 1982 August: 18–19.
Marty is one of the announced nominees. A brief biography is included.

Country club'n [news column]. *Music City News;* 1982 August; 20(2): 20.
The column announces that Ronny Robbins has started his own fan club under the direction of Nancy Van Putte.

Futty, John. Marty Robbins in great form. *Mansfield News Journal* (OH); 1982 August 11.
Note: Illus.
Concert review and photo. The reviewer notes, "Although the friendly conversation was welcome, the concert could have used a little less talking and a little more singing. Even those familiar with Robbins' custom of conversing with the audience must have grown weary of watching him make small talk with the endless stream of women who approached the stage to hand notes to the singer. Otherwise, it was a relaxed, satisfying concert in which the 56-year-old singer showed a large crowd why his name has become legendary in the country music field." The reviewer goes on to say, "Although he is nearly 57 and has suffered heart problems, he continues to perform with a relentless vigor and good cheer. Not only did he acknowledge every woman who brought a note or gift to the stage, he also encouraged those with cameras to come up to the stage to snap photos."

Music City News Awards. *Country Music People;* 1982 August; 13(8): 9.
Note: Illus.
Marty won Male Vocalist of the Year award. Photo of Marty with article.

Hicks, Tommy. Fans, excitement spur Robbins on. *The Advertiser-Journal* (Montgomery,AL); 1982 August 13. Note: Illus.
Interview covers MCN Awards, fans (Marty's Army), and auto racing. When asked about winning the MCN Award for Male Vocalist of the Year, Marty said it was special because it was voted by the readers of the magazine. "It's like knowing you have friends. I don't think I should have won the award this year. But I accepted it because of the fans. I didn't have a real big record this past year. So obviously the fans did it. That makes me happy."

[Photograph]. *Country Music People;* 1982 August; 13(8): 8.
Photo of Marty and others at the All American Country Games during Fan Fair, June, 1982.

Skaggs, Nelson lead CMA nominees. *The Tennessean;* 1982 August 20; (Friday): 56.
Marty included in the list as a nominee for the Hall of Fame.

Robinson, Tom. The sound of silence. *Nashville* [magazine]; 1982 August: 16,18.
Note: Illus.
The article is about the closing of the old CBS recording studio. Included is a photo of Marty and quotes from him about current economic problems of the recording industry.

Vincent, Charlie. His anthem: roar of engines provide a backup for Marty Robbins. *Detroit Free Press;* 1982 August 21; (Saturday).
Long racing article and interview from Brooklyn, Michigan, where Marty will race Sunday in the Champion Spark Plug 400 NASCAR Grand National race if he qualifies. Talking about racing, Marty says, "I don't play golf, hunt or fish. This is my rifle, golf cart and boat all in one. . . . I just do it for fun. It's like catching a fish and throwing it back in. Some people just fish for the fun of it, not for the fish." He also explains why he doesn't maintain radio contact with his pit crew: "I don't use ear plugs . . . my ears ring for three or four days, and I can't have that happening when I've got a [personal appearance] date coming up in the next couple of days. So I've got to count on pit boards instead of a radio."

[Advertisement]. *Country Rhythms;* 1982 September; (9): 23.
One-half-page ad for the album "Come back to me."

Come back to me. *Country Music People;* 1982 September; 13(9): 34.
Album review.

Country corner picks: Come back to me. *Country Music Roundup* [England]; 1982 September: 14.
Note: Illus.
Album review of "Come back to me."

Harris, Pat. Marty Robbins, candid. *Country Song Roundup;* 1982 September; 34(278): 26–27. Note: Illus.
Interview takes place in Marty's Nashville office and covers such topics as how he got into singing, his early career, his faith, his fans, and auto racing. An interesting description of his office, cluttered with western memorabilia, is included.

Oakley, Bill. Robbins, Skaggs bring fans to feet in Marshall show. *The Paducah Sun* (KY); 1982 September 3.
Note: Illus.
Concert review.

Marty at a race in Brooklyn, MI, August 1982. (Photo by Elmer Kappell)

Palmer, Barry. Country music beat [review column]. *The Union News-Leader* [Manchester, NH]; 1982 September 3; (Friday): 23.
Note: Illus.
Album review of "Come back to me."

Manley, Terry. Marty Robbins, singin' cowboy, has always been a straight shooter. *The Des Moines Register;* 1982 September 7: C1.
Note: Illus.
Performance review and interview. The reviewer says, "Marty Robbins stood on stage at the Franklin County Fair, mixing business with pleasure for the umpteenth time in his 30-year career. His familiar mischievous look surveyed the huge crowd, which included an abundance of lawmen. Obviously they were expecting some other country music entertainer, he said, acting all indignant while proceeding to make up one of his spontaneous tales about how they even brought a police dog on board his bus, 'sniffing for drugs or something.' That brought a roar from his followers. . . . Actually, the only thing he could be charged with is constantly violating the unwritten law of extracting more fun out of life than one person should be allowed." The reviewer notes, however, that his stage style sometimes raises questions: ". . . strangely, even his clowning had its repercussions when one of the sheriff's deputies wondered aloud whether the singer had been drinking before going on stage. Robbins had discussed that very irony during an interview before his performance, admitting that others have drawn the same mistaken conclusion during his happy-go-lucky career. He shrugs it off as no big deal, vowing his format will continue to be the kick-off-your-shoes approach that makes his audiences feel so at home." Marty said most people know him well enough to know he doesn't drink or do dope, that he's just having a good time.

[Performance review]. *Variety;* 1982 September 15: 78.
Favorable review of his show at the Dane County Coliseum in Madison, Wisconsin. The review notes that "Nearing 57, Robbins has been enjoying a comeback this past year, as shown by his stunning victory last month over formidables Kenny Rogers and Conway Twitty as best male singer in the annual Music City News poll, and his top 15 tune, 'Some Memories Just Won't Die'."

A pilot presides over C.A.B.'s demise. *New York Times;* 1982 September 28: 10.
This article about Civil Aeronautics Board Chairperson Dan McKinnon also covers his background in country music as a concert promoter and radio station owner; McKinnon mentions that he booked Marty and considers him to be a great entertainer.

[Advertisement]. *Music City News;* 1982 October; 20(4): 13.
Full-page ad for Marty Robbins Enterprises.

CMA announces award finalists. *Music City News;* 1982 October; 20(4): 4.
Marty nominated for the Hall of Fame Award.

Labels push "Greatest Hits" sets. *Billboard;* 1982 October 2; 94(39): 33,40.

Moody, Carter. CBS offers low-priced "Hits" tapes. *Billboard;* 1982 October 2; 94(39): 3.
Marty included on list of artists to be highlighted.

[Editorial note: Marty won the Hall of Fame award the night of October 11, 1982 during the broadcast of the Country Music Association Awards on CBS-TV.]

O'Donnell, Red. Alabama spells CMA top winners. *Nashville Banner;* 1982 October 12; (Tuesday): A1,8.
Note: Illus.
The CMA Awards, presented the night of October 11, included the presentation of the Hall of Fame Award to Marty. Large photo of Eddy Arnold presenting the award to Marty on page 8.

Oermann, Robert K.; Neese, Sandy. Alabama, Skaggs take top CMA Awards. *The Tennessean;* 1982 October 12; (Tuesday): 1,4.
Note: Illus.
Article includes Marty's Hall of Fame Award.

[Program booklet from the Grand Ole Opry]. The 57th Birthday Celebration of the Grand Ole Opry, official agenda for shows October 12–16.
Marty appeared on the special Opry show Tuesday night, October 12th. It was the day after he won the Hall of Fame award.

Billboard. The World of Country Music. Special issue of the magazine. *Billboard;* 1982 October 16: WCOM-22.
Note: Illus.
The annual special Billboard Country Awards included naming Marty for the "Artist Resurgence Award," the performer who has seen the greatest career revival during the past year.

Marty at the CMA Talent Buyers Seminar, October 10, 1982. (Photo by Barbara Pruett)

Come back to me. *Country Gazette;* 1982 October; (104): 40.
Album review.

Come back to me. *Country Rhythms;* 1982 October; (10): 18.
Album review.

Talent Buyer's Seminar acts, panelists confirmed. *CMA Close-up;* 1982 October: 10.
Marty to be on the artist's panel: "When you're hot, you're hot." The panel will represent the artists' viewpoints. To be held Sunday, October 10.

Fan Fair '82. *Country Rhythms;* 1982 October; (10): 62–66.
Note: Illus.
Pages of photos from Fan Fair; photo of Marty at the CBS Booth on p.
64.

Hayakawa, Alan. Marty Robbins a delight to his fans. *The Oregonian;*
1982 October 22; (Friday): G 11.
Concert review. The review in part says, ". . . Robbins' performance
experience of 25 years and more showed in his easy rapport with the
audience and his delight in its familiarity with his music. As singers go,
Robbins is not too bad a stand-up comic, and as singers go his humor is
cleaner than most, thank heaven. But . . . I wish he had cut the comedy
and dished out the music in his allotted hour and a half."

Music previews [news column]. *Seattle Post* (WA); 1982 October 22.
Note: Illus.
The paper notes that Marty and Eddy Raven will perform at the Seattle
Center Opera House tomorrow night.

Kirby, Kip. Alabama, Skaggs, Fricke are big winners at CMA Awards.
Billboard; 1982 October 23: 55.
Comments that Marty was a favorite at the show in winning the Hall of
Fame Award.

Kirby, Kip; Moody, Carter. Attendance holds steady for country music
week. *Billboard;* 1982 October 23: 3, 84.
The article notes that one of the highlights of the week was Marty
winning the Hall of Fame Award.

Morris, Edward; Moody, Carter. Talent Buyers Seminar tackles hard
times. *Billboard;* 1982 October 23: 59–60.
Note: Illus.
Marty was one of the members of the Artists Panel; panel photo
included.

[Photograph]. *Billboard;* 1982 October 23: 58.
Photo of Eddy Arnold presenting the Hall of Fame Award to Marty at
the CMA Awards Show.

[Photograph]. *Country Rhythms;* 1982 October; (10): 64.
Photo of Marty at the CBS booth during Fan Fair, June, 1982.

Marty Robbins. *Inside Country Music;* 1982 October: 58–60.
Note: Illus. Photos by John Carnes.

The interview covers in depth his plans to make and market his own records, his views on the recording industry, and the problems involved. Marty talks fondly about performing on the Grand Ole Opry and recalls that it was in 1968 that he started staying longer on stage than he was allowed. It happened because he cut short a race at the Nashville speedway to make his Opry show, only to find out that the Opry show was running late. He decided to take all of the time he wanted on stage and a new tradition was started. He also talks about the night he started cheering himself on stage (to the delight of the audience) and the reaction of the radio audience: "And all the time the people out there listening did not know that it was me making all the noise on stage, yelling for me and whistling. They thought it was the audience, so when they came to town they wanted to get in on it, so THEY started whistling and yelling. It was kind of a chain reaction."

Myers, Bob. Bobby wins the Firecracker. *Stock Car Racing;* 1982 October: 42–44+.
Note: Illus.
Photos and article include Marty. Good photo of Marty by race photographer Robert Alexander.

[Photograph]. *Country Gazette;* 1982 October; (104): 45.
Photo of Marty during a performance.

Allison beats Waltrip for Atlanta 500 title. *Athens Daily News* [GA]; 1982 November 8 (Monday).
Marty spun twice early in the race Sunday before going out. Photo of Marty in the crash with Travis Tiller on the 120th lap that caused him to go out. [Ed. note: this was Marty's last race.]

Triple promotion set for "Honkytonk Man" 's track. *Billboard;* 1982 November 13: 6, 52.
Promotion of music from the movie. Marty recorded the title song.

Picks and pans [brief review section]. *People;* 1982 November 22: 10.
A photo of Loni Anderson from the TV film "Country Gold" in a performing outfit. [Ed. note: Her suit was designed by Nudie and patterned after Marty's stage outfits.]

Fallstrom, Bob. Marty Robbins; his music, his machines. *Decatur Herald & Review* (IL); 1982 November 28.
Note: Illus.
One of his last interviews. It takes place backstage at the Nashville North in Taylorville and includes personal stories and racing background.

Marty in the pit area of his last race at Atlanta in November 1982. (Photo by Elmer Kappell)

The Nashville Connection [album by Ray Conniff]. *Country Music People;* 1982 November: 35.
Album review. Marty has one cut on the album: "We had it all."

Linedecker, Cliff. Marty Robbins: I know I have lived before. *National Examiner;* 1982 November 30; 19(48): 26.
Note: Illus.
Most of the article centers around the writing of "El Paso" and "El Paso City."

Pond, Neil. Alabama, Skaggs, Fricke take honors at CMA Awards. *Music City News;* 1982 November; 20(5): 4.
Note: Illus.
Marty was elected to the Hall of Fame at the October awards program.

Come back to me. *Country Song Roundup;* 1982 December; 34(281): 42.
Album review.

Marty with Bobby Jones on the "Bobby Jones Gospel" show, his last television appearance, November 1982. (Photo by Tom Lawson)

Highlights of the 11th Annual Talent Buyers Seminar. *CMA Close-up;* 1982 December: 12–13.
Note: Illus.
Photo of Marty and others from the Artists Panel on page 12.

New faces score at CMA awards. *Country Music People;* 1982 December; 13(12): 12–13.
Article about CMA awards; Marty's Hall of Fame Award included.

Newest Hall of Famer. *Country Music People;* 1982 December; 13(12): 4.
Note: Illus.
Brief article about Hall of Fame Award from CMA, October, 1982. Includes photo of Eddy Arnold presenting the award to Marty.

Marty Robbins: his bus keeps him going. *Destinations* [monthly publication of the American Bus Association]; 1982 December: 7.
Note: Illus.

[Photograph]. *Country Hotline News;* 1982 December; 13(10): 2.
Caption to the photo identifies Marty as the newest member of the Hall of Fame.

Marty Robbins. *CRS Annual (Country Song Roundup)*; 1982 Winter: 46–47. Note: Illus.

Star gazing [news column]. *Music City News;* 1982 December; 20(6): 7.
Marty recently completed a photo session at the Nashville Speedway for St. Thomas Hospital. The photo will be used on the cover of their annual report.

[Editorial Note: Marty's last concert was the night of December 1, 1982 for the American Tour Bus Association in Cincinnati, Ohio. He performed at the concert and returned home to Nashville. The next morning he awoke at his home with chest pains and entered St. Thomas Hospital around 11:30 a.m..]

Neese, Sandy. Marty Robbins stable but critical. *The Tennessean;* 1982 December 3: 31,34.

Oermann, Robert K. Superstar Marty Robbins in critical condition. *The Tennessean;* 1982 December 3.

Snyder, Bill; O'Donnell, Red. Marty Robbins still critical after 2nd heart operation. *Nashville Banner;* 1982 December 3.

Bartley, Diane. Opry stars share concern and prayers. *The Tennessean;* 1982 December 4: 31.

Robbins takes turn for the worse. *Nashville Banner;* 1982 December 4.

Prognosis improves for Marty Robbins. *Chicago Tribune;* 1982 December 5.
Note: Illus.

Marty Robbins' condition drops. *The Tennessean;* 1982 December 5.

Singer Marty Robbins kept alive by doctors' "gargantuan" effort. *The Atlanta Journal;* 1982 December 6; (Monday): 3 A.
Note: Illus.

Snyder, Bill. Pump aids Marty Robbins' heart. *Nashville Banner;* 1982 December 6: C2.

Snyder, Bill. Doctor: odds against Marty Robbins' recovery. *Nashville Banner;* 1982 December 6.

Marty Robbins reported still in critical condition. *The Tennessean;* 1982 December 6.

Marty Robbins still "extremely critical." *Chicago Tribune;* 1982 December 6.

Snyder, Bill. Robbins' condition worsens during night. *Nashville Banner;* 1982 December 7: A1.

Neese, Sandy. Doctor's still concerned over Marty's condition. *The Tennessean;* 1982 December 7.

Marty Robbins weakening in fight for life. *Madison Capital Times* (WI); 1982 December 7.

Oermann, Robert K. Marty Robbins has reasonably stable day. *The Tennessean;* 1982 December 8.

Snyder, Bill. Marty Robbins "just holding on." *Nashville Banner;* 1982 December 8.

Snyder, Bill. Robbins' pump rate to be cut. *Nashville Banner;* 1982 December 8.

Bays, Warren. Marty Robbins; performer more than just a singer. *The Intelligencer* [Wheeling, WV]; 1982 December 8; (Wednesday). Illus. Tribute article.

[St. Thomas Hospital Annual Report]. *The Tennessean;* 1982 December 8; (Special Supplement).
Color photo of Marty on the cover, taken October 13 at the Nashville International Raceway. Printed with permission of his family.

Oermann, Robert K. Country superstar Marty Robbins dies. *The Tennessean;* 1982 December 9: 1,11.
Note: Illus.
Marty died near midnight, December 8th.

[Woodlawn Funeral Home notice]. *Nashville Banner;* 1982 December 9.

Normand, Tom; Snyder, Bill. Funeral is set Saturday for Opry's Marty Robbins. *Nashville Banner;* 1982 December 9: 1,18.
Note: Illus.

A legacy of hits. *Nashville Tennessean;* 1982 December 9.
A list of hits compiled from *Billboard,* giving the titles, years, and chart numbers.

O'Donnell, Red. Humor was Robbins' hallmark [in: 'Round the Clock' feature column]. *Nashville Banner;* 1982 December 9: A1,A13.
Long personal tribute with stories about their friendship.

O'Donnell, Red. Opry pals will miss Marty. *Nashville Banner;* 1982 December 9: C1.
Note: Illus.
Personal memories of working with Marty from Opry members includes photo of Marty and Tammy Wynette.

Editorial: Marty Robbins' music will live on. *Nashville Banner;* 1982 December 9: A-20.

Marty Robbins dies of cardiac arrest. *USA Today;* 1982 December 9: 3A.

Singer Marty Robbins dies of heart ailments. *Louisville Times;* 1982 December 9: 1, back page.
Note: Illus.

Singer Robbins dies. *The Oregonian* (Portland, OR); 1982 December 9.

Trott, Walt. Marty Robbins couldn't climb last mountain. *The Capital Times;* 1982 December 9; (Thursday): 30.
Career review and tribute.

Fans grieve for Robbins. *El Paso Herald-Post;* 1982 December 9.

Kever, Jeannie. "El Paso" crooner Marty Robbins dies in Nashville. *El Paso Times;* 1982 December 9.
Note: Illus.

Marty Robbins, 57, dies following his third heart attack in 13 years. *The Atlanta Journal;* 1982 December 9: 3A.
Note: Illus.

Pareles, Jon. Marty Robbins, singer, 57; won a Grammy for "El Paso." *New York Times;* 1982 December 10.

Country music mourns Robbins. *New York Post;* 1982 December 10; (Friday): 20 A.
Note: Illus.

Top country singer Marty Robbins dies at 57. *Washington Post;* 1982 December 10: B10.
Note: Illus.

Edwards, Joe. Country music fans, stars mourn singer-songwriter Marty Robbins. *The Courier-Journal* [Louisville, KY]; 1982 December 10; (Friday): A 14.
Note: Illus.

Snyder, Bill. Scores file by Robbins' casket today. *Nashville Banner;* 1982 December 10: A1,16.
Note: Illus.

Mr. Robbins more than a superstar [Editorial]. *The Tennessean;* 1982 December 10: Ed. page.
Tribute.

Singer helped buy Sadat photo from S.C. teen. *The Charlotte Observer;* 1982 December 10; (Friday).
A businessman who bought an autographed photo of Sadat from a teen who needed money said that part of the money came from Marty.

Country king Marty Robbins dead at 57. *The Charlotte Observer;* 1982 December 10; (Friday): 7B.
Note: Illus.

Pepinsky, Pete. His singing could convert a skeptic into a country fan. *The Charlotte Observer;* 1982 December 10; (Friday): 7B.
Note: Illus.
Personal tribute.

Neese, Sandy. Marty's memories won't die. *The Tennessean;* 1982 December 10: 37,38.
Note: Illus.
Industry friends remember Marty.

Hayman, Ed. Singer Marty Robbins dies at 57; star of country, pop, rock music. *Detroit News;* 1982 December 10: 1.
Review of life and career.

Marty Robbins. *Charlotte News* (NC); 1982 December 10: Ed. pg.
Tribute commentary.

Marty Robbins mourned by country music world. *Detroit Free Press* (MI); 1982 December 10.
Personal memories from fellow performers.

McNamara, Tom. Memories of Robbins won't die. *USA Today;* 1982 December 10.
Note: Illus.

Stars mourn Marty Robbins. *White Plains Reporter-Dispatch;* 1982 December 10.

Surber, Art. Robbins was "friend" of Ocean Opry. *Panama City News-Herald* (FL); 1982 December 10.
Personal memories from the owner of the Ocean Opry, Wayne Rader.

Woody, Larry. Marty: on or off the race track, Robbins was true champ. *The Tennessean;* 1982 December 10: 51,57 (Front, Sports).

Note: Illus.
Racing tributes from NASCAR drivers; photo of Marty and Richard Petty at 1982 Daytona.

Easterling, Bill. Editorial: Marty lived. *Huntsville Times* (AL); 1982 December 10.

Editorial: Marty Robbins. *Charlotte News* (NC); 1982 December 10.

Editorial: Marty Robbins. *El Paso Herald-Post;* 1982 December 10.

Rush, Diane Samms. Wichita opened singer's career. *Wichita Eagle Beacon* (KS); 1982 December 10.
Interview and personal memories of Marty from Hap Peebles.

Sandvold, Jon. Fans of Marty Robbins plan memorials in FW. *Fort Worth Star Telegram;* 1982 December 10.
About a planned tribute in Forth Worth.

Siegel, Eric. Cowboy touch in music is Marty Robbins legacy. *Baltimore Sun;* 1982 December 10.
Note: Illus.

Edwards, Joe. Death of Robbins mourned by peers. *The Oregonian* (Portland); 1982 December 10.

Robbins called "true country," is praised as an entertainer. *Richmond Times* (VA); 1982 December 10.
Note: Illus.

Neese, Sandy; Oermann, Robert K. Producer remembers last days with Marty. *The Tennessean;* 1982 December 11: 29,32.
Interview with Bob Montgomery, who was working with Marty on his last album.

Robbins suffers third heart attack. *Cashbox;* 1982 December 11: 8.

Meeker, Frances. Marty's songs "touched soul of America." *Nashville Banner;* 1982 December 11: A1,6.
Note: Illus.
Coverage of Marty's funeral.

Grand Ole Opry plans tribute to late singer. *Houston Post;* 1982 December 11.

Note: Illus.
The Opry will pay tribute to Marty Saturday night.

Dilworth, Billy. Today, the country mourns Marty. *Banner-Herald/Daily News* [Athens, GA]; 1982 December 11; (Saturday).
Tribute article.

Claypool, Bob. Country star Marty Robbins; his distinctive voice will be deeply missed. *Houston Post;* 1982 December 11.
Note: Illus.
Long personal tribute.

Leach, Hugh. Robbins' work was really "play." *Lansing State Journal* (MI); 1982 December 11: 85,95.
Tribute, with quotes from Marty about his appreciation of life and his faith.

Marty Robbins; a minstrel of extraordinary talent. *Durham Morning Herald* (NC); 1982 December 11.
Tribute.

Pembrake, J. Garland. Marty Robbins: a hit in many areas. *Atlanta Journal;* 1982 December 11.
Note: Illus.

Strom, Susan. Festival seeks substitute for Marty Robbins. *East Hillsborough Tribune* (FL); 1982 December 11; (Saturday): 2-EH.
Marty's death mourned. He had been a regular at the Plant City Strawberry Festival.

Oermann, Robert K. Hundreds pay tribute to Robbins at funeral. *The Tennessean;* 1982 December 12: 1,12.
Note: Illus.

Hurst, Jack. The Old West's favorite son; Marty Robbins had the sort of spirit that couldn't stand fences. *The Orlando Sentinel* [FL]; 1982 December 12; (Sunday): D1,6.
Note: Illus.
Long personal tribute and historical piece.

[Photograph]. *Chicago Tribune;* 1982 December 12.
Note: Photo from Marty's funeral; text gives some information.

Glick, Shav. Racing; special to Marty. *Charlotte Observer;* 1982 December 12; (Sunday): 1D,14D.
Note: Illus.

Glick, Shav. Marty Robbins' flip side: racing. *Los Angeles Times;* 1982 December 12; (Sunday): Sec. III, p.3, col 1.
Interview, history.

Marty Robbins buried. *Denver Post;* 1982 December 12.
Note: Illus.

Cowboy farewell. *Forth Worth Star-Telegram;* 1982 December 12.
Note: Illus.
Tribute to Marty was held in Forth Worth.

Huffman, Jim. Stock car racing fraternity will miss Marty Robbins. *Omaha World-Herald;* 1982 December 12.
Tribute includes quotes from Marty.

Rhodes, Don. Marty Robbins leaves Opry memories. *Augusta Chronicle* (GA); 1982 December 12.
Note: Illus.
Tribute with personal memories.

Nichols, Judy. Friends in Valley fondly recall good days with Marty Robbins. *Arizona Republic;* 1982 December 13: 1+.
Note: Illus.
Remembrances of people in Arizona who knew Marty.

Marty Robbins will be in film he never saw. *USA Today;* 1982 December 13: 2D.
Note: Illus.
Comments regarding the film "Honkytonk Man."

[Photograph]. *Nashville Banner;* 1982 December 13.
Photo of workers changing a large billboard on Briley Parkway that had an ad with Marty's picture on it.

Zipf, Walter. Country star was just folks. *Mesa Tribune* (AZ); 1982 December 14.
Personal tribute.

Robbins took long road to Nashville, *The Glendale Star* [AZ]; 1982 December 15; (Wednesday).
Remembrances of people who knew Marty in Glendale, where he was born and grew up.

Lyon, Marc. Residents recall "good neighbor" Robbins. *Brentwood Journal* (TN); 1982 December 15: 1.
Comments and tributes by Marty's neighbors in Brentwood.

Nichols, Judy. Friends in Glendale remember award-winning singing star. *The Arizona Republic;* 1982 December 15: Wednesday.
Note: Illus.
Tribute comments from people who knew Marty when he was growing up in Glendale, Arizona.

[Photograph]. *Area Auto Racing News;* 1982 December 15.
Photo of Marty at his last stock car race in November.

Fielden, Greg. Heart attack claims Marty Robbins. *Southern Auto Racing;* 1982 December 16: 3,30.
Detailed review of Marty's racing career.

McCredie, Gary. Driver/singer Marty Robbins dies at 57. *Grand National Scene;* 1982 December 16: 1.
Note: Illus.
Quotes from drivers, general review of racing career.

Booth, Jim. Marty Robbins: he never quit. *Erie Morning News* (PA); 1982 December 16.
Note: Illus.
Personal tribute with quotes from past interviews.

Marty Robbins' entire estate goes to wife. *The Tennessean;* 1982 December 17; (Friday): 24.
Probate of Marty's will indicates that he left everything to Marizona, his wife.

Marty Robbins' will names wife sole heir. *Nashville Banner;* 1982 December 17.

Kirby, Kip. Entertainer Marty Robbins dies in Nashville at 57. *Billboard;* 1982 December 18: 8.

Robbins, 57, dies from cardiac arrest. *Cashbox;* 1982 December 18: 22,27.

[Advertisement]. *Billboard;* 1982 December 18: 41.
Full-page ad for the movie "Honkytonk Man," featuring the title song and a photo of Marty from the movie.

[Full-page memorial tribute]. *Billboard;* 1982 December 18: 61.
Full-page tribute to Marty from Clint Eastwood.

Maves, Sherry. Life was worth living for Marty Robbins. *Journal-Standard* [Hendersonville, TN]; 1982 December 18–24: 28.
Note: Illus.
Personal tribute.

Hurst, Jack. Rugged individualism: the legacy of Marty Robbins. *Chicago Tribune;* 1982 December 19: Arts & Books Section.
Two-page review of Marty's life and career, with quotes from past interviews.

Marty Robbins' style made a fan of reluctant visitor to Opry. *Louisville Courier-Journal* (KY); 1982 December 19: H4.
Note: Illus.
Personal comments from the writer, who saw Marty for the first time at what was his last Opry appearance in August.

Fallstrom, Bob. Marty; his memory will live on. *Decatur Herald & Review* (IL); 1982 December 19. Note: Illus.
Tributes and memories from local fans.

PM Magazine [TV series]. *TV Guide* [Charlotte, NC edition]; 1982 December 22: A-71.
The evening broadcast will show a scheduled piece on Marty taped early in the fall.

Faria, Manny. Robbins earned his spot in Nashville. *Danbury News Times* (CT); 1982 December 23.
Tribute.

"Mr. Teardrop." *Richmond News-Leader* (VA); 1982 December 23.
Tribute.

Kirby, Kip. Nashville Scene [news column]. *Billboard;* 1982 December 25: 68,69.
Note: Illus.
Personal tribute to Marty and commentary about what he meant to fans and industry friends alike. Photo was taken at Marty's last radio interview.

Mervyn Conn returns to roots. *Billboard;* 1982 December 25: 66.
Article about Conn's 1983 UK Festival plans includes words of tribute to Marty.

[Photograph]. *Amusement Business Weekly;* 1982 December 25.
Photo of Marty and his record producer, Bob Montgomery, with the caption, "Some memories just won't die."

Brave Marty Robbins would never give up. *Globe;* 1982 December 28.

Grizzard, Lewis. A musical question of age. *Dallas Times Herald;* 1982 December 29; (Wednesday): 2 E.
A commentary about John Lennon ends with a note about Marty.

Nelson, Vern. Country music and stage review [news column]. *South Pasadena Review* (CA); 1982 December 29: 7.
General tribute, including personal stories.

BIBLIOGRAPHY, 1983–88

[Photograph]. *Music City News;* 1983 January; 20(7): [back cover] p.32.
Large color photo of Marty and Barbara Mandrell, used as an ad for MCN.

In memoriam. *CMA Close-up;* 1983 January: 6.
Tribute to Marty includes a photo from the Hall of Fame Award presentation.

Allen, Bob. Marty Robbins. *Country Rhythms;* 1983 January; (12): 33–38.
Note: Illus.
Written before Marty's death, this extensive interview covers in detail such topics as Marty's heart attacks, working with Bob Montgomery on a new album, his religious beliefs, and life attitudes.

Axelsson, Hans; Axelsson, Ingegird. Marty Robbins som vi minns honom. *Kountry Korral;* 1983; 16(1): 42–48.
Note: Illus.
Long tribute article with photos.

Clint Eastwood. *Music City News;* 1983 January; 20(7): 8.
Article about the movie, "Honkytonk Man"; includes photo of Marty and Clint from the movie.

Comments [by editor]. *Country Music People;* 1983 January; 14(1): 3.
Memorial to Marty.

Country music mourns Robbins. *Music City News;* 1983 January; 20(7): 4.

Country music world mourns the death of superstar Marty Robbins. *Country Hotline News;* 1983 January; 13(11): 2.
Note: Illus.

Eastwood stars in "Honkytonk Man". *Country Hotline News;* 1983 January; 13(11): 3.
Note: Illus.
Movie review.

Granger, Gene. Shadowing the stocks [news column]. *Grand National Scene;* 1983 January 6.
Personal tribute, with racing stories.

Keeler, Terry. Marty Robbins; the final interview. *Country Music Roundup;* 1983 January; 7(2).
Note: Cover photo., Illus.
The interview covered his performances in England and his love of performing for British audiences.

Letters to the editor [monthly feature]. *Country Rhythms;* 1983 January; (12): 30.
A poem, by Jacqueline Short, "The ballad of Marty Robbins."

Marty Robbins. *International Musician Monthly;* 1983 January.

Marty Robbins discography. *Kountry Korral;* 1983; 16(1): 49.

Marty Robbins: 1925–1982. *Little Nashville Express* (IN); 1983 January/February: 6–7.

Note: Illus.
Two-page tribute with concert photos.

Marty Robbins: 1925–1982. *Destinations* [American Bus Association]; 1983 January: 10.
Note: Illus.
Brief review of Marty's last concert (before the ABA) and a photo from the concert.

Marty Robbins: vital contributor to music. *Country Music People;* 1983 January; 14(1): 4.
Tribute article.

Rockin' rollin' Robbins. *Country Music People;* 1983 January; 14(1): 34.
Album review.

Rock'n roll'n Robbins. *Country Gazette;* 1983 January: 43.
Album review.

Rockin' rollin' Robbins. *Kountry Korral;* 1983; 16(1): 64.
Album review.

van Dam, Hans. [Series of concert photos and a memorial to Marty]. *Country Gazette;* 1983 January; (107): 2.

Vogel, Manfred. We miss you, Marty Robbins. *Country Corner;* 1983 January: 10–11. Note: Illus.
Article in German.

Winters reunion gathers tonight. *The Tennessean;* 1983 January 21: 11-D.
Note: Illus.
The article includes several stories from Don Winters about working with Marty.

Music City News. Program book; Top Country Hits of the Year Awards Show; Broadcast January 24, 1983.
Program and book included a long tribute to Marty.

Oermann, Robert K. "Wino" is top song, fans say. *The Tennessean;* 1983 January 25: D 1.
MCN Top Country Hits televised awards show contained a tribute section to Marty.

[Advertisement]. *Music City News;* 1983 February; 20(8): 12.
Full-page ad for older Marty Robbins record albums.

Allan, David. The David Allan Page; "Marty's old west." *Country Music People;* 1983 February; 14(2): 11.
Tribute and comments from past interview. Allan quotes Marty as wanting his recordings released after his death.

Allen, Bob. Billy Sherrill; spinning tales. *Country Song Roundup;* 1983 February; 35(283): 15–17,26. Note: Illus.
Interview includes comments about working with Marty.

Byworth, Tony. Marty: always the crowd pleaser. *Country Music People;* 1983 February; 14(2): 17.
Note: Illus.

Cackett, Alan. Marty Robbins: 26.9.1925 to 8.12.1982; a tribute. *Country Music People;* 1983 February; 14(2): 16–19.
Note: Cover photo, illus.
Covers Marty's career and notes song titles Marty had said he had recorded but never released.

Letters [to the editor]. *Music City News;* 1983 February 20(8): 3.
Letters from fans regarding Marty's death.

Marty Robbins: 1925–1982. *Rolling Stone;* 1983 February 3: 38.
Note: Illus.
Tribute article.

Edwards, Joe. Son to complete concert dates Robbins scheduled. *The Youngstown Daily Vindicator* [OH]; 1983 February 3.
Ronny Robbins will fulfill some dates Marty had booked before his death.

Edwards, Joe. Ronny Robbins fills in for late father. *Houston Chronicle;* 1983 February 5.

Leach, Hugh. Tears for late, great Marty. *Lansing State Journal* (MI); 1983 February 5.
Review of the January issue of *Music City News*, a tribute issue to Marty.

Edwards, Joe. Robbins not trying to fill dad's shoes. *Austin American-Statesman* (TX); 1983 February 10: B 14.
Interview with Ronny Robbins.

Letters [to the editor]. *Country Music People;* 1983 February; 14(2): 44.
Note: Cover photo.
Several tribute letters from fans.

[Photograph]. *Country Rhythms;* 1983 February; (13): 53.
Photo of Marty Robbins and Eddy Arnold during the Hall of Fame
presentation on the CMA Awards telecast.

[Photograph]. *Country Rhythms;* 1983 February; (13): 54–55.
Photo of Marty and Janie Fricke at the CBS party during Country Music
Week, October, 1982.

Pond, Neil. Memories that just won't die; a special tribute to Marty
Robbins. *Music City News;* 1983 February; 20(8): 16–22.
Note: Illus.
Stories, photos, and tributes to Marty from family and associates.

Robbins' son to fill some dates. *Country Hotline News;* 1983 February.

Show tribute to Robbins. *The Kansian* (Kansas City, KS); 1983 February 24.
ary 24.
Note: Illus.

Star gazing [news column]. *Music City News;* 1983 February; 20(8): 6.
Notes that Ronny will tour with his father's band.

[Tribute issue to Marty]. *Music City News;* 1983 February; 20(8): various paging.
ous paging.
Note: Cover photo., illus.
Coverage includes: p.3, Letters to the editor; p. 12, full-page ad for
records; p.6, Star gazing [monthly column] says Ronny will tour with
his father's Band.

The David Allan Page [news column]. *Country Music People;* 1983
March; 14(3): 9.
Tribute. Also covers a radio tribute that was done in England.

Edwards, Joe. Son tries to carry on father's music. *Daytona Beach
Morning Journal;* 1983 March 5 (Saturday): 13D.
Note: Illus.
Interview with Ronny.

Letters [to the editor]. *Music City News;* 1983 March; 20(9): 3.
Letters from fans regarding Marty's death and remembering him.

Letters [to the editor]. *Music City News;* 1983 March; 20(9): 2.
Letters from fans about Marty's death.

Marty Robbins files, v. 1 and v. 2. *Kountry Korral;* 1983; 16(2): 54.
Album reviews.

Neese, Sandy. CBS Records show features 41 album covers. *The Tennessean;* 1983 March 4: 2 D.
Note: Illus.
The reception for latest exhibit at the Hall of Fame. A large record album cover design exhibit includes one of Marty's albums. Photo with the article is of Chet Atkins and photographer Beverly Parker, who took the photos for Marty's last album covers.

Oermann, Robert K. "Superstar of tomorrow" lights up rooms today. *The Tennessean;* 1983 March 31: 22 C.
The article is about Bobby Springfield, who wrote "Some memories just won't die."

Rector, Lee. Jeanne Pruett has new duet with Marty Robbins. *Music City News;* 1983 March; 20(9): 30.
Note: Illus.
New version of "Love me" has Marty and Jeanne singing duet. Recorded in early 1981.

Reverberations [news column]. *Country Music People;* 1983 March; 14(3): 21.
Part of column covers album release, "Rock 'n' roll Robbins."

Rowe, W. J. Marty's mountain. *Music City News;* 1983 March: [39].
The words and music to a tribute song to Marty.

Settlement reached on Pruett-Robbins duet. *Nashville Banner;* 1983 March 29: A 1.
The single involved in the suit with CBS Records was "Love me."

West Texas town honors Marty Robbins. *Nashville Banner;* 1983 March 31.
The El Paso City Council voted to name a 30-acre park after Marty.

[Advertisement]. *Country Music Inquirer;* 1983 April; 2(1): 2.
Note: Illus.
Large ad for a tribute record to Marty, "Tribute to Marty," written by Bettye Cole and recorded by Phil Speer.

[Advertisement]. *Country Rhythms;* 1983 April: 19.
Full-page ad for the album, "Number 1 Cowboy."

Oermann, Robert K. The death of Marty Robbins. *Country Rhythms;*
1983 April: 30–31. Note: Illus.
Detailed career review.

Allen, Bob. Marty Robbins; a final tribute. *Country Rhythms;* 1983
April: 32–33.
Note: Illus.
Personal tribute recalls Marty's faith and love of life. Photos by Joan
and Gordy Goodwin.

Oermann, Robert K. Pruett-Robbins duet is touching tribute. *The Tennessean;* 1983 April 1: 2-D.
Note: Illus.
Article about Jeanne's new single, a duet with Marty named "Love
me." Jeanne is quoted as saying that Marty told her that he hoped
someone would care enough to keep his music alive after he's gone.

Millard, Bob. May 7 stock car race to honor Marty Robbins. *Nashville
Banner;* 1983 April 7. Note: Illus.
A NASCAR race will be held at the Nashville Speedway to honor
Marty. Photo of Ronny Robbins and Nashville Speedway President
Gary Baker.

Woody, Larry. Race to be in Robbins' honor. *The Tennessean;* 1983
April 7: Sports (p.1,2).
The Marty Robbins 420 NASCAR stock care race will be held May 7th
at the Nashville Speedway.

Nashville race now the Marty Robbins 420. *Grand National Scene;*
1983 April 14.
Article about the special tribute race to be held in May at the Nashville
Speedway. To be broadcast on The Nashville Network.

Stone, Ted. Robbins album reflects career of country giant. *Winnipeg
Free Press* (MA/CAN); 1983 April 16.
Note: Illus.
Album review for "Marty Robbins: 20 golden memories."

Carrigan, Shaun. Suit filed on Marty Robbins duet. *Nashville Banner;*
1983 April 22.

The suit is by CBS Records to stop the sales and distribution of "Love me," the duet with Marty and Jeanne Pruett.

Suit filed to halt Robbins-Pruett duet record. *Nashville Banner;* 1983 April 22.

Oermann, Robert K. Suit would halt sale of Robbins, Pruett duet disc. *The Tennessean;* 1983 April 23.

Carrigan, Shaun. Judge denies CBS request to halt record. *Nashville Banner;* 1983 April 25.

[Advertisement]. *The Tennessean;* 1983 April 25.
Ad for the Marty Robbins 420 stock car race to be held at the Nashville International Speedway May 7, 1983.

Cunniff, Al. Marty Robbins; sometimes in the third person. *Country Song Roundup;* 1983 April; 35(285): 8–12.
Note: Illus.

Duet single release features Jeanne Pruett and Marty Robbins. *Country Hotline News;* 1983 April.
Note: Illus.
About the recording "Love me," a single from Audiograph Records.

Letters [to the editor]. *Country Rhythms;* 1983 April: 17.
Letter from Marty sent to Country Rhythms shortly before he died, thanking them for publishing an article about him.

Letters [to the editor]. *Country Rhythms;* 1983 April: 17.
Note: Illus.
Two poems remembering Marty: 1) Dedication to Marty, by Judy Brose; 2) Marty's gone, by Mary C. Ensley.

Marty Robbins. *Country Music Inquirer;* 1983 April; 2(1): 14.
Note: Illus.
Tribute article.

Ronny Robbins. *Country Music Inquirer;* 1983 April; 2(1): 14.
Note: Illus.

[Photograph]. *Bus Tours Magazine;* 1983 April: 58.
Photo of Marty at his last public appearance.

Grand National race named for Robbins. *Country Hotline News;* 1983 May; 14(3): 14.
Note: Illus.
The Marty Robbins 420 will be held May 7, 1983.

Newsline [news column]. *CMA Close-up;* 1983 May: 23.
Marty is being honored by CBS Records and the Nashville International Speedway with a May 7, 1983 NASCAR race, the "Marty Robbins 420."

[Photograph]. *CMA Close-up;* 1983 May: 8.
A photo of Marty and other participants at the June, 1982 All-American Games held during Fan Fair.

Rowe, Norman. Robbins album displays affection for the west. *Richmond Times-Dispatch* (VA); 1983 May 1.
Album review for "Some memories just won't die."

Fisher, Kitty. Robbins-Pruett "Love Me" duet distribution to be continued. *The Tennessean;* 1983 May 2.
Settlement reached on lawsuit by CBS Records against Jeanne's record company.

Woody, Larry. Marty Robbins 420 area's richest sports event. *The Tennessean;* 1983 May 5.

Woody, Larry. Waltrip nips Bonnett to gain 420 pole. *The Tennessean;* 1983 May 7: Sports 1,3.
Note: Illus.

Caldwell, Joe. Waltrip tries for 4th NIR win in row. *Nashville Banner;* 1983 May 7; (Saturday): B1,3.
Note: Illus.

Woody, Larry. Rain, rivals can't halt Waltrip win. *The Tennessean;* 1983 May 8: Sports 1,2.
Note: Illus.
Darrell Waltrip won the Marty Robbins 420.

Caldwell, Joe. Darrell makes it the "Waltrip 420." *Nashville Banner;* 1983 May 9: D1,2.
Note: Illus.
Article includes photo of the trophy being presented to the winner of the Marty Robbins 420.

Woody, Larry. Home sweet home; Waltrip makes winning look easy. *The Tennessean;* 1983 May 9: Sports (p.1,3).
Note: Illus.
Darrell Waltrip won the Marty Robbins 420.

Easy Robbins 420 victory for Waltrip at Nashville. *Midwest Racing News* [Milwaukee, WI]; 1983 May 12; 24(4): 1,3.
Note: Illus.
Headlines and article about the race.

Academy of Country Music Awards Program. *TV Guide.* 1983 May 9. The 18th annual awards show was telecast on NBC-TV. Rex Allen did a brief tribute to Marty and announced that the ACM has named its annual charity golf tourney in Marty's name.

Robbins remembered in special trophy. *Grand National Scene;* 1983 May 12: 5.
The trophy presented to Darrell Waltrip upon winning the "Marty Robbins 420" was designed to represent Marty and the respect given to him by the racing and recording communities. It consisted of one of Marty's racing suits, a picture of him, and two gold records encased in glass. Waltrip, who had been a friend of Marty's, indicated he planned to keep the trophy rather than donate it to a museum because of the way he felt about Marty.

Easy Robbins 420 Victory for Waltrip at Nashville [Headlines for the newspaper]. *Midwest Racing News;* 1983 May 12; 15(4): 1,3.

CBS, Indigo resolve dispute over Robbins 45. *Billboard;* 1983 May 14. Indigo retains the right to continue distribution of the release.

[Advertisement]. *Billboard;* 1983 May 14.
Ad for the Marty Robbins/Jeanne Pruett single, "Love me."

Record briefs [reviews]. *New York Daily News;* 1983 May 15; (Sunday).
Album review of "Some memories just won't die."

Millard, Bob. Robbins museum will be built at Twitty complex. *Nashville Banner;* 1983 May 18.
A reception was held Tuesday evening to announce plans for the museum.

Nashvillans' preferences probed. *Billboard;* 1983 May 21: 40.
Marty listed as one of the favorites in a radio poll.

Kirby, Kip. Nashville Scene [news column]. *Billboard;* 1983 May 21.
Mentions the Academy of Country Music golf tournament named to
honor Marty. Announcement was made on their awards show.

Honky Tonk Man [soundtrack]. *Country Rhythms;* 1983 May; (15): 19–
20.
Album review. Marty does the title song and one other on the album.

"Howdy, Conway." *Ford Times;* 1983 May; 76(2): 4–8.
Note: Illus.
Article about Fan Fair includes photo of Marty.

Letters to the editor [monthly feature]. *Country Rhythms;* 1983 May;
(15): 28.
Letters about Marty included.

Marty Robbins files, volume 1. *Country Gazette;* 1983 May; (111): 44.
Album review.

Robbins on Bear. *Country Music People;* 1983 May; 14(5): 5.
Gives listing of albums Bear Family Records plans to release.

Rockin' rollin' Robbins, volume 2. *Country Gazette;* 1983 May; (111):
43.
Album review.

ACM Awards Show issue. *Academy of Country Music [Newsletter];*
1983 June; 12(6): 1+.
Note: Illus.
Review of award show activities. The May 9th broadcast included a
tribute to Marty by Rex Allen and the announcement that the ACM
would name its annual charity golf tourney in Marty's name.

[Advertisement]. *Music City News;* 1983 June; 20(12): 25.
One-half-page ad for the album, "Some memories just won't die."

[Advertisement]. *Country Song Roundup;* 1983 June; 35(287): 51.
Full-page ad for the album, "No. 1 Cowboy."

Honky tonk man soundtrack. *Country Song Roundup;* 1983 June;
35(287): 37,48.
Album review.

[Advertisement]. *Music City News;* 1983 June; 20(12): 27.
One-half-page ad from Marty Robbins Enterprises featuring Ronny.

Awards sponsor stays silent on its winners. *The News and Observer* [Raleigh, NC]; 1983 June 6: 7 B.
Note: Illus.
Article about the MCN Awards show features Marty in a photo and notes that he is nominated for seven of the 14 awards.

Oermann, Robert K.; Neese, Sandy. Gone, not forgotten: Marty still tops. *The Tennessean;* 1983 June 7; (Tuesday): D1,4.
Note: Illus.
Marty was the big winner at the MCN Awards, receiving three.

Country fans honor late Marty Robbins. *The Raleigh Times* [NC]; 1983 June 7: 5 B.
Note: Illus.
Marty won three awards at the MCN Awards Show that was telecast last night. Photo of Ronny and Marizona receiving the awards.

The late Marty Robbins wins 3 country music awards. *The Des Moines Register;* 1983 June 7: 8-T.
Note: Illus.
Awards from the Music City News Awards.

Marty Robbins wins music awards. *Washington Post;* 1983 June 7: Show (p.2).

Marty Robbins wins three awards. *Yonkers Herald Statesman* (NY); 1983 June 7.
Coverage of the MCN Awards.

O'Donnell, Red. Fans vote 3 major awards to Robbins. *Nashville Banner;* 1983 June 7; (Sec.C): C 1.
Marty won three awards at the MCN Awards last night: Single of the Year, Album of the Year, and Male Vocalist of the Year.

Oermann, Robert K. Barbara's blues country games champs again. *The Tennessean;* 1983 June 8: (Wednesday): 8 D.
Note: Illus.
Article about the All-American Country Games. Barbara Mandrell took the time at the end of the game to remember Marty and his part in the games last year.

[Photograph]. *Glendale Star;* 1983 June 8: 1.
Photo of Mamie Minotto, Marty's twin sister, receiving a proclamation from the Glendale, Arizona Mayor naming the 4th of July as "Marty

Robbins Day." In one of the events, Marty will be named the first member of the Arizona Songwriters Hall of Fame.

[Photograph]. *The Phoenix Gazette;* 1983 June 8: NW-8.
Photo of Mamie Minotto receiving proclamation from Mayor of Glendale, Arizona making July 4th "Marty Robbins Day." The Proclamation will be given to the Hall of Fame in Nashville.

Mulholland, David. Robbins' records live on. *The Windsor Star* (ON, Canada); 1983 June 10. Note: Illus.
Album review of "Some memories just won't die."

Oermann, Robert K. Shrines to the stars of country. *USA Today;* 1983 June 15: 6D.
Note: Illus.
Article includes the Marty Robbins Memorial Showcase; photo of Ronny with the Panther DeVille.

Morris, Edward. Marty Robbins the big story at Music City News Awards. *Billboard;* 1983 June 18: 39.
Marty won: Album of the Year, Single of the Year, and Male Vocalist of the Year.

Kirby, Kip. Nashville Scene [news column]. *Billboard;* 1983 June 18: 45.
The column mentions the Marty Robbins 420.

City prepares for all-day 4th celebration. *The Glendale Star;* 1983 June 29: 1.
Detailed schedule of events for "Marty Robbins Day."

Country corner [news column]. *Watertown Daily News* (NY); 1983 June 30.
Covers the MCN Awards and notes that Marty was the big winner.

Letters [monthly feature]. *Country Gazette;* 1983 June; (112): 23.
Note: Illus.
Letters about Marty and an editorial response.

Marty Robbins files, volume 1 and volume 2. *Country Music People;* 1983 June; 14(7): 36.
Album reviews.

Marty Robbins memorial benefit set. *Bay City News* (MI); 1983 June 25.

Note: Illus.
Ronny Robbins and the Band will perform at a concert in Michigan.

Music, movies mix in new H of F exhibit. *Music City News;* 1983 June;
20(12): 56.
One of the exhibits in the Hall of Fame includes a clip from one of
Marty's movies.

[Photograph]. *Music City News;* 1983 June; 20(12): 14.
Photo of Marty from the 1982 MCN Awards show.

Some memories just won't die. *Country Gazette;* 1983 June; (112): 40.
Album review.

Some memories just won't die. *Kountry Korral;* 1983; 16(3): 60.
Album review.

Twentieth century drifter. *Country Rhythms;* 1983 June; (16): 22.
Album review.

Woody, Larry. Ronny Robbins runs wet track. *The Tennessean;* 1983
June 30: 7D.
Note: Illus.
Story about Ronny's speedboat racing activities in comparison to Marty's auto racing.

Wilde, Jim. July 4 in Glendale sparkled! It was Marty Robbins Day.
The Glendale Star; 1983 July 6.
Note: Illus.
Text and photos of the day. Includes photo of Mamie with picture of
Marty at the induction for the Arizona Songwriters Hall of Fame.

Marty Robbins Day; 4th of July celebration in Glendale. *Gila Bend,
Arizona Sun;* 1983 July 7: 6–7.
Note: Illus.
Two full pages of text and photos includes photo of Mamie at the
Arizona Songwriter's Association induction of Marty as the first member of their Hall of Fame.

[Advertisement]. *Music City News;* 1983 July; 21(1): 15.
Full-page ad featuring Ronny and Marizona.

[Advertisement]. *Inside Country Music;* 1983 July; 1(10): Inside back
cover.
Full-page ad for the album "No. 1 cowboy."

Courtney, Myrna L. Marty Robbins: the Marty Robbins Museum, "Some memories just won't die." *Inside Country Music;* 1983 July; 1(10): 46–48.
Note: Cover photo., Illus.
Article about the 1982–83 museum at Hermitage Landing. The museum was opened in June of 1982 and closed in early 1983.

Fans & stars [monthly feature]. *Country Rhythms;* 1983 July; (17): 34.
Photo of Marty with a fan.

A fond farewell to a country music legend, Marty Robbins: 1925–1982. *Country Song Roundup;* 1983 July; 35(288): Tribute issue.
Note: Issue title. Cover photo.
Special issue of CSR in memory of Marty.

Hall, Claude. They don't even remember. *Tune-in;* 1983 July: 11,14.
Memories of Marty and Bob Nolan.

Honky tonk man. *Country Music People;* 1983 July; 14(7): 10.
Film review. Mentions Marty's part.

Letters [to the editor]. *Country Song Roundup;* 1983 July; 35(288): 48.
Note: Cover photo.
Fan letters in memory of Marty.

Letters [to the editor]. *Country Rhythms;* 1983 July; (17): 50.
Letters about Marty from fans.

Marty Robbins. *Country Music People;* 1983 July; 14(7): 40.
Album review for "Biggest hits." CBS 32301.

Oermann, Robert K.; Allen, Bob. Marty Robbins: 1925–1982. *Country Song Roundup;* 1983 July; 35(288): 11–17, 26–28.
Note: Cover photo. Illus.
Memorial articles; detailed review of his career.

Pitts, Michael R. Marty Robbins filmography. *Classic Images;* 1983 July; (97): 73.
Note: Illus.
Article about Marty's movies.

The reader's page [monthly feature]. *Country Rhythms;* 1983 July; (17): 28–29.

Two poems about Marty: 1) Tribute to Marty Robbins, by Louise Mayer; and 2) My loyal fan, by Joni.

Robbins, Alabama and Skaggs top MCN Country Awards. *Music City News;* 1983 July; 21(1): 20–23.
Note: Illus.
Marty won three awards: Album of the Year, Single of the Year, and Male Vocalist of the Year. The awards were accepted by Ronny and Marizona.

Some memories just won't die. *Country Music People;* 1983 July; 14(7): 40.
Album review.

Arizona songwriters induct Robbins. *Music City News;* 1983 August; 21(2): 4.

Letters to the editor [monthly feature]. *Country Rhythms;* 1983 August; (18): 19.
Fan letter.

A lifetime of song, 1951–1982. *Cash Box;* 1983 August 27: 23.
Album review.

Marty Robbins Memorial Golf Classic. *Academy of Country Music [Newsletter]*; 1983 August; 12(8): 1,7.
The golf classic was a success. Details of the event.

In search of. . . *Academy of Country Music [Newsletter]*; 1983 August; 12(8): 5.
Article detailing the information Marty Robbins Enterprises (with the aid of Barbara Pruett) is trying to collect about Marty.

Byworth, Tony. Marty's memory lives on at MCN Awards. *Country Music People;* 1983 August; 14(8): 23.
Note: Illus.
Marty won three awards at the June awards: Male Vocalist, Single of the Year, and Album of the Year. Photo of Marizona and Ronny included.

Reader's page [monthly feature]. *Country Rhythms;* 1983 August; (18): 26.
Poem: "Memories of Marty," by Peggie Blakenship.

Rowe, Norman. Tribute to Marty Robbins has all his old favorites. *Richmond Times-Dispatch;* 1983 August 28.
Note: Illus.
Album review for "A lifetime of song, 1951–1982" includes background information on Marty.

Oermann, Robert K. Double-LP pays high tribute to Marty Robbins. *The Tennessean;* 1983 September 2: 2D.
Note: Illus.
Album review of "A lifetime of song, 1951–1982."

Rhodes, Don. Singer Marty Robbins to be honored by fans. *The Augusta Chronicle, Augusta Herald;* 1983 September 4; (Sunday): E 6.
Note: Illus.
The article mentions several ways Marty is being remembered and quotes from the *ACM Newsletter* about the attempts to collect information about Marty.

[Advertisement]. *Music City News;* 1983 September: 7.
Note: Illus.
¾-page ad for the album, "A lifetime of song, 1951–1982."

Allen, Bob. Marty Robbins. *Country Music;* 1983 September/October; (103): 18–22.
Note: Illus.
Quotes from past interviews include previous heart attacks, his feelings about death, and beliefs about how to lead his life. Article includes a tribute letter from Johnny Cash.

Country lovin', volume 1. *Country Music People;* 1983 September; 14(9): 14.
Album review. Various artists; Marty has two cuts on the album: "Love me" and "It's not love (but it's not bad)."

Marty Robbins Files, volumes 2 and 3. *Country Gazette;* 1983 September; (114): 43.
Album reviews.

Jerold, Jane. Marty Robbins. *Good News* [Madison/Inglewood, TN]; 1983 September 26: 9. Note: Illus.
General review of Marty's career and information on the Memorial Showcase in Hendersonville.

Sharpe, Jerry. Album revives hits of Marty Robbins. *Pittsburgh Press;* 1983 September 25.
Album review of "A lifetime of song, 1951–1982."

Millard, Bob. Groundbreaking begins work on Marty Robbins museum. *Nashville Banner;* 1983 September 26.
The Marty Robbins Memorial Showcase in Hendersonville was started with a groundbreaking and reception.

Nashville lowdown [news column]. *Country Rhythms;* 1983 September; (19): 8.
Marty dominated the 17th Annual Music City News Awards, winning the Best Male Vocalist, Best Album, and Best Single awards.
[Editorial note: the Awards were held in June.]

[Advertisement]. *Music City News;* 1983 October; 21(4): 35.
Ad from Marty Robbins Enterprises featuring Ronny.

[Advertisement]. *Country Rhythms;* 1983 October; (20): 3.
Full-page ad for the album "A lifetime of song, 1951–1982."

Biggest hits. *Country Gazette;* 1983 October; (115): 38–39.
Note: Illus.
Album review.

[Photograph]. *The Tennessean;* 1983 October 1: 4D.
A photo of the groundbreaking ceremonies of the Showcase. Photo shows Marizona, Ronny, and the developer holding a painting of the planned museum.

Jerold, Jana. Memories don't die. *Good News* [Madison/Inglewood, TN]; 1983 October 10: 6.
Note: Illus.
Article about the Marty Robbins Memorial Showcase in Hendersonville.

Campaign to name Phoenix street for Marty Robbins gets under way. *Arizona Republic;* 1983 October 30; (Sunday).

Country: favorites of a polished entertainer. *Detroit Free Press;* 1983 October 30.
Album review of "A lifetime of song, 1951–1982."

Fan time [news column]. *Country Song Roundup;* 1983 October; 35(291): 38–39.
Note: Illus.
The column says that the city of El Paso has a plaque in the airport thanking Marty for helping publicize the city; it now plans to name a 33-acre park after him.

Letters to the editor [monthly feature]. *Country Song Roundup;* 1983 October; 35(291): 35.
Letters from fans in memory of Marty.

Pond, Neil. Ronny Robbins carries on the family business. *Music City News;* 1983 October; 21(4): 35.
Note: Illus.

TNN adds variety to new fall programming. *Country News;* 1983 October: 3.
Article about programming lists the fall appearance of Marizona on a two-part interview on "Yesteryear in Nashville" with Archie Campbell.

Weed, Gene. First annual Marty Robbins Memorial Classic a huge success. *The Chronicle of Country Music* [Academy of Country Music]; 1983 October; 12(10): 1,7.
The golf tourney was held September 12th and raised over $9,000 for the American Heart Association.

Battle, Bob. Forum [regular column]. *Nashville Banner;* 1983 November 21.
Note: Illus.
Column titled "New Billy Walker song pays tribute to Robbins." About the new release, "He sang the songs about El Paso."

Down memory lane with Frankie Starr. *Paradise Valley Voice* [AZ]; 1983 November 23.
Note: Illus.
The article notes that Frankie helped Marty get started. He says he has 13 songs written by Marty in the early days, a gift from Marty.

Fan time [news column]. *Country Song Roundup;* 1983 November; 35(292): 54.
Note: Illus.
The column mentions the Time-Life three-album set and booklet titled "Marty Robbins."

Frederick, Elise. Brentwood honors its hometown heros. *Nashville Banner;* 1983 November 18.
Note: Illus.
Marty one of four performers honored; Ronny represented the family.

Humphrey, Nancy. Brentwood salutes music stars. *Nashville Banner;* 1983 November 10.
Note: Illus.
Marty one of four Hall of Fame stars honored who lived in Brentwood, Tennessee.

Letters to the editor [monthly feature]. *Country Song Roundup;* 1983 November; 35(292): 51.
Fan letters.

Love and family. *Country Music;* 1983 November/December; (104): 9.
Brief article about Ronny and his concert activities following his father's death. Notes he appeared on television show "Yesteryear in Nashville" in September and is working with the Marty Robbins Band.

Lyon, Marc. Chamber salutes Opry stars. *Brentwood Journal* [TN]; 1983 November 16; (Wednesday): 3A.
Marty was one of the country music stars honored by the Brentwood Chamber of Commerce. [Ed. note: His home was in Brentwood.]

Marty Robbins museum to showcase his entire lifetime. *Country Hotline News;* 1983 November; 14(9): 2.
Note: Illus.
Groundbreaking ceremonies, article and photo.

The Master's call. *Country Music People;* 1983 November; 14(11): 12.
Note: Illus.
Album review.

Nashville Scene [news column]. *Billboard;* 1983 November 26.
The column contains a note about Chet Walker in Phoenix and his effort to get a highway named after Marty.

[Advertisement]. *Music City News;* 1983 December: 9.
Color ad for the Marty Robbins commemorative collector's plate. Same ad appears in the November issue on page 9.

[Advertisement]. *Country Rhythms;* 1983 December; (22): 19.
Note: Cover photo.
Small ad for the book, *The Marty Robbins Songbook.*

[Classified ad section]. *Music City News;* 1983 December; 21(6): 31.
Several personal tributes in memory of Marty.

Country Rhythms first Annual International Awards. *Country Rhythms;*
1983 December; (22): 52–53.
Note: Illus.
Marty won the Memorial Award.

Dixon-Harden, Lydia. Billy Walker offers a tribute to Marty Robbins.
Music City News; 1983 December; 21(6): 12.
Article about Billy Walker's new release, "He sang the songs about El
Paso."

Marty Robbins gone, not forgotten. *The Grand Rapids Press* [MI];
1983 December 8; (Thursday).
Note: Illus.
A review of the past year and an interview with Don Winters. Photo of
Don Winters and Jack Pruett.

Some memories just won't die. *Gila Bend Sun* (AZ); 1983 December 8:
8–9. Illus.
Two pages of text and photos of activities honoring Marty during the
past year includes the tribute at the Grand Ole Opry, the Marty Robbins
420, groundbreaking for the museum, and the induction into the Arizona Songwriters Hall of Fame.

Edwards, Joe. On country [column]. *San Gabriel Valley Daily Tribune*
(West Covina, CA); 1983 December 9.
Article about the year since Marty died. Quotes Don Winters.

Edwards, Joe. Fans still venerate Robbins' memory. *The Houston Post;*
1983 December 12; (Wednesday): 4 B. Note: Illus.
Article about the ways Marty has been remembered during the last year.

Maves, Sherry. Singer Marty Robbins remembered. *Journal-Standard*
[TN]; 1983 December 17–23: 28.
Note: Illus.
Interview with Don Winters; information about the Memorial
Showcase.

Hardy, John M.; Cox, Donald E. The legend of Marty Robbins. *Country Song Roundup;* 1983 December; 35(293): 37.
Lyrics to a tribute song about Marty.

My favorite singer is. . . *Country Music People;* 1983 December; 14(12): 15–18.
Marty one of several singers noted in article.

Nash, Alanna. Marty Robbins, a never before published interview. Part 1. *Country Rhythms;* 1983 December; (22): 60–65.
Note: Cover photo., Illus.
The article covers performing, religion, philosophy, and health problems. Part 2 will appear in the January issue.

The readers page [monthly feature]. *Country Rhythms;* 1983 December; (22): 27.
Note: Cover photo.
Tribute poem to Marty, "Good-bye Marty" by Jackie Kovac.

Axelsson, Ingegard. Ronny Robbins and the Marty Robbins Band. *Kountry Korral;* 1984; 17(1): 17. Illus.

Fan time [news column]. *Country Song Roundup;* 1984 January; 36(294): 54.
The column notes that the Marty Robbins Memorial Showcase will be built.

Geneson, Paul. In search of Rosa's Cantina. *Paso del Norte;* 1984 January: 46–49. Note: Illus.

Hardy, John M.; Cox, Donald E. The legend of Marty Robbins. *Country Song Roundup;* 1984 January; 36(294): 36.
Lyrics to a tribute song about Marty.

Joe Knight. *Country Heritage;* 1984 January; 10(6): 5–10,14–22.
Note: Cover photo., illus.
Article covers Joe Knight's career. He played on Marty's first recordings; photos of Marty's first recording session included.

Letters to the editor [monthly feature]. *Country Song Roundup;* 1984 January; 36(294): 49.
Fan letters.

Loggins, Kirk. . . . so you want to be a disc jockey. *The Tennessean;* 1984 January 12.
A listener threatened to kill WSM-AM radio DJ after calling a number of times demanding to hear "A white sport coat."

Lomax III, John. Nashville lowdown [monthly feature]. *Country Rhythms;* 1984 January; (23): 11.
Comments about the museum to be built.

Nash, Alanna. The Marty Robbins interview, part 2. *Country Rhythms;* 1984 January; (23): 64–69.
Note: Cover photo., illus.
Detailed interview includes stories about his childhood.

Powel, Bob. Country tracks [record review column]. *Country Music People;* 1984 January; 15(1): 35.
Album review of "Just me and my guitar."

[Special tribute issue to Marty Robbins]. *Country Music Inquirer;* 1984 January; 2(?): Special issue.
Note: Illus. Cover photo.
Special tribute issue to Marty includes several articles and a number of photos. [Editorial note: Because of the popularity of this issue, the material on Marty was reproduced completely in the April issue.]

Construction under way at Music Village USA. *The Tennessean;* 1984 February 9: 8E.

Kenton, Gary. [Record album reviews]. *Country Rhythms;* 1984 February; (24): 24–25.
Album reviews for "A lifetime of song, 1951–1982," from CBS Records, and "The Marty Robbins files," volumes 1,2, and 3 from Bear Family Records.

Marty honoured in Phoenix. *Country Music People;* 1984 February; 15(2): 7.

Nash, A. A lifetime of song. *Stereo Review;* 1984 February; 48: 86.
Note: Illus.
Album review.

A lifetime of song, 1951–1982 [Album review]. *Country Song Round-up;* 1984 February; 36(295): 51.
Album review.

Fans & stars [monthly photo feature]. *Country Rhythms;* 1984 March; (25).
Photo of Marty with fans.

Hofer, Betty. Ronny Robbins; more than a famous name. *Country Song Roundup;* 1984 March; 35(296): 24–25. Note: Illus.
Contents page says February, 1984.

Ronny Robbins, *Kountry Korral;* 1984; 17(2): 32–33, back cover.
Note: Illus.

Up front [news column]. *Country Song Roundup;* 1984 March; 35(296): 8.
Contents page has February, 1984 as date of issue. The news page is about the Marty Robbins Memorial Showcase.

Fans & stars [monthly photo feature]. *Country Rhythms;* 1984 April; (26): 32,33.
Two photos of Marty with fans.

"Friends of Marty Robbins" strikes sour note with family. *Arizona Republic;* 1984 April 29.
The Arizona Memorial Foundation is not approved by Marty's family.

The Marty Robbins story. *Country Music Inquirer;* 1984 April; 3(1): Various paging.
Note: Cover title reads: Special Marty Robbins issue. Pages 18–27, The Marty Robbins story; pages 26–27, Discography; page 24, the words to "Marty, we love you" by Liz Lyndell.

Means, Andrew. Singer keeps Marty Robbins' memory alive with jam session. *Arizona Republic;* 1984 April 22.
Article about Chet Walker and the Marty Robbins Foundation he started.

Ronny Robbins: filling the shoes of a great man isn't easy. *Country Music People;* 1984 April; 15(4): 30–32.
Note: Illus.
Article includes photos of both Marty and Ronny.

[Advertisement]. *Reader's Digest;* 1984 May.
Three-page ad for a five-album set of Marty's recordings, "Marty Robbins; his greatest hits and finest performances."

Harris, Stacy. Bargaining with the stars. *Country Rhythms;* 1984 May; (27): 26–28.
Note: Illus.
Includes photo and short story about Marty buying a guitar for $100.

A jam for Marty: Robbins remembered in music. *Glendale Star* (AZ); 1984 May 9.
A one-page collection of photos from the jam.

[Photograph]. *Country Rhythms;* 1984 May; (27): 33.
Photo of Marty with a fan.

[Program]. Music City News Awards. 1984 June 4.
The front cover of the awards program features the jacket from Marty's white (with flowers) performing suit.

Biggest hits. *Country Music People;* 1984 June; 14(6): 36.
Album review. Cuts on British album vary from U.S. release. Liner notes on back cover written by Marty Robbins.

Byworth, Tony. Broad range of country music at 16th Wembley Fest. *Billboard;* 1984 May 5: 63.
Article takes note of Glen Campbell's tribute to Marty and Ronny Robbins' selection of Marty's songs.

[Advertisement]. *Music City News;* 1984 June: 26.
A ¾-page ad from Marty Robbins Enterprises thanking fans for the award nominations for the MCN Awards received by Marty and Ronny.

Hackett, Vernell. Ronny Robbins says touring is necessary, but enjoyable. *Country News;* 1984 June: 1,4.
Note: Illus.
Interview with Ronny about touring after his father's death.

Honick, Bruce. Country stars are real sports. *Country News;* 1984 June: 6,7.
The article includes comments about Marty's auto racing.

Hall, Claude. Are you sure it's really country music that you're listening to? *Tune-in;* 1984 June; 2(6): 14,20–21.
Extensive article about Marty and the range of music styles he recorded.

Letters to the editor [monthly feature]. *Country Song Roundup;* 1984 June; 35(299): 51.
Fan letter.

Oermann, Robert K. Shrines to the stars of country. *USA Today;* 1984
June 15; (Friday): 5D.
Note: Illus.
The article about museums includes the Marty Robbins Memorial
Showcase. Photo of Ronny with the Panther DeVille.

Silk Cut Festival. *Country Music People;* 1984 June; 15(6): 24–29, 35.
Note: Illus.
Ronny's performance mentioned on p. 24; also noted, how popular
Marty had been at the festival in England over the years.

[Advertisement]. *Country Music People;* 1984 July; 15(7): 44.
Ad for video tape of movie, "From Nashville with Music."

Faces 'n' places [news column]. *Country Music People;* 1984 July;
14(7): 13.
Notes the Jeanne Pruett/Marty Robbins single "Love me" suit settled
out of court with CBS.

A lifetime of song. *Country Music People;* 1984 July; 15(7): 10.
Album review.

Country Music [news section]. *Billboard;* 1984 July 14.
The news column notes that a group called the "Friends of Marty
Robbins" in Arizona has ceased operations due to the objection of the
Robbins family.

Marty's memorial. *Country Music People;* 1984 July; 15(7): 4.
Announcement of the Museum to be built.

Newsline [column]. *CMA Close-up;* 1984 July: 5.
A news note about a "Friends of Marty Robbins" group formed in
Glendale, Arizona.

Russell, Dennis. Street name change dies. *Glendale Star* (AZ); 1984
July 4.
Article goes into detail regarding problems of the foundation started by
Chet Walker and lack of support from Robbins' family.

Street won't carry Robbins' name. *The Tennessean;* 1984 July 1.
Note: Illus.

[Advertisement]. *Country Music People;* 1984 August; 15(8): 44.
Full-page ad for eight Marty Robbins albums from Bear Records.

Marizona Robinson during Ronny's fan club party, 1984. (Photo by
Barbara Pruett)

[Advertisement]. *Country Song Roundup;* 1984 August; 35(301): Inside
back cover.
Full-page ad for the Marty Robbins Memorial Showcase.

Delaney, Kelly. Marty Robbins; alive for all time. *Country Song Roundup;* 1984 August; 35(301): 10–13.
Note: Illus.
Interviews with friends and family remembering Marty. Extensive interview with Marizona.

Guitar great, Grady Martin. *Country Song Roundup;* 1984 August; 35(301): 50–51, 57–58.
Note: Illus.
Career review by Grady includes comments about working with Marty.

Littleton, Bill. Ronny Robbins. *Country Rhythms;* 1984 August; (30): 46–49.
Note: Illus.
In-depth article covers Marty Robbins Enterprises business activities, touring with his father's band, etc.

[Advertisement]. *Country Music People;* 1984 September; 15(9).
Full-page ad for Marty Robbins albums from Bear Records.

The reader's page [monthly feature]. *Country Rhythms;* 1984 September; (31): 59.
Note: Illus.
Photo and poem: "My singing cowboy," by Gloria Zimprich.

Sooner pair helps keep traditional country music alive. *The Sunday Oklahoman;* 1984 September 30: 3.
Note: Illus.
Article about Beverly King and Joe Knight. Mentions that Joe played on Marty's early recordings.

Daens, Sandy. Studio spotlight [monthly feature]. *Country Music Parade;* 1984 October/November; 1(3): 11.
Interview with Bob Montgomery.

Smith, Bobbi. Exclusive report from Nashville [monthly column]. *Country Music Parade;* 1984 October/November; 1(3): 4.
Note: Illus.
Interview with Marizona. Large publicity photo of Marizona included.

[Advertisement]. *Country Music People;* 1984 November; 15(11): 8.
Full-page ad for the Marty Robbins albums from Bear Records.

Marty after midnight. *Country Music People;* 1984 November; 15(11): 12–13.
Note: Illus.
Album review.

Second Robbins golf classic set. *Billboard;* 1984 November 3.

[Advertisement]. *Country Music People;* 1984 December; 15(12): 34.
Ad for video tape of the movie, "From Nashville with Music."

[Advertisement]. *Country Rhythms;* 1984 December; (34): 14.
Full-page ad for the Memorial plate.

Marty Robbins Memorial Golf Classic—a huge success! *Academy of Country Music* [monthly newsletter]; 1984 December; 13(11): 1,2.
Note: Illus.
The event was held November 5th.

The reader's page [monthly feature]. *Country Rhythms;* 1984 December; (34): 62.
Poem: "A tribute to Marty," by Margaret Conley.

Sharpe, Jerry. Albums revive songs of Robbins, Haggard. *The Pittsburgh Press;* 1984 December 5.
Album review of "Long, long ago."

[Book review]. *Billboard;* 1985 January 26.
A review of the book: *Country Music Buyers-Sellers Reference Book and Price Guide,* by Jerry Osborne.

Ernest Tubb: the legend and the legacy. Volume 1. *Country Music;* 1985 January/February; (111): 67.
Album review. Marty has two duets on the album: 1) "Rainbow at midnight," and 2) "Journey's end."

Letters to the editor [monthly feature]. *Country Song Roundup;* 1985 January; 36(306): 6.
Fan letter.

Marty Robbins; at every turn. *Country Music Inquirer;* 5; 1(12–15).
Note: Cover photo., Illus.
Review of Marty's life and career. Photos from his youth.

Ronny Robbins: doing it his way. *Country Music Inquirer;* 1985 January; 5(1): 17–18. Note: Illus.
Article about Ronny includes a photo of Ronny with Marty.

Satterfield, LaWayne. Marizona; more than just Mrs. Marty Robbins. *Country Music Inquirer;* 1985 January; 5(1): 16.
Note: Illus.

The article highlights her strong religious faith and her life with Marty. She was 15 and working in an ice cream shop when she first met Marty. He told his friends the first time he saw her that he would marry her. They married three years later. She also recalls a conversation she had with Marty, just a short time before his last heart attack, in which he told her he knew he was going to Heaven when he died. Since Marty's death, she has been learning about how to run the business and is in demand as a speaker by religious groups.

Myers, Bob. Marty's magnum. *Petersen's Circle Track;* 1985 January; 4(1): 62–65.
Note: Illus.
Story about Marty's stock car, a '78 Dodge Magnum. The car has been donated to the International Motorsports Hall of Fame and Museum at Talladega. Photos included of car no. 42.

[Photograph]. *Country Music;* 1985 January/February; (111): 44.
Early photo of Marty, Carl Smith, Ernest Tubb, and Faron Young playing golf.

Radio/TV [news column]. *Music City News;* 1985 January; 22(7): 40.
KRPT in Oklahoma gave Willie Nelson and Ernest Tubb "Marty Robbins Lifetime Achievement Awards."

Seideman, Tony. Two companies introduce video titles for below $10. *Billboard;* 1985 January 26: 1,82.
"Road to Nashville" listed.

Send in blanks, get film videos for $5.95 each via VCI mail. *Variety;* 1985 January 23: 43.
"Road to Nashville" one of the films listed.

Kirby, Kip. Nashville scene [news column]. *Billboard;* 1985 February 2.
In writing about the MCN awards, she notes that Marty dominated the MCN Awards during his lifetime.

May celebration to honor singer Marty Robbins' fans. *Douglas Dispatch* [Arizona]; 1985 February 11.
Douglas will hold a special weekend, "Marty Robbins Days," May 18–19. The Douglas Cemetery Committee has received $2600 from Marty's fans for trees to be planted in his memory and the cemetery will dedicate a "Marty Robbins Trail." The celebration is in part a "thank

you" to the fans as well as a tribute to him. Two of Marty's sisters live in Douglas and will take part in the event.

[Advertisement]. *Country Rhythms;* 1985 March; (37): [17].
Full-page ad for the Marty Robbins commemorative collectors plate.

Kirby, Kip. Nashville scene [news column]. *Billboard;* 1985 March 2.
The ACM's 2nd annual Marty Robbins Memorial Golf Tournament raised $15,000 for the LA Chapter of the American Heart Association.

Marty Robbins files, volume 4 and volume 5. *Country Music People;* 1985 March; 16(3): 16–17.
Note: Illus.
Album review of new Bear Family Record albums, "Marty Robbins files, v. 4" and "Marty Robbins files, v. 5."

TNN sales impact: mixed results. *Billboard;* 1985 March 30: 52,56.
The article is about marketing records by ads on The Nashville Network. Marty is one of the artists who benefited most by this type of approach.

Granger, Gene. Commentary [regular column]. *Grand National Scene;* 1985 April 25; 8(43): 4.
Title of column: "Robbins would enjoy Elliotts' success." The story centers around Marty's friendship with the three Elliott Brothers and their enjoyment of racing.

Long, long ago. *Country Music People;* 1985 April; 16(4): 33.
Album review.

Statlers dominate Music City News nominations. *Billboard;* 1985 May 4.
Marty nominated for Album of the Year Award for "Long, long ago."

[Advertisement]. *Music City News;* 1985 June; 22(12): [43].
¾-page ad for "Long, long ago" from Marty Robbins Enterprises thanking fans for the nomination.

Kartes unleashes barrage of $9.95 titles. *Billboard;* 1985 June 8: 29,32.
The Indianapolis firm will release series of "Country Classics" videos; Marty among those listed. Film to be used is from the "Classic Country" television series of 1950s Opry shows.

Kirby, Kip. Fulfillment firm finds big CD demand. *Billboard;* 1985 June 8: 51,56.
Manager Bill VernDick of The Music Shop telemarketing firm was Marty's chief engineer in 1979 and got his idea working for Marty.

Oermann, Robert K. Marty Robbins remembered as ambassador. *The Tennessean;* 1985 June 16: 1,12.
Note: Headline article on front page.
Marty was awarded the city's Metronome Award; the first time it has been awarded posthumously. The Award was presented at the IFCO Show at the Fairgrounds the last day of Fan Fair by Mayor Richard Fulton and accepted by Marizona and Ronny.

Metronome Award goes to Marty Robbins. *Nashville Banner;* 1985 June 17: A 2.
Special award from the city of Nashville.

[Reviews for new releases]. *Billboard;* 1985 June 29: 67.
Single review of a tribute release by the Nashville Nightshift called "Nightshift." The review says it is a Commodores song redone as a tribute to Marty.

The nominees are. . . *Music City News;* 1985 June; 22(12): 40,42,44.
Photos and information about MCN Award nominees. Marty on p. [42].

Oermann, Robert K. 1960: El Paso elevates Marty Robbins to superstardom. *Country Song Roundup;* 1985 June; 37(311): 43.
A historical look at the popularity of "El Paso" when it was released and the importance it played in Marty's career.

Our past winners, 1967–1984. *Music City News;* 1985 June; 22(12): [58–60].
Complete list of previous MCN Awards winners.

Country video [feature]. *Country Rhythms;* 1985 July; (41): 42–43.
Note: Illus.
Review of the movie "Honkytonk Man."

Goldsmith, Thomas. Nice guy Ronny Robbins giving career best shot. *The Tennessean;* 1985 July 28.
Interview and career review.

Marty Robbins; alive for all time. *Country Song Roundup Yearbook;* 1985 Summer: 14–17.
Note: Cover photo. Illus.
Extensive quotes from Marizona and industry friends, Minnie Pearl and Hal Durham.

Neese, Sandy. Ronny Robbins. *Country Rhythms;* 1985 July; (41): 52–55.
Note: Illus.
Interview and career review. Photos include Ronny, his wife Kathy, and Marizona.

Fan clubs [monthly feature]. *Music City News;* 1985 August; 23(2): 19.
Notes that Marty was presented with the Metronome Award.

Who's gonna fill their shoes. *Tune-in;* 1985 August: 9.
Note: Illus.
A review of George Jones' new video of his new single release, "Who's gonna fill their shoes," a song that covers country music greats (reference to Marty is included in the song and video).

Barber, Joe. Marty Robbins: his memory won't ever die. *West Coast Country Music Reporter;* 1985 September/October: 8–9.
Note: Cover photo. Illus.

Radio featured programming [news column]. *Billboard;* 1985 November 23, 1985: 18.
The Creative Radio Network, of California, has a two-hour special called "Marty Robbins remembered" available for radio play.

Kienzle, Rich. The essential collector [Marty Robbins: the legend continued]. *Country Music;* 1986 January/February; (117): 66–67.
Note: Illus.
Album reviews for the 17-album series of Marty's recordings recently issued by Bear Family Records.

The Marty Robbins story. *Country Music Parade;* 1986 Jan/Feb 3(1): 18–23.
Note: Cover photo, illus.
Long review of Marty's career with a number of photos spanning his life.

[Advertisement]. *Country Music;* 1986 January/February; (117): 20,34.
Note: Illus.
Ads for the albums issued by Bear Family Records.

The 60th Anniversary of the Grand Ole Opry. *TV Guide.* 1986 January
14.
This television special included a brief tribute to Marty and showed a
film clip of him singing "El Paso."

Awards. *Close-up* [Country Music Association]; 1986 January; 20(1):
18.
The Marty Robbins Lifetime Achievement Award (from KRPT radio in
Anadarko, Oklahoma) was presented this year to Loretta Lynn and
Marty Robbins.

DeLaney, Donnie. The stars reflect on Christmas. *Country Song Round-
up;* 1986 February; 37(319): 9–10,12–13,56.
Note: Illus.
A personal story from Marty, as remembered by a friend, is included.

A tribute to country greatness. *TV Guide.* 1986 March 8.
This television special was shown on a number of PBS stations around
the country during March. It was hosted by Glen Campbell and Minnie
Pearl and paid tribute to country music greats. One segment paid tribute
to Marty. Ronny Robbins appeared.

Anderson, Bill. Questions and answers [monthly feature]. *Country
Song Roundup;* 1986 March; 37(320): 10.
A fan asked if any books were available on Marty. She was referred to
Mamie Minotto's book.

Oermann, Robert K. Country acts pay tribute to Robbins. *The Tennessean;* 1986 May 10; 81(54): 1 D.
Note: 1 A: photo with caption, "A tribute to Marty"; p.1D: Details
about the two-hour TV special under production by Multimedia called
"Marty Robbins—Super Legend." The special will be available in late
summer.

Wood, Gerry. Nashville scene [news column]. *Billboard;* 1986 May 31;
98(22).
Information about the two-hour special, "Marty Robbins—Super Legend," and the artists who will be on the show.

[Program listing]. *TV Guide* (Detroit Edition); 1986 May 31; A-32. The program, "Rocky Mountain Inn," featured Ronny Robbins and showed a video of Marty singing "El Paso."

Multimedia produces Marty Robbins special. *Country Music Parade*. 1986 Jul-Sep: 3(4) 22–23.
Article about the making of the television special, "Marty Robbins—Superlegend," with comments and photos from the program.

Pugh, Ronnie. Marty Robbins: a salute to "The Twentieth Century Drifter." *Country Sounds*. 1986 August: 30–32.
Note: Illus.
Article reviews Marty's career and calls him a "Renaissance man" of country music.

Marty Robbins, In the Wild West, part 3. *The Big Reel*. 1986 November: 45.
Album review.

Hillinger, Charles. Nashville museums 2nd only to the music. *The Journal Times* (Racine, WI); 1986 December 28 (Sunday); 1D-2D.
Note: Illus.
An article about the country music museums in Nashville includes mention of Marty's museum.

Marty Robbins: Just me and my guitar. *Country Sounds;* 1987 January: 33.
Review of the album, "Just me and my guitar."

Video reviews [review column]. *Video;* 1987 January: 79.
The magazine reviews two videos about Marty: "Marty Robbins—His Legacy" and "Marty Robbins—For Fans Only."

Video reviews [column]. *Video Review;* 1987 January: 94–95.
The magazine reviews two videos: "His Legacy" and "For Fans Only."

[Video reviews]. *Washington Post;* 1987 February 8 (Sunday TV Section for Feb. 8–14).
Note: Illus.
Reviews of two videos: "Marty Robbins—His legacy" and "Marty Robbins—For Fans Only."

Country music questions [monthly news column]. *Country Music People;* 1987 July: 16.

Most of the page is devoted to a large photo of Marty and a discussion of Marty's hit recordings in England (both singles and albums). It also includes an interesting list of other artists who have had success on the charts in England with songs Marty wrote.

Ralph Emery: Nashville's super host. *The Examiner;* 1987 July 21. Interview. Ralph is quoted, "I'd probably have to say Marty Robbins and Merle Haggard were the best country singers ever, day after day, record after record."

Have a Marty Christmas. *USA Today;* 1987 November 11. A brief news note that announces Marty's new Christmas album and gives the address of Marty Robbins Enterprises for ordering the product.

[Advertisement]. *Music City News;* 1987 November. The ad is for the sale of a videotape of the television special, "Marty Robbins—Superlegend," with additional footage not seen on the TV version.

Kienzle, Rich. Legends of country music: Marty Robbins. *CMSA Newsletter* [Country Music Society of America], published as an insert section of *Country Music* that is available to CMSA members only; 1987 November/December: 38F–38G. Note: Illus. Additional photos on page 38A. A detailed review of Marty's career.

Price, Deborah Evans. A Christmas remembered. *Country Music-USA;* 1987 December: 7(11): 4–5. Note: Cover photo, Illus. Cover photo and inside story about the new Christmas album that has just been released called "A Christmas Remembered." Interview with Ronny includes stories about Marty at Christmas.

Veereman, Luc. Some memories just won't die. *Nashville Tennessee Magazine* [Holland]; 1987 December: 45–47. Note: Illus. Photos by Sandy Daens. The text of the article in Dutch.

[Television show]. The Country Music Association's 30th Anniversary. CBS-TV: 1988 January 23. The show included a brief clip of Marty from a 1970 show.

[Photograph]. *Music City News;* 1988 January :29(7) 52.
Photo of Marty included in a section of pictures from 25 years ago. The
photo is of Marty and Ronny (in uniform) as Ronny is leaving for Army
duty in Germany in 1969.

Marty Robbins: Superlegend. *Video Review:* 1988 February.
Review of the video.

Gates, David. Nashville's shrines: memories, stars and famous guitars.
The Smithsonian; 1988 March: 84–93.
Note: Illustrated.
The article covers the museums, gift shops, and tourist spots devoted to
country music stars. It includes mention of Marty's Showcase; a photo
of Marty from the Wax Museum is also used. One of the fans interviewed recalled Marty's performance at the old Opry House and the fact
that he would go out in the lobby afterwards, with his pot of coffee, and
sign autographs.

Hofer, Betty. Marty Robbins remembered. *Country Song Roundup;*
1988 April: 39(345) 6–11.
Cover photo, Illus.
Long review of Marty's life and career.

Powel, Bob. The Marty Robbins memorial interview. *Country Music
People* [London, England]; 1988 April: 22–26.
Note: Illus.
The article is an interview which was conducted with Marty in Nashville
in early 1982. Marty talks in detail about the first time he ever heard
himself on the radio, his thoughts and fears about the Vietnam war, his
auto racing experiences, and his extreme hay fever and pollen allergies.

Marty Robbins drifts again in home vid series. *Billboard;* 1988 May 14:
41.
A short article announces the release of the 13-episode "The Drifter"
series on video tape. Originally filmed in 1965–66 in black-and-white,
the series episodes are a half-hour in length and were shown in only a
few markets at the time they were made.

Edwards, Joe. Marty Robbins, "fan's favorite," on 60s videotape. *The
News-Times* [Danbury, Ct.]; Friday 1988 July 1; pg. 36.
A long review about "The Drifter" video tape.

Marty Robbins' lost TV series now available on video. *Country Song Roundup;* 1988 September; 39(350); 6–7.
Note: Illus.
The article provides photos and background about Marty's 1965–66 series, "The Drifter." Only 13 episodes were made and these are being made available on video tape.

7

PAT GALVIN TALKS ABOUT MARTY ROBBINS TV SPECIAL

Pat Galvin (scriptwriter for the "Marty Robbins—Super Legend" TV special) and her husband, Billy Galvin, are a husband/wife team who together have written and produced some of the most memorable country music television specials to come out of Nashville. They are programs you have all seen. They write and produce the "MCN Country Awards Show" that is seen by all of us each June. They are also the people who did the Statlers specials and the Conway Twitty special. The MCN Songwriters Awards program was their concept. They work mainly for Jim Owens Productions and Multimedia, the company that produced the "Marty Robbins—Super Legend" program. Billy is a producer as well as a writer. Pat's a friendly, attractive woman with shoulder-length dark curly hair.

I first met her at the Country Music Foundation Library in March of 1986 while I was there doing my own research and she was starting her first day of research on the Marty special. Ronnie Pugh, the Head Reference Librarian, walked her over to the table where I was working and said: "The two of you need to know each other." And he was right. As luck would have it, I had brought along a computer print-out of my research on Marty, and Pat spent most of the next several days going through the information to find what she needed. This, in turn, served as the background for her work in writing the script. Of course, we kept in touch over the next several weeks as work on the special progressed and as more, and different, information was required.

I also recommended several other names to her as resource people.

Pat agreed to be interviewed regarding how the Marty special was created and the steps it took to complete production. The look behind the scenes is indeed an interesting story.

BP: How about giving our readers an idea about how a television special like this is created.

Pat: First, the idea has to originate in someone's mind. And that someone has to be in a position to "sell" the idea to a production company . . . to be able to get the financial backing to get the show made. In this case, you have to secure permission from those in authority (Marty's family), and it's always helpful to have the cooperation of those closest to the personality the show is about. After that comes the financial backing. A show like this will cost $2 or 3 million dollars to produce. Once all of the necessary permissions are secured and the production company has committed the project, then the detailed work starts. And this often moves very quickly.

First, there will be a meeting of all of the people involved . . . the producer, director, writers, etc. They discuss how to present the concept of the show; This is the idea . . . how do we present it? What will the approach be? Who will go on the list of guests? How many do we have time for? Will there be music? An orchestra? Will there be a live audience? Will we use film or tape? How will we find out what's available? All of these things have to be determined, the approach to the show, before you can do any of the other work.

BP: Then what happens?

Pat: Many people contribute to a show. Time schedules for various activities and areas of responsibilities are established each step of the way. The schedules for this production were very tight; we had just a little over three months before post production work.

BP: How were the guests selected?

Pat: It's a combination of who is best suited to be a guest from the viewpoint of the perspective we are trying to present, and who is actually available.

People may wonder why one person or another wasn't on the show. It wasn't because they couldn't contribute, but because of the time factor. Maybe a particular artist we would like to have had as a guest couldn't be available at the time of the taping; or there just wasn't enough time on the show to include more people. In the case of the Marty Robbins Special, there were so many people we could have used!

BP: Once you have the budget approved, the producer, director, and the writer selected, the initial decisions made, how much time do you have to get things done on time?

Pat: When you know who is going to be on the show, what approaches to take, what ideas to develop, then you can proceed with the writing of the script. Then you can do your first real draft.

BP: And then?

Pat: Then there are more meetings with the director. How much time in the show will involve the performances of the guests or of Marty himself? Will locations be used for any part of the show? What historical film or tape might be available and what are we going to try to find and use? By this, I mean who owns the rights to the film and will they let us use it? How much will each rights owner (that we can find) want in terms of money for the right to use it? All of these things will affect the script and how it is written.

BP: Once you have a direction, what do you have to go after?

Pat: With Marty, we were trying to show the different phases of his life. And his personality. We divided the show into different segments that would identify these areas fully. For example, in the racing segment we went after the people who were involved in racing with him. People who had been there and who could come to the studio and talk with our host (John Schneider). And we had actual film footage of Marty racing and some of the events the drivers were talking about. We tried to show how Marty's racing progressed and the important part it played in his life. Once we knew who would appear from the racing society, we could gear the script to what these people might have to say. We could develop the questions to prompt people about the stories they had to tell. We didn't want to write the script to include the actual stories people had to tell, because we wanted them to tell the stories naturally, in their own words. But this part of the script could be written to include questions worded in a way that it would support the guests and lead the conversation in a natural way.

That's just one segment, but each one was developed in the same way. We worked with the people to show Marty as he was at that point.

BP: You have to have permission to use every photo and/or piece of film on the show?

Pat: That's right. For any kind of film or any photograph. There might be a particular piece of film that is very good, but you may not be able to use it. *Any time* you see a show that uses historical film or past performances, this will be the case. You have to get the rights to use every single thing you see on the screen. And there is always an expense involved. The owners have the right to be reimbursed for the use of that material. And sometimes people refuse use or request so much money that it's prohibitive. The cost for the right to use just a two- or three-minute piece of film can range anywhere from "free" to $20,000 or more. And if you can't actually find the person or company who owns the rights to the film, you can't use it. Or, if it costs too much, or the rights owner simply says "No," that film can't be used.

But a writer is not concerned with the financial problems; that's the job of someone else. The writer is the member of the team who has the primary responsibility for the presentation of the subject of the program. But all of these things we've just discussed can influence what can be used on the show, and therefore, how a writer can put together a script.

BP: How do you put together the questions that are used to interview people on the show?

Pat: It goes back to the use of research. To the lists and lists of references you gave me to all of the articles. I didn't have access to the people we were going to interview on the program at that early a stage, so I read all of those articles . . . or as much as I could. Then I put together questions I felt would bring out those comments or stories in a conversational way. We didn't want this to be in an "educational" tone; we wanted it to be entertaining. And we wanted it informal. The questions then went to John Schneider.

BP: How did John feel about hosting the Special?

Pat: John was delighted to have the opportunity to do the special because he was a fan of Marty's. And he shared with him the love of racing. He told us about when he was in California, Marty would come into the shop John had out there then. And that story is in the show. So he was happy to be involved and his affection for Marty shows up, I think, in the show. He was a little apprehensive about the interviewing because his background is as an actor and he hadn't interviewed people before. But after he got a chance to do some of it, he did a marvelous job and relaxed and enjoyed it. His interest really showed and he enhanced the questions with his approach.

BP: Do you work in the post-production phase too?

Pat: No, not usually. My husband and I are a writing team and he's the associate producer for this show. He frequently works in the post-production end. He's produced a number of other shows.

And together, we do the MCN Awards show in June of each year. Of course, we knew Marty because we had worked with him on these shows.

BP: As a script writer, what do you like best about the job?

Pat: I like the behind-the-scenes part of it. The developing of a concept, or a variety of different ideas. When it comes to the actual technical production, I'm happy to turn that part over to the others. The writing of each show is really like doing something new that no one has ever done before.

It's amazing to me the things you turn up when you're doing research, to see the things people have overcome and/or the amount of work people have done in their lives. Or to find a story that really explains the personality of the artist you are researching. It's always satisfying to find a well written story or something that is especially well done.

BP: What is your favorite kind of writing?

Pat: My favorite kind of writing is theme writing and comedy. And doing specials. I've done quite a bit of work with the Statlers. We put together their TV specials. I enjoy working with them; they have a quick wit and good delivery. We also did the Conway Twitty special and I had a chance to go on location for that one because of the use of the riverboats. I like to go on location when I get the chance.

BP: And now you're getting into writing and producing videos?

Pat: Yes. That's a new avenue. It comes back to theme writing. What is the idea? What are you talking about? Who is the performer and what is his personality? The producer of the video usually has an idea of what he wants, and often the artist will too. But the artist is often on the road and doesn't get involved in the early stages of the development of the video concept. Usually, it's up to the producer and the writer to develop the idea.

BP: Did you feel you learned anything new about Marty from doing the Special?

Pat: Yes! Lots! Of course, we had worked with Marty on the MCN shows, but doing the Special added so much depth! A lot about his racing was new to me. You could see parts of his life developing. I came away with a sense of continuity I didn't have before.

BP: What do you hope the viewers got from the program?

Pat: What we tried to do was give the viewer a feeling for what he was really like. We wanted to reach people who may not have been knowledgeable about his life, and show them why he was such a special person and why he was so successful. The "fan" thing was so special with him; that was one of the ideas we tried to present. We've already discussed some of the others. We wanted to present the total picture of the man.

BP: What do you think would have been his favorite part of the show?

Pat: Oh! The racing part, no doubt about that! He would have been interested in hearing what the drivers had to say about him.

8

BOOKS, TELEVISION, AND OTHER MEDIA

BOOKS

Byworth, Tony. *The History of Country & Western Music*. New York: Exeter Books, 1984. 224 pp., illus.

The Encyclopedia of Folk, Country & Western Music. New York: St. Martin's Press, undated [circa 1984]. 902 p.

Hemphill, Paul. *The Nashville Sound; bright lights and country music*. New York: Simon & Schuster, 1970. Also available from Pocket Books, 1971. xi, 209 p.

The Illustrated Encyclopedia of Country Music. New York: Harmony Books, 1977. 256 pp. Originally published in England.
A review of Marty's career primarily from a British viewpoint and a brief discography listing his British releases.

The Johnny Cash Discography, compiled by John L. Smith. With Forewords by Johnny Cash and Johnny Western. Westport, CT.: Greenwood Press, 1985. 203 pp.
Contains information about Johnny's television show, including Marty's appearances on the series.

Linedecker, Cliff. *Country Music Stars and the Supernatural*. New York: Dell, 1979. 317 pp.
The book includes comments about "El Paso City," a song Marty wrote in which reincarnation plays a central part. It also includes comments from Marty about songwriting as well as a couple of his personal experiences.

Marty Robbins. New York: Hill and Range Songs, 1970. 63 pp., illus. [Currently out of print.]
A songbook containing 27 songs written by Marty.

Marty Robbins Discography. Nashville: Marty Robbins Enterprises, 1982. unpaged.
A complete listings of Marty's recordings through 1981. It also includes a listing of the recordings of Ronny Robbins.

Marty Robbins Discography; volume 2. Nashville: Marty Robbins Enterprises, 1983. 100 pp.
Updates the previous publication and expands the scope of information to include additional material about Marty: awards he received, a racing history, and a list of television and film work.

The Marty Robbins Songbook. Milwaukee, WI.: Hal Leonard Publishing Corporation, undated [circa 1983]. 48 pp.
Sixteen songs written and/or recorded by Marty.

The New Grove Dictionary of American Music, edited by Hitchcock, H. Wiley, and Stanley Sadie. 4 volumes. New York: Grove's Dictionaries 1986. 2700 pp.

Osborne, Jerry. *Country Music Buyers-Sellers Reference Book & Buyers Guide*. Tempe, AZ: Osborne Enterprises, 1985. 320 pp.
Discographies and prices of country performers, including Marty. Recordings listed in alphabetical order with recording information, date of release, and estimated dollar value to collectors.

Robbins, Marty. *The Small Man*. Nashville: Marty Robbins Enterprises, 1966. 108 pp., paperback.
A western novel written by Marty. Still in print and available from publisher.

Robinson-Minotto, Mamie. *Marty Robbins Photographic Journal*. 1985. 30 pp., illus. Available through Robinson's Books, P.O. Box 1901, Glendale, AZ 85311.

Shestack, Melvin. *The Country Music Encyclopedia*. New York: Thomas Y. Crowell, 1974. xii, 410 p.
Long article, with photos. Quotes from other articles and covers Marty's racing as well as his entertainment activities.

Stambler, Irwin. *Encyclopedia of Pop, Rock, and Soul*. New York: St. Martin's Press, 1974. 609 p.

Yeatman, Ted T. and Eng, Steve. *The Tennessee Wild West*. Nashville: Rutledge Hill Press, 1988.

The book contains information about Marty's western songs, films, and television series.

TELEVISION SERIES

Marty made several television series over the years, beginning with the two he had in Phoenix when he was first starting out. Regretfully, no tapes of these earliest programs exist. Once he moved to Nashville, he appeared frequently in the mid-1950s as a guest or host of a show that is currently being telecast around the country under the title, "Classic Country." Then, in 1965, he made thirteen episodes of "The Drifter," and most of these are now available on video tape. Marty followed that in 1969 with 39 episodes of "The Marty Robbins Show." His last series, made in 1978 and 1979, became his most popular one, "Marty Robbins' Spotlight." It is still being shown in some parts of the country. Listed below are Marty's credits on two of these programs. My thanks to Multimedia Entertainment in Nashville for supplying the information about "Marty Robbins' Spotlight."

"CLASSIC COUNTRY" PROGRAMS

The "Classic Country" programs were originally shown on television in the mid-1950s as half-hour, black/white episodes under the title, "Stars of the Grand Ole Opry." It was later shown under several titles, including "Country Caravan." The producer of the program had a great deal of foresight, however, and all of the episodes were actually filmed in color. They are marketed today throughout the United States as "Classic Country" and are usually shown in hour-long episodes that combine two of the half-hour programs. Marty was a frequent guest on the program and sometimes the host. Because the series contains film of Marty singing so many of his earliest hit recordings, I've decided to list his appearances on the program. Also on several programs was Okie Jones, who later gave up his singing career and spent many years as Marty's tour bus driver. Researchers looking for film of early country music stars might want to contact the Country Music Foundation Library because a nearly-complete set of the film from this series has been donated to its collection.

The episodes on which Marty appeared are listed by host, along with other guests.

Jimmy Dickens, host. Guests: Marty Robbins, Simon Crum (Ferlin Huskey), Bill Monroe, Old Hickory Quartet, Rod Brassfield, Minnie Pearl, and Cowboy Copus. Marty sang "Time goes by."

Jimmy Dickens, host. Guests: Marty Robbins, Ray Price, June Carter, Okie Jones, Rod Brassfield, and Lonzo & Oscar. Marty sang "I couldn't keep from crying."

Ernest Tubb, host. Guests: Marty Robbins, Grandpa Jones, The Jordanaires, Jean Shepard, Chet Atkins. Marty sang "Call me up and I'll come calling on you," and "Pretty words."

Marty Robbins, host. Guests: Ernest Tubb, The Duke of Paducah, Kitty Wells, and Johnny & Jack. Marty sang "Time goes by," "At the end of a long, lonely day," and the closing song with the cast, "She'll be coming around the mountain."

Marty Robbins, host. Guests: Webb Pierce, Johnny & Jack, Ernest Tubb, The Duke of Paducah, and Kitty Wells. Marty sang "Pretty Mama" and "At the end of a long, lonely day."

Ernest Tubb, host. Guests: Marty Robbins, Cousin Jody, Grandpa Jones, Rita Faye. Marty sang "Tennessee Toddy" and "Don't let me hang around."

Jim Reeves, host. Guests: Marty Robbins, Cousin Jodie & Odie, and Goldie Hill. Marty sang "Mr. Teardrop," and "Half way chance with you."

Jim Reeves, host. Guests: Marty Robbins, Grandpa Jones, Rita Faye, The Duke of Paducah. Marty sang "I'll go on alone," and "That's alright, Mama."

Carl Smith, host. Guests: Marty Robbins, Minnie Pearl, Del Wood, Goldie Hill. Marty sang: "Pretty words," and "Maybellene."

Faron Young, host. Guests: Marty Robbins, Carl Smith, Goldie Hill, Rod Brassfield, Minnie Pearl, Sam & Kirk McGee, and June Carter. Marty sang "Gossip."

Faron Young, host. Guests: Marty Robbins, Minnie Pearl, Jimmy Dickens, and Rod Brassfield. Marty sang "I couldn't keep from crying" and That's alright, Mama."

Ray Price, host. Guests: Marty Robbins, Goldie Hill, Rod Brassfield, Carl Smith, and Van Howard (with Ray Price). Marty sang "Maybellene."

Marty Robbins, host. Guests: June Carter, Lonzo & Oscar, and Webb Pierce. Marty sang "Singing the blues" and "Time goes by."

Webb Pierce, host. Guests: Marty Robbins, June Carter, and Lonzo & Oscar. Marty sang "I'll go one alone" and "Half way chance with you."

Ray Price, host. Guests: Marty Robbins, June Carter, Arty Inman, and Grandpa Jones. Marty sang "Pretty words" and "Don't let me hang around."

Marty Robbins, host. Guests: Ernest Tubb, Rita Faye, Carl Smith, June Carter, and Lonzo & Oscar. Marty sang "I can't quit, I've gone too far," and "Castle in the sky."

Marty Robbins, host. Guests: Jimmy Dickens, Carter Family, June Carter, and Gordon Terry. Marty sang "Tennessee Toddy" and "I pay with every breath."

Carl Smith, host. Guests: Marty Robbins, June Carter, Chet Atkins, and The Carter Family. Marty sang "I couldn't keep from crying" and "Sugaree."

Webb Pierce, host. Guests: Marty Robbins, June Carter, Carl Smith, Ray Price, The Jordanaires, and Goldie Hill. Marty sang "Lucky, lucky someone else." Marty, Webb, and Carl sang "Why, baby, why" together.

Marty Robbins, host. Cast: Carl Smith, June Carter, Webb Pierce, and Goldie Hill. Marty sang: "Call me up and I'll come calling on you" and "You don't owe me a thing."

Marty Robbins, host. Guests: Jimmy Dickens, The Carter Family, Lonzo & Oscar, and Webb Pierce. Marty sang "Tennessee Toddy" and "Time goes by.

MARTY ROBBINS' SPOTLIGHT

SHOWS TAPED IN 1977 (Show Number/Guests)

101.   Brenda Lee (Steve Allen, Mel Tillis, Sonny James).

SONGS

Marty	Big Boss Man
Brenda	I'm Sorry
Marty & Brenda	Dynamite
Brenda	Sweet Nothings/ Too Many Rivers/ All Alone Am I/ Jambalaya
Marty	Don't Worry
Brenda	One Step at a Time
(Group)	My Window Faces the South

102.   Hank Williams, Jr. (Merle Kilgore, Billy Walker).

SONGS

Marty	I Washed My Hands in Muddy Water
Hank Jr.	All By Myself
Marty	Adios Amigo
Marty & Hank	My Woman, My Woman, My Wife/ Call Me/ Devil Woman/ Living Proof
Hank Jr.	Mansion on the Hill/ Hey Good Looking/ I Can't Help It/ Jambalaya
Billy Walker	Word Games
Merle Kilgore	Wolverton Mountain

103.   Ruth Buzzi (Henry Gibson, JoAnn Worley, Roger Bowling).

SONGS

Marty	Singing the Blues
Marty & Ruth	My Happiness/ Mockingbird Hill/ I Don't Know Why/ Biding My Time

Ruth	You Oughta Hear the Song
Marty	White Sport Coat
Ruth	'57 Chevrolet
Marty & Ruth	Rocky Top/ House of Bryant

104. Dottie West (Chet Atkins, Jeannie Seely).

SONGS

Marty	My Blue Heaven
Dottie	Country Sunshine
Marty & Dottie	Would You Hold It Against Me/ Here Comes My Baby/ El Paso/ Love Is Blue/ Last Time I Saw Him
Dottie	Every Word I Write
Marty	You Gave Me a Mountain
Jeannie	Don't Touch Me
(Group)	Walkin' in the Sunshine

105. Ray Stevens.

SONGS

Marty	Good Hearted Woman
Ray	Feel the Music
Marty & Ray	Raindrops Keep Falling on My Head/ Pretend/ I Write the Songs/ Release Me/ Tell Me What I say
Marty	Falling Out of Love
Ray	Honky Tonk/ Misty
Marty & Ray	Everything is Beautiful/ El Paso/ Goodbye

106. Tom T. Hall (Jeannie C. Riley, Bobby Bare).

SONGS

Marty	Country Is
Tom T.	Old Dogs, Children, and Watermelon Wine
Marty & Tom T.	Ravishing Ruby/ Begging to You/ Ballad of Forty Dollars/ White Sport Coat/ Shoe Shine Man
Marty	Eighteen Yellow Roses
Tom T.	I Love/ Sneaky Snake
Tom & Jeannie	Harper Valley PTA
(Group)	Travel On

107.   Carol Channing (Hank Locklin, Jimmy C. Newman).

SONGS

Marty	Don't Worry
Marty & Carol	Hello Dolly/ Little Girl from Little Rock/ Hey Good Looking/ Help Me Make It Through the Night/ Doggone, How I Love Them Old Songs
Carol	One's on the Way
Carol & Hank	Everywhere We Go
Marty	Inspiration for a Song
Marty & Carol	You Are My Sunshine
(Group)	Cotton Fields

108.   Johnny Rodriguez (Bobby Bare, Tom T. Hall).

SONGS

Marty	Ribbon of Darkness
Johnny	Pass Me By
Marty & Johnny	Ridin' My Thumb to Mexico/ Yours/ Hillbilly Heart/ The Hanging Tree/ Desperado
Marty	Tree in the Meadow
Johnny	La Paloma/ If Practice Makes Perfect
(Group)	Take Me Back to Tulsa

109.   Jim Ed Brown (Helen Cornelious, Bob Ferguson, Maxine Brown).

SONGS

Marty	Deep Water
Jim Ed & Helen	Born Believers
Marty	Maria Elena
Marty/Jim/Helen	What'll I Do/ Pop-a-Top/ How's the World Treating You/ I Don't Want to Have to Marry You/ I Don't Know Why
Jim/Maxine/Helen	Morning
(Group)	Tumbling Tumbleweeds
Jim Ed/ Helen	If It Ain't Love By Now
(Group)	I Believe in Music

110.   Jack Green (Jeannie Seely, Ernest Tubb).

SONGS

Marty	There's a Big Rock in the Road
Jack/Jeannie	I Wish I Didn't Have to Miss You
Marty/Jack/Jeannie	Don't Touch Me/ White Sport Coat/ Statue of a Fool/ It Just Doesn't Seem to Matter/ Don't Worry/ Can I Sleep in Your Arms Tonight/ I'm Not a Good Woman's Man
Marty	No Letter Today
Jack	There Goes My Everything
Jeannie	We're Still Hangin' in there, Ain't We Jessie
(Group)	San Antonio Rose

111.   Barbara Mandrell (Irby Mandrell, Joe Maphis).

SONGS

Marty	If You Got The Money, I've Got the Time
Barbara	Midnight Oil
Marty/Barbara	Standing Room Only/ Ribbon of Darkness/ Midnight Angel/ Love Me
Marty	Born to Lose
Barbara	Married, But Not to Each Other
Marty/Barbara	Columbus Stockade Blues

112.   George Jones, Faron Young

SONGS

Marty	Heartaches by the Number
George	The Race Is On
Marty & George	White Lightening/ Don't Take Your Love to Town/ The Door/ I Walk Alone/ The Grand Tour/ It's A Sin
Marty	Anytime
George	If I Could Put Them All Together I'd Have You
Marty/George/Faron	Tender Years/ Wabash Cannonball

113.   Donna Fargo (Tommy Overstreet, Jim Fogelsong).

SONGS

Marty	Lovesick Blues
Donna	Happiest Girl in the Whole USA
Marty & Donna	You Can't Be a Beacon/ Make the World Go Away/ Superman/ Just Married/ Mockingbird Hill/ Funny Face
Marty	I Can't Stop Loving You
Donna	That Was Yesterday
(Group)	Do Lord

114.   Mickey Gilley (Eddie Kilroy, Carl Smith).

SONGS

Marty	Blue, Blue Day
Mickey	Room Full of Roses
Marty & Mickey	The Girls Get Prettier at Closing Time/ Helen/ Bring It On Home/ Tonight Carmen/ Lawdy Miss Clawdy/ She's Pulling Me Back Again/ I Can't Help It
Marty	The Story of My Life
Mickey	Honky Tonk Memories
(Group)	Roly Poly

115.   Billy "Crash" Craddock (Mickey Gilley, Dale Morrie).

SONGS

Marty	Oh Lonesome Me
Crash	Easy as Pie
Marty & Crash	Broken Down in Tiny Pieces/ Crazy Arms/ Knock Three Times/ Walking Piece of Heaven/ Ruby Baby/ Sunshine on My Shoulders/ Rub It In
Marty	Harbor Lights
Crash	A Tear Fell
Marty & Crash	Country Roads

116.   Larry Gatlin (Dottie West, Johnny Rodriguez).

SONGS

Marty	Honeycomb
Larry	Broken Lady
Marty & Larry	Practice Makes Perfect/ Just a Little Loving/ The Heart/ I Walk the Line/ Penny Annie/ Blueberry Hill/ Statues Without Hearts
Marty	How's The World Treating You
Larry	I Don't Want to Cry
(Group)	Abilene

117.   Johnny Paycheck (Larry Gatlin, Billy "Crash" Craddock).

SONGS

Marty	That's All Right Mama
Johnny	She's All I Got
Marty & Johnny	Someone to Give My Love to/ Mr. Lovemaker/ My Shoes Keep Walkin' Back to You/ I Love You Because/ Song and Dance Man/ Folsom Prison Blues/ Slide off Your Satin Sheets
Marty	Chained to a Memory
Johnny	I'm the Only Hell My Mama Ever Raised
(Group)	Let's All Go Down to the River

118.   Bill Anderson (Mary Lou Turner, Bill Goodwin).

SONGS

Marty	Talk Back Tremblin' Lips
Bill	Still
Marty & Bill	City Lights/ Bouquet of Roses/ Po Folks/ Wild Weekend/ Take These Chains from My Heart/ Beyond the Reef/ Liars One, Believers Zero
Marty	Almost
Bill	Head to Toe
Marty & Bill	Roly Poly

119.   Ray Price (Daryl McCall, Bill Anderson).

SONGS

Marty	Singing the Blues
Ray	For the Good Times
Marty & Ray	Crazy Arms/ You Gave Me a Mountain/ Heartaches by the Number/ Solamente Una Vez (You Belong to My Heart)/ Help Me Make It Through the Night/
Marty	You'll Never Walk Alone
Ray	Born to Love Me
Marty & Ray	Release Me

120.   Bobby Bare (Harland Howard, Chet Atkins).

SONGS

Marty	I've Got a Tiger by the Tail
Bobby	Detroit City
Marty & Bobby	Shame on Me/ Cry/ The Streets of Baltimore/ Candy Kisses/ Four Strong Winds/ Your Cheatin' Heart/ Five Hundred Miles from Home
Marty	Makin' Believe
Bobby	Marie Laveau
Marty & Bobby	Ride Me Down Easy

121.   Bob Luman (Bobby Bare, Norell Wilson).

SONGS

Marty	When My Blue Moon Turns to Gold
Bob	Let's Think About Living
Marty & Bob	Lonely Women Make Good Lovers/ To Each His Own/ Satisfied Mind/ Worried Mind/ Still Loving You/ Down Where the Trade Winds Play/ Don't Worry
Marty	Half As Much
Bob	I'm A Honky Tonk Woman's Man
Marty/Bob	Hey Good Looking

122. Don Gibson (Wesley Rose).

SONGS

Marty	It Keeps Right on a Hurtin'
Don	I Can't Stop Loving You
Marty & Don	Who Cares/ Blue, Blue Day/ Lonesome Number One/ Just One Time/ Don't Tell Me Your Troubles/ Sweet Dreams/ I'll Be a Legend in My Time
Marty	Green, Green Grass of Home
Don	If You Ever Get to Houston
Marty & Don	Oh Lonesome Me

123. Billie Jo Spears (Ralph Emery, Bobby Borchers)

SONGS

Marty	I Get the Blues When It Rains
Billie Jo	Blanket on the Ground
Marty/Billie Jo	Misty Blue/ I Walk Alone/ What I've Got in Mind/ Penny for Your Thoughts/ If You Want Me/ Someday/ I'm Not Easy
Marty	Roses (I Send You Roses)
Billie Jo	Too Much Is Not Enough
Marty/Billy Jo	Hey Good Looking

124. Rex Allen, Sr. (Rex Allen, Jr.).

SONGS

Marty	El Paso
Rex	Streets of Laredo
Marty/Rex Sr. & Rex Jr.	Along the Navajo Trail/ Big Iron/ Little Joe the Wrangler/ Kin to the Wind/ Teardrops in My Heart/ Tumblin' Tumbleweeds
Marty	Bend in the River
Rex Jr.	Can You Hear Those Pioneers
(Group)	Cool Water

SHOWS TAPED IN 1978

201.   Roy Acuff (Bashful Brother Oswald, Bud Wendell, Minnie Pearl).

SONGS

Marty	If You've Got the Money
Roy	Wabash Cannonball
Marty & Roy	Blue Eyes Crying in The Rain/ I'll Hold You in My Heart/ No One Will Ever Know/ Each Minute Seems a Million Years/ Waltz of the Wind
Marty	Yesterday's Roses
Roy	Great Speckled Bird
(Band)	Bud's Bounce

202.   Stella Parton (Even Stevens, Jim Malloy).

SONGS

Marty	Who's Sorry Now
Stella	Standard Lie Number One
Marty & Stella	The Danger of a Stranger/ I'm Not That Good at Goodbye/ Jealous/ This Cold War With You/ I'm in the Mood for Love/ I Want to Hold You In My Dreams Tonight/ Charlie's Baby
Marty	Makin' Believe
Stella	Four Little Letters
Marty & Stella	Sugarfoot Rag

203.   Faron Young (Roy Acuff, Merle Kilgore).

SONGS

Marty	Dear Hearts and Gentle People
Faron	Hello Walls
Marty & Faron	I Miss You Already and You're Not Even Gone/ Tears on My Pillow/ Four in the Morning/ Let Me Go Lover/ This Little Girl of Mine/ Makes No Difference Now/ Alone With You
Marty	You'll Never Know
Faron	Wine Me Up
(Band)	High Voltage

204. Billy Walker (Faron Young, Ray Pennington).

SONGS

Marty	Okie From Muskogee
Billy	Funny How Time Slips Away
Marty & Billy	Things/ Trail Dreaming/ I'd Climb The Highest Mountain/ Word Games/ Cross the Brazos of Waco
Marty	The Way I Loved Her Best
Billy	Charlie's Shoes
(Band)	Short Circuit

205. David Houston (Barbara Mandrell, Glen Sutton).

SONGS

Marty	That's All Right Mama
David	Almost Persuaded
Marty & David	I Do My Swingin' At Home/ Many Tears Ago/ Together Again/ Living in a House Full of Love/ You Mean the World to Me/ Bouquet of Roses/ It's Started All Over Again
Marty	It's No Sin
David	No Tell Motel
(Band)	Remington Ride

206. Don Williams (Charlie Pride, Jim Halsey).

SONGS

Marty	Night Train to Memphis
Don	You're My Best Friend
Marty & Don	Amanda/ Live and Let Live/ Some Broken Hearts Never Mend/ I Wonder Who's Kissing Her Now/ The Shelter of Your Eyes/ You Know How Talk Gets Around
Marty	To Get to You
Don	I've Got a Winner in You

207. Sammi Smith (Bob Luman, Harland Howard).

SONGS

Marty	For Me and My Gal
Sammi	Help Me Make It Through the Night
Marty & Sami	All I Ever Need Is You/ For the Good Times/ Foggy River/ I Ain't Got the Time to Rock No Babies/ You Are So Beautiful/ Too Young/ They'll Never Take His Love from Me
Marty	To Each His Own
Sammi	It Just Won't Feel Like Cheatin' with You
(Band)	Help Me Make It Through the Night

208. Hank Snow (Ernest Tubb, Joe Talbot).

SONGS

Marty	Ruby Ann
Hank	I'm Movin' On
Marty & Hank	I Don't Hurt Anymore/ Waitin' for a Train/ Love Me/ Guess I've Been Asleep All These Years/ Blue Moon of Kentucky/ A Fool Such As I/ A Faded Petal from a Beautiful Bouquet
Marty	To Think You've Chosen Me to Be Your Own
Hank	I've Done At Least One Thing That Was Good in My Life
(Band)	I'm Movin' On

209. Porter Wagoner (Bill Graham, Speck Rhodes).

SONGS

Marty	Wabash Cannonball
Porter	Carroll County Accident
Marty & Porter	Old Slew Foot/ I'll Step Aside/ Highway Headin' South/ Born to Lose/ Tennessee Saturday Night/ Someday/ I've Enjoyed As Much of This As I Can Stand
Marty	Today I Started Loving You Again
Porter	Big Wind
(Band)	Tennessee Saturday

210.   Chet Atkins (June Carter Cash, Ray Stevens).

SONGS

Marty	Truck Drivin' Man
Chet	Stars and Stripes Forever
Marty & Chet	Windy and Warm/ I Feel Another Heartbreak Comin' On/ This String/ Take These Chains from My Heart/ Tiger Rag
Marty	Roses
Chet & Ray	Frog Kissin'
(Band)	Wildwood Flower

211.   Eddie Rabbit (Bill Anderson, Ralph Emery).

SONGS

Marty	Six Days on the Road
Eddie	Rocky Mountain Music
Marty & Eddie	Two Dollars in a Juke Box/ No Letter Today/ Pure Love/ Hearts on Fire/ I Can't Begin to Tell You/ Crazy/ Drinkin' My Baby Off My Mind
Marty	Foggy, Foggy Dew
Eddie	You Don't Love Me Anymore
(Band)	Orange Blossom Special

212.   Jimmie Dean (Mike Douglas, Alex Houston).

SONGS

Marty	Honky Tonk Man
Jimmy	Big Bad John
Marty & Jimmy	I Know What It Means to Be Lonely/ Blues in My Heart/ The First Thing Every Morning/ Make the World Go Away/ Glad Rags/ How's the World Treating You
Jimmy	To a Sleeping Beauty
(Band)	Rocky Top

213. Freddy Fender (Jim Ed Brown, Huey Meaux).

SONGS

Marty	I Can't Quit
Freddie	Before the Next Teardrop Falls
Marty & Freddie	Wasted Days and Wasted Nights/ Many Tears Ago/ Lookin' for a Fool/ A Petal for a Faded Rose/ Secret Love/ The Hands You're Holding Now/ I Love My Rancho Grande
Marty	You Win the Bride
Freddie	Talk to Me
(Band)	Columbus Stockade Blues

214. Carl Perkins (Porter Wagoner, Harold Reid).

SONGS

Marty	Long Gone Lonesome Blues
Carl	Blue Suede Shoes
Marty & Carl	Match Box Blues/ Is There Anything Left I Can Say?/ Honey Don't/ Help Me Make It Through the Night/ Turn Around/ You Know How Talk Gets Around/ Country Boy's Dream
Marty	This Love of Mine
Carl	Good Night Irene
(Band)	Blue Suede Shoes

215. Charlie Daniels (Joe Sullivan).

SONGS

Marty	Mountain Dew
Charlie	The South's Gonna Do It Again
Marty & Charlie	Long Haired Country Boy/ Maria Teresa/ Caballo Diablo/ You're an Angel Disguised as a Girl/ She Thinks I Still Care
Marty	If I Want To
Charlie	Orange Blossom Special
(Band)	The South's Gonna Do It Again

216.   Statler Brothers (Carl Perkins, Mel Tillis).

SONGS

Marty	I'm Back in the Saddle Again
Statlers	I'll Go to My Grave Loving You
Marty & Statlers	Flowers on the Wall/ I'll Go on Alone/ Class of '57/ It Keeps Right on a Hurtin'/ Don't Let Me Touch You/ Whatever Happened to Randolph Scott/ Do You Remember These
Marty	I'm Wanting to
Statlers	Do You Know You Are My Sunshine?
Marty & Statlers	No One Will Ever Know
(Band)	San Antonio Rose

217.   Mel Tillis (Minnie Pearl, Maggie Ward).

SONGS

Marty	Folsom Prison Blues
Mel	Ain't No California
Marty & Mel	Ruby Don't Take Your Love to Town/ After the Storm/ Detroit City/ There's No More You and Me/ Good Woman Blues
Marty	Life
Mel	I Believe in You
(Band)	Tom Cattin'

218.   Barbara Fairchild (Jerry Crutchfield, Connie Smith).

SONGS

Marty	South of the Border
Barbara	Teddy Bear Song
Marty & Barbara	Under Your Spell Again/ Worried Mind/ Kid's Stuff/ Just out of Reach/ Oh Lonesome Me/ Among My Souvenirs/ Standing in Your Line
Marty	Holding on to You
Barbara	I'll Meet You on the Other Side of the Morning
(Band)	Hey Good Looking

219.   Boots Randolph (Chet Atkins, Floyd Cramer).

SONGS

Marty	Singing the Blues
Boots	Yakety Sax
Marty & Boots	Big Daddy/ Farther and Farther Apart/ Honky Tonk/ My Best to You/ Southern Nights/ Old Joe Clark/ Send Me the Pillow That You Dream On
Marty	I'm So Afraid of Losing You
(Band)	Foggy Mountain Breakdown

220.   Ernest Tubb (Carl Smith, Jack Greene).

SONGS

Marty	Don't Be Ashamed of Your Age
Ernest	Walkin' the Floor Over You
Marty & Ernest	You Nearly Lose Your Mind/ Tomorrow Never Comes/ I'll Always Be Glad to Take You Back/ Let's Say Goodbye Like We Said Hello/ Try Me One More Time/ When the World Turns You Down/ I Wonder Why You Said Goodbye
Marty	Make the World Go Away
Ernest	Waltz Across Texas
(Group)	Thanks a Lot

221.   Connie Smith (Bill Anderson, Jeannie C. Riley).

SONGS

Marty	Margie
Connie	Lovin' You Baby
Marty & Connie	Ribbon Of Darkness/ Girl of My Dreams/ Then and Only Then/ Thinkin' Tonight of My Blue Eyes/ Just for What I Am/ Almost/ Once a Day
Marty	Lonely Street
Connie	You've Got Me Right Where You Want Me
(Band)	Mountain Dew

222. Jerry Reed (Ray Stevens, Jerry Clower).

SONGS

Marty	Blue Moon of Kentucky
Jerry	East Bound and Down
Marty & Jerry	When My Blue Moon Turns to Gold Again/ I'm Ragged But I'm Loud/ Take These Chains from My Heart/ Uncle Pen/ Wedding Bells/ Please Don't Let Me Love You
Marty	It's Crying Time Again
Jerry	Stars and Stripes Forever
(Band)	Old Joe Clark

223. The Kendalls (Barbara Mandrell, Jay Diamond).

SONGS

Marty	Break My Mind
Kendalls	Heaven's Just a Sin Away
Marty & Kendalls	Leavin' on a Jet Plane/ Crystal Chandeliers/ Don't Let Me Cross Over/ Kiss Me Once, Kiss Me Twice/ Don't Feel Like Sinning to Me/ Makes No Difference/ Old Fashioned Love
Marty	Am I That Easy to Forget
Kendalls	Sweet Desire
(Band)	They Say Country Music's Gone to Town

224. Marty's Western Show (Jeanne Pruett, Ronny Robbins, Don Winters, Bobby Sykes).

SONGS

Marty	Strawberry Roan
Ronny	White Sport Coat
Marty	Pay Day
Marty	Home on the Range
Marty	El Paso City
Marty & Jeanne	Love Me
Marty/Trio	El Paso

Films by Marty Robbins

Atoka (unreleased at this time; made in 1979). It was made in Oklahoma and had a concert setting with a number of country stars.

The Badge of Marshal Brennan. 1957; 74 minutes, b/w. Produced and directed by Albert C. Gannaway, written by Thomas G. Hubbard. Cast: Jim Davis, Arleen Whelan, Lee Van Cleef, Carl Smith, Marty Robbins, and others.
A western in which Marty plays a Mexican outlaw and Carl Smith is a sheriff.

Ballad of a Gunfighter. August, 1963; 84 minutes, color. A Bill Ward Production (produced, directed, and written by Bill Ward). Distributed by Parade Pictures. Cast: Marty Robbins, Joyce Reed, Bob Barron, Traveler (a white horse), and others. "San Angelo," written and sung by Marty Robbins. "El Paso," written by Marty Robbins (not sung in the film).
A western film loosely based on Marty's song, "El Paso."

Buffalo Gun. Made in 1958 [Released May,1961], 72 min., b/w. Produced and written by A. R. Milton, directed by Albert C. Gannaway for A. R. Milton-Gannaway Productions. Distributed by Globe Pictures. Cast: Marty Robbins, Webb Pierce, Carl Smith, Wayne Morris, Mary Ellen Kay, Don "Red" Barry, Douglas Fowley, and The Jordanaires. Marty sings "The Same Two Lips," and "Clementine." Webb Pierce, Carl Smith, and The Jordanaires also sing.
A western in which Marty, Webb, and Carl play lawmen fighting outlaws who have stolen shipments of supplies destined for the Indians.

Country hits. 1976, Super 8mm, Columbia Pictures (possibly a 10-minute "short"). Has songs performed by Marty, Faron Young, Ernest Tubb, and Webb Pierce. (Source of information: OCLC record: 6652146.)

Country Music. September, 1972; 93 minutes, color. Universal Pictures. Produced and directed by Robert Hinkle. Cast: Marty Robbins, Sammy Jackson; with appearances by Barbara Mandrell, Dottie West, Don Winters, Bobby Sykes, Ralph Emery, Carl Smith, Bobby Allison, Richard Petty, Ronny Robbins, and others.
The film follows Marty through several weeks of performances and visits on his tour schedule. It also includes some auto racing scenes and ends with one of Marty's performances on the stage of the Grand Ole Opry.

Country Music Caravan. (The film was also shown under the title, *Country Music Carnival.*) September,1964; 83 minutes, color. Colorama Roadshows. Cast: Marty Robbins, Jim Reeves, Ray Price, Minnie Pearl, Ernest Tubb, Faron Young, others.
Musical review movie with country stars singing their hits.

From Nashville with Music. July, 1969; 87 minutes, color. John C. Bradford Productions; distributed by Craddock Films. Produced and directed by Eddie Crandall and Robert Patrick. Cast: Marty Robbins, Leo G. Carroll, Marilyn Maxwell; with appearances by Merle Haggard, Buck Owens, Charlie Pride, Tammy Wynette, George Jones, and others. Marty sings, "Tonight, Carmen," "The Shoe Goes on the Other Foot Tonight," and "Singing the Blues."
Comedy with music, set in Nashville and the Grand Ole Opry.

Guns of a Stranger. 1973; 91 minutes, color. Universal Pictures. Produced and directed by Robert Hinkle, written by Charles W. Aldridge. Cast: Marty Robbins, Chill Wills, Dovie Beams, Charlie Aldridge, Ronny Robbins, and Melody Hinkle.
A singing cowboy picture. Music written and sung by Marty Robbins. He plays a drifter named Mathew Roberts who helps save the ranch of father and daughter from takeover by a town businessman.

Hell on Wheels. 1967; 97 minutes, color. Crown-International. Produced by Robert Patrick, directed by Will Zens, written by Wesley Cox. Cast: Marty Robbins, John Ashley, and others. Two songs, "Fly, Butterfly, Fly," and "No Tears, Milady" were written and sung by Marty. The story revolves around two auto racing brothers and their problems with moonshiners.

Honkytonk Man. December,1982; 122 minutes, color. Warner Brothers. Cast: Clint Eastwood and others.
Marty makes a special appearance near the end of the film as Smokey, a recording session singer who finishes recording the title song when Eastwood's character collapses in the middle of the session. Marty's recording of the title song, "Honkytonk Man," was the version released in conjunction with the film. It was Marty's last movie appearance.

The Nashville Story. 1960s (?), Donald A. Davis Productions

Raiders of Old California. 1957; 72 minutes, b/w. Distributed by Republic Pictures. Produced and directed by Albert C. Gannaway, written by Sam Roeca and Thomas C. Hubbard. Cast: Jim Davis, Arleen Whelan, Faron Young, Marty Robbins, Lee Van Cleef, and others.

Much of the same cast (and some of the same film) as in *The Badge of Marshal Brennan*. Faron Young is a lawman and Marty one of the outlaws.

Road to Nashville. September, 1966; 109 minutes, color. Distributed by Crown International for Robert Patrick Productions. Produced by Robert Patrick; Associate producer, Marty Robbins. Written and directed by Will Zens. Cast: Marty Robbins, Richard Arlen, Doodles Weaver; appearances by: Connie Smith, Webb Pierce, The Stonemans, Waylon Jennings, Johnny Cash, The Carter Family, Lefty Frizzell, Porter Wagoner, Hank Snow, Faron Young, Bill Anderson, and others. The film, a musical comedy, centers around the problems of signing singers for a country music film. Marty sings "El Paso," "Devil Woman," "Begging to You," "Working My Way Through a Heartache," and "Count Me Out." Don Winters sings, "Annie Lou," and Bobby Sykes sings, "I Hope You'll Learn."

Tennessee Jamboree. September, 1964; 75 minutes, color. Distributed by Colorama Roadshows. Produced and directed by Albert C. Gannaway. Cast: Jim Reeves, Marty Robbins, Webb Pierce, Little Jimmy Dickens, Minnie Pearl, Carl Smith, Ray Price, Chet Atkins, others. The film is a musical review of country music stars.

Films in Which Marty Sang But Did Not Appear

The Alamo (Marty sang the theme song).

The Hanging Tree. 1959; 106 minutes, color. Warner Brothers. Cast: Gary Cooper, Maria Schell, and others.
Marty sang the theme song, "The Hanging Tree."

Emperor of the North Pole. 1973; 132 minutes, Fox, color. Cast: Lee Marvin, Ernest Borgnine, and others.
Marty sang the theme, "A Man and a Train."

Moonfire. 1970; 107 minutes, color. Distributed by Hollywood Continental; directed by Michael Parkhurst. Cast: Richard Egan, Sonny Liston, and others.
Marty sang "Wheel of Life" and "Get You off My Mind."

The Young Rounders (Marty sang "Red River Valley"). 1960s.

FILMS IN CHRONOLOGICAL ORDER

Badge of Marshal Brennan, 1957
Raiders of Old California, 1957
Buffalo Gun, 1958
Country Music Jubilee, 1960
Ballad of a Gunfighter, 1963
Country Music Caravan, 1964
Tennessee Jamboree, 1964
The Nashville Story, 1960s (?)
Road to Nashville, 1966
Hell on Wheels, 1967
From Nashville with Music, 1969
Country Music, 1972
Guns of a Stranger, 1973
Country Hits, 1976
Atoka, 1979
Honkytonk Man, 1982

Others: The Alamo
Moonfire
The Hanging Tree
Emperor of the North Pole
The Young Rounders

VIDEO TAPE AVAILABLE

Marty Robbins . . . His Legacy. 64 minutes, color, 1986. Distributed by Andrew Thompson, Inc.
Contents: concert footage from a 1981 performance in West Palm Beach, Florida, along with some film of Marty on his farm.

For Fans Only. 30 minutes, color, 1986. Distributed by Andrew Thompson, Inc.
Contents: noted on the videotape case as "the lighter side of Marty Robbins," this tape contains outtakes and additional concert footage from the West Palm Beach, Florida concert.

Marty Robbins: Super Legend. 120 minutes, color, 1987. Available from Multimedia Entertainment, Inc.
Contents: a videotape release of the 1986 televised tribute of the same title, with additional footage added.

The Drifter; volume 1. 78 minutes, black and white, 1988. Available from Marty Robbins Incorporated, Nashville, Tennessee.
Contents: the video contains three episodes from Marty's 1965 television series. Included here are "General Store," with Tex Ritter as a guest; "Trapper's Cabin," with Grandpa Jones as a guest; and "Virginia."
The series is developed around the singing cowboy concept, with each episode presenting a number of songs in a western setting. It is anticipated that the three additional volumes will contain the rest of the episodes.

Road to Nashville. Approximately 120 minutes, color, 1967. Distributed by Niets International, P. O. Box 916028, Longwood, FL 32791-6028.
The movie includes Marty and a number of other country music stars.

Marty also appears in the video tape of the film, *Honkytonk Man.* In addition, it is still possible to find copies of one of Marty's old westerns, *Ballad of a Gunfighter.*

AUDIO TAPES

Several audio tapes of Marty have been marketed since his death. All are worth hearing because of the insight they provide and the rare historical material they contain.

The Country Music Association's 11th Annual Talent Buyers Seminar. Artist's Panel (held Sunday, October 10th): "When You're Hot, You're Hot." Recorded for CMA by Beaverwood Recording Studio, Nashville. Marty was one of the performers who participated on the panel, which dealt with artists' viewpoints about life on the road, working with talent buyers, and career development. Other artists on the panel included Dottie West, Gary Morris, and Janie Fricke. An audio tape of the session is available from Beaverwood Recording Studio, 133 Walton Ferry Road, Hendersonville, TN 37075. Phone: (615) 824-2820. The Beaverwood Studios frequently tape country music industry seminars and meetings. The tapes are available for sale to the public and include a wealth of valuable information and conversation from leading performers and industry executives over the last ten years. The collection provides an excellent, and little known, source of primary research material for researchers and writers.

Bill Mack "Marty Party" tapes. 2 volumes. Available from Bill Mack Productions, P.O. Box 8777, Forth Worth, TX 76124. Bill Mack was a long-time friend of Marty's who had a late night radio show for WBAP. Marty would stop in and visit with Bill and his listeners for hours when he was in the area, bringing his guitar with him and singing whatever people wanted to hear. A brief reenactment of one of these visits to WBAP radio with Bill Mack appears in Marty's movie, *Country Music*. The two tapes contain excerpts from these visits and include both interview segments and music. Of special interest to researchers is the inclusion of Marty's brief performance of some unrecorded material, especially another song about El Paso, called "The Mystery of El Paso."

The Frankie Starr tapes. 2 audio tapes. Available from Frankie Starr, 12834 North 29th Place, Phoenix, AZ 85023. Frankie was one of the first people to help Marty get started singing. The time was 1947 and Frankie gave Marty a job as a guitar player in his band. Frankie marketed two tapes in 1983 and 1984 informally. Neither tape was a commercial production, i.e., they arrived without printed labels or other identifying marks. As far as I know, they were never sold in stores. One tape was identified as Ron Hall singing several songs written by Marty Robbins. The literature which accompanied the tape explained that Marty had given Ron 13 songs he had written in his youth and some of these songs were on the Hall recording. The second tape is a recording of Marty from 1947 singing three songs and of Frankie singing additional songs written by Marty.

RESOURCE PEOPLE AND ORGANIZATIONS

ORGANIZATIONS

Library of Congress
Music Division
Madison Building
Washington, D.C. 20540

Ronnie Pugh, Jay Orr, Alan Stoker, and Bob Pinson
Country Music Foundation Library
4 Music Square East
Nashville, TN 37203
(615) 256-1639

National Cowboy Hall of Fame & Western Heritage Center
1700 N.E. 63rd Street
Oklahoma City, OK 73111
(405) 478-2250

For information on "Marty Robbins' Spotlight":
Multimedia Entertainment
75 Rockefeller Plaza
22nd Floor
New York, NY 10019
(212) 484-7025
  Nashville office:
  3401 West End Avenue
  Nashville, TN 37203

Mr. Richard Weize
Bear Family Records
Achtern Dahl 30
2864 Vollersode
West Germany
Has complete list of Marty's early recording sessions.

SOURCES FOR PHOTOGRAPHS

Pat Bird
P.O. Box 307
Wauzeka, WI 53826
Concert photos, of Marty and other country music stars.

David and Kim Chobat
10430 Albemarle Road, #25
Charlotte, NC 28212
Racing photos of Marty and other drivers.

Country Music Association
7 Music Circle North
P.O. Box 22299
Nashville, TN 37202
(615) 244-2840
Hall of Fame award photos (October, 1982)

Sandy Daens
301 Wallace Road
Nashville, TN 37211
(615) 834-7728
Racing, concert photos of Marty. Photos of other country music artists.

Jasper Daily
3000 Castle Heights Avenue
Los Angeles, CA 90034
Concert and backstage photos. Photos from television programs. Photographer for many of the Academy of Country Music award programs. Photos of Marty and many other country stars who have toured the West Coast. Also: Sonny & Cher, Rick Nelson, Herb Alpert, Jerry Lee Lewis and more.

Joan & Gordy Goodwin
2751 Haymeadow Dr.
York, PA 17402
(717) 848-4684
Good selection of concert photos of Marty and many other country music artists. Some back stage photos and press conferences. The photos have been used in the tour books of many artists and are published regularly in country music periodicals.

Andrew A. Hanson
P.O. Box 140192
Dallas, TX 75214
Good selection of country music performers in concert around the west. He's a press photographer who has photos available of other public people in addition to performers.

Rick Henson Photography
P.O. Box 9994
Austin, TX 78766
Excellent candid photos (close-ups). Currently is George Strait's official photographer.

Donnie Jennings
R.R. 2, Box 97
Blackwell, OK 74631
Concert and candid photos of Marty and other performers.

Elmer C. Kappell
Route 2, Box 164
1013 Colesburg Road
Lebanon Junction, KY 40150
Excellent selection of racing photos of Marty, particularly from Atlanta
(November, 1982) and the June Marty Party. A racing photographer, he
has good photos of many other drivers.

Lucky Photo
P.O. Box 8262
Ft. Lauderdale, FL 33310-8262
(305) 753-1781
Concert photos of Marty and other performers. Some backstage and
television photos.

Richard Mischell
P.O. Box 64
Okeana, OH 45053
(513) 738-2801 or 1241
Concert photos of Marty and other performers.

Milton Moore, Jr.
P.O. Box 140280
Dallas, TX 75214-0280
Film stills.

Music City News
Lydia Dixon Harden, Editor
P.O. Box 22975
Nashville, TN 37202
(615) 329-2200
Photos from MCN Awards programs: receiving awards as well as per-
formances on the shows.

Harold Newton
300J North Withers
Liberty, MO 64068
Concert photos.

Don Putnam Photographers
16 Music Circle South
Nashville, TN 37203
(615) 242-7325

The official photographer for many of CMA's programs as well as many other music industry meetings around Nashville. He has photos from the 1982 Talent Buyers Seminar.

Beverly Parker
P.O. Box 211
New York, NY 10012
Took photos for Marty's last album cover.

Hope Powell
4700 Trusdale Drive
Nashville, TN 37211
(615) 833-4673
Portrait and candid photos of superior quality from 1970 to 1980s. The official photographer for "Marty Robbins' Spotlight."

Jim & Pat Rawlings
P.O. Box 1205
Gallatin, TN 37066
Concert and television photos.

Jean Scotte
716 Brighton Blvd.
Zanesville, OH 43701
1950s photos of Marty at office and race track.

Smile Photo
P.O. Box 15293
Chesapeake, VA 23320
Concert photos.

Don VanPutte
12006 Falls of Neuse Road
Wake Forest, NC 27587
Concert and candid photos of Marty and a large number of other country music performers.

MUSEUMS AND SOURCES OF PRODUCTS

Marty Robbins Memorial Showcase
2613 McGavock Pike
Nashville, TN 37214

(615) 885-1515
A museum and gift shop. Exhibits cover all phases of Marty's life.
Photographs of his family and childhood, clips from his films, cases of
awards and citations, his stage suits and jewelry, and racing memorabilia make up the main sections of the museum. Of special interest are
three of his favorite cars: the white Panther DeVille, his NASCAR
racing car, and a black Cadillac. The gift shop offers a variety of
products with his picture on them.

Marty Robbins, Inc.
713 18th Avenue, South
Nashville, TN 37203
(615) 327-3752
The business office and music publishing address for Mariposa Music.
Currently managed by Ronny Robbins. Some products are sold through
the office. The video tape of "The Drifter" series is marketed from this
address.

SOURCES FOR USED RECORDS

Larry Blevins
8436 West Rugby Road
Manassas, VA 22111

Donnie Jennings
R.R. 2, Box 97
Blackwell, OK 74631

Dave Kressley
P.O. Box 463
New Tripoli, PA 18066

9

NASCAR RACING HISTORY

This NASCAR racing history is compiled from News Bulletins and Newsletters of NASCAR (National Association for Stock Car Auto Racing, Inc.). In addition to the information listed below, the NASCAR records show that Marty competed in the Grand American Series in 1968, starting in five events and finishing in the top ten twice. He also finished 12th in the NASCAR Charlotte 500 in 1968, a Grand National race, winning $1525.

RACE TITLE, LOCATION, AND DATE

NASCAR Grand National Championship Circuit Race No. 36, 1966 Season (200 miles, ½-mile track, paved); Fairgrounds Speedway, Nashville, TN. July 30, 1966.

Finished: 25   *Laps*: 48
Started: 17   *$ won*: 100
Car no.: 53   *Reason out of*
Model: 64 Ford   *race*: oil pressure

NASCAR Grand National Championship Circuit Race No. 44, 1970 Season, "National 500" (500 miles, 1.5-mile track, paved). Charlotte Motor Speedway, Charlotte, NC. October 11, 1970.

Finished: 32   *Laps*: 105
Started: 33   *$ won*: 1160
Car no.: 42   *Reason out of*
Model: 69 Dodge   *race*: engine failure

Marty at the Daytona International Speedway for the "Firecracker 400," July 4, 1982. (Photo by Sandy Daens)

NASCAR Grand National Championship Circuit Race No. 21, 1971 Season, "World 600" (600 miles, 1.5-mile track, paved). Charlotte Motor Speedway, Charlotte, NC. May 30, 1971.

Finished: 15   *Laps*: 376
Started: 19   *$ won*: 1800
Car no.: 42   *Reason out of*
Model: 69 Dodge   *race*: running

NASCAR Grand National Championship Circuit Race No. 33, 1971 Season, "Dixie 500" (500 miles, 1.522-mile track, paved). Atlanta International Raceway, Atlanta, GA. August 1, 1971.

Finished: 13   *Laps*: 309
Started: 17   *$ won*: 1350
Car no.: 42   *Reason out of*
Model: 69 Dodge   *race*: running

NASCAR Grand National Championship Circuit Race No. 40, 1971 Season, "Southern 500" (500 miles, 1.366-mile track, paved). Darlington International Raceway, Darlington, SC. September 6, 1971.

Finished: 7   *Laps*: 339
Started: 18   *$ won*: 2550
Car no.: 42   *Reason out of*
Model: 69 Dodge   *race*: running

NASCAR Grand National Championship Circuit Race No. 42, 1971 Season, "National 500" (357 miles, 1.5-mile track, paved. Race halted on lap 238 due to rain and darkness). Charlotte Motor Speedway, Charlotte, NC. October 10, 1971.

Finished: 37   *Laps*: 97
Started: 15   *$ won*: 812
Car no.: 42   *Reason out of*
Model: 69 Dodge   *race*: steering

NASCAR Grand National Championship Circuit Race No. 48, 1971 Season, "Texas 500" (500 miles, 2-mile track, paved). Texas World Speedway, Byran-College Station, TX. December 12, 1971.

Finished: 25   *Laps*: 175
Started: 20   *$ won*: 640
Car no.: 42   *Reason out of*
Model: 71 Dodge   *race*: eng. failure

Winston Cup Grand National Championship Race No. 4, 1972 Season, "Miller High Life 500" (500 miles, 2.5-mile track, paved). Ontario Motor Speedway, Ontario, CA. March 5, 1972.

Finished: 8   *Laps*: 190
Started: 22   *$ won*: 3445
Car no.: 42   *Reason out of*
Model: 72 Dodge   *race*: running

Winston Cup Grand National Championship Race No. 11, 1972 Season, "Winston 500" (500 miles, 2.66-mile track, paved). Alabama International Motor Speedway, Talladega, Alabama. May 7, 1972.

Finished: *50   *Laps*: 179
Started: 9   *$ won*: 745
Car no.: 42   *Reason out of*
Model: 72 Dodge   *race*: running

*Note accompanying the race results: Marty Robbins was dropped to last position because of a carburetor rule infraction.

Winston Cup Grand National Championship Race No. 16, 1972 Season, "Lone Star 500" (500 miles, 2-mile track, paved). Texas World Speedway, College Station, Texas. June 25, 1972.

Finished: 40   *Laps*: 56
Started: 10   *$ won*: 595
Car no.: 42   *Reason out of*
Model: 72 Dodge   *race*: eng. failure

Winston Cup Grand National Championship Race No. 24, 1972 Season, "Southern 500" (500 miles, 1.366-mile track, paved). Darlington International Raceway, Darlington, SC. September 4, 1972.

Finished: 9   *Laps*: 339
Started: 21   *$ won*: 2465
Car no.: 42   *Reason out of*
Model: 71 Dodge   *race*: running

Winston Cup Grand National Championship Race No. 30, 1972 Season, "American 500" (500 miles, 1.017-mile track, paved). North Carolina Motor Speedway, Rockingham, NC. October 22, 1972.

Finished: 26   *Laps*: 332
Started: 34   *$ won*: 700
Car no.: 42   *Reason out of*
Model: 72 Dodge   *race*: battery

Wintson Cup Grand National Championship Race No. 2, 1973 Season, "Daytona 500" (500 miles, 2.5-mile track, paved). Daytona International Speedway, Daytona Beach, FL. February 18, 1973.

Finished: 34   *Laps*: 63
Started: 37   *$ won*: 1515
Car no.: 42   *Reason out of*
Model: 72 Dodge   *race*: wrecked

Winston Cup Grand National Championship Race No. 14, 1973 Season, "Alamo 500" (500 miles, 2-mile track, paved). Texas World Speedway, College Station, TX. June 10, 1973.

Finished: 29   *Laps*: 38
Started: 10   *$ won*: 1115
Car no.: 42   *Reason out of*
Model: 73 Dodge   *race*: bkn. exhaust

Winston Cup Grand National Championship Race No. 17, 1973 Season, "Metal of Honor Firecracker 400" (400 miles, 2.5-mile track, paved). Daytona International Speedway, Daytona Beach, FL. July 4, 1973.

Finished: 8   *Laps*: 153
Started: 36   *$ won*: 1500
Car no.: 42   *Reason out of*
Model: 73 Dodge   *race*: running

Winston Cup Grand National Championship Race No. 20, 1973 Season, "Talladega 500" (500 miles, 2.66-mile track, paved). Alabama International Motor Speedway, Talladega, AL. August 12, 1973.

Marty in the garage area during a 1974 race. (Photo from NASCAR News Bureau)

Finished: 36   *Laps*: 80
Started: 10   *$ won*: 1265
Car no.: 42   *Reason out of*
Model: 73 Dodge   *race*: ignition

Note: Marty is listed as being the lap leader for lap 15.

Winston Cup Grand National Championship Race No. 10, 1974 Season, "Winston 500" (500 miles, 2.66-mile track, paved). Alabama International Motor Speedway, Talladega, AL. May 5, 1974.

Finished: 15   *Laps*: 185
Started: 15   *$ won*: 1950
Car no.: 42   *Reason out of*
Model: 73 Dodge   *race*: running

Winston Cup Grand National Championship Race No. 16, "Motorstate 400" (400 miles, 2-mile track, paved). Michigan International Speedway, Irish Hills, MI. June 16, 1974.

Finished: 5   *Laps*: 178
Started: 22   *$ won*: 2050
Car no.: 42   *Reason out of*
Model: 74 Dodge   *race*: running

Winston Cup Grand National Race No. 21, "Talladega 500" (2.66-mile track, paved). Alabama International Motor Speedway, Talladega, AL. August 11, 1974.

Finished: 9   *Laps*: 185
Started: 16   *$ won*: 1085
Car no.: 42   *Reason out of*
Model: 73 Dodge   *race*: running

Winston Cup Grand National Race No. 28, "National 500" (1.5-mile track, paved). Charlotte Motor Speedway, Charlotte, NC. October 6, 1974.

Finished: 42   *Laps*: 2
Started: 42   *$ won*: 649
Car no.: 42   *Reason out of*
Model: 74 Dodge   *race*: wrecked

Winston Cup Grand National Race No. 2, 1975 Season, "Daytona 500" (500 miles, 2.5-mile track, paved). Daytona International Speedway, Daytona Beach, FL. February 16, 1975.

Finished: 39   *Laps*: 3
Started: 28   *$ won*: 1125
Car no.: 42   *Reason out of*
Model: Dodge   *race*: wrecked

Winston Cup Grand National Race No. 10, 1975 Season, "Winston 500" (500 miles, 2.66-mile track). Alabama International Motor Speedway, Talladega, AL. May 4, 1975.

Finished: 31   *Laps*: 62
Started: 17   *$ won*: 1455
Car no.: 42   *Reason out of*
Model: Dodge   *race*: wrecked

Note: Marty was listed as the lap leader for laps 49 and 50 before he wrecked. After this, his third wreck in a row, he announced he was giving up racing.

Winston Cup Grand National Race No. 15, "CAM2 Motor Oil 400" (400 miles, 2-mile track). Michigan International Speedway, Brooklyn, MI. June 19, 1977.

Finished: 13	*Laps*: 193
Started: 33	*$ won*: 1500
Car no.: 42	*Reason out of*
Model: Dodge	*race*: running

Winston Cup Grand National Race No. 19, "Talladega 500" (500 miles, 2.66-mile track). Alabama International Motor Speedway, Talladega, AL. August 7, 1977.

Finished: 38	*Laps*: 36
Started: 28	*$ won*: 1090
Car no.: 42	*Reason out of*
Model: Dodge	*race*: transmission

Winston Cup Grand National Race No. 19, "Talladega 500" (500 miles, 2.66-mile track). Alabama International Motor Speedway, Talladega, AL. August 6, 1978.

Finished: 18	*Laps*: 171
Started: 38	*$ won*: 2240
Car no.: 42	*Reason out of*
Model: Dodge	*race*: running

Winston Cup Grand National Race No. 16, "Gabriel 400" (400 miles, 2-mile track). Michigan International Speedway, Brooklyn, MI. June 17, 1979.

Finished: 35	*Laps*: 64
Started: 29	*$ won*: 970
Car no.: 42	*Reason out of*
Model: Dodge	*race*: bkn. conn. rod

Winston Cup Grand National Race No. 20, "Talladega 500" (500 miles, 2.66-mile track). Alabama International Motor Speedway, Talladega, AL. August 5, 1979.

Finished: 32   *Laps*: 75
Started: 40   *$ won*: 1325
Car no.: 36   *Reason out of*
Model: Dodge   *race*: eng. failure

Winston Cup Grand National Race No. 21, "Champion Spark Plug 400" (400 miles, 2-mile track). Michigan International Speedway, Brooklyn, MI. August 19, 1979.

Finished: 27   *Laps*: 96
Started: 33   *$ won*: 825
Car no.: 6   *Reason out of*
Model: Dodge   *race*: cracked cyl. head

Winston Cup Grand National Race No. 10, "Winston 500" (500 miles, 2.66-mile track). Alabama International Motor Speedway, Talladega, AL. May 4, 1980.

Finished: 33   *Laps*: 54
Started: 36   *$ won*: 1470
Car no.: 6   *Reason out of*
Model: Dodge   *race*: eng. failure

Winston Cup Grand National Race No. 17, "Firecracker 400" (400 miles, 2.5-mile track). Daytona International Speedway, Daytona Beach, FL. July 4, 1980.

Finished: 30   *Laps*: 131
Started: 31   *$ won*: 2285
Car no.: 79   *Reason out of*
Model: Dodge   *race*: eng. failure

Winston Cup Grand National Race No. 20, "Talladega 500" (500 miles, 2.66-mile track). Alabama International Motor Speedway, Talladega, AL. August 3, 1980.

Finished: 13   *Laps*: 173
Started: 37   *$ won*: 2765
Car no.: 6   *Reason out of*
Model: Dodge   *race*: running

Winston Cup Grand National Race No. 28, "National 500" (500 miles, 1.5-mile track). Charlotte Motor Speedway, Charlotte, NC. October 5, 1980.

Finished: 32   *Laps*: 171
Started: 30   *$ won*: 1000
Car no.: 6   *Reason out of*
Model: Chevy   *race*: accident

Winston Cup Grand National Race No. 16, 1982 Season, "Firecracker 400" (400 miles, 2.5-mile track). Daytona International Speedway, Daytona Beach, FL. July 4, 1982.

Finished: 37   *Laps*: 45
Started: 31   *$ won*: 1260
Car no.: 22   *Reason out of*
Model: Buick   *race*: eng. failure

Winston Cup Grand National Race No. 29, 1982 Season, "Atlanta Journal 500" (500 miles, 1.522-mile track). Atlanta International Raceway, Atlanta, Georgia. November 7, 1982.

Finished: 33   *Laps*: 89
Started: 36   *$ won*: 795
Car no.: 22   *Reason out of*
Model: Buick   *race*: accident

PART II

MARTY AND HIS MUSIC
(Including Discography)

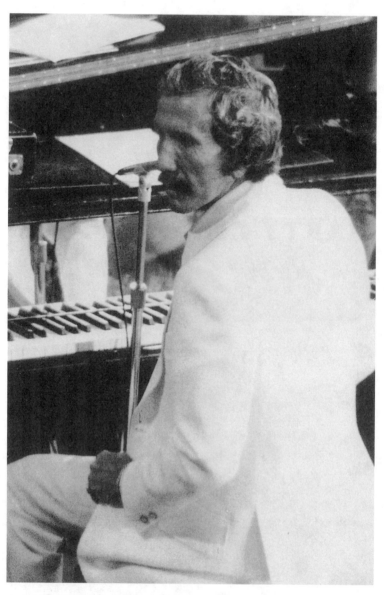

Marty at the piano. (Photo by Don VanPutte)

10

JEANNE PRUETT TALKS ABOUT MARTY'S MUSIC

Jeanne and I had been trying to get together all week, but it was during a DJ/Music Industry Seminar event and we both were having trouble finding some free time. Finally, she suggested we meet backstage at the Grand Ole Opry after her performance and talk about Marty's music and what it was like to work with him over the years.

I chatted with her briefly as she waited to go on stage and was able to catch her performance as I was sitting on the bleachers behind the Opry Band. She had an enthusiastic audience and it brought forth fond memories to see the fans move forward to take her photo while she sang—an Opry tradition. She really "comes alive" on stage, really glows!

She's wearing gold slacks and a rose-colored top that complement each other beautifully. At the end of her signature song, "Satin Sheets," she gets tremendous applause and starts to exit, but returns for another bow as the clapping continues. As she comes backstage, she takes hold of my arm and we start walking quickly back toward the dressing rooms, only to be approached several times along the way by people wanting photos or brief interviews. We both keep walking and she nicely (and patiently) explains to each one that she has promised me her time first. If they want to wait, she says, she will see them after we are finished. She decides to stop and see if the office of the Opry manager is empty, and finding it vacant she suggests we do the interview there where it's quiet. We sit down on the sofa and start to relax.

She speaks softly, barely above a whisper, but intently and sincerely. She starts talking, saying she thinks of Marty as "family" because of the intertwining of their lives.

BP: What was Marty like as a person?

JP: Even though he belonged to the world, he was a very private man and those of us who knew him and worked with him respected that, and abided by Marty's wishes. There were some people Marty liked to work with and he called them "My People." I was lucky enough to be one of them.

BP: Tell me about the first time you met Marty.

JP: My relationship with Marty goes so far back, it was really before I was involved with music. When I first met him I used to come up to the Friday night Opry with my (then) husband Jack; he was playing lead guitar for Marty at the time. Jack was instrumental in taking some of the lyrics I had written way back in the 1960s or so to Marty. Marty looked over the lyrics; I think there were seven songs in the group (he eventually recorded five of the seven). He called me and said he thought I really had a gifted way with words and a good way of putting lyrics together. He said he was going to put together a publishing company and he would like me to write for it! And that's how I first began the association with him.

I wasn't singing yet, I was still staying home. Jack and I had two children together and I was a mother and a housewife. The songwriting started out as a hobby that I loved dearly, and eventually it became a way of life and a real money-making venture for me.

BP: Does music come naturally to you? Can you play instruments?

JP: I can. I play a little guitar, some piano, and have been able to write successfully for myself and others. Most of the time I wrote exclusively for Marty. He would call me up and say something like, "Jeanne, I'm doing a Christmas album and I'd like two or three songs from you." And this would be in the middle of May or June! I'd write them and then submit them to him personally and he would pick and choose what he wanted. Of course, I wasn't a recording artist at that time and he always had first choice of my material.

I said one time in an interview—and I didn't realize at the time what a true statement it was—that "Every song I ever wrote, I wrote for Marty Robbins to sing." Isn't that strange? And a great many things I did write for Marty he did sing and record. Marty always sang the lyrics and melodies so much like they were his own. He told me one time, "When an artist sings a song like he writes it for himself, that's a real compliment to the writer." And I always felt like that was a special pat on the back from him.

BP: What did Marty look for in a song?

JP: In a word, simplicity. He didn't like hard-to-follow melodies and he didn't care too much for lyrics that were too flowery or involved. He loved story songs and this showed up in his own writing, like "El Paso" and the gunfighter ballads. The key phrase was "simplicity."

BP: You wrote "Love Me" for Marty.

JP: Yes. And I recorded the song before he did. But, like I said, everything I ever wrote I wrote for him to sing.

I had an opportunity to record about the time I wrote "Love Me" and it really opened up a lot of doors for me. And Marty kind of decided to record it as an afterthought more than anything else. I'd sent over another song for him to use and I put a copy of "Love Me" in the same envelope. He started playing around with it and decided he liked it so well he would do it. I'd had a hit on it the same year and then Marty recorded it and had a big hit on it. So it was kind of an accident, but it turned out to be one of the big songs of his career.

BP: Was it a song you sat down and wrote all at one time?

JP: I write everything that way. I'm not the kind to sit down and work awhile and then come back tomorrow and work at it some more. I'm not a 9 to 5 writer; I can't get up in the morning and say, "I'm going to write two or three songs today." I like to say my songs have "been sent" to me. I have to be motivated to write; I need that inspiration. And I've written very few songs from personal experience. Most of the things I write come about through someone else's experience or from my own imagination because I've read something.

BP: Was that true of Marty too?

JP: It depended on the song. I think that at times Marty worked great long periods over songs. He labored hours over some of his wonderful story songs. He wrote over a period of time. And both of us always wrote on the road and on the bus. I think the late hours he spent when he couldn't sleep were some of the most productive hours he had. Ideas would come to him then. He always thought he just couldn't sleep. But I think that the music inside of him had to come out, and it chose the nighttime hours because Marty was such a nighttime person. And maybe because he was supposed to be up and about with his music.

BP: He only slept two or three hours a night at the most?

JP: That's right. He told me one time he was sure he had not gotten more than four hours of sleep at night for twenty years. And he used to go out late, in the wee hours of the night, and ramble around the city. In fact, he used to go up and visit the late night DJs when he couldn't sleep: Chuck Morgan, Hairl Hensley, and Ralph Emery—all of them hosted late night WSM shows at one time. He'd call them and pretend to be totally someone else, a stranger! Some of our fondest memories are that kind. Because he was such a humorous man! Marty was *so alive!* He was not only very "viable" but a very visible man; he was so dynamic off stage too. His personality was just magnetic! He drew people to him who didn't even know him, who didn't even know what he did for a living. They would pass him on the sidewalk and do a doubletake because of his personality. He had what we in the business call "the magic." He had Lady Luck sitting on his shoulder most of the time during his career and he also had "the magic." His music was able to transcend all barriers. His music never was just for country music fans, because Marty was one of the few people in our business who had the ability and the talent to be able to do it all! He did an album one time called "Marty after Midnight." It was pop all the way from beginning to end. I'd put it up along side anybody's pop album anywhere, anytime. He did a religious album one time, too, that was the same way. And Christmas music. And Hawaiian. He did such a variety of music!

[Jeanne stops suddenly and laughs at herself, hearing herself talking with such emotion and so rapidly.]

JP: You wouldn't know that I'm a Marty Robbins fan, would you!

[She's delighted at the thought. But then her mood turns softer, melancholy, and she speaks more quietly.]

JP: I talk to fans every day who still miss him and still love his music.

BP: What do you miss most about him?

JP: Just him.

BP: Those are the exact words Bobby Sykes used when I asked him that question, "Just him."

JP: The sad thing about it is that as time goes on, it gets harder. They say that when you lose someone you care about, and Marty was family to me for 25 years, it gets easier with time. But I miss Marty more today than I did the first year. And I've talked to Don Winters and Bobby Sykes and Louis Dunn, people who were associated with him for 30 years, and they all say the same thing. It gets harder instead of easier.

BP: How do you think Marty would have liked to be remembered? You've just said that everyone misses him; do you think he would like to have known that?

JP: Yes. I think he *does know* that.

I think he had the kind of relationships with his friends that he was bound to know. I think that if one of us had gone before he did, he would have missed us in the same way. He would have missed *the person*. Don't get me wrong, *I miss his music!* But more than anything else, I miss the person. I miss the live performances, and I do not mind admitting that to anyone in the world. I *loved* his shows. And a lot of joy in the music business has gone for a lot of us who looked forward to the Opry at 11:30 on a Saturday night when Marty did his shows.

That was Marty's show. I worked it with him for ten years. It was *his* show and I was honored to be on it with him as the supporting act. And that hour held magic like no other part of the Opry! He was just a tremendous talent!

BP: Your record company recently released a recording of you and Marty singing "Love Me" together. When did the two of you record it?

JP: About six months before his death. In fact, "Love Me" was Marty's idea; that was the song he chose. We had talked about making some records together. It came about because Ralph Emery used to do the late-night radio show and I would co-host occasionally (on his show or on Chuck Morgan's show), and Marty would come up and be on the show with us. And he would sit at the piano and play. Just Marty, without the band. He'd be at the piano and once in a while I would go over and do harmony with him. "Love Me" was one of the things Marty liked to do so well. And one night he kinda motioned me over and I went over and sat by the piano and did the harmony parts with him. And Ralph Emery just about had a fit! He loved it! Both Ralph and Chuck said, "You ought to cut some songs together." And that's how it came about.

Marty chose a song and I chose one. My choice was "Walking Piece of Heaven"; we also recorded that. It hasn't been released yet. I hope someday it will be out, for Marty's fans and mine. I think if they released both cuts on the same single, it would be a hit. One of the reasons would be because Marty never did any other duets. And I think his fans would accept our duet together.

BP: Marty was always close to his fans and believed in the power of his fans.

JP: He sure did! That's how the phrase "Marty's Army" came to be. Because he had such an army of fans and once they made up their minds that things had to be a certain way, they worked to see that it happened! They would do anything for him, and he for them. Marty's fans were in such close harmony with him and his music.

BP: How would *you* have Marty remembered?

JP: I'd like to see his music played at the beginning and end of each day by country radio stations. And I'd like to see more articles about him, even though he's gone. And I'd like to see his music continued to be released.

I usually say in my concerts, "I made a promise I'd do everything I could to keep Marty's music alive," and I've been true to that promise.

BP: What was he like to work with?

JP: Well, you always knew that Marty was going to be the star of the show. It didn't matter what stature you had. No one could ever close the show behind Marty Robbins! I always knew how to work with Marty, knew his likes and dislikes about other artists. And Marty never liked another artist on stage to crowd him, as far as his being with his fans. After a show, he'd be sittin' on the stage signing those autographs, and the people were around Marty because they wanted to be *around* Marty. The fans didn't want anyone else near him. So, I always had my way of signing for my fans at one end of the stage and Marty had the other section for himself. The only time we ever really signed autographs together in close proximity was when we did the Opry on Saturday night and would go over to the park afterwards. We would sign autographs at the Hospitality Suite: 200, 300, 500 fans would show up at a time and he would stay until the last one left. He would always take hours.

It's one of the things I learned from Marty very early on in my career. When the fans have taken the time and the effort to come to the concert, they deserve everything you can give them. Not only the performance, but the "performance" also of taking photos with their children, taking photos with them, signing special things: boots, belt-buckles, whatever they call special in their life. They deserve to have that with you because not one of us knows when we ever have the opportunity to share with our fans another song, another handshake, or another photo. So, it never mattered to me that I see people every day who must have many pictures of me and a hundred things already signed. Everything they want, I try to give them. And I learned that from Marty Robbins.

BP: Do you have Marty's autograph?

JP: I do. Marty autographed a copy of his *The Small Man* book for me.

Also—I have to tell you this story—I got in line after a concert with the fans to get his autograph, to tease him, in Birmingham, Alabama. I got in line like I was a fan and had a scarf over my hair and my coat collar pulled up so he wouldn't see me coming. When I got up to him, I slid my paper under his pen. And, without looking up, he drew a little picture of a person and put big eyes and big ears on it and then wrote "Marty to Maudie," to tease me back! (Maude was his pet name for me.) He knew I was in that line all of the time!

I recall being in Las Vegas the first time Marty played there, and it was so strange to see fans line up at 4:00 in the afternoon to get into an 8:00 pm performance, in a casino area where gambling was the main rule of the day. And it was really neat to see fans lined up five and six and ten deep between the slot machines to get in to see Marty Robbins. I think Marty might have been the first country artist to cross the barriers in Vegas, and it was tremendous to see the response, to see the fans lined up.

BP: Were you performing with him at the time?

JP: No one was! Nobody! He needed nobody! He was "King of the Hill" when it came to performing for the fans in Las Vegas.

BP: Tell me about traveling on the road. He loved to travel, didn't he?

JP: Yes! I think the long hours on the road were good times. After Marty's health problems began, he had to take a lot of his own food along, because he wasn't allowed to have certain things. And so many of his band members had been with him for 15 or 20 years. In fact, I'm sure some of the musicians were as close to him as family, because they spent so much time together. Marty would tour 150–175 days a year. Add one or two travel days to each trip and you're talking about most of the year!

BP: Do performers ever get used to sleeping on a tour bus?

JP: You get to the point where you can't sleep anywhere else except on the bus! When you're used to doing the concert tour and doing 500 miles between shows, you jump on the bus, take off your make-up, get into something comfortable and head for the next place. You can relax and sleep, expecially if you have a competent bus driver. The drivers are some of the people who don't get much recognition, but they're one of the keys to the business.

BP: Do you ever "lose" people on the road?

JP: Yes! Oh, yes! You do. When we're at a stop and band members wake up and leave the bus. If they don't put a note on the driver's seat or turn their lights on, we'll just drive off and leave them.

It happens to everybody! In every traveling unit in the business. We have to have the "missing persons" flown in; or, sometimes a highway patrolman stops you down the road and says: "Does this guy belong to you?" You can get those stories from every artist. Eventually they catch up to you somewhere along the line.

BP: How did Marty feel about winning the Hall of Fame Award? This was just two months before he died. Did he expect to win it?

JP: No, he didn't. I don't think he was ready for that award at that particular time. He had mixed emotions. Marty felt like other awards should have come before that one, that perhaps that one should have come later. He felt like he missed out on all of the other awards that should have led up to confirmation into the Hall of Fame. There were many times when he should have had Male Artist, Album of the Year, or Entertainer of the Year awards— awards that precede the Hall of Fame Award. It's just that he felt he had other things coming to him before that.

BP: Do you think that he realized how sick he was?

JP: I don't know. I think Marty knew more about it than he told people. But as far as knowing he would die, I don't think so. He was used to hard work and he probably wanted to carry on like he was used to doing. I feel like the happiest time of his life was when he was on the stage. He gave everything he had to give to his audience. When he was on, he had peace of mind.

I think the last three years of his life, he was known to do extended performances. Instead of doing an hour show, he would do two hours. And I think it was because he was so in love with the stage and with life. He was so happy and in control of the situation.

BP: He loved a live audience.

JP: He sure did. And occasionally he would get in a melancholy mood and go sit down at the piano, and the band would sort of be dismissed from his mind, and he'd sing one great song after another, maybe for as long as 45 minutes to an hour. He could electrify a crowd and he could go way back and do the real early songs. Some of the old Eddy Arnold or Ernest Tubb songs. He could do "The Great Speckled Bird." He would do something "off the wall" that nobody was expecting, and that's what made him so fresh and so new.

BP: He could always remember the words.

JP: Oh, he *never* forgot the words! It might be five years since he sang a song, and all of a sudden it would come to his heart and his mind and he could sit down at a piano and *do* it. I've seen it happen in a concert situation many times, and here at the Opry during his late show. Millions of fans have watched him from the audience when he would just sit down at the piano and pull one great song after another from his mind. If the band joined in, fine. And if they didn't, that was all right too, because he was in his own world at that point. And he was with "his people." That was Marty Robbins.

11

MARTY ROBBINS DISCOGRAPHY

ALBUMS IN CHRONOLOGICAL ORDER

carl, lefty and marty. House Party Series ed. Marty Robbins, Carl Smith, and Lefty Frizzell. Information taken from Mono CL 2544 (House Party Series, "Lp" 35430 and "Lp" 35431): Columbia Records; First released in 1956; 33⅓ rpm. (10-inch LP released in Mono only).
Note: Carl Smith and Lefty Frizzell are the other two artists. The names of the singers and songwriters for each tune are on the record label.
　Album contents. Side 1: Let old mother nature have her way (Carl Smith; Southerland, L. Clark)/ Sing me something sentimental (Marty Robbins; Robbins)/ Always late (with your kisses) (Lefty Frizzell; Frizzell and Crawford); Side 2: If you've got the money, I've got the time (Lefty Frizzell; Frizzell and Beck)/ I couldn't keep from crying (Marty Robbins; Robbins)/ Hey Joe! (Carl Smith; B. Bryant).

Rock'n roll'n Robbins. House Party Series CL 2601 (Side 1: "Lp" 38558; Side 2: "Lp" 38559): Columbia Records; 1956; 33⅓ rpm. (10-inch LP released in Mono only).
　Album contents. Side 1: Long tall Sally (E. Johnson)/ Tennessee Toddy (Robbins)/ Maybelline (C. Berry); Side 2: Respectfully Miss Brooks (Robbins)/ Mean Mama blues (Robbins)/ Long gone lonesome blues (H. Williams).

Rock and roll Robbins. Bella Records 1002; no date; 33⅓ rpm. (Album).
　Album contents. Side A: Long gone lonesome blues/ That's allright/ Long tall Sally/ Mr. Teardrop/ Pretty mama/ Just married/ Maybelline/ Grown-up tears/ Mean mama blues; Side B: Please don't blame me/ Tennessee Toddy/ Teenage dream/ Respectfully, Miss

Brooks/ Stairway of love/ Teenager's dad/ Cap and gown/ Ruby Ann/ I'll know you're gone.

The Song of Robbins. Information taken from LE 10578 Stereo (Columbia Limited Edition. Cover photo: Dirone. Side 1: XSM 116299; Side 2: XSM 116300). Additional releases are numbered Mono CL 976, Stereo CS 9421: Columbia Records; First issued April, 1957; 33⅓ rpm. (Album). Photo for CL 976: Don Cravens/Black Star.
    Album contents. Side 1: Lovesick blues (I. Mills, Friend; 2:33, ASCAP)/ I'm so lonesome I could cry (H. Williams; 2:44, BMI)/ It's too late now (to worry anymore) (Pope; 2:17, BMI)/ Rose of ol' Pawnee (F. Rose; 3:16, ASCAP)/ I never let you cross my mind (F. Rose; 2:59, ASCAP)/ I hang my head and cry (Autry, F. Rose, Whitley; 2:15, ASCAP)/. Side 2: You only want me when you're lonely (Autry, S. Nelson; 2:30, BMI)/ Moanin' the blues (H. Williams; 1:59, BMI)/ I'll step aside (Bond; 2:15, BMI)/ All the world is lonely now (Foree; 2:12, BMI)/ Bouquet of roses (S. Nelson, Hilliard; 2:16, BMI)/ Have I told you lately that I love you (Autry, Wiseman; 3:07, BMI).

Song of the Islands. Mono CL 1087 (Side 1: xLP 42300; side 2: xLP 42300), Stereo 9425: Columbia Records; October, 1957; 33⅓ rpm. (Album).
Note: back of cover of CL 1087 says "Songs of the Islands."
    Album contents. Side 1: Song of the islands (C. King, 2:56, E. B. Marks Music Co., ASCAP)/ Don't sing Aloha when I go (Smith, B. Black & Moret, 1:49, Robbins Music Corp., ASCAP)/ Beyond the reef (Pitman, 2:29, Laurel Music Corp., ASCAP)/ Crying steel guitar waltz (S. Long, 1:58, Tannen Music Inc., BMI)/ My isle of golden dreams (Kahn, Blaufuss, 2:51, Remick Music Corp., ASCAP)/ Now is the hour (Maori farewell song) (Kaihan, C. Scott, D. Stewart, 2:29, Leeds Music Corp., ASCAP); Side 2: Sweet Leilani (H. Owens, 1:47, Joy Music Inc., ASCAP)/ Down where the trade winds blow (H. Owens, 2:27, Joy Music Inc., ASCAP)/ Constancy (Ua like No a like) (J. Noble, Berger, 3:09, Miller Music Corp., ASCAP)/ Island echoes (Kessel, 3:37, Be-Are Publishing Co., BMI)/ Moonland (Byrd, 2:44, Acuff-Rose, BMI)/ Aloha Oe (Farewell to thee) (Liliukalani, 2:26, Public domain).

Marty Robbins. Information taken from Mono CL 1189 (Side 1: x "Lp" 43580; Side 2: x "Lp" 43581): Columbia Records; December, 1958; 33⅓ rpm. (Album).

Note: one song titled "Judy" on the album face is listed as "Jodie" on the sleeve. No times are listed for the cuts on either the record or the sleeve.

Album contents. Side 1: Kaw-liga (H. Williams, F. Rose)/ Judy (Stokes)/ Nothing but sweet lies (M. Robbins)/ Oh, how I miss you (since you went away) (Cassell, Taylor)/ Baby I need you (like you need me) (M. Robbins)/ Shackles and chains (J. Davis); Side 2: Waltz of the wind (F. Rose)/ Paper-face (Locklin, S. Williams)/ Then I turned and walked slowly away (Fortner, E. Arnold)/ Wedding bells (C. Boone)/ A house with everything but love (M. Robbins)/ The hands you're holding now (M. Robbins).

Marty's greatest hits. Information taken from Stereo CS 8639 (Side 1: XSM 55972; Side 2: XSM 55973). Additional releases are numbered Mono CL 1325, PC 8639, and LC 11222: Columbia Records; First released April, 1959; 33⅓ rpm. (Album).

Album contents. Side 1: A white sport coat (and a pink carnation) (Robbins)/ The story of my life (H. David, B. Bacharach)/ Ain't I the lucky one (Endsley)/ The last time I saw my heart (H. David, Bacharach)/ Long tall Sally (E. Johnson)/ The blues country style (M. David, J. Livingston); Side 2: The hanging tree (From the Warner Bros. picture "The Hanging Tree," M. David, J. Livingston)/ Sittin' in a tree house (H. David, Bacharach)/ She was only seventeen (he was one year more) (Robbins)/ Singing the blues (Endsley)/ Knee deep in the blues (Endsley)/ Aloha Oe (Farewell to thee) (Liliukalani).

Gunfighter ballads and trail songs. Information taken from Stereo CS 8158 (Side 1: XSM 47135; Side 2: XSM 47136). Additional releases have numbers Mono CL 1349, PC 8158: Columbia Records; First released September, 1959; 33⅓ rpm. (Album).

Album contents. Side 1: Big iron (Robbins)/ Cool water (Nolan)/ Billy the Kid (public domain)/ A hundred and sixty acres (Kapp)/ They're hanging me tonight (Low, Wolpert)/ Strawberry Roan (public domain); Side 2: El Paso (Robbins)/ In the valley (Robbins)/ The Master's call (Robbins)/ Running gun (Tom Glaser, Tim Glaser)/ The little green valley (Robison)/ Utah Carol (public domain). Note: One title on the record, "The little green valley," is titled "Down in the little green valley" on the record jacket.

More gunfighter ballads and trail songs. Information taken from Stereo PC 8272 (Side 1: XSM 49962; Side 2: XSM 49963). Additional release numbers are Mono CL 1481, Stereo CS 8272: Columbia Records; First released September, 1960; 33⅓ rpm. (Album).

Album contents. Side 1: San Angelo (M. Robbins)/ Prairie fire (J. Babcock)/ Streets of Laredo (public domain)/ Song of the bandit (B. Nolan)/ I've got no use for the women (public domain); Side 2: Five brothers (T. Glaser)/ Little Joe the wrangler (public domain)/ Ride, cowboy ride (L. Emerson)/ This peaceful sod (J. Glaser)/ She was young and she was pretty (M. Robbins)/ My love (M. Robbins).

More greatest hits. Information taken from Stereo CS 8435 (Side 1: XSM 52909; Side 2: XSM 52910). Additional releases numbered Mono CL 1635, PC 3485: Columbia Records; Album first released June, 1961; 33⅓ rpm. (Album).
Album contents. Side 1: El Paso (M. Robbins, 4:22, Marty's Music Inc., BMI)/ Like all the other times (L. Emerson, J. Glaser, 2:26, Marizona Music Inc, BMI)/ Is there any chance (M. Robbins, 2:10, Marizona Music Inc., BMI)/ Ride, cowboy ride (L. Emerson, 3:15, Marizona Music Inc., BMI)/ A time and a place for everything (B. Joy, 1:51, Marizona Music Inc., BMI)/ Red River Valley (public domain, 2:24); Side 2: Don't worry (M. Robbins, 3:14, Marty's Music Inc., BMI)/ Streets of Laredo (public domain, 2:47)/ Saddle tramp (M. Robbins, 2:47, Marty's Music Inc., BMI)/ Ballad of the Alamo (From the Batjac Prod. "The Alamo," P. F. Webster, D. Tiomkin, 3:41, Leo Feist Inc., ASCAP)/ I told my heart (M. Robbins, 2:04, Marizona Music Inc., BMI)/ Big iron (M. Robbins, 3:57, Marty's Music Inc., BMI).

Just a little sentimental. Information taken from Stereo CS 8466 (Side 1: XSM 53534; Side 2: XSM 53535). Additional release numbers: Mono CL 1666: Columbia Records; First released October, 1961; 33⅓ rpm. (Album).
Note: Back cover reads "Marty Robbins with the Jordanaires." Cover photo: Don Hunstein.
Album contents. Side 1: A little sentimental (J. Babcock, 2:57, Marty's Music Inc, BMI)/ Hurt (Crane, Jacobs, 2:53, Miller Music Corp., ASCAP)/ To each his own (J. Livingston, R. Evans, 1:52, Paramount Music Corp., ASCAP)/ I can't help it (if I'm still in love with you) (H. Williams, 2:12, Acuff-Rose Pub., BMI)/ Answer me my love (C. Sigman, G. Winkler, 2:10, Bourne Inc., ASCAP)/ Clara (M. Robbins, 1:30, Marty's Music Inc., BMI); Side 2: Half as much (C. Williams, 2:04, Acuff-Rose Pub., BMI)/ Unchained melody (H. Zaret, H. North, 2:19, Frank Music Corp., ASCAP)/ Are you sincere? (W. Walker, 2:30, Cedarwood Pub. Co., BMI)/ Guess I'll be going (M. Robbins, 2:03, Marty's Music Inc., BMI)/ To think you've chosen me (B. Benjamin, G. Weiss, 2:05, Valando Music

Corp., ASCAP)/ Too young (S. Dee, S. Lippman, 2:40, Jefferson Music Corp., ASCAP).

Portrait of Marty. Information taken from CL 1855. Also issued as a re-release Limited Edition LE 10022 (Side 1: XSM 56254; Side 2: XSM 56255). Other issue numbers: Stereo 8655: Columbia Records; First released July, 1962; 33⅓ rpm. (Album). CL 1855 contained a special souvenir framed portrait of Marty in the package.
Note: Produced by Don Law and Frank Jones.
   Album contents. Side 1: The bend in the river (M. Robbins, 2:32, Marty's Music, BMI)/ Abilene Rose (J. B. Hosale, 2:59, Marty's Music, BMI)/ Lolene (M. Robbins, 3:55, Marty's Music, BMI)/ Foggy Foggy Dew (public domain, 2:15)/ Beyond the reef (J. Pitman, 3:05, Laurel Music Co., BMI)/ Ka-Lu-a (K. Darby, 2:21, T. B. Harms Co., ASCAP); Side 2: Yours (Quiereme Mucho) (A. Gamse, G. Roig, 2:38, E. B. Marks Music Corp., BMI)/ Dusty Winds (J. Babcock, 1:51, Marizona Music, BMI)/ No one will ever know (M. Foree, F. Rose, 2:12, Milene Music, ASCAP)/ The nearness of you (N. Washington, H. Carmichael, 3:03, Famous Music Corp., ASCAP)/ All the way (S. Cahn, J. Van Heusen, 2:56, Maraville Music Corp., ASCAP)/ I'll walk alone (S. Cahn, J. Styne, 2:55, Mayfair Music Corp., ASCAP).

Marty after midnight. Information taken from CS 8601 (Side 1: XSM 56179, Side 2: XSM 56180). Other release numbers: Mono CL 1801, Cameo reissue (1984, Stereo CBS 32421): Columbia Records; First released September, 1962; 33⅓ rpm. (Album).
Note: Produced by Don Law and Frank Jones. Back cover has credit: "With the Jordanaires." Liner notes indicate Marty has five Golden Guitar awards (for "Don't worry," "El Paso," "Big Iron," "Singing the blues," and "A white sport coat." Cover photo from Henry Parker of Columbia Records Photo Studio.
   Album contents. Side 1: I'm in the mood for love (J. McHugh, D. Fields, 3:24, Robbins Music Corp, ASCAP)/ Misty (J. Burke, E. Garner, 3:22, Vernon Music Corp., ASCAP)/ Looking back (C. Otis, B. Benton, B. Hendricks, 3:11, Eden Music, Inc. and Sweco Music Corp., BMI)/ September in the rain (A. Dubin, H. Warren, 2:00, Remick Music Corp., ASCAP)/ Don't throw me away (M. Robbins, 3:24, Marty's Music, BMI)/ Pennies from heaven (J. Burke, A. Johnston, 2:07, Joy Music, ASCAP); Side 2: Summertime (D. Heyward, G. Gershwin, 2:32, Gershwin Pub. Corp., ASCAP)/ All the way (S. Cahn, J. Van Heusen, 2:56, Maraville Music Corp., ASCAP)/ It had to be you (G. Kahn, I. Jones, 2:23, Remick Music

Corp., ASCAP)/ I'm having a ball (L. Phillips, 2:05, Marizona Music, BMI)/ If I could cry (J. Babcock, 2:47, Marizona Music, BMI)/ On the sunny side of the street (D. Fields, J. McHugh, 1:83, Shapiro, Bernstein, & Co., ASCAP).

Devil woman. Information taken from the re-release Limited Edition LE 10579 (Side 1: XSM 57536; Side 2: XSM 57537). Other release numbers: Mono CL 1918, Stereo CS 8718: Columbia Records; First released November, 1962; 33⅓ rpm. (Album).
Note: Produced by Don Law and Frank Jones. Cover photo (of girl and car) by Joe Rudis; front cover inset photo and back cover photo of Marty by Henry Parker. All published by Marty's Music, Inc., BMI, except for "In the ashes of an old love affair," published by Marizona Music, BMI.
Album contents. Side 1: Devil woman (M. Robbins, 2:52)/ Ain't life a crying shame (T. Senn, H. McDowell, 2:28)/ Time can't make me forget (M. Robbins, 2:36)/ In the ashes of an old love affair (L. Douglas, 2:02)/ The hands you're holding now (M. Robbins, 3:02)/ Worried (M. Robbins, 2:05); Side 2: Little rich girl (M. Robbins, 2:29)/ Progressive love (M. Robbins, 2:01)/ I'm beginning to forget (M. Robbins, 2:43)/ Love is a hurting thing (J. Clay, 2:25)/ Kinda halfway feel (M. Robbins, 2:43)/ The wine flowed freely (J. Babcock, 2:11).

Hawaii's calling me. Information taken from Stereo CS 8840. Additional release numbers: Mono CL 2040, Air Force issue P-8438: Columbia Records; First released October, 1963; 33⅓ rpm. (Album).
Note: Produced by Don Law and Frank Jones. Liner notes by Jerry Byrd. Cover photo by Ray Manley from Shastal.
Album contents. Side 1: Lovely hula hands (R. A. Anderson, 2:28, Miller Music Corp., ASCAP)/ The sea and me (J. Byrd, 3:04, Maricana Music, BMI)/ Ka-lu-a (A. Caldwell, J. Kern, 2:21, T. B. Harms C.., ASCAP)/ The night I came ashore (C. Robinson, 3:03, Maricana Music, BMI)/ Echo Island (H. Robinson, 2:30, Marty's Music, BMI)/ Kuu Ipo Lani (My sweetheart, Lani) (J. Byrd, 3:08, Marty's Music, BMI); Side 2: The Hawaiian Wedding Song (C. King, 2:14, Pickwick Music Corp., ASCAP)/ Drowsy waters (Wailana) (J. Byrd, 2:08, Maricana Music, BMI)/ Hawaiian Bells (J. Byrd, 3:30, Marty's Music, BMI)/ My wonderful one (J. Sweeney, 2:48, Marty's Music, BMI)/ Blue Sand (J. Byrd, 2:55, Marty's Music, BMI)/ Hawaii's calling me (J. B. Hosale, 3:03, Marizona Music).

Return of the gunfighter. Information taken from Stereo CS 8872 (Side 1: XSM 75125; Side 2: XSM 75126). Other numbers: Mono CL 2072: Columbia Records; First released November, 1963; 33⅓ rpm. (Album). Note: Produced by Don Law and Frank Jones. Liner notes by Carol Endeman. Cover photo by Byron Shaw. Cover photo for CL 2220 is by Joe Rudis.

    Album contents. Side 1: San Angelo (Robbins, 5:32, Marizona Music, BMI)/ Man walks among us (Robbins, 3:03, Marizona Music, BMI)/ Tall handsome stranger (Dorrough, 2:05, Maricana Music, BMI)/ Dusty winds (Babcock, 1:51, Marizona Music, BMI)/ The Master's call (Robbins, 2:53, Marty's Music)/ The fastest gun around (Pruett, Glaser, 1:45, Marty's Music); Side 2: Old Red (Robbins, 3:09, Marty's Music)/ The bend in the river (Robbins, 2:32, Marty's Music)/ Johnny Fedavo (Babcock, 3:01, Maricana Music, BMI)/ Abilene Rose (Hosale, 2:59, Marty's Music)/ Doggone cowboy (Babcock, 2:08, Marizona Music, BMI)/ The Red Hills of Utah (Robbins, 2:05, Marty's Music).

Island woman. Information taken from Stereo CSRP 8976 (Columbia Special Products, Century Series. Side 1: XSM 76755; Side 2: XSM 76756). Other release numbers: Mono CL 2176, Stereo 8976: Columbia Records; June, 1964; 33⅓ rpm. (Album). Note: Produced by Don Law and Frank Jones. Cover photo: Horn/Griner.

    Album contents. Side 1: The mango song (1:52, Marty's Music, BMI)/ Girl from Spanish town (2:55, Marty's Music, BMI)/ Blue sea (2:03, Marty's Music, BMI)/ Calypso vacation (2:11, Marizona Music, BMI)/ Calypso girl (3:37, Maricana Music, BMI)/ Native girl (1:42, Marty's Music, BMI); Side 2: Bahama mama (2:06, Marizona Music, BMI)/ Tahitian boy (2:56, Marizona and Starday Music, BMI)/ Kingston girl (2:01, Marizona Music, BMI)/ Back to Montego Bay (1:38, Marty's Music, BMI)/ A woman gets her way (2:16, Maricana Music)/ Sweet bird of paradise (2:47, Maricana Music).

R.F.D. Information taken from Stereo CS 9020 (Side 1: XSM 77575; Side 2: XSM 77576). Additional release numbers: Mono CL 2220: Columbia Records; October, 1964; 33⅓ rpm. (Album). Note: Produced by Don Law and Frank Jones. Cover photo by Henry Parker, Columbia Records Photo Studio.

    Album contents. Side 1: Melba from Melbourne (Robbins, 2:10, Maricana Music, BMI)/ Change that dial (Winters, 2:16, Marizona Music, BMI)/ Only a picture stops time (Dorrough, 2:47, Maricana Music, BMI)/ Southern Dixie Flyer (Babcock, 3:28, Maricana Music, BMI)/ Everybody's darlin' plus mine (Hur, 2:16, Maricopa Music, SESAC)/ She means nothing to me now (Greff, 2:25, Marizona Music, BMI); Side 2: Making excuses (P. Binkley, B. Binkley, 2:09, Marty's Music, BMI)/ Rainbow (Jones, 2:11, Maricana Music, BMI)/ I lived a lifetime in a day (Worth, 2:33, Marty's Music, BMI)/ You won't have her long (Talley, 2:31, Marizona Music, BMI)/ The things that I don't know (Pruitt, 2:14, Marty's Music, BMI)/ Urgently needed (Johnson, 2:30, Marizona Music).

Turn the lights down low. Information taken from Stereo CS 9104 (Side 1: XSM 78960; Side 2: XSM 78961). Additional release numbers: Mono CL 2304, LE 10145. Also available on cassette: LET 10545: Columbia Records; First released March, 1965; 33⅓ rpm. (Album). Note: Produced by Don Law and Frank Jones. Cover photo by Don Hunstein.

Album contents. Side 1: Turn the lights down low (Babcock, 2:25, Maricana Music, BMI)/ Forever yours (Winters, 2:34, Marizona Music, BMI)/ You're not the only one (B. Binkley, P. Binkley, 2:58, Mariposa Music, BMI)/ I don't care (if you don't care for me) (B. Binkley, P. Binkley, 2:41, Marizona Music, BMI)/ But only in my dreams (Babcock, 2:44, Maricana Music, BMI)/ If you see my heart today (Babcock, 2:44, Maricana Music, BMI); Side 2: When your love was mine (Babcock, 2:51, Maricana Music, BMI)/ Up in the air (Robbins, 2:31, Mariposa Music, BMI)/ No tears, no regrets (Sweeney, 2:52, Maricana Music, BMI)/ Refer him to me (B. Binkley, P. Binkley, 2:25, Marizona Music, BMI)/ Can I help it (B. Binkley, P. Binkley, 2:33, Mariposa Music, BMI)/ I'll be all right (David, Cordle, 2:27, Maricana Music).

What God has done. Information taken from Stereo ACS 9248 (Collectors' Series. Side 1: XSM 111688; Side 2: XSM 111689). Other release numbers: Mono CL 2448, Stereo CS 9248. A reissue for 1986 is numbered: FC 40348: Columbia Records; First released May, 1965; 33⅓ rpm. (Album).

Note: Original release produced by Don Law and Frank Jones; liner notes by Ren Grevatt. A special 1986 edition of the album has a color portrait illustration of Marty on the cover and a scenic illustration on the back cover by Bill Imhoff. Liner notes are personal memories by Marizona Robinson, in which she acknowledges that she (with some help from son Ronny) wrote the title song.

Album contents. Side 1: When the roll is called up yonder (J. M. Black, 2:03, Public Domain)/ An evening prayer (C. M. Battersby, C. Gabriel, 3:43, The Rodeheaver Co., ASCAP)/ A little spot in heaven (M. Robbins, 3:24, Marty's Music and Noma Music, BMI)/

What God has done (M. Robinson, R. Robinson, 2:48, Marizona Music and Noma Music, BMI)/ You gotta climb (M. Yeargin, 2:09, Marty's Music, Elvis Presley Music, and Noma Music, BMI)/ Almost persuaded (P. P. Bliss, 2:38, public domain); Side 2: There's power in the blood (L. E. Jones, 2:00, public domain)/ With his hand on my shoulder (M. Robbins, 3:20, Noma Music and Marty's Music, BMI)/ The great speckled bird (3:17, public domain)/ Will the circle be unbroken? (A. Habershon, C. Gabriel, 3:01, The Rodeheaver Co., ASCAP)/ Who at my door is standing (E. Arnold, 2:58, Hill & Range Songs, BMI)/ Have thine own way, Lord (2:16, public domain).

The drifter. Information taken from Stereo CS 9327. Other release numbers: Mono CL 2527: Columbia Records; First released August, 1966; 33⅓ rpm. (Album).
Note: Produced by Don Law and Frank Jones. Liner notes by Don Richardson, Sr. The cover also notes the songs are selected from Marty's television series, "The Drifter."
　Album contents. Side 1: Meet me tonight in Laredo (M. Cordle, R. Robinson, 3:23)/ The wind goes (M. Robbins, 1:43)/ Cry Stampede (B. D. Johnson, 2:16)/ Feleena (from El Paso) (M. Robbins, 8:17); Side 2: Never tie me down (M. Robbins, 1:29)/ Cottonwood tree (B. Sykes, 3:56)/ Oh, Virginia (M. Robbins, 3:40)/ Mr. Shorty (M. Robbins, 5:01)/ Take me back to the prairie (B. Sykes, 2:19).

Saddle tramp. Information taken from Stereo P2S 5098/DS 237 (Columbia Record Club Exclusive. Side 1: XSM 116131; Side 2: XSM 116132). Additional release numbers: Mono D 237, Stereo DS 237: Columbia Records; First released in 1966.; 33⅓ rpm. (Album).
　Album contents. Side 1: I'm gonna be a cowboy/ Billy Venero/ Saddle tramp/ Johnny Fedavo/ La Paloma; Side 2: The cowboy in the continental suit/ Jimmy Martinez/ When the work's all done this fall/ The roving gambler/ Maria Elena.

My kind of country. Information taken from Stereo LE 10033 (Columbia Limited Edition. Side 1: XSM 116824; Side 2: XSM 116825). Additional release numbers: Mono 2645, CS 9445: Columbia Records; First released March, 1967; 33⅓ rpm. (Album).
Note: Produced by Don Law and Frank Jones. Cover photo by Henry Parker, Columbia Records Photo Studio.
　Album contents. Side 1: I'll have to make some changes (B. Johnson, 2:10)/ Nine-tenths of the law (R. Robinson, C. Babcock, 2:32, SESAC)/ Sorting memories (J. Pruett, 2:40)/ Hello heartache (M. Cor-

dell, J. Beard, 3:59)/ One window, four walls (M. Cordell, A. Russell, 3:32)/ Working my way through a heartache (B. Mize, 2:51); side 2: Would you take me back again (B. Sykes, 2:38)/ Do me a favor (D. Winters, 2:35)/ Sixteen weeks (M. Robbins, 2:53)/ Seconds to remember (B. Johnson, 2:52)/ Another lost week-end (D. Winters, 2:07).

Tonight Carmen. Information taken from Mono CL 2725 (Side 1: XLP 118860; Side 2: XLP 118861). Other release numbers: Stereo CS 9525, Columbia Limited Edition (Stereo LE 10189): Columbia Records; First released March, 1967; 33⅓ rpm. (Album).
Note: Produced by Bob Johnston. Cover photo by New World Photo. Liner notes by Bob Johnston. Music arranged by Bill McElhiney, Bill Walker, and Bob Johnston.
Album contents. Side 1: Tonight Carmen (M. Robbins, 2:45)/ Waiting in Reno (J. Pruett, 2:26)/ Is there anything left I can say (M. Robbins, 1:59)/ Loves gone away (B. Binkley, P. Binkley, 2:13)/ Bound for old Mexico (J. Lebsock, 3:00)/ Don't go away Senor (J. Sweeney, 2:37); Side 2: The girl with gardenias in her hair (J. Byers, B. Tubert, 2:35)/ In the valley of the Rio Grande (A. Russell, 2:23)/ The mission in Guadalajara (L. Emerson, 2:35)/ Chapel bells chime (B. Binkley, P. Binkley, 2:51)/ Spanish lullaby (B. Johnston, 3:23).

Christmas with Marty Robbins. Information from Stereo CS 9535 (Side 1: XSM 118911; Side 2: XSM 118912. Other release numbers: Mono CL 2735, C-10980, P-13358: Columbia Records; First released October, 1967; 33⅓ rpm. (Album). CL 2735 contains the music publishers and licensing agents for each song in addition to the information provided below.
Note: Produced by Bob Johnston; cover photo by New world photo.
Album contents. Side 1: O little town of Bethlehem (public domain, 3:11)/ Christmas is for kids (J. Pruett, 2:48)/ Christmas time is here again (H. Robinson, 2:18)/ Many Christmases ago (P. Binkley, B. Binkley, 3:23)/ The joy of Christmas (P. Binkley, B. Binkley, 2:15)/ Little stranger (in a manger) (T. Connor, 1:59); Side 2: Hark! The herald angels sing (public domain, 3:06)/ One of you (in every size) (J. Pruett, 1:37)/ Christmas kisses (B. Johnson, 2:24)/ Merry Christmas to you from me (M. Robbins, 2:35)/ A Christmas prayer (M. Robbins, 3:15).

By the time I get to Phoenix. Information taken from Columbia Limited Edition LE 10045 (Side 1: XSM 135713; Side 2: XSM 135714). Other

release numbers: Stereo 10045, CS 9617, C 11311, P 11513: Columbia Records; [1968]; 33⅓ rpm. (Album).
Note: Produced by Bob Johnston, arranged and conducted by Robert Mersey. One song, "Oh Virginia," is listed as "Virginia" on the album cover. Cover photo by Robert Hinkle, Hollywood, California.
   Album contents. Side 1: By the time I get to Phoenix (J. Webb)/ Am I that easy to forget (C. Belew, W. S. Stevenson)/ Love is blue (L'Amour est bleu) (Blackburn, C. Cour, A. Popp)/ Oh Virginia (M. Robbins)/ Until we meet again (M. Robbins, B. Mersey)/ Yesterday (J. Lennon, Paul McCartney); Side 2: Love is in the air (M. Robbins)/ As time goes by (H. Hupfeld)/ That old feeling (L. Brown, S. Fain)/ To be in love with her (M. Robbins)/ You made me love you (J. V. Monaco, J. McCarthy).

*Bend in the river.*Information taken from a reissue, Columbia Musical Treasuries Stereo DS 445 (Side 1: XSM 137822; Side 2: XSM 137823). Other release numbers: Mono D 445 (Side 1: XLP 137820; Side 2: XLP 137821), Stereo DS 445: Columbia Records; First released October, 1968; 33⅓ rpm. (Album). Mfg. by Columbia Record Club.
   Album contents. Side 1: The bend in the river/ Tonight Carmen/ Devil woman/ Big iron/ El Paso; Side 2: The girl with gardenias in her hair/ Mr. Shorty/ I'll step aside/ Bouquet of roses/ Abilene Rose.

I walk alone. Information taken from Stereo CS 9725 (Side 1: XSM 137953; Side 2: XSM 137954).: Columbia Records; First released October, 1968; 33⅓ rpm. (Album).
Note: Produced by Bob Johnston, cover photo by Leonard of Sweden.
   Album contents. Side 1: I walk alone (H. Wilson)/ Today I started loving you again (M. Haggard, B. Owens) I can't help it (if I'm still in love with you) (H. Williams)/ They'll never take her love from me (L. Payne)/ Begging to you (M. Robbins)/ She thinks I still care (D. Lee); Side 2: The last letter (R. Griffin)/ Lily of the Valley (J. Pruett)/ I feel another heartbreak coming on (M. Robbins)/ Windows have pains (W. Buchanan)/ Let me live in your world (K. Russell).

It's a sin. Information taken from Stereo LE 10030 (Side 1: XSM 139689; Side 2: XSM 139690). Other release numbers: CS 9811: Columbia Records; First released June, 1969; 33⅓ rpm. (Album).
Note: Produced by Bob Johnston. Titles listed on record cover are not in the same order as they are on the recording itself.
   Album contents. Side 1: I can't say goodby (R. Hardin, J. Byers)/ It's a sin (F. Rose, Z. Turner)/ Hello Daily News (J. Easterly)/ If I want to (B. Mize)/ You gave me a mountain (M. Robbins); Side 2: When

my turn comes around (J. Sweeney)/ We're getting mighty close (K. Russell)/ Rainbows (O. Jones)/ Times have changed (P. Binkley, B. Binkley)/ This song (J. Pruett)/ Fresh out of tears (F. Laine, R. Morgan).

Marty's country. 2-album set. Information taken from records CS 9894/CS 9895 (Record 1: GP 15, CS 9894; Side 1: XSM 150579; Side 2: XSM 150580. Record 2: GP 15, CS 9895; Side 1: XSM 150581; Side 2: XSM 150582): Columbia Records; First released in 1969; 33⅓ rpm. (Album). Other release numbers: Stereo CG 15.
Note: Previously released material. Cover photo by Lee Friedlander. Album contents for Record 1. Side 1: Kaw-liga (H. Williams, F. Rose)/ Yours (Quiereme Mucho) (A. Gamse, G. Roig)/ Half as much (C. Williams)/ I can't help it (if I'm still in love with you) (H. Williams)/ Streets of Laredo; Side 2: Devil woman (M. Robbins)/ Red River Valley/ The hanging tree (M. David, J. Livingston from the Warner Bros. Picture "The Hanging Tree")/ Singing the blues (Endsley)/ Cool water (Nolan). Album contents for Record 2. Side 1: Amor (S. Skylar, R. L. Mendez, G. Ruiz)/ Are you sincere? (W. Walker)/ The great speckled bird/ Have I told you lately that I love you? (Autry, Wiseman)/ I'm so lonesome I could cry (H. Williams)/ Hello heartache (M. Cordell, J. Beard); Record 2, Side 2: The Strawberry roan/ Little Joe the wrangler/ The Hawaiian wedding song (C. King)/ Long tall Sally (E. Johnson).

Singing the blues. Information taken from Stereo Harmony, HS 11338 (Side 1: XSM 139903; Side 2: XSM 139904): Columbia Records; First released October, 1969; 33⅓ rpm. (Album).
Note: Cover photo by Lee Friedlander. Notes by Russ Barnard. Album contents. Side 1: Singing the blues (Endsley)/ The hands you're holding now (M. Robbins)/ Ruby Ann (R. Bellamy)/ The Master's call (Robbins)/ Have I told you lately that I love you? (Autry, Wiseman); Side 2: I can't help it (if I'm still in love with you) (H. Williams)/ Shackles and chains (J. Davis)/ Hello heartache (M. Cordell, J. Beard)/ Begging to you (M. Robbins).

Heart of Marty Robbins. 2-album set. STS 2016 (STS 1015/1016: Columbia Records; Columbia Star Series; October, 1969, 33⅓ rpm. (Album).
Album contents. Record STS 1015, Side 1 (XSM 139389): Love is blue (L'amour est bleu)/ Bouquet of roses/ The girl with gardenias in her hair/ Pennies from heaven/ The great speckled bird; Side 2 (XSM 139390): The nearness of you/ The last time I saw my heart/ Big

iron/ Devil woman/ Begging to you. Record STS 1016, Side 1 (XSM 139391: Foggy foggy dew/ El Paso/ The story of my life/ Who at my door is standing/ Sittin' in a tree house; Side 2 (XSM 139392): A white sport coat (and a pink carnation)/ I'll step aside/ Ride, cowboy ride/ Saddle tramp/ The last letter.

My woman, my woman, my wife. Information taken from Stereo CS 9978 (Side 1: XSM 151854; Side 2: XSM 151855): Columbia Records; First released May, 1970; 33⅓ rpm. (Album).
Note: Produced by Bob Johnston. Cover photo by Bill Grimes. Cover notes by Don DeVito and Jim Wiles.
   Album contents. Side 1: My woman, my woman, my wife (M. Robbins)/ Can't help falling in love (G. Weiss, H. Peretti, L. Creatore)/ Love me tender (E. Presley, V. Matson)/ I've got a woman's love (M. Robbins)/ Three little words (M. Robinson)/ Maria (if I could) (C. E. Daniels); Side 2: The Master's touch (H. Hanewinkel, T. Lang)/ My happy heart sings (J. B. Hosale)/ Without you to love (D. Winters)/ A very special way (M. Robbins) Martha Ellen Jenkins (P. Binkley, B. Binkley).

The story of my life. Information taken from LE 10577 (Side 1: XSM 152992; Side 2: 152993). Other release numbers: Stereo HS 11409: Columbia Records; First released June, 1970; 33⅓ rpm. (Album).
Note: Liner notes by Bill Dobbins; cover photo by Lee Friedlander.
   Album contents. Side 1: The story of my life (H. David, Bacharach, 2:31)/ Are you sincere? (W. Walker, 2:30)/ The hands you're holding now (M. Robbins, 3:02)/ Hurt (Crane, Jacobs, 2:52)/ To each his own (J. Livingston, R. Evans, 1:51); Side 2: Answer me my love (C. Sigman, G. Winkler, 2:08)/ She thinks I still care (D. Lee, 3:19)/ Meet me tonight in Laredo (M. Cordle, R. Robinson, 3:23)/ Lovesick blues (J. Mills, Friend, 2:33).

El Paso. Information taken from Stereo PC 30316 (Side 1: AL 30316; Side 2: BL 30316). Other release numbers: Harmony Headliner Series KH 30316: Columbia Records; Released December, 1970; 33⅓ rpm. (Album).
Note: Cover photos by Al Clayton, cover design by Jim Cook. Notes by Marguerite Renz. "The nearness of you" is misspelled on the album cover.
   Album contents. Side 1: El Paso (M. Robbins)/ The wine flowed freely (J. Babcock)/ Streets of Laredo/ The hanging tree (M. David, Jerry Livingston)/ Bouquet of roses (S. Nelson, Hilliard); Side 2: Hello Heartaches (M. Cordell, J. Beard)/ Forever yours (D. Win-

ters)/ The nearness of you (N. Washington, H. Carmichael)/ My wonderful one (J. Sweeney)/ Love is in the air (M. Robbins).

Greatest Hits, Vol. III. Information taken from Stereo C 30571 (Side 1: AL 30571; Side 2: BL 30571). Other release numbers: PC 30571: Columbia Records; First released April, 1971; 33⅓ rpm. (Album).
Note: Cover photo by Al Clayton. Album notes by Don DeVito.
   Album contents. Side 1: Devil woman (M. Robbins, 2:52)/ Love is blue (L'Amour est bleu) (Blackburn, P. Cour, A. Popp, 2:24)/ You gave me a mountain (M. Robbins, 4:02)/ I walk alone (H. Wilson, 3:17)/ Ribbon of darkness (G. Lightfoot, 2:30); Side 2: It's a sin (F. Rose, Z. Turner, 2:48)/ Padre (A. Romans, P. F. Webster, 3:17)/ The girl with gardenias in her hair (J. Byers, B. Turbert, 2:35)/ Jolie girl (B. Fowler, 2:43)/ My woman, my woman, my wife (M. Robbins, 3:30)/ Tonight Carmen (M. Robbins, 2:45).

From the heart. Information taken from Columbia Limited Edition LE 10575 (Side 1: AL 30756; Side 2: BL 30756). Other release numbers: Stereo Harmony Headliner Series KH 30756: Columbia Records; Album first released September, 1971; 33⅓ rpm. (Album).
Note: J. Pruett's name is misspelled (as Pruitt) in the credits. Cover design by Ron Coro; cover photo by Al Clayton.
   Album contents. Side 1: I'm so lonesome I could cry (H. Williams, 2:45)/ I never let you cross my mind (F. Rose, 3:00)/ Lolene (M. Robbins, 3:56)/ The things that I don't know (J. Pruitt, 2:17)/ I can't say goodbye (R. Hardin, J. Byers, 3:01); Side 2: Half as much (C. Williams, 2:05)/ Oh, Virginia (M. Robbins, 3:41)/ I feel another heartbreak coming on (M. Robbins, 3:15)/ Love's gone away (B. Binkley, P. Binkley, 2:14)/ Would you take me back again? (B. Sykes, 2:38).

Today. Information taken from Columbia Limited Edition Stereo LE 10046 (Side 1: AL 30816; Side 2: BL 30816). Other release numbers: C 30816: Columbia Records; First released August, 1971; 33⅓ rpm. (Album).
Note: Produced by Marty Robbins, arranged by Bill McElhiney. Cover Photo by Pal Parker, cover design by Ron Coro. Cover liner notes by race driver Bobby Allison and editor Noel Coppage.
   Album contents. Side 1: Early morning sunshine (J. Marshall)/ Late great lover (B. D. Johnson)/ I'm not blaming you (B. Mize)/ Another day has gone by (D. Winters Jr., D. Winters)/ Thanks, but no thanks, thanks to you (C. Harwell II)/ Quiet shadows (C. Blanchard, B. Blanchard); Side 2: Too many places (D. Winters)/ You say it's over

(J. Sweeney)/ Put a little rainbow in your pocket (B. Binkley, P. Binkley)/ Seventeen years (M. Robbins)/ The chair (M. Robbins).

The World of Marty Robbins. A 2-album set. Information taken from Stereo CG 30881: G 30881 and C 30882 (Side 1: AL 30882; Side 2: AL 30883; Side 3: BL 30883; Side 4: BL 30882): Columbia Records; October, 1971; 33⅓ rpm. (Album).
Note: Cover art and design by Karenlee Grant. Liner notes by Noel Coppage.
Album contents. Side 1: The story of my life (H. David, Bacharach, 2:31)/ She was young and she was pretty (M. Robbins, 2:58)/ Ride, cowboy ride (L. Emerson, 3:15)/ I'm beginning to forget (M. Robbins, 2:43)/ The blues country style (M. David, J. Livingston, 2:35); Side 2: Lovesick blues (I. Mills, C. Friend, 2:35)/ Tall handsome stranger (H. Dorrough, 2:06)/ I hang my head and cry (G. Autry, F. Rose, R. Whitley, 2:15)/ All the world is lonely now (M. Foree, 2:13)/ Have I told you lately that I love you? (G. Autry, S. Wiseman, 3:08); Side 3: Long tall Sally (E. Johnson, 2:06)/ The wine flowed freely (J. Babcock, 2:12)/ The Hawaiian wedding song (C. King, 2:15)/ I'm so lonesome I could cry (H. Williams, 2:45)/ Singing the blues (M. Endsley, 2:25); Side 4: In the valley of the Rio Grande (A. Russell, 2:23)/ One window, four walls (M. Cordell, A. Russell, 3:34)/ I feel another heartbreak coming on (M. Robbins, 3:15)/ The mission in Guadalajara (L. Emerson, 2:35)/ The last letter (R. Griffin, 3:56).

Marty Robbins favorites. Information taken from Columbia/Harmony House Headliner Series release Stereo KH 31257 (Side 1: AL 31257; Side 2: BL 31257): Columbia Records, Harmony House; June, 1972; 33⅓ rpm. (Album).
Note: Cover photo by Baron Wolman, back cover photo by Jim Marshall. Liner notes by Mart Goode.
Album contents. Side 1: Almost persuaded (P. P. Bliss)/ You're not the only one (B. Binkley, P. Binkley)/ I don't care (if you don't care for me) (B. Binkley, P. Binkley)/ When your love was mine (J. Babcock)/ Would you take me back again (B. Sykes); Side 2: The great speckled bird (public domain)/ No tears, no regrets (J. Sweeney)/ Refer him to me (B. Binkley, P. Binkley)/ Forever yours (D. Winters)/ I'll be alright (M. David, M. Cordle).

Song of the islands. Information taken from Stereo Harmony H 31258 (Side 1: AL 31258; Side 2; BL 31258): Harmony; a product of Columbia Records; Released September, 1972; 33⅓ rpm. (Album). Additional release numbers: CL 1087, CS 9425.

Note: Cover design by Bill Barnes. Cover photo by Baron Wolman, Garry Langham. Liner notes by Ed Lawson.
    Album contents. Side 1: Song of the islands (C. King)/ Don't sing aloha when I go (W. Smith, B. Black, Moret)/ My isle of golden dreams (Kahn, Blaufuss)/ Now is the hour (Maori farewell song) (Kalhan, C. Scott, D. Stewart); Side 2: Sweet Leilani (H. Owens)/ Down where the trade winds blow (H. Owens)/ Island echoes (Kessel)/ Moonland (Byrd)/ Aloha Oe (Farewell to thee) (Liliuokalani).

All time greatest hits. A 2-album set. Information taken from CG 31361: KG 31361 and C 31362 (Side 1: AL 31362; Side 2: AL 31363; Side 3: BL 31363; Side 4: BL 31362): Columbia Records; 1972; 33⅓ rpm. (Album).
Note: "Joli girl" is spelled "Jolie girl" on other recordings. Liner notes by Jay Hoffer. Cover photo by Hope Powell. Produced in part by Bob Johnson, Don Law, and Frank Jones.
    Album contents. Side 1: El Paso (M. Robbins, 4:22)/ Streets of Laredo (2:47)/ Ribbon of darkness (G. Lightfoot, 2:30)/ Love is blue (L'Amour est bleu) (Blackburn, P. Cour, A. Popp, 2:26)/ Big iron (Robbins, 3:58); Side 2: Devil woman (M. Robbins, 2:52)/ Don't worry (M. Robbins, 3:14)/ Tonight Carmen (M. Robbins, 2:45)/ You gave me a mountain (M. Robbins, 4:02)/ Kaw-liga (H. Williams, F. Rose, 2:30); Side 3: My woman, my woman, my wife (M. Robbins, 3:30)/ Padre (A. Romans, P. F. Webster, 3:17)/ The hanging tree (M. David, J. Livingston, 2:52)/ Red River Valley (2:24)/ Joli girl (B. Fowler, 2:43); Side 4: The girl with gardenias in her hair (J. Byers, B. Tubert, 2:35)/ It's a sin (F. Rose, Z. Turner, 2:48)/ Maria (if I could) (C. E. Daniels, 2:32)/ I walk alone (H. Wilson, 2:59)/ Aloha Oe (Farewell to thee) (Liliukalani, 2:28).

Bound for old Mexico. Stereo KC 31341, Harmony HC 15026: Columbia Records; 1972; 33⅓ rpm. (Album). Australia release numbers: HC 15026; cassette TCHC 15026.
Note: Cover photos by Slick Lawson and Al Clayton.
    Album contents. Side 1: Camelia/ La Paloma/ Is there anything else I can say/ You belong to my heart/ San Angelo; Side 2: Girl from Spanish town/ Maria Elena/ Bound for Old Mexico/ Adios, Mariquita Linda/ La Borrachita/ Amor.

Bound for old Mexico (great hits from south of the border). Information taken from Stereo HC 15026 (KC 31341. Side 1: MX 203309; Side 2: MX 203310). Other release numbers: Cassette TCHC 15026: Made in Australia. Harmony Records/CBS; First released in the United States in 1972 as Stereo KC 31341; c1972; 33⅓ rpm. (Australian album release).

Note: Produced by Don Law and Frank Jones; some cuts produced by Bob Johnston.

Album contents. Side 1: Carmelia (M. Robbins, 2:41, Belinda)/ La Paloma (Yradier, 2:59, MCPS)/ Is there anything else I can say (M. Robbins, 1:58, Acuff-Rose)/ You belong to my heart (R. Gilbert, A. Lara, 1:57, Allans)/ San Angelo (M. Robbins, 5:31, Acuff-Rose/Belinda); Side 2: Girl from Spanish town (M. Robbins, 2:53, Acuff-Rose/Belinda)/ Maria Elena (S. K. Russell, L. Barcelata, 2:48, Allans)/ Bound for old Mexico (J. Slaton, 3:00, Acuff-Rose)/ Adios, Mariquita Linda (M. A. Jiminez, 2:55, Allans)/ La Borrachita (T. Nacho, 1:56, Southern)/ Amor (S. Skylar, G. Ruiz, 1:53, Allans).

I've got a woman's love. Information taken from Stereo KC 31628: Columbia Records; Released November, 1972; 33⅓ rpm. (Album). Note: Various cuts produced by Marty Robbins, Bob Johnston, and Don Law/Frank Jones. Album contains previously released material. Cover photo by Al Clayton, back cover photo by Sandy Speiser. Liner notes by Earl James Carter.

Album contents. Side 1: I've got a woman's love (M. Robbins, 2:23)/ It had to be you (G. Kahn, I. Jones, 2:24)/ I'm in the mood for love (J. McHugh, D. Fields, 3:25)/ Janet (M. Robbins, 2:21)/ Misty (J. Burke, E. Garner, 3:24)/ The best part of living (B. D. Johnson, 2:52); Side 2: The city (M. Robbins, 4:37)/ Don't throw me away (M. Robbins, 3:23)/ Gone with the wind (B. Sykes, W. P. Walker, 3:23)/ At times (M. Robbins, 2:45)/ A little spot in heaven (M. Robbins, 2:46).

Joy of Christmas. "Featuring Marty Robbins and his friends." Information taken from Stereo C 11087: Created by Columbia Special Products in association with Continental Production Company, a Division of Continental Dynamics, Inc.; Released November, 1972; 33⅓ rpm. (Album).

Note: Marty recorded side one of the album.

Album contents. Side one (all songs recorded by Marty): The joy of Christmas/ O little town of Bethlehem/ Little stranger (in a manger)/ Hark! The herald angels sing/ A christmas prayer; Side 2 (recorded by various artists): Soon it will be Christmas day/ It came upon a midnight clear/ Joy to the world/ The first Noel/ Silent night, holy night.

Marty! A Columbia Musical Treasury (P5S, 5812). 5-record album set. Record 1, DS 989 (Side 1: XSM 156793; Side 2: XSM 156794); Record 2, DS 990 (Side 1: XSM 156795; Side 2: XSM 156796); Record 3, DS

991 (Side 1: XSM 156797; Side 2: XSM 156798); Record 4, DS 992 (Side 1: XSM 156799, Side 2: XSM 156800); Record 5, DS 993 (Side 1: XSM 156801; Side 2: XSM 156802): Columbia House, Columbia Records; 1972; 33⅓ rpm. (Album).

Contents of albums. Record 1 (side 1): Love is blue (L'Amour est bleu)/ A white sport coat (and a pink carnation)/ Streets of Laredo/ Love is a hurting thing/ Tonight Carmen; Record 1 (Side 2): My woman, my woman, my wife/ It's a sin/ Tall handsome stranger/ Bouquet of roses; Record 2 (side 1): Ballad of the Alamo/ The hanging tree/ When the roll is called up yonder/ You gave me a mountain/ San Angelo; Record 2 (side 2): El Paso/ The Strawberry roan/ She was only seventeen (he was one year more)/ The girl with gardenias in her hair/ Little rich girl; Record 3 (side 1): Red River Valley/ Cool water/ Old Red/ I'm so lonesome I could cry/ Devil woman; Record 3 (side 2): Saddle tramp/ Singing the blues/ The Hawaiian wedding song/ What God has done/ The valley of the Rio Grande; Record 4 (side 1): Ribbon of darkness/ Song of Kalua/ They're hanging me tonight/ Lovely hula hands/ With his hand on my shoulder; Record 4 (side 2): By the time I get to Phoenix/ Joli girl/ Long tall Sally/ Little Joe the Wrangler/ Ride cowboy ride; Record 5 (side 1): I walk alone/ Big iron/ Time can't make me forget/ Maria (if I could)/ Padre; Record 5 (side 2): The great speckled bird/ Song of the bandit/ Knee deep in the blues/ Kaw-liga/ Aloha oe (farewell to thee).

This much a man. Information taken from Stereo MCA DL 7-5389 (Side 1: 7-13124, MCA-61; Side 2: 7-13125, MCA-61): MCA Records; Released November, 1972; 33⅓ rpm. (Album).

Note: Produced by Marty Robbins. Cover photo by Hope Powell. Liner notes by Sammy Jackson.

Album contents. Side 1: This much a man (Marty Robbins, 2:56, Mariposa Music, BMI)/ Funny face (Donna Fargo, 2:56, Prima-Donna Music Company, BMI)/ Franklin, Tennessee (Marty Robbins, 3:03, Mariposa Music, BMI)/ She's too good to be true (Johnny Duncan, 2:54, Pi-Gem Music, BMI)/ You don't really know (Jim Easterling, 3:16, Mariposa Music, BMI)/ Leaving is a whole lot harder (Bill D. Johnson, 2:39, Mariposa Music BMI); Side 2: Over-hurt and underloved (Buddy Mize, 2:55, Mariposa Music, BMI)/ It's not love (but it's not bad) (Glenn Martin, Hank Cochran, 3:47, Tree Publishing Company, BMI)/ Eyes (Marty Robbins, Karen Russell, 3:03, Mariposa Music, BMI)/ Making the most of a heartache (Phoebe Binkley, Bob Binkley, 2:55, Mariposa Music, BMI)/ Guess I'll just stand here looking dumb (Larry Locke, Johnny Holland, 2:15, Mariposa Music, BMI).

Best of Marty Robbins. Information taken from Stereo LPC 110-LD
Side 1: LPC 644 LD; Side 2: LPC 644 LD): Artco; March, 1973; 33⅓
rpm. (Album).
Note: The album and cover both have "From the HALL OF FAME
motion picture soundtrack."
  Album contents. Side 1: I can't quit, I've gone too far/ I pay with
  every breath/ Tennessee Toddy/ Mr. Teardrop/ I'll go on alone/ Time
  goes by; Side 2: I couldn't keep from crying/ At the end of a long
  lonely day/ Pretty words/ Castle in the sky/ Gossip/ Pretty Mama.

Streets of Laredo and other ballads of the old west. Information taken
from Columbia Limited Edition, LE 10576 (Side 1: AL32286; Side 2:
BL 32286). Other release numbers: Stereo Harmony KH 32286: Colum-
bia Records; First released August, 1973; 33⅓ rpm. (Album).
Note: Liner notes by Ed Lawson.
  Album contents. Side 1: Red River Valley (public domain, 2:25)/ A
  hundred and sixty acres (Kapp, 1:42)/ Five brothers (J. Glaser, 2:13)/
  Ride, cowboy ride (L. Emerson, 3:16)/ Streets of Laredo (public
  domain, 2:47); Side 2: Big iron (Robbins, 3:59)/ The hanging tree
  (M. David, L. Livingston, 2:53)/ The cowboy in the continental suit
  (M. Robbins, 2:54)/ The fastest gun around (J. Pruett, J. Glaser,
  1:46)/ Cool water (Nolan, 3:11).

Marty Robbins. Information taken from MCA 342 (Side 1: MCA-176;
Side 2: MCA-177): MCA Records; August, 1973; 33⅓ rpm. (Album).
  Album contents. Side 1: A man and a train (from the 20th Century-
  Fox film "Emperor of the North Pole," Hal David, Frank de Vol,
  3:05, ASCAP)/ Las Vegas, Nevada (Lobo Rainey, 2:47, Mariposa
  Music, BMI)/ Pretend (Parman, Douglas, Lavere, Belloc, 2:27,
  Brandom Music Co., ASCAP)/ Crawling on my knees (Marty Rob-
  bins, 2:28, Mariposa Music, BMI)/ Up to my shoulders in a heart-
  ache (Marty Robbins, 2:29, Noma Music, Elvis Presley Music, Mo-
  jave Music, BMI)/ Walking piece of heaven (Marty Robbins, 2:02,
  Mariposa Music, BMI); Side 2: Love me (Jeanne Pruett, 4:16, Moss
  Rose Publications, BMI)/ The taker (Kris Kristofferson, Shel Silver-
  stein, 2:17, Evil Eye Music, Inc. BMI)/ San Francisco teardrops
  (Marty Robbins, 2:58, Mariposa Music, BMI)/ If there's still another
  mountain (Marty Robbins, 2:48, Mariposa Music, BMI)/ Martha, oh
  Martha (Marty Robbins, 2:28, Mariposa Music, BMI).

Marty Robbins. Information taken from SPC 3742: Pickwick International; 1973, 1980; 33⅓ rpm. (Album).
Note: This album is essentially the same as MCA 342 (previous entry),

with the exception of two songs that have been deleted ("Pretend" and "Up to my shoulders in a heartache"). The front covers are the same, the back covers differ.

Album contents. Side 1: A man and a train (from the film "Emperor of the North Pole," H. David, F. deVol, 3:05)/ Las Vegas, Nevada (L. Rainey, 2:47)/ The taker (K. Kristofferson, S. Silverstein, 2:17)/ Crawling on my knees (M. Robbins, 2:28)/ Walking piece of heaven (M. Robbins, 3:02); Side 2: Love me (J. Pruett, 4:16)/ San Francisco teardrops (M. Robbins, 2:58)/ If there's still another mountain (M. Robbins, 2:48)/ Martha, oh Martha (M. Robbins, 2:28).

Good 'n country. Information taken from Stereo MCA 421 (Side 1: MCA 462; Side 2: MCA 463): MCA Records; June, 1974; 33⅓ rpm. (Album).
Note: Liner notes by Marty Robbins dedicating the song "Twentieth Century Drifter" to all of the people connected with racing.

Album contents. Side 1: Twentieth century drifter (Marty Robbins, 2:59, Mariposa Music, BMI)/ I'm wanting to (Ronny Robbins, Karen Russell, 2:48, Mariposa Music, BMI)/ I heard the bluebirds sing (Hod Pharis, 2:52, Peer International Corp., BMI)/ The way I'm needing you (Hank Cochran, Jane Kinsey, 3:23, Tree Publishing, BMI)/ I couldn't believe it was true (Wallace Fowler, Eddy Arnold, 2:32, Vogue Music, BMI)/ You're an angel disguised as a girl (Jimmy Sweeney, 2:20, Mariposa Music, BMI); Side 2: Georgia blood (Marty Robbins, 5:04, Mariposa Music, BMI)/ Don't you think (Marty Robbins, 2:53, Mariposa Music, BMI)/ Mother knows best (Marty Robbins, 2:01, Mariposa Music, BMI)/ Darling come home (Donnie Winters, Dennis Winters, 2:40, Mariposa Music, BMI)/ Love needs (Bill D. Johnson, 2:54, Mariposa Music, BMI).

Marty Robbins' own favorites. Cover reads: Vaseline Hair Tonic presents Marty Robbins' Own Favorites. Information taken from Columbia Special Products Stereo P 12416 (Side 1: AS 12416; Side 2: BS 12416): Columbia Records; July, 1974; 33⅓ rpm. (Album).
Note: Editorial note: this was a special record for promotional purposes by Vaseline Hair Tonic.

Album contents. Side 1: Big iron/ Don't worry/ Ruby Ann/ It's your world/ My woman, my woman, my wife; Side 2: A white sport coat/ By the time I get to Phoenix/ El Paso/ Love me tender/ Devil woman.

Have I told you lately that I love you? Information taken from Stereo C 32586 (Side 1: AL 32586; Side 2: BL 32586): Columbia Records; First released March, 1974; 33⅓ rpm. (Album).

Note: Cover design by Bill Barnes; back cover photo by Al Clayton. Liner notes by Barry Levine.

Album contents. Side 1: Tonight Carmen (M. Robbins, 2:45)/ Moanin' the blues (H. Williams, 1:59)/ I'll step aside (Bond, 2:16)/ The girl with gardenias in her hair (J. Byers, B. Tubert, 2:35)/ Have I told you lately that I love you? (Autry, Wiseman, 3:09); Side 2: I'm so lonesome I could cry (H. Williams, 2:45)/ Lovesick blues (I. Mills, Friend, 2:33)/ You only want me when you're lonely (Autry, S. Nelson, 2:28)/ I hang my head and cry (Autry, F. Rose, Whitley, 2:16)/ Loves gone away (B. Binkley, P. Binkley, 2:13).

Marty Robbins gold. Information taken from Stereo NU 9060/P12935 (Side 1: AS 12935; Side 2: BS 12935). Other release numbers: CSPS 890: K-Tel; 1975; 33⅓ rpm. (Album).
Note: Album cover notes "20 original hits" and "As advertised on TV." Writer and publisher credits given on back cover.

Album contents. Side 1: El Paso/ Gone with the wind/ Singing the blues/ My woman, my woman, my wife/ Big iron/ It's a sin/ A white sport coat (and a pink carnation)/ I walk alone/ The hanging tree/ Just married; Side 2: Ballad of the Alamo/ Devil woman/ Tonight Carmen/ Don't worry/ Saddle tramp/ You gave me a mountain/ The story of my life/ She was only seventeen (he was one year more)/ Ribbon of darkness/ The cowboy in the continental suit.

My woman, my woman, my wife/ Gunfighter ballads. 2-album set packaged and sold together ed. Stereo CG 33630: Columbia Records; 1976; 33⅓ rpm. (Album).
Note: This combined set contains the two albums previously issued separately. Four photos are inside the gatefold cover.

Legendary music man. P 2-14035 (A 2-album set): Candelite; 1976, 1977; 33⅓ rpm. (Album).
Note: Cover reads: Candlelite Music, Inc. is proud to present: "The Legendary Music Man, Marty Robbins." An authentic Golden Treasure Collectors Edition.

Album contents. Record 1 (P 14036), side 1 (AS 14036): A white sport coat (and a pink carnation)/ Are you sincere?/ Laura (what's he got that I ain't got)/ My woman, my woman, my wife/ Singing the blues; side 2 (BS 14036): Ruby Ann/ The Hawaiian wedding song/ The shoe goes on the other foot tonight/ I walk alone/ Ribbon of Darkness. Record 2 (P 14037), side 1 (AS 14037): You gave me a mountain/ Have I told you lately that I love you/ Tonight Carmen/ It's a sin/ El Paso; Side 2 (BS 14037): Devil woman/ Begging to you/ Padre/ Am I that easy to forget/ Don't worry.

No signs of loneliness here. Information taken from Stereo C 33476: Columbia Records; 1976; 33⅓ rpm. (Album).
Note: Produced by Don Law and Frank Jones. Cover by Bill Barnes. Liner notes by Michael Garfield.
  Album contents. Side 1: Fly Butterfly fly (M. Robbins, 2:51)/ No tears milady (M. Robbins, 1:53)/ The shoe goes on the other foot tonight (B. Mize, 2:07)/ Count me out (J. Pruett, 2:31)/ While you're dancing (B. Braddock, 2:27); Side 2: Matilda (B. Braddock, 2:29)/ Begging to you (M. Robbins, 2:37)/ The cowboy in the continental suit (M. Robbins, 2:55)/ I hope you learn a lot (B. Sykes, 3:05)/ No signs of loneliness here (L. Emerson, 2:03).

Two Gun Daddy. MCF 2757; MCA; 1976; 33⅓ rpm. (Album).
Note: Album not seen. Information taken from a record review in *Country Music People,* October, 1976 (v. 7, no. 10), page 22. The review says the album is a reissue of the *This much a man* album with three songs added: "Two gun daddy," "Queen of the big rodeo," and "Life."
  Album contents: Two gun daddy/ Queen of the big rodeo/ Overhurt and underloved/ It's not love (but it's not bad)/ Eyes/ Making the most of a heartache/ Guess I'll just stand here looking dumb/ This much a man/ Funny face/ Franklin, Tennessee/ She's too good to be true/ You don't really know (how far you can go)/ Leaving is a whole lot harder/ Life.

El Paso city. Information taken from Stereo KC 34303 (Side 1: AL 34303; Side 2: BL 34303). Other release numbers: PC 34303: Columbia Records; First released August, 1976; 33⅓ rpm. (Album).
Note: Produced by Billy Sherrill, photography by Jim McGuire.
  Album contents. Side 1: El Paso city (M. Robbins, 4:13)/ Ava Maria Morales (M. Robbins, 4:20)/ I'm gonna miss you when you go (M. Robbins, 2:27)/ Kin to the wind (R. Robbins, 2:05)/ Way out there (B. Nolan, 2:15); Side 2: The ballad of Bill Thaxton (B. Sykes, 4:56)/ Trail dreamin' (B. Nolan, 1:41)/ I did what I did for Maria (M. Murray, P. Callander, 2:22)/ She's just a drifter (M. Robbins, 2:48)/ Among my souvenirs (E. Leslie, H. Nicholls, 2:32).

The best of Marty Robbins. Information taken from CSP 014 (Side 1: MX177716; Side 2: MX177717). Other release numbers: Cassette CSC 014: Made in Australia. CBS Records; c1976; 33⅓ rpm. (Album).
  Album contents. Side 1: El Paso (Robbins, Belinda/Acuff-Rose)/ A hundred and sixty acres (Kapp, Control)/ You belong to my heart (R. Gilbert, A. Lara, Allans)/ The fastest gun around (J. Pruett, J. Glaser, Acuff-Rose/Belinda)/ I walk alone (H. Wilson, Chappell)/ The hanging tree (M. David, J. Livingston, from the Warner Bros.

picture, "The Hanging Tree," Warner Bros.)/ Bound for old Mexico
(J. Slaton, Acuff-Rose)/ Cool water (Nolan, Nicholsons)/ My wom-
an, my woman, my wife (M. Robbins, Acuff-Rose)/ Billy the Kid
(P.D.); Side 2: Streets of Laredo (P.D.)/ Devil woman (M. Robbins,
Belinda/Acuff-Rose)/ Song of the bandit (B. Nolan, Albert)/ Love is
blue (L'amour est bleu) (Blackburn, P. Cour, A. Popp,
Leeds/BIEM)/ Kaw-liga (H. Williams, F. Rose, Acuff-Rose)/ A
white sport coat (and a pink carnation) (Robbins, Acuff-Rose)/
They're hanging me tonight (Low, Wolpert, Belinda)/ Red River
Valley (P.D.)/ Tonight Carmen (M. Robbins, Belinda)/ Maria Elena
(S. K. Russell, L. Barcelata, Allans).

Adios Amigo. Information taken from Stereo PC 34448 (Side 1: AL
34448; Side 2: BL 34448): Columbia Records; First released February,
1977; 33⅓ rpm. (Album).
Note: Various cuts produced by Billy Sherrill and Marty Robbins. Photography by Jim McGuire.
   Album contents. Side 1: Adios Amigo (B. Vinton, R. Girado, 3:35)/
18 yellow roses (B. Darin, 2:33)/ Falling out of love (M. Robbins,
2:50)/ I've never loved anyone more (L. Hargrove, M. Nesmith,
2:54)/ Helen (J. Ouzts, R. Robbins, 3:19); Side 2: I don't know why
(I just do) (R. Turk, E. Ahlert, 2:23)/ My happiness (B. Bergantine,
B. Peterson, 2:31)/ My blue heaven (G. Whiting, W. Donaldson,
2:26)/ Inspiration for a song (R. C. Bannon, 2:39)/ After the storm
(D. Noe, 2:40).

The greatest hits. WC 334: K-Tel; As advertised on TV; 1977; 33⅓
rpm. (Album). Made in Canada.
   Album contents. Side 1: CSPS 1251 (CSPS 1251A): El Paso city/
Adios Amigo/ Ribbon of darkness/ Ruby Ann/ The chair/ The shoe
goes on the other foot tonight/ I can't say goodbye/ The best part of
living/ My woman, my woman, my wife/ Among my souvenirs; Side
2: CSPS 1251 (CSPS 1251B): Don't worry/ Devil woman/ Padre/
Begging to you/ That's all right/ Jolie girl/ Early morning sunshine/
One of these days/ It's your world/ Knee deep in the blues.

Don't let me touch you. Information taken from Stereo KC 35040 Side
1: AL 35040; Side 2: BL 35040): Columbia Records; Released December, 1977; 33⅓ rpm. (Album).
Note: Produced by Billy Sherrill, photography by Jim McGuire.
   Album contents. Side 1: Don't let me touch you (M. Robbins, B.
Sherrill, 2:48)/ There's no more you and me (B. Jadin, 3:11)/ To get
to you (J. Chapel, 3:15)/ The way I loved you best (M. Robbins,

2:50)/ Try a little tenderness (H. Woods, J. Campbell, R. Connelly, 3:22); Side 2: Return to me (C. Lombardo, D. DiMinno, 2:55)/ Harbor lights (J. Kennedy, H. Williams, 2:27)/ More than anything I miss you (R. Robbins, 2:27)/ A tree in the meadow (B. Reid, 2:54)/ Tomorrow, tomorrow, tomorrow (M. Robbins, 2:29).

The greatest hits of Marty Robbins; 20 greatest hits. Information taken from WC334 (CSPS 1251): Distributed by K-tel International. Made & litho'd in Canada; Released in 1977; 33⅓ rpm. (A Canadian album release).
Note: Advertised on TV. Additional recording information given on the album cover: music publisher, licensing organization, and the date of initial release for each song.
   Album contents. Side 1: El Paso city (Robbins)/ Adios Amigo (Vinton, Girado)/ Ribbon of darkness (Lightfoot)/ Ruby Ann (Bellamy)/ The chair (Robbins)/ The shoe goes on the other foot tonight (Mize)/ I can't say goodbye (Hardin, Byers)/ The best part of living (Johnson)/ My woman, my woman, my wife (Robbins)/ Among my souvenirs (Leslie, Nicholls); Side 2: Don't worry (Robbins)/ Devil woman (Robbins)/ Padre (Romans, Webster)/ Begging to you (Robbins)/ That's all right (Crudup)/ Jolie girl (Fowler)/ Early morning sunshine (Marshall)/ One of these days (Montgomery)/ It's your world (Robbins)/ Knee deep in the blues (Endsley).

Border town affair. Information taken from Stereo CBS 31536: Embassy-CBS Records-United Kingdom; c1977; 33⅓ rpm. (British Album release). Also: Stereo EMB-31391.
Note: Liner notes by Nigel Hunter.
   Album contents. Side 1: El Paso (M. Robbins, 4:22)/ Tonight Carmen (M. Robbins, 2:45)/ Gardenias in her hair (J. Byers, R. F. Tubert, 2:35)/ Have I told you lately that I love you (Scott Wiseman, 3:07)/ La Paloma (Yradier, Ardo, 2:59)/ Girl from Spanish town (M. Robbins, 3:00); Side 2: Maria Elena (L. Barcelate, 2:48)/ Camelia (M. Robbins, 2:41)/ Bound for old Mexico (Slaton, 3:00)/ Spanish lullaby (B. Johnston, 3:23)/ In the valley of the Rio Grande (Ann Russell, 2:23)/ Feleena (from El Paso) (M. Robbins, 8:17).

Greatest hits, volume IV. Information taken from Stereo KC 35629: Columbia Records; Released October, 1978; 33⅓ rpm. (Album).
Note: Cover photo by Jim McGuire.
   Album contents. Side 1: El Paso (M. Robbins, 4:20)/ Adios Amigo (V. Vinton, R. Girado, 3:35)/ Devil woman (M. Robbins, 2:51)/ Return to me (C. Lombardo, D. DiMinno, 2:55)/ El Paso City (M.

Robbins, 4:13); Side 2: I don't know why (I just do) (R. Turk, F. Ahlert, 2:23)/ Don't let me touch you (M. Robbins, B. Sherrill, 2:48)/ Among my souvenirs (E. Leslie, H. Nicholls, 2:32)/ Try a little tenderness (H. Woods, J. Campbell, R. Connelly, 3:22)/ My woman, my woman, my wife (M. Robbins, 3:30).

Best of Marty Robbins. [TV Offer] ed. Information taken from P 14613 (Side 1: AS 14613; Side 2: BS 14613): Manufactured by CBS Records for Green Valley Record Store, Inc., Nashville, Tennessee; 1978; 33⅓ rpm. (Album).
　Album contents. Side 1: Singing the blues/ Don't worry/ My woman, my woman, my wife/ El Paso/ Ribbon of darkness/ Laura (what's he got I ain't got)/ The shoe goes on the other foot tonight/ Tonight Carmen/ Are you sincere/ Have I told you lately that I love you; Side 2: A white sport coat (and a pink carnation)/ Devil woman/ You gave me a mountain/ Ruby Ann/ I walk alone/ It's a sin/ Begging to you/ Padre/ The Hawaiian wedding song/ Am I that easy to forget.

The performer. Information taken from Stereo KC 35446 (Side 1: AL 35446; Side 2: BL 35446). Other release numbers: PC 35446: Columbia Records; Released in March, 1979; 33⅓ rpm. (Album).
Note: Produced by Billy Sherrill, photography by Slick Lawson.
　Album contents. Side 1: Please don't play a love song (B. Sherrill, S. Davis, 3:04)/ Confused and lonely (M. Robbins, 2:37)/ Look what you've done (S. Gibb, 2:30)/ You're not ready for me yet (M. Robbins, 3:07)/ Another pack of cigarettes, another glass of wine (M. Robbins, 3:00); Side 2: My elusive dreams (C. Putnam, B. Sherrill, 3:42)/ Jenny (C. Davies, 3:00), Oh, Regina (M. Robbins, 2:24)/ Touch me with magic (S. Bogard, M. Utley, 2:41)/ The performer (M. Robbins, 3:20).

All around cowboy. Information taken from Stereo 36085: Columbia Records; Released in September, 1979; 33⅓ rpm. (Album).
Note: Produced by Billy Sherrill; photographs by Slick Lawson.
　Album contents. Side 1: All around cowboy (M. Robbins, 3:03)/ The dreamer (M. Robbins, 4:00)/ Pride and the badge (M. Robbins, 5:52)/ Restless cattle (M. Robbins, 2:32)/ When I'm gone (M. Robbins, 2:10); Side 2: Buenos Dias Argentina (B. Raleigh, U. Jurgens, 3:12)/ Lonely old bunkhouse (M. Robbins, 2:14)/ San Angelo (M. Robbins, 4:34)/ Tumbling tumbleweeds (B. Nolan, 3:50)/ The ballad of a small man (M. Robbins, 4:01).

Souvenir Album. CSP 097 (Side 1: MX188050; Side 2: MX188051). Other release numbers: Cassette CSC097, Cartridge CST097: CBS Records Australia; c1979; 33⅓ rpm. (Australian album release.)

Album contents. Side 1: The story of my life (H. David, B. Bacharach, 2:25, Belinda)/ Adios amigo (B. Vinton, R. Giraldo, 3:35, Castle)/ My elusive dreams (C. Putman, B. Sherrill, 3:42, Sydney Tree)/ My blue heaven (G. Whiting, W. Donaldson, 2:26, Allan)/ I don't know why (I just do) (R. Turk, F. Ahlert, 2:23, Allan)/ Cool water (Nolen, 3:11, Nicholsons)/ The girl with gardenias in her hair (J. Byers, B. Tubert, 2:35, Belinda)/ Try a little tenderness (H. Woods, J. Campbell, R. Connelly, 3:22, Chappell)/ My happiness (B. Bergantine, B. Peterson, 2:31, Sterling)/ I did what I did for Maria (M. Murray, P. Callander, 2:22, April); Side 2: Just married (DeVorzon, A. Allen, 2:07, Control)/ Among my souvenirs (E. Leslie, H. Nicholls, 2:32, Allan)/ 18 yellow roses (B. Darin, 2:33, T.M.)/ Hawaiian wedding song (C. King, 2:16, Leeds)/ Kaw-liga (H. Williams, F. Rose, 2:30, Acuff-Rose)/ Return to me (C. Lombardo, D. DiMinno, 2:55, Southern)/ El Paso city (M. Robbins, 4:13, Acuff-Rose, Control)/ Harbour lights (J. Kennedy, H. Williams, 2:27, Chappell)/ Amor (S. Skylar, G. Ruiz, 1:53, Allan)/ Padre (A. Romans, P. F. Webster, 3:17, Aberbach).

With love. Information taken from Stereo JC 36507: Columbia Records; June, 1980; 33⅓ rpm. (Album).
Note: Produced by Marty Robbins. Photography by Bruno of Hollywood.

Album contents. Side 1: She's made of faith (M. Robbins, 3:18)/ I can't wait until tomorrow (D. M. Scott, 2:52)/ Slipping from me (L. Ray, 4:27)/ One man's trash (is another man's treasure) (D. Winters, D. Winters Jr., 2:58)/ All I want to do (D. Winters, D. Winters, Jr., 2:09); Side 2: Sometimes when we touch (B. Mann, D. Hill, 4:41)/ I'll go to pieces (C. Noddin, 2:30)/ Wonderful world of you (A. Cunniff, 2:39)/ Misery in my soul (D. Winters, D. Winters Jr., 3:03)/ Oh my papa (J. Turner, G. Parsons, P. Burkhard, 3:44).

No. 1 cowboy. Special TV offer ed. Information taken from P 15594: Manufactured by CBS Records for Gusto Records; 1980; 33⅓ rpm. (Album).
Note: Also briefly sold under the title, "All around cowboy." Released with two different album covers.

Album contents. Side 1: El Paso/ El Paso city/ The hanging tree/ Red River Valley/ Streets of Laredo/ San Angelo/ All around cowboy/ Tumbling tumbleweeds/ The fastest gun around/ Meet me tonight in

Laredo; Side 2: Mr. Shorty/ They're hanging me tonight/ Cool water/ Strawberry roan/ Ballad of the Alamo/ Big iron/ Running gun/ Five brothers/ The cowboy in the continental suit/ Old red.

Everything I've always wanted. Information taken from Stereo, JC 36860. Other release numbers: PC 36860: Columbia Records; First released January, 1981; 33⅓ rpm. (Album).
Note: Produced by Eddie Kilroy. Photography by Jim McGuire.
   Album contents. Side 1: The woman in my bed (E. Kilroy, N. Martin, 3:13)/ Completely out of love (M. Robbins, 3:05)/ There's no wings on my angel (C. Coben, I. Melsher, E. Arnold, 2:40)/ Holding on to you (L. Buchanan, 3:36)/ Gene Autry, my hero (M. Robbins, 3:14); Side 2: My greatest memory (B. Taylor, B. Moore, M. Capps, 3:14)/ I'll go on alone (M. Robbins, 3:12)/ Another cup of coffee (M. Robbins, 3:15)/ An occasional rose (D. Burgess, 3:07)/ Crossroads of life (M. Robbins, 3:22).

A collection of his greatest hits. GS-4003: Sunrise Media; 1981; Series: The History of Country Music; 33⅓ rpm. (Album).
   Album contents: Singing the blues/ Devil woman/ She was only seventeen/ Knee deep in the blues/ The story of my life/ Ain't I the lucky one/ Tonight Carmen/ Big iron/ A white sport coat/ El Paso.

Country Music. Information taken from Stereo P 15832 STW-109: Time-Life Records; Country Music Series. 1981; 33⅓ rpm. (Album).
Note: Cover portrait by Reid L. Icard. Liner notes by Charles K. Wolfe.
   Album contents. Side 1: I'll go on alone (Robbins)/ Singing the blues (Endsley)/ Knee deep in the blues (Endsley)/ A white sport coat (Robbins)/ El Paso (Robbins); Side 2: Devil woman (Robbins)/ Ribbon of darkness (Lightfoot)/ My woman, my woman, my wife (Robbins)/ El Paso City (Robbins).

Encore. Information taken from FC 37353: Columbia Records; July, 1981; 33⅓ rpm. (Album).
Note: Illustration by Barry Buxkamper.
   Album contents. Side 1: Touch me with magic (S. Bogard, M. Utley, 2:41, BMI)/ Please don't play a love song (B. Sherrill, S. Davis, 3:06, BMI)/ Buenos Dias Argentina (B. Raleigh, U. Jurgens, 3:12, ASCAP)/ Sometimes when we touch (B. Mann, D. Hill, 4:41, ASCAP, BMI)/ El Paso city (M. Robbins, 4:13, BMI); Side 2: She's made of faith (M. Robbins, 3:18, BMI)/ My woman, my woman, my wife (M. Robbins, 3:30, BMI)/ All around cowboy (M. Robbins, 3:03, BMI)/ My elusive dreams (C. Putman, B. Sherrill, 3:42, BMI)/ 18 yellow roses (B. Darin, 2:33, BMI).

The legend. Information taken from Stereo FC 37541: Columbia Records; September, 1981; 33⅓ rpm. (Album).
Note: Produced by Marty Robbins and Eddy Fox. Photography by Larry Williams.
   Album contents. Side 1: Jumper cable man (M. Robbins, 2:46, BMI)/ Lady, I love you (Z. Van Arsdale, 3:34, BMI)/ It's not too hard (M. Robbins, 3:14, BMI)/ Good hearted woman (W. Jennings, W. Nelson, 4:05, BMI)/ The air that I breathe (M. Hazelwood, A. Hammond, 4:09, ASCAP); Side 2: My all time high (M. Robbins, 3:00, BMI)/ Honeycombe (B. Merrill, 2:49, ASCAP)/ Simple little love song (R. Robbins, E. Webb, 3:09, BMI)/ I'm just here to get my baby out of jail (K. Davis, H. Taylor, 3:33, BMI)/ Teardrops in my heart (V. Horton, 3:16, ASCAP).

Marty Robbins' best hits. Information taken from PT 15812: CSP, A Service of CBS Records; 1981; 33⅓ rpm. (Audio cassette).
[Editorial note: for the song "You gave me a mountain," both the album cover and the record itself cite the title incorrectly as "You give me a mountain."]
   Album contents. Side 1: Singing the blues/ My woman, my woman, my wife/ El Paso/ Ribbon of Darkness/ The shoe goes on the other foot tonight/ Tonight Carmen/ Have I told you lately that I love you?; Side 2: A white sport coat (and a pink carnation)/ Devil woman/ You give me a mountain/ Ruby Ann/ I walk alone/ The Hawaiian wedding song/ Am I that easy to forget?

Reflections. Information taken from P 16561: CSP, a service of CBS Records; c1982; 33⅓ rpm. (Album).
   Album contents. Side 1: Bouquet of roses/ The things that I don't know/ Begging to you/ El Paso; Side 2: Lovesick blues/ The hands you're holding now/ Are you sincere?/ Devil woman.

Marty Robbins/Conway Twitty Through the years. A 2-record set. The Franklin Mint Record Society, vol. 19/20; 1982.
Note: Marty is on one side of each of the two records (Record number 19A and 20A).
   Albums contents for Marty's songs. Record 19, side A: Singing the blues/ A white sport coat/ El Paso/ Don't worry/ Love me; Record 20, Side A: My woman, my woman, my wife/ El Paso City.

Come back to me. Information taken from Stereo FC 37995: Columbia Records; Released in Spring, 1982; 33⅓ rpm. (Album).
Note: Produced by Bob Montgomery. Photography by Beverly Parker. Session musicians and recording studios listed on the back cover.

Album contents. Side 1: Some memories just won't die (B. Springfield, 3:21, BMI)/ It's not all over (R. Sharp, 3:19, BMI)/ The American dream (B. McDill, 2:49, BMI)/ Here your memory comes again (T. Dubois, W. Newton, 2:22, BMI)/ The first song that wasn't the blues (C. Putman, S. Pippin, M. Kosser, 3:09, BMI); Side 2: Prayin' for rain (C. Lester, A. L. Owens, 3:10, BMI/ASCAP)/ That's all she wrote (J. Fuller, 3:32, BMI)/ Tie your dreams to mine (T. Dubois, 2:52, BMI)/ If her blue eyes don't get you (C. Putman, S. Pippin, D. Hill, BMI)/ Lover, lover (M. Robbins, 4:01, BMI).

Biggest hits. Information taken from FC 38309: Columbia Records; Released in 1982; 33⅓ rpm. (Album).
Note: Liner notes by Marty Robbins include his reasons for writing or selecting the songs on the album. Photography by Beverly Parker.
Album contents. Side 1: Ribbon of darkness (G. Lightfoot, 2:34, ASCAP)/ An occasional rose (D. Burgess, 3:07, BMI)/ She's just a drifter (M. Robbins, 2:48, BMI)/ My greatest memory (B. Taylor, B. Moore, M. Capps, 3:14, BMI)/ Padre (A. Romans, P. F. Webster, 3:20, ASCAP); Side 2: El Paso (M. Robbins, 4:20, BMI)/ Completely out of love (M. Robbins, 3:05, BMI)/ Jenny (C. Davies, 3:00, BMI)/ Teardrops in my heart (V. Horton, 3:16, ASCAP)/ You gave me a mountain (M. Robbins, 4:02, BMI).

The Master's call. Word-WST. 1983; British release. 33⅓ rpm. (Album).
Note: Album not seen. Information taken from an album review in *Country Music People,* November, 1983 (v. 14, no. 11); page 12.
Album contents: The performer/ There's power in the blood/ The wonderful world of you/ What God has done/ My love/ An evening prayer/ You gotta climb/ The great speckled bird/ Almost persuaded/ Who at my door is standing/ The Master's call/ Have thine own way Lord/ With his hand on my shoulder/ Will the circle be unbroken/ When the roll is called up yonder/ A little spot in heaven.

Just me and my guitar. Information taken from BFX 15119 (LSP 15388): Bear Family Records; Released in 1983; 33⅓ rpm. (Album).
Note: Liner notes by Ronnie Pugh. All but four of these songs are previously unissued. The four (The little rosewood casket, The letter edged in black, The convict and the rose, and The dream of the miner's child) were released in an EP, Columbia B-2153, *Marty Robbins sings The letter edged in black.*
Album contents. Side 1: The little rosewood casket (Public domain, 2:52)/ The letter edged in black (Public domain, 2:54)/ Twenty one

years (Public domain, 2:26)/ The convict and the rose (B. McDonald, R. King, 2:50)/ The dream of the miner's child (A. Jenkins, 3:15)/ The little box of pine on the 7:29 (Etllinger, Brown, Lee, 3:35)/ The wreck of the Number Nine (Carson Robison, 2:38)/ The sad lover (Public domain, 2:07); Side 2: The little shirt my mother made for me (Harry Wincott, 2:41)/ My mother was a lady (Joseph W. Stem, Edward B. Marks, 3:08)/ When it's lamplighting time in the valley (Lyons, Hart, Poulton, Goodman, Upson, 2:23)/ The wreck of the 1256 (Carson Robison, 2:02)/ Just before the battle Mother (Public domain, 3:58)/ Long, long ago (Public domain, 3:15)/ Beautiful dreamer (Public domain, 1:54).

Rock' n roll' n Robbins. Information taken from BFX 15045 House Party Series (LSP 15287): Bear Family Records; Released March, 1983; c1982; 33⅓ rpm. (Album).
Note: Four songs were previously unissued.
Album contents. Side 1: Footprints in the snow (Traditional, 2:11)/ It's driving me crazy (Ray Edenton, 2:12, Acuff-Rose)/ Baby, I need you (like you need me) (Marty Robbins, 2:05, Acuff-Rose)/ Mean mama blues (Marty Robbins, 2:11, Acuff-Rose)/ That's allright (Arthur Crudup, 2:32, Wabash Music)/ Maybelline (Chuck Berry, 2:30, ARC Music, BMI)/ Pretty mama (Marty Robbins, 2:40, Acuff-Rose)/ I can't quit (I've gone too far) (Marty Robbins, 2:24, Acuff-Rose); Side 2: Long tall Sally (E. Johnson, R. Penniman, O. Blackwell, 2:07, Venice Music, BMI)/ Singing the blues (Melvin Endsley, 2:24, Acuff-Rose)/ Knee deep in the blues (Melvin Endsley, 2:09, Acuff-Rose)/ Respectfully Miss Brooks (Marty Robbins, 2:58, Acuff-Rose)/ Mister Teardrop (Marty Robbins, 2:42, Acuff-Rose)/ Tennessee Toddy (Marty Robbins, 3:14, Acuff-Rose)/ Pain and misery (Mean mama blues) (vocals by Ray Edenton, Roy "Junior" Huskey, and Marty Robbins, written by Marty Robbins, 2:16, Acuff-Rose)/ You don't owe me a thing (Marty Robbins, 2:45, Acuff-Rose)/ Long gone lonesome blues (Hank Williams, 2:29, Acuff-Rose).

Rockin' rollin' Robbins, volume 2. (The Ray Conniff recordings) ed. Information taken from BFX 15105. House Party Series (LSP 15298): Bear Family Records; March, 1983; c1982; 33⅓ rpm. (Album).
Note: A typed note inserted in the package with the album states that one title listed on the record jacket for Side 1 ("Foolish decision") is not actually on the record because the master could not be found. One song previously unissued.
Album contents. Side 1: Jeannie and Johnnie (2:25)/ Just married (DeVorzon, A. Allen, 2:06)/ Stairway of love (Tepper, R. C. Ben-

nett, 2:02)/ Please don't blame me (Marty Robbins, 2:20)/ Grown up tears (Conniff, Weismantel, Schell, 2:16)/ Teen age dream (Marty Robbins, 1:50)/ Once-a-week date (Marty Robbins, 2:20); Side 2: The story of my life (Hal David, Burt Bacharach, 2:29)/ A white sport coat (and a pink carnation) (Marty Robbins, 2:30)/ Ain't I the lucky one (Melvin Endsley, 2:14)/ The hanging tree (M. David, J. Livingstone, 2:52)/ Sittin' in a tree house (Hal David, Bert Bacharach, 2:16)/ She was only seventeen (and he was one year more) (2:20)/ The last time I saw my heart (Hal David, Bert Bacharach, 2:35)/ The blues country style (M. David, J. Livingstone, 2:33).

Rockin' Rollin' Robbins, Vol. 3 (Rockin' Ruby Ann). House Party Series ed. BFX 15184 (LSP 15752): Bear Family Records; 1985; 33⅓ rpm. (Album).
Note: Two songs were previously unissued and there are two versions of "Ruby Ann" (one of which was previously unissued). The back album cover has recording session and additional record number information.
  Album contents. Side 1: Ruby Ann (R. Bellamy, 2:05, Acuff-Rose Music, KG)/ Sometimes I'm tempted (Marty Robbins, 2:20, Marty's Music, BMI)/ No signs of loneliness here (Lee Emerson, 2:02, Marty's Music Corp., BMI)/ While you're dancing (B. Braddock, 2:27, Marty's Music Corp., BMI)/ Teenager's dad (H. Dorrough, 1:49, Marty's Music Corp., BMI)/ Ruby Ann (R. Bellamy, 1:59, Acuff-Rose Music, KG); Side 2: Cap and Gown (Sid Tepper, R. C. Bennett, 2:05, Aberbach)/ Last night about this time (Marty Robbins, 2:25, Marty's Music Corp., BMI)/ I hope you learn a lot (Bobby Sykes, 3:03, Marty's Music Corp., BMI)/ Love can't wait (Marty Robbins, 2:46, Marty's Music Corp., BMI)/ Cigarettes and coffee blues (Marty Robbins, 2:41, Marty's Music Corp., BMI)/ Little rich girl (Marty Robbins, 3:00, Marty's Music Corp., BMI).

The Marty Robbins files, volume 1, (1951–1953). Information taken from BFX 15095 (LSP 15299): Bear Family Records; Record released April, 1983; c1982; 33⅓ rpm. (Album).
Note: Four cuts are previously unissued. Detailed liner notes by Ronnie Pugh provide historical information about the individual songs and the recording sessions. Editorial note: Marty's name is misspelled on the back cover; it reads "Robertson" instead of "Robinson."
  Album contents. Side 1: Tomorrow you'll be gone (Marty Robbins, 2:45)/ I wished somebody loved me (Marty Robbins, 2:55)/ Love me or leave me alone (Marty Robbins, 2:41)/ Crying 'cause I love you (Marty Robbins, 2:35)/ I'll go on alone (Marty Robbins, 2:39)/ Pretty words (Marty Robbins, 2:32)/ You're breaking my heart (while

you're holding my hand) (Marty Robbins, 2:50)/ I can get along (without you very well) (Marty Robbins, 2:41); Side 2: I couldn't keep from crying (Marty Robbins, 2:43)/ Just in time (Marty Robbins, 2:55)/ Crazy little heart (Marty Robbins, 2:45)/ After you leave me (Marty Robbins, 2:27)/ Lorelei (1:49)/ A castle in the sky (Marty Robbins, 2:58)/ Your heart's turn to break (Marty Robbins, 2:42)/ Why keep wishing (you don't care) (Marty Robbins, 2:35)/ A half-way chance with you (Marty Robbins, 2:30).

The Marty Robbins files, volume 2, (1953–1954). Information taken from BFX 15096 (LSP 15300): Bear Family Records; 1983; 33⅓ rpm. (Album).
Note: Five cuts are previously unreleased, although Marty's role in three of these songs (with vocals by Ray Edenton and Roy M. "Junior" Huskey) is uncertain. Detailed liner notes by Ronnie Pugh provide information about the songs and recording sessions.
Album contents. Side 1: Sing me something sentimental (Marty Robbins, 2:51)/ At the end of a long, lonely day (Marty Robbins, 2:30)/ Blessed Jesus, should I fall don't let me lay (Marty Robbins, 2:55)/ Kneel and let the Lord take your load (Marty Robbins, 2:52)/ Don't make me ashamed (Marty Robbins, 2:45)/ It's a long, long ride (Marty Robbins, 1:54)/ It looks like I'm just in your way (Marty Robbins, 2:42)/ I'm happy 'cause you're hurtin' (2:20); Side 2: My isle of golden dreams (Kahn, Blaufuss, 2:20)/ Have thine own way, Lord (Public domain, 2:40)/ God understands (Marty Robbins, 3:00)/ Aloha oe (farewell to thee) (Public domain, 2:23)/ What made you change your mind (& vocals by Ray Edenton and Roy M. "Junior" Huskey, 2:41)/ Way of a hopeless love (& vocals by Ray Edenton and Roy M. "Junior" Huskey, 2:52)/ Juarez (& vocals by Ray Edenton and Roy M. "Junior" Huskey, 2:34)/ I'm too big to cry (Marty Robbins, 2:53).

The Marty Robbins files, vol. 3, (1954–1956). Information taken from BFX 15118 (LSP 15387): Bear Family Records; Released in 1983; 33⅓ rpm. (Album).
Note: Liner notes by Ronnie Pugh provide detail about individual songs and recording sessions. Two songs are previously unissued.
Album contents. Side 1: Call me up (and I'll come calling on you) (Marty Robbins, 2:05)/ It's a pity what money can do (Marty Robbins, 2:17)/ Time goes by (Marty Robbins, 2:20)/ This broken heart of mine (Marty Robbins, 2:19)/ It looks like I'm just in your way (Marty Robbins, 2:33)/ I'll love you till the day I die (Marty Robbins, 2:33)/ Don't let me hang around (if you don't care) (Marty

Robbins, 2:17)/ Pray for me mother of mine (Marty Robbins, 2:50); Side 2: Daddy loves you (Marty Robbins, 2:40)/ Gossip (Marty Robbins, 2:40)/ I'll know you're gone (recorded with Lee Emerson, written by Lee Emerson, 1:45)/ How long will it be (recorded with Lee Emerson, written by Lee Emerson, 2:20)/ Where d'ja go (recorded with Lee Emerson, written by Lee Emerson, 2:01)/ Most of the time (2:53)/ The same two lips (Marty Robbins, 3:04)/ Your heart of blue is showing through (Lee Emerson, 2:45).

The Marty Robbins files, vol. 4, (1957–1958). Information taken from BFX 15138 (LSP 15561): Bear Family Records; Released in 1984; 33⅓ rpm. (Album).
Note: Liner notes by Ronnie Pugh provide information about the songs and recording sessions. Two cuts on the album are previously unissued.
Album contents. Side 1: It's too late now (to worry anymore) (Pope, 2:17)/ I never let you cross my mind (Fred Rose, 2:59)/ I'll step aside (Bond, 2:15)/ Bouquet of roses (S. Nelson, Hilliard, 2:16)/ I'm so lonesome I could cry (Hank Williams, 2:44)/ Lovesick blues (I. Mills, S. Friend, 2:33)/ Moanin' the blues (Hank Williams, 1:59)/ Rose of Ol' Pawnee (Fred Rose, 3:16); Side 2: I hang my head and cry (G. Autry, F. Rose, R. Whitley, 2:15)/ Have I told you lately that I love you (G. Autry, S. Wiseman, 3:07)/ All the world is lonely now (Mel Foree, 2:12)/ You only want me when you're lonely (G. Autry, S. Nelson, 2:30)/ Beautiful Ohio (Ballard, McDonald, Mary Earl, 1:56)/ A faded petal from a beautiful bouquet (Hank Snow, 2:42)/ Then I turned and slowly walked away (Fortner, E. Arnold, 2:15)/ Judy (Jodie) (Stokes, 2:25).

The Marty Robbins files, volume 5, (1958/1959/1962). Information taken from BFX 15139 (LSP 15562): Bear Family Records; Released in 1983; 33⅓ rpm. (Album).
Note: Liner notes by Ronnie Pugh provide detailed information about individual songs and the recording sessions at which they were recorded. Six of the cuts were previously unissued.
Album contents. Side 1: A house with everything but love (Marty Robbins, 3:02)/ Nothing but sweet lies (Marty Robbins, 1:47)/ Baby, I need you (like you need me) (Marty Robbins, 2:26)/ Kaw-liga (Hank Williams, Fred Rose, 2:27)/ Paper face (H. Locklin, S. Williams, 2:15)/ Many tears ago (Jenny Lou Carson, 2:16)/ Address unknown (G. Autry, Horton, Darling, 2:45)/ Waltz of the wind (Fred Rose, 2:12); Side 2: The hands you're holding now (Marty Robbins, 2:57)/ Shackles and chains (Jimmie Davis, 2:16)/ Oh, how I miss you (since you went away) (Cassell, Taylor, 2:04)/ Wedding bells (C. Boone, 2:10)/ Sweet Cora (Marty Robbins, 3:18)/ Ain't life a crying

shame (Harry McDowell, 2:59)/ Silence and tears (Tompall Glaser, 2:17)/ The roving gambler (Traditional/Public domain, 2:07).

Twentieth century drifter. Information taken from MCA 27060 (Side 1: MCA 3271; Side 2: MCA 3272): MCA Records; Released January, 1983; 33⅓ rpm. (Album).
Note: Side 1: All selections written by Marty Robbins and published by Mariposa Music (BMI), except "Love me" written by Jeanne Pruett and published by Moss-Rose Publications (BMI). Produced by Marty Robbins, except "Love me" and "Crawling on my knees," produced by Walter Haynes. Side 2: All selections written by Marty Robbins and published by Mariposa Music (BMI), except "A man and a train" written by Hal David & Frank de Vol and published by 20th Century Music Corp. (ASCAP). Produced by Marty Robbins. All selections previously released on the MCA/DECCA labels. Compiled by Steve Hoffman.
   Album contents. Side 1: Twentieth century drifter (2:59)/ This much a man (2:56)/ Love me (2:45)/ Don't you think (2:53)/ Crawling on my knees (2:48); Side 2: Walking piece of heaven (3:02)/ A man and a train (3:05)/ Two gun daddy (2:44)/ It takes faith (3:07)/

Some memories just won't die. Stereo FC 38603: Columbia Records; This was Marty Robbins' last recording. Recorded in December 1982; released April, 1983; 33⅓ rpm. (Album).
Note: Produced by Bob Montgomery; cover illustrations by Bill Imhoff. "Honkytonk man" produced by Snuff Garrett from the soundtrack of the film of the same name. Liner notes by Rick Blackburn.
   Album contents. Side 1: Some memories just won't die (B. Springfield, 3:20, BMI)/ Change of heart (R. Sharp, 3:09, BMI)/ What if I said I love you (C. Black, T. Rocco, 2:47, BMI)/ I'm saving all the good times for you (J. Slate, L. Henley, L. Keith, 3:35, BMI)/ Devil in a cowboy hat (J. D. Hoag, 3:18, BMI); Side 2: Angelina (J. Bettis, J. Photoglo, B. Neary, 4:11, ASCAP)/ I miss you the most (B. Springfield, 3:19, BMI)/ How to make love to a woman (B. Springfield, S. Allen, 3:19, BMI/ASCAP)/ Baby that's love (G. Adams, D. Adams, 2:29, BMI)/ Honkytonk man (D. Blackwell, 2:50, BMI).

Marty Robbins. Country & western classics series; 3-album set. TLCW-10. Series Number: P3 16578 (Sides 1&2: P 16579; Sides 3&4: P 16580; Sides 5&6: P 16581): Time-Life Records; May, 1983; 33⅓ rpm.
Note: Contains booklet, "Marty Robbins," written by Patricia Hall; notes on the music by Ronnie Pugh (24 pages, Time-Life Records, illus., c 1983). The booklet contains an overview of Robbins' life and a

detailed discussion of the music contained in the set. Two covers were used; one had swinging bar doors and another one had a photo of Marty.

Album contents. Side 1: Tomorrow you'll be gone (Marty Robbins)/ I'll go on alone (Marty Robbins)/ I can get along (without you very well) (Marty Robbins)/ I couldn't keep from crying (Marty Robbins)/ Sing me something sentimental (Marty Robbins)/ At the end of a long, lonely day (Marty Robbins)/ Don't make me ashamed (Marty Robbins); Side 2: My isle of golden dreams (Gus Kahn, Walter Blaufuss)/ Time goes by (Marty Robbins)/ That's all right (Arthur Crudup)/ Gossip (Marty Robbins)/ Singing the blues (Melvin Endsley)/ Long tall Sally (Enotris Johnson, Richard Penniman, Robert Blackwell)/ Knee deep in the blues (Melvin Endsley); Side 3: The wreck of Number Nine (Carson J. Robison)/ A white sport coat (Marty Robbins)/ The story of my life (Hal David, Burt F. Bacharach/ Sweet Leilani (Harry Owens)/ Moonland (Jerry Byrd)/ Just married (Barry DeVorzon, Al Allen); Side 4: El Paso (Marty Robbins)/ Big iron (Marty Robbins)/ Silence and tears (Tompall Glaser)/ Billy Venero (Traditional)/ Don't worry (Marty Robbins)/ Ruby Ann (Roberta Bellamy)/ Devil woman (Marty Robbins); Side 5: Lovely hula hands (Robert Alexander Anderson)/ Begging to you (Marty Robbins)/ The cowboy in the continental suit (Marty Robbins)/ Ribbon of darkness (Gordon Lightfoot)/ Tonight Carmen (Marty Robbins)/ I walk alone (Herbert W. Wilson)/ You gave me a mountain (Marty Robbins); Side 6: My woman, my woman, my wife (Marty Robbins)/ El Paso city (Marty Robbins)/ Trail dreamin' (Bob Nolan)/ Among my souvenirs (Edgar Leslie, Horatio Nicholls)/ All around cowboy (Marty Robbins)/ The performer (Marty Robbins).

A lifetime of song, 1951–1982. C2 38870 (Record 1 contains sides 1 & 3: C 38871; Record 2 contains sides 2 & 4: C 38872): Columbia Records; August, 1983; 33⅓ rpm. (2-album set).
Note: Liner notes by Marizona Robbins (Robinson) and others. Cover photography by Beverly Parker; insert photos in foldout cover by others. Producers and original release date for each song is listed in credits on back cover.

Album contents. Side 1: Tomorrow you'll be gone (M. Robbins, 2:43, BMI)/ I'll go on alone (M. Robbins, 2:40, BMI)/ That's all right (A. Crudup, 2:34, BMI)/ Knee deep in the blues (M. Endsley, 2:12, BMI)/ Singing the blues (M. Endsley, 2:23, BMI); Side 2: A white sport coat (and a pink carnation) (M. Robbins, 2:29, BMI)/ The story of my life (H. David, B. Bacharach, 2:34, ASCAP)/ Don't worry (M. Robbins, 3:10, BMI)/ Ruby Ann (R. Bellamy, 2:00, BMI)/ Devil woman (M. Robbins, 2:52, BMI); Side 3: El Paso (M.

Robbins, 4:39, BMI)/ Big iron (M. Robbins, 3:56, BMI)/ The hanging tree (M. David, J. Livingston, 2:54, ASCAP)/ Ribbon of darkness (G. Lightfoot, 2:32, ASCAP)/ El Paso city (M. Robbins, 4:16, BMI); Side 4: I walk alone (H. Wilson, 3:15, BMI)/ My woman, my woman, my wife (M. Robbins, 3:30, BMI)/ Among my souvenirs (E. Leslie, H. Nicholls, 2:31, ASCAP)/ Return to me (C. Lombardo, D. DiMinno, 2:50, ASCAP)/ Some memories just won't die (B. Springfield, 3:20, BMI).

Golden collection. Stereo WH 5009: Lotus Records. Produced in association with CBS Records (Made in England); Distributed by K-Tel Int., c1983; 33⅓ rpm. (Album).

Album contents. Side 1: Devil woman (Robbins, Acuff-Rose Music)/ Streets of Laredo (Traditional, public domain)/ My blue heaven (G. Whiting, W. Donaldson, Francis Day & Hunter)/ The bend in the river (Robbins, Acuff-Rose Music)/ Abilene rose (Hosdale, Acuff-Rose Music)/ Little rich girl (Robbins, Acuff-Rose Music)/ Adios Amigo (R. Girado, Ardmore & Beechwood/Britico)/ She's just a drifter (Robbins, Acuff-Rose)/ Billy the Kid (Traditional, public domain)/ El Paso (Robbins, Acuff-Rose Music); Side 2: Ruby Ann (R. Bellamy, Starday Music)/ After the storm (Dale No, Campbell Connelly)/ 18 yellow roses (B. Darin, Carlin Music)/ Kin to the wind (Robbins, Acuff-Rose Music)/ She was young and she was pretty (Robbins, Acuff-Rose Music)/ Is there any chance (Robbins, Acuff-Rose Music)/ I told my heart (Robbins, Acuff-Rose Music)/ Saddle tramp (Robbins, Acuff-Rose Music)/ Doggone cowboy (Babcock, Acuff-Rose Music)/ Big iron (Robbins, Acuff-Rose Music).

Bouquet of songs. RB 17138: Orbit/CBS Records. Manufactured for Summit Productions; Released in 1983; 33⅓ rpm. (Album).

Album contents. Side 1: All the way/ Bouquet of roses/ Love me tender/ Summertime; Side 2: Have I told you lately that I love you?/ Too young/ It's a sin/ Misty.

Country classics. P 16914: Columbia Records, CSP; 1983; 33⅓ rpm. (Album).

Note: The song "You gave me a mountain" is mistitled on both the record and the album cover as "Lord, you gave me a mountain."

Album contents. Side 1: Lovesick blues/ The hands you're holding now/ Are you sincere?/ Devil woman/ Lord, you gave me a mountain; Side 2: Bouquet of roses/ The things that I don't know/ Begging to you/ El Paso/ Among my souvenirs.

Country cowboy. Information taken from RB 17209: Orbit/CBS Records. Manufactured for Cowboy Productions; Released in 1983; 33⅓ rpm. (Album).
Note: Editorial note: The song "Change that dial" is mistitled on the album cover as "Change the dial."
   Album contents. Side 1: The hands you're holding now/ I'll step aside/ Nothing but sweet lies/ I lived a lifetime in a day; Side 2: Ribbon of darkness/ Pennies from heaven/ Change that dial/ Tonight Carmen.

Forever yours. Information taken from Stereo RB 17136: Orbit/CBS Records. Manufactured for Arthur Sharf; Released in 1983; 33⅓ rpm. (Album).
   Album contents. Side 1: Forever yours/ Answer me my love/ Sorting memories/ Unchained melody; Side 2: To each his own/ All the world is lonely now/ As time goes by/ Hurt.

The legendary Marty Robbins. Information taken from Stereo RB 17206: Orbit/CBS Records. Manufactured for Investment Sounds; 1983; 33⅓ rpm. (Album).
   Album contents. Side A: Singing the blues/ I can't help it (if I'm still in love with you)/ It's a sin/ Kaw-liga; Side B: Ruby Ann/ She thinks I still care/ Rainbow/ A white sport coat (and a pink carnation).

Sincerely. Information taken from RB 17120: Orbit/CBS Records. Manufactured for Northern Ohio Productions; 1983; 33⅓ rpm. (Album).
   Album contents. Side 1: Hello heartache/ Up in the air/ If you see my heart today/ This song; Side 2: The girl with gardenias in her hair/ You made me love you/ Are you sincere?/ Can't help fallin' in love.

That country feeling. Information taken from RB 17137: Orbit/CBS Records. Manufactured for Memory Lane Associates; 1983; 33⅓ rpm. (Album).
   Album contents. Side 1: Don't worry/ Love is blue (L'amour est bleu)/ Oh how I miss you (since you went away)/ Urgently needed; Side 2: But only in my dreams/ She thinks I still care/ Times have changed/ Devil woman.

A song for every mood. Information taken from Stereo P 17628: CSP, CBS Special Products. Manufactured for Moody Cowboy Productions; Released in 1983; 33⅓ rpm. (Album).
   Album contents. Side 1: I couldn't keep from crying/ One window, four walls/ Let me live in your world/ Love's gone away; Side 2: Girl

from Spanish town/ Rainbow/ Three little words/ You gave me a mountain.

Memories in song. (2-record set) ed. Information taken from P2 19162 (Record 1: P 19163; Record 2: P 19164): CBS Special Products. Manufactured for S.L.H. Productions Company; Released in 1983; 33⅓ rpm. (Album).
Album contents. Record 1, side 1: Up in the air/ Beyond the reef/ Five brothers/ Unchained melody/ A white sport coat (and a pink carnation); Record 1, side 2: Don't throw me away/ Running gun/ Paper face/ Hurt. Record 2, side 1: Mr. Teardrop/ Oh how I miss you (since you went away)/ Refer him to me/ To each his own/ El Paso; Record 2, side 2: Kingston girl/ The blues country style/ Too young/ Big iron.

Ray Price/Marty Robbins: Brothers in song. (A 2-record set). Information taken from P2 19197 (Ray Price record: P 19198; Marty Robbins record: P 19199): CBS Special Products; c1983; 33⅓ rpm. (2-album set).
Note: Ray Price is on Record One, Marty Robbins is on Record Two.
Album contents. Record 1, side 1: Night life/ Release me/ Let me talk to you/ Take me as I am (or let me go); Record 1, side 2: I've gotta have my baby back/ The last letter/ One more time/ My baby's gone. Record 2, Side 1: Lord you gave me a mountain/ Padre/ Can't help falling in love/ Are you sincere?; Record 2, Side 2: You made me love you/ The girl with gardenias in her hair/ This song/ If you see my heart today.

20 golden memories. (2-record set) ed. Information taken from Stereo CDM 2-048 (Record 1: CDM1-49; Record 2: CDM 1-50): CBS Records, Canada; c1983; 33⅓ rpm. (Album).
Note: Editorial note: there are a number of mistakes on the album and cover. R. Ballamy should be R. Bellamy; "Don't worry 'bout me" should be "Don't worry"; and "A white sports coat" should not have the "s" on the end of "sport."
Album contents. Record 1, side 1: El Paso (M. Robbins)/ Singing the blues (Endsley)/ Devil woman (M. Robbins)/ Ruby Ann (R. Ballamy)/ Among my souvenirs (E. Leslie, H. Nicholls); Record 1, side 2: My woman, my woman, my wife (M. Robbins)/ Ribbon of darkness (G. Lightfoot)/ Cool water (Nolan)/ Tonight Carmen (M. Robbins)/ Don't worry 'bout me (M. Robbins). Record 2, side 1: A white sports coat (M. Robbins)/ Begging to you (M. Robbins)/ My elusive dream (C. Putman, B. Sherrill)/ Big iron (M. Robbins)/ El Paso city (M. Robbins); Record 2, side 2: The story of my life (H.

David, B. Bacharach)/ You gave me a mountain (M. Robbins)/ Almost persuaded (P. P. Bliss)/ Have I told you lately that I love you (G. Autry, S. Wiseman)/ I walk alone (H. Wilson).

The great Marty Robbins; 18 songs you'll always love. Information taken from P 17159: Advertised and distributed by Suffolk Marketing, Inc. [Smithtown, NY]; c1983; 33⅓ rpm.
Note: TV advertisement.
   Album contents. Side 1: Bouquet of roses/ Half as much/ Have I told you lately that I love you/ A white sport coat (and a pink carnation)/ Streets of Laredo/ Red River Valley/ Cool water/ El Paso; Side 2: My elusive dreams/ Am I that easy to forget/ Among my souvenirs/ My blue heaven/ Tonight Carmen/ She thinks I still care/ Devil woman/ My happiness/ My woman, my woman, my wife.

Hawaii's calling me. BFX 15123 (LSP 15499): Bear Family Records; Released in 1983; 33⅓ rpm. (Album).
Note: There are two versions of "The Hawaiian wedding song" on the album, one of which was previously unissued. The back cover contains recording session information and record numbers of previously released material.
   Album contents. Side 1: Lovely hula hands (R. A. Anderson, 2:28, Miller Music Corp., ASCAP)/ The sea and me (Jerry Byrd, Maricana Music, BMI)/ Ka-lu-a (A. Caldwell, 2:21, Miller Music Corp., ASCAP)/ The night I came ashore (C. Robinson, 3:03, Maricana Music, BMI)/ Echo island (H. Robinson, 2:30, Marty's Music, BMI)/ Kuu Ipo Lani (my sweetheart, Lani) (Jerry Bird, 3:08, Marty's Music, BMI)/ Beyond the reef (J. Pitman, 3:05, Marty's Music, BMI); Side 2: The Hawaiian wedding song (C. King, 2:14, Pickwick Music Corp, ASCAP)/ Drowsy waters (Wailana) (Jerry Bird, 2:08, Maricana, BMI)/ Hawaiian bells (Jerry Byrd, 3:30, Marty's Music, BMI)/ My wonderful one (J. Sweeney, 2:48, Marty's Music, BMI)/ Blue sand (Jerry Byrd, 2:55, Marty's Music, BMI)/ Hawaii's calling me (J. B. Hosale, 3:03, Marizona Music, BMI)/ The Hawaiian wedding song (C. King, 2:47, Pickwick Music Corp., ASCAP).

Song of the islands. Information taken from BFX 15130 (LSP 15500): Bear Family Records; Released in 1983; 33⅓ rpm. (Album).
Note: Liner note: "All titles were recorded October 3, 1957." Session members are identified as Hillous Buttram, James Farmer, Jack Pruett, Floyd T. "Lightin' " Chance, Louis Dunn, Powell Hassell.
   Album contents. Side 1: Song of the islands (C. King, 2:56, Marks Music Corp, BMI)/ Don't sing aloha when I go (W. Smith, B. Black,

Moret, 1:49, Charles N. Daniels and Jerry Vogel Music Co., AS-CAP)/ Beyond the reef (Pitman, 2:29, Laurel Music Corp., ASCAP)/ Crying steel guitar waltz (S. Long, 1:58, Mamy Music Corp., BMI)/ My isle of golden dreams (Kahn, Blaufuss, 2:51, Remick Music Corp., ASCAP)/ Now is the hour (Maori farewell song) (Kaihan, C. Scott, D. Stewart, 2:29, Leeds Music Corp. & Southern Music Pub. Co., ASCAP); Side 2: Sweet Leilani (H. Owens, 1:47, Ann Rachael Music Corp., ASCAP)/ Down where the tradewinds blow (H. Owens, 2:27, Royal Music Publishers, ASCAP)/ Constancy (ua like no a like) (J. Noble, Berger, 3:09, Miller Music Corp., ASCAP)/ Island echoes (Kessel, 3:37, Be-Are Pub. Co., BMI)/ Moonland (Byrd, 2:44, Acuff-Rose Pub., BMI)/ Aloha oe (farewell to thee) (Traditional, Liliuo Kalani, 2:26).

Songs of the islands. Information taken from P 17367: CBS Records. Distributed exclusively by The Good Music Record Company. Released in 1983; 33⅓ rpm. (Album).

Album contents. Side 1: Lovely hula hands/ Don't sing aloha when I go/ Beyond the reef/ Now is the hour (Maori farewell song)/ Drowsy waters (Wailana)/ Song of the islands/ Constancy (Ua like no a like)/ Kuu upo Lani (My sweetheart, Lani)/ The Hawaiian wedding song; Side 2: My isle of golden dreams/ The sea and me/ Crying steel guitar waltz/ Hawaiian bells/ Sweet Leilani/ Down where the trade winds blow/ Love songs of Kalua/ Harbor lights/ Aloha oe.

Marty Robbins. Information taken from Stereo SPR 8506. Additional releases: Cassette SPC 8506: Spot Records/Pickwick International; c1983; 33⅓ rpm. (British album release).

Note: the date on the record is 1976, album cover is dated 1983. The list of songs on the album cover is not in the same order as they appear on the record label.

Album contents. Side 1: El Paso city (M. Robbins, Acuff-Rose Music)/ Ava Maria Morales (M. Robbins, Acuff-Rose Music)/ Trail dreamin' (B. Nolan, B. Feldman)/ I did what I did for Maria (M. Murray, P. Callander, Intune Ltd.)/ Way out there (B. Nolan, B. Feldman); Side 2: The ballad of Bill Thaxton (B. Sykes, Acuff-Rose Music)/ I'm gonna miss you when you go (M. Robbins, Acuff-Rose Music)/ Kin to the wind (M. Robbins, Acuff-Rose Music)/ She's just a drifter (M. Robbins, Acuff-Rose Music)/ Among my souvenirs (E. Leslie, H. Nicholls, Lawrence Wright Music).

His greatest hits and finest performances. RB4-054. A 5-record set with each record having its own title and record number. Record 1, RB4-

054-1: "El Paso/Marty's Greatest hits" (Side 1: AS17185; Side 2: BS17185). Record 2, RB4-054-2: (Side 1 is titled "Sweet Leilana/Hawaiian memories", AS17186; Side 2 is titled "Tumbling tumbleweeds/Country and western classics," BS17186). Record 3, RB4-054-3 (Side 1 is titled "Love is blue," AS17187; Side 2 is titled: "You made me love you/Golden favorites of yesteryear," BS17187). Record 4, RB4-054-4 (Side 1 is titled "Ruby Ann/The girls in Marty's life," AS17188; Side 2 is titled "You gave me a mountain/Marty's favorites," BS17188). Record 5, RB4-054-5 (Side 1 is titled "Big iron/Gunfighter ballads and trail songs," AS17189; Side 2 is titled "Some memories just won't die/Songs of unforgettable love," BS17189): Reader's Digest. Made for Reader's Digest by Columbia Special Products; 1983; 33⅓ (5-album set); Stereo. (Album).
Note: An illustrated booklet accompanies the set.
  Album contents: Record 1, side 1: Singing the blues/ A white sport coat (and a pink carnation)/ The story of my life/ Don't worry/ El Paso; Record 1, Side 2: My woman, my woman, my wife/ Ribbon of darkness/ Among my souvenirs/ El Paso city/ I walk alone; Record 2, Side 1: The Hawaiian wedding song/ Lovely hula hands/ Sweet Leilani/ My wonderful one/ Aloha oe (Farewell to thee); Record 2, Side 2: Lovesick blues/ Kaw-liga/ Have I told you lately that I love you/ Bouquet of roses/ The Red River Valley/ Tumbling tumbleweeds; Record 3, Side 1: Love is blue (L'amour est bleu)/ By the time I get to Phoenix/ Yesterday/ The air that I breathe/ Can't help falling in love; Record 3, Side 2: Try a little tenderness/ You made me love you/ All the way/ Love me tender/ It had to be you/ Misty; Record 4, Side 1: Devil woman/ Tonight Carmen/ Maria Elena/ Ruby Ann/ A good hearted woman; Record 4, Side 2: You gave me a mountain/ Just married/ Stairway of love/ Begging to you/ Knee deep in the blues/ Long tall Sally; Record 5, Side 1: Big iron/ Cool water/ The hanging tree/ Billy the kid/ The strawberry roan/ The streets of Laredo; Record 5, Side 2: Adios Amigo/ 18 yellow roses/ Falling out of love/ Return to me/ My elusive dreams/ Some memories just won't die.

The great love songs. Information taken from Stereo RLRP17730: CBS Special Products. Distributed exclusively by the Good Music Record Co.; Released in 1984; 33⅓ rpm. (Album).
  Album contents. Side 1: My happiness/ You made me love you/ As time goes by/ I'm in the mood for love/ My blue heaven/ Love me tender/ Answer me my love/ Unchained melody/ Too young; Side 2: I don't know why (I just do)/ That old feeling/ To each his own/ Return to me/ The nearness of you/ Misty/ Try a little tenderness/ Are you sincere/ It had to be you.

'Cause I love you. Information taken from Stereo P 19738: CBS Special Products. Manufactured for FY-CY-R Enterprises/Courtesy of CBS Inc.; Released in 1984; 33⅓ rpm. (Album).

Album contents. Side 1: Windows have pains/ Crying 'cause I love you/ Don't go away senor/ Ain't I the lucky one; Side 2: The story of my life/ Answer me my love/ Let me live in your world/ Padre.

The best of Marty Robbins. CBS Special Products. Manufactured especially for Reader's Digest (Bonus offer RB4-214-1; 1984.

Album contents. Side 1 (AS 17729): Singing the blues/ A white sport coat (and a pink carnation)/ Big iron/ The story of my life/ Among my souvenirs/ El Paso; Side 2 (BS 17729): My woman, my woman, my wife/ Don't worry/ Ruby Ann/ Knee deep in the blues/ Devil woman/ Some memories just won't die.

Long, long ago. KC2 39575 (Sides 1&4: C 39606; Sides 2&3: C 39607)): Columbia Records; c1984; 33⅓ rpm. (2-album set).

Note: Inside of gatefold record jacket has five early publicity photos by Walton S. Fabry of Nashville. Back cover photo by Beverly Parker. Liner notes have tributes by Jack Hurst and Chip Young. Back cover credits give the date each song was recorded.

Album contents. Side 1: Long, long ago (Arranged and adapted by M. Robbins, 3:08, BMI)/ It finally happened (M. Robbins, 2:45, BMI)/ Reach for me (M. Robbins, 2:16, BMI)/ Peoples valley (M. Robbins, 2:45, BMI)/ When the work's all done this fall (Arranged and adapted by M. Robbins, 2:30, BMI); Side 2: Ghost riders in the sky (S. Jones, 3:40, ASCAP)/ Baby, talk to me (F. Rose, A. Heath, 1:53, ASCAP)/ Night time on the desert (M. Robbins, 2:16, BMI)/ To be in love with her (M. Robbins, 3:27, BMI)/ Wind (B. Nolan, 2:55, BMI); Side 3: The roving gambler (C. Houston, 2:10, BMI)/ Yesterday's roses (G. Autry, F. Rose, 2:42, ASCAP)/ This song (J. Pruett, 2:51, BMI)/ Beautiful dreamer (S. Foster, Arr. & adapted by M. Robbins, 1:52, BMI)/ Chant of the wanderer (B. Nolan, 2:04, BMI); Side 4: I'm gonna be a cowboy (M. Robbins, 1:49, BMI)/ Last night about this time (M. Robbins, 2:39, BMI)/ Address unknown (C. Lombardo, J. Marks, D. L. Hill, 2:49, ASCAP)/ Lonely old bunkhouse (M. Robbins, 2:55)/ Where could I go (but to the Lord) (J. B. Coats, 3:07).

Pieces of your heart. BFX 15212 (LSP 15753): Bear Family Records; 1985; 33⅓ rpm. (Album).

Note: Eight cuts on the album are previously unissued, including one of the two versions of "Girl from Spanish town." Recording session information given on the back of the album cover. Publishers listed for side one only.

Album contents. Side 1: Ribbon of darkness (Gordon Lightfoot, 2:29, Whitmark & Sons, ASCAP)/ Pieces of your heart (Marty Robbins, 3:00, Marty's Music Corp., BMI)/ I'm not ready yet (Marty Robbins, 2:50, Marty's Music, BMI)/ I feel another heartbreak coming on (Marty Robbins, 2:17, Marty's Music Corp., BMI)/ Too far gone (Marty Robbins, 3:07, Marty's Music Corp., BMI)/ Not so long ago (Marty Robbins, 2:03, Marty's Music Corp., BMI); Side 2: Ain't I right (Marty Robbins, 3:17)/ My own native land (Marty Robbins, 2:52)/ Girl from Spanish town (Marty Robbins, 2:41)/ Kingston Girl (Don Winters, 2:09)/ Girl from Spanish town (Marty Robbins, 2:37)/ Never look back (Marty Robbins, 2:46).

In the wild west, part 1. BFX 15145 (LSP 15702): Bear Family Records; 1985; 33⅓ rpm.

Note: One song, "Feleena (from El Paso)," is only identified as "Feleena" on the record itself. Recording session information and original release numbers on on the back of the album cover.

Album contents. Side 1: Cool water (Bob Nolan, 3:06, American Music, BMI)/ In the valley (Marty Robbins, 1:48, Marizona Music, BMI)/ Running gun (Marty Robbins, 2:10, Marizona Music, BMI)/ El Paso (Marty Robbins, 4:37, Marizona Music, BMI)/ Feleena (Marty Robbins, 8:17, Marizona Music, BMI)/ El Paso city (Marty Robbins, 2:42, Marizona Music); Side 2: Big iron (Marty Robbins, 3:53, Marizona Music, BMI)/ The Master's call (Marty Robbins, 3:05, Marizona Music, BMI)/ The little green valley (Carson Robison, 2:25, Mayfair Music Corp)/ A hundred and sixty acres (Kapp, 1:43, Garland Music, Inc.)/ Billy the Kid (2:23, public domain)/ They're hanging me tonight (Low, Wolpert, 3:05, Sure Music, Inc.)/ Utah Carol (3:11, public domain).

In the wild west, part 2. BFX 15146 (LSP 15615): Bear Family Records; 1984; 33⅓ rpm. (Album).

Note: The album contains two previously unissued cuts.

Album contents. Side 1: Utah Carol (3:11, Trad.)/ Saddle tramp (Marty Robbins, 2:00, Marty's Music)/ She was young and she was pretty (Marty Robbins, 2:58, Marty's Music)/ Streets of Laredo (2:47, Trad.)/ Little Joe, the wrangler (4:07, Trad.)/ I've got no use for the women (3:21, Trad.)/ Billy Venero (3:47, Trad.)/ This peaceful sod (Jim Glaser, 1:47, Marizona Music)/ Side 2: Five brothers (Jim Glaser, 2:13, Marizona Music)/ San Angelo (Marty Robbins, 5:41, Marizona Music)/ Song of the bandit (Bob Nolan, 2:30, American Music)/ Wind (Bob Nolan, 2:53, American Music)/ Prairie fire (J. Babcock, 2:14, Marizona Music)/ My love (Marty Robbins, 1:45, Marizona Music)/ Ride cowboy ride (Lee Emerson, 3:15, Marizona Music)/ Red River Valley (2:20, Trad.).

In the wild west, part 3. BFX 15147 (LSP 15703): Bear Family Records; 1985; 33⅓ rpm. (Album).
Note: Recording session information on the back of the album cover.
Album contents. Side 1: The ballad of the Alamo (Webster, Dimitri, Tiomkin, 3:44, Leo Feist Music Co., ASCAP)/ The bend in the river (Marty Robbins, 2:32, Marizona Music, BMI)/ Abilene rose (J. B. Hosale, 2:59, Marizona Music, BMI)/ Dusty winds (J. Babcock, 1:51, Marizona Music, BMI)/ Doggone cowboy (J. Babcock, 2:08, Marizona Music, BMI)/ The Red Hills of Utah (Marty Robbins, 2:05, Marizona Music, BMI)/ Tall handsome stranger (H. Dourough, 2:05, Marizona Music, BMI); Side 2: Jimmie Martinez (Marty Robbins, 3:24)/ Ghost train (J. Babcock, 3:05)/ The fastest gun around (J. Pruett, J. Glaser, 1:45)/ San Angelo (Marty Robbins, 5:32)/ Old Red (Marty Robbins, 3:03)/ Johnny Fedavo (J. Babcock, 3:01)/ Man walks among us (Marty Robbins, 3:04, Marizona Music, BMI).

In the wild west, part 4. BFX 15183 (LSP 15750): Bear Family Records; 1985; 33⅓ rpm. (Album).
Note: The album contains seven previously unissued songs. Recording session information and original release numbers are on the back of the album cover. The album contains two versions of "When the work's all done this fall." The song, "Rich man, poor man," is titled "Rich man, rich man" on the album cover.
Album contents. Side 1: When the work's all done this fall (2:37, Trad.)/ Old Red (Marty Robbins, 2:56, Marty's Music Corp., BMI)/ I'm gonna be a cowboy (Marty Robbins, 1:49, Marty's Music Corp., BMI)/ Rich man, poor man (2:58, Copyright Control)/ I've got a woman's love (Marty Robbins, 2:10, Marty's Music Corp., BMI)/ Small man (Tom Perry, Bill Perry, 4:19, Marty's Music Corp., BMI); Side 2: The hanging tree (David, Livingston, 2:52, Whitmark & Sons, ASCAP)/ When the work's all done this fall (2:30, Trad.)/ Lonely old bunkhouse (Marty Robbins, 2:55, Marty's Music Corp., BMI)/ Night time on the desert (Marty Robbins, 2:16, Marty's Music Corp., BMI)/ Yours (Quiereme mucho) (A. Gamse, G. Roig, 2:23, Edward B. Marks Music)/ Adios Marquita Linda (M. A. Jiminez, 2:22, BMI).

In the wild west, part 5. BFX 15213 (LSP 15751): Bear Family Records; 1985; 33⅓ rpm. (Album).

Note: Recording session information and original release numbers for individual cuts are listed on the back of the album cover.

   Album contents. Side 1: The Master's call (Marty Robbins, 2:53)/ The cowboy in the continental suit (Robbins, 2:54)/ Cry stampede (B. D. Johnson, 2:16)/ Oh, Virginia (Marty Robbins, 3:40)/ Meet me tonight in Laredo (M. Cordle, R. Robinson, 3:23)/ Take me back to the prairie (B. Sykes, 2:19, Marizona Music, BMI); Side 2: The wind goes (Marty Robbins, 1:43, Marizona Music, BMI)/ Never tie me down (Marty Robbins, 1:29, Marizona Music, BMI)/ Cottonwood tree (Bobby Sykes, 3:56, Marizona Music, BMI)/ Mister Shorty (Marty Robbins, 5:01, Marizona Music, BMI)/ Chant of the wanderer (Bob Nolan, 2:04, American & Hill & Range, BMI)/ Ghost-riders in the sky (Stan Jones, 3:40, E. H. Morris & Co., ASCAP).

Marty Robbins' best loved hits. P 18825 (HL 1024); CBS; Heartland Music; 1985.
Note: Cover photo by Jim McGuire.
   Album contents. Side 1 (AS 18825): A white sport coat (and a pink carnation)/ The story of my life/ I'm so lonesome I could cry/ Devil woman/ Begging to you/ El Paso; Side 2 (BS 18825): Are you sincere/ I walk alone/ My happiness/ Don't worry/ Ribbon of darkness/ My woman, my woman, my wife.

Golden memories. P 18826, HL 1025; CBS; Heartland Music, 1985.
Note: Cover photo by Jim McGuire.
   Album contents. Side 1 (AS 18826): Singing the blues/ Half as much/ Cool water/ Have I told you lately that I love you/ To each his own/ Good hearted woman; Side 2 (BS 18826): Love me tender/ Return to me/ Unchained melody/ I don't know why, I just do/ Misty/ Can't help falling in love (with you).

What God has done. FC 40348: CBS Records; c1986; 33⅓ rpm. (Album).
Note: Album originally released as CS 9248.
   See previous listing for album contents.

A Christmas remembered. Information taken from TRC 2202 (Side 1: 2202-A; Side 2: 2202-B): Thunder Records; First released October, 1987.
Note: Produced by Marty Robbins. Liner notes by Gene Autry and Ronny Robbins. Cover design and artwork by J. William Myers from a photo by Paul "Paparu" Ruchti.
   Album contents. Side 1: Christmas time's a comin' (Red Simpson, Buck Owens, 2:07, Central Songs, BMI)/ Merry little Christmas

bells (Phoebe & Carolyn Binkley, 2:38, Mariposa Music, BMI)/ Don't hang the mistletoe (Bob & Phoebe Binkley, 2:50, Mariposa Music, BMI)/ Rudolph the red nosed reindeer (Johnny Marks, 2:05, St. Nicholas Music, ASCAP)/ If we make it through December (Merle Haggard, 2:27, Shade Tree Music, BMI); Side 2: Jingle bell rock (Joseph Carleton Beal, James Booth, 1:54, Intersong Music, ASCAP)/ Pretty paper (Willie Nelson, 2:45, Tree International, BMI)/ Santa Claus is coming to town (Haven Gillespie, Fred Coots, 1:59, S. B. K. Feist Catalog, ASCAP)/ Nestor the long-eared Christmas donkey (Gene Autry, Dave Burgess, Don Pfrimmer, 3:50, Golden West Melody & Singletree, BMI)/ I'll be home for Christmas (Kim Gannon, Walter Kent, 2:27, Gannon & Kent Music, ASCAP).

The great years. Stereo SHM 3208. Also available on cassette: HSC 3208: Hallmark Records. Made in England. A product of Pickwick International, Inc. Licensed from MCA Records; Released in 1987; 33⅓ rpm. (Album).
Note: This compilation, 1974 MCA Records, Inc.
   Album contents. Side 1: Twentieth century drifter (Marty Robbins, Acuff-Rose/Opryland Music)/ Mother knows best (Marty Robbins, Acuff-Rose/Opryland Music)/ I heard the bluebirds sing (Hod Pharis, Southern Music)/ The way I'm needing you (H. Cochran, Jane Kinsey, EMI Music)/ Darling come home (Donnie Winters, Dennis Winters, Acuff-Rose/Opryland Music)/ You're an angel disguised as a girl (Jimmy Sweeney, Acuff-Rose/Opryland Music); Side 2: Georgia blood (Marty Robbins, Acuff-Rose/Opryland Music)/ Don't you think (Marty Robbins, Acuff-Rose/Opryland Music)/ I'm wanting to (Ronny Robbins, Karen Russell, Acuff-Rose/Opryland Music)/ I couldn't believe it was true (Wallace Fowler, Eddy Arnold, Chappell-Morris Music)/ Love needs (Bill D. Johnson, Acuff-Rose/Opryland Music).

ALBUMS MARTY APPEARED ON AS A GUEST

Ernest Tubb. *The Legend and the legacy.* Volume 1. First Generation Records. TeeVee Records for Cachet Records; FGLP-0002. 1978, 1979.
Note: Marty appeared on two songs with Ernest; "Journey's end" (recorded with Marty, Ernest, and the Wilburn Brothers), and "Rainbow at midnight."

Bob Nolan. *The sound of a pioneer.* Electra/Asylum Records; 6E-212; 1979.
Note: Marty sings with Bob on one song, "Man walks among us."

Soundtrack music from the Clint Eastwood film Honkytonk Man Sound-track. Warner Bros./Viva Records, 1- 23739. 1982.
Note: Marty has two songs on the album: "Honkytonk man," and "In the jailhouse now" (sung by Marty, John Anderson, David Frizzell, and Clint Eastwood).

Columbia Records presents Marty Robbins, Jr.; Columbia Records; CS 9944. [1967].
This was Ronny Robbins' first album (he briefly went under the stage name of Marty Robbins, Jr.). Marty sang harmony with him on two of the songs. "Big mouthin' around," and "It finally happened."

Johnny Cash. *Encore.* Columbia Records; PC 37355. 1981. Marty sings harmony with Johnny on "Song of the patriot."

45s, 78s, AND EPs

MARTY ROBBINS 45 RPM SINGLE RECORDINGS

Love me or leave me alone/Tomorrow you'll be gone. 4-20925: Columbia Records; March 24, 1952; 45 rpm. (Single).
Note: Vocal with string band acc.
Love me or leave me alone (Robbins, RZSP 10040); Tomorrow you'll be gone (Robbins, RZSP 10038).

Crying 'cause I love you/I wished somebody loved me. 4-20965: Columbia Records; June 27, 1952; 45 rpm. (Single).
Note: Vocal with string band acc.
Crying 'cause I love you (M. Robbins, RZSP 10041); I wished somebody loved me (M. Robbins, RZSP 10039).

I'll go on alone/You're breaking my heart (while you're holding my hand). 4-21022: Columbia Records; October 10, 1952; 45 rpm. (Single).
Note: Vocal with string band acc.
I'll go on alone (Robbins, ZSP 9959); You're breaking my heart (while you're holding my hand) (Robbins, ZSP 9961).

I couldn't keep from crying/After you leave. 4-21075: Columbia Records; February 20, 1953; 45 rpm. (Single).

Note: Vocal with string band acc.
I couldn't keep from crying (M. Robbins, ZSP 12803); After you leave (M. Robbins, ZSP 12806).

A castle in the sky/A half-way chance with you. 4-21111: Columbia Records; May 15, 1953; 45 rpm. (Single).
Note: Vocal with string band acc.
A castle in the sky (M. Robbins, ZSP 13987); A half-way chance with you (M. Robbins, ZSP 13990).

Sing me something sentimental/At the end of a long, lonely day. 4-21145: Columbia Records; August 3, 1953; 45 rpm. (Single).
Note: Vocal with string band acc.
Sing me something sentimental (M. Robbins, ZSP 14673); At the end of a long, lonely day (M. Robbins, ZSP 14674).

Blessed Jesus, should I fall don't let me lay/Kneel and let the Lord take your load. 4-21172-s: Columbia Records (Columbia Sacred Series); October 12, 1953; 45 rpm. (Single).
Note: Record has a purple center label. Credit reads: Vocal with string band acc.
Blessed Jesus, should I fall don't let me lay (Robbins, ZSP 14675); Kneel and let the Lord take your load (Robbins, ZSP 14676).

Don't make me ashamed/It's a long, long ride. 4-21176: Columbia Records; October 12, 1953; 45 rpm. (Single).
Note: Vocal with string band acc.
Don't make me ashamed (M. Robbins, ZSP 30047); It's a long, long ride (M. Robbins, ZSP 30048).

My isle of golden dreams/Aloha oe. 4-21213: Columbia Records; January 25, 1954; 45 rpm. (Single).
Note: Vocal with instrumental acc.
My isle of golden dreams (Kahn-Blaufuss, ZSP 30679); Aloha oe (Liliuokalani, ZSP 30682).

Your heart's turn to break/Pretty words. 4-21246: Columbia Records; May 3, 1954; 45 rpm. (Single).
Note: Vocal with instrumental acc.
Your heart's turn to break (Robbins, ZSP 13988); Pretty words (Robbins, ZSP 9960).

I'm too big to cry/Call me up (and I'll come calling on you). 4-21291: Columbia Records; August, 1954; 45 rpm. (Single).

Note: Vocal with instrumental acc.
I'm too big to cry (Robbins, ZSP 32245); Call me up (and I'll come calling on you) (Robbins, ZSP 32246).

I'm too big to cry/Call me up (and I'll come calling on you). Promotion Record 4-21291: Columbia Records; August 2, 1954; 45 rpm. (Single).
Note: Vocal with instrumental acc.
I'm too big to cry (Robbins, 2:52, Acuff-Rose, BMI, ZSP 32245); Call me up (and I'll come calling on you) (Robbins, 2:05, Acuff-Rose, BMI, ZSP 32246).

It's a pity what money can do/Time goes by. 4-21324: Columbia Records; October 25, 1954; 45 rpm. (Single).
Note: Vocal with instrumental acc.
It's a pity what money can do (Robbins, ZSP 32247); Time goes by (Robbins, ZSP 32248).

It's a pity what money can do/Time goes by. Promotion Record 4-21324: Columbia Records; October 25, 1954; 45 rpm. (Single).
Note: Vocal with instrumental acc.
It's a pity what money can do (Robbins, 2:17, BMI, Acuff-Rose, ZSP 32247); Time goes by (Robbins, 2:20, BMI, Acuff-Rose, ZSP 32248).

That's all right/Gossip. 4-21351: Columbia Records; December 27, 1954; 45 rpm. (Single).
That's all right (Crudup, ZSP 34865); Gossip (Robbins, ZSP 34866).

That's all right/Gossip. Promotion Record 4-21351: Columbia Records; December 27, 1954; 45 rpm. (Single).
That's all right (Crudup, 2:32, Wabash Music Co., ZSP 34865); Gossip (Robbins, 2:40, BMI, Acuff-Rose, ZSP 34866).

God understands/Have thine own way. 4-21352-s: Columbia Records; January 10, 1955; 45 rpm. (Single).
God understands (Robbins, ZSP 30681); Have thine own way (Pollard-Stebbins, ZSP 30680).

God understands/Have thine own way, Lord. Promotion Record 4-21352-s: Columbia Records; January 10, 1955; 45 rpm. (Single).
God understands (Robbins, 2:58, BMI, Acuff-Rose Pub., ZSP 30681).
Have thine own way, Lord (Pollard-Stebbins, 2:40, public domain, ZSP 30680).

Pray for me mother of mine/Daddy loves you. 4-21388: Columbia Records; April 11, 1955; 45 rpm. (Single).
Pray for me mother of mine (Robbins, ZSP 34863); Daddy loves you (Robbins, ZSP 34864).

Pray for me mother of mine/Daddy loves you. Promotion Record 4-21388: Columbia Records; April 11, 1955; 45 rpm. (Single).
Pray for me mother of mine (Robbins, 2:46, BMI, Acuff-Rose, ZSP 34863); Daddy loves you (Robbins, 2:37, BMI, Acuff-Rose, ZSP 34864).

It looks like I'm just in your way/I'll love you till the day I die. 4-21414: Columbia Records; June 27, 1955; 45 rpm. (Single).
It looks like I'm just in your way [Robbins], ZSP 34701; I'll love you till the day I die [Robbins], ZSP 34702.

It looks like I'm just in your way/I'll love you till the day I die. Promotion Record 4-21414: Columbia Records; June 27, 1955; 45 rpm. (Single).
It looks like I'm just in your way (Robbins, 2:33, BMI, Acuff-Rose, ZSP 34701); I'll love you till the day I die (Robbins, 2:33, BMI, Acuff-Rose, ZSP 34702).

Maybelline/This broken heart of mine. 4-21446: Columbia Records; August 15, 1955; 45 rpm. (Single).
Maybelline (Chuck Berry, ZSP 36895); This broken heart of mine (Robbins, ZSP 34700).

Maybelline/This broken heart of mine. Promotion Record 4-21446: Columbia Records; August 15, 1955; 45 rpm. (Single).
Maybelline (Chuck Berry, 2:30, BMI, Arc Music Corp., JZSP 36895); This broken heart of mine (Robbins, 2:19, BMI, Acuff-Rose Pub., JZSP 34700).

Pretty mama/Don't let me hang around (if you don't care). 4-21461: Columbia Records; October 17, 1955; 45 rpm. (Single).
Pretty mama (Robbins, ZSP 36896); Don't let me hang around (if you don't care) (Robbins, ZSP 34703).

Pretty mama/Don't let me hang around (if you don't care). Promotion Record 4-21461: Columbia Records; October 17, 1955; 45 rpm. (Single).

Pretty mama (Robbins, 2:40, BMI, Acuff-Rose, Pub., JZSP 36896); Don't let me hang around (if you don't care) ([Robbins], 2:17, BMI, Acuff-Rose Pub., JSZP 34703).

Tennessee Toddy/Mean mama blues. 4-21477: Columbia Records; December 19, 1955; 45 rpm. (Single).
Tennessee Toddy (M. Robbins, ZSP 37383); Mean mama blues (M. Robbins, ZSP 36897).

Tennessee Toddy/Mean mama blues. 4-21477: Columbia Records; December 19, 1955; 45 rpm. (Single).
Tennessee Toddy (M. Robbins, 3:14, BMI, Acuff-Rose, ZSP 37383); Mean mama blues (M. Robbins, 2:11, BMI, Acuff-Rose, ZSP 36897).

Mr. Teardrop/Long tall Sally. 4-40679: Columbia Records; March 26, 1956; 45 rpm. (Single).
Mr. Teardrop (Robbins, ZSP 38100); Long tall Sally (E. Johnson, ZSP 38099).

Mr. Teardrop/Long tall Sally. Promotion Record 4-40679: Columbia Records; March 26, 1956; 45 rpm. (Single).
Mr. Teardrop (Robbins, 2:42, BMI, Acuff-Rose Pub., JZSP 38100); Long tall Sally (E. Johnson, 2:02, BMI, Venice Music Inc., JZSP 38099).

I'll know you're gone/How long will it be. 4-21525: Columbia Records; June 25, 1956; 45 rpm. (Single).
Note: Performer credit given on both sides as: Lee Emerson and Marty Robbins.
I'll know you're gone (Emerson, JZSP 38257); How long will it be (Emerson, JZSP 38258).

I'll know you're gone/How long will it be. Promotion Record 4-21525: Columbia Records; June 25, 1956; 45 rpm. (Single).
Note: Performer credit given on both sides as: Lee Emerson and Marty Robbins.
I'll know you're gone (Emerson, 1:47, BMI, Golden West Melodies Inc., JZSP 38257); How long will it be (Emerson, 2:05, BMI, Golden West Melodies Inc., JZSP 38258).

Respectfully Miss Brooks/You don't owe me a thing. 4-40706: Columbia Records; June 11, 1956; 45 rpm. (Single).

Respectfully Miss Brooks (Robbins, JZSP 38101); You don't owe me a thing (Robbins, JZSP 38102).

Respectfully Miss Brooks/You don't owe me a thing. Promotion Record 4-40706: Columbia Records; June 11, 1956; 45 rpm. (Single). Respectfully Miss Brooks (Robbins, 2:54, BMI, Acuff-Rose Pub., JZSP 38101); You don't owe me a thing (Robbins, 2:41, BMI, Acuff-Rose, Pub., JZSP 38102).

Singing the blues/I can't quit (I've gone too far). 4-21545: Columbia Records; August 6, 1956; 45 rpm. (Single). Singing the blues (Endsley, JZSP 37382); I can't quit (I've gone too far) (M. Robbins, JZSP 37379).

Singing the blues/I can't quit (I've gone too far). Promotion Record 4-21545: Columbia Records; August 6, 1956; 45 rpm. (Single). Singing the blues (Endsley, 2:24, BMI, Acuff-Rose, JZSP 37382); I can't quit (I've gone too far) (M. Robbins, 2:24, BMI, Acuff-Rose, JZSP 37379).

Knee deep in the blues/The same two lips. 4-40815-c: Columbia Records; December 17, 1956; rpm. (Single). Knee deep in the blues (Ensley, JZSP 39197); The same two lips (M. Robbins, JZSP 39195).

Knee deep in the blues/The same two lips. Promotion Record 4-40815-c: Columbia Records; December 17, 1956; 45 rpm. (Single). Knee deep in the blues (Ensley, 2:09, BMI, Acuff-Rose, JZSP 39197); The same two lips (Robbins, 2:59, BMI, Acuff-rose, JZSP 39195).

A white sport coat (and a pink carnation)/Grown-up tears. 4-40864: Columbia Records; March 4, 1957; 45 rpm. (Single). Note: Performer credit reads: Marty Robbins with Ray Conniff. A white sport coat (and a pink carnation) (Robbins, ZSP 39892); Grown-up tears (Conniff-Weismantel-Schell, ZSP 39893).

A white sport coat (and a pink carnation)/Grown-up tears. Promotion Record 4-40864: Columbia Records; March 4, 1957; 45 rpm. (Single). Note: Performer credit reads: Marty Robbins with Ray Conniff. A white sport coat (and a pink carnation) (Robbins, 2:30, BMI, Acuff-Rose, ZSP 39892); Grown-up tears (Conniff, Weismantel, Schell, 2:04, BMI, Blackwood Music, ZSP 39893).

Where d'ja go?/I cried like a baby. 4-40868-c: Columbia Records; March 11, 1957; 45 rpm. (Single).
Note: Performer credits: Lee Emerson and Marty Robbins are listed on "Where d'ja go?"; only Lee Emerson is credited on "I cried like a baby."
Where d'ja go? (Emerson, JZSP 39190); I cried like a baby (Emerson, JZSP 38256).

Where d'ja go?/I cried like a baby. Promotion Record 4-40868-c: Columbia Records; March 11, 1957; 45 rpm. (Single).
Note: Performer credits: Lee Emerson and Marty Robbins are listed on "Where d'ja go?"; only Lee Emerson is credited on "I cried like a baby."
Where d'ja go? (Emerson, 1:58, Be-Are Pub. Co., JZSP 39190); I cried like a baby (Emerson, 2:13, BMI, Cedarwood Pub., JZSP 38256).

Teen-age dream/Please don't blame me. 4-40969: Columbia Records; July 15, 1957; 45 rpm. (Single).
Note: Performer credits read: Marty Robbins with Ray Conniff and his Orch.
Teen-age dream (M. Robbins, ZSP 41741); Please don't blame me (M. Robbins, ZSP 41740).

Teen-age dream/Please don't blame me. Promotion Record 4-40969: Columbia Records; July 15, 1957; 45 rpm. (Single).
Note: Performer credits read: Marty Robbins with Ray Conniff and his Orch.
Teen-age dream (M. Robbins, 2:20, BMI, Acuff-Rose Pub., ZSP 41741); Please don't blame me (M. Robbins, 2:20, BMI, Acuff-Rose, ZSP 41740).

The story of my life/Once-a-week date. 4-41013: Columbia Records; September 30, 1957; 45 rpm. (Single).
Note: Performer credits read: Marty Robbins with Ray Conniff and his Orchestra. Issued with picture sleeve.
The story of my life (H. David/Bacharach, ZSP 42-189); Once-a-week date (Robbins, ZSP 42190).

The story of my life/Once-a-week date. Promotion Record 4-41013: Columbia Records; September 30, 1957; 45 rpm. (Single).
Note: Performer credits read: Marty Robbins with Ray Conniff and his Orchestra. Issued with picture sleeve.
The story of my life (H. David/Bacharach, 2:25, ASCAP, Famous

Music Corp., ZSP 42-189); Once-a-week date (Robbins, 2:20, BMI, Acuff-Rose, ZSP 42190).

Just married/Stairway of love. 4-41143: Columbia Records; March 10, 1958; 45 rpm. (Single).
Note: Performer credits read: Marty Robbins with Ray Conniff and his Orch.
Just married (B. Devorzon/A. Allen, ZSP 43164); Stairway of love (S. Tepper/C. Bennett, ZSP 43163).

Just married/Stairway of love. Promotion Record 4-41143: Columbia Records; March 10, 1958; 45 rpm. (Single).
Note: Performer credits read: Marty Robbins with Ray Conniff and his Orch.
Just married (B. Devorzon/A. Allen, 2:06, BMI, DeVorzon Music, ZSP 43164); Stairway of love (S. Tepper/C. Bennett, 2:02, ASCAP, Planetary Music Pub, Corp., ZSP 43163).

She was only seventeen (he was one year more)/Sittin' in a tree house. 4-41208: Columbia Records; July 7, 1958; 45 rpm. (Single).
Note: Performer credits read: Marty Robbins with Ray Conniff and his Orch.
She was only seventeen (he was one year more) (Robbins, ZSP 44045); Sittin' in a tree house (H. David/Bacharach, ZSP 44046).

She was only seventeen (he was one year more)/Sittin' in a tree house. Promotion Record 4-41208: Columbia Records; July 7, 1958; 45 rpm. (Single).
Note: Performer credits read: Marty Robbins with Ray Conniff and his Orch.
She was only seventeen (he was one year more) (Robbins, 2:35, BMI, Acuff-Rose, ZSP 44045); Sittin' in a tree house (H. David, Bacharach, 2:30, ASCAP, Famous Music Corp., ZSP 44046).

Ain't I the lucky one/The last time I saw my heart. 4-41282: Columbia Records; June 18, 1958; 45 rpm. (Single).
Note: Performer credits read: Marty Robbins with Ray Conniff and his Orch.
Ain't I the lucky one (Endsley, ZSP 44780); The last time I saw my heart (H. David, Bacharach, ZSP 44779).

Ain't I the lucky one/The last time I saw my heart. Promotion Record 4-41282: Columbia Records; June 18, 1958; 45 rpm. (Single).

Note: Performer credits read: Marty Robbins with Ray Conniff and his Orch.
Ain't I the lucky one (Endsley, 2:14, BMI, Acuff-Rose, ZSP 44780); The last time I saw my heart (H. David, Bacharach, 2:35, ASCAP, Famous Music Corp., ZSP 44779).

The hanging tree/The blues country style. 4-41325: Columbia Records; January 12, 1959; 45 rpm. (Single).
Note: Performer credits read: Marty Robbins with Ray Conniff and his Orchestra.
The hanging tree (M. David, Jerry Livingston, from the Warner Bros. picture "The Hanging Tree," RZSP 40990); The blues country style (M. David, Jerry Livingston, RZSP 40991).

The hanging tree/The blues country style. Promotion Record 4-41325: Columbia Records; January 12, 1959; 45 rpm. (Single).
Note: Performer credits read: Marty Robbins with Ray Conniff and his Orchestra.
The hanging tree (M. David, Jerry Livingston, from the Warner Bros. picture "The Hanging Tree," 2:52, ASCAP, M. Witmark & Sons, RZSP 40990); The blues country style (M. David, Jerry Livingston, 2:53, ASCAP, Advanced Music, Corp., RZSP 40991).

Cap and gown/Last night about this time. 4-41408: Columbia Records; May 25, 1959; 45 rpm. (Single).
Cap and gown (Tepper, R. Bennett, ZSP 47642); Last night about this time (Robbins, ZSP 47641).

Cap and gown/Last night about this time. Promotion Record 4-41408: Columbia Records; May 25, 1959; 45 rpm. (Single).
Cap and gown (Tepper, R. Bennett, 2:05, ASCAP, Aberbach Canada Ltd., ZSP 47642); Last night about this time (Robbins, 2:25, BMI, Marty's Music, ZSP 47641).

El Paso/Running gun. 4-41511: Columbia Records; October 26, 1959; 45 rpm. (Single).
Note: From the album "Gunfighter ballads and trail songs." Issued with picture sleeve.
El Paso (Robbins, ZSP 48863); Running gun (Tom Glaser, Tim Glaser, ZSP 48875).

El Paso/Running gun. Promotion Record 4-41511: Columbia Records; October 26, 1959; 45 rpm. (Single).

Note: From the album "Gunfighter ballads and trail songs." Issued with picture sleeve.
El Paso (Robbins, 4:37, BMI, Marty's Music, ZSP 48863); Running gun (Tom Glaser, Tim Glaser, 2:10, BMI, Marty's Music, ZSP 48875).

El Paso/El Paso. Promotion record: Columbia Records; 45 rpm. (Single).
Note: From the album "Gunfighter ballads and trail songs." El Paso [Robbins], (2:58, BMI, Marty's Music), JZSP 49158; El Paso [Robbins], (4:37, BMI, Marty's Music), JZSP 48863.

Big iron/Saddle tramp. 4-41589: Columbia Records; February 22, 1960; 45 rpm. (Single).
Note: Issued with picture sleeve.
Big iron (M. Robbins, ZSP 48864); Saddle tramp (M. Robbins, ZSP 49502).

Big iron/Saddle tramp. Promotion Record 4-41589: Columbia Records; February 22, 1960; 45 rpm. (Single).
Note: Issued with picture sleeve.
Big iron (M. Robbins, 3:53, BMI, Marty's Music, ZSP 48864); Saddle tramp (M. Robbins, 2:03, BMI, Marty's Music, ZSP 49502).

Is there any chance/I told my heart. 4-41686: Columbia Records; May 16, 1960; 45 rpm. (Single).
Is there any chance (M. Robbins, ZSP 50430); I told my heart (M. Robbins, ZSP 50431).

Is there any chance/I told my heart. Promotion Record 4-41686: Columbia Records; May 16, 1960; 45 rpm. (Single).
Is there any chance (M. Robbins, 2:08, BMI, Marizona Music Inc., ZSP 50430); I told my heart (M. Robbins, 2:04, BMI, Marizona Music Inc., ZSP 50431).

Five brothers/Ride, cowboy ride. 4-41771: Columbia Records; August 15, 1960; 45 rpm. (Single).
Note: Issued with picture sleeve. From the Columbia LP, "More gunfighter ballads and trail songs."
Five brothers (T. Glaser, ZSP 51244); Ride, cowboy ride (L. Emerson, ZSP 51243).

Five brothers/Ride, cowboy ride. Radio Station Copy 4-41771: Columbia Records; August 15, 1960; 45 rpm. (Single).

Note: From the Columbia LP, "More gunfighter ballads and trail songs."
Five brothers (T. Glaser, 2:10, BMI, Marizona Music, JZSP 51244); Ride, cowboy ride (L. Emerson, 3:12, Marizona Music Inc., JZSP 51243).

Ballad of the Alamo/A time and a place for everything. 4-41809: Columbia Records; September 19, 1960; 45 rpm. (Single).
Note: Credit for "The ballad of the Alamo" reads: From the Batjac Production, "The Alamo." Issued with picture sleeve.
Ballad of the Alamo (P. F. Webster, D. Tiomkin, ZSP 51733); A time and a place for everything (B. Joy, ZSP 51222).

Ballad of the Alamo/A time and a place for everything. Radio Station Copy 4-41809: Columbia Records; September 19, 1960; 45 rpm. (Single).
Note: Credit for "The ballad of the Alamo" reads: From the Batjac Production, "The Alamo." Issued with picture sleeve.
Ballad of the Alamo (P. F. Webster, D. Tiomkin, 3:38, ASCAP, Leo Feist Inc., ZSP 51733); A time and a place for everything (B. Joy, 1:49, BMI, Marizona Music Inc., ZSP 51222).

Don't worry/Like all the other times. 4-41922: Columbia Records; December 23, 1960; 45 rpm. (Single).
Note: Issued with picture sleeve.
Don't worry (M. Robbins, ZSP 51221); Like all the other times (L. Emerson, J. Glaser, ZSP 52411).

Don't worry/Like all the other times. Radio Station Copy 4-41922: Columbia Records; December 23, 1960; 45 rpm. (Single).
Note: Issued with picture sleeve.
Don't worry (M. Robbins, 3:10, BMI, Marty's Music, ZSP 51221); Like all the other times (L. Emerson, J. Glaser, 2:23, BMI, Marizona Music Inc., ZSP 52411).

Jimmy Martinez/Ghost train. 4-42008: Columbia Records; May 1, 1961; 45 rpm. (Single).
Note: Issued with picture sleeve.
Jimmy Martinez (M. Robbins, ZSP 53699); Ghost train (J. Babcock, ZSP 53700).

Jimmy Martinez/Ghost train. Radio Station Copy 4-42008: Columbia Records; May 1, 1961; 45 rpm. (Single).

Note: Issued with picture sleeve.
Jimmy Martinez (M. Robbins, 3:25, BMI, Marizona Music Inc., ZSP 53699); Ghost train (J. Babcock, 3:05, BMI, Marty's Music, ZSP 53700).

It's your world/You told me so. 4-42065: Columbia Records; July 28, 1961; 45 rpm. (Single).
Note: Issued with picture sleeve.
It's your world (M. Robbins, 2:43, ZSP 54448); You told me so (M. Robbins, 2:47, ZSP 54484).

It's your world/You told me so. Radio Station Copy 4-42065: Columbia Records; July 28, 1961; 45 rpm. (Single).
Note: Issued with picture sleeve.
It's your world (M. Robbins, 2:43, BMI, Marizona Music Inc., ZSP 54448); You told me so (M. Robbins, 2:47, BMI, Marizona Music, ZSP 54484).

I told the brook/Sometimes I'm tempted. 4-42246: Columbia Records; November 24, 1961; 45 rpm. (Single).
Note: Issued with picture sleeve.
I told the brook (M. Robbins, JZSP 55445); Sometimes I'm tempted (M. Robbins, JZSP 55446).

I told the brook/Sometimes I'm tempted. Radio Station Copy 4-42246: Columbia Records; November 24, 1961; 45 rpm. (Single).
Note: Issued with picture sleeve.
I told the brook (M. Robbins, 2:55, BMI, Marty's Music, JZSP 55445); Sometimes I'm tempted (M. Robbins, 2:20, BMI, Marizona Music Inc., JZSP 55446).

Love can't wait/Too far gone. 4-42375: Columbia Records; March 16, 1962; 45 rpm. (Single).
Note: Issued with picture sleeve.
Love can't wait (M. Robbins, ZSP 56386); Too far gone (M. Robbins, ZSP 56385).

Love can't wait/Too far gone. Radio Station Copy 4-42375: Columbia Records; March 16, 1962; 45 rpm. (Single).
Love can't wait (M. Robbins, 2:46, BMI, Marty's Music, JZSP 56386); Too far gone (M. Robbins, 3:07, BMI, Marizona Music, JZSP 56385).

Devil woman/April fool's day. 4-42486: Columbia Records; June 22, 1962; 45 rpm. (Single).

Note: Issued with two different picture sleeves. Produced by Don Law. Devil woman (M. Robbins, ZSP 57156); April fool's day (J. Winters, ZSP 57155).

Devil woman/April fool's day. Radio Station Copy 4-42486: Columbia Records; June 22, 1962; 45 rpm. (Single).
Note: Issued with two different picture sleeves. Produced by Don Law. Devil woman (M. Robbins, 2:58, BMI, Marty's Music, ZSP 57156); April fool's day (J. Winters, 2:43, BMI, Marty's Music, ZSP 57155).
Ruby Ann/Won't you forgive. 4-42614: Columbia Records; October 26, 1962; 45 rpm. (Single).
Note: Issued with picture sleeve. Prod. by Don Law and Frank Jones. Ruby Ann (R. Bellamy, ZSP 58214); Won't you forgive (J. Babcock, ZSP 58215).

Ruby Ann/Won't you forgive. Radio Station Copy 4-42614: Columbia Records; October 26, 1962; 45 rpm. (Single).
Note: Issued with picture sleeve. Prod. by Don Law and Frank Jones. Ruby Ann (R. Bellamy, 1:58, BMI, Marizona Music, ZSP 58214); Won't you forgive (J. Babcock, 2:45, BMI, Maricana Music, ZSP 58215).

Hawaii's calling me/Ka lu a. 4-42672: Columbia Records; June 9, 1962; 45 rpm. (Single). Printed in Canada.
Note: Produced by Don Law and Frank Jones.
Hawaii's calling me (J. B. Hosale, ZSP 56870)/Ka lu a (A. Caldwell, J. Kern, ZSP 58869).

Teenager's dad/Cigarettes and coffee blues. 4-42701: Columbia Records; February 8, 1963; 45 rpm. (Single).
Note: Issued with picture sleeve. Prod. by Don Law and Frank Jones. Teenager's dad (H. Dorrough, ZSP 59236); Cigarettes and coffee blues (M. Robbins, ZSP 59237).

Teenager's dad/Cigarettes and coffee blues. Radio Station Copy 4-42701: Columbia Records; February 8, 1963; 45 rpm. (Single).
Note: Issued with picture sleeve. Prod. by Don Law and Frank Jones. Teenager's dad (H. Dorrough, 1:49, BMI, Maricana Music, ZSP 59236); Cigarettes and coffee blues (M. Robbins, 2:41, BMI, Marty's Music, ZSP 59237).

Teenager's dad/Cigarettes and coffee blues. AAG 141 (4-42701): Columbia Records; 45 rpm. (Single).

Note: Issued in England. Produced by Don Law and Frank Jones. Additional credit: Acuff-Rose Pubs.
Teenager's dad (H. Dorrough); Cigarettes and coffee blues (M. Robbins).

No signs of loneliness here/I'm not ready yet. 4-42781: Columbia Records; April 19, 1963; 45 rpm. (Single).
Note: Issued with two different picture sleeves. Prod. by Don Law and Frank Jones.
No signs of loneliness here (L. Emerson, ZSP 59758); I'm not ready yet (M. Robbins, ZSP 59759).

No signs of loneliness here/I'm not ready yet. Radio Station Copy 4-42781: Columbia Records; April 19, 1963; 45 rpm. (Single).
Note: Prod. by Don Law and Frank Jones.
No signs of loneliness here (L. Emerson, 2:02, BMI, Marizona Music, JZSP 4-59758); I'm not ready yet (M. Robbins, 2:50, BMI, Marty's Music, JZSP 59759).

Not so long ago/I hope you learn a lot. 4-42831: Columbia Records; July 23, 1963; 45 rpm. (Single).
Note: Prod. by Don Law and Frank Jones.
Not so long ago (M. Robbins, ZSP 75617); I hope you learn a lot (B. Sykes, ZSP 75618).

Not so long ago/I hope you learn a lot. Radio Station Copy 4-42831: Columbia Records; July 23, 1963; 45 rpm. (Single).
Note: Prod. by Don Law and Frank Jones.
Not so long ago (M. Robbins, 2:03, BMI, Marty's Music, ZSP 75617); I hope you learn a lot (B. Sykes, 3:03, BMI, Maricana Music, ZSP 75618).

Begging to you/Over high mountain. 4-42890: Columbia Records; October 8, 1963; 45 rpm. (Single).
Note: Produced by Don Law and Frank Jones.
Begging to you (Marty Robbins, ZSP 76080); Over high mountain (Marty Robbins, ZSP 76093).

Begging to you/Over high mountain. Radio Station Copy 4-42890: Columbia Records; October 8, 1963; 45 rpm. (Single).
Note: Produced by Don Law and Frank Jones.
Begging to you (Marty Robbins, 2:26, BMI, Marty's Music, ZSP 76080); Over high mountain (Marty Robbins, 2:23, BMI, Maricana Music, ZSP 76093).

Girl from Spanish town/Kingston Girl. 4-42968: Columbia Records; January 28, 1964; 45 rpm. (Single).
Note: Prod. by Don Law and Frank Jones.
Girl from Spanish town (M. Robbins, ZSP 76798); Kingston Girl (D. Winters, ZSP 76799).

Girl from Spanish town/Kingston Girl. Radio Station Copy 4-42968: Columbia Records; January 28, 1964; 45 rpm. (Single).
Note: Prod. by Don Law and Frank Jones.
Girl from Spanish town (M. Robbins, 2:53, BMI, Marty's Music, ZSP 76798); Kingston Girl (D. Winters, 2:01, BMI, Marizona Music, ZSP 76799).

The cowboy in the continental suit/Man walks among us. 4-43049: Columbia Records; May 19, 1964; 45 rpm. (Single).
Note: Prod. by Don Law and Frank Jones.
The cowboy in the continental suit (M. Robbins, 2:54, ZSP 77637); Man walks among us (M. Robbins, 3:04, ZSP 77636).

The cowboy in the continental suit/Man walks among us. Radio Station Copy 4-43049: Columbia Records; May 19, 1964; 45 rpm. (Single).
Note: Prod. by Don Law and Frank Jones.
The cowboy in the continental suit (M. Robbins, 2:54, BMI, Marizona Music, ZSP 77637); Man walks among us (M. Robbins, 3:04, BMI, Marizona Music, ZSP 77636).

One of these days/Up in the air. 4-43134: Columbia Records; September 15, 1964; 45 rpm. (Single).
Note: Prod. by Don Law and Frank Jones.
One of these days (M. Robbins, 3:32, ZSP 78519); Up in the air (M. Robbins, 2:31, ZSP 78518).

One of these days/Up in the air. Radio Station Copy 4-43134: Columbia Records; September 15, 1964; 45 rpm. (Single).
Note: Prod. by Don Law and Frank Jones.
One of these days (M. Robbins, 3:32, BMI, Mariposa Music, Inc., JZSP 78519); Up in the air (M. Robbins, 2:31, BMI, Mariposa Music Inc., JZSP 78518).

I-eish-tay-mah-su (I love you)/A whole lot easier. 4-43196: Columbia Records; December 28, 1964; 45 rpm. (Single).
Note: Prod. by Don Law and Frank Jones.
I-eish-tay-mah-su (I love you) (M. Robbins, 2:28, ZSP 79541); A whole lot easier (M. Robbins, 2:02, ZSP 79540).

I-eish-tay-mah-su (I love you)/A whole lot easier. Radio Station Copy 4-43196: Columbia Records; December 28, 1964; 45 rpm. (Single). Note: Prod. by Don Law and Frank Jones.
I-eish-tay-mah-su (I love you) (M. Robbins, 2:28, BMI, Mariposa Music, ZSP 79541); A whole lot easier (M. Robbins, 2:02, BMI, Mariposa Music, ZSP 79540).

Ribbon of darkness/Little Robin. 4-43258: Columbia Records; March 22, 1965; 45 rpm. (Single).
Note: Produced by Don Law and Frank Jones.
Ribbon of darkness (G. Lightfoot, 2:29, ZSP 110047); Little Robin (J. Robinson, 2:08, ZSP 110048).

Ribbon of darkness/Little Robin. Radio Station Copy 4-43258: Columbia Records; March 22, 1965; 45 rpm. (Single).
Note: Produced by Don Law and Frank Jones.
Ribbon of darkness (G. Lightfoot, 2:29, ASCAP, M. Witmark & Sons, ZSP 110047); Little Robin (J. Robinson, 2:08, BMI, Majove Music and Noma Music, ZSP 110048).

Old Red/Matilda. 4-43377: Columbia Records; August 23, 1965; 45 rpm. (Single).
Old Red (M. Robbins, 3:03, ZSP 111334); Matilda (J. Braddock, 2:28, ZSP 111333).

Old Red/Matilda. Radio Station Copy 4-43377: Columbia Records; August 23, 1965; 45 rpm. (Single).
Note: From the Columbia LP, "The return of the gunfighter." Prod. by Don Law and Frank Jones.
Old Red (M. Robbins, 3:03, BMI, Marty's Music Corp., JZSP 111334); Matilda (B. Braddock, 2:28, BMI, Mariposa Music Inc., JZSP 111335).

While you're dancing/Lonely too long. 4-43428: Columbia Records; October 18, 1965; 45 rpm. (Single).
While you're dancing (2:27, B. Babcock, ZSP 111820); Lonely too long (2:33, M. Robbins, ZSP 111821).

While you're dancing/Lonely too long. Radio Station Copy 4-43428: Columbia Records; October 18, 1965; 45 rpm. (Single).
Note: Produced by Don Law & Frank Jones.
While you're dancing (B. Braddock, 2:27, BMI, Mariposa Music, Inc., JZSP 111820); Lonely too long (M. Robbins, 2:33, BMI, Mojave Music, Inc., JZSP 111821).

Private Wilson White/Count me out. 4-43500: Columbia Records; January 17, 1966; 45 rpm. (Single).
Note: Produced by Don Law & Frank Jones.
Private Wilson White (M. Robbins, 2:14, ZSP 112681); Count me out (J. Pruett, 2:29, ZSP 112682).

Private Wilson White/Count me out. Radio Station Copy 4-43500: Columbia Records; January 17, 1966; 45 rpm. (Single).
Note: Produced by Don Law & Frank Jones.
Private Wilson White (M. Robbins, 2:14, BMI, Mojave Music Inc., ZSP 112681); Count me out (J. Pruett, 2:29, BMI, Mariposa Music, ZSP 112682).

The shoe goes on the other foot tonight/It kind of reminds me of me. 4-43680: Columbia Records; June 6, 1966; 45 rpm. (Single).
Note: Produced by Don Law & Frank Jones.
The shoe goes on the other foot tonight (B. Mize, 2:00, ZSP 114408); It kind of reminds me of me (M. Robbins, 2:30, ZSP 114407).

The shoe goes on the other foot tonight/It kind of reminds me of me. Radio Station Copy 4-43680: Columbia Records; June 6, 1966; 45 rpm. (Single).
Note: Produced by Don Law & Frank Jones.
The shoe goes on the other foot tonight (B. Mize, 2:00, BMI, Mariposa Music Inc., ZSP 114408); It kind of reminds me of me (M. Robbins, 2:30, BMI, Mojave Music Inc., ZSP 114407).

No tears milady/Fly butterfly fly. 4-43845: Columbia Records; January 9, 1967; 45 rpm. (Single).
Note: Prod. by Don Law & Frank Jones.
No tears milady (M. Robbins, 1:51, ZSP 115984); Fly butterfly fly (M. Robbins, 2:49, ZSP 115985).

No tears milady/Fly butterfly fly. Radio Station Copy 4-43845: Columbia Records; January 9, 1967; 45 rpm. (Single).
Note: Prod. by Don Law & Frank Jones.
No tears milady (M. Robbins, 1:51, BMI, Mojave Music Inc. and Noma Music Inc., ZSP 115984); Fly butterfly fly (M. Robbins, 2:49, BMI, Mariposa Music, ZSP 115985).

Mr. Shorty/Tall handsome stranger. 4-43870: Columbia Records; April 7, 1966; 45 rpm. (Single).

Note: Produced by Don Law & Frank Jones.
Mr. Shorty (M. Robbins, 5:01, ZSP 116031); Tall handsome stranger
(H. Dorrough, 2:04, ZSP 116030).

Mr. Shorty/Tall handsome stranger. Radio Station Copy 4-43870: Co-
lumbia Records; April 7, 1966; 45 rpm. (Single).
Note: Produced by Don Law & Frank Jones.
Mr. Shorty (M. Robbins, 5:01, BMI, Mariposa Music, ZSP 116031);
Tall handsome stranger (H. Dorrough, 2:04, BMI, Maricana Music,
ZSP 116030).

Tonight Carmen/Waiting in Reno. 4-44128: Columbia Records; May 1,
1967; 45 rpm. (Single).
Note: Arranged by Bill McElhiney; Produced by Bob Johnston.
Tonight Carmen (M. Robbins, 2:39, ZSP 118444); Waiting in Reno (J.
Pruett, 2:27, ZSP 118445).

Tonight Carmen/Waiting in Reno. Radio Station Copy 4-44128: Colum-
bia Records; May 1, 1967; 45 rpm. (Single).
Note: Arranged by Bill McElhiney; Produced by Bob Johnston.
Tonight Carmen (M. Robbins, 2:39, BMI, Mojave Music Inc. and
Noma Music Inc., ZSP 118444); Waiting in Reno (J. Pruett, 2:27, BMI,
Mariposa Music Inc., ZSP 118445).

Gardenias in her hair/In the valley of the Rio Grande. 4-44271: Columbia Records; August 15, 1967; 45 rpm. (Single).
Note: Arranged by Bill Walker; Produced by Bob Johnston.
Gardenias in her hair (J. Byers, B. Tubert, 2:35, ZSP 119422); In the
valley of the Rio Grande (A. Russell, 2:23, ZSP 119421).

Gardenias in her hair/In the valley of the Rio Grande. Radio Station
Copy 4-44271: Columbia Records; August 15, 1967; 45 rpm. (Single).
Note: Arranged by Bill Walker; Produced by Bob Johnston.
Gardenias in her hair (J. Byers, B. Tubert, 2:35, BMI, Hill & Range
Songs and Mariposa Music Inc., ZSP 119422); In the valley of the Rio
Grande (A. Russell, 2:23, BMI, Mojave Music Inc. and Noma-Elvis
Presley Music ZSP 119421).

Love is in the air/I've been leaving every day. 4-44509: Columbia
Records; April 2, 1968; 45 rpm. (Single).
Note: Produced by Bob Johnston.
Love is in the air (M. Robbins, 2:03, ZSP 136850); I've been leaving
every day (W. Buchanan, 2:38, ZSP 136849).

Love is in the air/I've been leaving every day. Radio Station Copy 4-44509: Columbia Records; April 2, 1968; 45 rpm. (Single).
Note: Produced by Bob Johnston.
Love is in the air (M. Robbins, 2:03, BMI, Weedville Music, ZSP 136850); I've been leaving every day (W. Buchanan, 2:38, BMI, Airborne Music, ZSP 136849).

I walk alone/Lily of the valley. 4-44633: Columbia Records; August 27, 1968; 45 rpm. (Single).
Note: Produced by Bob Johnston.
I walk alone (H. Wilson, 2:59, ZSP 138182); Lily of the valley (J. Pruett, 2:39, ZSP 138183).

I walk alone/I walk alone. Radio Station Copy 4-44633: Columbia Records; August 27, 1968; 45 rpm. (Single).
Note: Produced by Bob Johnston. Radio Station copy has "I walk alone" on both sides.
I walk alone (H. Wilson, 2:59, BMI, Adams-Vee & Abbott Inc., ZSP 138182).

Big mouthin' around/It finally happened. 4-44641: Columbia Records; 1968; 45 rpm. (Single).
Note: [Editorial note: Artist credited is Marty Robbins, Jr. Marty sang harmony on both sides of this single release by his son Ronny.] Produced by Bob Johnston.
Big mouthin' around (M. Robbins, 1:47, ZSP 138185); It finally happened (M. Robbins, 2:22, ZSP 138184).

It's a sin/I feel another heartbreak coming on. 4-44739: Columbia Records; December 31, 1968; 45 rpm. (Single).
Note: Produced by Bob Johnston.
It's a sin (F. Rose, Z. Turner, 2:48, ZSP 138806); I feel another heartbreak coming on (M. Robbins, 3:22, from the Columbia LP, "I walk alone," CS 9725, ZSP 138805).

It's a sin/I feel another heartbreak coming on. Radio Station Copy 4-44739: Columbia Records; December 31, 1968; 45 rpm. (Single).
Note: Produced by Bob Johnston.
It's a sin (F. Rose, Z. Turner, 2:48, ASCAP, Milene Music Inc., ZSP 138806); I feel another heartbreak coming on (M. Robbins, 3:22, from the Columbia LP, "I walk alone," CS 9725, BMI, Mariposa Music Inc., ZSP 138805).

Hello Daily News/I can't say goodbye. 4-44895: Columbia Records; June 2, 1969; 45 rpm. (Single).
Note: Produced by Bob Johnston.
I can't say goodbye (R. Hardin, J. Byers, 2:57, JZSP 150024); Hello Daily News (J. Easterly, 2:06, JZSP 150023).

Hello Daily News/I can't say goodbye. Radio Station Copy 4-44895: Columbia Records; June 2, 1969; 45 rpm. (Single).
Note: Produced by Bob Johnston.
I can't say goodbye (R. Hardin, J. Byers, 2:57, BMI, Noma Music, Inc., JZSP 150024); Hello Daily News (J. Easterly, 2:06, BMI, Mariposa Music, Inc., JZSP 150023).

Camelia/Virginia. 4-45024: Columbia Records; October 21, 1969; 45 rpm. (Single).
Note: Produced by Bob Johnston.
Camelia (M. Robbins, 2:39, JZSP 151084); Virginia (M. Robbins, 2:34, from the Columbia LP, "By the time I get to Phoenix," CS9617, JZSP 151083).

Camelia/Virginia. Radio Station Copy 4-45024: Columbia Records; October 21, 1969; 45 rpm. (Single).
Note: Produced by Bob Johnston.
Camelia (M. Robbins, 2:39, BMI, Weedville Music & Noma Music, Inc., JZSP 151084); Virginia (M. Robbins, 2:34, BMI, Mariposa Music, Inc., from the Columbia LP, "By the time I get to Phoenix," CS 9617, JZSP 151083).

My woman, my woman, my wife/Martha Ellen Jenkins. 4-45091: Columbia Records; January 23, 1970; 45 rpm. (Single).
Note: Produced by Bob Johnston; Arranged by Bill Walker.
My woman, my woman, my wife (M. Robbins, 3:29, ZSP 151144); Martha Ellen Jenkins (P. Binkley, B. Binkley, 2:41, ZSP 151145).

My woman, my woman, my wife/My woman, my woman, my wife. Radio Station Copy 4-45091: Columbia Records; January 23, 1970; 45 rpm. (Single).
Note: Produced by Bob Johnston; Arranged by Bill Walker.
My woman, my woman, my wife (M. Robbins, 3:29, BMI, Mariposa Music, JZSP 151144).

Jolie girl/The city. 4-45215: Columbia Records; August 11, 1970; Stereo, 45 rpm. (Single).

Note: Arranged and conducted by Bill Walker; Produced by Bob Johnston.
Jolie girl (B. Fowler, 2:42, ZSP 152775); The city (M. Robbins, 4:37, ZSP 152774).

Jolie girl/The city. Radio Station Copy 4-45215: Columbia Records; August 11, 1970; Stereo, 45 rpm. (Single).
Note: Arranged and conducted by Bill Walker; Produced by Bob Johnston.
Jolie girl (B. Fowler, 2:42, ZSP 152775); The city (M. Robbins, 4:37, ZSP 152774).
[Editorial note: There were two different Radio Station copies distributed, one in stereo and one in mono. The center labels have different designs and colors.]

Padre/At times. 4-45273: Columbia Records; November 13, 1970; Stereo, 45 rpm. (Single).
Note: Arranged by Bill Walker; Produced by Bob Johnston.
Padre (J. Romans, P. F. Webster, 3:17, ZSS 152868); At times (M. Robbins, 2:44, ZSS 152869).

Padre/At times. Radio Station Copy 4-45273: Columbia Records; November 13, 1970; Stereo, 45 rpm. (Single).
Note: Arranged by Bill Walker; Produced by Bob Johnston.
Padre (J. Romans, P. F. Webster, 3:17, ASCAP, Anne-Rachael Music Corp., ZSS 152868); At times (M. Robbins, 2:44, BMI, Mariposa Music Inc., ZSS 152869).

Little spot in heaven/Wait a little longer please Jesus. 4-45346: Mfg by Columbia Records of Canada, Ltd.; March, 1971; Stereo, 45 rpm. (Single).
Note: Arranged by Bill Walker; produced by Marty Robbins.
Little spot in heaven (M. Robbins, 2:46, ZSS 154178); Wait a little longer please Jesus (C. Smith, H. Houair, 2:48, ZSS 154177).

The chair/Seventeen years. 4-45377: Columbia Records; April 22, 1971; Stereo, 45 rpm. (Single).
Note: Arranged by William McElhiney; Produced by Marty Robbins.
The chair (M. Robbins, 4:11, ZSS 154200); Seventeen years (M. Robbins, 2:30, ZSS 154201).

The chair/Seventeen years. Radio Station Copy 4-45377: Columbia Records; April 22, 1971; Stereo, 45 rpm. (Single).

Note: Arranged by William McElhiney; Produced by Marty Robbins. The chair (M. Robbins, 4:11, BMI, Mariposa Music, ZSS 154200); Seventeen years (M. Robbins, 2:30, BMI, Mariposa Music, ZSS 154201).

Early morning sunshine/Another day has gone by. 4-45442: Columbia Records; August 12, 1971; Stereo, 45 rpm. (Single).
Note: Arranged by Bill McElhiney; Produced by Marty Robbins.
Early morning sunshine (J. Marshall, 2:43, ZSS 154295); Another day has gone by (Don Winters, Jr., Dennis Winters, 2:59, ZSS 154296).

Early morning sunshine. Radio Station Copy 4-45442: Columbia Records; August 12, 1971; 45 rpm. (Single). Same song on both sides. Stereo: JZSS 154295; Mono: JZSP 154294.
Note: Arranged by Bill McElhiney; Produced by Marty Robbins.
Early morning sunshine (J. Marshall, 2:43, BMI, Mariposa Music).

The best part of living/Gone with the wind. 4-45520: Columbia Records; November 24, 1971; Stereo, 45 rpm. (Single).
Note: Arranged by Bill McElhiney; Produced by Marty Robbins.
The best part of living (B. D. Johnson, 2:56, ZSS 155413); Gone with the wind (B. Sykes, W. P. Walker, 3:24, ZSS 155412).

The best part of living. Radio Station Copy 4-45520: Columbia Records; November 24, 1971; Stereo, 45 rpm. (Single). Same song on both sides. Stereo: ZSS 154413; Mono: ZSP 154413.
Note: Arranged by Bill McElhiney; Produced by Marty Robbins.
The best part of living (B. D. Johnson, 2:56, BMI, Mariposa Music).

I've got a woman's love/A little spot in heaven. 4-45668: Columbia Records; August 7, 1972; Stereo, 45 rpm. (Single).
Note: Arranged by Bill Walker; Produced by Bob Johnston.
I've got a woman's love (M. Robbins, 2:23, ZSS 156591); A little spot in heaven (M. Robbins, 2:46, ZSS 156590).

I've got a woman's love. Radio Station Copy 4-45668: Columbia Records; August 7, 1972; Stereo, 45 rpm. (Single). Same song on both sides. Stereo: ZSS 156591; Mono: ZSP 156592.
Note: Arranged by Bill Walker; Produced by Bob Johnston.
I've got a woman's love (M. Robbins, 2:23, BMI, Acuff-Rose).

Laura (what's he got that I ain't got)/It kind of reminds me of me. 4-45775: Columbia Records; January 10, 1973; Stereo, 45 rpm. (Single).

Note: Strings arranged by Bill McElhiney; Produced by Bob Johnston. Laura (what's he got that I ain't got) (L. Ashley, M. Singleton, 3:40, ZSS 157115); It kind of reminds me of me (M. Robbins, 2:25, ZSS 157114).

Laura (what's he got that I ain't got). Radio Station Copy 4-45775: Columbia Records; January 10, 1973; Stereo, 45 rpm. (Single). Same song on both sides. Stereo: ZSS 157115; Mono: ZSP 157116.
Note: Strings arranged by Bill McElhiney; Produced by Bob Johnston. Laura (what's he got that I ain't got) (L. Ashley, M. Singleton, 3:40, BMI, Al Gallico Music Corp.).

This much a man/Guess I'll just stand here looking dumb. 33006: Decca Records (MCA Records); 1972; 45 rpm. (Single).
Note: Engineer: Mike Figlio.
This much a man (Marty Robbins, 2:56, BMI, Mariposa Music, Inc., 7-123,989); Guess I'll just stand here looking dumb (Larry Locke, Johnny Holland, 2:15, BMI, Mariposa Music, Inc., 7-123,990).

This much a man/Guess I'll just stand here looking dumb. Promotion Copy 33006: Decca Records (MCA Records); 1972; Mono: 45 rpm. (Single).
Note: Engineer: Mike Figlio.
This much a man (Marty Robbins, 2:56, BMI, Mariposa Music, Inc., 7-123,989); Guess I'll just stand here looking dumb (Larry Locke, Johnny Holland, 2:15, BMI, Mariposa Music, Inc., 7-123,990).

Walking piece of heaven/Franklin, Tennessee. MCA-40012: MCA Records; 1972, 1973; 45 rpm. (Single).
Walking piece of heaven (Marty Robbins, 3:02, BMI, Mariposa Music Inc., 7-124,099); Franklin, Tennessee (Marty Robbins, 3:03, from Decca LP, DL 75389, "This much a man," BMI, Mariposa Music Inc., 7-124,096).

Walking piece of heaven/Franklin, Tennessee. Promotion Copy MCA-40012: MCA Records; 1972, 1973; Stereo: 45 rpm. (Single).
Walking piece of heaven (Marty Robbins, 3:02, BMI, Mariposa Music Inc., 7-124,099); Franklin, Tennessee (Marty Robbins, 3:03, from Decca LP, DL 75389, "This much a man," BMI, Mariposa Music Inc., 7-124,096).

A man and a train/Las Vegas, Nevada. MCA-40067: MCA Records; 1973; Stereo, 45 rpm. (Single).

A man and a train ([Lyrics by Hal David/Music by Frank de Vol], 3:05, from the 20th Century-Fox film, "Emperor of the North Pole," ASCAP, 20th Century Music Corp., MC1630); Las Vegas, Nevada (Lobo Rainey, 2:47, BMI, Mariposa Music, Inc., MC1070).

A man and a train/Las Vegas, Nevada. Promotion Copy MCA-40067: MCA Records; 1973; Stereo, 45 rpm. (Single).
A man and a train ([Lyrics by Hal David/Music by Frank de Vol], 3:05, from the 20th Century-Fox film, "Emperor of the North Pole," ASCAP, 20th Century Music Corp., MC1630); Las Vegas, Nevada (Lobo Rainey, 2:47, BMI, Mariposa Music, Inc., MC1070).

Love me/Crawling on my knees. MCA-40134: MCA Records; 1973; 45 rpm. (Single).
Note: Produced by Walter Haynes. From the MCA LP MCA-342.
Love me (Jeanne Pruett, 2:45, BMI, Moss Rose Publications, Inc., MC2064); Crawling on my knees (Marty Robbins, 2:48, BMI, Mariposa Music Inc., 7-124,098).

Love me/Crawling on my knees. Promotion Copy MCA-40134: MCA Records; 1973; Stereo, 45 rpm. (Single).
Note: Produced by Walter Haynes. From MCA LP MCA-342.
Love me (Jeanne Pruett, 2:45, BMI, Moss Rose Publications, Inc., MC2064); Crawling on my knees (Marty Robbins), 2:48, BMI, Mariposa Music Inc., 7-124,098).

Twentieth century drifter/I'm wanting to. MCA-40172: MCA Records; 1973; 45 rpm. (Single).
Note: Produced by Marty Robbins.
Twentieth century drifter (Marty Robbins, 2:59, BMI, Mariposa Music Inc., MC2398); I'm wanting to (Ronny Robbins, Karen Russell, 2:48, BMI, Mariposa Music Inc., MC2431).

Twentieth century drifter/I'm wanting to. Promotion Copy MCA-40172: MCA Records; 1973; Stereo: 45 rpm. (Single).
Note: Produced by Marty Robbins.
Twentieth century drifter (Marty Robbins, 2:59, BMI, Mariposa Music Inc., MC2398); I'm wanting to (Ronny Robbins, Karen Russell, 2:48, BMI, Mariposa Music Inc., MC2431).

Don't you think/I couldn't believe it was true. MCA-40236: MCA Records; 1974; 45 rpm. (Single).
Note: Produced by Marty Robbins.

Don't you think (Marty Robbins, 2:53, BMI, Mariposa Music, Inc., MC 2397); I couldn't believe it was true (Wallace Fowler, Eddy Arnold, 2:32, BMI, Vogue Music, Inc., MC2432).

Don't you think/I couldn't believe it was true. Promotion Copy MCA-40236: MCA Records; 1974; Stereo, 45 rpm. (Single).
Note: Produced by Marty Robbins.
Don't you think (Marty Robbins, 2:53, BMI, Mariposa Music, Inc., MC2397); I couldn't believe it was true (Wallace Fowler, Eddy Arnold], (2:32, BMI, Vogue Music Inc., MC2432).

Two gun daddy/Queen of the big rodeo. MCA-40296: MCA Records; 1974; 45 rpm. (Single).
Note: Produced by Marty Robbins.
Two gun daddy (Marty Robbins, 2:44, BMI, Mariposa Music, Inc., MC3055); Queen of the big rodeo (Marty Robbins, 2:53, BMI, Mariposa Music Inc., MC3308).

Two gun daddy/Queen of the big rodeo. Promotion Copy MCA-40296: MCA Records; 1974; Stereo; 45 rpm. (Single).
Note: Produced by Marty Robbins.
Two gun daddy (Marty Robbins, 2:44, BMI, Mariposa Music, Inc., MC3055); Queen of the big rodeo (Marty Robbins, 2:53, BMI, Mariposa Music Inc., MC3308).

Life/It takes faith. MCA-40342: MCA Records; 1974; 45 rpm. (Single).
Note: Produced by Marty Robbins.
Life (Marty Robbins, 2:27, BMI, Mariposa Music Inc., MC3572); It takes faith (Marty Robbins, 3:07, BMI, Mariposa Music Inc., MC3573).

Life/It takes faith. Promotion Copy MCA-40342: MCA Records; 1974; Stereo, 45 rpm. (Single).
Note: Produced by Marty Robbins.
Life (Marty Robbins, 2:27, BMI, Mariposa Music Inc., MC3572); It takes faith (Marty Robbins, 3:07, BMI, Mariposa Music Inc., MC3573).

Shotgun rider/These are my souvenirs. MCA-40425: MCA Records; 1975; 45 rpm. (Single).
Note: Produced by Marty Robbins.
Shotgun rider (Donnie & Dennis Winters, 2:58, BMI, Mariposa Music, MC4005); These are my souvenirs (Marty Robbins, 2:44, BMI, Mariposa Music Inc., MC4010).

Shotgun rider/These are my souvenirs. Promotion Copy MCA-40425: MCA Records; 1975; Stereo, 45 rpm. (Single).
Note: Produced by Marty Robbins.
Shotgun rider (Donnie & Dennis Winters, 2:58, BMI, Mariposa Music Inc., MC4005); These are my souvenirs (Marty Robbins, 2:44, BMI, Mariposa Music Inc., MC4010).

El Paso City/When I'm gone. 3-10305: Columbia Records; 1976; Stereo, 45 rpm. (Single).
Note: "El Paso city" produced by Billy Sherrill; "When I'm gone" produced by Marty Robbins.
El Paso City (M. Robbins, 4:13, ZSS 161496); When I'm gone (M. Robbins, 2:08, ZSS 161497).

El Paso City. Demonstration copy 3-10305: Columbia Records; 1976; Stereo, 45 rpm. (Single). Promotion copy has same song on both sides. Stereo: 161496; Mono: ZSS 161495.
Note: "El Paso City" produced by Billy Sherrill.
El Paso City (M. Robbins, 4:13, BMI, Mariposa Music Inc., ZSS 161496).

Among my souvenirs/She's just a drifter. 3-10396: Columbia Records; August, 1976; Stereo, 45 rpm. (Single).
Note: Produced by Billy Sherrill. Taken from the Columbia LP, "El Paso City," KC 34303.
Among my souvenirs (E. Leslie, H. Nicholls, 2:32, ZSS 161738); She's just a drifter (M. Robbins, 2:48, ZSS 161739).

Among my souvenirs. Demonstration copy 3-10396: Columbia Records; August, 1976; Stereo, 45 rpm. (Single). Promotion copy has same song on both sides. Stereo: ZSS 161738; Mono: 161737.
Note: Produced by Billy Sherrill. Taken from the Columbia LP, "El Paso City," KC 34303.
Among my souvenirs (E. Leslie, H. Nicholls, 2:32, ASCAP, Chappell & Co).

Adios Amigo/Helen. 3-10472: Columbia Records; January 13, 1977; Stereo, 45 rpm. (Single).
Note: Taken from the Columbia LP, "Adios Amigo," KC 34448. "Adios Amigo" strings arranged by Bergen White, produced by Billy Sherrill. "Helen" produced by Marty Robbins.
Adios Amigo (B. Vinton, R. Girado, 3:35, ZSS 161865); Helen (J. Ouzts, R. Robbins, 3:19, ZSS 161866).

Adios Amigo. Demonstration copy 3-10472: Columbia Records; January 13, 1977; Stereo, 45 rpm. (Single). Promotion copy has same song on both sides. Stereo: ZSS 161865; Mono, 161864.
Note: Taken from the Columbia LP, "Adios Amigo," KC 34448. "Adios Amigo" strings arranged by Bergen White, produced by Billy Sherrill.
Adios Amigo (B. Vinton, R. Girado, 3:35, BMI, Al Gallico Music Corp. and Algee Music Corp.).

I don't know why (I just do)/Inspiration for a song. 3-10536: Columbia Records; April 26, 1977; Stereo, 45 rpm. (Single).
Note: Taken from the Columbia LP, "Adios Amigo," KC 34448. "I don't know why (I just do)" produced by Billy Sherrill. "Inspiration for a song" produced by Marty Robbins.
I don't know why (I just do) (R. Turk, F. Ahlert, 2:23, Pencil Mark, Tro-Cromwell, ASCAP, ZSS 162747); Inspiration for a song (R. C. Bannon, 2:39, ZSS 162748).

I don't know why (I just do). Demonstration copy 3-10536: Columbia Records; April 26, 1977; Stereo, 45 rpm. (Single). Promotion copy has same song on both sides. Stereo: ZSS 162747; Mono: ZSS 162746.
Note: Taken from the Columbia LP, "Adios Amigo," KC 34448. "I don't know why (I just do)" produced by Billy Sherrill.
I don't know why (I just do) (R. Turk, F. Ahlert, 2:23, ASCAP).

Don't let me touch you/Tomorrow, tomorrow, tomorrow. 3-10629: Columbia Records; September 23, 1977; Stereo, 45 rpm. (Single).
Note: "Don't let me touch you" strings arranged by Bill McElhiney, produced by Billy Sherrill. "Tomorrow, tomorrow, tomorrow" strings arranged by Billy Strange, produced by Marty Robbins.
Don't let me touch you (M. Robbins, B. Sherrill, 2:48, ZSS 163771); Tomorrow, tomorrow, tomorrow (M. Robbins, 2:29, ZSS 163772).

Don't let me touch you. Demonstration copy P3-10629: Columbia Records; September 23, 1977; Stereo, 45 rpm. (Single). Promotion copy has same song on both sides. Stereo: ZSS 163771; Mono: ZSS 163770.
Note: "Don't let me touch you" strings arranged by Bill McElhiney, produced by Billy Sherrill.
Don't let me touch you (M. Robbins, B. Sherrill, 2:48, BMI, Mariposa Music).

Return to me/More than anything I miss you. 3-10673: Columbia Records; January 5, 1978; Stereo, 45 rpm. (Single).
Note: Taken from the Columbia LP, "Don't let me touch you," KC

35040. "Return to me" strings arranged by Bergen White, produced by Billy Sherrill. "More than anything I miss you" produced by Billy Sherrill.

Return to me (C. Lombardo, D. DiMinno, 2:55, ZSS 163856); More than anything I miss you (R. Robbins, 2:27, ZSS 163857).

Return to me. Demonstration copy 3-10673: Columbia Records; January 5, 1978; Stereo, 45 rpm. (Single). Promotion record has same song on both sides. Stereo: ZSS 163856; Mono: ZSS 163855.

Note: Taken from the Columbia LP, "Don't let me touch you," KC 35040. "Return to me" strings arranged by Bergen White, produced by Billy Sherrill.

Return to me (C. Lombardo, D. DiMinno, 2:55, ASCAP, Southern Music Pub. Co.)

Please don't play a love song/Jenny. 3-10821: Columbia Records; October 10, 1978; Stereo, 45 rpm.

Note: Produced by Billy Sherrill.

Please don't play a love song (B. Sherrill, S. Davis, 3:04, ZSS 164640); Jenny (C. Davis, 3:00, ZSS 164617).

Please don't play a love song. Demonstration copy 3-10821: Columbia Records; October 10, 1978; Stereo, 45 rpm. Promotion copy has same song on both sides. Stereo: ZSS 164640; Mono: ZSP 164639.

Note: Produced by Billy Sherrill.

Please don't play a love song (B. Sherrill, S. Davis, 3:04, BMI, Algee Music Corp.).

Touch me with magic/Confused and lonely. 3-10905: Columbia Records; January 23, 1979; 45 rpm. (Single).

Note: Produced by Billy Sherrill.

Touch me with magic (S. Bogard, M. Utley, 2:41, ZSS 165521); Confused and lonely (M. Robbins, ZSS 165522).

Touch me with magic. Demonstration Copy 3-10905: Columbia Records; January 23, 1979; 45 rpm. (Single). Promotion copy has same song on both sides. Stereo: ZSS 165521; Mono: ZSP 165520.

Note: Produced by Billy Sherrill.

Touch me with magic (S. Bogard, M. Utley, 2:41, BMI, Lyn-Lou Music Inc. and Algee Music Corp.).

All around cowboy/The dreamer. 3-11016: Columbia Records; May 30, 1979; Stereo, 45 rpm. (Single).

Note: Produced by Billy Sherrill.

All around cowboy (M. Robbins, 3:03, ZSS 165607); The dreamer (M. Robbins, 4:00, ZSS 165608).

All around cowboy. Demonstration copy 3-11016: Columbia Records; May 30, 1979; Stereo, 45 rpm. (Single). Promotion record has same song on both sides. Stereo: ZSS 165607; Mono: ZSP 165606.
Note: Produced by Billy Sherrill.
All around cowboy (M. Robbins, 3:03, BMI, Mariposa Music).

Buenos Dias Argentina/Ballad of a small man. 1-11102: Columbia Records; September 18, 1979; Stereo, 45 rpm. (Single).
Note: Produced by Billy Sherrill. Taken from the Columbia LP, "All Around Cowboy," JC 36085.
Buenos Dias Argentina (B. Raleigh, U. Jurgens, 3:02, ZSS 165654); Ballad of a small man (M. Robbins, 4:01, ZSS 165655).

Buenos Dias Argentina. 1-11102: Columbia Records; September 18, 1979; 45 rpm. (Single). Promotion copy has same song on both sides. Stereo: ZSS 165654.
Note: Produced by Billy Sherrill. Taken from the Columbia LP, "All Around Cowboy," JC 36085.
Buenos Dias Argentina (B. Raleigh, U. Jurgens, 3:02, ASCAP, F.A. Music Co. Inc.).

She's made of faith/Misery in my soul. 1-11240: Columbia Records; March 13, 1980; Stereo, 45 rpm. (Single).
Note: Produced by Marty Robbins.
She's made of faith (M. Robbins, 3:18, ZSS 166958); Misery in my soul (D. Winters, D. Winters, Jr., 3:03, ZSS 166959).

She's made of faith. Demonstration copy 1-11240: Columbia Records; March 13, 1980; Stereo, 45 rpm. (Single). Promotion record has same song on both sides.
Note: Produced by Marty Robbins.
She's made of faith (M. Robbins, 3:18, BMI, Mariposa Music, ZSS 166958).

Song of the patriot/She's a go-er. 1-11283: Columbia Records; 1980; Stereo, 45 rpm. (Single). Recording artist: Johnny Cash.
Note: Produced by Earl Ball; engineer: Gene Eichelberger.
Song of the patriot (M. Robbins—S. Milete, 3:27, vocal harmony Marty Robbins, ZSS 167000); She's a go-er (J. P. Cash, 2:28, vocal harmony Joe Allen, ZSS 167001).

Song of the patriot. Demonstration copy 1-11283: Columbia Records; 1980; Stereo, 45 rpm. (Single). Recording artist: Johnny Cash. Promotion copy has same songs on both sides.
Note: Produced by Earl Ball; engineer: Gene Eichelberger.
Song of the patriot (M. Robbins—S. Milete, 3:27, vocal harmony Marty Robbins, BMI, Kaysey Music and Mariposa Music, ZSS 167000).

One man's trash (is another man's treasure)/I can't wait until tomorrow. 1-11291: Columbia Records; June 5, 1980; Stereo, 45 rpm. (Single).
Note: Produced by Marty Robbins. Taken from the Columbia LP, "With love, Marty Robbins," JC 36507.
One man's trash (is another man's treasure) (D. Winters, D. Winters, Jr., 2:58, ZSS 167008); I can't wait until tomorrow (D. M. Scott, 2:52, ZSS 167009).

One man's trash (is another man's treasure). Demonstration copy 1-11291: Columbia Records; June 5, 1980; Stereo, 45 rpm. (Single). Promotion copy has same song on both sides.
Note: Produced by Marty Robbins. Taken from the Columbia LP, "With love, Marty Robbins," JC 36507.
One man's trash (is another man's treasure) (D. Winters, D. Winters, Jr., 2:58, BMI, Mariposa Music, ZSS 167008).

An occasional rose/Holding on to you. 1-11372: Columbia Records; October 2, 1980; Stereo, 45 rpm. (Single).
Note: Produced by Eddie Kilroy.
An occasional rose (D. Burgess, 3:07, ZSS 167072); Holding on to you (L. Buchanan, 3:36, ZSS 167073).

An occasional rose. Demonstration copy 1-11372: Columbia Records; October 2, 1980; Stereo, 45 rpm. (Single). Promotion copy has same song on both sides.
Note: Produced by Eddie Kilroy.
An occasional rose (D. Burgess, 3:07, BMI, Singletree Music, ZSS 167072).

Completely out of love/Another cup of coffee. 11-11425: Columbia Records; January 8, 1981; Stereo, 45 rpm. (Single).
Note: Produced by Eddie Kilroy for Shaggy Dog Productions. Taken from the Columbia album, "Everything I've Always Wanted," JC 36860.
Completely out of love (M. Robbins, 3:05, ZSS 167869); Another cup of coffee (M. Robbins, 3:15, ZSS 167870).

Completely out of love. Demonstration copy 11-11425: Columbia Records; January 8, 1981; Stereo, 45 rpm. (Single). Promotion copy has same song on both sides.
Note: Produced by Eddie Kilroy for Shaggy Dog Productions. Taken from the Columbia album, "Everything I've Always Wanted," JC 36860.
Completely out of love (M. Robbins, 3:05, BMI, Mariposa Music, ZSS 167869).

Jumper cable man/Good hearted woman. 18-02444: Columbia Records; July, 1981; Stereo, 45 rpm. (Single).
Note: Produced by Marty Robbins and Eddie Fox.
Jumper cable man (M. Robbins, 2:40, ZSS 167981); Good hearted woman (W. Jennings, W. Nelson, 4:03, ZSS 167982).

Jumper cable man. Demonstration copy 18-02444: Columbia Records; July, 1981; Stereo, 45 rpm. (Single). Promotion record has same song on both sides.
Note: Produced by Marty Robbins and Eddie Fox.
Jumper cable man (M. Robbins, 2:40, BMI, Mariposa Music, ZSS 167981).

Teardrops in my heart/Honeycombe. 18-02575: Columbia Records; 1981; Stereo, 45 rpm. (Single).
Note: Taken from the Columbia LP, "The Legend," FC 37541. Produced by Marty Robbins and Eddy Fox.
Teardrops in my heart (V. Horton, 3:16, ZSS 168014); Honeycombe (B. Merrill, 2:49, ZSS 168015).

Some memories just won't die/Lover, lover. 18-02854: Columbia Records; April 6, 1982; Stereo, 45 rpm. (Single).
Some memories just won't die (B. Springfield, 3:20, ZSS 170452); Lover, lover (M. Robbins, 3:52, ZSS 170453).

Tie your dreams to mine/That's all she wrote. 38-03236: Columbia Records; August 13, 1982; Stereo, 45 rpm. (Single).
Note: Produced by Bob Montgomery. Taken from the Columbia LP, "Come back to me."
Tie your dreams to mine (T. DuBois—V. Stephenson—S. Lorber—J. Silbar, 2:50, ZSS 170554); That's all she wrote (J. Fuller, 3:18, ZSS 170555).

Tie your dreams to mine. Demonstration copy 38-03236: Columbia Records; August 13, 1982; Stereo, 45 rpm. (Single). Promotion copy has same song on both sides.

Note: Produced by Bob Montgomery. Taken from the Columbia LP, "Come back to me."
Tie your dreams to mine (T. DuBois—V. Stephenson—S. Lorber—J. Silbar, 2:50, House of Gold Music [BMI], Bobby Goldsboro Music [ASCAP], ZSS 170554).

Honkytonk man/Shotgun rag. 7-29847: Viva/Warner Brothers; December, 1982; 45 rpm. (Single).
Note: Honkytonk man, recorded by Marty Robbins; produced by Snuff Garrett. Shotgun rag, recorded by Johnny Gimble & the Texas Playboys, produced by Snuff Garrett. From the soundtrack of the Clint Eastwood film, "Honkytonk man."
Honkytonk man [D. Blackwell], (2:46), ACA 1995S; Shotgun rag [C. Crofford/S. Dorff/S. Garrett], (1:58), ACA 1994S.

Change of heart/Devil in a cowboy hat. 38-03789: Columbia Records; February 14, 1983; Stereo, 45 rpm. (Single).
Note: Taken from the Columbia LP, "Some memories just won't die," FC 38603. Produced by Bob Montgomery for Bob Montgomery Productions.
Change of heart [R. Sharp], (3:07), ZSS 170639; Devil in a cowboy hat [J. D. Hoag], (3:15), ZSS 170640.

Love me/Safely in the arms of Jesus. AG 45-454: Audiograph; 1983; Stereo, 45 rpm. (Single).
Note: Love me, recorded by Marty Robbins and Jeanne Pruett; Safely in the arms of Jesus, recorded by Jeanne Pruett. Produced by Walter Haynes. Marty Robbins courtesy of CBS Records.
Love me (Jeanne Pruett, 3:14); Safely in the arms of Jesus (Sonny Throckmorton, 3:26).

Love me. Promotion copy AG 45-454: Audiograph; 1983; Stereo, 45 rpm. (Single). Promotion copy has same song on both sides. Stereo: AG 45-454; Mono: AG 45-454.
Note: Love me, recorded by Marty Robbins and Jeanne Pruett; Marty Robbins courtesy of CBS Records. Distributed by Indigo Music Corp.
Love me (Jeanne Pruett, 3:14, BMI, Johnny Beinstock Music).

Life/Two gun daddy. MCA-52197: MCA Records; 1983; 45 rpm. (Single).
Note: Produced by Marty Robbins. From the MCA LP, MCA-27060, "20th Century Drifter."
Life [Marty Robbins], (2:27, BMI, Mariposa Music, Inc.) MC 13945R; Two gun daddy [Marty Robbins], (2:44, BMI, Mariposa Music, Inc.), MC 3055.

What if I said I love you/Baby that's love. 38-03927: Columbia Records; 1983; Stereo, 45 rpm. (Single).

What if I said I love you. Demonstration copy 38-03927: Columbia Records; April 29, 1983; Stereo, 45 rpm. (Single). Promotion copy has same song on both sides.
Note: Arranged by Ron Oates; produced by Bob Montgomery for Bob Montgomery Productions.
What if I said I love you (C. Black, T. Rocco, 2:44, ASCAP, Chappell Music and Intersong Music).

"COLUMBIA HALL OF FAME" SPECIAL RELEASES

I couldn't keep from crying/Sing me something sentimental. 4-52004: Columbia Records; Hall of Fame series; 45 rpm. (Single).
I couldn't keep from crying (Robbins, ZSP 12803); Sing me something sentimental (Robbins, ZSP 14673).

I couldn't keep from crying/Sing me something sentimental. Radio Station Copy 4-52004: Columbia Records; Hall of Fame series; 45 rpm. (Single).
Note: Vocal with String Band Acc.
I couldn't keep from crying (Robbins, 2:43, BMI, Acuff-Rose, ZSP 12803); Sing me something sentimental (Robbins, 2:51, BMI, Acuff-Rose, ZSP 14673).

El Paso/A white sport coat (and a pink carnation). Columbia Hall of Fame ed. 13-33013 (also released as 4-33015): Columbia Records; 45 rpm. (Single).
Note: A white sport coat (and a pink carnation), recorded by Marty Robbins with Ray Conniff.
El Paso (M. Robbins, 4:37, October 1951, ZSP 48863); A white sport coat (and a pink carnation) (M. Robbins, 2:30, March 1957, ZSP 39892).

Singing the blues/Big iron. Columbia Hall of Fame ed. 13-33045 (also released as 4-33013); Columbia Records; 45 rpm. (Single).
Singing the blues (M. Endsley, 2:24, March 1956, ZSP 37382); Big iron (M. Robbins, 3:53, February 1960, ZSP 48864).

Don't worry/Devil woman. Columbia Hall of Fame ed. 13-33070 (also released as 4-33070): Columbia Records; 45 rpm. (Single).
Note: Prod. by Don Law and Frank Jones.
Don't worry (M. Robbins, 3:09, December 1960; ZSP 51221); Devil woman (M. Robbins, 2:52, June 1962, ZSP 57156).

It's a sin/I walk alone. Columbia Hall of Fame ed. 13-33151 (also released as 4-33151): Columbia Records; May 20, 1969; 45 rpm. (Single).
Note: Produced by Bob Johnston.
It's a sin (F. Rose/Z. Turner, 2:48, December 1968, ZSP 138806); I walk alone (H. Wilson, 2:59, August 1968, ZSP 138182).

The hanging tree/The story of my life. Columbia Hall of Fame ed. 13-33231: Columbia Records; April 25, 1973; 45 rpm. (Single).
Note: Marty Robbins With Ray Conniff and his Orchestra.
The hanging tree (M. David, J. Livingston, 2:52, ZSP 40990); The story of my life (H. David, B. Bacharach, 2:25, September 1957, ZSP 42189).

Ruby Ann/Is there any chance. Columbia Hall of Fame ed. 13-33230 (also released as 4-33230): Columbia Records; April 25, 1973; 45 rpm. (Single).
Note: Ruby Ann, produced by Don Law and Frank Jones.
Ruby Ann (R. Bellamy, 1:58, October 1962, ZSP 58214); Is there any chance (M. Robbins, 2:08, May 1960, ZSP 13-33230).

Tonight Carmen/Gardenias in her hair. Columbia Hall of Fame ed. 13-33122: Columbia Records; December 26, 1967; 45 rpm. (Single).
Note: Tonight Carmen, arranged by Bill McElhiney and produced by Bob Johnston. Gardenias in her hair, arranged by Bill Walker and produced by Bob Johnston.
Tonight Carmen (M. Robbins, 2:39, May 1967, ZSP 118444); Gardenias in her hair (J. Byers, B. Tubert, 2:39, August 1967, ZSP 119422).

El Paso City/Among my souvenirs. Columbia Hall of Fame ed. 13-33341: Columbia Records; 1976; 45 rpm. (Single).
El Paso City (M. Robbins, 4:13, March, 1976, ZSS 161496); Among my souvenirs (E. Leslie, H. Nicholls, 2:32, August, 1976, ZSS 161738).

Adios Amigo/Don't let me touch you. Columbia Hall of Fame ed. 13-33370: Columbia Records; January, 1979; 45 rpm. (Single).
Note: Produced by Billy Sherrill. Strings arranged by Bill McElhiney.
Adios Amigo (B. Vinton, R. Girado, 3:35, January, 1977, ZSS 161865); Don't let me touch you (M. Robbins, B. Sherrill, 2:48, September, 1977, ZSS 163771).

Among my souvenirs/Return to me. Columbia Hall of Fame ed. 13-33371: Columbia Records; January 9, 1979; 45 rpm. (Single).

Note: Produced by Billy Sherrill. For "Return to me," strings arranged by Bergen White.
Among my souvenirs (E. Leslie, H. Nicholls, 2:32, August, 1976, ZSS 161738); Return to me (C. Combardo, D. DiMinno, 2:55, January, 1978, ZSS 163856).

PALOMINO RECORDS

Wheel of life/Get you off my mind. Promotional copy only. MP 469: Palomino Records; 1972; Mono 45 rpm. (Single).
Note: Arranged by Jimmy Haskill. Music from the film "Moonfire." From the original soundtrack.
Wheel of life/Get you off my mind [both songs composed by Norm Anderson].

PICTURE RECORDS

El Paso/A white sportcoat. 45 rpm. The cover side of the recording has a photo of Marty that is frequently used with "El Paso" publicity (he's in a black western outfit, kneeling by a tree and holding a gun). The publisher credit reads: Maybellene 33. The recording title reads: "Marty Robbins. This side, El Paso; other side, A white sportcoat." The verso of the recording has a color drawing of three western riders firing guns and the following information printed at the bottom of the record: ncb: made in E.E.C.. All rights reserved. First released 1987. Special Collectors Item. Limited Edition 1000 cps.

MARTY ROBBINS 78 RPM RECORDS

Love me or leave me alone/Tomorrow you'll be gone. 20925: Columbia Records; March 24, 1952; 78 rpm. (Single).
Note: Vocal with String Band Acc.
Love me or leave me alone (Robbins, RHCO 10040)/Tomorrow you'll be gone (Robbins, RHCO 10038).

Love me or leave me alone/Tomorrow you'll be gone. Special Record for Radio Stations 20925: Columbia Records; March 24, 1952; 78 rpm. (Single).
Note: Vocal with String Band Acc.
Love me or leave me alone (Robbins, 2:32, RHCO 10040)/Tomorrow you'll be gone (Robbins, 2:45, RHCO 10038).

Crying 'cause I love you/I wish somebody loved me. 20965: Columbia Records; June 27, 1952; 78 rpm. (Single).
Note: Vocal with String Band Acc.
Crying 'cause I love you (M. Robbins, RHCO 10041)/I wish somebody loved me (M. Robbins, RHCO 10039).

Crying 'cause I love you/I wish somebody loved me. Special Record for Radio Stations, 20965: Columbia Records; June, 1952; 78 rpm. (Single).
Note: Vocal with String Band Acc.
Crying 'cause I love you (M. Robbins, 2:35, RHCO 10041)/I wish somebody loved me (M. Robbins, 2:47, RHCO 10039).

I'll go on alone/You're breaking my heart (while you're holding my hand). 21022: Columbia Records; October 10, 1952; 78 rpm. (Single).
Note: Vocal with String Band Acc.
I'll go on alone (Robbins, CO 48023)/You're breaking my heart (while you're holding my hand) (Robbins, CO 48025).

I'll go on alone/You're breaking my heart (while you're holding my hand). Special Record for Radio Stations 21022: Columbia Records; October 10, 1952; 78 rpm. (Single).
Note: Vocal with String Band Acc.
I'll go on alone (Robbins, 2:39, BMI, Acuff-Rose, CO 48023)/You're breaking my heart (while you're holding my hand) (Robbins, BMI, Brenner Music, Inc., CO 48025).

Blessed Jesus, should I fall don't let me lay/Kneel and let the lord take your load. 21172: Columbia Records; October 12, 1953; 78 rpm. (Single).
Note: Vocal with String Band Acc.
Blessed Jesus, should I fall don't let me lay (Robbins)/Kneel and let the lord take your load (Robbins).

Blessed Jesus, should I fall don't let me lay/Kneel and let the lord take your load. Sacred Series, 21172-s: Columbia Records; October, 1953; 78 rpm. (Single).
Note: Vocal with String Band Acc.
Blessed Jesus, should I fall don't let me lay (Robbins, 2:53, Acuff-Rose Pub., BMI)/Kneel and let the lord take your load (Robbins, 2:50, Acuff-Rose, BMI).

Don't make me ashamed/It's a long, long ride. 21176: Columbia Records; October 12, 1953; 78 rpm. (Single).

Note: Vocal with String Band Acc.
Don't make me ashamed (M. Robbins, CO 49964)/It's a long, long ride (M. Robbins, CO 49965).

Don't make me ashamed/It's a long, long ride. Promotion Record, 21176: Columbia Records; October, 1953; 78 rpm. (Single).
Note: Vocal with String Band Acc.
Don't make me ashamed (M. Robbins, 2:45, Acuff-Rose, BMI, CO 49964)/It's a long, long ride (M. Robbins, 1:54, Acuff-Rose, BMI, CO 49965).

I couldn't keep from crying/After you leave. 21075: Columbia Records; February 20, 1953; 78 rpm. (Single).
Note: Vocal with String Band Acc.
I couldn't keep from crying (M. Robbins, CO 48487)/After you leave (M. Robbins, CO 48490).

I couldn't keep from crying/After you leave. Special Record for Radio Stations, 21075: Columbia Records; 1953; 78 rpm. (Single).
Note: Vocal with String Band Acc.
I couldn't keep from crying (M. Robbins, 2:43, Acuff-Rose, BMI, CO 48487)/After you leave (M. Robbins, 2:27, Acuff-Rose, BMI, CO 48490).

A castle in the sky/A half way chance with you. 21111: Columbia Records; May 15, 1953; 78 rpm. (Single).
Note: Vocal with String Band Acc.
A castle in the sky (M. Robbins, CO 49152)/A half way chance with you (M. Robbins, CO 49155).

A castle in the sky/A half way chance with you. Special Record for Radio Stations 21111: Columbia Records; May 15, 1953; 78 rpm. (Single).
Note: Vocal with String Band Acc.
A castle in the sky (M. Robbins, 2:55, BMI, Acuff-Rose, CO 49152)/A half way chance with you (M. Robbins, 2:30, BMI, Acuff-Rose, CO 49155).

Sing me something sentimental/At the end of a long, lonely day. 21145: Columbia Records; August 3, 1953; 78 rpm. (Single).
Note: Vocal with String Band Acc.
Sing me something sentimental (M. Robbins, CO 49515)/At the end of a long, lonely day (M. Robbins, CO 49516).

Sing me something sentimental/At the end of a long, lonely day. Columbia Promotion Record 21145: Columbia Records; August 3, 1953; 78 rpm. (Single).
Note: Vocal with String Band Acc.
Sing me something sentimental (M. Robbins, 2:51, BMI, Acuff-Rose, CO 49515)/At the end of a long, lonely day (M. Robbins, 2:30, BMI, Acuff-Rose, CO 49516).

My isle of golden dreams/Aloha oe (Farewell to thee). 21213: Columbia Records; January 25, 1954; 78 rpm. (Single).
Note: Vocal with Instrumental Acc.
My isle of golden dreams (Kahn, Blaufuss, CO 50668)/Aloha oe (Farewell to thee) (Liliuokalani, CO 50671).

My isle of golden dreams/Aloha oe (Farewell to thee). Columbia Promotion Record, 21213: Columbia Records; 1954; 78 rpm. (Single).
Note: Vocal with Instrumental Acc.
My isle of golden dreams (Kahn, Blaufuss, 2:41, Remick Music Corp., ASCAP, CO 50668)/Aloha oe (Farewell to thee) (Liliuokalani, 2:20, Public Domain, CO 50671).

Your heart's turn to break/Pretty words. 21246: Columbia Records; May 3, 1954; 78 rpm. (Single).
Note: Vocal with String Band Acc.
Your heart's turn to break (Robbins, CO 49153)/Pretty words (Robbins, CO 48024).

Your heart's turn to break/Pretty words. Promotion Record 21246: Columbia Records; May 3, 1954; 78 rpm. (Single).
Note: Vocal with String Band Acc.
Your heart's turn to break (Robbins, 2:42, BMI, Acuff-Rose, CO 49153)/Pretty words (Robbins, 2:52, BMI, Acuff-Rose, CO 48024).

I'm too big to cry/Call me up (and I'll come calling on you). 21291: Columbia Records; August 4, 1954; 78 rpm. (Single).
Note: Vocal with Instrumental Acc.
I'm too big to cry (Robbins, CO 51616)/Call me up (and I'll come calling on you) (Robbins, CO 51617).

I couldn't keep from crying/Sing me something sentimental. Hall of Fame Special ed. 52004: Columbia Records; August 2, 1954; 78 rpm. (Single).
Note: Vocal with String Band Acc.

I couldn't keep from crying (Robbins, CO 48487)/Sing me something sentimental (Robbins, 49515).

It's a pity what money can do/Time goes by. 21324: Columbia Records; October 25, 1954; 78 rpm. (Single).
Note: Vocal with Instrumental Acc.
It's a pity what money can do (Robbins, CO 51618)/Time goes by (Robbins, CO 51619).

That's all right/Gossip. 21351: Columbia Records; December 27, 1954; 78 rpm. (Single).
That's all right (Crudup, CO 52857)/Gossip (Robbins, CO 52858).

It looks like I'm just in your way/I'll love you till the day I die. 21414: Columbia Records; June 27, 1955; 78 rpm. (Single).
It looks like I'm just in your way/I'll love you till the day I die.

Maybelline/This broken heart of mine. 21446: Columbia Records; August 15, 1955; 78 rpm. (Single).
Maybelline/This broken heart of mine.

Pretty mama/Don't let me hang around. 21461: Columbia Records; October 17, 1955; 78 rpm. (Single).
Pretty mama (Robbins, CO 53740)/Don't let me hang around (Robbins, 52813).

Have thine own way, Lord/God understands. 21352-s: Columbia Records; January 10, 1955; 78 rpm. (Single).
Have thine own way, Lord (Pollard/Stebbins, CO 50669)/God understands (Robbins, CO 50670).

Pray for me mother of mine/Daddy loves you. 21388: Columbia Records; April 11, 1955; 78 rpm. (Single).
Pray for me mother of mine (Robbins, CO 52855)/Daddy loves you (Robbins, CO 52856).

Tennessee Toddy/Mean mama blues. 21477: Columbia Records; December 19, 1955; 78 rpm. (Single).
Tennessee Toddy (M. Robbins, CO 54287)/Mean mama blues (M. Robbins, CO 53741).

Singing the blues/I can't quit (I've gone too far). 21545: Columbia Records; August 6, 1956; 78 rpm. (Single).

Singing the blues (Endsley, CO 54286)/I can't quit (I've gone too far) (M. Robbins, CO 54285).

Long tall Sally/Mr. Teardrop. 40679: Columbia Records; March 26, 1956; 78 rpm. (Single).
Long tall Sally (Johnson, CO 55593)/Mr. Teardrop (Robbins, CO 55594).

Respectfully Miss Brooks/You don't owe me a thing. 40706: Columbia Records; June 11, 1956; 78 rpm. (Single).
Respectfully Miss Brooks/You don't owe me a thing.

I'll know you're gone/How long will it be. 21525: Columbia Records; June 25, 1956; 78 rpm. (Single).
Note: Performer credits for both sides read: Lee Emerson and Marty Robbins.
I'll know you're gone (Emerson, CO 55833)/How long will it be (Emerson, CO 55834).

Knee deep in the blues/The same two lips. 40815-c: Columbia Records; December 17, 1956; 78 rpm. (Single).
Knee deep in the blues (Endsley, CO 56872)/The same two lips (M. Robbins, CO 56870).

A white sport coat (and a pink carnation)/Grown-up tears. 40864: Columbia Records; March 4, 1957; 78 rpm. (Single).
Note: Artist credits for both sides read: Marty Robbins with Ray Conniff.
A white sport coat (and a pink carnation) (Robbins, CO 57240)/Grown-up tears (Conniff, Weismantel, Schell, CO 57241).

Please don't blame me/Teen age dream. 40969: Columbia Records; July 15, 1957; 78 rpm. (Single).
Note: Artist credits for both sides read: Marty Robbins with Ray Conniff.
Please don't blame me (Robbins, CO 57238)/Teen age dream (Robbins, CO 57239).

The story of my life/Once a week date. 41013: Columbia Records; September 30, 1957; 78 rpm. (Single).
The story of my life (H. David, Bacharach, CO 58370)/Once a week date (Robbins, CO 58371).

The story of my life/Once a week date. 41013: Columbia Records; Promotion Record. September 30, 1957; 78 rpm. (Single).
The story of my life (H. David, Bacharach, 2:25, CO 58370)/Once a week date (Robbins, 2:20, Acuff-Rose, CO 58371).

Where d'ja go/I cried like a baby. 40868c; Columbia Records; March 11, 1957; 78 rpm. (Single).
Note: Both Marty and Lee are credited as artists on "Where d'ja go"; only Lee Emerson is credited on "I cried like a baby."
Where d'ja go (Emerson)/I cried like a baby (Emerson).

MARTY ROBBINS EP RECORDINGS
(7-inch, 45 rpm, Extended Play)

Marty Robbins. H-1785: Columbia Records; November 9, 1953; 45 rpm. (EP). Issued with picture sleeve.
Note: Vocals with String Band Acc.
EP contents. Side ZEP 15020: I'll go on alone (Robbins)/Crying 'cause I love you (Robbins); Side ZEP 15021: I couldn't keep from crying (Robbins)/A half-way chance with you (Robbins).

Marty Robbins. H-2069: Columbia Records (Hall of Fame Series); April 25, 1955; 45 rpm. (EP). Issued with picture sleeve.
Note: Two songs by George Morgan also included.
EP contents: I couldn't keep from crying/Sing me something sentimental.

Singing the blues. B-2116: Columbia Records; November 5, 1956; 45 rpm. (EP). Issued with picture sleeve.
Note: The title is on the sleeve, but not on the record itself.
EP contents. Side ZEP 39130: Singing the blues (Endsley)/I can't quit (I've gone too far) (Robbins); Side ZEP 37131: Long gone lonesome blues (H. Williams)/Lorelei (C. Walker).

A white sport coat; and other favorites. B-2134: Columbia Records; April 15, 1957; 45 rpm. (EP). Issued with picture sleeve.
Note: The title is on the sleeve, but not on the record itself. The songs "A white sport coat" and "Grown-up tears" are noted as recorded with Ray Conniff.
EP contents. Side ZEP 39955: A white sport coat (and a pink carnation) (Marty Robbins)/Mean mama blues (Marty Robbins); Side ZEP 39956: Grown-up tears (Conniff-Weismantel-Schell)/Long tall Sally (E. Johnson).

4 big hits! B-2152: Columbia Records; 45 rpm. (EP). Issued with picture sleeve.
Note: Marty has one song on the EP.
EP contents: Side 1: Johnny Cash, Don't take your guns to town (Cash)/ Marty Robbins, The hanging tree (David/Livingston); Side 2: Johnny Horton, When it's springtime in Alaska (it's forty below) (T. Franks)/ Charlie Walker, Pick me up on your way down (H. Howard).

The letter edged in black. B 2153: Columbia Records; 45 rpm. (EP). Issued with picture sleeve.
EP contents. Side ZEP 45675: The letter edged in black (Nevada)/ The little rosewood casket (Traditional); Side ZEP 45676: The dream of the miner's child (A. Jenkins)/ The convict and the rose (B. Macdonald/R. King).

Marty Robbins. Hall of Fame Series ed. B-2808: Columbia Records; September 16, 1957; 45 rpm. (EP). Issued with picture sleeve.
Note: The title and series are on the sleeve, but not on the record itself.
EP contents. Side ZEP 41464: I couldn't keep from crying (M. Robbins)/ Sing me something sentimental (M. Robbins); Side ZEP 41465: Tennessee Toddy (M. Robbins)/ You don't owe me a thing (M. Robbins).

Marty Robbins. B-2814: Columbia Records (Hall of Fame Series); 1957; 45 rpm. (EP). Issued with picture sleeve.
Note: The title is on the sleeve but not on the record itself.
EP contents. Side ZEP 43568: A white sport coat (and a pink carnation) (Robbins)/ Singing the blues (Endsley); Side ZEP 43569: The story of my life (H. David, Bacharach. Marty Robbins, Ray Conniff and his Orch.)/ I'm so lonesome I could cry (H. Williams).

The Song of Robbins. Volume 1. B-9761: Columbia Records; April 29, 1957; 45 rpm. (EP). Issued with picture sleeve.
Note: The title and volume number appear on the cover, but not on the record itself.
EP contents. Side ZEP 41013: Lovesick blues (I. Mills, Friend)/ I'm so lonesome I could cry (H. Williams); Side ZEP 41014: It's too late now (to worry anymore) (Pope)/ Rose of Ol' Pawnee (F. Rose).

The song of Robbins. Volume 2. B-9762: Columbia Records; April 29, 1957; 45 rpm. (EP). Issued with picture sleeve.
Note: The title and volume number appear on the sleeve, but not the record itself.

EP contents. ZEP 41015: I never let you cross my mind (F. Rose)/ I hang my head and cry (Autry, F. Rose, Whitley); Side ZEP 41016: You only want me when you're lonely (Autry, S. Nelson)/ Moanin' the blues (H. Williams).

The Song of Robbins. Volume 3. B-9763: Columbia Records; April 29, 1957; 45 rpm. (EP). Issued with picture sleeve.
Note: Title and volume number appear on the cover but not on the record itself.
EP contents. Side ZEP 41017: I'll step aside (J. Bond)/ All the world is lonely now (Foree); Side ZEP 41018: Bouquet of roses (S. Nelson)/ Have I told you lately that I love you? (Autry, Wiseman).

Song of the islands. B-10871: Columbia Records; December 30, 1957; 45 rpm. (EP). Issued with picture sleeve.
Note: The title appears on the sleeve but not on the record itself.
EP contents. Side ZEP 42301: Song of the islands (C. King)/ Now is the hour (Maori farewell song) (Kaihan-C., Scott-D. Stewart); Side ZEP 42302: Sweet Leilani (H. Owens)/ Aloha oe (farewell to thee) (Liliukalani).

Marty Robbins. B-11891: Columbia Records; 1958; 45 rpm. (EP). Issued with picture sleeve.
Note: Title is on sleeve but not on the record itself.
EP contents. Side ZEP 43582: Kaw-liga (H. Williams, F. Rose)/ Waltz of the wind (F. Rose); Side ZEP 43583: Then I turned and walked slowly away (Fortner, E. Arnold)/ A house with everything but love (M. Robbins).

Gunfighter ballads and trail songs; volume 1. B-13491: Columbia Records; October 26, 1959; 45 rpm. (EP). Issued with picture sleeve.
Note: Title is on the sleeve but not on the record itself.
EP contents. Side ZEP 47137: El Paso (Robbins)/ A hundred and sixty acres (Kapp); Side ZEP 47138: They're hanging me tonight (Low, Wolpert)/ The strawberry roan (Public domain).

Gunfighter ballads and trail songs; volume 2. B-13492: Columbia Records; October 26, 1959; 45 rpm. (EP). Issued with picture sleeve.
Note: Title is on the sleeve but not on the record itself.
EP contents. Side ZEP 47139: Big iron (Robbins)/ In the valley (Robbins); Side ZEP 47140: Running gun (Tom Glaser, Tim Glaser)/ Utah Carol.

Gunfighter ballads and trail songs; volume 3. B 13493: Columbia Records; October 26, 1959; 45 rpm. (EP). Issued with picture sleeve.
Note: Title is on the sleeve but not on the record itself.
EP contents. Side ZEP 47141: Cool water (Nolan)/ The Master's call (Robbins); Side ZEP 47142: Billy the Kid (Public domain)/ The little green valley (Robison).

More gunfighter ballads and trail songs; volume 1. B-14811: Columbia Records; August 15, 1960; 45 rpm. (EP). Issued with picture sleeve.
Note: Volume is incorrectly spelled as "volumm" on the sleeve.
EP contents. Side ZEP 49968: San Angelo (M. Robbins); Side ZEP 49969: Prairie fire (J. Babcock)/ Streets of Laredo.

More gunfighter ballads and trail songs; volume 2. B 14812: Columbia Records; August 15, 1960; 45 rpm. (EP). Issued with picture sleeve.
EP contents. Side ZEP 49970: Song of the bandit (B. Nolan)/ I've got no use for the women; Side ZEP 49971: Five brothers (T. Glaser)/ Little Joe the Wrangler.

More gunfighter ballads and trail songs; volume 3. B 14813: Columbia Records; August 15, 1960; 45 rpm. (EP). Issued with picture sleeve.
EP contents. Side ZEP 49972: Ride, cowboy, ride (M. Robbins)/ This peaceful sod (J. Glaser); Side ZEP 49973: She was young and she was pretty (M. Robbins)/ My love (M. Robbins).

12

COPYRIGHT RECORDS OF MARTY'S MUSIC

This chapter results from a search of the Copyright Office records and is a compilation of all songs copyrighted by Marty Robbins. Arranged in alphabetical order by title, the titles range from *H-E-A-R-T-S-I-C-K* in 1950 to music recently copyrighted by Marty Robbins Enterprises. Much of the music was copyrighted under Marty's personal name, Martin David Robinson, or variations of his stage and personal names. The entries are presented as they were found on the official Copyright Office records. If there is some inconsistency, it's because the cards were inconsistent. Information on these records was taken directly from the paperwork that was filed; the office makes no effort to research apparent problems (such as name spellings) or to correct spelling errors. On copyright forms, the claimant is legally different from the author of the work. Because of this, while the name of the writer of the song is nearly always "Marty Robbins," the name of the person claiming ownership of the work is seen in several different forms, depending upon how Marty or his representative signed his name on that particular piece of paper. That's why his name appears as claimant in several different forms: Marty Robbins, Martin D. Robinson, Martin David Robinson, etc.

Eight titles were found under the pseudonym of Lobo Rainey. Five of them were co-authored with Karen Russell. Marty wrote music under that name for two of his early films, "Road to Nashville" in 1966 and "Hell on Wheels" in 1967. The songs with Karen Russell were all copyrighted on the same date in November of 1969. The last song registered under this name was

476

Las Vegas, Nevada in December of 1982. This song appears on his MCA album, *Marty Robbins.*

Most of his earlier music (from the 1950s) was written for the Acuff-Rose Publishing firm. While Marty later established his own publishing firms, he also sold these publishing houses to Chappell Music which currently owns much of his work, including *El Paso.* Mariposa Music remains in the family today as part of Marty Robbins Enterprises and owns the music written during the last years of his life.

Because of the numerous changes in the ownership of the music, I have included the current rights owner as well as the original claimant of each work when I could identify the company.

It is still possible to buy sheet music of songs Marty wrote from Acuff-Rose and Marty Robbins Enterprises. Hal Leonard has published a Marty Robbins songbook and some of Marty's most popular works (such as *El Paso*) are continually available in music stores.

INFORMATION FROM COPYRIGHT OFFICE RECORDS
(Alphabetized by Song Title)

Robinson, Martin, claimant. *After you leave.* Marty Robbins, [pseud.].
Nashville: Acuff-Rose; 1953; c27Feb53; (EP69791).
RE 80-161; 9Jan81.

Robbins, Marty, claimant. *Ain't I right?* Noma Music, Mojave Music,
& Elvis Presley Music; 1966; c8Aug66; (EU951777).
Current holder: Chappell Music.

Robbins, Marty, claimant. *The all around cowboy.* Nashville: Mariposa
Music; 1979; c2Apr79; (PA-29-178).

Robbins, Marty, claimant. *Allegheny airlines.* previously titled: *Fly me
back to Tennessee.* Nashville: Mariposa Music.

Robbins, Marty, claimant. *An old friend misses you.* Nashville: Mariposa Music.
Previous title: *An old pal, a real pal.*

Robinson, Martin D., claimant. *An old pal, a real pal.* By: Marty Robbins, [pseud.]. Nashville: Mariposa Music; 1966; c31Mar66; (EP216984).
Title changed to: *An old friend misses you.*

Robbins, Marty, claimant. *Another cup of coffee.* Nashville: Mariposa Music; 1978; c24Mar78; (PA-1-932).

Robbins, Marty, claimant. *Another pack of cigarettes, another glass of wine.* Nashville: Mariposa Music; 1976; c16Jan76; (EP347774).

Robinson, Martin, claimant. *At the end of a long, lonely day.* Marty Robbins [pseud.]. Nashville: Acuff-Rose; 1953; c19Oct53; (EP75066). RE 80-137; 9Jan81.

Robbins, Marty, claimant. *At times.* Nashville: Mariposa Music; 1970; c21Apr70; (EP271494).

Robbins, Marty, claimant. *Ava Maria Morales.* Nashville: Mariposa Music; 1974; c5Dec74; (EP331393).

Robbins, Marty, claimant. *Baby, I need you.* Nashville: Acuff-Rose; 1959; c6Apr59; (EP128931).

Robbins, Marty. *Ballad of a small man.*
See title: *Small man.*

Robinson, Martin D, claimant. *Begging to you.* By: Marty Robbins, [pseud.]. Nashville: Marty's Music; 1963; c23Sep63; (EP179426).
Current holder: Chappell Music.

Robbins, Marty, claimant. *The beginning of goodbye.* Nashville: Mariposa Music; 1969; c20Nov69; (EP274426).

Robinson, Martin D, claimant. *The bend in the river.* By: Marty Robbins, [pseud.]. Nashville: Marty's Music; 1962; c30Jul62; (EP165748).
Current holder: Chappell Music.

Robbins, Marty, claimant. *Big iron.* Be-Are Music; 1958; c13Oct58; (EP124200).
Current holder: Chappell Music.

Robbins, Marty, claimant. *Big mouthin' around*. Nashville, New York: Mojave Music, Noma Music, & Elvis Presley Music; 1968; c2Jan68; (EU29709).
Current holder: Chappell Music.

Robbins, Martin D, claimant. *Black coat*. Robbins, Marty, [pseud.]. Nashville: Marty's Music; 1959; c10Dec59; (EP136766).
Current holder: Chappell Music.

Robinson, Martin, claimant. *Blessed Jesus, should I fall, don't let me lay*. By: Marty Robbins, [pseud.]. Nashville: Acuff-Rose; 1953; c25Nov53; (EP76061).
RE 80-139; 9Jan81.

Robinson, Martin D, claimant. *Bobby darlin'*. By: Marty Robbins [pseud.]. Nashville: Mariposa Music; 1965; c28Jan65; (EP197905).

Robinson, Martin D.; McAlpin, Vic, claimants. *Breakfast with the blues*. Words by: Martin David [pseud. of Martin D. Robinson]; music by Vic McAlpin. Nashville: Maricana Music; 1963; c2Aug63; (EP177976).
Current holder: Mariposa Music.

Robinson, Martin, claimant. *Call me up and I'll come calling on you*. By: Marty Robbins [pseud.]. Nashville: Acuff-Rose; 1954; c1Oct54; (EP83659).
RE 113-924; 4Jan82. Renewal title reads: *Call me up (and I'll come calling on you)*.

Robbins, Marty, claimant. *Camelia*. Noma Music & Weedville Music; 1968; c16Aug68; (EU69551).
Second registration by Noma Music & Weedville Music, 2Jan70; EP267493. Current holder: Chappell Music.

Robinson, Martin, claimant. *Castle in the sky*. By: Marty Robbins [pseud.]. Nashville: Acuff-Rose; 1953; c19May53; (EP71793).
RE 80-148; 9Jan81.

Robbins, Marty, claimant. *The Chair*. Nashville: Mariposa Music; 1970; c6Apr70; (EP271202).

Robbins, Marty, claimant. *A Christmas prayer*. Nashville: Mojave Music, Noma Music, & Elvis Presley Music; 1967; c20Oct67; (EU20398).

Robbins, Marty, claimant. *Christmas time*. Nashville: Marty's Music; 1962; c4Oct62; (EP167727).
Current holder: Mariposa Music. Alternate title: *Christmas time is here again*.

Robbins, Marty. *Christmas time is here again*.
See title: *Christmas time*.

Robbins, Marty. *Cigarettes and coffee blues*.
See title: *Smokin' cigarettes and drinkin' coffee blues*.

Robbins, Marty, claimant. *The city*. Nashville: Mariposa Music; 1970; c6Apr70; (EP271203).

Robbins, Marty, claimant. *Clara*. Nashville: Marty's Music; 1961; c10Jul61; (EP153849).
Current holder: Chappell Music.

Robinson, Martin D., claimant. *Come go with me*. By: Marty Robbins [pseud.]. Nashville: Marty's Music; 1959; c24Dec59; (EP137313).
Current holder: Chappell Music.

Robbins, Marty, claimant. *Completely out of love*. Nashville: Mariposa Music; 1976; c16Jan76; (EP347775).

Robbins, Marty, claimant. *Confused and lonely*. Nashville: Mariposa Music; 1978; c26May78; (PA-5-736).

Robinson, Martin D., claimant. *The cowboy in the continental suit*. Nashville: Marizona Music; 1964; c13Feb64; (EP186354).
Current holder: Chappell Music.

Robbins, Marty, claimant. *Crawling on my knees*. Nashville: Mariposa Music; 1972; c3Mar72; (EP296777).

Robbins, Marty, claimant. *Crossroads of life*. Nashville: Mariposa Music; 1974; c4Nov74; (EP330447).
Also: 20Nov80 (PA-87-107).

Robbins, Marty, claimant. *Crying 'cause I love you*. Hollywood, CA: Ridgeway Music; 1952; c22Sep52; (EU288686).

Robinson, Martin, claimant. *Daddy loves you*. By: Marty Robbins [pseud.]. Nashville: Acuff-Rose; 1955; c20Apr55; (EP89212).
RE 184-120; 24Aug83.

Robinson, Martin D., claimant. *Devil woman.* By: Marty Robbins [pseud.]. Nashville: Marty's Music; 1962; c24Apr62; (EP162708). Current holder: Chappell Music.

Robinson, Martin, claimant. *Don't let me hang around if you don't care.* By: Marty Robbins [pseud.]. Nashville: Acuff-Rose; 1955; c12Dec55; (EP95137).
RE 184-123; 24Aug83.

Robbins, Marty, claimant. *Don't let me touch you.* Words and music by Marty Robbins and Billy Sherrill. Nashville: Mariposa Music; 1977; c8Sep77; (EP373582).

Robinson, Martin, claimant. *Don't make me ashamed.* By: Marty Robbins, [pseud.]. Nashville: Acuff-Rose; 1953; c25Nov53; (EP76063).
RE 80-141; 9Jan81.

Robinson, Martin D., claimant. *Don't take him from me, devil woman.* By: Marty Robbins [pseud.]. Nashville: Marty's Music; 1962; c24Apr62; (EP168033).
Parody of *Devil Woman;* new words, same music. Current holder: Chappell music.

Robinson, Martin D., claimant. *Don't throw me away.* By: Marty Robbins, [pseud.]. Nashville: Marty's Music; 1962; c16Apr62; (EP162366).
Current holder: Chappell Music.

Robinson, Martin D., claimant. *Don't worry.* By: Marty Robbins [pseud.]. Nashville: Marty's Music; 1960; c25Jul60; (EP142980). Current holder: Chappell Music.

Robbins, Marty, claimant. *Don't you think.* Nashville: Mariposa Music; 1973; c12Dec73; (EP319119).

Robinson, Martin D., claimant. *The dreamer.* By: Marty Robbins, [pseud.]. Nashville: Mariposa Music; 1966; c31Oct66; (EP223437).

Robbins, Marty, claimant. *The drifter.* Nashville: Mariposa Music; 1971; c3Feb71; (EP282756).

Robinson, Martin D., claimant. *Each time I hear "Don't worry 'bout me".* By: Marty Robbins [pseud.]. Nashville: Marty's Music; 1961; c18Jan61; (EP148239).
Current holder: Chappell Music.

Robinson, Martin D., claimant. *Eight feet long*. By: Marty Robbins [pseud.]. Nashville: Marizona Music; 1963; c11Feb63; (EP172078). Current holder: Chappell Music.

Robinson, Martin D., claimant. *El Paso*. By: Marty Robbins [pseud.]. Nashville: Marty's Music; 1959; c29May59; (EU578937). Current holder: Chappell Music.

Robbins, Marty, claimant. *El Paso, city*. Nashville: Mariposa Music; 1976; c13Feb76; (EP348877).

Robbins, Marty, claimant. *Eternal life giver*. Nashville: Mariposa Music; 1974; c15Jan74; (EP321257).

Robbins, Marty, claimant. *Ever since my baby went away*. Noma Music & Mojave Music; 1965; c18Mar65; (EU872770). Current holder: Chappell Music.

Robbins, Marty; Russell, Karen, claimants. *Eyes*. Music by Marty Robbins; words by Karen Russell. Nashville: Mariposa Music; 1971; c23Feb71; (EP283306).

Robinson, Martin D., claimant. *Faleena* (from El Paso). By: Marty Robbins, [pseud.]. Nashville: Mariposa Music; 1966; c10May66; (EP217187).

Robbins, Marty, claimant. *Falling out of love*. Nashville: Mariposa Music; 1976; c29Dec76; (EP363240).

Robbins, Marty, claimant. *A favorite song*. Nashville: Mariposa Music; 1984; c21Aug84; (PA-222-607).

Robbins, Marty; Milete, Sherrill, claimants. *A flag-waving patriotic nephew of my Uncle Sam*. Nashville: Mariposa Music & Kaysey Music; 1980; c24Mar80; (PA-62-723). Alternate title registered: *Song of the patriot*. 19Aug80, PA-77-693. See also this title.

Robinson, Martin D., claimant. *Fly, butterfly, fly*. By: Marty Robbins, [pseud.]. Nashville: Mariposa Music; 1964; c25Aug64; (EP191491).

Robbins, Marty, claimant. *Fly me back to Tennessee*. Nashville: Mariposa Music; 1976; c16Jan76; (EP347773). Title changed to: *Allegheny Airlines*.

Robbins, Marty, claimant. *Franklin, Tennessee.* Nashville: Mariposa Music; 1970; c10Aug70; (EP276258).

Robbins, Marty, claimant. *Gene Autry, my hero.* Nashville: Mariposa Music; 1980; c22Sep80; (PA-80-941).

Robbins, Marty, claimant. *Georgia blood.* Nashville: Mariposa Music; 1969; c5Nov69; (EP267463).

Robinson, Martin D., claimant. *Girl from Spanish town.* By: Marty Robbins [pseud.]. Nashville: Marty's Music; 1963; c28Jan63; (EP171733).
Current holder: Chappell Music.

Robinson, Martin, claimant. *God understands.* By: Marty Robbins [pseud.]. Nashville: Acuff-Rose; 1955; c23Mar55; (EP88923).
RE 184-118; 24Aug83.

Robinson, Martin, claimant. *Gossip.* By: Marty Robbins [pseud.]. Nashville: Acuff-Rose; 1955; c1Mar55; (EP87861).
RE 184-117; 24Aug83.

Robbins, Marty, claimant. *Graduation's almost here.* Nashville: Mojave Music & Noma Music; 1965; c21Apr65; (EU879633).
Current holder: Chappell Music.

Robinson, Martin, claimant. *A half way chance with you.* By: Marty Robbins [pseud.]. Nashville: Acuff-Rose; 1953; c19May53; (EP71794).
RE 80-149; 9Jan81.

Robbins, Marty, claimant. *The hands you're holding now.* Canada: Be-Are Music; 1958; c17Jun58; (EP120705).
Current holder: Chappell Music.

Robbins, Marty, claimant. *Harley Rutledge.* Nashville: Mariposa Music; 1972; c26Dec72; (EP306816).

Robinson, Martin David, claimant. *H-E-A-R-T-S-I-C-K.* Words, music, & copyright by: Martin David Robinson; 1950; c20Jul50; (EU210108).

Robbins, Marty, claimant. *A heel that time will wound.* Nashville: Noma Music, Elvis Presley Music, & Mojave Music; 1968; c6Nov68; (EU83257).
Current holder: Chappell Music.

Rainey, Lobo, claimant. *Hell on wheels.* Nashville: Mariposa Music; 1967; c7Jul67; (EP233480).
Note: Music only.
Lobo Rainey [pseud. of Martin D. Robinson].

Robinson, Martin D., claimant. *Hello, baby.* By: Marty Robbins [pseud.]. Nashville: Maricana Music; 1964; c22May64; (EP187886).
Current holder: Mariposa Music.

Robbins, Marty, claimant. *A house with everything but love.* Canada: Be-Are Music; 1958; c17Jun58; (EP120707).
Current holder: Chappell Music.

Robinson, Martin D., claimant. *How well do I remember.* By: Marty Robbins [pseud.]. Nashville: Marty's Music; 1959; c1Jul59; (EP134194).
Current holder: Chappell Music.

Robbins, Marty, claimant. *I can get along without you very well.* Brenner Music; 1952; c8Dec52; (EU297223).
RE 46-476; 7Jan80. Current holder: Chappell Music.

Robinson, Martin, claimant. *I can't quit, I've gone too far.* By: Marty Robbins [pseud.]. Nashville: Acuff-Rose; 1956; c8Aug56; (EP101367).
RE 196-836; 21Feb84.

Robinson, Martin, claimant. *I couldn't keep from crying.* By: Marty Robbins [pseud.]. Nashville: Acuff-Rose; 1953; c13Feb53; (EP69358).
RE 80-160; 9Jan81.

Robbins, Marty, claimant. *I-eish-tay-mah-su.* Nashville: Mariposa Music; 1964; c23Dec64; (EP196384).
Translation: I love you. English words.

Robinson, Martin D., claimant. *I feel another heartbreak coming on.* By: Marty Robbins [pseud.]. Nashville: Marty's Music; 1963; c11Feb63; (EP173297).
Current holder: Mariposa Music.

Robbins, Marty, claimant. *I gave everything (a girl in love should never give).* Nashville: Mariposa Music; 1973; c9Jul73 (in notice: 1972); (EP313974).

Robinson, Martin D., claimant. *I guess I'll be going*. By: Marty Robbins [pseud.]. Nashville: Marty's Music; 1961; c9Aug61; (EP154785). Current holder: Chappell Music.

Rainey, Lobo; Russell, Karen, claimants. *I learned it all from you*. Words by Karen Russell; Music by Lobo Rainey. Nashville: Mariposa Music; 1969; c20Nov69; (EP274424).
Lobo Rainey [unregistered pseud. of Martin D. Robinson].

Robinson, Martin, claimant. *I saw you, I saw you*. By: Marty Robbins [pseud.]. Nashville: Acuff-Rose; 1957; c3June57; (EP109494).
RE 239-025; 8Mar85.

Robinson, Martin D., claimant. *I told my heart*. By: Marty Robbins [pseud.]. Nashville: Marty's Music; 1960; c22Mar60; (EP139250). Current holder: Chappell Music.

Robinson, Martin D., claimant. *I told the brook*. By: Marty Robbins [pseud.]. Nashville: Marty's Music; 1961; c4Dec61; (EP158194). Current holder: Chappell Music.

Robinson, Martin David, claimant. *I wish somebody loved me*. Martin David Robinson; 1950; c20Jul50; (EU210107).
Personal copyright; no publisher listed. Same title copyrighted 22Sep52 by Ridgeway Music: EU288685.

Robbins, Marty, claimant. *I wish somebody loved me*. Hollywood, CA: Ridgeway Music; 1952; c22Sep52; (EU288685).
RE 66-998; 29Sep80. Previously copyrighted in 1950 by Martin David Robinson: EU210107.

Robbins, Marty, claimant. *If there's still another mountain*. Nashville: Mariposa Music; 1973; c4May73; (EP311714).

Robbins, Marty, claimant. *If this is love*. Nashville: Mariposa Music; 1974; c29May74; (EP325324).

David, Martin; Cordle, Mable, claimants. *I'll be allright*. Music by Martin David; words by Mable Cordle. Nashville: Maricana Music; 1964; c2Sep64; (EP191835).
Martin David [unregistered pseud. of Martin D. Robinson]. Current holder: Mariposa Music.

Robinson, Martin, claimant. *I'll go on alone*. By: Marty Robbins [pseud.]. Nashville: Acuff-Rose; 1952; c6Oct52; (EP66225).
RE 63-639; 15Jul80. First copyright; a second copyright, with new words, was made in 1953 (EP69357).

Robinson, Martin, claimant. *I'll go on alone*. By: Marty Robbins [pseud.]. Nashville: Acuff-Rose; 1953; c13Feb53; (EP69357).
Note: Copyright on new words.
RE 80-159; 9Jan81. Previously copyrighted, with original words, in 6Oct52 (EP66225).

Robinson, Martin, claimant. *I'll love you till the day I die*. By: Marty Robbins [pseud.]. Nashville: Acuff-Rose; 1955; c10Aug55; (EP91951).
RE 184-121; 24Aug83.

Robinson, Martin D., claimant. *I'm beginning to forget*. By: Marty Robbins [pseud.]. Nashville: Marizona Music; 1962; c27Aug62; (EP169902).
Current holder: Chappell Music.

Robinson, Martin D., claimant. *I'm gonna be a cowboy*. By: Marty Robbins [pseud.]. Nashville: Mariposa Music; 1964; c25Aug64; (EP191492).

Robbins, Marty, claimant. *I'm gonna miss you when you go*. Nashville: Mariposa Music; 1974; c15Jan74; (EP321253).

Robinson, Martin, claimant. *I'm happy cause you're hurtin'*. Nashville: Acuff-Rose; 1983, 1985; c8Feb85; (PA-239-715).
DCRE 1978; DPUB 29Jan85.

Robinson, Martin D., claimant. *I'm not ready yet*. By: Marty Robbins [pseud.]. Nashville: Marty's Music; 1963; c4Apr63; (EP174024).
Current holder: Chappell Music.

Robinson, Martin, claimant. *I'm too big to cry*. By: Marty Robbins [pseud.]. Nashville: Acuff-Rose; 1954; c7Oct54; (EP83810).
RE 113-925; 4Jan82.

Robbins, Marty, claimant. *In the morning*. Noma Music & Weedville Music; 1969; c8Dec69; (EU151202).
Current holder: Chappell Music.

Robinson, Martin D., claimant. *In the valley.* By: Marty Robbins [pseud.]. Nashville: Marty's Music; 1959; c29May59; (EU578939).
Current holder: Chappell Music.

Robbins, Marty, claimant. *In this corner.* Nashville: Mariposa Music; 1969; c20Nov69; (EP274425).

Robinson, Martin D., claimant. *Is it asking too much?* By: Marty Robbins [pseud.]. Nashville: Maricana Music; 1962; c28Dec62; (EP170435).
Current holder: Chappell Music.

Robinson, Martin D., claimant. *Is there any chance.* By: Marty Robbins [pseud.]. Nashville: Marizona Music; 1960; c23Mar60; (EP139260).
Current holder: Chappell Music.

Robinson, Martin D., claimant. *Is there any reason?* By: Marty Robbins [pseud.]. Nashville: Marizona Music; 1963; c27Aug63; (EP178712).
Current holder: Chappell Music.

Robbins, Marty, claimant. *Is there anything left I can say?* Mojave Music, Noma Music, & Elvis Presley Music; 1967; c13Jun67; (EU403).
Current holder: Chappell Music.

Robbins, Marty, claimant. *It finally happened.* Nashville: Mariposa Music; 1964; c20Nov64; (EP195036).

Robbins, Marty, claimant. *It kinda reminds me of me.* Noma Music, Mojave Music, & Elvis Presley Music; 1966; c31Mar66; (EU930376).
Current holder: Chappell Music.

Robinson, Martin, claimant. *It looks like I'm just in your way.* By: Marty Robbins [pseud.]. Nashville: Acuff-Rose; 1954; c4Mar54; (EP78678).
RE 113-918; 4Jan82.

Robbins, Marty, claimant. *It may take awhile.* Nashville: Marty's Music; 1961; c10Jul61 (in notice: 1959); (EP153848).
Current holder: Chappell Music.

Robbins, Marty, claimant. *It must be nice to be wanted.* Noma Music, Mojave Music; 1965; c7Oct65; (EU905871).
Current holder: Chappell Music.

Robbins, Marty, claimant. *It takes faith.* Nashville: Mariposa Music; 1974; c16Sep74; (EP328918).

Robbins, Marty, claimant. *It was worth it all.* Nashville: Mariposa Music; 1973; c12Dec73; (EP319118).

Robinson, Martin, claimant. *It won't do no good.* By: Marty Robbins [pseud.]. Nashville: Acuff-Rose; 1956; c29Mar56; (EP98214).
RE 196-831; 21Feb84.

Robinson, Martin, claimant. *It's a long, long ride.* By: Marty Robbins [pseud.]. Nashville: Acuff-Rose; 1953; c13Nov53; (EP75785).
RE 80-138; 9Jan81.

Robinson, Martin, claimant. *It's a pity what money can do.* By: Marty Robbins [pseud.]. Nashville: Acuff-Rose; 1954; c28Dec54; (EP86086).
RE 113-930; 4Jan82.

Robbins, Marty, claimant. *It's not too hard.* Nashville: Mariposa Music; 1980; c17Nov80; (PA-86-645).

Robinson, Martin D., claimant. *It's your world.* By: Marty Robbins [pseud.]. Nashville: Marizona Music; 1961; c21Mar61; (EP150093).
Current holder: Chappell Music.

Robinson, Martin, claimant. *I've got a woman's love.* By: Marty Robbins [pseud.]. Nashville: Acuff-Rose; 1953; c8Jul53; (EP72888).
RE 80-154; 9Jan81.

Robbins, Marty, claimant. *Janet.* Nashville: Mariposa Music; 1972; c23Oct72; (EP304854).

Robbins, Marty, claimant. *Jimmy and me.* Nashville: Mariposa Music; 1981; c30Jan81; (PAU-265-211).

Robbins, Marty, claimant. *Jimmy Martinez.* Nashville: Marizona Music; 1961; c25Apr61; (EP152302).
Current holder: Chappell Music.

Robbins, Marty, claimant. *Jumper cable man*. Nashville: Mariposa Music; 1981; c23Jul81; (PA-110-565).

Robinson, Martin, claimant. *Just in time*. By: Marty Robbins [pseud.]. Nashville: Acuff-Rose; 1953; c23Mar53; (EP70613). RE 80-162; 9Jan81.

Robbins, Marty, claimant. *Kate*. Nashville: Mariposa Music; 1972; c22Feb72; (EP296435).

Robinson, Martin D., claimant. *Kind' a half way feel*. By: Marty Robbins [pseud.]. Nashville: Marty's Music; 1962; c16Apr62; (EP162364). Current holder: Chappell Music.

Robinson, Martin, claimant. *Kneel and let the Lord take your load*. By: Marty Robbins [pseud.]. Nashville: Acuff-Rose; 1953; c8Dec53; (EP76423). RE 80-142; 9Jan81.

Rainey, Lobo, claimant. *Las Vegas, Nevada*. Nashville: Mariposa Music; 1972; c26Dec72; (EP306817). Lobo Rainey [unregistered pseud. of Martin D. Robinson].

Robinson, Martin D., claimant. *Last night about this time*. By: Marty Robbins, [pseud.]. Nashville: Marty's Music; 1959; c14May59; (EP130159). Current holder: Chappell Music.

Robbins, Marty, claimant. *Let me hear from you*. Blackwood Music; 1955; c25Mar55; (Eu392151). DREG: 28Dec83.

Robbins, Marty, claimant. *Life*. Nashville: Mariposa Music; 1974; c16Sep74; (EP328917).

Robinson, Martin D., claimant. *Little rich girl*. By: Marty Robbins [pseud.]. Nashville: Marizona Music; 1962; c27Aug62; (EP169903). Current holder: Chappell Music.

Robinson, Martin D., claimant. *A little spot in heaven*. By: Marty Robbins [pseud.]. Nashville: Marty's Music; 1963; c18Jul63; (EP177489). Current holder: Mariposa Music.

Robbins, Marty, claimant. *Lolean.* Nashville: Marty's Music; 1962; c16Apr62; (EP162365).
Current holder: Chappell Music.

Robinson, Martin D., claimant. *Lonely old bunkhouse.* By: Marty Robbins [pseud.]. Nashville: Mariposa Music; 1966; c22Apr66; (EP216626).

Robbins, Marty, claimant. *Lonely too long.* Noma Music, Mojave Music, & Elvis Presley Music; 1965; c22Oct65; (EU909367).
Current holder: Chappell Music.

Robbins, Marty, claimant. *Look at that tree.* Mojave Music, Noma Music, & Elvis Presley Music; 1968; c2Jan68; (EU29708).
Current holder: Chappell Music.

Robinson, Martin D., claimant. *Love can't wait.* By: Marty Robbins [pseud.]. Nashville: Marty's Music; 1959; c1Jul59; (EP134196).
Current holder: Chappell Music.

Robbins, Marty, claimant. *Love is in the air.* Noma Music, Weedville Music; 1968; c15Apr68; (EU47948).
Current holder: Chappell Music. A second registration was made on the same song, by the same publishers, 26June68 (EP247463).

Robbins, Marty, claimant. *Lover, lover.* Nashville: Mariposa Music; 1982; c15Mar82; (PA-131-660).

Robinson, Martin, claimant. *Lucky, lucky someone else.* By: Marty Robbins [pseud.]: Acuff-Rose; 1956; c15Jun56; (EP100267).
RE 196-833; 21Feb84.

Robbins, Marty, claimant. *Make believe cowboy.* Nashville: Mariposa Music; 1980; c10Dec80; (PA-88-587).

Robinson, Martin D., claimant. *Man walks among us.* By: Marty Robbins [pseud.]. Nashville: Marizona Music; 1963; c10Apr63; (EP174307).
Current holder: Chappell Music.

Robbins, Marty, claimant. *Martha, Oh Martha.* Nashville: Mariposa Music; 1972; c26Dec72; (EP306818).

Robinson, Martin D., claimant. *The Master's call.* By: Marty Robbins [pseud.]. Nashville: Marty's Music; 1959; c9Jun59; (EP130984).
Current holder: Chappell Music.

Robinson, Martin, claimant. *Mean mama blues.* By: Marty Robbins [pseud.]. Nashville: Acuff-Rose; 1956; c7Feb56; (EP96992). RE 196-828; 21Feb84.

Robinson, Martin D., claimant. *Melba from Melbourne.* By: Marty Robbins [pseud.]. Nashville: Maricana Music; 1963; c13Feb63; (EP172165). Current holder: Mariposa Music.

Robinson, Martin D., claimant. *Merry Christmas to you from me.* By: Marty Robbins [pseud.]. Nashville: Mariposa Music; 1964; c25Aug64; (EP191490).

Robinson, Martin, claimant. *Miss me just a little.* By: Marty Robbins [pseud.]. Nashville: Acuff-Rose; 1953; c24Apr53; (EP71126). RE 80-165; 9Jan81.

Robinson, Martin D., claimant. *Mister Shorty.* By: Marty Robbins [pseud.]. Nashville: Mariposa Music; 1966; c2May66; (EP219465).

Robinson, Martin, claimant. *Mister Teardrop.* By: Marty Robbins [pseud.]. Nashville: Acuff-Rose; 1956; c25Apr56; (EP98904). RE 196-832; 21Feb84.

Robinson, Martin D., claimant. *Mother knows best.* By: Marty Robbins [pseud.]. Nashville: Marty's Music; 1964; c24Mar64; (EP185862). Current holder: Mariposa Music.

Robbins, Marty, claimant. *My all time high.* Nashville: Mariposa Music; 1981; c23Jul81; (PA-110-567).

Robbins, Marty, claimant. *My friend Jim.* Mojave Music, Noma Music, & Elvis Presley Music; 1968; c2Jan68; (EU29707). Current holder: Chappell Music.

Robinson, Martin D., claimant. *My heart has a mind of its own.* By: Marty Robbins [pseud.]. Nashville: Marty's Music; 1959; c1Jul59; (EP134195). Current holder: Mariposa Music.

Robinson, Martin D., claimant. *My love.* By: Marty Robbins [pseud.]. Nashville: Marty's Music; 1960; c22Feb60; (EP138814). Current holder: Chappell Music.

Robbins, Marty, claimant. *My own native land.* Nashville: Noma Music, Mojave Music, & Elvis Presley Music; 1966; c20Oct66; (EU960936).
Current holder: Chappell Music.

Robbins, Marty, claimant. *My woman, my woman, my wife.* Nashville: Mariposa Music; 1969; c16Dec69; (EP267250).

Robinson, Martin D., claimant. *Never look back.* By: Marty Robbins [pseud.]. Nashville: Marizona Music; 1961; c2Feb61; (EP148718).
Current holder: Chappell Music.

Robinson, Martin D., claimant. *Never say devil woman.* By: Marty Robbins [pseud.]. Nashville: Marty's Music; 1962; c24Apr62; (EP168032).
Note: NM: new words. Parody of *Devil Woman.*
Current holder: Chappell Music.

Robinson, Martin D., claimant. *Never tie me down.* By: Marty Robbins [pseud.]. Nashville: Mariposa Music; 1966; c22Apr66; (EP216624).

Robinson, Martin D., claimant. *Night time on the desert.* By: Marty Robbins [pseud.]. Nashville: Mariposa Music; 1966; c22Apr66; (EP216627).

Robinson, Martin D., claimant. *Nineteen years ago.* By: Marty Robbins [pseud.]. Nashville: Marty's Music; 1963; c13Dec63; (EP182882).
Current holder: Mariposa Music.

Robbins, Marty, claimant. *No tears, milady.* Nashville: Mojave Music, Noma Music, & Elvis Presley Music; 1966; c14Oct66; (EU960943).
Current holder: Chappell Music.

Robinson, Martin D., claimant. *Not so long ago.* By: Marty Robbins [pseud.]. Nashville: Marty's Music; 1963; c13Jun63; (EP176469).
Current holder: Chappell Music.

Robbins, Marty, claimant. *Oh, Regena.* Nashville: Mariposa Music; 1978; c24Nov78; (PA-27-700).

Robinson, Martin D., claimant. *Oh, Virginia.* By: Marty Robbins [pseud.]. Nashville: Mariposa Music; 1966; c31Aug66; (EP221435).

Robinson, Martin D., claimant. *Old Red.* By: Marty Robbins [pseud.].
Nashville: Marty's Music; 1962; c23Mar62; (EP161737).
Current holder: Chappell Music.

Robinson, Martin, claimant. *Once a week date.* By: Marty Robbins
[pseud.]. Nashville: Acuff-Rose; 1957; c21Nov57; (EP114248).
RE 239-029; 8Mar85.

Rainey, Lobo; Russell, Karen, claimants. *One more time.* Music by
Lobo Rainey [pseud. of Martin D. Robinson]; Words by Karen Russell.
Nashville: Mariposa Music; 1969; c20Nov69; (EP274433).
Lobo Rainey [unregistered pseud. of Martin D. Robinson].

Robinson, Martin D., claimant. *One of these days.* By: Marty Robbins
[pseud.]. Nashville: Mariposa Music; 1964; c27Aug64; (EP191542).

Robbins, Marty, claimant. *The one, the only King.* Nashville: Mariposa
Music; 1973; c12Dec73; (EP319116).

Robbins, Marty, claimant. *Our last goodbye.* Nashville: Mariposa Music; 1973; c12Dec73; (EP319115).

Robbins, Marty, claimant. *The outlaws.* Nashville: Mariposa Music;
1974; c5Dec74; (EP331392).

Robinson, Martin D., claimant. *Over high mountain.* By: Marty Robbins [pseud.]. Nashville: Maricana Music; 1963; c4Oct63; (EP179784).
Current holder: Mariposa Music.

Robbins, Marty, claimant. *Pain and misery.* Nashville: Mariposa Music; 1982; c9Nov82; (PA-156-039).

Robinson, Martin D., claimant. *Peoples valley.* By: Marty Robbins
[pseud.]. Nashville: Mariposa Music; 1966; c19Apr66; (EP216333).

Robbins, Marty, claimant. *The performer.* Nashville: Mariposa Music;
1978; c18Oct78; (PA-15-271).

Robbins, Marty, claimant. *Pieces of your heart.* Nashville: Maricana
Music; 1963; c25Oct63; (EP180642).
Current holder: Mariposa Music.

Robinson, Martin, claimant. *Please don't blame me*. By: Marty Robbins [pseud.]. Nashville: Acuff-Rose; 1957; c26Aug57; (EP111601). RE 239-027; 8Mar85.

Robinson, Martin, claimant. *Pray for me, mother of mine*. By: Marty Robbins [pseud.]. Nashville: Acuff-Rose; 1955; c20Apr55; (EP89210). RE 184-119; 24Aug83.

Robinson, Martin, claimant. *Pretty mama*. By: Marty Robbins [pseud.]. Nashville: Acuff-Rose; 1955; c22Dec55; (EP95509). RE 184-124; 24Aug83.

Robinson, Martin, claimant. *Pretty words*. By: Marty Robbins [pseud.]. Nashville: Acuff-Rose; 1952; c6Oct52; (EP66228). RE 63-641; 15Jul80.

Robbins, Marty, claimant. *Pride and the badge*. Nashville: Mariposa Music; 1973; c16Feb73; (EP310260).

Robbins, Marty, claimant. *Private Wilson White*. Nashville: Mojave Music, Noma Music, & Elvis Presley Music; 1966; c20Jan66; (EU922940).
Second copyright made 30Mar66 (EP214919) on same title by same publishers.

Robinson, Martin D., claimant. *Progressive love*. By: Marty Robbins [pseud.]. Nashville: Maricana Music; 1962; c17Aug62; (EP166344). Current holder: Mariposa Music.

Robbins, Marty, claimant. *Queen of the big rodeo*. Nashville: Mariposa Music; 1974; c13Aug74; (EP328883).

Robbins, Marty, claimant. *Reach for me*. Nashville: Mariposa Music; 1984; c20Aug84; (PA-222-552).
DPUB 15Aug84.

Robinson, Martin D., claimant. *The Red Hills of Utah*. By: Marty Robbins [pseud.]. Nashville: Marty's Music; 1962; c24Aug62; (EP166443).
Current holder: Chappell Music.

Robinson, Martin, claimant. *Respectfully, Miss Brooks*. By: Marty Robbins [pseud.]. Nashville: Acuff-Rose; 1956; c3Aug56; (EP101307). RE 196-835; 21Feb84.

Robinson, Martin D., claimant. *Restless cattle.* By: Marty Robbins [pseud.]. Nashville: Mariposa Music; 1966; c31Oct66; (EP223438).

Robinson, Martin D., claimant. *Rich man, rich man.* By: Marty Robbins [pseud.]. Nashville: Marty's Music; 1962; c29May62; (EP163824). Current holder: Mariposa Music.

Rainey, Lobo, claimant. *Road to Nashville.* Nashville: Mariposa Music; 1966; c23May66; (EP217554). Lobo Rainey [unregistered pseud. of Martin D. Robinson].

Robinson, Martin D., claimant. *Saddle tramp.* By: Marty Robbins [pseud.]. Nashville: Marty's Music; 1960; c22Feb60; (EP138815). Current holder: Chappell Music.

Robinson, Martin, claimant. *The same two lips.* By: Marty Robbins [pseud.]. Nashville: Acuff-Rose; 1957; c16Jan57; (EP105514). RE 239-021; 8Mar85.

Robinson, Martin D., claimant. *San Angelo.* By: Marty Robbins [pseud.]. Nashville: Marty's Music; 1960; c22Mar60; (EP139249). Current holder: Chappell Music.

Robbins, Marty, claimant. *San Francisco teardrops.* Nashville: Mariposa Music; 1973; c4May73; (EP311715).

Robbins, Marty, claimant. *Seventeen years.* Nashville: Mariposa Music; 1971; c2Apr71; (EP284691).

Robbins, Marty, claimant. *She liked the way I loved her best.* Nashville: Mariposa Music; 1974; c13Aug74; (EP328881). Also titled: *The way I loved you best.*

Robinson, Martin, claimant. *She was only seventeen, he was one year more.* By: Marty Robbins [pseud.]. Nashville: Acuff-Rose; 1958; c15Aug58; (EP121850).

Robinson, Martin D., claimant. *She was young.* By: Marty Robbins [pseud.]. Nashville: Marty's Music; 1959; c29May59; (EU578940). Current holder: Chappell Music.

Robbins, Marty, claimant. *She's just a drifter.* Nashville: Mariposa Music; 1976; c3Jun76; (EP353542).

Robbins, Marty, claimant. *She's made of faith*. Nashville: Mariposa Music; 1980; c5Mar80; (PA-61-037).

Robbins, Marty, claimant. *Since you've gone*. Nashville: Marty's Music; 1960; c29Sep60; (EP145039).
Current holder: Chappell Music.

Robinson, Martin, claimant. *Sing me something sentimental*. By: Marty Robbins [pseud.]. Nashville: Acuff-Rose; 1953; c21Aug53; (EP73773). RE 80-155; 9Jan81.

Robinson, Martin D., claimant. *Sixteen weeks*. By: Marty Robbins [pseud.]. Nashville: Marty's Music; 1964; c26Mar64; (EP185888).
Current holder: Mariposa Music.

Robinson, Martin D., claimant. *Small man*. By: Marty Robbins [pseud.]. Nashville: Marizona Music; 1962; c27Aug62; (EP169904).
Current holder: Mariposa Music.

Robbins, Marty, claimant. *Smokin' cigarettes and drinkin' coffee blues*. Be-Are Music Publications; 1958; c29Sep58; (EP123131).
Note: Also titled: *Cigarettes and coffee blues*.
Current holder: Chappell Music.

Robinson, Martin D., claimant. *Sometimes I'm tempted*. By: Marty Robbins [pseud.]. Nashville: Marizona Music; 1961; c4Dec61; (EP158193).
Current holder: Chappell Music.

Robbins, Marty, claimant. *Sometimes love*. Nashville: Mariposa Music; 1975; c20Jan75; (EP335022).

Robbins, Marty; Milete, Sherrill, claimants. *Song of the patriot*. Nashville: Mariposa Music, Kaysey Music; 1980; c19Aug80; (PA-77-693).
Note: Title change.
Previous title: *A flag-waving patriotic nephew of my Uncle Sam;* previous copyright registration 24Mar80 (PA-62-723).

Robinson, Martin D., claimant. *Standing in each other's way*. By: Marty Robbins [pseud.]. Nashville: Marty's Music; 1962; c28Dec62; (EP170437).
Current holder: Mariposa Music.

Robinson, Martin, claimant. *Sugaree*. By: Marty Robbins [pseud.].
Nashville: Acuff-Rose; 1957; c22Jan57; (EP105520).
RE 239-022; 8Mar85.

Robinson, Martin D., claimant. *Sweet Cora*. By: Marty Robbins
[pseud.]. Nashville: Marizona Music; 1960; c13Apr60, in notice: 1959;
(EP139830).
Current holder: Chappell Music.

Robinson, Martin, claimant. *Sweet lies*. By: Marty Robbins [pseud.].
Nashville: Acuff-Rose; 1956; c20Mar56; (EP97915).
RE 196-830; 21Feb84.

Robinson, Martin, claimant. *The tears behind the smile*. By: Marty
Robbins [pseud.]. Nashville: Acuff-Rose; 1957; c4Apr57; (EP107644).
RE 239-024; 8Mar85.

Robinson, Martin, claimant. *Teen age dream*. By: Marty Robbins
[pseud.]. Nashville: Acuff-Rose; 1957; c26Aug57; (EP111600).
RE 239-026; 8Mar85.

Robbins, Marty, claimant. *Tennessee teardrops*. Nashville: Marty's
Music; 1962; c24Oct62; (EP169599).
Current holder: Chappell Music.

Robinson, Martin, claimant. *Tennessee Toddy*. By: Marty Robbins
[pseud.]. Nashville: Acuff-Rose; 1956; c15Feb56; (EP97143).
RE 196-829; 21Feb84.

Robbins, Marty, claimant. *These are my souvenirs*. Nashville: Mariposa
Music; 1975; c18Apr75; (EP338149).

Robinson, Martin, claimant. *This broken heart of mine*. By: Marty
Robbins [pseud.]. Nashville: Acuff-Rose; 1955; c21Oct55; (EP93829).
RE 184-122; 24Aug83.

Robbins, Marty, claimant. *This much a man*. Nashville: Mariposa Music; 1972; c7Apr72; (EP297861).

Robbins, Marty; Milete, Shirl, claimants. *Three quarter time*.
Nashville: Mariposa Music, Kaysey Music; 1981; c21Dec81;
(PA-123-866).

Robbins, Marty, claimant. *'Til hell freezes over*. Nashville: Mariposa Music; 1984; c27Aug84; (PA-222-929).

Robinson, Martin D., claimant. *Time can't make me forget*. By: Marty Robbins [pseud.]. Nashville: Marty's Music; 1962; c7Sep62; (EP166829).
Current holder: Chappell Music.

Robinson, Martin, claimant. *Time goes by*. By: Marty Robbins [pseud.]. Nashville: Acuff-Rose; 1954; c28Dec54; (EP86085).
RE 113-929; 4Jan82.

Robinson, Martin D., claimant. *To be in love with her*. By: Marty Robbins [pseud.]. Nashville: Mariposa Music; 1966; c31Mar66; (EP216979).

Rainey, Lobo; Russell, Karen, claimants. *To live again*. Music by: Lobo Rainey; Words by Karen Russell. Nashville: Mariposa Music; 1969; c20Nov69; (EP274434).
Lobo Rainey [unregistered pseud. of Martin D. Robinson].

Robbins, Marty, claimant. *Tomorrow, tomorrow, tomorrow*. Nashville: Mariposa Music; 1975; c10Jul75; in notice: 1974.; (EP340352).

Robbins, Marty, claimant. *Tonight Carmen*. Nashville: Mojave Music, Noma Music, & Elvis Presley Music; 1967; c15Sep67; (EP235937).
Previous registration: 13Jun67 (EU402).

Robbins, Marty, claimant. *Too far*. Nashville: Mariposa Music; 1969; c16Dec69; (EP267254).

Robinson, Martin D., claimant. *Too far gone*. By: Marty Robbins [pseud.]. Nashville: Marizona Music; 1962; c20Feb62; (EP160784).
Current holder: Chappell Music.

Robbins, Marty, claimant. *Twentieth century drifter*. Nashville: Mariposa Music; 1973; c31Jul73; (EP315657).

Robbins, Marty, claimant. *Twenty dollar Jim*. Nashville: Mariposa Music; 1982; c10May82; (PA-137-224).

Robbins, Marty, claimant. *Two gun daddy*. Nashville: Mariposa Music; 1974; c13Aug74; (EP328880).

Robbins, Marty; Russell, Karen, claimants. *Two of a kind.* Music by: Marty Robbins; Words by Karen Russell. Nashville: Mariposa Music; 1971; c23Feb71; (EP283307).

Robbins, Marty; Mersey, Bob, claimant. *Until we meet again.* Words and music by: Marty Robbins and Bob Mersey. Nashville: Mojave Music, Noma Music, & Elvis Presley Music; 1968; c2Jan68; (EU29706). Current holder: Chappell Music.

Robinson, Martin D., claimant. *Up in the air.* By: Marty Robbins [pseud.]. Nashville: Mariposa Music; 1964; c27Aug64; (EP191543).

Robbins, Marty, claimant. *Up to my shoulders in a heartache.* Nashville: Mojave Music, Noma Music, & Elvis Presley Music; 1968; c2Jan68; (EU29705). Current holder: Chappell Music.

Robbins, Marty, claimant. *A very special way.* Nashville: Mariposa Music; 1969; c29Dec69; (EP266796).

Robbins, Marty, claimant. *Walking piece of heaven.* Nashville: Mariposa Music; 1972; c6Sep72; (EP303189).

Robbins, Marty. *The way I loved you best.*
See: *She liked the way I loved her best.*

Rainey, Lobo; Russell, Karen, claimants. *What do I do until then?* Music by: Lobo Rainey; Words by Karen Russell. Nashville: Mariposa Music; 1969; c20Nov69; (EP274421).
Lobo Rainey [unregistered pseud. of Martin D. Robinson].

Rainey, Lobo; Russell, Karen, claimants. *What I don't want to know.* Music by: Lobo Rainey; Words by Karen Russell. Nashville: Mariposa Music; 1969; c20Nov69; (EP274432).
Lobo Rainey [unregistered pseud. of Martin D. Robinson].

Robbins, Marty, claimant. *When I'm gone.* Nashville: Mariposa Music; 1973; c12Dec73; (EP319120).

Robinson, Martin, claimant. *A white sport coat and a pink carnation.* By: Marty Robbins [pseud.]. Nashville: Acuff-Rose; 1957; c1Apr57; (EP107590).
RE 239-023; 8Mar85.

Robbins, Marty, claimant. *A whole lot easier.* Nashville: Mariposa Music; 1964; c20Nov64; (EP195033).

Robinson, Martin, claimant. *Why keep wishing?* By: Marty Robbins [pseud.]. Nashville: Acuff-Rose; 1953; c29Jun53; (EP72683). RE 80-153; 9Jan81.

Robinson, Martin D., claimant. *The winds go.* By: Marty Robbins [pseud.]. Nashville: Mariposa Music; 1966; c31Mar66; (EP216981).

Robinson, Martin D., claimant. *With his hand on my shoulder.* By: Marty Robbins [pseud.]. Nashville: Marty's Music; 1964; c21May64; (EP187873).
Current holder: Mariposa Music.

Robbins, Marty, claimant. *The world needs a leader.* Nashville: Mariposa Music; 1977; c7Nov77; (EP375826).

Robinson, Martin D., claimant. *Worried.* By: Marty Robbins [pseud.]. Nashville: Marty's Music; 1960; c19Jul60; (EP142780).
Current holder: Chappell Music.

Robinson, Martin, claimant. *You came to the prom alone.* By: Marty Robbins [pseud.]. Nashville: Acuff-Rose; 1957; c8Oct57; (EP112879). RE 239-028; 8Mar85.

Robinson, Martin, claimant. *You don't owe me a thing.* By: Marty Robbins [pseud.]. Nashville: Acuff-Rose; 1956; c1Aug56; (EP101256). RE 196-834; 21Feb84.

Robbins, Marty, claimant. *You gave me a mountain.* Nashville: Noma Music, Elvis Presley Music, & Mojave Music; 1969; c19Feb69; (EP255668).
Previous Copyright registration: 6Nov68 (EU83256).

Robbins, Marty, claimant. *You put me here.* Nashville: Mariposa Music; 1972; c2Feb72; (EP295819).

Robbins, Marty, claimant. *You told me so.* Nashville: Marizona Music; 1961; c25Apr61; (EP152303).
Current holder: Chappell Music.

Robinson, Martin, claimant. *Your heart's turn to break.* By: Marty Robbins [pseud.]. Nashville: Acuff-Rose; 1953; c11Jun53; (EP72337). RE 80-152; 9Jan81.

Robbins, Marty, claimant. *You're breaking my heart while you're holding my hand:* Brenner Music; 1952; c10Oct52; (EU292604).
Current holder: Chappell Music. Renewed by Chappell: RE 46-472; 7Jan80.

Robbins, Marty, claimant. *You're not ready for me yet.* Nashville: Mariposa Music; 1974; c15Jan74; (EP321251).

Robbins, Marty, claimant. *You've been so busy.* Nashville: Mojave Music, Elvis Presley Music, & Noma Music; 1967; c18Dec67; (EU29284).
Current holder: Chappell Music.

13

MARTY IN CONCERT

No review of Marty's career would be complete without pictures from a Marty Robbins concert. After all, it is the performer we are remembering. He was a showman: smooth and relaxed, playing a Spanish guitar (photo B); funny and charming (photo C); wild and wacky (photo D); a crooner and a comedian. A combination of arrogance and humility. The man with the "Golden Throat." The modern day drifter who knew how to run a concert like an old-fashioned medicine show and leave the audience happy but begging for more.

Marty frequently played county fairs throughout the Midwest in the summer, and dinner theatres and concert halls at other times. For evening and indoor performances, he usually wore the brightly embroidered and sequined costumes he designed himself (and which were made by Nudie in California), but at times he wore a tailored business suit. In the hot and humid summer, for outdoors concerts he would wear jeans and a western shirt. The photos included in the following pages of Marty in concert have been selected to show the many faces and styles of Marty Robbins during his moments in the spotlight.

THE CONCERT

The lights dim, the crowd gets quiet. The band is in place and wearing black suits and white shirts (pleats and ruffles but no ties); they start playing the opening notes of *Singing the blues* and

A. Photo by Joan Goodwin

Marty bounds from behind a curtain on the right and strolls quickly to center stage. By the time he reaches the microphone, he's got the rapt attention of the audience. He's resplendent in a brilliant white stage suit splashed with brightly colored Spanish designs of flowers and birds that have been embroidered over the shoulders and arms of the jacket as well as on the slacks. The boots match the suit right down to the flowers and the rhinestones.

A band member hands him a small Martin acoustic guitar. Unlike most singers, Marty wears no shoulder strap with it. To keep it level, he cradles it in one arm as he strums it . . . and you wonder how he keeps it there (photo E). Sometimes it almost looks as though it is suspended in space. When he stops to talk, he tucks it under his arm like a newspaper or holds the neck of it in one hand. At other times it becomes a prop: he uses it like an oar and pretends he's paddling a boat as he struts around the stage. No one has ever seen him drop it.

By the time the crowd realizes he's there, he's finished *Singing*

B. Photo by Andrew A. Hanson

Photos C (above) and D (below) by Joan Goodwin

E. Photo by Andrew A. Hanson

F. Photo by Joan Goodwin

the blues, and continues on without a pause through *Ribbon of darkness* and *A white sport coat.* The bolder fans are already moving up to the edge of the stage to take pictures—and Marty has started to mug for them. When he finishes this opening group of songs, he stops and steps forward to acknowledge the enthusiastic welcome. He smiles modestly, and holds up his hands as if to quiet the crowd (photo F). "Oh, please, don't," he says several times; then pauses just long enough before saying, "Please, don't stop." It brings his first laugh of the evening.

He's excited to be there. He yells at the audience, "My friends!" They yell back. There's a constant chatter between Marty and the audience. Some entertainers would be angered or thrown off stride by the constant requests and shouted comments. Not Marty. He takes the interruptions and works them into funny one-liners or the flow of the show. He relishes this audience repartee and is adept at keeping a light upper hand throughout it all.

As the concert settles down into a familiar rhythm, more and more fans approach the stage with their cameras, until there's a constant flash of bulbs from Polaroids and Instamatics. He tells one woman when her flash has failed to go off, and another one when to take the best picture. And he reminds all of them that it's fine to take as many pictures as they want as long as they remain knelt down by the stage apron so that they don't obstruct the view of the other audience members.

He stops after the next song to tell an admiring fan about his suit and to show off his matching boots. He pauses while the fan takes a photo of the boots, and holds the pose a little longer as others scamper up with their cameras to get pictures too (photo G). "Get one you'll remember for life," he says. Then, turning slightly, he instructs, "Get one over here."

G. Photo by Joan Goodwin

Photo H (above left) by Andrew A. Hanson; photos I (above right) and J (below) by Joan Goodwin

Other times, he will wait until the split second a fan presses the button for a perfect picture and make a face filled with horror, wink, or cross his eyes (photos H and I). And all of this while singing; he never misses a beat.

Marty loves to clown. In fact, he's shameless about it. The humor is spontaneous and unpredictable. He's a man of contrasts. Offstage, he seems quiet and humble, bright but self-effacing. On stage he plays the clown with the big ego. One review (*Lincoln Courier*, 8/2/82) called him the Mohammed Ali of the country music world, saying, "He'll handle a song in grand fashion, then be the first to applaud. He literally struts and prances on stage, and yells, 'Ain't it great!' " (photo J). At times he has the manner of a hep Black comic jive, standing with his hip at an angle and the back of his hand resting on it, and talking in street slang: "Hey, baby . . ." (photo K). Or he'll cry out, "Aw-w-w ri-i-ight! I'm on, baby!"

He's a tease. He says that he's enjoyed the show, but that the thing he's enjoyed most about it is that he didn't have to pay to get in! He starts one song, feigns disappointment at the response, and stops the band (photo L). The audience sits at confused attention. "I usually get just a little more applause on this one," he says. He tells the audience he's not going to waste his time or theirs on a song they don't want to hear, because he's got a lot of songs and they can go on to another one. He starts again and gets his applause.

He's an entertainer and a man who handles many styles of music (photo M). Blessed with a clear and distinctive voice, by the time the evening is over he'll sing love songs, cowboy story songs, rock music, and a couple of his old Hawaiian hits. He has the talent to sing well without appearing to try too hard. He is the last of the cowboy singers, an unabashed lover of the Old West. The trumpets add a mariachi, south-of-the-border flavor to the music. *Devil woman, Buenos Días, Argentina,* and *Tonight Carmen* shine with the brass of the horns. He's been known to do humorous (and accurate) imitations of Merle Haggard, Hank Snow, and Johnny Cash.

This is turning into one of the "request nights," when the

Photos K (above left) and L (above right) by Joan Goodwin; photo M (below) by Andrew A. Hanson

N. Photo by Andrew A. Hanson

audience knows what it wants and constantly calls out the names of songs they want to hear. Marty tries his darndest to oblige. He's operated that way from the very beginning. He never decides what to sing until he gets on the stage and gauges the mood and temper of the audience. He has no set show, but he does have songs he knows he will have to do for every audience. The band follows along as best it can. There are certain cues in his talk and physical movements that alert them to what he plans to sing next, but sometimes, like tonight, the audience may cry out for little-known songs that the older band members haven't played in years and the new ones have never heard of.

Marty says he doesn't remember all of the words, but he'll give it a try and launches into it. The band picks up the song after Marty begins. He gets through the whole thing, able to remember

Photos O (above left) and P (above right) by Joan Goodwin; photo Q (below) by Andrew A. Hanson

the words after all, and turns to the band with a smug look and a slight nod of satisfaction (photo N). Sometimes, if a band member recalls the words when Marty can't, he will whisper them in Marty's ear while he sings. It's a little unorthodox perhaps, but it gets the job done, and to the delight of everyone. And some of the songs aren't even ones Marty has recorded; they just happen to be favorite tunes of the requesters. It's a loose show, like having the performance in your living room. It makes for a friendly and familiar evening. He's one of the family, and as such, can get away with telling a persistently raucous fan to sit down and shut up without creating tension or wrecking the mood of the show.

Between songs, the fans approach the stage. Some hesitantly and shyly, others with eager anticipation. Notes are handed to him, and he silently reads them and reacts with funny faces and perhaps an innuendo to the audience (photo O). Occasionally one scrap of paper will get stuffed into the small center hole of his guitar. Other people bring gifts: pink carnations, yellow roses. unusual gifts (photo P). Each one is acknowledged (photo Q).

Marty's fans come in all ages, shapes, and sizes. Many of them have traveled into late middle-age along with Marty. Men are fans as well as women; you see lots of couples. There are several generations of a family sitting together, grandparents with their kids and grandkids. An older man of 80 might be just as likely to approach the stage with a request as a timid little girl of eight. They both get what they want.

As the show progresses, Marty gets emotionally higher. He struts, prances, and does an occasional mock bump-and-grind. Songs are performed with vigor and good cheer (photo R). He likes rock and roll and sings, *That's alright mama* and *Good hearted woman*. He is blatantly uninhibited one second and tenderly kind the next. He displays a quick wit in repartee with the more vocal fans.

R. Photo by Andrew A. Hanson

Photo S (left) by Andrew A. Hanson; photo T (right) by Joan Goodwin

The high spirits can be contagious. More than once, he's con-
vulsed in laughing fits over his own jokes (photo S) or breaks up
at the actions of one of the fans at the edge of the stage in front of
him (photo T). This, in turn, sends the audience back into the
giggles. He's on their wavelength and in control; he can now send
parts of the audience into laughter simply with a look or a subtle
movement.

At the halfway point, he stops to introduce the band. The
introductions are affectionate, but irreverent, and sometimes a
little ribald (depending on the band member he's talking about).
Marty has firmly instructed the audience that they are to give *one
hand-clap only* as he introduces each band member, and must
hold their final applause until the end. To ensure this, he leads the
hand-clap after each introduction, turning in mock seriousness to
reprimand the audience each time he hears more. The audience
giggles. At the end, the audience, finally free of his control,
cheers the band heartily.

Marty leaves the stage for a few minutes to let the band members display their skills. Each gets a brief solo performance that

shows what he can do and why, together, they were named "Band of the Year" at the 1981 MCN Awards. Don Winters steps out of his role as back-up singer and pleases the crowd with his yodeling, an almost-lost art.

Marty returns and sits at the piano. It's easy to see he loves it. The antics are temporarily abandoned and the audience calms. Now he's a balladeer. He plays and sings love songs—*Love me, 18 yellow roses, Tonight Carmen, Among my souvenirs,* and a special crowd favorite, *My woman, my woman, my wife.* The sincerity of each song is conveyed simply and with emotion. A romantic interlude.

And then he gets up and goes back to the center of the stage and his guitar. *You gave me a mountain* and *Don't worry* are next. The show is nearing the end, and he changes the pace. This time he sings harmony with Don Winters and Bobby Sykes through a series of western songs: *Tumbling tumbleweed, Big iron,* and *Streets of Laredo* (photo U). Marty ends the concert as he always does by singing his favorite song by his favorite song-writer ("I remember the day I wrote it," he says). The song, of course, is *El Paso.*

U. Photo by Andrew A. Hanson

V. Photo by Don VanPutte

As it ends, he strolls off stage to a standing ovation. He's kept the audience enthralled for nearly two hours. He takes his time, smiling and shaking hands with fans who have crowded the edge of the stage as he goes. He's showed the crowd why he is a legend.

And when it's all over, he heads for his bus, takes a shower and changes clothes, rests for a few minutes, and steps out of his tour bus to greet the fans who have lingered after the show. He stays around to talk with them and sign autographs until the last one has been satisfied.

The sign on the front of his tour bus says, "Nobody you've heard of" (photo V).

14

THE BOB ALLEN INTERVIEW
WITH MARTY

MARTY ROBBINS IN HIS OWN WORDS

The following interview with Marty Robbins is provided through the courtesy of Bob Allen, a writer whose credits include articles written for *Country Music, Country Song Roundup, and Music City News*. He's also the author of the book, *George Jones; the saga of an American singer* (Doubleday & Co., 1984).

I have taken the following material from Bob's transcript of a long, multi-part interview Marty gave Allen in early 1981. Their series of conversations took place in a variety of locations: on Marty's farm, in his Nashville office, at a local Brentwood, Tennessee restaurant and on his tour bus. Because of the length of the interview and the informality of the settings, the number of topics covered in random order (as they came to mind), the repetition of the same stories, and the occasionally confusing language, I have rearranged the conversation so that comments about particular topics are grouped together into a more orderly narrative. Therefore, remarks about Marty's heart attacks, his youth and early career, his auto racing experiences, and his feelings about the music industry are grouped together in their respective sections. Other than that, the transcript remains unchanged. The words are Marty's own. And I've retained much of the description provided by Bob of the physical surroundings and his personal impressions of Marty because they provide visual images and emotional feelings that accompany the words being spoken.

The interview is an unusually candid and reflective look at

Marty's life and career; it is filled with humor, and emotion. It's simple, honest, and direct. I think the most telling thing about the interview is the background it provides to enable the reader to follow the roads Marty traveled during his life; you can see the real measure of the success he achieved against tremendous odds. When one understands the problems he faced, it makes his accomplishments even more impressive. He didn't live an easy life. And yet, he was known by everybody as an upbeat person who loved life and looked forward with genuine enthusiasm to every day.

The conversation is punctuated with a mix of auto racing slang, music industry terms, and Marty's own rhythm and style of speaking. Sometimes it's hard to follow. Readers should be aware of the fact that the series of interview sessions took place about six weeks after Marty had a mild heart attack in the first days of January, 1981. Marty was off the road for nearly three months recovering from the illness and was anxious to return to the concert trail; in fact, the last interview of the series took place on his tour bus as he was traveling to his first performance upon his return to the stage.

When Marty talks about "this attack," he means the 1981 attack. When he talks about "the first time," he means the 1969/1970 one. (Even though he reveals that he probably suffered a heart attack during a stock car race in 1968, this one never really figures in other parts of the conversation.) Although it is usually spoken about as one event, the 1969 attack actually consisted of two separate medical conditions that occurred over a six-month period covering the last part of 1969 and the early part of 1970. Marty suffered a heart attack while on tour in Ohio at the end of July, 1969 and spent several weeks in hospitals in Ohio and Nashville before recuperating at home. Although he remained ill, he returned to performing by the end of the year. Then, in January of 1970 he entered the hospital for tests relating to his heart condition and it was discovered that the arteries to his heart were almost completely blocked. Bypass surgery was performed immediately and another period of recovery followed.

Marty's childhood was characterized by abject poverty and a

broken home. It was something he never talked much about until the last few years of his life. Although he spoke lovingly about his mother, and retained familial relationships with his brothers and sisters, he spoke with pain and anger about a father who hated him even when he was a child too young to have done anything to create that dislike. But he stood in awe of his grandfather, who became a major influence in his life and the impetus for his love of the Old West. His youth was clearly troubled. By his own admission, before he had reached his teens meaningful schooling had ended and he had become incorrigible and uncontrollable, a wild kid with no future, headed for jail. What saved him at that time was the chance to enter the Navy. Although less abrasive and more settled on his return from the Navy after World War II ended, he still drifted from job to job with no goal or direction. What saved him this time was music. He discovered he could sing. And his life changed permanently.

A CONVERSATION WITH MARTY ROBBINS

MID-FEBRUARY, 1981

Bob Allen: The interview began at Marty's office in a renovated two-story frame house just off the Music Row area in Nashville. The office has a disheveled look: performing suits and other clothing lay over the sofa, about eight brown grocery bags filled to overflowing with unopened mail, a huge old wooden office desk (also full of unopened mail). The shelves along the walls are full of books about the Old West and mementos given to him by fans and friends—among other things, a picture of Gene Autry, little race cars, several photos.

Marty owns several other properties up and down the block that were bought for a song some years back. Now this Music Row real estate is the hottest thing since oil.

Robbins is a ruggedly handsome man, soft-spoken but intense. His handsome features are made more poignant—rather than marred—by the barely discernible scar that runs down the right side of his forehead to his eye and the dent in his nose that are reminders of a spectacular wreck a few years ago at Talladega.

He is an outdoors guy and looks ten years younger than his age, sort of self-centered in an innocent kind of way, occasionally hard-headed, believes in himself. Intensely private, religious. And he's also recovering from a heart attack suffered just a month ago. Of course, the first question is about his health.

Marty: I've been off now since the 18th of December (this is February 12th). That's the longest I've *ever* been off. That's a *long* time! Except maybe when I had the heart attack before. Whew! (he shakes his head) I'll be glad to get going again! I thrive on it. Because, if it wasn't for the people, you know, where would I be?

You have to learn to be able to talk to the people and not talk over them. A lot of performers do that . . . they are not really making that audience part of the show. You don't have to do that, but it's a whole lot more fun when you can. Some people just cannot do that. But if you can make the audience feel more appreciated, the better it works. Man, I like to kid with 'em and have a big time with 'em, carry on a conversation with 'em.

When we go to England, it's like request night! I get requests for songs I did 20 years ago. I get requests for songs I didn't even do. But if you make a real genuine effort to play them and make them part of the show, it'll work. But if you're tryin' to put one over, they can spot you in a second. If you don't have anything goin' out through the air to them, they can tell. I signed autographs until three in the morning one night in Georgia. I'm not a tightwad.

FAMILY LIFE AND CHILDHOOD

Bob Allen: Marty's office is practically wallpapered with music awards. Tons of western books sent by fans. A postcard nearly as big as a door, nearly ten feet high. Son Ronny is 31; daughter Janet is 22. He has read extensively about the West.

Marty: I've always liked to read about outlaws. They were my heroes, even though they weren't really the Robin Hoods they were made out to be.

This is my grandfather here. (He points to an old sepia black & white photo in a battered frame; one of the few mementos rescued from his mother's house when it burned down. The man in the photo has flowing strands of silver hair, mustache, looks much like Wild Bill Cody or other heroes of the old west.) He was a Texas Ranger . . . or so he told me. He died when I was six, but I remember him very well. He was a poet. He wrote two little books of poetry. He was a real story-teller. He was a drummer boy in the civil war—or so he told me. And sold patent medicine. My love for the West came from him. He died when he was 86. That photo is what he looked like about the time he died. A face from the Old West.

Bob Allen: His grandmother had coal black hair. She had quite a bit of Paiute Indian in her. Marty is part Indian; she was almost full-blooded. His mother was mostly Indian, with a little Mexican. His father was Polish.

Marty: I was born and raised in the desert; *on* the desert. I was 12 years old when we moved to town, to Glendale, when my mother and father got divorced.

My mother would wash clothes for the neighbors and I would do odd jobs. That's how we got by. We lived in a shack by the railroad tracks, across the street from a big feed company. My father did odd jobs . . . when he could find them. I could tell you how we used to live, but I have brothers and sisters still living and it would embarrass them. But I'll just tell you this much: people who think they're poor now never had it any worse than I did. Never. I sympathize with 'em, but I know what it is to be laughed at because your shoe doesn't have a sole in it and because your pants have a hole in them. Not only other kids, but I know what it's like to be ridiculed by teachers. That used to hurt me so much. I was poor and there was nothing I could do about it.

Bob Allen: Marty only saw his father two times after he was twelve years old. He says he lost track of him altogether after that.

Marty: I wasn't one of his favorites. All together, counting half-brothers and sisters, there were nine of us.

He would whip me for nothing! I remember one time. His favorite was one of my younger brothers. He and I were getting into it and he called for my father. My Dad had a bad temper. I ran away and I wouldn't come back. He chased me and threw a hammer at me like a tomahawk. I picked it up and threw it back as hard as I could and hit him in the chest with it. He never bothered me after that.

I would get letters once in a while from people that claimed they had seen somebody who claimed to be my father, but I never really checked into it. (He says this indifferently.) I'm not sure what became of him. I never did look into it. My mother was the one who took care of me. I was able to buy her a small house in Phoenix.

Bob Allen: It would be 120 degrees in the desert, with young Marty working in the ditches. He used to pick cotton for 50 cents a hundred pounds. Made a dollar a week at that. Shined shoes. Ran a con by cutting his shoe polish with water.

Marty: Everybody else charged ten cents, and I only charged a nickel, but I wouldn't put any wax on them. I tell you, I was a bad kid. I'd get the liquid shine and put half water in it and make two bottles for one. I was only interested in volume! (laughs)

Bob Allen: Marty ran with a rough crowd, just one step away from reform school. He only weighed about 105 pounds, but would gang up with his friends and take on much older kids. One of these kids ended up in the hospital; it was the last in a long string of petty burglaries and run-ins he had with the cops. The fight started when one older kid accused them of being thieves. Two of them, Marty and a friend, took him on and sent him to the hospital. After the fight, he told his mother what had happened and was spirited off to the country to the farm of his mother's friend. He left town one step ahead of the law.

Marty: I left right then, with nothin' but what I had on my back. They didn't pay nothing, but it got me out of town.

I got in trouble a lot (he admits hesitantly, very guarded about his past). In fact, I almost went to reform school. I mean, I was "gone." Then my mother asked this friend of mine who lived on a farm about 15 miles away, if I could stay there until things kinda cooled off. Oh, man, I'm not proud of the things I did, you see. Well, uh, I'd better not tell some of the things because I could still get in trouble for them now.

I herded goats up in the mountains. I got to where I could outrun the goats and throw a good sailing rock a 150 yards and come within ten feet of what I wanted to hit. When I was 11 or 12, I could throw a baseball 296 feet and I was only 5'2" and weighed 105 pounds.

I had a little round of telephone booths that I used to make. I'd stuff napkins up inside so people wouldn't get their money back—nickels, dimes, quarters—and I had about 15 or 20 telephone booths I had rigged up like that, that I worked for about ten months or so. Make my rounds, get 60 to 75 cents out of each one. (Laughs)

In a town of 4000 people it was pretty hard to get away with this, but I did. I sold newspapers. You bought them for three cents apiece and sold them for five. But there's always a stack of day-old ones. And when I decided I was gonna quit, on the last day, I bought about three new ones and grabbed a whole stack of old ones and ran out the back door. I'd just scream out the headlines and keep the new ones on top. I got rid of every one of those damned old papers! (Laughs) Sold them all.

The police were always talking to me about something. They had payoff pinball machines in a lot of the stores in town. So me and my friends would take an icepick and drill through the sides of the machines and we'd rack up games at five cents a game. And we'd go back there, like we were really playing, keeping our eyes open. Then we'd take a piece of gum that was the same color as the machine, and cover up the hole, and nobody ever caught us. We had eight or ten machines that we rigged up like this. We were careful; we'd only get about a dollar a night from each machine. We were only 14. But they were beginning to catch up with us.

I had one year of high school, and didn't even complete enough credits to be a freshman. All my friends were poor, mostly Mexicans and Indians. I can identify with them and I know what they're still going through today.

Down in the South you can at least grow something, but you can't out in the desert where there's no water. When we lived in the desert, we only lived in a house two times. I won't tell you how we lived the other times. I mentioned one time on the "Dinah Shore Show" how I once picked cotton to get the money to go see Gene Autry at the movies because that was the only way I could go see them. And my sister said that I embarrassed her, that I never did that. But I picked lots of cotton. I used to herd goats with my brother up in the Bradshaw Mountains north of Phoenix. I used to dig ditches and clean irrigation ditches, which is a man's job, when I was 11 years old. And they paid me ten cents a day.

I was digging ditches most every day; I wouldn't even bother going to school. Went to high school for three years without passing a single subject. I'd be working or would catch a freight up to Prescott, a hundred miles away. Got kicked out of school repeatedly, spent most of the time in pool halls. I could not pass freshman English; I could not understand it. I needed three years of it and I couldn't even get through one year. At the time there didn't seem to be much future.

What I wanted to do was join the Navy, but my mother wouldn't let me. Finally, when I was 17, I gave up on school and joined the Navy. After the Navy, I came back and got all those other jobs. I'm a lazy person and I'm not afraid to admit it. I just don't like to work.

GENE AUTRY

Bob Allen: Marty has an autographed book from Gene Autry. He likes to talk about Autry.

Marty: I wrote a song about him called *Gene Autry, my hero*. I called him up first and asked him if it would be alright to write it, because he really is a hero to me still. He said, "Go ahead, write whatever you want." Then I sent him a copy and he called me up and told me how great it was, and then he played it for someone else and called me up again (Marty chuckles); I think he called me three times, just to tell me how much he liked it!

He called me in the hospital and invited me to come out to his hotel in Palm Springs and spend a week. I don't get to see him very often. I got to see him about two years ago and I got to sit and talk to him for 45 minutes, longer than I've ever gotten to before. He knows he's my favorite singer, but he told me I was his favorite. I never expected to hear that!

The first time I ever saw him, I was about 15 years old. He came to our high school in Arizona. Then I met him in 1952, just to say hello, in Hollywood at Columbia Records. Don Law, who produced me, took me down to meet him because he knew I'd always wanted to meet him. Gene was working on a television show or something. I've met him about two or three times down here in Nashville. He really is a nice person. He's probably a billionaire. I know that eight or ten years ago I saw a list of the wealthiest people in California and I think he was second to Howard Hughes. He was worth $900 million at the time.

When I was little, that's what I wanted to be: Gene Autry.

EARLY YEARS IN THE BUSINESS IN PHOENIX

Bob Allen: After Marty got out of the Navy, he returned to the Phoenix area.

Marty: I had never considered anything close to work, because I didn't like work. I had eight jobs in six months. I only got fired from the last one (driving the brick truck), I quit all of the others. I'd only work long enough for a payday. I just didn't like to get up in the morning. I just didn't like getting up at five o'clock and going to get a load of bricks at all! I was a mechanics helper in a garage, electrician's helper, worked on a milk truck, on a well drilling rig, on an ice truck carrying 100-pound chunks of ice up several flights of stairs, and farmed.

I never knew what I wanted. I would daydream about being a singer, but I never thought about trying it myself . . . not until I heard this guy on the radio. Earlier, I had worked as a guitar player for this guy named Frankie Starr. I didn't have a guitar and I didn't have an amplifier, but this guy who worked for him did have. I couldn't play very well at all. But I could play better than Frankie, so he thought I was pretty good. So he asked me one night when I was listening to him sing at this radio station if I wanted to work that night. He gave me $10 for three hours work! That was a lot of money to me. I had only been making a dollar an hour driving that brick truck. So I went back over to him and said, "Frankie, you gave me too much money, didn't you?" He said, "No, that's union scale." His guitar player never showed up and I played three nights in a row and made 30 bucks. That was great, getting paid that much for doing something I loved! Pretty soon I was making 60 bucks a week. No way I could've made that much otherwise. I really wasn't skilled labor. I eventually went out and got a job of my own in another place as a lead vocalist.

Bob Allen: His opportunity came one night when Frankie was sick and Marty had to carry the show himself.

Marty: The boss said to me, "Can you sing?" I was so embarrassed to get up and sing, I couldn't. I just held my head down, I couldn't look up at the people because I thought they were all making fun of me. But I had to sing that night when he didn't show up.

Frankie really knew how to meet people and how to talk to an audience. And there's tricks to getting people to come back and see you a second time, and I learned from watching him. And, luckily, it's stayed with me. That's what makes it so easy to do shows now. Because I learned early how to treat an audience.

Sometimes I still put on bad shows, because it's so easy. I

mean, if the lights aren't just right, and I think they should be right every time, and the sound system should be right every time. But as soon as something little like that happens, the audience can sense you're mad. But, of course, they think you're stuffy or you're being a little stuck up, and after that, you can't get back on their side. The best entertainers in the business have been heckled. I don't care who it is. I've seen Dean Martin, Frankie Laine, and people like that in Las Vegas; there's always somebody drunk in the audience who is gonna mess up their show, or at least try and bend it out of shape.

But if you get started right, and the first three or four minutes are great, *then* you can relax. But if you get off on a bad start, that's it. I've had it happen to me a couple of times. I'll get up there and on the very first song, the very first note, a string will break on my guitar (grimaces) . . . that's all it takes.

I like to get a crowd's attention just as soon as I get out there. That's why I wear flashy outfits. That's why I don't wear jeans, even though a lot of people do. I design my own clothes and I have Nudie make all my clothes for the stage. I've worn suits and coats, but I get a lot of response from the start when I wear a flashy outfit. They're $2000 each; I've got a closet full of them.

I was really shy, I didn't know how to talk to people. I couldn't get up (in front of them), but I knew that's what I had to do. After Frankie, I worked for another guy; he was the leader even though I was the singer. Gradually, I learned how to do it, how to perform and how to meet people. Even in the last 15 years I've learned a lot. First, you have to want to. Some people don't sign autographs, but the only reason I don't is if we've done two shows that night and have 600 miles to go to the next one. But if I can't sign autographs, I'll usually try and lay on an extra 15 minutes of music and that seems to satisfy people.

Bob Allen: Marty got into this business full time when he replaced a singer at a local radio station.

Marty: I was driving a brick truck, and I had stopped at this little open air market along the highway where I stopped every day at

12 o'clock. This guy had had a half-hour show. But he really wasn't very good. One time, he got right in the middle of his song and he forgot the words and didn't know what to do. And I thought, "Man, this guy has got to be making a living doing this. He's not doing this for nothing, I know."

So, I told the boss that Monday that I had to go to Phoenix to see the dentist and he gave me the day off (Marty smiles at this deception).

I had a motorcycle and I jumped on and strapped my guitar on the back and headed for that radio station. I didn't know who I was supposed to see so I asked for the owner, and the receptionist said, "The owner isn't here, he lives in Colorado. What would you like?" And I told her I wanted to be a singer, and she sent me back to the program director. I told him I wanted to be a cowboy singer on his radio station. He said, "We already have one." I told him, "Yeh, and he's not very good either." (Marty laughs) When you're young, you say a lot of things. But I was so sincere when I said it that he said, "Well, can you do better?" I said "Yeh." I sang one song for him, *Strawberry Roan,* and he gave me the job and fired the other guy.

Bob Allen: Marty was 22 or 23 when he went into the radio station for the first time. He was also working at a small club in the city and doing shows around the area.

Marty: The first road show, I did everything: western songs, Perry Como songs, Johnny Ray, Ernest Tubb songs, Roy Acuff, Eddy Arnold. Everybody's songs. It was just a little three-piece group that worked at this club. The club wasn't very big. It wouldn't hold more than a hundred people. But every night, for three years, it was packed. They'd stand in line outside waiting for somebody to come out so they could go in. FRED KARES was the name of the club. I was about 24 or 25 years old. That came after the TV appearances, It's been so long ago that I hardly remember. I didn't think I'd ever be asked.

I had a television show, just me and my guitar. But I had my name on the guitar! The way I got that, I had an early morning show (on the radio) and I also worked in the club. I taped the morning radio show. And one day the program director said, "How would you like to do some television?" And I said, "Oh, no. I don't want to do any television." Because it scared me. He said he needed me that afternoon, that they had fifteen minutes where they didn't have anything to run. But I kept telling him I couldn't do it. He finally said, "Well, if you want to keep your radio show, you'll do it." And that scared me to death! I didn't know what to do. I didn't have any fancy clothes to wear on TV. Just a cowboy shirt and levi's.

So I went on and told 'em who I was. I had a list of songs in my shirt pocket, and all I could do was look at my pocket and say, "And for my next song, I'd like to do. . ." And in fifteen minutes I must have done ten songs because I couldn't talk. But it went over so big (shakes his head in wonder). I guess maybe the people were feeling sorry for me, because I was really shy and embarrassed-looking, you know. They liked it so well that he made me do fifteen minutes a week by myself from then on.

I'd be so nervous sometimes that I just could not make it. A couple of times I threw up just before the show. Then I'd get through the show and I'd be so relieved and I'd sleep so good that night! But then the next morning, I couldn't sleep again, a-knowing I had to go through that same thing the next Friday. I never did get used to live television. I still can't do it. I'm not a perfectionist, but I always like that second chance to do it right. I just could never handle live television.

So many people hate their jobs; I think that's what turns so many people into alcoholics. It's sad. After they reach a certain age and all of the parties have been had, and all you have to look forward to is getting up in the morning at a certain time and going to work.

My parents didn't want me to be what I am today. I guarantee it! I wouldn't even tell my mother what I did for a long time. I went under another name, as Jack Robinson, when I first started playing on the radio. My real name is Robinson, you see, Martin Robinson. I played pop music on my first radio appearances. I really didn't know very many country songs. I knew some of the country artists like Roy Acuff or Ernest Tubb because they were such big names then. And if you went down to the Chinese restaurant in Glendale where all the kids would go, they would have an Ernest Tubb or a Gene Autry record on the juke box. Gene Autry, to me, was more of a cowboy singer, and that's what I love about him.

Bob Allen: The scene shifts to Marty's farm. He has a 240-acre farm. Grows a few crops, has a few head of horses. He wrote a song about one of them called *The Cowboy in the Continental Suit*. It's a good looking buckskin horse, 22 years old now, but you would never know it to look at him. The song's on the *All around cowboy* album.

Marty: I only ride him about once every two or three years anymore. It got to be just like everything else . . . just monotonous to have to catch him, get him in a corner, put the bridle and saddle on and then ride him a while and rub him down . . . and on and on. Anything that gets to be a job, I don't like to do it anymore. That's the way I feel about the road; when it becomes a job, I'm not going to do it. But it's not a job, you see, I enjoy it.

Bob Allen: What about your early years? What happened to get your career going on the national level?

Marty: I was spotted on the TV show by Little Jimmy Dickens, who came through town and came on the show to plug his show date. And he just stood there and listened. There wasn't even an audience in the studio. Just a little space in front of the camera. I had a little television show at 5:15 in the evening. It was just me and the guitar. Jimmy was big with Columbia Records at the time and he heard me and he liked me, and when he got back to California, he told the people at Columbia they should come hear me. So they came out and saw my show and signed me. The manager of the station where I worked in Phoenix was a former manager of WSM (the Opry station in Nashville). So they brought me directly to the Grand Ole Opry. They thought I would be good enough for it.

Bob Allen: Were you shocked?

Marty: Well, I was young at the time and I had a lot of confidence in myself, y'see. And I knew what I wanted in life. And I knew I was going to get it . . . if I worked.

There was another guy who came through, whose name I can't remember, but he was big on the West Coast at the time (Marty adds a sharpness to his voice). He came through, came on the show while I was singing, and never even looked at me. Never said hello, never said anything. And I was hurt. Because I wanted to meet him. And he just walked right on by. And I got through and he never said hello, never said goodbye, never said anything. I made it and he didn't.

At the time, I had a lot of confidence, but I didn't know how I was going to get on records or become a recording star. But I never worried about it. Because I had found what I wanted and I didn't really see how I could fail. So I knew it had to happen, that there could be no other way.

So, Jimmy Dickens was the start of it. He told people with Columbia in California about me. They sent a man over and signed me. And several months later I began recording.

I tell you, I had so much confidence that I thought I was making all the money that could ever be made working in Phoenix at the television station, the radio station, and the night club (he laughs). I just thought, how could I make more money than I'm already making? I was making maybe $750 a month. That was a lot of money in 1952.

I recorded my first session in Dallas. Even after I moved to Nashville, I used to go to Dallas to record. I liked the studio there. And there was only one studio in Nashville. I finally started recording in Nashville, and even went to New York. But it really doesn't make much difference where you record, if you have the right song. If you have the right song, you can record right out here (he points to his lake).

One man took me to Los Angeles to record me the first time. Art Slattery and another person who was involved had sent about twenty songs to me, to pick out about four of them to record. But I wrote songs, and I said to myself, my songs are better than these. So I just didn't bother to learn them. None of them fit me or my style. But then, when we got to the recording session, the guy asked me how I was coming along learning those songs, and I told him I didn't like the songs at all. I mostly said that because I thought I was already making all the money a person could make, so why worry. I told the man I had four of my own songs that were better. And he didn't like that at all. Right before the session started, he called me to one side and says, "Before the session starts, I gotta tell you that you've got to give me half of these songs." I said, "What do you mean?" He said, "I mean you've got to put my name on there as a co-writer." I just said I couldn't do that, and he said, "Well, that's the only way we can record you." So, I had three guys from Phoenix with me who were going to be on the session, and I just said, "OK, you guys, get your things. We're going home." Really, it didn't mean a thing for me to record. I wasn't that concerned. But then the guy said, "Oh, uh, wait just a minute. It's all right, you can record."

Most of my early hits I wrote myself: *El Paso, Devil Woman, Don't Worry, A White Sport Coat.* I've been writing since I was about 16 years old. My first chart song was in 1953, with a song I wrote myself. Webb Pierce covered me on it. He was the hottest thing going then and he had a Number 1 (with the record), but I still managed to get into the top ten with it. It was a song called *I'll Go On Alone.* I just recorded it again and put it on my new album. It may give some of the people who bought my albums a long time ago something to compare it with. The voice is more mature, I think, but the same kind of feeling is there. The arrangements are a little different; but really, it's about the same.

Don Law produced me for about ten years, from 1953 until about 1963. I went to New York for maybe two sessions with

Mitch Miller and Ray Conniff, but he did the rest. Don Law; why isn't he in the Hall of Fame?

Bob Allen: Was the adjustment difficult when you moved to Nashville?

Marty: When I first moved to the South, you couldn't see. You couldn't see one mile down the road. They were crooked, trees everywhere. I felt trapped down here. I almost went back to Arizona. And I couldn't handle the cold weather down here; I couldn't take the humidity.

To me, the West really starts in El Paso, Texas. There are a lot of ranches and a lot of cowboys before you get to El Paso, but to me that's where it starts. If you're riding in an airplane, it almost changes color after you pass over into New Mexico and Arizona. To me, that *is* the Old West, even though the old gunfighters were from all over the country. *To me* it's great, even though some people don't like it. I like to drive where you can just see for miles and miles. *That's God's country!* I don't care anything for hills. I think they're beautiful, but they're blockin' my view!

I still like to go back to Arizona in June or July and walk across the desert. I rent a car sometimes. I still have people (relatives) out there and I go see them. And I like to just drive and drive. I wrote a song called *Man walks among us* a long, long time ago. I went out in the desert. I used to go out to where there was nothing for ten or 15 miles.

Bob Allen: The conversation turns to his early days in Nashville.

Marty: When I first got here, it was like starting all over. Because, while I was in Phoenix on the radio and television shows, I had learned to talk to audiences a little bit. But when I moved to Nashville, I met stars, and I was just absolutely tongue-tied. I couldn't say anything on the stage. It took me about three or four years to get over that. I was so impressed with people like Jimmy Dickens, Eddy Arnold, George Morgan, Red Foley, Roy Acuff. It took me a long time. It really made me nervous.

Very few people do strictly country music, because it doesn't get the airplay any more. It's a different style of music (today). It's called country music, and it won't be the same five years from now; it'll be different. And so you just swim along, you know, go on, and hope that you can hang in there.

When I first got here, I didn't get much road work. In fact, it got to the point where I was ready to go back to Arizona because I really wasn't doing very good. Everybody here had a little clique, and I never belonged to any of them. Still don't. But there was one man who controlled all the bookings for the Opry and he saw to it that I didn't get any work, or at least bad work. If I did get anything, I'd have to drive 700 miles to do one night's work and coming back, and I wasn't getting much money for it either. And there were no interstates then. He'd book me, say, one night in Washington, D.C., and I had to drive there and back and carry four people, so I wasn't making any money. I finally got kind of mad about that, and I told him, "Some of these days, I'm going to have a hit, and when I do, I'm really going to make it tough on you." He said, "You're never going to have a hit." (He laughs gleefully.) And about six weeks later, *Singing the blues* broke. Oh, boy! He'd offer me jobs and I'd tell him where to shove it! Because then, everybody wanted to book Marty Robbins. And it's been no problem since then. I had two more songs in 1953, and then nothing else until 1956; then, in 1957, *A white sport coat*. But for a while there, I couldn't get nothing. Couldn't work anywhere.

Things have really just happened for me. I didn't try to make them happen.

Before *Singing the blues* I had another number one, *That's Alright Mama*. Elvis had recorded it first and then I did a version with Columbia and got a number one, even though I didn't do it near as well. I did Chuck Berry tunes, Little Richard tunes: I wrote some R & B songs. I even did some shows with some rock people even though, really, I was just country. Elvis, Frankie

Avalon, Orbison. A lot of them are forgotten now. Sometimes, I don't even remember them 'til I see a "songs of the 50s" record ad on TV or something.

HEART ATTACKS

Marty: When I had my first heart attack eleven years ago, I got 22,000 pieces of mail and telegrams. The heart attack was mainly due to a high cholesterol level; my blood pressure, heart rate, etc. are OK. I was the sixteenth in the world to have a three-vein bypass. Today they do 300 of them in one month just here in Nashville. It was a 7½ hour operation and I was in the hospital nine days. I think the only reason the doctor let me out that soon was that he was afraid I might commit suicide, because I wanted out so bad. And I thought—you know, I was on the fourth floor—it would have really been simple just to dive through that glass (he laughs at the thought). He was going to let me out on a Friday and he came on that Friday and said, "I'm going to have to keep you till Monday." Well, that's just about as close as I've ever come to giving up. I just wanted to get out . . . just like I wanta get out now. But I can't because I know it's not healed yet. Already, I've done more than I'm supposed to do. But it takes time to heal, just like a cut on your arm.

At one time I weighed 190 pounds. The problem was that I would eat what I wanted. And that was part of the same problem this time. I had started drinking a lot of milk and eating butter and cream. I was taking milk and whipped cream and putting it on my cereal and I'd be up at three and four in the morning and eat three or four bowls of that and a couple more during the day. God, I'd eat pork chops, fat . . . I had just gotten into the habit.

Bob Allen: We stop at a little country store along a narrow old two-lane highway near Marty's farm. You can buy fresh bologna there and they'll cut it as thick as you want it. An elderly man and woman run it. They're friends with Marty and inquire about his health. He buys a Snickers bar and we move on.

Marty: I have a lot of cholesterol in the blood, and I've never really followed the diet that I should have followed. I just have a natural high cholesterol count. This is the first candy bar I've had. Before the heart attack I was on a strict low sodium, low fat diet.

I'm not supposed to have these (the Snickers bar), but it's the first one I've had since my heart attack. The same doctor treated me this time. And the same doctor was ready to operate if I needed it. They were standing by to move me right into the operation if I needed it.

The first heart attack, I was up in Ohio to do a show date. Now, I don't smoke, I don't drink, and I don't take dope. I don't care what other people do, but it's just that I didn't, see. I thought I was in pretty good shape. And we're driving along in the bus and I've got this *terrible* pain. It was an hour from any town of any size. We finally got to this little town and I went into the hospital, and it was such a small hospital that all they had was one portable cardiogram, and it was out being used. So, they couldn't take a cardiogram. The doctor told me I'd had a heart attack, and a bad one too. I couldn't believe it and I couldn't really accept it, even though I was in really bad pain right while I was talking to him. And I just told him, "No, that's impossible." And I told him all of the things I didn't do. He said, "That doesn't make any difference, that's what it is. We're going to have to keep you here." I said, "No, I've got a show date."

He wanted me to stay there three days. I finally talked him into giving me something for the pain. He gave me a shot and some pills, and the pain went away, and I thought I was all right. So, I asked him, "If I take a plane straight from Cleveland back to Nashville and go straight to a hospital there, will you let me go?" He said, "If you promise you'll do that, I'll release you." But I didn't do that. I went ahead and did the show date.

I didn't believe the doctor. In fact, I didn't believe it until I went in the hospital in Cleveland. I couldn't figure out how I could have a heart attack. Because I wasn't overweight, I weighed about 157, I was in pretty good shape, so I thought. *But it had stopped the bottom part of my heart from beating,* and I went on and *did a show that night.* And I was jumping around on the stage having a big time, just because the pain killers had taken the pain away, and I still didn't believe.

Then, later, coming back through Cleveland after the show (and on the way to the next one), the shot and the medicine began wearing off, so I told the bus driver we'd better stop by a hospital. Then I finally started realizing that maybe I was having a heart attack. So, I went in and told them I thought I was having a heart attack and they checked me right through from the electrocardiograph unit into intensive care. The bottom of my heart had actually stopped beating. They had to run a wire from my arm, all the way around to the bottom of my heart to give it an electric shock to get it started beating again. (Smiles.) I hope I can tell the same story fifty years from now.

It was a thousand times more pain than I had this time. I'm really lucky to be alive. I happen to thank God for that.

I was given a 50-50 chance just of getting out of the Cleveland hospital. They didn't know if I was going to live or not. I thank God that I did.

I spent 15 days in the hospital in Cleveland, then WSM got their plane and flew me back to Nashville where I stayed in the hospital 18 more days. That was in September (1969). Part of August and part of September. Then I got out. I was really in bad shape and didn't know it. Then I found out in January that I had to have the operation. And it was really such a dangerous operation.

That was in July, but I wanted to race, see. And I couldn't race until I found out if I needed an operation. And they wanted to wait until May to give me the arteriogram, but I talked them into giving it to me in January. When I took it, it showed that of the three leading arteries, two of them were 100% blocked and the other was 80% blocked. It was so bad, it scared the doctor when he saw it!

It really was dangerous. I was on a medication that thinned my blood, but in order to do the operation, they had to get my blood back up to its original thickness . . . and at that time, of the three leading arteries, two were 100% stopped and one was 80% stopped. So, it was really serious. Any little part of cholesterol that could've jarred loose some way would have done it. But they managed to get my blood back to normal and then they did the operation.

But because I was on the kind of medication that would thin your blood, and that's the only reason I'm alive, because I was only getting 20% out of one artery. So, *that scared me then!* So, I said, "How long do I have? I'd like to think about it." Boy, he was serious! He said, "If it was me or my wife or my children, I'd say do it today." Well, that scared me again! I said, "How long will I live if I don't have the operation?" He said, "You might live six weeks or you might live six months." And he wouldn't make me any promises about that, either. In fact, he wouldn't even promise that I would get off the operating table . . . and that really scared me worse!

I've always been pretty religious, as far as believing. I don't do all of the things I should do, I never have. But I tell you, that night I prayed and prayed. But I knew I was not getting through. Finally, I realized that *living* was not the most important thing there was. Because I believe in heaven and hell. Maybe you do, maybe you don't. But that's your business. I finally realized that it wasn't life that mattered. So, I just prayed that regardless of what happened, my soul would be saved. And I prayed that in the morning when I woke up that I would have the answer. Well, the next morning when I did wake up, everything was peaceful. I had the answer. The rest was no problem. I told the doctor I wanted to have the operation just as soon as I could. And I never worried after that.

Even after they took me off the medication, it still hadn't dawned on me how serious it really was. My only thought was racing. I asked one of the doctors if I'd ever be able to race again, because that was very important to me and he said, "No, you'll never race again. You're going to have to live a very quiet life." And, boy, that really hit me hard! Even if that were true, I don't think he should have told me that. (An uncharacteristic tone of bitterness in his voice.) Even if it were true, I don't think he should have told me that. No, he didn't have any right to tell me that.

Well, I started praying then. I prayed that He would let me race again! (Laughs.) Well, I should have been praying for much more important things than racing. And he later told me I did die on the operating table. After it was all over, I thanked the doctor, and he just smiled and said, "I think God had a little bit to do with it." All the worldly things that I have, I prayed for and received them. Everything that I am, I am because I *asked* to be. I don't know if you understand that or not.

People sometimes ask me why I don't talk like this on stage (preach religion), but I can't talk like this on stage. People come to forget their problems, to forget reality, to enjoy an hour or so of this show. But if somebody asks me while I'm on stage, I'll tell them. Because people have to see it themselves.

Bob Allen: Do you ever feel sorry that you have this problem, when others don't?

Marty: No. (He says this firmly.) I know that a lot of things don't seem to be fair in life, but it all depends on how you believe and if you accept life.

That's probably the scaredest I've ever been, up until then. Then, later, I was on the farm and a bull chased me under the fence. That was just a month or so after the operation. He really charged me and I was only about ten feet away from the fence and I dived under it, tore all the skin off the side of my face. The ground was frozen. I was going to kill the bull! I'd just bought it the day before for $2500. The doctor had told me just before that, "Don't get excited about anything." (He laughs.)

Bob Allen: A car wreck in Phoenix in his younger days was so bad that the local newspaper ran a picture of the wreckage and wondered at the fact that anyone walked away from it without being crushed to death.

Marty: When I first felt that car turn over, I just said, "Not yet, God," just like I've said many times since then at race tracks. I had wrecks at 187 miles per hour and I've always had time to say, "Not yet." It's nice if you can take a long time to pray; but, sometimes, a real quick prayer will do.

I know, when I had the heart attack, when I felt like I was in hell burning, man it's a bad feeling and I knew the flames were up to *here* (his chin), and I felt like I was a hot dog, getting ready to pop, and I said, "God, please don't! Let me live to testify." And at that very moment, the flames went down.

I prayed so hard this last one, that I *wanted* to have the operation (again). You see, the doctors can cut and sew, but it's up to God and you to put your body back together. I was almost disappointed that I didn't have to have the operation this time because I was so ready for it. And I admit that's a dumb feeling, a stupid feeling.

Bob Allen: Marty had this latest attack New Year's Day. He had done three shows the night before on New Year's Eve.

Marty: It was kind of embarrassing and it was as big a surprise to me as anybody. I hadn't even been to the doctor for a year.

New Year's Day, I'd been watching television all day . . . all the bowl games . . . and I had a bad headache. The worst one I've ever had in my life. It felt like my eyes were comin' out of my head. I took about six aspirin and that relieved it, and some painkiller that I had for something else. Then I felt the pain in my chest and I just thought it was indigestion. I didn't even go to the doctor until the following Monday. I just thought it was indigestion because it was nothing like the first heart attack. I waited five days. I wasn't even going to go in then, but the doctor told me when I explained what I was feeling, "Get over here right now!" And when I got there, he put me right in an ambulance and sent me to the hospital and the intensive care unit. I couldn't believe it was happening, just like the other time. I started to get up and the doctor said, "Sit down there!" I said, "You're kidding me!" He said, "No, you're going to the hospital right now!" (Laughs.) I really was embarrassed. They rolled me right through that front office on a stretcher in my boots, my cowboy hat on my chest. I still had my boots on!

But it'll heal and I'll be back as good as I ever was.

Bob Allen: Marty's supposed to be on a skim milk, low butterfat diet.

Marty: The last year, I was taking milk and whipping cream and sugar, and mixing it with cereal and eating five or six bowls a day.

I don't sleep well, you see. I can't go to bed until . . . I can go to bed at ten and be back up at 12. And what can I do? Then I go back to sleep around four o'clock and sleep until 7:30. That's another big problem I have, and I think it's also hard on the heart. Your body gets enough rest, but your mind doesn't.

My problem started in 1952, on the first long tour I took. I lived in Phoenix, Arizona, and I went through Texas by myself. I was working with strange bands and making all those long jumps overnight. I would have to work 'til two or three o'clock in the morning and then drive four or five hundred miles to the next place. I was doing nothing but driving, drinking coffee, and taking No-Doz tablets. The last jump I made was from Shreveport, Louisiana to Phoenix, nonstop. Hell, when I got home around three o'clock in the morning, I couldn't even close my eyes. I'd close 'em and they'd pop open, like they were gonna pop outa my head.

So, I just got in the habit of not needing a lot of sleep, but I'm sure I could get by if I could just get four hours of sleep a night at one time. I would never need any more than that. It's just that my mind's always running, is always wondering what I can do to-morrow to have fun. I'm happy. What kind of show is it gonna be tonight? And if it's a good show, I can't sleep. That's why we travel at night.

I used to weigh 187, looked like Rocky Marciano. Had a big thick neck, big old arms. There was one point after I got out of the hospital after the operation that I weighed 130 pounds. Now, I'm about 145 or so.

Bob Allen: And the cause of this second heart attack?

Marty: Well, after that I figured if I've had a heart attack, it's on account of the same thing that happened before. If there's the same kind of blockage, I'm going to have to have the operation. Now, nobody wants to be operated on, you know. But I'd already figured this means another operation. Well, I took the arteriogram and they found out where the blockage was and it was down at the end, near the bottom of the heart. It had actually killed a little part of the heart. Just like if you have a cut on your hand and it's open.

I've been doing light exercise all the time now. I've been doing light exercise all along. Just enough to do something, you know. The last four or five years, I have not done all of the exercises I should have been doing.

I wish I could just sleep the hours, four until eight, because I can't stand to sleep the day away. I like to be up and see what's going on. I know what's happening at night. If it's a beautiful day and the sun's shining, I want to swim if I can. I don't want to just sit back and watch a good day go by. I hope I never have to do that.

It's like racing. I looked forward to racing so much and I only got to do it four or five times a year. But I'd get so excited that when that day would finally get there, where I could get out on the track, I can't *tell* you the excitement I'd feel. It's just like going before a good crowd.

Now, at the house, I've got weights, a chinning bar, walker, in-place bicycle, piano, tape player. I play the piano a while, lift weights a while. I ride a bicycle some. I'm on a low-sodium, low-fat diet. I've learned to eat things without salt.

Allen: He travels on his own bus, usually only four or five days at a time.

Marty: I have one refrigerator on the bus for me and one for the guys in the band now, so I can pre-cook things at home. It won't be a problem; it's going to be fun. Food's really a problem (on the road). The food in most hotels is bad. I've only ever been in one that served a good steak, and that was in Ann Arbor, Michigan. A lot of times, there's no place open. If you play a small county fair, you finish and there's nothing open. And if one of the guys didn't run out to the fair and get some of those foot-long hot dogs (laughing), there was nothing to eat. But we would usually buy a lot of canned goods and stock up on those just in case. We can heat food on the bus. But sometimes we'd forget and run out of canned goods and there might not be anything but a can of corn or beanie weenies or something.

I travel on the bus. It's just that (the other way) you can't get any rest. Up, down, in and out of airports. I used to fly my whole band commercial. And I even thought about buying my own plane for a while. But I was sort of afraid I might end up with a pilot that liked to party too much. Now I have two bus drivers. For me, it's the easier way to travel.

I cannot sleep at home, I hardly ever get to sleep before one or two o'clock in the morning. We can leave a town where we worked that night and usually it's anywhere from 500 to 650 miles to the next show and, oh, my driver likes to drive at night. So, by the time we get there, the rooms are ready and we can have breakfast, it's about nine o'clock. We can sleep until afternoon and then, if it's summer, we can lay around the pool. I party in the daytime. Some people like to party at night, but I don't like that, because there's a lot more to think of than just having a good time.

There's a picture of me on one of my album covers that was taken after I got out of the hospital after my first operation (in 1970). I looked like *death*. I was down to 130 pounds; I looked terrible!

The first attack, the bottom of my heart was dead. So, they had to insert an electric wire and put it across my chest and into the heart to touch the bottom of the heart and start it beating.

So, I put on a show with half a heart, even though it was wholeheartedly! (He laughs.)

This time, I'm taking it easy for three months.

Bob Allen: They took the veins out of his legs and put them in, in place of the arteries. The veins are smaller than arteries. Takes medicine to pressurize the blood.

Marty: After the operation, awww! I've had a lot of pain in my life and it's hard to say which one is worse. But when they sew you back up, you've got about 900 stitches on the inside and about 60 stitches on the outside. They have to put the breast bone back together with wire stitches. Have to go through five layers of tissue. It would hurt so bad! (Sighs.) I was in terrible pain! I just said to God—I was still in intensive care, and I just said— "Oh, God, I just don't think I can take it any more. Just take me right now!" (Laughs painfully.) But as soon as I said that, I realized what I'd said, and I said, "God, I didn't mean that! (Laughs.) I'll just take all the pain, if you just let me live!" And you know, it wasn't 45 minutes 'til the pain was gone. The wire you can still see when I go in to get an X-ray.

Strange things have happened in my life. There's been so many times, I have experienced death so many times, I should be dead. When I had the wreck in Charlotte, I hit that wall at 150 miles an hour head on! See the car scars on my face. I had four broken ribs and a broken tailbone; 150 miles, head on, into a wall. I hit that wall with such force that by all rights, the seat belt should have been torn loose and I should have been killed. When you have a wreck at 150 miles an hour and it totals the car and nothing happens to you, like I did in Daytona, you've got to think that somebody's looking after you.

If the doctor were to tell me I couldn't do any more road work, I'd just have to accept that (he says sadly). But then, there goes the band . . . I've got 17 people who work with me . . . I sure hope it never happens.

After I was operated on, it seemed like it took me back 15

years, as far as being able to do things. I mean, I could hit notes I hadn't been able to hit in years, and my reflexes were a lot better.

I'd had a bad heart for a long time before. I've had three heart attacks, really. I had the first one driving a race car in Charlotte, North Carolina. First time I'd ever raced on a big track. I thought I had indigestion, but it hurt almost as bad as the one that later caused me to have the operation. It was during a 500-mile race, and I got out of the car for about an hour and a half. I could not breathe deep; I had no idea what was wrong. I didn't even go to the doctor with that one. I had no idea it was my heart. That one healed itself. And it was almost as bad as the one I had a year later, before I had the operation. I didn't know! There I was, driving a race car at 155 miles an hour with a heart attack going on! I didn't know. I didn't slow down, I just got back in the car and finished it. But later, when they X-rayed my heart, they could see the scar. So, you see, somebody is taking care of me.

I hope it doesn't happen to me again, because I kind of like life. I've lived a lot of it, but not as much as I'd like to!

STOCK CAR RACING

Racing was a passion in Marty Robbins' life. Even he referred to it as an addiction. The desire to race saved his life when it was the cause of his seeking the 1970 tests that led to his bypass operation. The same passion also nearly cost him his life in three consecutive breathtaking wrecks at NASCAR tracks in the mid-1970s. And even though he talks here (in this 1981 interview) as if he assumes he will never race again, he did, in fact, return to NASCAR racing in 1982. His last race was on November 8, 1982. Only three weeks before his final heart attack.

Marty on race driving: I never cared about winning. I just loved to drive. I just loved to compete against the people who made a living doing it, because I knew that somewhere in that field was somebody who was just about my match and we could race all day, him and I. I just completely forgot about Richard Petty and Cale Yarborough and the Bakers and Pearsons because I knew I wasn't gonna beat them.

And I never did put a lot of money in the car. The only way I could have done that would have been to run in every race for a whole year and then pick one track where I was going to win. But every week I would take off to go to a race, because it takes a week, that was a week that I wasn't making any money. And the bills kept right on coming in. It's expensive. It got to where the last couple of years I was outlasting the cars. And that cost some money! That's just the way racing is, you can pay $15,000 for an engine and it can blow up while you're warming it up. And there's no insurance on that!

I had three bad wrecks in a row and none of them were my fault. And I had more publicity than anybody in the world! The first time was four years ago this last October, in Charlotte. I flew in the day before and qualified almost without any practice laps. (During the race), eight or ten cars piled up into a cloud of smoke. "I'm not going to be able to go through this" (all this goes through your mind in a fraction of a second). "I can't stop on the infield; you can't stop on grass. If I locked up, I'm not going to stop before I go into all that smoke and hit somebody." All in a flash of a second, it went through my mind that all I could do was hit the wall and hopefully bounce off the wall and maybe take some of that speed out, ricochet, because I was doing about 150 mph at the time. And when I turned that right, it went right so quick that I locked it up and hit the wall at about 150 mph.

Allen: His face hit the steering wheel, his goggles were ground into his forehead and split his forehead and eyelid open, broke his nose. His chest hit the steering column with massive force.

Marty: Oh, man, it hurt so bad. I didn't care if I was dying. There was blood all over. I got 37 stitches and later had to have some surgery done to straighten my nose back out. I have never

This 1981 close-up of Marty clearly shows the scar on his forehead received from his racing accident. (Photo by Neil Pond/Music City News)

gone back and got it fixed right. That's why I still have this little dent right in my nose (he points to the long, light scar down his forehead all the way to his right eye).

That was in October. The next time was down in Daytona. That was the next race I could get to. I wanted to make Daytona because it was a big track and I liked the speed. You could get going 190 mph down there, you know. I made the field and this one car was up ahead of me doing about 200 and he started smoking and I'd already decided I didn't want any more collisions. So I had decided ahead what I would do in this case. I decided if it happened again I would turn left and hit the brakes and get down in the infield, regardless. Because I had all of the steering wheel I wanted. So I decided I've gotta pass this guy because he's gonna blow and I'm gonna be in his oil and there is no way you can control it then, not when you're going 175, 180 miles per hour. So, I just stepped on the gas. I was taking it easy up 'til then, 'cause I was still kind of shellshocked from the last time. I got down on it and was doing close to 190 mph, trying to catch this guy. You're traveling nearly 100 feet a second. And just then I see him hit the wall. There was nothing I could do in the turn going that fast. You can't lock up or you'll hit the wall. But I'd always heard that you should go where you saw the car last, because it won't be there, so I tried that, and it worked because he wasn't there. He had already hit the wall and ricocheted off. But what I didn't know was that there was another eight cars involved. Coming out of the smoke, I'd already gotten back down on it, and here's this car sittin' right in front of me . . . stopped. I turn left and let up on the gas, but it didn't do a lot of good. It tore both cars up, but I didn't get hurt.

The next race I ran was down in Talladega. You can get big speeds there. You see, I like big tracks. And I was doing pretty good. I was drafting a guy and we're going into the turn doing maybe 192, 193. He qualified four or five miles an hour faster than me, but I was draftin' him. I was really driving a good race, taking advantage of all the drafts that I could get, running late when I could and just doing all of the right things. But, man, he blew his engine right in the middle of that turn, all that flame and smoke. And I hit the brakes and turned left, and the tires just went pop, pop, pop—all four of them blew, just like that. We got sideways and slowed down to maybe 150 mph sideways and here comes another one and, man, he's haulin' ass. He hit me so hard, it snapped my head over to the side of the car and knocked me out. I never even got turned around. I got hit four more times before I ever got off the track. I don't even remember getting out of the car. I don't remember anything 'til they got me to the hospital. I couldn't remember where I was. People would come in and see me and they would disappear and somebody else would be there. I knew *who* I was and what business I was in. All I could think of was, "You've really done it this time. I've messed up my mind and I wouldn't be able to remember the words to my songs." That's really what haunted me. I told the doctor I didn't want to see anybody, and he told me to just sit there and rest. And I sat there and said all of the words to *El Paso* to myself. And that's when I knew I was going to be all right, then!

I'd had four ribs broken and a broken tailbone in the race in Charlotte. We worked that Tuesday (the race was on Sunday). I played all in bandages and black eyes and stitches, you know, in front of 250 of the world's leading surgeons! Never even went to the hospital. I'd go to sit down and I'd miss the chair. I'd already had two concussions and the doctor told me, "Your head can only stand so much of this!"

Last October [in 1980] I was running up in Charlotte, and I was running real good. I would've finished in the top ten, I'm sure, when the right front wheel broke off coming into the turn and threw me into the wall, and I ricocheted back out into the middle of the track. But on three wheels that car went down the straightaway as smoothly as if it had four wheels. And there was a lot of traffic because we were on a re-start. I had, then, some more thoughts about racing. I thought, "We all have those accidents I've had and I haven't been seriously hurt, but . . ." And I thought, "Maybe somebody's trying' to tell me something."

Even in that half second, there's time to get scared! This last time in Charlotte there was time, because I couldn't get that car to turn left and I had just about one-half of a second to realize that I was gonna hit that guard rail. And I thought, "What if part of that guard rail gets inside the car?" That's the only time I have ever been scared. In fact, that time I hit the wall, I was mad! I was mad when I hit the wall because I knew I wasn't gonna get to race, and I'd been looking forward to it for two or three months. I got so mad! But then that steering column hit me in the chest and I couldn't breathe!

My car is outdated now, even though it's a 1979 model.

Then I had this heart attack, and I knew it would be no use to go back to running because they surely wouldn't let me run again. And I won't run again, even though I know I could still pass any physical they put me through. I'd always take a physical at the race track down at Daytona and the doctor would always tell me, "You're as good as anybody else." I would do it still, but I'm sure they would find a reason not to let me do it. It bothers me, because I really want to, even though I know I'm not going to get to. But I'll just do something else (he shrugs). It's just the challenge of seeing how well you can do at something you don't do regularly. People like Allison and Petty, they have more time on pit row than I do on the track. And anybody who has gotten in a full season on the NASCAR circuit has more competition miles than I have for my whole career. Even though I don't have the experience or the horsepower that those guys did, I didn't ever let up.

I never went there thinking I was gonna win. I never took the chances that people who did it for a living took because I know it hurts to be hurt. And it costs a lot of money to get a car running again. It costs me a lot of money to rebuild a car, and I totaled three in three wrecks.

It's kind of like walking a tightrope. You can't just watch the car in front of you, you've got to watch way ahead, you've got to watch everything and everybody. You've got to watch in back of you and know who's back there and how far back they are.

I don't think I was ever in anybody's way. I think most of the drivers will tell you they didn't mind racing against me. There was a lot of people I would pass and a lot of people that would pass me. I'm not saying I could never have been a winner. But the top cars had at least 555 horsepower; I only had 440 horsepower. In a field of 40 cars at 187 mph, I'm sittin' in the 36th spot. They were all faster.

I want to race to see the guys, because man, I love them all. I respect and admire anybody who can strap himself into a car— and I was never trying to be *one* of them. I just wanted to be *among* them. I'm not a race car driver. I did it for a hobby, for fun, not to make a living. I never ever thought that I could win a race. Only one time, I had just had the wreck in Daytona and we had built a brand new car. They set it up in Spartanburg, South Carolina. I didn't get any qualifying laps, because I'm always late for those. This time, I got in only ¾ of a lap in practice when they started qualifying. It was a two-mile track and it's easy to get hurt on them. I qualified and I made 10th spot, without the car being set up. It was set up in the garage. We had two days to work on it and it was the fastest car out there. So I started in tenth. It was Richard, Buddy Baker, Cale Yarborough, Darrell Waltrip, and some others all in front of me. In seven laps, I was in fourth, right on Cale's bumper, looking at his eyes in the mirror (smiles)! It's such a great feeling, you know! He was right on Buddy's bumper and he was right on Petty's bumper and there we were, the first time I'd ever run up there. I had a lot of power and the car was running right. Well, I ran about three more laps and the distributor broke and it quit running (he shakes his head). But my car had to be at least three miles faster than any car out there that day. That's the only time I was ever close to winning.

I used to go as a spectator to the races here in Nashville, and I ran my first race at that little dirt track out at Ridgetop. I raced two years out there and three years at the Nashville track. I had the heart attack, and then in 1971 I started racing again.

The first time I ran at Darlington I finished seventh, and that's a hard track to run. I finished eighth out at Ontario. I started somewhere in the last ten at Daytona and finished eighth at the Firecracker 400.

It's still show business, you see, because there's people up there looking, but they're not just looking at me. It's still a performance. I'm so high when I start to race, it's just like I'm so high when I go out on stage. But as a race goes on, you settle down, you have a particular spot in that race and sometimes the excitement wears off when you're running seven or eight laps and there's nobody there I'm trying to pass and nobody trying to pass me. But on stage it's there for the whole hour and fifteen minutes. It *stays* there. That's why I have a problem sleeping. I can't go to sleep until three or four in the morning, just because of that. That's part of my problem. I get so excited; I can't get over a good show. Even after all these years, it takes me a long time to get over it. That's why I would rather leave one place and drive all night to the next show, because I can't sleep after a good show.

Bob Allen: What about the annual Marty Robbins at the Nashville Speedway a few years back? Held in October.

Marty: It was at the wrong time of year. We got plenty of cars, but the people just didn't want to come out. Had it for three years. I wasn't really involved; they just used my name.

Bob Allen: Marty was popular at the races for another reason: he would hold impromptu concerts around the motel swimming pool for the drivers and mechanics. They sometimes would go all night; word would spread until the place was packed. It's the most fun when it's not planned, when somebody just has a guitar and it just happens.

Marty: I got my first car from Bobby Allison. We traded around. (Laughs.) Traded some cars and cows and trucks. That was in 1971 when I got my first race car. I've known Bobby for a long time. Used to watch him race before I started. I started racing at 37 or 38; when most people are ready to stop, I started. I've always liked racing, but I never had the money to have a race car. Finally, I had a little car built to run on dirt tracks and I used to run on Friday nights. Later, I decided I wanted to run on asphalt.

I ran at the Nashville Speedway for three or four years, then had the heart attack in 1969. I had a Dodge Dart, brand new, never got to run it.

I didn't start racing the Grand National [NASCAR racing] until after the heart attack. My doctors couldn't understand why I would want to race. I suppose they probably play golf. I never have asked what they do. Finally they said if you want to, go ahead, you're strong enough. I passed the physical in Daytona; they said I was in as good a shape as anyone else.

Nobody wanted me to race. In fact, now that I've said that I won't do it anymore, a lot of people have told me that they're really glad because they were worried about me. The people I did business with; naturally they didn't like it. Because it's a dangerous sport and I've had a couple of bad wrecks.

I would do it now if I could, because I know I could pass the physical. But I would feel that other drivers wouldn't feel safe, because when you say "heart attack" that's serious. Still, I might run some short tracks again. . . .

My wife never did like it, never liked it at all. And everybody that worked with me didn't like it. It was costing them money. Because, if I was running in a race, that was a whole week that they couldn't book me. Because it takes a week, you see, what with the time trials and qualifications.

I never had more than six races in one year in the Grand Nationals and that's not really much experience. Somebody like Richard Petty probably has close to 185,000 competition miles; Allison has over 100,000. I have between 7,000 and 8,000, and that's not very much. Some of those guys get in more miles in one season than I have altogether. So, I wasn't that experienced.

It's real exciting to race a car! Even if I'm out there running by myself. When I go to a track, I'll almost wear an engine out just practicing, just playing. Now, I know that I'm not going to win; I just go to have a good time and play and do the best I can. It's just really exciting to me to do that. I don't know what I could ever find that would even be half as exciting. I can't think of anything. I don't know what it would be. Even though I've enjoyed my career. It has always been a kind of relief. It was still show business, you see, you still had people there, looking. I don't care what they call it, it's still show business. I look at it all from the standpoint of someone who buys records. I watch television quite a bit and if I see an advertisement of a record I want, I'll buy it.

Racing was a thrill to me, it was like being on the stage, only it was a different kind of excitement. I can't think of another sport that I could get really involved in like that. I don't know what it would be. I don't even like to go to races because I want to be in them so bad. (Says with a trace of dejection.). I couldn't even watch the Daytona 500 this year because I wanted to be there so bad. It'll take a while to get over that.

Only difference with racing is there's more competition there. When I get up on a stage, I feel that I'm as good as anybody in the world and I don't say that in a bragging manner. I just have that much confidence in what I do. I've been in this business a long time and there's a lot of tricks to giving a good performance, just like there's a lot of tricks to driving a race car.

The first time I met Bobby and Donnie Allison was when they came to one of my shows down in Florida. Later on, they would come to Nashville and race, and eventually they became friends. Bobby let me drive his car one time up in Charlotte, North Carolina.

If I had started earlier and had the money, I might have done it professionally. But if I had any choice at all about it, I'd be what I am now. I'd be singing. As much as I love racing, I could never trade it for this. I guess that's why people become suicides and alcoholics, because they don't like the job they have. I wouldn't trade places with anybody.

Maybe that might have even hurt my career in the music business because I've never had a car manager. From 1963 to up until the past couple of years, I almost worked my road dates around my racing dates. Because I liked it so much. If I'd concentrated on something else, who knows? I could be doing bigger show dates, or be in movies. I had film offers that I turned down on

Marty in his race car at Atlanta. (Photo by Elmer Kappell)

account of the racing. I might have let that get in my way a little bit. But still, I'm not sorry. Because I did something that made me happy.

Anybody that's not contented with what they're doing, they're going to look for something else. When it's not as much of a challenge anymore—and I feel in a way, like I have won everything, I'm not trying to prove anything to anybody—but I wanted to try something else that was a different type of excitement. Some people might want to drop out of an airplane at 30,000 feet; I just liked to race. I don't know, I think hang gliding might be exciting!

Just to be that free! I think that's what I felt in racing. I was free. I didn't worry about beating anybody. I just did the best I could. And I never ran a slow lap in my life. If I had started early,

I might have been a better-than-average driver. I finished seventh at Darlington, ninth at Darlington, eighth at Daytona, eighth out at Ontario. I've had some decent finishes for somebody who is just an amateur, which is all I am.

Bob Allen: This part of the interview also took place on Marty's farm, 240 acres about 25 miles south of Nashville: rolling hills, horses, 200 head of cattle, bass in a small lake. He used to live on the farm, but now lives closer to Nashville in a house in Brentwood with his wife. A farm hand lives on the place now, and Marty comes out whenever he can. Marty's dressed in blue jeans, jacket, boots. Gray skies, light rain. He steers a four-wheel-drive Chevy pickup through mud almost up to the axles in the cow pasture.

THE RECORDING INDUSTRY

Bob Allen: Marty has had his own recording studio now for about a year and a half (located across the alley from the back door of his office). Eddie Kilroy produced his last album.

Marty: I don't believe in real expensive albums. I don't believe in a lot of overdubbing and stuff the producer does when it's not his money. Usually, if it were a producer's own money he would produce it for about twenty-five, thirty thousand less than what most of them end up costing. But some producers just go wild. I don't think that the sound makes a record sell. I think that I can sing well enough that I don't need a particular sound to sell. I can sell a record myself and I don't have to have funky sound to sell it. I don't sing that kind of music; I never did. I don't want to start now and lose the fans I have.

Marty [talking about the farm]: The guy that takes care of the place for me sings. Sometimes I'll bring my dobro out here and we'll sit in the garage where I like to work on my race cars and sing all day, have a big time!

Bob Allen: There's a little mobile home no bigger than a horse trailer.

Marty: That's a place for me to come out and sit and play and be alone and write songs if I want to. I just wrote a song the night before last. One of the finest I've written in the last two or three years. I wrote it around two o'clock in the morning. I'd been thinking about the idea for three or four days. I like to come out here and mess around, work on the farm.

Bob Allen: Marty plays guitar, piano, dobro, harmonica, and a little Spanish guitar.

Marty: Every night late is when I play. That's when I really enjoy playing, when nobody else is around. I play every night. I used to play from 11 o'clock at night until three or four in the morning. Every night. I can't do that now where I live now. The neighbors are too close!

I was on Columbia all but three years, when I got mad and left. I don't think I've made but one big mistake since I've been in this business and that was when I left Columbia and went with another label. But I was mad, I got my feelings hurt. That was about 1971 to '74; I came back to Columbia in 1975. It was the same old story. I didn't feel like my records were being placed right in the record stores. I got a good contract when I came back, but not as good a one as I had because I asked to come back, and that's different from when they ask you.

I just needed a change [to Kilroy] because I wasn't really satisfied with the way I was going with Columbia. Most every song, to me, was beginning to sound alike. Billy Sherrill was the producer. I like him, and he's one of the best producers to ever come to Nashville, but I wanted another sound. I wanted to go back to more country, and we did.

Marty about the record charts: I knew one time when a song was number one and only sold 12,000. I've seen ones that get in the charts that didn't sell one copy. And I know what I'm talking about.

I like to handle the production end of it. Produce it myself and then sell the finished album to the record company for a certain price, plus royalties. See, a person doesn't make as much money as the public believes. If you have a gold record every time out, you're making money, sure. And I used to make money like that, and I published and wrote and recorded the songs myself, so I made a lot of money. But the competition today is just like the rock music business was back in the '50s. If you stay number one more than two or three weeks, boy, then you've got a hit! These days, they'll be number one for one week, maybe two, and then it falls right down. Webb Pierce once had a song that was number one for 18 weeks. You don't see that any more.

Bob Allen: Marty has gold and platinum albums; some of them are from Canada, also Australia and New Zealand. And England. He's toured worldwide.

Marty: One album on K-Tel did more than 400,000. That was part of my complaint with Columbia. I know I can sell records. I know from the letters I get. But sometimes they don't put them out [in the stores]. But they don't worry about people like Marty Robbins anymore. They're worried about Willie Nelson and Crystal Gayle. But they shouldn't be worried about them. Their records will sell if they just put them out there, because they're hot right now. But I really can't complain. I signed a good contract with both Columbia and MCA. I made enough money just off the contracts.

I'm not bragging but I know more about the music business—and you can print this—than anybody who's in the business. I don't care if it's the president of Columbia Records, or Billy Sherrill, or who it is. I know what a good record is and I know how to make a good record. But I can't sell that record if it's not out there in the record store.

I've been a member of the Grand Ole Opry since 1953. I've never signed a contract with them. I just go when I feel like it.

Bob Allen: Marty recently did a syndicated television series for two years ("Marty Robbins' Spotlight") but ended it on his own accord. Not only did it take him away from the concert trail, but he was also impatient with the production requirements. He wanted more spontaneity than he felt he was allowed to have.

Marty: It was a good show, but it was not country enough. It was done right. It was a good show, but I had to dress up and wear a tie and everything.

"Cut 48": it was really hard for me to do that, and I'm not putting anybody down, but I know it wasn't my fault. They would do retake, retake, retake, retake. If you said anything funny and got any kind of response from the audience, they'd make you do it over again. And I'm not going to repeat a joke. Not to the same crowd. Because you're never gonna get no laugh, and I won't have anybody cranking up my laughter. I never had somebody out there saying, "Let's have a nice hand for Marty!" If I see a disc jockey or somebody doing that at one of my shows, I'll send somebody out to get him off there! I want them to clap for me when they want to. That's the only way I can tell when to get off the stage. If they've had enough of me, I'll get off!

We did 48 half-hour shows. We could only work three days at a time on it. The first one, it took from twelve o'clock noon until four o'clock the next morning to do one half-hour show! Then it got better. We could do one in six hours. And I had to buy new clothes. I only wore the same suit three times. I bought 45 brand-new tailored suits and that cost plenty of money.

FANS

Bob Allen: We stopped at a comfortable, family-style restaurant on the main boulevard into Brentwood, an exclusive suburb south of Nashville. Marty is known here and his wife is a regular. The elderly waitress fawns on him and other patrons greet him by name. He orders a cup of Sanka and some unbuttered whole wheat toast and goes over to their tables to inquire about their health. Naturally, they've all read the papers and they're concerned about his. One of the younger waitresses from the back section comes and asks him for three autographs: one for her, and one for each of her two friends. "Mr. Robbins, will you give me three autographs?" she asks. "My sister's name is Karen, and mine's Brenda. My neighbor's sitting down there and he would like one too." "I've only got one left," he kids her gently as he signs the three pieces of paper. These people like him and welcome him as one of their own, and he obviously enjoys the attention, almost basks in the warmth. The older waitress comes over and reminds him, "You remember that Lincoln Continental you had one time and you couldn't get into the trunk?" Marty laughs and shakes his head, "Finally got into it with a torch. Yeh, I remember."

Marty: Yeh, that happens a lot [people asking for autographs]. I get a kick out of it. Especially when I fly. My ears are tuned for "Marty Robbins." For some reason, I can hear people whisper "Marty Robbins" a hundred yards away—whisper, whisper, "Hey, is that Marty Robbins?" and I won't even look, see. Finally, someone will get up the nerve to say, "Are you who we think you are?" And I'll say (His eyes light up, trace of boyish devilment in his voice), "I know who you think I am, you think I'm Marty Robbins. I've been told that three times a day! I wish I was Marty Robbins, but I'm not." So, then, I'd get a conversation going and I'll say something like, "He is my favorite singer, though," really building Marty Robbins up. And then, when they finally get ready to walk away, I'll say, "Hey, I was just kidding, I really am Marty Robbins." (Laughs.)

I really don't know a lot of people around Nashville here, except people from my wife's church and a lot of the people I see on Saturday nights when I play on the Opry. My wife will sometimes have someone over from her church, but not too often. Relatives might visit once every three or four years. Most of the people I see are the fans. (He smiles.) I would rather get to meet a lot of the fans than I would more people in the business. I just like personal appearances, I like show dates, and I'll be glad to get back.

I got one guy so mad, I wouldn't tell him I was Marty Robbins. We'd played at this fair and afterwards we went out on the midway and just wandered around and we got acquainted with all the carnival people. It was just a small county fair. They had a big time following us around and we were having a big time. It was really nice to get to know those people at the carnival because they're in show business too.

Maybe six weeks later, we played another fair nearby. So, that night I went out to the fair with Don Winters, who yodels on the show and who is kinda my best friend. He's worked with me for 20 years. So, we were walkin' around and all of a sudden I hear somebody yell, "Hey, Marty Robbins!" And I didn't look up. I just looked around like I was looking for Marty Robbins too. He kept at it, "Hey, Marty! Hey, don't you remember me!" And it was one of these guys from the fair before. By this time, there were ten or 15 people who started looking, and by this time I *couldn't* say who I was. He kept asking me what I was doing there, and I kept telling him that I was a farmer who lived nearby. He said, "Don't you remember me?" And I said, "No, this is my first night at the fair." And he said, "You are Marty Robbins." And I kept saying, "No, I'm not." And so he started cussing and got real mad. I had to leave then, and I was afraid if I told him the truth then, he'd wanta fight or something. I figured he'd yell, "Hey Rube!" and I'd have to fight everybody. And then there was this guy broadcasting live on the radio out of a booth nearby, and he started in too. He yelled, "Hey, there goes Marty Robbins!" over the air. And I just kept looking to see where Marty Robbins was. That was the only time I ever really let it pass.

I enjoy being recognized. Absolutely. Sometimes I'll pass people in airports and they'll say, "Hey, there's Marty Robbins!" and I'll look back and say, "Where?" (Chuckles.) I like to play with them.

And you'll be surprised at the people who ask for autographs. People from ten to 80. One day this little kid came up to the front of the stage and gave me his little pocket knife. Gave it to me. After the show, his grandfather brought him back. It turned out that *El Paso* was his favorite song and that I was his grandfather's favorite singer and the little boy's favorite too. (He says this with warm pride, not brash egotism. He was genuinely moved by this.)

There are very few artists who have loyal fans. Young artists today don't have loyal fans. We have one family, there's a grandmother, a daughter, and a grandaughter and every time we get within 300 miles, we'll see them.

PERFORMING ON STAGE

Marty: When I'm not on the road, I don't wanta be around anybody, because that just makes me that much hungrier for the road. And during the day, I don't want to do interviews or go to radio stations. I lock myself in my room and stay there. And, then, at night when they unchain me (laughing) and I head for the stage, I'm wild and ready! (Laughs.) But I don't wanta see anybody. That's why I hate to go on last. I don't care who . . . I wanta play the audience first. I've got to get them right away! I want 'em to know who's there right away!

I don't want anybody messing with me before a show. I'm really kinda hard to get along with right before a show. I don't do interviews or talk to anyone. Because all that does is take away what I've built up all day. I've been just waiting for that moment to *see* somebody! (Voice gets intense.) It's real easy just to lose everything you've been saving up.

I want 'em to know who's there! I do a good show (he says bluntly). I want to make 'em go away from there saying they've just seen the best show they've even seen in their life! And every time I go out there, I do my very best I can to make them say that!

I've been to the Wembley festival in England three or four

times. I think the third time I went there, I went on before intermission, and I got through with my part and went back to my dressing room. And they were stompin' and yellin'. Never happened to me before. I felt like Presley or the Beatles. There was just a roar. They were standing and yelling (slightly amazed). That was exciting!

Bob Allen: What does it take to stay in the business a long time?

Marty: Longevity—well (his eyes twinkle), I think I have a little secret, you know, but I would never tell anybody (he chuckles, with a little bit of pride). So far, it has worked out the right way. I think the key to it with most anybody, though, is good material and good performances, and *making* performances. Television contact, if done the right way, is great. But too much of it is bad for you; it can kill you in a hurry. It's the live contact with people that keeps you going.

If you try too hard to put on an act, it shows. I've found it's best not to try to be professional, but just try to be "down-home."

The Palomino Club (in Los Angeles): I used to play out there and there was no back stage door. You had to walk through the crowd to get to the stage. A setup like that ruins it, because the excitement is gone before you get to the stage. Well, they [the managers] didn't want you to stop when you got off stage, between the first and second show. They wanted you to go straight back [to the dressing room] so they could get everybody out and get ready for the next show. The promoter said, "Don't stop and talk." But what he didn't realize is that when I don't do that, the people don't get mad at the guy who runs the Palomino, they get mad at Marty Robbins. I did that a couple of times and heard some people say things like, "Oh, so you're too good to come over and sign this," or something like that. So I decided not to play there anymore. He kept asking me to come back, and I said I would, just as soon as he cut a back door [in the wall behind the stage]. So, he finally cut a little door in the back and called it "The Marty Robbins Door."

SONG WRITING

Marty: I never read much about the West until I moved to the South. It was all there and I never thought that much of it until I moved away from it. That's the reason I wrote a lot of the cowboy songs, because I wanted to be in the West. But this is where I had to be. I used to have some bad problems with hay fever here, but I've gotten used to it, and the humidity. Now when I go out West, the dust will make me start sneezin', so I guess I'd better stay here.

Faleena from El Paso, eight minutes long, tells about her life, being born in the desert, and how she met this cowboy and how he got shot. It's a beautiful story, but it was too much too soon after *El Paso.* It came out within ten years after *El Paso.* But I wrote at least forty verses and I never could get the last line of the song right. I never could figure out the way I wanted it to end. I was in Phoenix and I said, "I'm going to finish this," so I flew to El Paso. I checked into a hotel that looked out over the mountains and wrote it just as fast as I could write it down. I still think it's one of the most beautiful songs I've ever written (softly recites the lyrics to the last two verses). I think the song is more beautiful than *El Paso.*

El Paso I wrote one day when I was driving through; I never even got it down on paper until I got to Phoenix the next day. But I couldn't forget it, because it was like a movie, and I didn't know how it was going to end. I must have been going 100 miles per hour when I ended it. It was so exciting. I did not know how it was going to end. But once I got started, it just rolled out. I never changed a word.

(About writing *El Paso City*): Every time I flew over El Paso, between Los Angeles and Dallas or wherever, and I was usually getting some sleep. Well, it never failed in the daytime, if I was sleeping, I would always wake up about five seconds before the pilot would say, ". . . and off to the left is the city of El Paso." So I had thought about writing that song for so long. And one time, I heard the pilot say that and I asked the stewardess for a pen and paper, and I had that song written before we even got across the state of New Mexico. By the time I got to L.A. I had the tune and everything. I called the guy who was going to come pick me up and told him to bring my guitar so I could keep it at the motel with me, and he listened to it and said, "Man, that's a hit!"

And I have another one called *The Mystery of El Paso.* I haven't recorded that yet. Maybe I'll do that, next album, in the fall.

I was just in El Paso for the Fiesta Bowl. I narrated a history of El Paso as they did the halftime festivities. I've had two "Marty Robbins Days" out there, and now I have a plaque up at the airport.

Don't Worry, I wrote that one night in the four miles that it takes to drive from the Grand Ole Opry to where I lived then. I had started it when I left, and had it finished before I ever got home. I went right in and played it on the piano. I never even put it down on paper until it was copyrighted.

I wrote *White Sport Coat* in 11 miles in 1956. We were driving somewhere in Ohio, and I just happened to look up and see this sign that said 11 miles to the next town. And I had the song finished by the time we got to that town. Where that idea came from, I have no idea. I'd never heard of a white sport coat and a pink carnation!

The only thing I've never won is Entertainer of the Year from CMA. Two Grammies; *first grammy ever given a country-western artist.*

I think I can entertain as well as anybody in the world. I have enough confidence that I'll follow anybody in the world; only person I wouldn't follow is if Elvis came back. Elvis would be a hard act to follow. I did a tour with Elvis down in Texas; he was pretty hot, but at that time I was still the star of the show. But I was smart enough to know. I toured with Elvis, Hank Snow, others. Colonel Tom Parker, there was a case of a manager that was worth his salt. Because he made Elvis the single biggest attraction, besides Christ, that's ever been on this earth.

Bob Allen: Marty had his own in-house booking agency, owned by a former band member of his. Marty completely controls his own bookings.

Marty: I had an income tax problem for eight or nine years. I never could catch up. Not counting personal appearances or performance royalties, I got two checks in one year, both for over $60,000 from Columbia. I just spent a lot of it before I paid the income tax (laughs). I just went over my head in business deals without thinking to save that tax money back. I probably made $500,000 that year [1960], and that was a lot of money back then!

That's when I got in trouble. I never had to sell anything, but I couldn't save anything. And I never got caught back up until about 1970. I did sell one little piece of property, but that was all. Everything else I still have.

Finally I got caught up and straightened up. I made so much money back in 1959, '60, '61 and '62 and I didn't even have a CPA. By the time I got one, it was already too late. I'd already spent a whole lot of my money and a whole lot of Uncle Sam's. When I really started to make and save money was in 1970, even though I had bought property and I never went without anything. If I had been the type of person who was always drinking and throwing parties, I wouldn't have the things that I have today. But I've only had two people over to my house in 20 years for any kind of dinner or anything. That was Eddy Arnold and a steel guitar player, Roy Wiggins. Those are the only times. I'm not much for having parties and that sort of thing.

Bob Allen: Today he has diversified holdings: a recording studio, publishing company, his farm, Music Row property. In 1958 he formed his own publishing company, published his own hits, but sold all the copyrights.

Marty: I didn't have a manager then, or even a CPA, that knew anything about the music industry, or I would have saved all those copyrights. But I just got so mad over paying all that income tax that I just sold them.

I now work about 120 days a year. I finally sat down and figured out how much it was going to cost me to have a band, how many dates a year I'd have to work, and how much I was going to have to give Uncle Sam and how much I was going to get to keep. I'd like to make more money, but I don't think I've ever overcharged. I won't tell you what I get, but my price has only changed $1000 in the last ten years. I pay the band goooood, gooood.

Bob Allen: The interview moved to the tour bus, on the way to his first performance since his heart attack, going to Saginaw, Michigan. (Marty tours extensively with Merle Haggard or Conway Twitty.)

Marty: Tonight is going to show me a lot as far as how much I can do. I don't need anybody to tell me if I'm getting tired, or if I'm doing something I shouldn't do. If I get tired, I just go lay down.

I don't know, I may have to do special exercises because I haven't been doing any singing. I really don't know what it's going to feel like tonight. I guess this is the longest I've ever gone in my life without singing. I mean, even when I was a little kid, I sang almost every day. I never practiced. I used to just sing for the enjoyment. After I had that heart attack back in 1969, I used to sing three or four hours a day. We lived out on a farm then. My wife would go to bed around eleven, and I would go to the other side of the house where the piano was, and she couldn't hear me, and I would play . . . many times . . . from 11 till four. I used to know at least one thousand songs by heart. I knew everybody's songs. I just enjoy it that much.

I've only written two songs since the first of the year, but they're both pretty good. I wrote one in the hospital and one at home.

I did my first tour in 1952, and that's when I was making all those long jumps by myself. And that's when this insomnia started: December of 1952. And I haven't slept good since then. When I was in the hospital, they'd sometimes have to give me a shot in the arm; regular sleeping capsules wouldn't work.

When I was in the hospital in Cleveland the first time, they thought I was a real good patient, because I slept all day. I was in an intensive care unit, and I had a tube that they put in my wrist—intravenous, they call it—and two wires were hooked up to me with an electrocardiogram, and they didn't really watch me too much. What they didn't know was that I could run around at night. I found out later that this is a very dangerous time, right after a heart attack, to be up and moving around like that. I was on some kind of medication—I don't know what it was; I wish I knew—and I wrote eight songs between ten and one o'clock in the morning. They were beautiful songs, all of them westerns except for one. I've recorded a couple of them.

The record companies really aren't interested in somebody anymore who's only going to sell 150,000 albums. They're interested in the big shots, the million sellers. They're not going to fool with somebody like me. They're gonna keep me because I can make money for them, but I can't make much money. I like Columbia Records and I understand that. They're a big outfit, and they can't afford to spend that much money on me. They have to put it on the new sound. And I can't forsake the people who have been loyal to me and try for a new sound when I'm not sure I could sell a new sound. But I can sell Marty Robbins. And I have to do what I think is right for Marty Robbins, and Columbia has to do what they think is right for Columbia. And I understand that. But, you know, I think there is a market for Marty Robbins in this world, or I wouldn't be singing today. I have already proven myself. I've been around for a long time and I don't have to prove anything to anybody. But I understand how they can only do so much for me.

Johnny Cash is an example of a guy that was into drugs real heavy and got out. I've never been into drugs, and I'm not saying that like I'm something special or anything. I used to drink a lot, many, many years ago, till I found out what drinking would do for you if you became an alcoholic. Nothing! I saw that movie,

The Rose, recently and I thought that it was a *great* picture. It really dealt with the problem. I think anybody who's in the music business could understand it. Some people think I take dope or get drunk on stage. But I'd never do that. It's just that I get so happy on stage sometimes, I get silly. I love it so much!

Bob Allen: You used to drink a lot, but quit?

Marty: I only drank for three years of my life, but I drank enough in those three years to last me the *rest* of my life. I haven't drank for years. It's a religious thing. I've been a believer all my life but I haven't always practiced it like I should. You see, I'm a believer and not a doer. I'm a Christian; I'm not a born-again Christian, but I'm a believer. I read the Bible but I don't pretend to understand it all. It's like a map or a puzzle, you have to study it and study it before you can really put it all together. (Laughs.) I don't like to get off on religion (almost apologetically); I know that's not the kind of thing you want to talk about, but those are my beliefs. I don't ask anybody else to believe the way I do, but no one else could ever change the way I feel.

Bob Allen: Much of Marty's home life revolves around religion. "Not too exciting, huh?" he jokes lightly. His wife is very religious, has been for 30 years. They've been married 32 years.

Marty: I was about 21. It's been 30 years last December that I stopped drinking. But I drank enough during those three or four years to do me the rest of my life. But it was a religious thing that made me stop drinking and I'll never start again . . . not one drop.

I don't care. People will tell you that I'm drunk on the stage, or on dope. But it's almost like you have to make them feel like that, to please them. It's just my way of having a good time, and if I'm having a good time on the stage, there's no way the audience can keep from having a good time.

My life has been a very exciting life (he says thoughtfully), I've done so many things. In my mind, I've just about done it all.

I was wild, baaad, I was *real* bad. *A real bad-ass.* I did anything I wanted to do, whatever I felt like. I was lucky enough that I never went to jail for anything. I found out real early what I could handle and what I couldn't handle.

I've drank as many as 24 bottles of beer between nine and one at night, and then at this one particular time, went to a party and drank whiskey. I was working in a club and I had won a case of beer. And I had all the beer I could drink anyway. People are always buying you drinks when you play those clubs. Then I went on to this party. After. Then I started drinking whiskey. After the party, I was driving along this four-lane highway about four o'clock in the morning and they had a lot of oleander trees along the highway. All of a sudden I wake up, my head is over the back seat and I was on the wrong side of the highway and had gone off the side into the emergency lane, going about 70 miles an hour and the trees are brushing the windshield. And this road is traveled by those big oil tankers. Only thing I remember is steering the car back over into my lane, and then the only thing I remember after that was running a red light in Glendale just as the policeman showed up. I forced him off to the side and wouldn't let him stop me. I went to my mother's house, ran inside. They waited out there for me. They didn't come in and get me. He gave me a ticket for reckless driving. He could've hauled me off to jail. I learned something in life from that. I was so lucky during those years that they never shipped me off to jail.

You never know (he muses quietly), I may become an evangelist. You never know. *Why had God kept me around this long . . . brought me through everything . . . did He do it for nothing?*

I've certainly had enough experiences in life to give a pretty good testimony.

It's the tries you make that count. Not the failures, the *tries.*

I've never had the feeling that I had it made. I never felt like I could get by on what I had. Somehow, I've always had this fear that it could all be taken away. Maybe that's what keeps me going, the feeling that it could all go away. Besides, I don't like to work. I'd rather be doing what I'm doing, because this is not work to me. (Smiles.) I like it so much, I feel ashamed that I'm getting paid for it!

Bob Allen: How do the audiences and fame affect you?

Marty: Because people like you, you can't let that change you. The more you like them, the more they're going to like you. If they want to place you up above them, let them! If they want to write you letters and tell you how great you are, read it and just be glad that somebody's telling you that, because that's what a person lives on. I love to get letters like that! But I don't let it bother me. I'm always thankful that I'm doing something I want to do.

When I first moved to Nashville, they had a television show every evening at four o'clock and I'd go down for it and do a little shopping. It was a WSM show and different artists would appear on it. I remember I was down there one day and a man in a shoe store told me, "You'll never make it. You're not country." But I guess I've done pretty well. People sometimes tell me I'm their favorite country singer. Well, I just love it. Whatever they want to tell me.

Because I had to please a lot of people when I was coming up in this business and working in nightclubs, I learned how to handle different types of songs. I was never a pure country singer. I think I've had 18 number one hits and only two have been pure country songs. The others were for the country market, but they were not country songs. I am Marty Robbins; I'm a singer by trade. I love music and that's how I make my living.

The other night, I watched the Metropolitan Opera on television and loved it. I didn't understand what they were saying, but I knew the emotions and feelings they put in the songs. They were coming across just like I wanted to come across to my audience.

Nobody knows what country is. I don't. And neither do people who call country music, country music. They only know what the public wants, but not until the public shows them. The industry is always one step behind the public. They find out what the public's going to accept and they give it to them. But they're not ahead of the public. They'll never be. That's what I mean when I say I know as much about the music business as the people at Columbia or anywhere else. I know what it takes to sell a record. They don't "push" Marty Robbins because they have a whole lot of younger people on the label they can push who will sell more. They're satisfied with that.

Bob Allen: Some people would say that Robbins is part of the Old Guard. He is, after having been in the business thirty years, and on the Opry nearly that long. But the business today is fast-paced and competitive; and there's a whole crop of young artists out there who have the same hunger that he had thirty years ago. And every day the market place is beginning to belong more and more to them. Some would say he's set in his ways, peaked. To this he answers:

Marty: There's more drive left in me to do more than what I'm doing. I don't know just how I will, but I will. I have plans to do more, to sell more records. And I will. I don't have any doubt in my mind. K-Tel leased an album of mine from Columbia and sold about 400,000 of them real quick. So I know that's the way to do it. But Columbia is not set up for that, for the mail order business. There's still a market out there for Marty Robbins and Marty Robbins' type of music.

I've been called "King of the Balladeers," probably because of the gunfighter ballads, but I don't want to be put in any category. I don't want to get in a rut. I've never been in one and I don't want to get in one. Now I can try one or two new type songs, of the new type of music on an album. But, I'll guarantee you, I'll get a bunch of letters saying, "You shouldn't have tried that!" But I've got to satisfy two different sources: I've got to satisfy the people who have been buying records from me all these years and I've also got to try and get Columbia Records interested enough in me that they will try and sell my product.

I venture to say I've got 250,000 ardent Marty Robbins fans in this world. And I'm going to find them in the next three years. I know a person can make money on an album and sell it for $6.00 and still pay the postage. An established artist can sell records through mail order. Judging from letters and the number of albums I sell at personal appearances, just to people who can't find my albums [in stores], I could sell 250,000 of every album I've made if I were organized right.

If I never made another record in my life, I can go on with what I've done for 15 more years. But I don't want that, I'm not satisfied at all with what I've done. I want to do more. I haven't lost the drive. If I was certain I could sell a half a million albums by cutting the kind of music they're cutting today, I might try it. But there's no guarantee that when I cut an album I can satisfy the people who put me where I am. And that is my main goal. I've been Marty Robbins too long. I'm not cutting the kind of stuff that is selling today and I can't cut that kind of stuff because that's not Marty Robbins, and I've been Marty Robbins too long to change. Not that I couldn't, but why change? Oh, if I were certain I could sell a half million. . .

Bob Allen: A description of Marty's bus: a Silver Eagle touring bus, worth $150,000. There are nine bunks in the bus. Marty doesn't have a separate compartment; he just sleeps in a bunk like the other band members. Coffee machine, microwave oven, Betamax.

Marty: They [the band members] can do whatever they want to; that's none of my business, as long as they do a good show and they're here when the bus pulls out. If they want to do a little drinkin' on the bus now and then, that's alright, as long as it doesn't turn into a brawl. And with these guys, it never does.

Marty about his early days: I was about 23 when I first made a full-time living on it [singing]. Before that, I didn't have any sense of direction. All I knew was that I didn't like what I was doing. And I tried a lot of things. And then I got a job playing music. I didn't sing at first, I was a guitar player. But right then I knew it was what I wanted because it fit my hours. I didn't have to go to work till nine o'clock at night and then get off at one o'clock. That was great! It suited me so much. I just couldn't believe it at first. That a person could make a *living* doing that. I knew that people could make good money making motion pictures, but I didn't know that they could make any money singing, unless they were in motion pictures. I didn't know you could make a living singing in a club. But when I found that out, I knew it was what I wanted. But I didn't know too much about music. I didn't even know some of the chords that I played [on the guitar]. Still don't.

I don't know, I think the great songs just come out. They are there in a person and they come out. I never rewrote *Devil Woman, El Paso,* or *You Gave Me a Mountain.* Songs that I rewrote and tried to make into better songs did nothing. So I've learned that if it comes quick, leave it the way it is.

THE FUTURE

Bob Allen: What about the future?

Marty: I'm not even close to being through in this business. I'm more interested in looking ahead at what I'm still going to do than I am at looking back at what I've already done. I still want to write a song that's better than *El Paso.* I don't feel like I'm through. And nobody knows, maybe I have seen my best years. Or, maybe I haven't even peaked yet. Who knows. *Because all along, I've let everything come to me. I've never even had a manager except for the first three years of my career.* If I'd ever taken all the small parts that have been offered to me in the movies in the last 20 years, I'd be a movie star by now (he says matter-of-factly).

I certainly don't feel like I have done everything that I'm going to do. If I did, then I wouldn't be on the road. I just feel that somewhere, something else is going to happen great for me. So I don't want to stop . . . *this.* Somebody might offer me a good part in a movie, I don't know. Because if I get a good part, I'm going to take it. I think I'm capable of playing just about any part, except the part of a real handsome Hollywood-type person. They couldn't make me look that good. But in a western, I could play the part of an outlaw, I could play the part of a marshal, I could do about anything. I could do about anything in a detective series. Anything that called for an ordinary person, I could do that. Now Hollywood is looking at a lot of the Tennessee people, so it could happen. Maybe it never will. But I'm not pushing it, so if it doesn't, I won't be disappointed. But that's what keeps me going; that there's always the possibility that I could do something else in the entertainment field that I haven't.

Urban Cowboy: I like it. I think it gave a lot of people a chance to be something. I don't necessarily mean be something other than themselves. But it gave them a chance to get away. It gave people in the big city—Los Angeles, Philadelphia, anywhere—a chance to get away. They had a hat on. They were part of something, part of a movement. And I think it was good. It helped the careers of a number of people. It's like disco music, it'll go away. But think of the fun that people have had wearing a straw hat, a pair of jeans, and a pair of boots. I'm gonna say it did more for this country than any movement I know of. It just released them.

For years, the only place you saw people wearing cowboy hats was in Texas. Now you can go into the biggest cities and see people wearing them (says warmly). It's just being part of the working part of America. They're doing what they want to do, shaping their own hats, wearing their jeans like they want to wear them.

All my uncles on my mother's side, with the exception of one, were cowboys. Real cowboys, chaps, hats.

I have to go on my own feelings as much as someone else's when I pick my material. Because when someone has been in the business as long as I have, I really have to rely on my own judgment. Because I don't think a record company will work with an artist who's been on the label as long as I have. They don't give the attention that a new artist is going to get. So I have to do what I want to sing and do what I like now. Because I owe it to the people who have bought my records all these years. And if I have a hit with a song I don't like, how can I go out there and sing it night after night if I don't like it?

So, I'd say 70% of the song singles I've recorded have been my own songs. I think I've had 18 number ones and 12 of them were songs I had written myself.

Bob Allen: Did you feel like you had really hit the big time?

Marty: No, I've never felt like I was something. I believe in myself. I believe I have the talent to sing songs, if they're the right songs. But I'm not foolish enough to believe I'm going to have a number one record every time. The only time I have made a big scene or told someone I was going to be a star of a show, was when I was rubbed wrong [by somebody]. I don't like to have somebody push me around.

I can look around and see what I've already done in this business. I don't have to go in the Hall of Fame to be remembered. I'm gonna be remembered for what I've already done. I could live, I could make personal appearances for the next 20 years off what I've already done, even if I never recorded again. It may sound like I'm bragging, but it's a fact. I don't want to stop making records though. I want them to be sold; I want them to be in the homes. But when I'm gone, 50 years from now, they'll still . . . because, you see, I have records of a guy who was in the business before I was even born, called Vernon Dalhart. I listened to him when I was five, six, seven years old and it brings back a lot of memories to hear him now. He had one of the first million sellers ever, *The Prisoner Song,* back in the '20s.

Bob Allen: You'd like that too, people playing your records 50, 60 years from now?

Marty: Sure! And they will, you know (smiles), if they don't wear out before then. And I know it will happen. It's already been proven.

I've never felt like I was on top of the world, because I always had the feeling that it could all change tomorrow. I still have that feeling. It doesn't scare me. I hope it never happens, but there's always the possibility. I don't feel like I have it made. I feel like I've got a long way to go before I can even feel safe. I don't let what I've already done affect me. It only makes me want to do more. It makes me want to do better . . . so, I keep going.

Appendix A

THE COUNTRY MUSIC FOUNDATION
LIBRARY AND MEDIA CENTER

The Country Music Foundation runs the Hall of Fame, the best known and busiest tourist attraction in Nashville. On display at the museum on Division Street are rooms full of country music history that tell the nation and the world about the roots of the music and the people who make it. But there's another wealth of country music history in the same building that isn't on display: the library and media center located in the basement of the complex. It may be out of sight, but it's not out of mind, especially to people in the entertainment industry and writers from such far away places as England, Australia, or Japan. It's the only library in the world devoted completely to country music, and as such, draws users from inside the industry and out, whose needs can only be fulfilled at this location.

Ronnie Pugh, Head of the Reference section of the library, is himself a country music enthusiast and scholar. He's proud of his library's collection and likes to talk about it.

BP: Ronnie, would you please tell us a little about the library and the people who use it.

RP: The library is available to users weekdays, from nine to five. As far as who can use it, just about anyone with a need. We don't have the space or the staff to provide services to anyone who just wants to come in and read, but people who are doing serious research are welcome. Appointments must be made ahead of time in order for us to reserve space in the reading room and prepare the materials that might be needed for that particular project. It's important that we know what topics a researcher wants to cover before he or she arrives, so that we can give the best assistance. We will also answer some questions over the phone if the researcher can't come in. We realize that it's not always possible for someone in another part of the country to come to Nashville, because of the expense.

Most of our users are industry people such as journalists, record company personnel, publicity people, and researchers for production companies, as well as fans, scholars, and students. A very interesting clientele!

BP: What kinds of collections do you have?

RP: Foremost in my mind is our extensive disk collection of over 110,000 items. We're *very* proud of that. We also have a large collection of historical photos. We have vertical files full of newspaper clippings, biographies, press releases, and fan club journals. We probably have something on just about every country music artist. Of course, we have more material on some than others. We also have general historical files about country music that cover subjects about the music rather than just the artists themselves.

Our stacks are "closed," which means that visitors must ask for the material instead of going after it themselves. The stack area contains the books, sheet music, and hundreds of magazine titles (and thousands of individual issues) that have been published about country music over the decades. We have a lot of old Grade-B movies, mostly westerns, and are now starting to get in some first-run films like *Coal Miner's Daughter*. Our collection of video tape and television programs is growing, but we can use a lot more of this type of thing.

As far as special collections, we have the Roy Acuff Collection. He gave us his collection of movies and print items some time ago and it's stored in our Roy Acuff Room. It was a very generous thing for him to do and has been extremely valuable to music historians. We also have the Session Sheet Contracts from the AFM-Nashville Local. We have them from 1970 on; they weren't saved before that, I'm sorry to say. Session sheets are the work records of recording sessions held in the studios around Nashville. They have the day, time, people involved (the musicians and technicians), titles of the songs recorded during the session, and the payment for the work. You can't copy them but they can be used in the Library. Right now, we are still trying to sort them all out by artist; it's a big job.

BP: How do you get most of the material you have here?

RP: By donation. Both fans and the industry have contributed. Fans have always played an important part in country music and this is an area where fans deserve a *lot* of credit. As far as the industry, we have had donations from the Country Music Association, the Musician's Union, from the performers themselves and their offices, music publishers, magazines, publicity agents, record companies, and radio and television stations.

Fans are big collectors; sometimes they have more than the artists themselves. They care enough about preserving the history of their favorite artist to donate their collection to us. There has to be a lot of caring to give something significant, such as a letter or other personal object that the fan may have received directly from the artist.

BP: What are some end uses for all of the information you have here?

RP: A huge number of magazine articles are published because of the work writers do here. We get writers from all over the world. We get researchers from TV quiz shows. People who need photos from the 1930s and 1940s for their books contact us. Movie companies want to know what songs were sung, or instruments played, years ago. A staff member from an artist may come in looking for information about the early part of that artist's career. Record companies ask us to research things for album covers. And television production companies send researchers and script writers to work on the background for television specials.

BP: What are some of the things you need most to enlarge your collection?

RP: Photos, local newspaper clippings, complete sets of periodicals. We especially need correspondence, letters from the artists themselves. We have very little of this and would be very interested in building up this part of our collection.

We ask people to contact us directly if they want to consider donating something. We try to keep from accepting duplicates of things we already have because we don't have the space or the staff to take care of multiple copies of the same thing. And it's not fair to people to let them donate something we can't use, especially if the item means a lot to them personally.

BP: Using Marty as an example, tell me what you have in various parts of your collection about him.

RP: Well, first we have many of his recordings; albums, 45s, ep's, and even some of the old 78s. We also have a nice selection of photos going back to the 1950s. We have most of the old fan club *Journals* and all of the *Pen Friends* issues, thanks to the fans who donated those. We do have some correspondence relating to his office from years ago, as well as hundreds of old newspaper clippings about his recordings, performances, and auto racing activities. We have the session sheets from the recording sessions he did here in Nashville (from 1970 on) and some song books and sheet music of the tunes he wrote. Of course, he's in a lot of the magazines we have. As you have found out, there's hundreds of articles over nearly forty years! Lately, we have been getting in some video tape and old film. Of course, he's in a couple of our old Grade-B westerns, but we have had those for some time. We just received most of the film of the old "Classic Country" television shows and Bobby Jones donated copies of Marty's appearances on his show. We have a copy of his interview on

"Miller & Company" that was done in 1981. We even have some tape of his British performances. When you put it all together, it comes to quite a bit.

BP: Could you draw from your various collections and put together that much information about other artists?

RP: Yes, for many of them. The longer the career of the artist, the more we are likely to have. Of course, part of that depends on the success the artist had and how much was written about him or her. Just by the nature of it, we will have more information about the biggest stars. But you would be surprised at what we do have. Sometimes someone will give us a whole collection about an artist for whom we had very little, and that means so much to all of us who deal in country music history. You never know what will happen tomorrow.

Appendix B

COUNTRY MUSIC FOUNDATION LIBRARY PERIODICALS

The following list of journals, prepared for me by Jay Orr, includes those most likely to contain information about Marty Robbins. The Library has holdings for each title listed.

Academy of Country and Western Music
Across Country (Australia)
American Music
American Sound
ASCAP Today
Association of Country Entertainers (newsnotes)
Austin Notes

BMI—News About Music and Writers
Bare Back (Japan)
Ben-Tone News
Big Beat (France)
Big Country News
Billboard
Brite Star Country
Buckeye Music News
Buddy

CMA Close-Up (Country Music Association)
California Country
Capital Country News (Canada)
Carwin Country
Cavalcade of Music
Chattanooga Country
Clark's Country Music News

Colorado Country Music Review
Colorado Country Weekly
Continental Country Music News
Cooper's Country Collage
Coor's Country Music Magazine
Country (Philadelphia)
Country and Blue Grass Roads (newsletter)
Country and Western (Japan)
Country and Western Hit Parade
Country and Western Jamboree
Country and Western Music
Country and Western Music (foreign)
Country and Western Music (magazine)
Country and Western Music Club Newsletter
Country and Western Music News Round-up (Canada)
Country and Western Music Society
Country and Western Music Stars
Country and Western News-Scene
Country and Western News-Scene (Upper Midwest)
Country and Western Press
Country and Western Record Review
Country and Western Review
Country and Western Roundabout
Country and Western Spotlight (Australia)
Country and Western Spotlight (New Zealand)
Country and Western World (New York)
Country and Western Yearbook
Country Billboard
Country Cannonball
Country Capers
Country Connection News
Country Corner
Country Corner (Germany)
Country Courier
Country Express (Denmark)
Country Fever
Country Gazette
Country Gazette (Netherlands)
Country Heritage
Country Hits
Country Hits of the 70's
Country Hot-Line
Country Hot-Line News

Country in the City
Country Informer Magazine
Country Life
Country Music
Country Music (England)
Country Music Ambassador
Country Music Beat
Country Music Club of Oregon
Country Music Digest
Country Music Express (Australia)
Country Music Extra (England)
Country Music Fan Club
Country Music Fan Fair
Country Music File (Japan)
Country Music Florida
Country Music Gazette (Minnesota)
Country Music Gazette (Virginia)
Country Music Herald
Country Music Hits
Country Music Inquirer
Country Music Life
Country Music Memorial (France)
Country Music Monthly
Country Music News (Canada)
Country Music News (Florida)
Country Music News (Ireland)
Country Music News (Oklahoma)
Country Music News (Pennsylvania)
Country Music News Magazine (Virginia Country Music Association)
Country Music News Roundup (also titled *Western Roundup*)
Country Music Parade
Country Music People (England)
Country Music Rag
Country Music Record
Country Music Report
Country Music Report (Country Music Association of Austria newsletter)
Country Music Reporter (Title later changed to *Music Reporter*)
Country Music Reporter (Canada)
Country Music Reporter (San Antonio, Tex.)
Country Music Review (London)
Country Music Review (Orange County, Calif.)
Country Music Review (Tulsa, Okla.)

Country Music Round Up (England)
Country Music Round Up and Fan Club Monitor
Country Music Scene
Country Music Scene (Iowa)
Country Music Special (England)
Country Music Special (Annual)
Country Music Spotlight
Country Music Star
Country Music Star Life
Country Music Star News
Country Music Stars
Country Music Tattler
Country Music Telegram
Country Music Time with Chaplain Paul (newsletter)
Country Music Times (Australia; newsletter)
Country Music Trail
Country Music USA (France)
Country Music World (England)
Country Music World (Ideal Series)
Country Music World News
Country News (formerly *Country Hotline News*)
Country News and Views (England, Australia)
Country News and Views Newsletter
Country People
Country Rambler
Country Recording Voice
Country Rhythms
Country Roads
Country Roundup
Country Scene USA
Country Sky
Country Song Roundup
Country Song Roundup Annual
Country Song Roundup Yearbook
Country Songs and Stars
Country Songwriter
Country Sounds (Germany)
Country Sounds of the Southwest
Country Star Review (Nashville)
Country Startime
Country Style (magazine)
Country Talk
Country 10/40

Country Tid-Bits
Country Time
Country Time Review
Country Times
Country Times (Kansas)
Country Traveler
Country Western Album
Country Western Express (England)
Country Western Gazette (Illinois)
Country Western Gazette (Minnesota)
Country Western Record Review
Country Western Stars
Countryside
CountryStyle
Country Music World
Cowboy Songs

Deejay
Disc—The Record Magazine
Disc and Music Echo
Downhome (Canada)

ECMA (European Country Music Association newsletter)
ESCMI (Eastern States Country Music Inc., newsletter)
East Side News (Country Music and News Magazine)
Entertainer (Several editions sold: Gold Coast [Ft. Lauderdale],
    Music City [Nashville], New York, West Coast [San Francisco])
Entertainers Variety Magazine

FICAP Voice (newsletter)
Fan Fair Country Music Magazine
Florida Country Music Foundation
Florida Country Music Magazine
Florida Country Music News
Folk and Country (Finland)
Folk and Country Songs
Frontier Country (Country and Western Digest)

Georgia World of Country Music
Giant Country
Gilly's Country Magazine
Grammy Pulse (NARAS)
Grand Ole Opry News
Grinder's Switch Gazette

Hayride—Jubilee Combination (Dutch)
Hayride Newsletter
Here's News About WSM's Grand Ole Opry
Hillbilly
Hillbilly (West Germany)
Hillbilly and Country Hit Parade
Hillbilly and Cowboy Hit Parade
Hillbilly and Western Review
Hillbilly and Western Scrapbook
The Hillbilly Folk (England)
Hillbilly Hit
Hillbilly Hit Parade
Hillbilly Western Songs
Hoedown
Hoedown (The Country Music Magazine)
Hoedown (Hillbilly and Western Stars)
Honky Tonk
Hootenanny
Houston Country Scene

Inside (Country Music)
Inside Country Music
Inside Nashville (National Tattler special)
International Music Review

Jamboree
Jamboree Magazine (Ventura, Calif.)
Jenny's Swingin' Country
Journal of American Culture
Journal of Country Music
Journal of Popular Culture

K-BAR-T Country Roundup
Keep It Country (New Zealand)
Keep It Country (South Africa Country Music Association)
Kommotion (England)
Kountry Karavan News
Kountry Korral (Sweden)
Kritik (Germany)

Lincolnshire Country Music Roundup (England)
Little Nashville Express (Nashville, IN)

Maine Country
Melody Maker (England)
Michigan Country News
Midem News (France)
Midlands Country Music Club—MCMC (England)
Midwestern Country and Western Association Newsletter
Milner's Country Roads (see *Country Roads*)
Mississippi Valley Country and Western Music Association newsletter
    (Chat Time)
Mississippi Valley Country Notes
Music (England)
Music Capital News (Washington, D.C., Maryland, Virginia,
    Pennsylvania newsletter)
Music Capital News Countryside
Music City Loafer
Music City News
Music City News Inquirer
Music City News Tradesheet (newsletter)
Music City TV Tempo
Music Country (continues *Muleskinner News*)
Music Country Network Closeup (newsletter)
Music Folio of Popular Western Songs
Music Galore
Music Labo (Japan)
Music Life (Japan)
Music Maker (Australia)
Music Makers
Music News
Music Reporter
Music Row
Music Scene
Music Spotlight
Music Views
Music World (England)
Music World (Grapevine Opry)
Musical Echoes
Musical Traditions (England)
My Country

Nashville
Nashville City Beat
Nashville Entertainer
Nashville Gazette

Nashville Magazine
Nashville Network Newsletter (see *The Wrap Sheet*)
Nashville Panorama
Nashville Reporter
Nashville Scene
Nashville Sound
Nashville Sound (Dutch)
Nashville Sound (Nashville)
Nashville Sound Country Music News (Sevierville, Tenn.)
Nashville Star Reporter
Nashville Voice
Nashville West
New England Country News
New England Country Times
New Frontier
New Kommotion (England)
New Zealand Country Music News
Not Fade Away (England)
Not Fade Away (Texas)

Okie (England)
Oklahoma Country Music Association Newsletter
O'Lunney's Country Music City News
Omaha Rainbow (England)
Opry (The Journal of Country Music)
Opry News (National Life)
Orange Blossom Special
Our Kinda Country (Australia)

Parade of Stars (newsletter)
Paragon Western Stars
Pony Express News
Popular Country Stars
Proud Country

Radio Stars
Record News
Renfro Valley Bugle
Rhinestone Rooster
Round-Up (France)
Round-Up (Hollywood)

Schwann (record catalog)
Schwann Country and Western Catalog
Sheridan's Quarterly
The Shindig in the Barn
Showman
Song and Saddle
Songmakers Almanac
Songs and Music
Songs and Shows
Songs and Stars
Songs of the West (newsletter)
Sounds (England)
Southern Country (England)
Southern Exposure
Southern Music News
Speek's Country Music News (Knoxville)
Spurs
Stand By
Star from Nashville West
Star News (Bear Family Records newsletter, Germany)
Stardust
Strictly Country (Germany)
Strictly Country (Netherlands)

Take One
Tall Timber Times
Tennessee Sunday Showcase
Texas Country
Texas Country Music News (newsletter)
Texas Country Western Magazine
Texas Music
Texas Music News
Texas Prairie Schooner
Texas Proud
Texas Ragg
Theme
Third Coast
Thursday
Trail
Twin States Country Music News

U.K. Country Music Guide (England)
Under Western Skies
Upper Midwest Country and Western News-Scene

Valley Jammer
Valley Music News
Virginia Country Music News

WSM Festival News
WSM Radio Newsletter
WWVA Jamboree (newsletter)
WWVA Jamboree-News with "The Wheeling Feeling"
WWVA/WCPI Newsletter
West Coast Country Music Sound (England)
Western and Country Music
Western Bulletin (Denmark)
Western Corral
Western Music
Western Music Picture Album (Japan)
Western News
Western Revue
Western Roundup
Western-Saloon News (Netherlands)
Western Songs (Sweden)
Western Star Digest
Western Star News (newsletter)
Western Trails
What's Doing in Nashville
What's Happening (Virginia Country Music Association)
Wheeling Feeling (Wheeling, W.Va.)
Whiskey, Women, and. . .
Who's Who in the Country and Western World
Who's Who in Western Stars
World of Country Music (Calif.)
World of Country Music (Canada)
The Wrap Sheet (Nashville Network Newsletter)

INDEX